Garfield

FAT CAT 3-PACK

VOLUME 20

Garfield
FAT CAT 3-PACK
VOLUME 20

BY
JIM DAVIS

BALLANTINE BOOKS • NEW YORK

Published in the United States by Ballantine Books, an imprint of Random House,
a division of Penguin Random House LLC, New York.

BALLANTINE and the HOUSE colophon are registered trademarks of Penguin Random House LLC.

NICKELODEON is a Trademark of Viacom International, Inc.

GARFIELD GOES TO HIS HAPPY PLACE was published separately by Ballantine Books, an imprint of
Random House, a division of Penguin Random House LLC, in 2014. GARFIELD THE BIG CHEESE and
GARFIELD CLEANS HIS PLATE were each published separately by Ballantine Books, an imprint of Random
House, a division of Penguin Random House LLC, New York, in 2015.

ISBN 978-0-425-28571-8

Printed in China on acid-free paper

randomhousebooks.com

10

Garfield
Goes to His Happy Place

BY JIM DAVIS

Ballantine Books ● New York

OODLES OF DOODLES

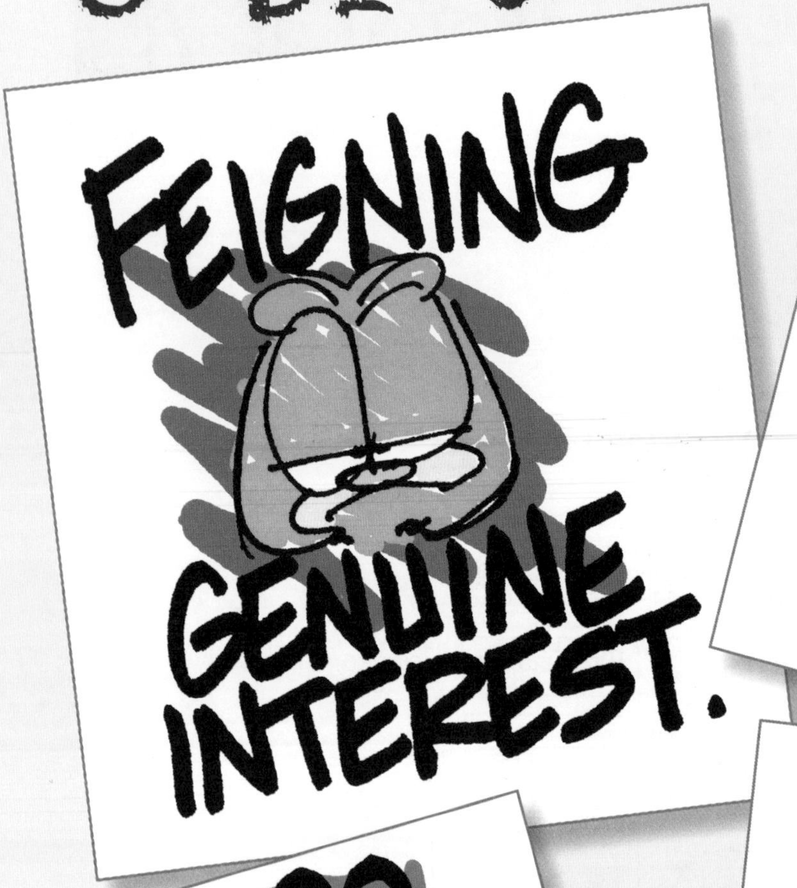
FEIGNING
GENUINE INTEREST.

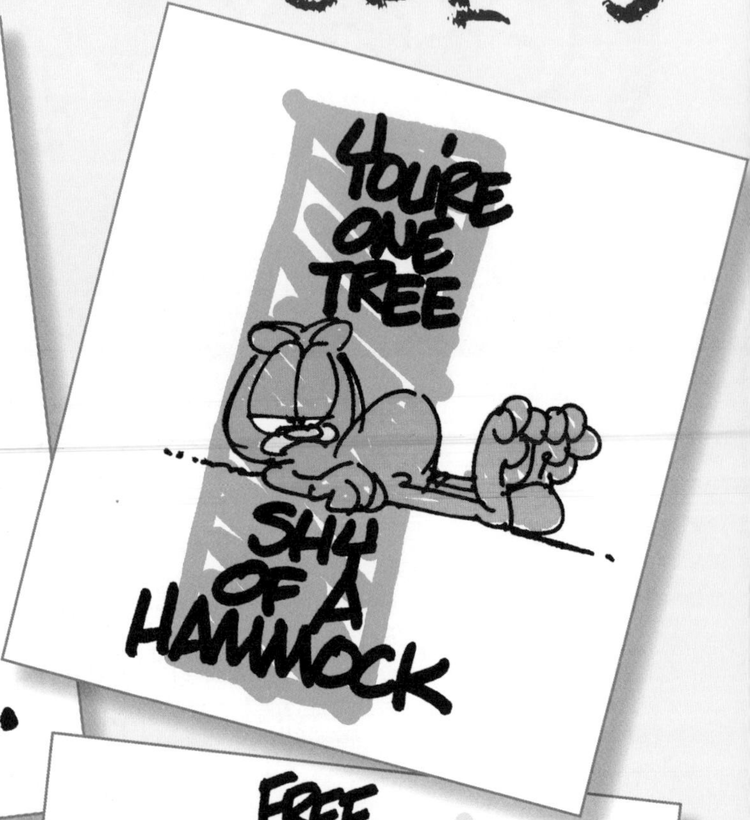
YOU'RE ONE TREE
SHY OF A HAMMOCK

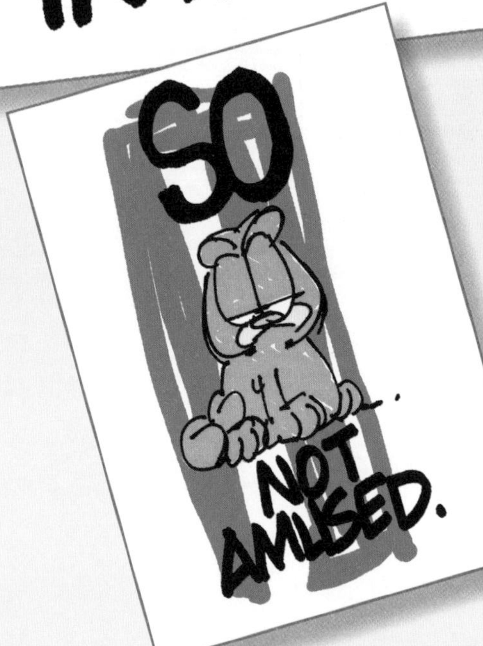
SO
NOT AMUSED.

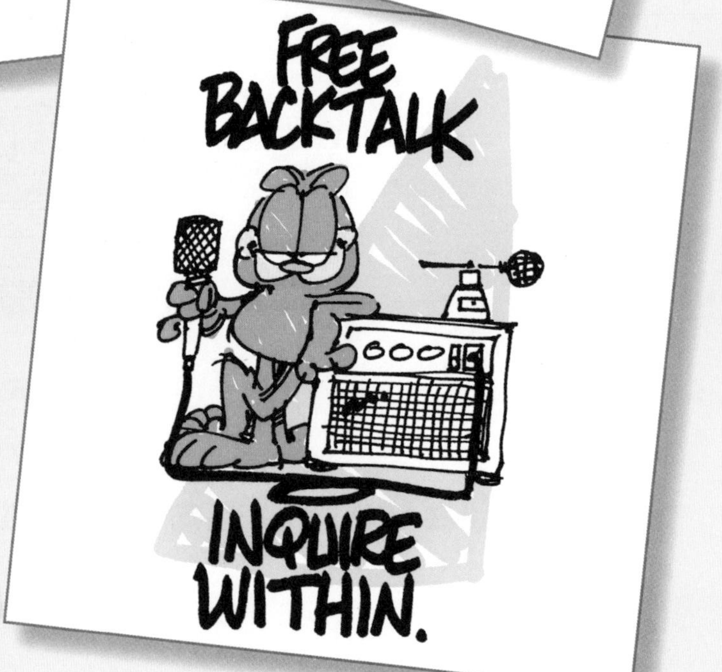
FREE BACKTALK
INQUIRE WITHIN.

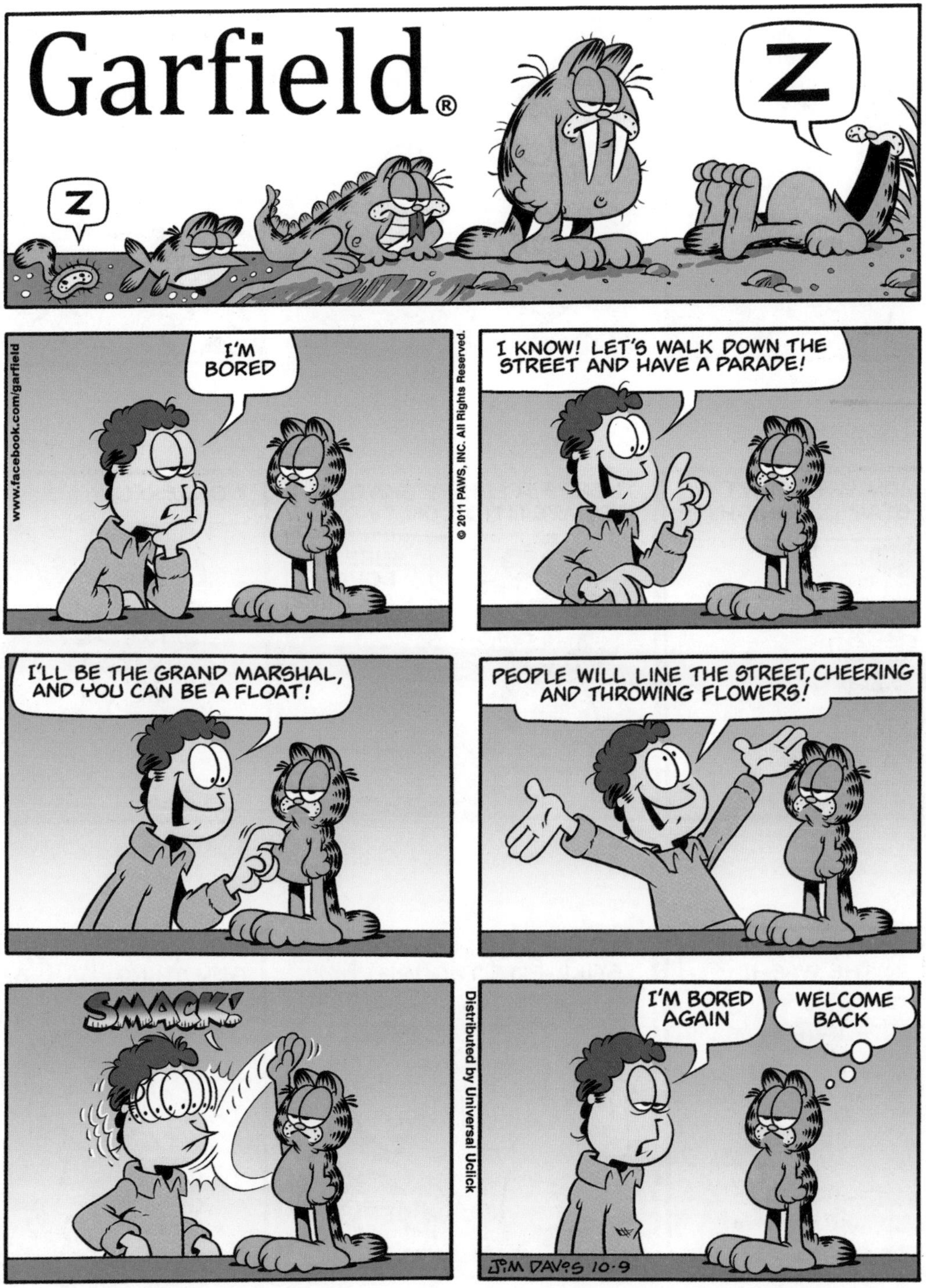
Garfield®
Z
Z
www.facebook.com/garfield
I'M BORED
© 2011 PAWS, INC. All Rights Reserved.
I KNOW! LET'S WALK DOWN THE STREET AND HAVE A PARADE!
I'LL BE THE GRAND MARSHAL, AND YOU CAN BE A FLOAT!
PEOPLE WILL LINE THE STREET, CHEERING AND THROWING FLOWERS!
SMACK!
Distributed by Universal Uclick
I'M BORED AGAIN
WELCOME BACK
JIM DAVIS 10-9

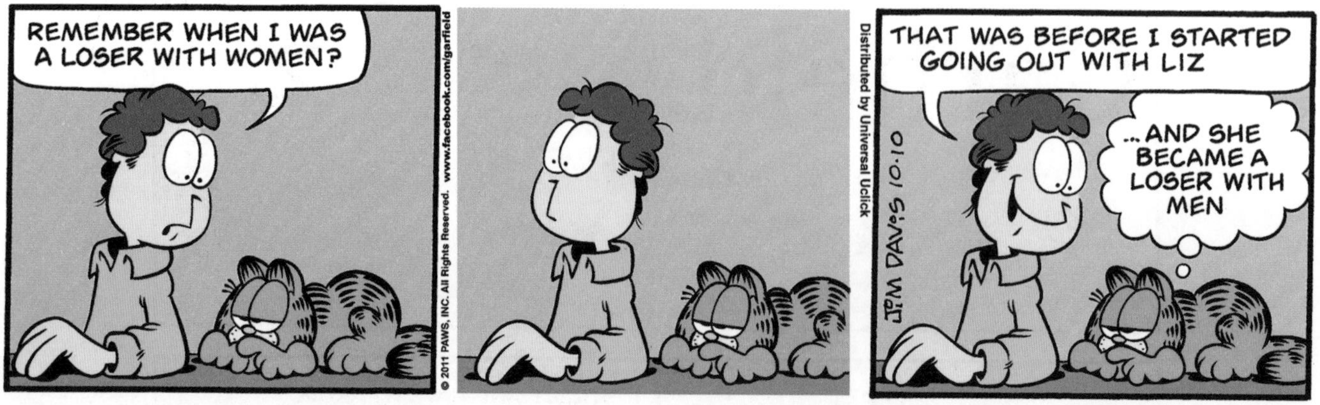
REMEMBER WHEN I WAS A LOSER WITH WOMEN?
© 2011 PAWS, INC. All Rights Reserved. www.facebook.com/garfield
Distributed by Universal Uclick
THAT WAS BEFORE I STARTED GOING OUT WITH LIZ
...AND SHE BECAME A LOSER WITH MEN

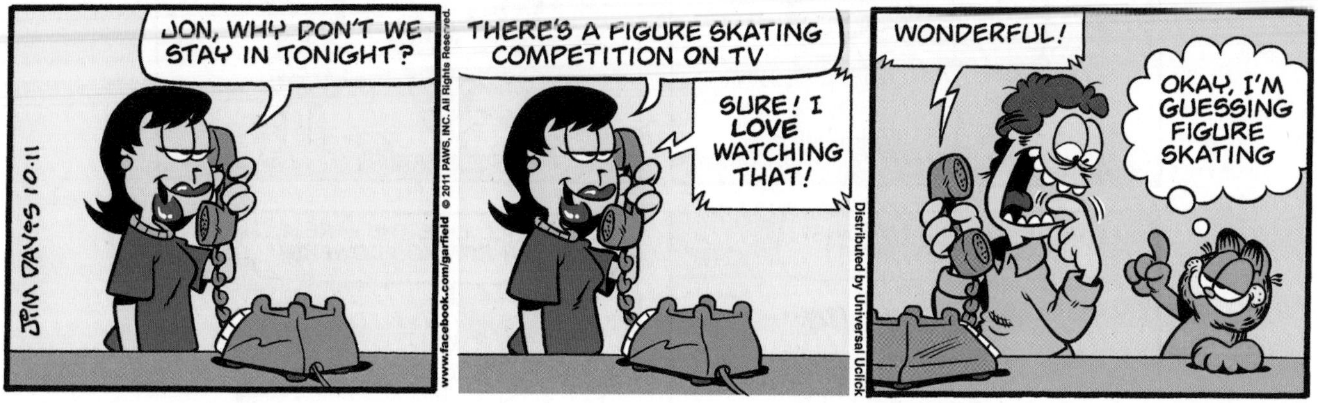
JON, WHY DON'T WE STAY IN TONIGHT?
© 2011 PAWS, INC. All Rights Reserved. www.facebook.com/garfield
THERE'S A FIGURE SKATING COMPETITION ON TV
SURE! I LOVE WATCHING THAT!
Distributed by Universal Uclick
WONDERFUL!
OKAY, I'M GUESSING FIGURE SKATING

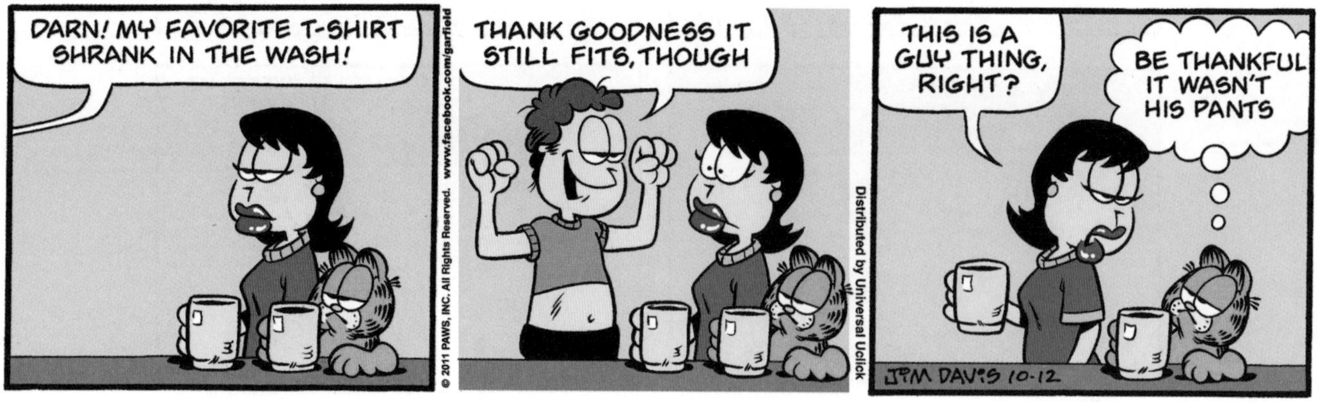
DARN! MY FAVORITE T-SHIRT SHRANK IN THE WASH!
© 2011 PAWS, INC. All Rights Reserved. www.facebook.com/garfield
THANK GOODNESS IT STILL FITS, THOUGH
Distributed by Universal Uclick
THIS IS A GUY THING, RIGHT?
BE THANKFUL IT WASN'T HIS PANTS

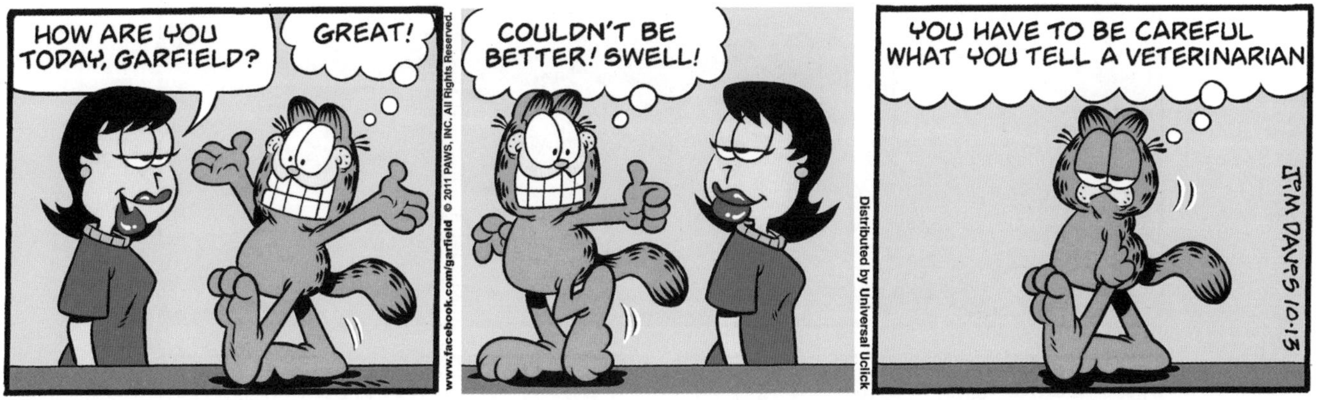
HOW ARE YOU TODAY, GARFIELD?
GREAT!
www.facebook.com/garfield © 2011 PAWS, INC. All Rights Reserved.
COULDN'T BE BETTER! SWELL!
Distributed by Universal Uclick
YOU HAVE TO BE CAREFUL WHAT YOU TELL A VETERINARIAN
JIM DAVIS 10-13

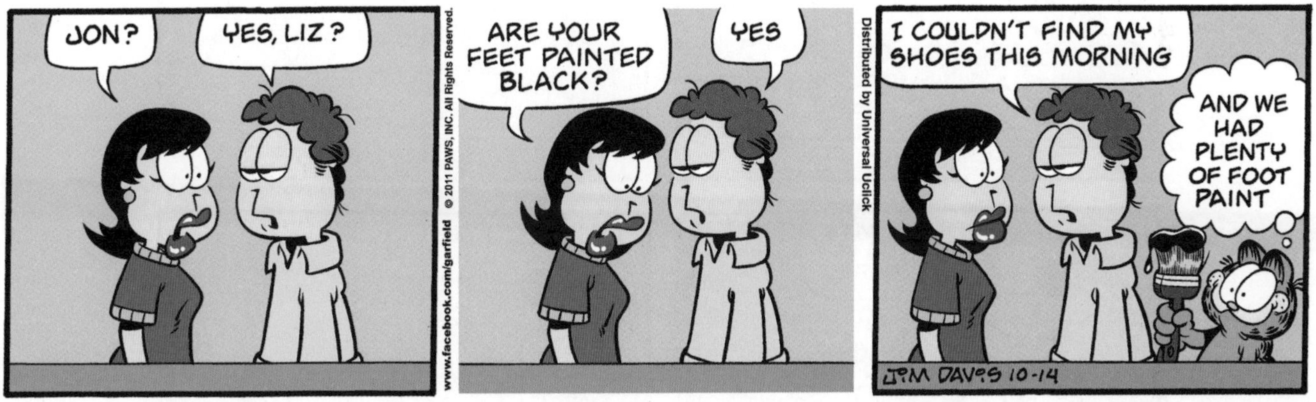
JON?
YES, LIZ?
www.facebook.com/garfield © 2011 PAWS, INC. All Rights Reserved.
ARE YOUR FEET PAINTED BLACK?
YES
Distributed by Universal Uclick
I COULDN'T FIND MY SHOES THIS MORNING
AND WE HAD PLENTY OF FOOT PAINT
JIM DAVIS 10-14

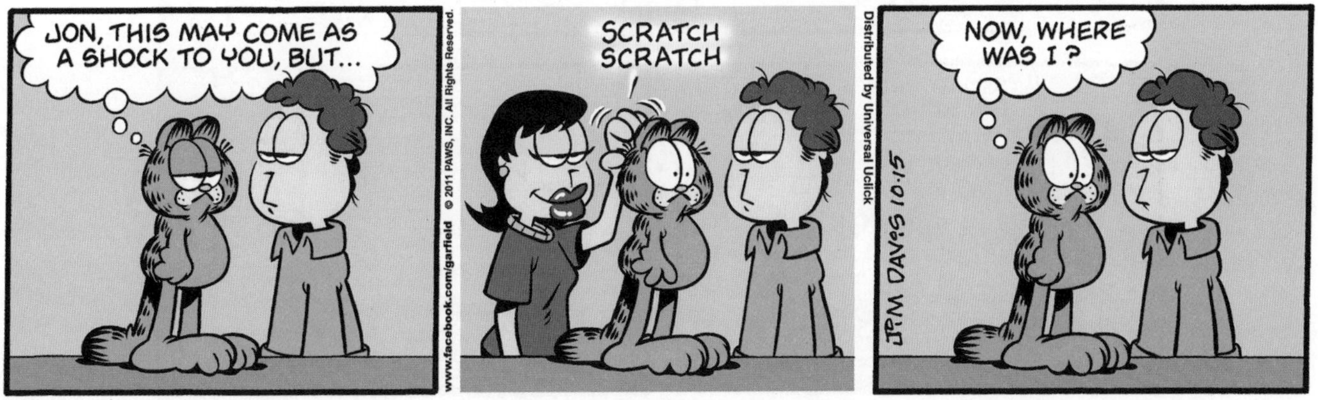
JON, THIS MAY COME AS A SHOCK TO YOU, BUT...
www.facebook.com/garfield © 2011 PAWS, INC. All Rights Reserved.
SCRATCH SCRATCH
Distributed by Universal Uclick
JIM DAVIS 10-15
NOW, WHERE WAS I?

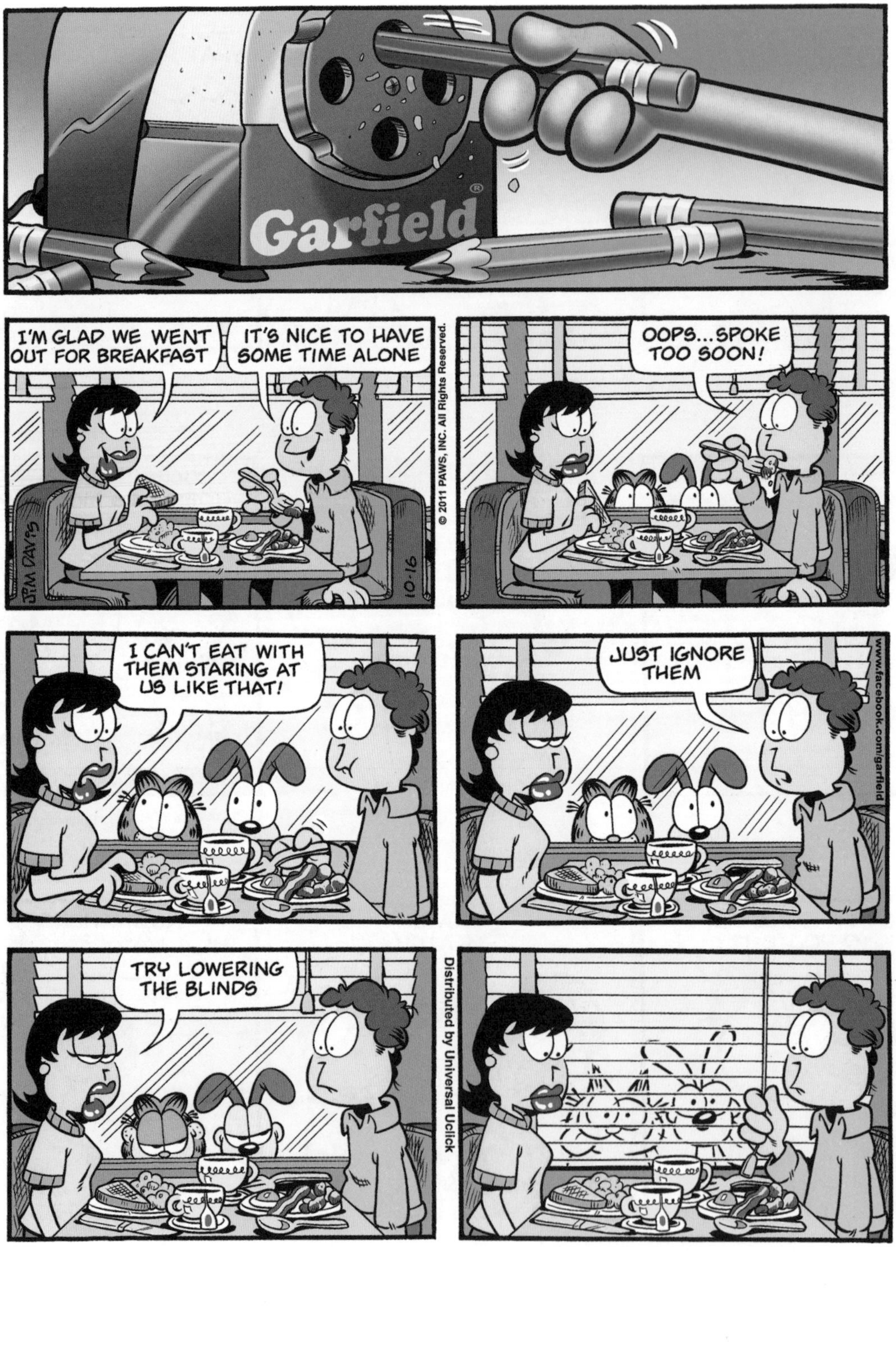
Garfield
I'M GLAD WE WENT OUT FOR BREAKFAST
IT'S NICE TO HAVE SOME TIME ALONE
JIM DAVIS
10-16
© 2011 PAWS, INC. All Rights Reserved.
OOPS...SPOKE TOO SOON!
I CAN'T EAT WITH THEM STARING AT US LIKE THAT!
JUST IGNORE THEM
www.facebook.com/garfield
TRY LOWERING THE BLINDS
Distributed by Universal Uclick

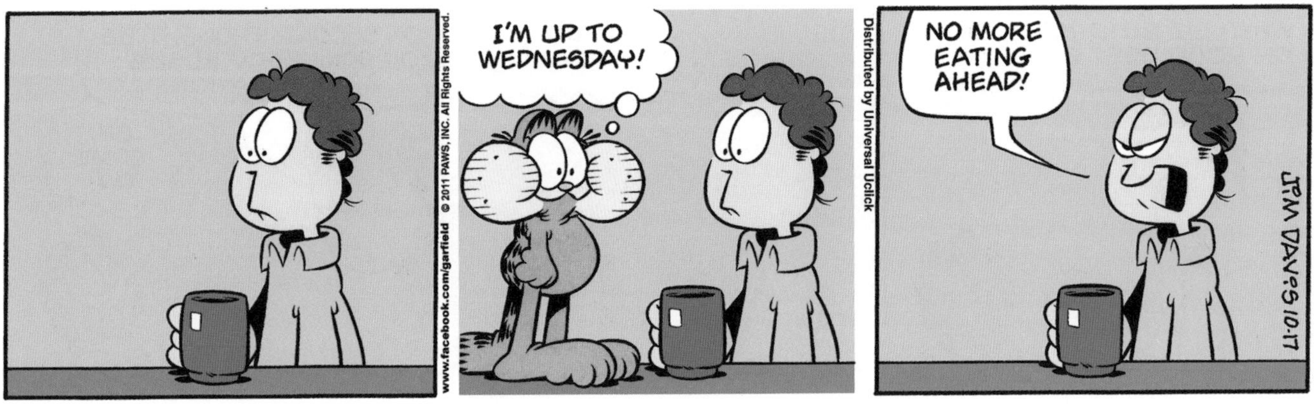
www.facebook.com/garfield © 2011 PAWS, INC. All Rights Reserved.
I'M UP TO WEDNESDAY!
Distributed by Universal Uclick
NO MORE EATING AHEAD!
JIM DAVIS 10-17

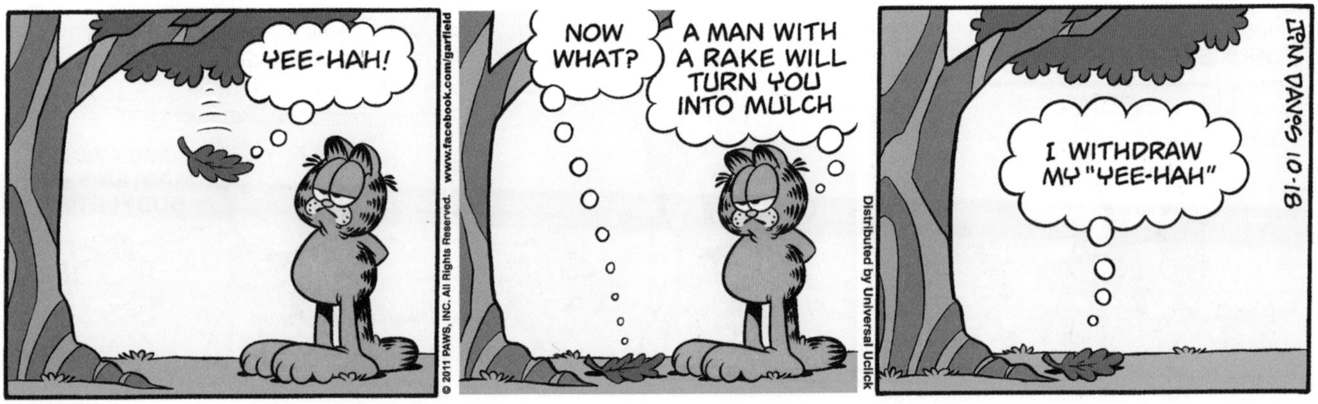
YEE-HAH!
© 2011 PAWS, INC. All Rights Reserved. www.facebook.com/garfield
NOW WHAT?
A MAN WITH A RAKE WILL TURN YOU INTO MULCH
Distributed by Universal Uclick
I WITHDRAW MY "YEE-HAH"
JIM DAVIS 10-18

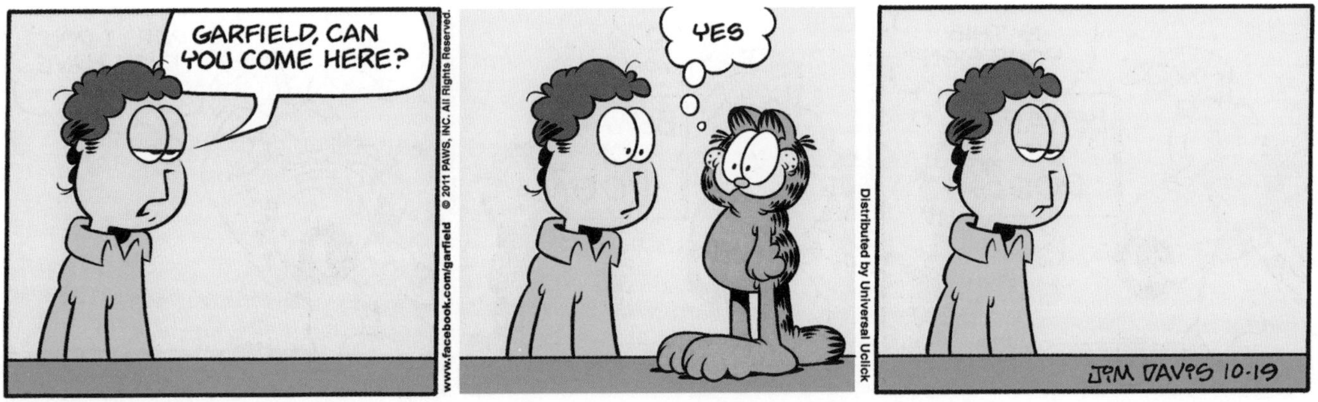
GARFIELD, CAN YOU COME HERE?
www.facebook.com/garfield © 2011 PAWS, INC. All Rights Reserved.
YES
Distributed by Universal Uclick
JIM DAVIS 10-19

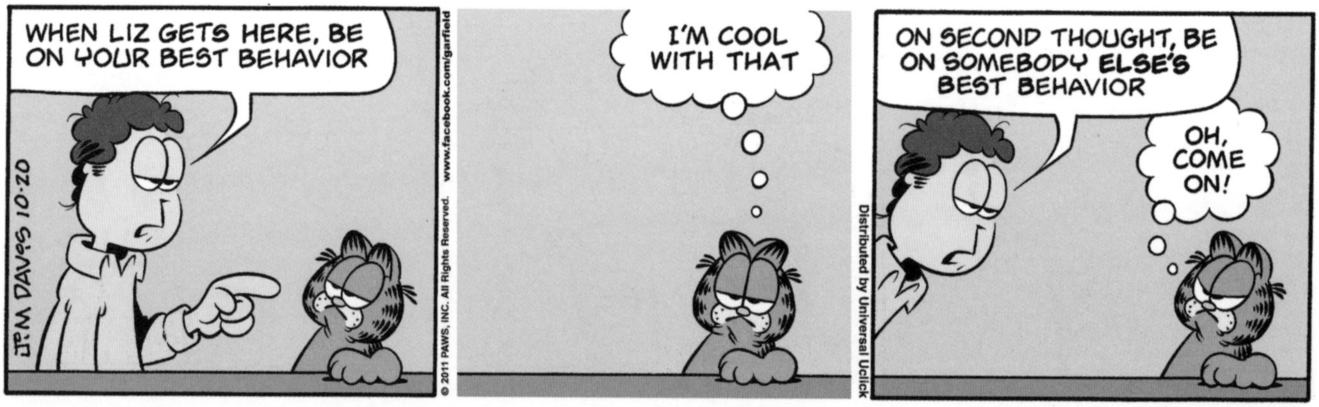
WHEN LIZ GETS HERE, BE ON YOUR BEST BEHAVIOR
JIM DAVIS 10-20
© 2011 PAWS, INC. All Rights Reserved. www.facebook.com/garfield
I'M COOL WITH THAT
Distributed by Universal Uclick
ON SECOND THOUGHT, BE ON SOMEBODY ELSE'S BEST BEHAVIOR
OH, COME ON!

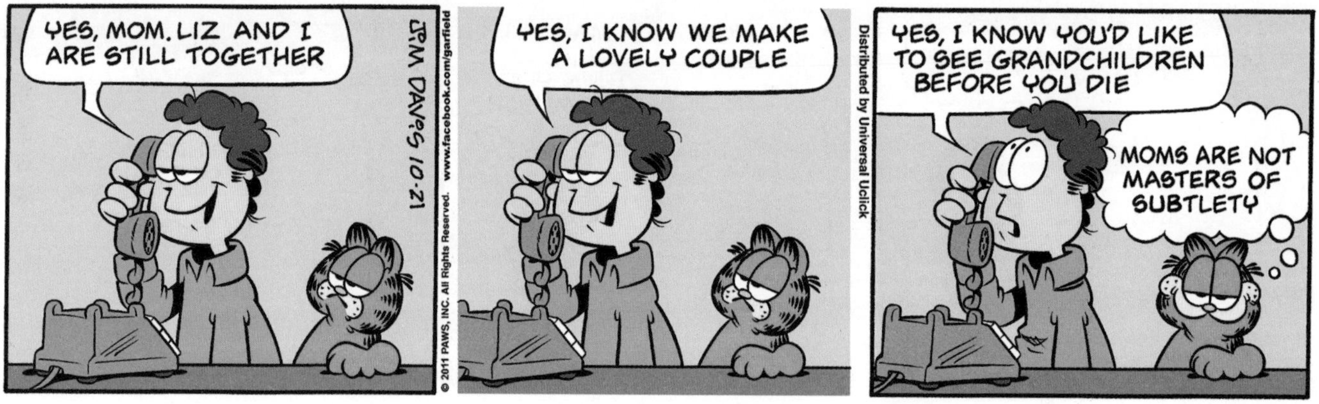
YES, MOM. LIZ AND I ARE STILL TOGETHER
JIM DAVIS 10-21
© 2011 PAWS, INC. All Rights Reserved. www.facebook.com/garfield
YES, I KNOW WE MAKE A LOVELY COUPLE
Distributed by Universal Uclick
YES, I KNOW YOU'D LIKE TO SEE GRANDCHILDREN BEFORE YOU DIE
MOMS ARE NOT MASTERS OF SUBTLETY

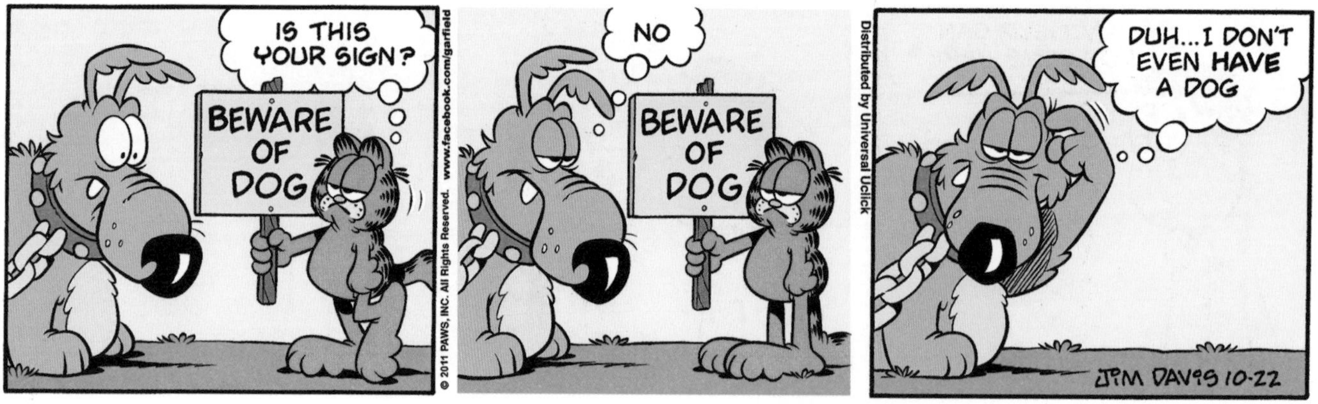
IS THIS YOUR SIGN?
BEWARE OF DOG
© 2011 PAWS, INC. All Rights Reserved. www.facebook.com/garfield
NO
BEWARE OF DOG
Distributed by Universal Uclick
DUH...I DON'T EVEN HAVE A DOG
JIM DAVIS 10-22

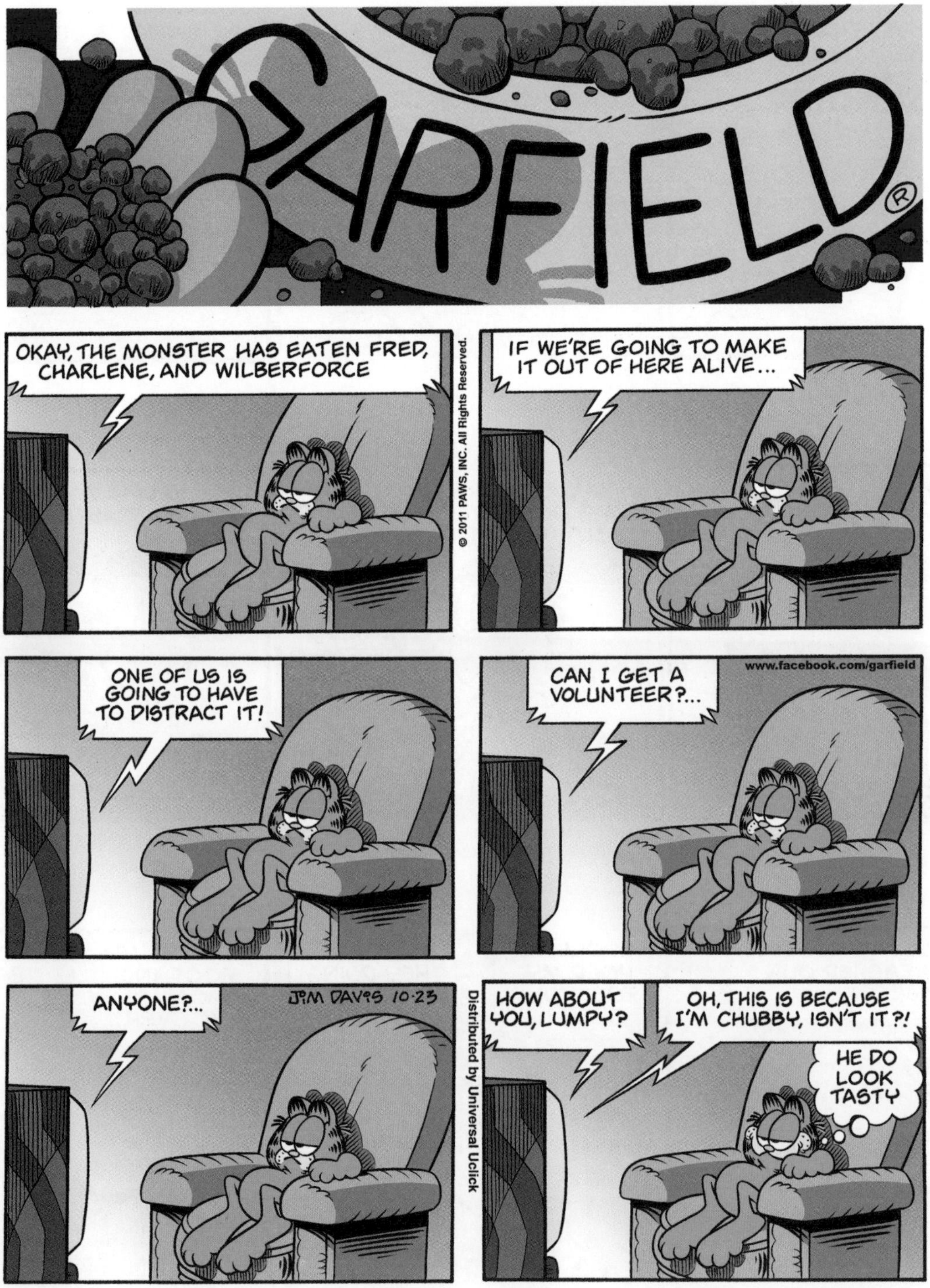
GARFIELD®
OKAY, THE MONSTER HAS EATEN FRED, CHARLENE, AND WILBERFORCE
© 2011 PAWS, INC. All Rights Reserved.
IF WE'RE GOING TO MAKE IT OUT OF HERE ALIVE...
ONE OF US IS GOING TO HAVE TO DISTRACT IT!
www.facebook.com/garfield
CAN I GET A VOLUNTEER?...
ANYONE?...
JIM DAVIS 10-23
Distributed by Universal Uclick
HOW ABOUT YOU, LUMPY?
OH, THIS IS BECAUSE I'M CHUBBY, ISN'T IT?!
HE DO LOOK TASTY

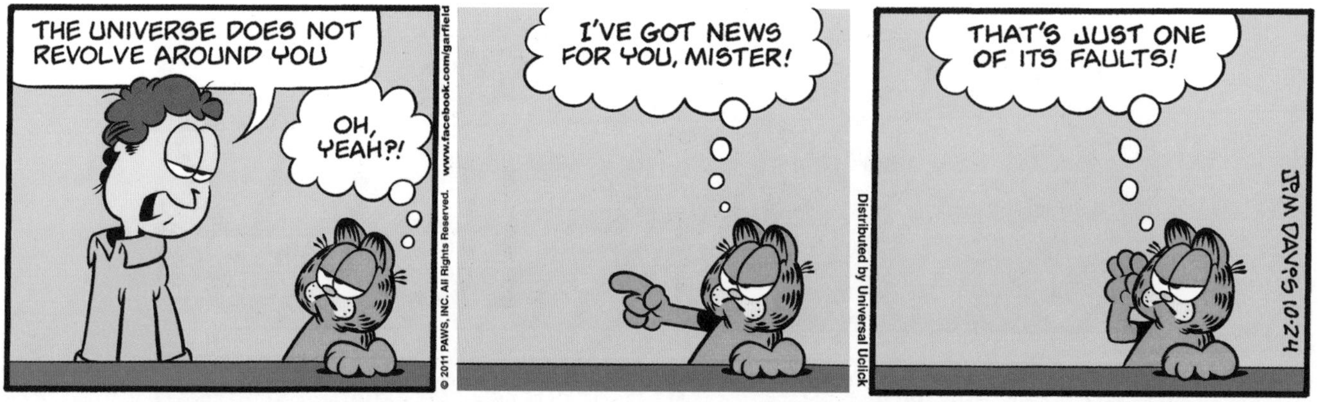
THE UNIVERSE DOES NOT REVOLVE AROUND YOU
OH, YEAH?!
I'VE GOT NEWS FOR YOU, MISTER!
THAT'S JUST ONE OF ITS FAULTS!
© 2011 PAWS, INC. All Rights Reserved. www.facebook.com/garfield
Distributed by Universal Uclick
JIM DAVIS 10-24

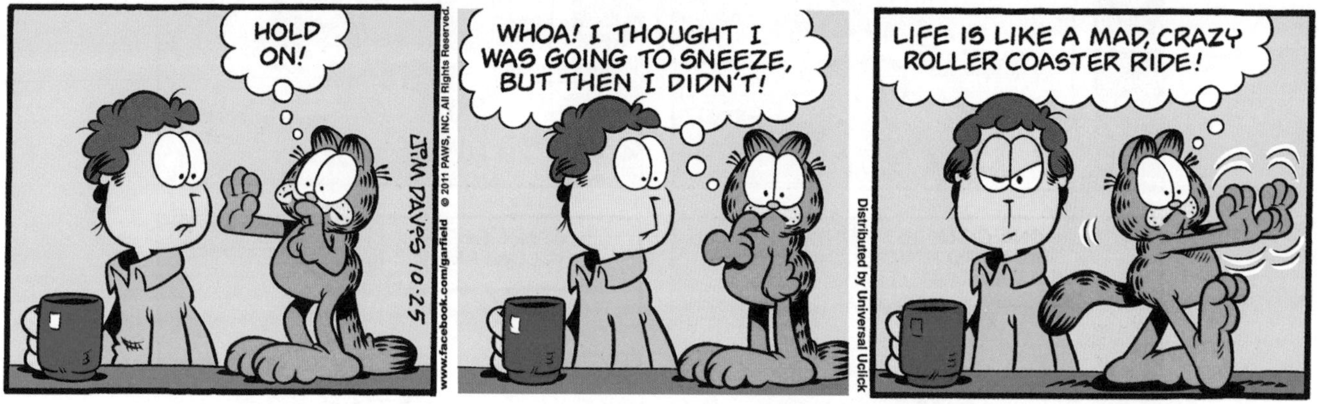
HOLD ON!
WHOA! I THOUGHT I WAS GOING TO SNEEZE, BUT THEN I DIDN'T!
LIFE IS LIKE A MAD, CRAZY ROLLER COASTER RIDE!
JIM DAVIS 10-25
www.facebook.com/garfield © 2011 PAWS, INC. All Rights Reserved.
Distributed by Universal Uclick

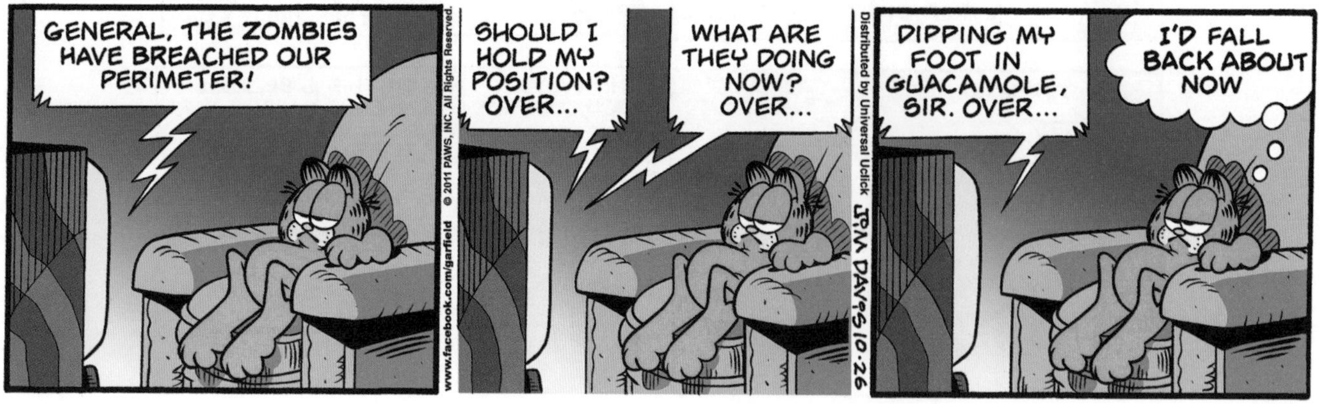
GENERAL, THE ZOMBIES HAVE BREACHED OUR PERIMETER!
SHOULD I HOLD MY POSITION? OVER...
WHAT ARE THEY DOING NOW? OVER...
DIPPING MY FOOT IN GUACAMOLE, SIR. OVER...
I'D FALL BACK ABOUT NOW
www.facebook.com/garfield © 2011 PAWS, INC. All Rights Reserved.
Distributed by Universal Uclick
JIM DAVIS 10-26

THE MONSTER IS COMING THIS WAY!

HA! LOOK HOW SLOW IT IS!

MY **GRANDMOTHER** COULD OUTRUN THAT MON—

EEEEK!

UM... CHECK THAT

MAW-MAW WENT WITH HER TRACK SHOES ON

JIM DAVIS 10-27

MR. MAYOR! A GIANT CHEESY FAKE RUBBER SPIDER IS INVADING THE CITY!

YOU CAN SEE THE WIRES AND EVERYTHING!

THEN CALL OUT THE TINY TOY TANKS!

PARDON ME, BUT YOUR BUDGET IS SHOWING

JIM DAVIS 10-28

GENERAL, THERE'S A GIANT MUTANT 98-YEAR-OLD LADY APPROACHING ON RADAR!

HOW BAD CAN THAT BE?

BAD, SIR

SHE'S DRIVING A 32-STORY 1965 BONNEVILLE!

WITH A 16-FOOT BLINKING LEFT TURN SIGNAL

JIM DAVIS 10-29

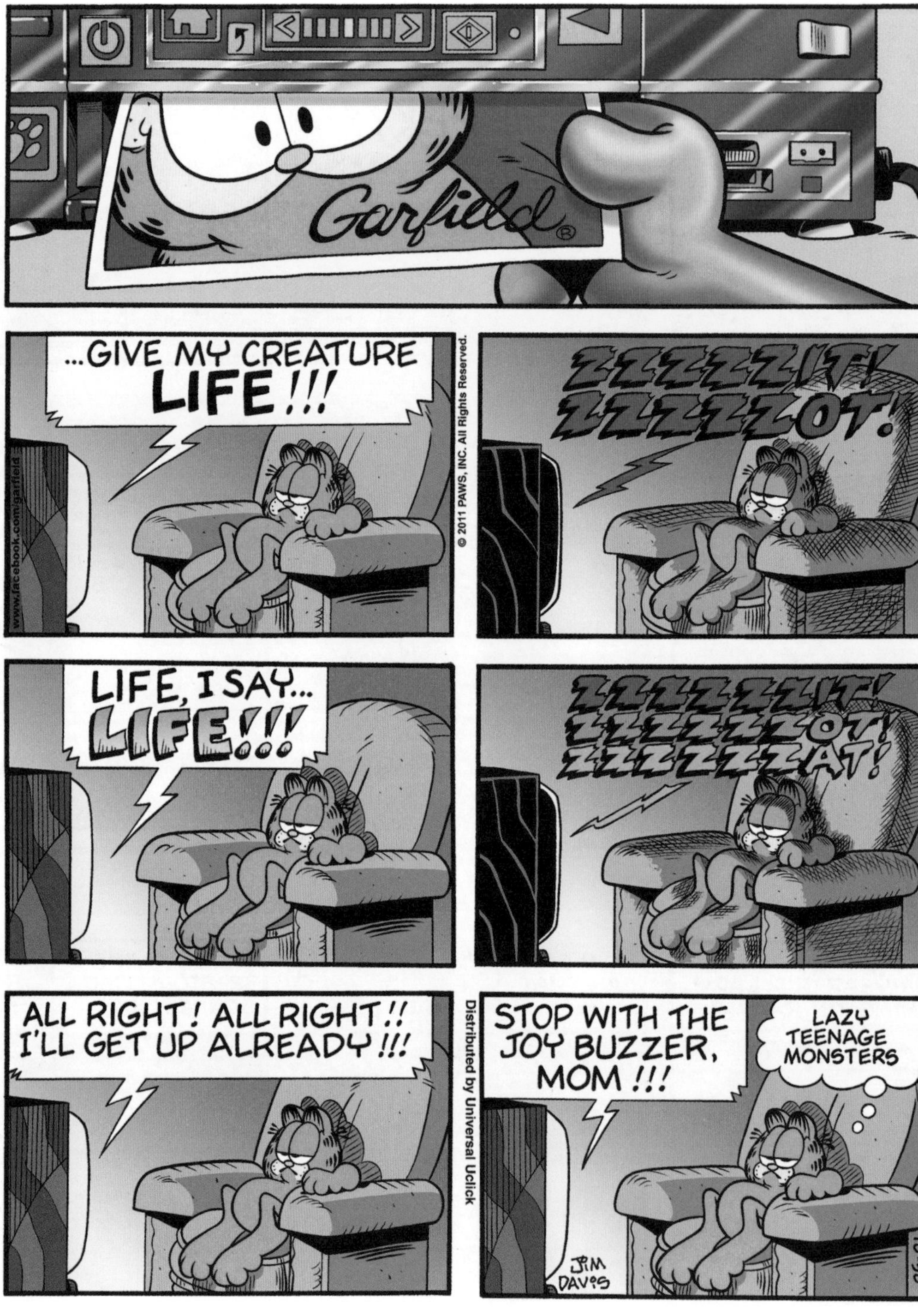

Garfield®
www.facebook.com/garfield
...GIVE MY CREATURE LIFE!!!
© 2011 PAWS, INC. All Rights Reserved.
ZZZZZZZIT! ZZZZZZZOT!
LIFE, I SAY... LIFE!!!
ZZZZZZZZIT! ZZZZZZZZOT! ZZZZZZZZAT!
ALL RIGHT! ALL RIGHT!! I'LL GET UP ALREADY!!!
Distributed by Universal Uclick
STOP WITH THE JOY BUZZER, MOM!!!
LAZY TEENAGE MONSTERS
JIM DAVIS
10-30

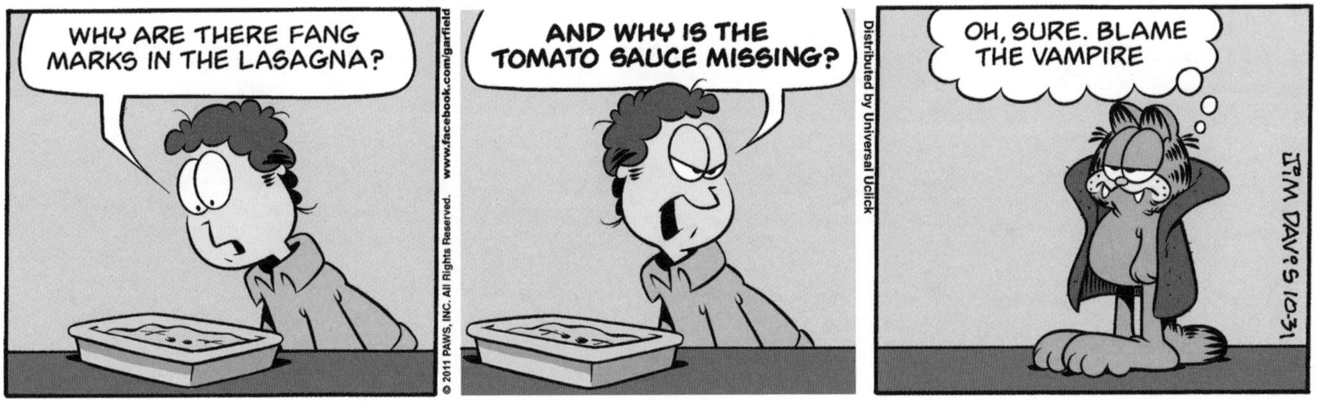
WHY ARE THERE FANG MARKS IN THE LASAGNA?
© 2011 PAWS, INC. All Rights Reserved. www.facebook.com/garfield
AND WHY IS THE TOMATO SAUCE MISSING?
Distributed by Universal Uclick
OH, SURE. BLAME THE VAMPIRE
JIM DAVIS 10-31

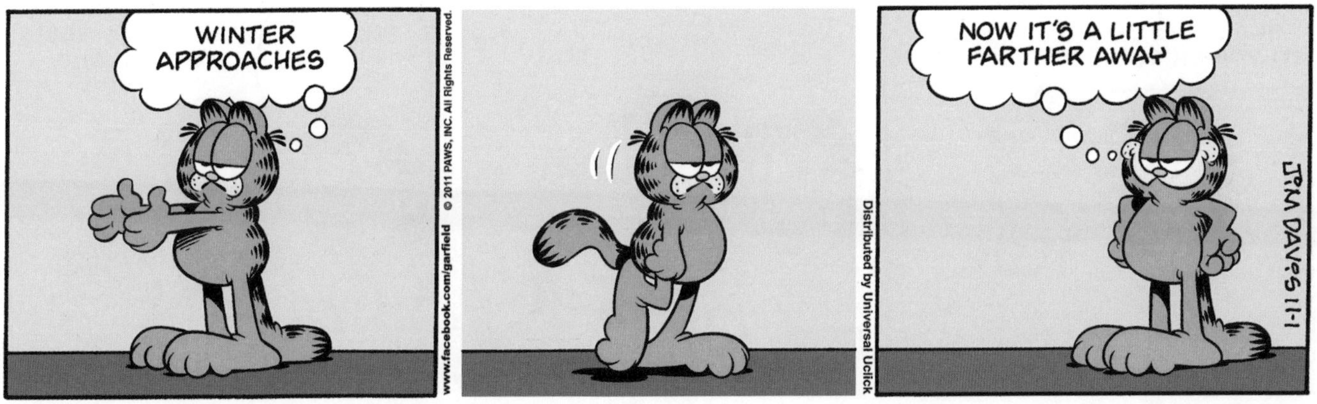
WINTER APPROACHES
www.facebook.com/garfield © 2011 PAWS, INC. All Rights Reserved.
Distributed by Universal Uclick
NOW IT'S A LITTLE FARTHER AWAY
JIM DAVIS 11-1

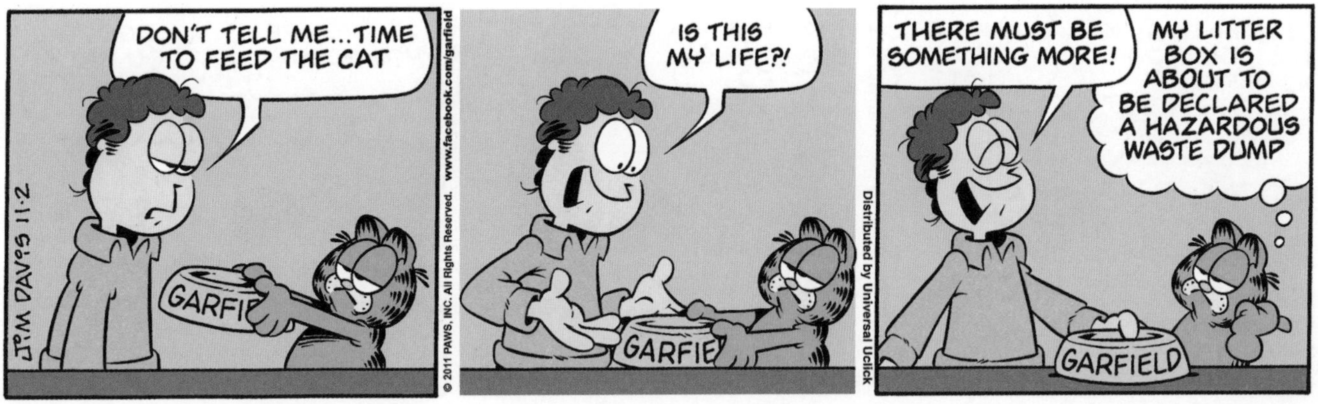
DON'T TELL ME...TIME TO FEED THE CAT
JIM DAVIS 11-2
GARFIE
© 2011 PAWS, INC. All Rights Reserved. www.facebook.com/garfield
IS THIS MY LIFE?!
GARFIE
Distributed by Universal Uclick
THERE MUST BE SOMETHING MORE!
MY LITTER BOX IS ABOUT TO BE DECLARED A HAZARDOUS WASTE DUMP
GARFIELD

SO, HOW'D YOU GET SO **FAT**?
EATING CHUBBY MICE
LET ME REPHRASE THAT
JIM DAVIS 11-3
© 2011 PAWS, INC. All Rights Reserved. www.facebook.com/garfield
Distributed by Universal Uclick

SHALL WE GO OUT TO DINNER TONIGHT?
OKAY!
SHE WAS TALKING TO ME!
VERY WELL, YOU MAY DRIVE
JIM DAVIS 11-4
© 2011 PAWS, INC. All Rights Reserved. www.facebook.com/garfield
Distributed by Universal Uclick

I'LL BE HOWLING AT THE MOON TONIGHT!
WHY DO YOU DO THAT?
OH, IT'S SOMETHING TO DO
THAT'S SILLY
WHERE ARE YOU GOING?
I GOTTA GO BAT A BALL OF YARN
JIM DAVIS 11-5
© 2011 PAWS, INC. All Rights Reserved. www.facebook.com/garfield
Distributed by Universal Uclick

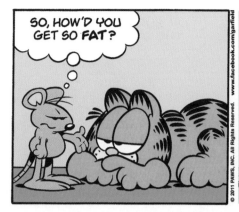

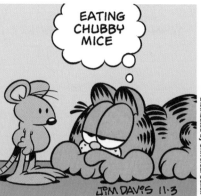

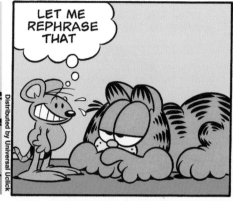

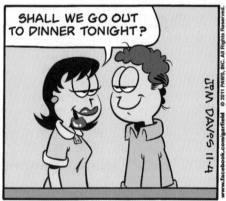

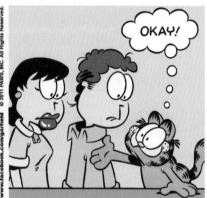

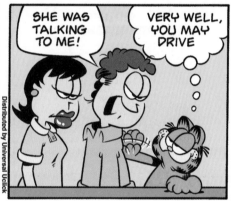

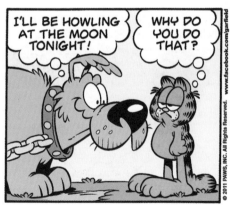

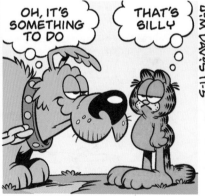

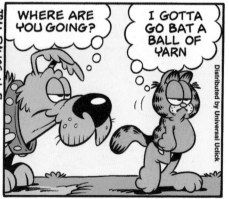

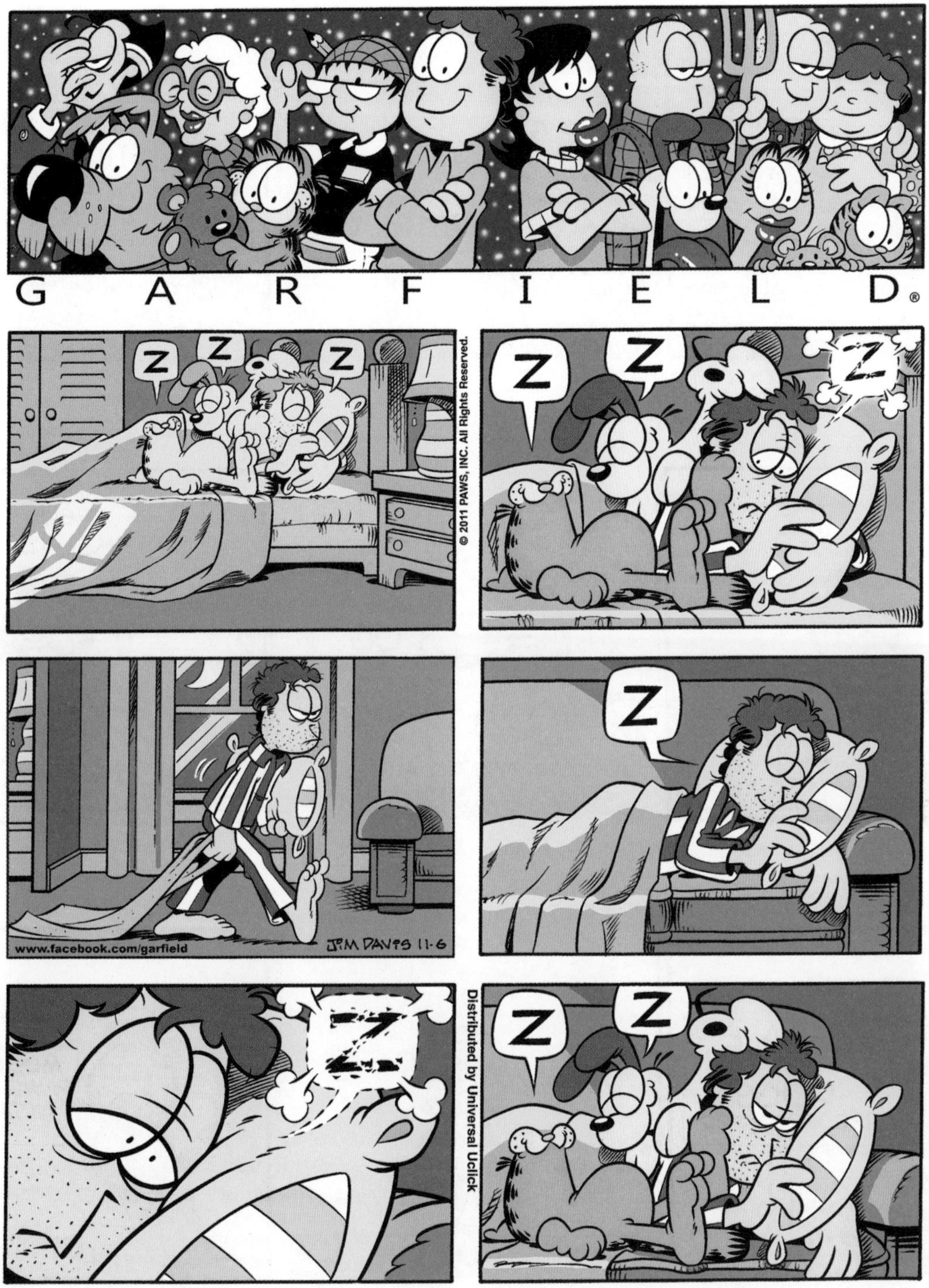
G A R F I E L D®
Z
Z
Z
Z
Z
Z
© 2011 PAWS, INC. All Rights Reserved.
www.facebook.com/garfield
JIM DAVIS 11-6
Z
Z
Distributed by Universal Uclick
Z
Z

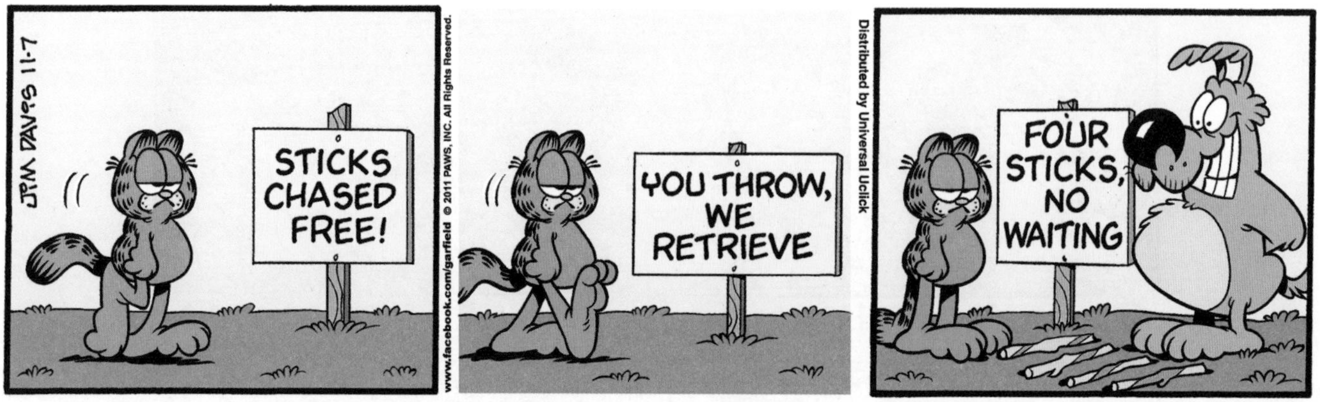
JIM DAVIS 11-7
STICKS CHASED FREE!
www.facebook.com/garfield © 2011 PAWS, INC. All Rights Reserved.
YOU THROW, WE RETRIEVE
Distributed by Universal Uclick
FOUR STICKS, NO WAITING

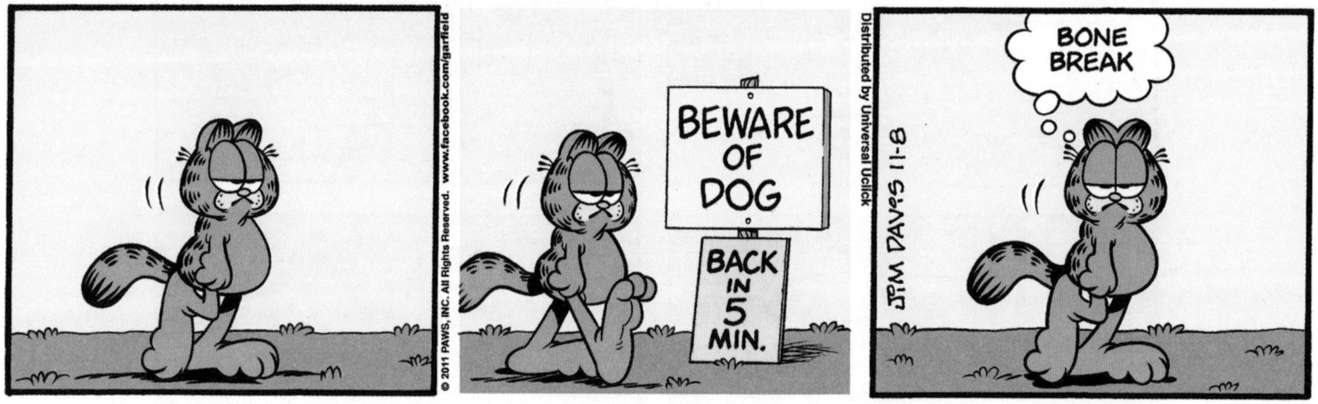
© 2011 PAWS, INC. All Rights Reserved. www.facebook.com/garfield
BEWARE OF DOG
BACK IN 5 MIN.
Distributed by Universal Uclick
JIM DAVIS 11-8
BONE BREAK

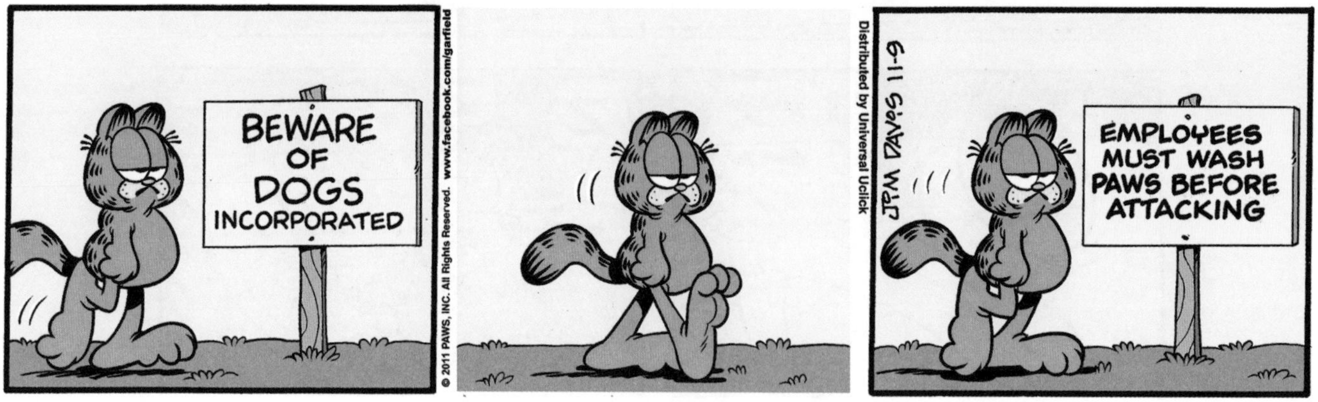
BEWARE OF DOGS INCORPORATED
© 2011 PAWS, INC. All Rights Reserved. www.facebook.com/garfield
Distributed by Universal Uclick
JIM DAVIS 11-9
EMPLOYEES MUST WASH PAWS BEFORE ATTACKING

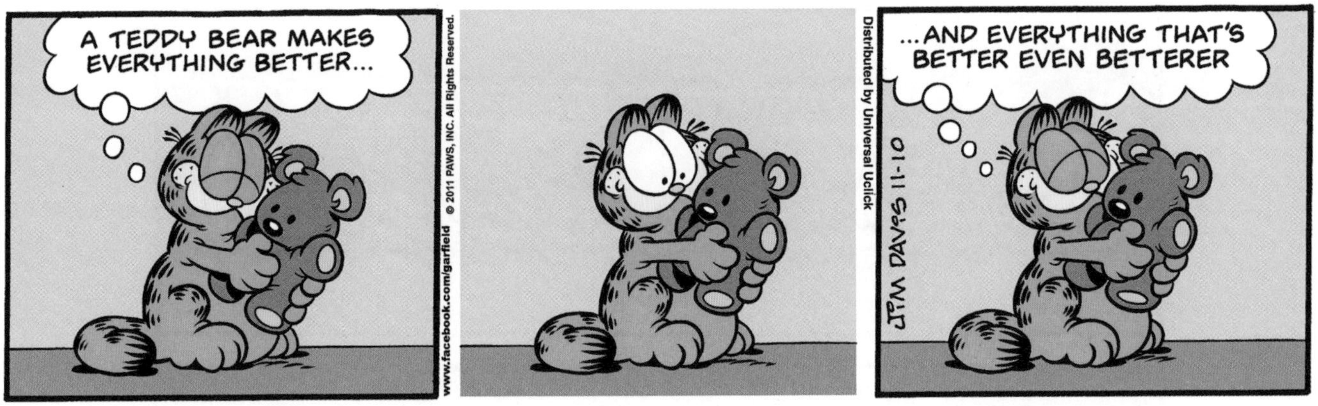
A TEDDY BEAR MAKES EVERYTHING BETTER...
www.facebook.com/garfield © 2011 PAWS, INC. All Rights Reserved.
Distributed by Universal Uclick
...AND EVERYTHING THAT'S BETTER EVEN BETTERER
JIM DAVIS 11-10

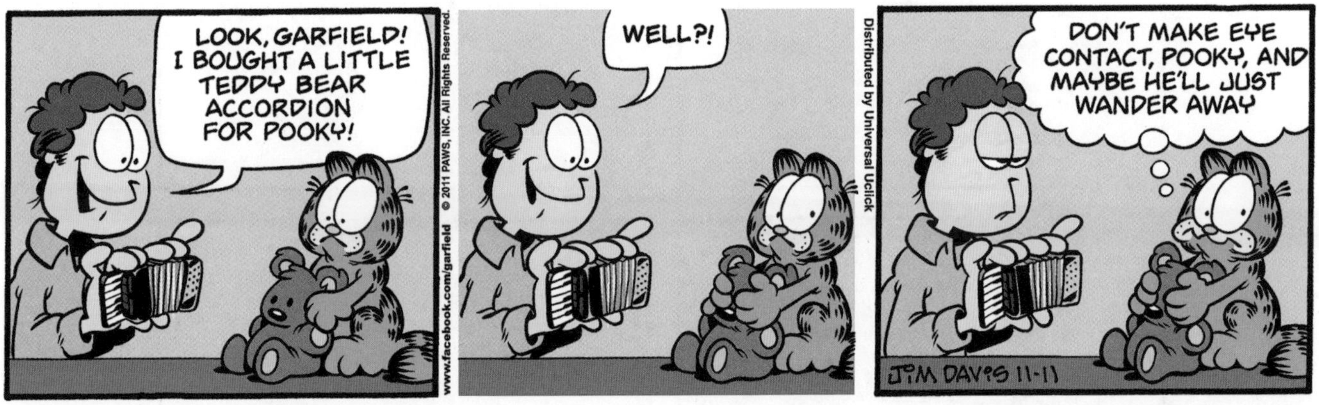
LOOK, GARFIELD! I BOUGHT A LITTLE TEDDY BEAR ACCORDION FOR POOKY!
www.facebook.com/garfield © 2011 PAWS, INC. All Rights Reserved.
WELL?!
Distributed by Universal Uclick
DON'T MAKE EYE CONTACT, POOKY, AND MAYBE HE'LL JUST WANDER AWAY
JIM DAVIS 11-11

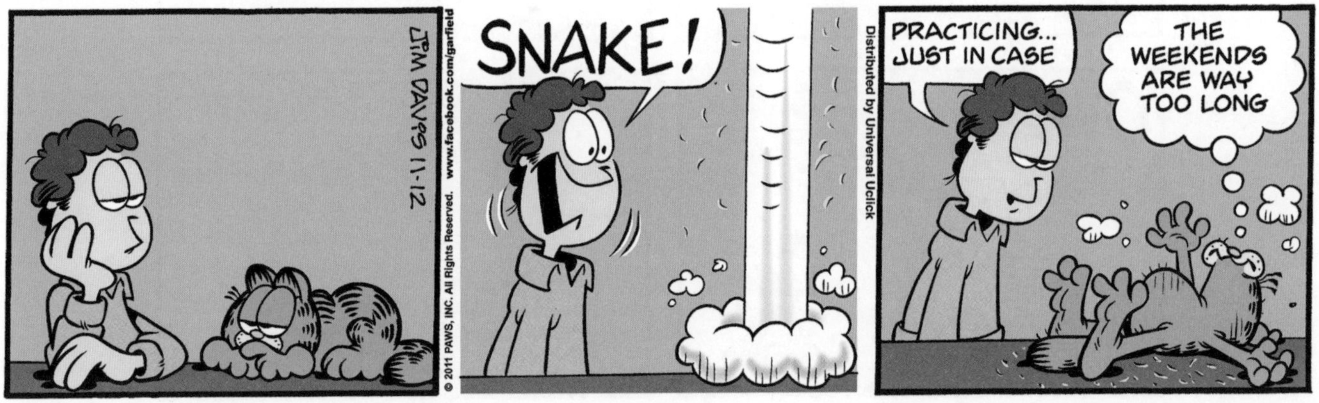
JIM DAVIS 11-12
© 2011 PAWS, INC. All Rights Reserved. www.facebook.com/garfield
SNAKE!
Distributed by Universal Uclick
PRACTICING... JUST IN CASE
THE WEEKENDS ARE WAY TOO LONG

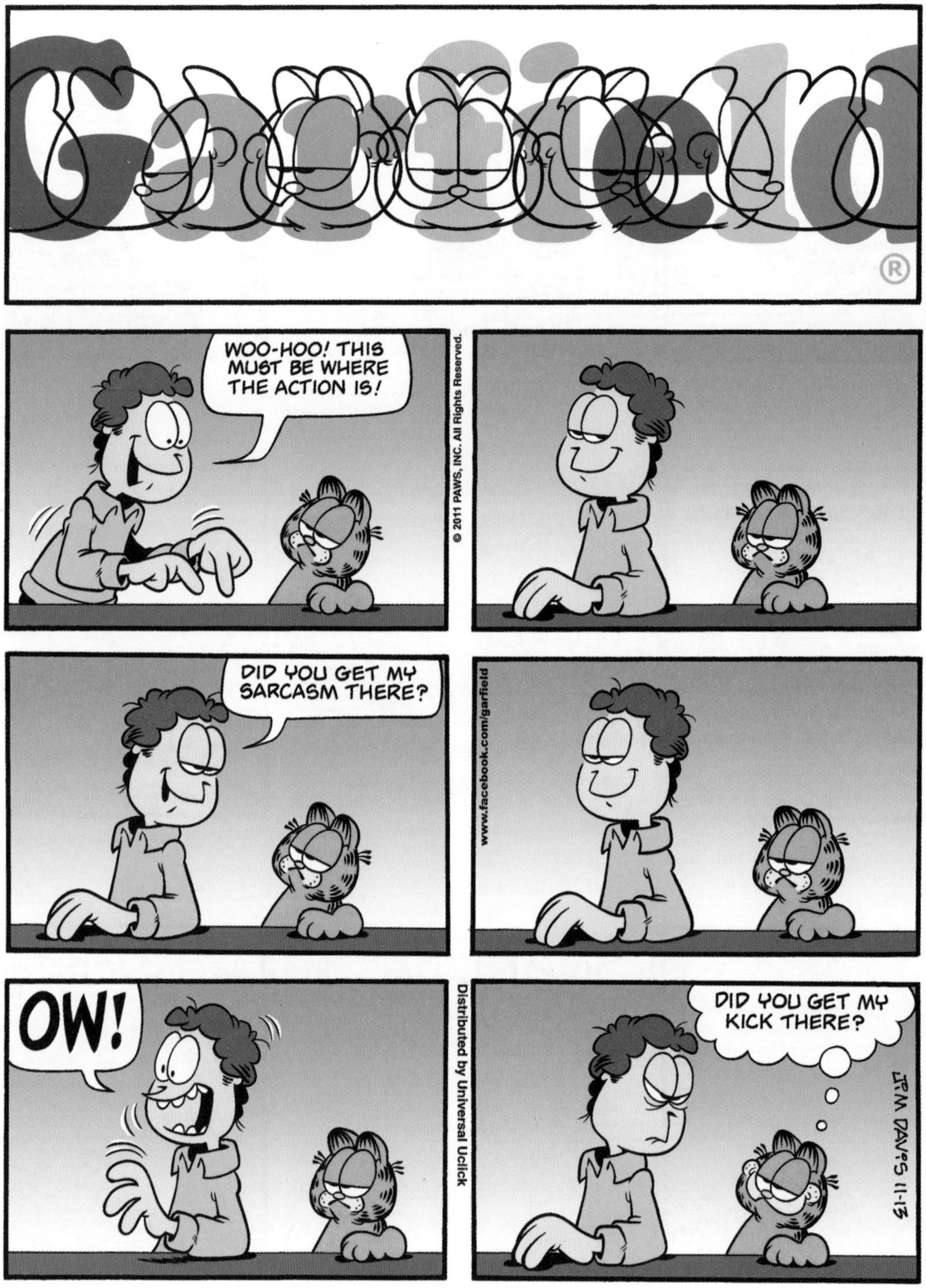
Garfield®
WOO-HOO! THIS MUST BE WHERE THE ACTION IS!
© 2011 PAWS, INC. All Rights Reserved.
DID YOU GET MY SARCASM THERE?
www.facebook.com/garfield
OW!
Distributed by Universal Uclick
DID YOU GET MY KICK THERE?
JIM DAVIS 11-13

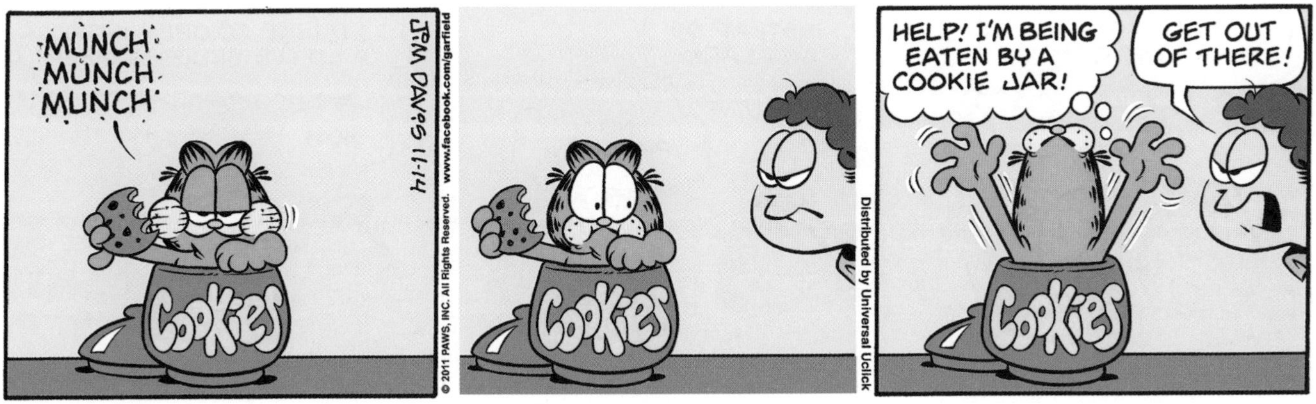
MUNCH MUNCH MUNCH
JIM DAVIS 11-14
© 2011 PAWS, INC. All Rights Reserved. www.facebook.com/garfield
Distributed by Universal Uclick
HELP! I'M BEING EATEN BY A COOKIE JAR!
GET OUT OF THERE!

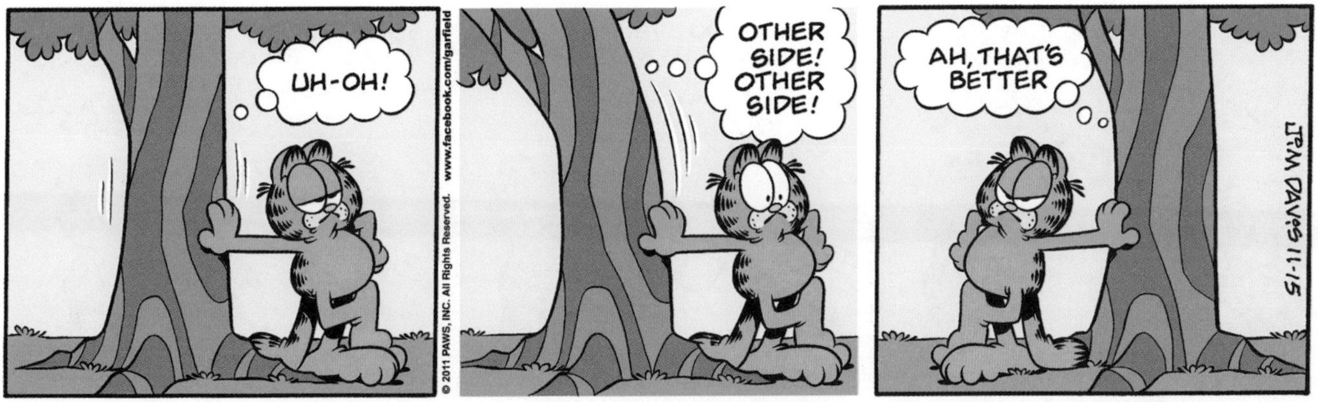
UH-OH!
© 2011 PAWS, INC. All Rights Reserved. www.facebook.com/garfield
OTHER SIDE! OTHER SIDE!
AH, THAT'S BETTER
JIM DAVIS 11-15

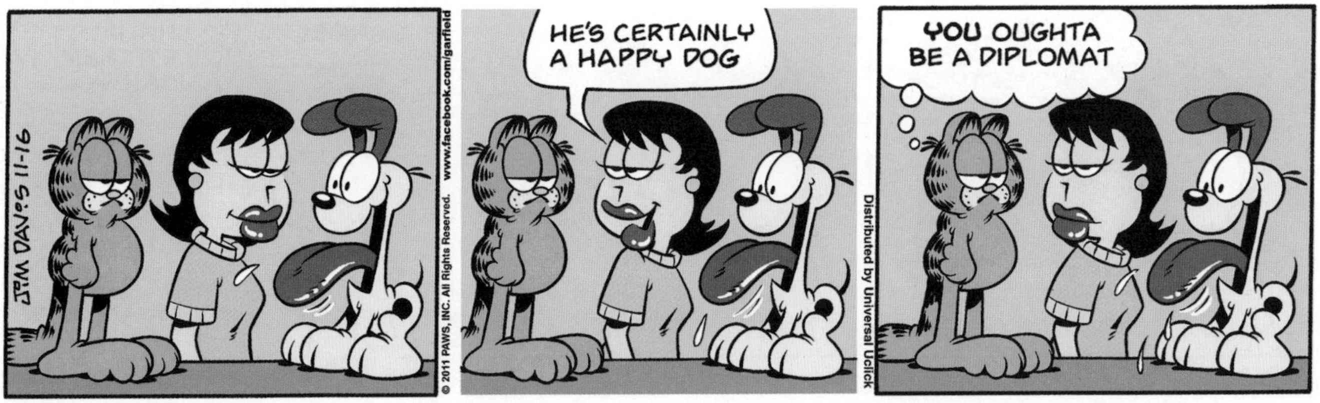
JIM DAVIS 11-16
© 2011 PAWS, INC. All Rights Reserved. www.facebook.com/garfield
HE'S CERTAINLY A HAPPY DOG
Distributed by Universal Uclick
YOU OUGHTA BE A DIPLOMAT

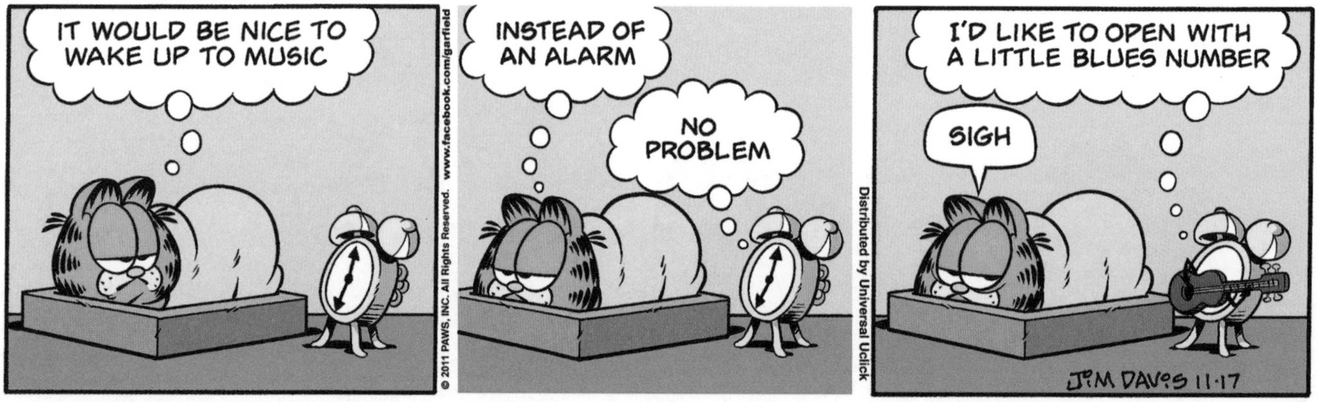
IT WOULD BE NICE TO WAKE UP TO MUSIC
© 2011 PAWS, INC. All Rights Reserved. www.facebook.com/garfield
INSTEAD OF AN ALARM
NO PROBLEM
Distributed by Universal Uclick
I'D LIKE TO OPEN WITH A LITTLE BLUES NUMBER
SIGH
JIM DAVIS 11-17

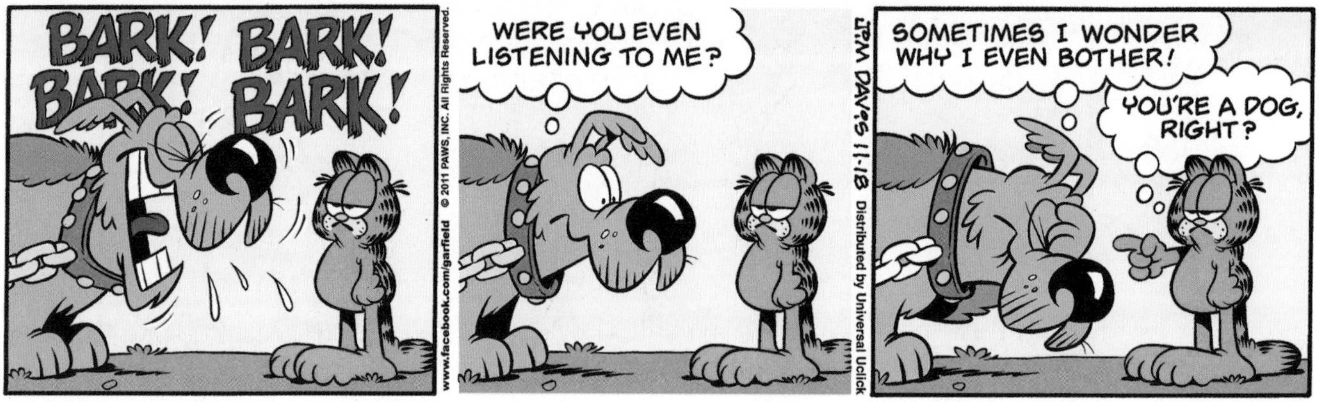
BARK! BARK! BARK! BARK!
© 2011 PAWS, INC. All Rights Reserved. www.facebook.com/garfield
WERE YOU EVEN LISTENING TO ME?
JIM DAVIS 11-18 Distributed by Universal Uclick
SOMETIMES I WONDER WHY I EVEN BOTHER!
YOU'RE A DOG, RIGHT?

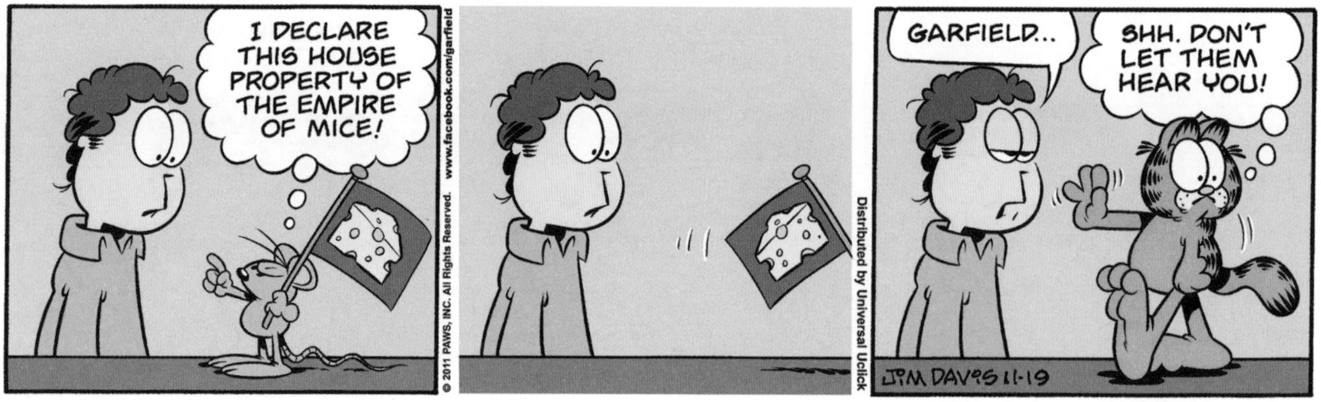
I DECLARE THIS HOUSE PROPERTY OF THE EMPIRE OF MICE!
© 2011 PAWS, INC. All Rights Reserved. www.facebook.com/garfield
Distributed by Universal Uclick
GARFIELD...
SHH. DON'T LET THEM HEAR YOU!
JIM DAVIS 11-19

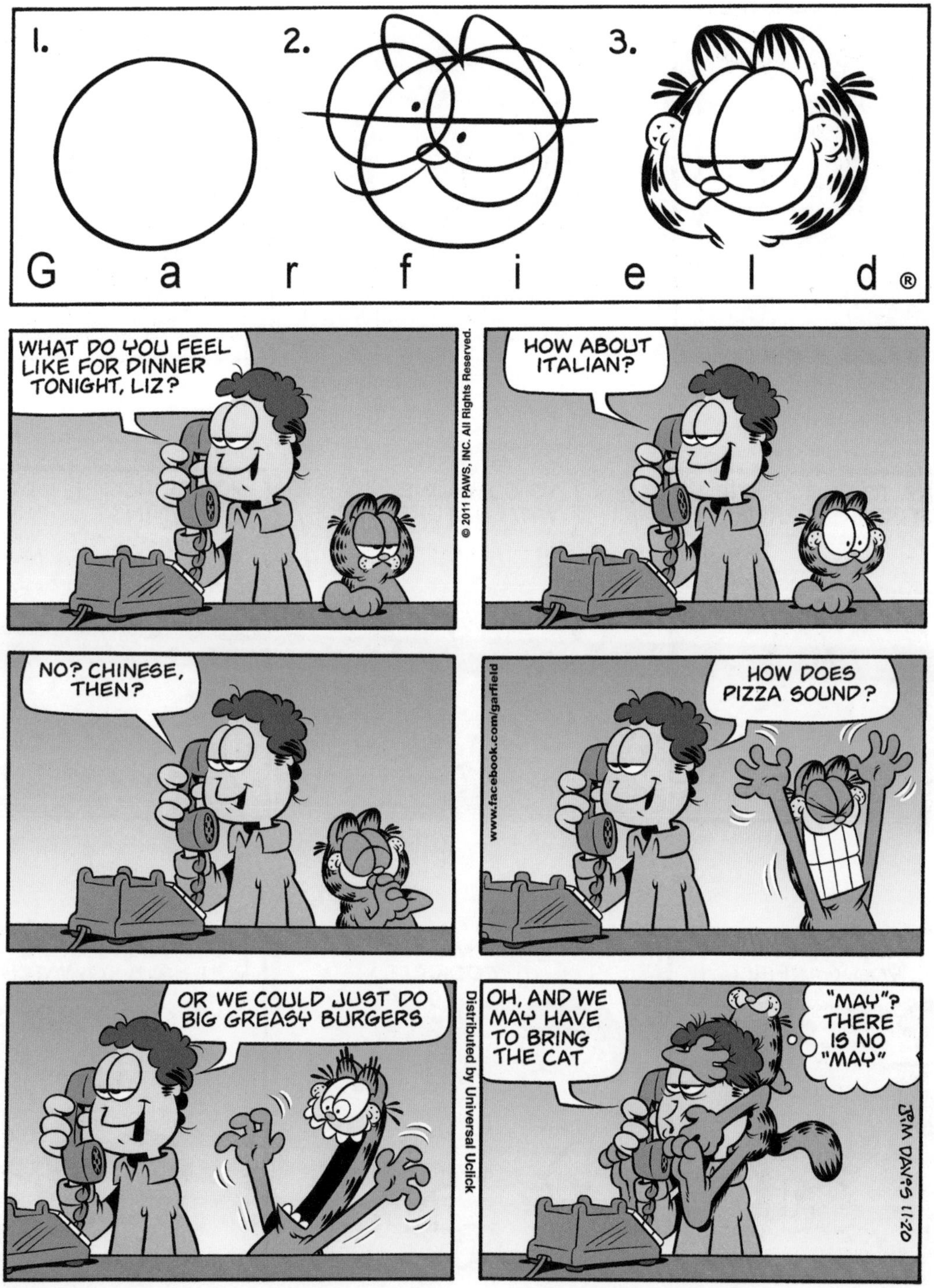
1.
2.
3.
Garfield®
WHAT DO YOU FEEL LIKE FOR DINNER TONIGHT, LIZ?
© 2011 PAWS, INC. All Rights Reserved.
HOW ABOUT ITALIAN?
NO? CHINESE, THEN?
www.facebook.com/garfield
HOW DOES PIZZA SOUND?
OR WE COULD JUST DO BIG GREASY BURGERS
Distributed by Universal Uclick
OH, AND WE MAY HAVE TO BRING THE CAT
"MAY"? THERE IS NO "MAY"
JIM DAVIS 11-20

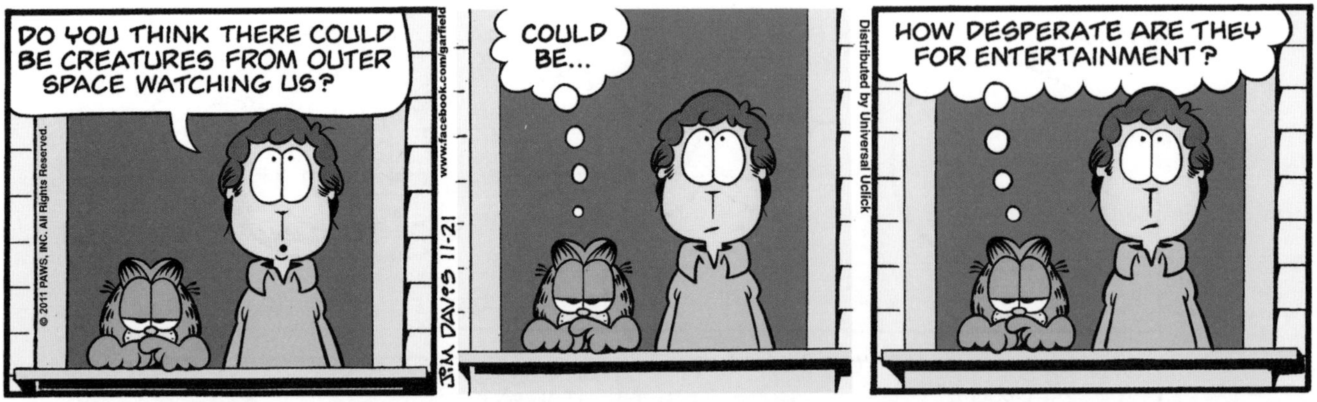
DO YOU THINK THERE COULD BE CREATURES FROM OUTER SPACE WATCHING US?
COULD BE...
HOW DESPERATE ARE THEY FOR ENTERTAINMENT?

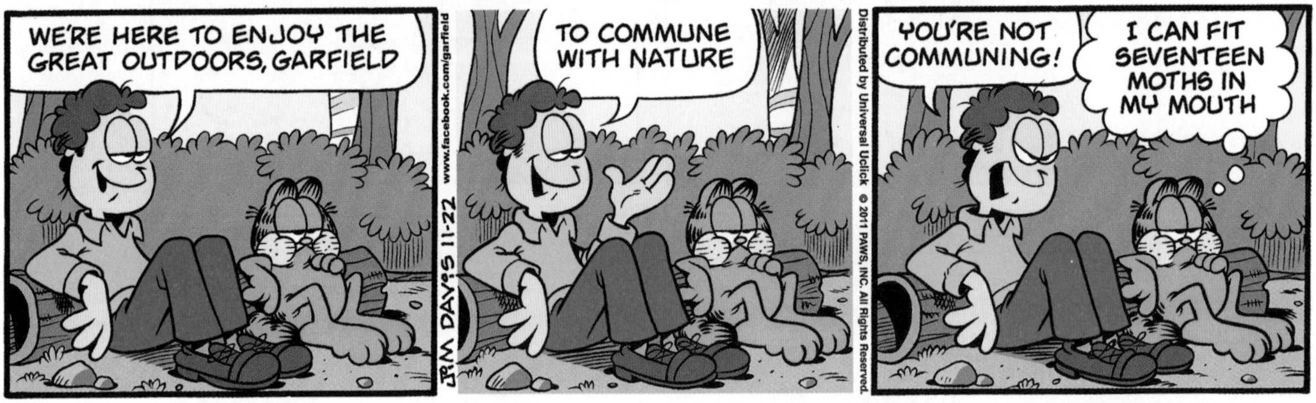
WE'RE HERE TO ENJOY THE GREAT OUTDOORS, GARFIELD
TO COMMUNE WITH NATURE
YOU'RE NOT COMMUNING!
I CAN FIT SEVENTEEN MOTHS IN MY MOUTH

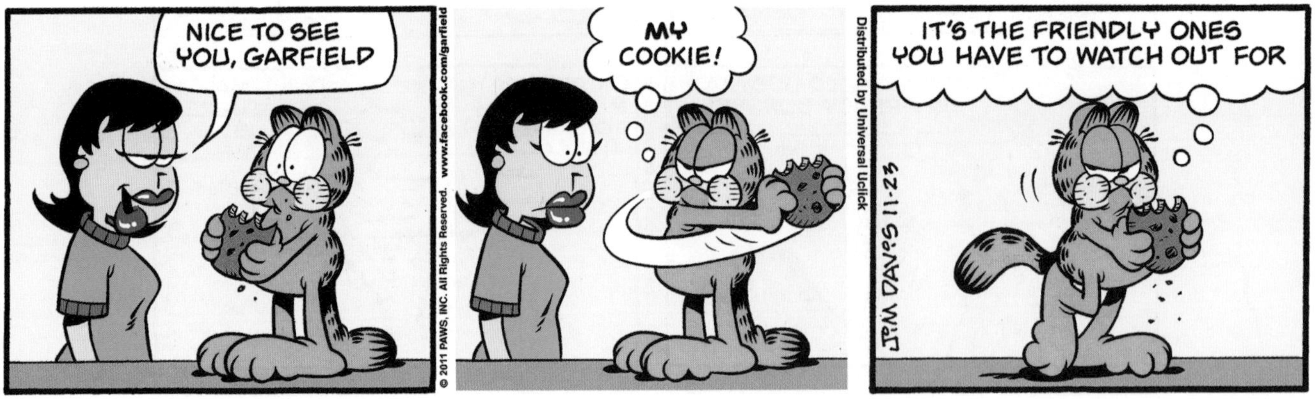
NICE TO SEE YOU, GARFIELD
MY COOKIE!
IT'S THE FRIENDLY ONES YOU HAVE TO WATCH OUT FOR

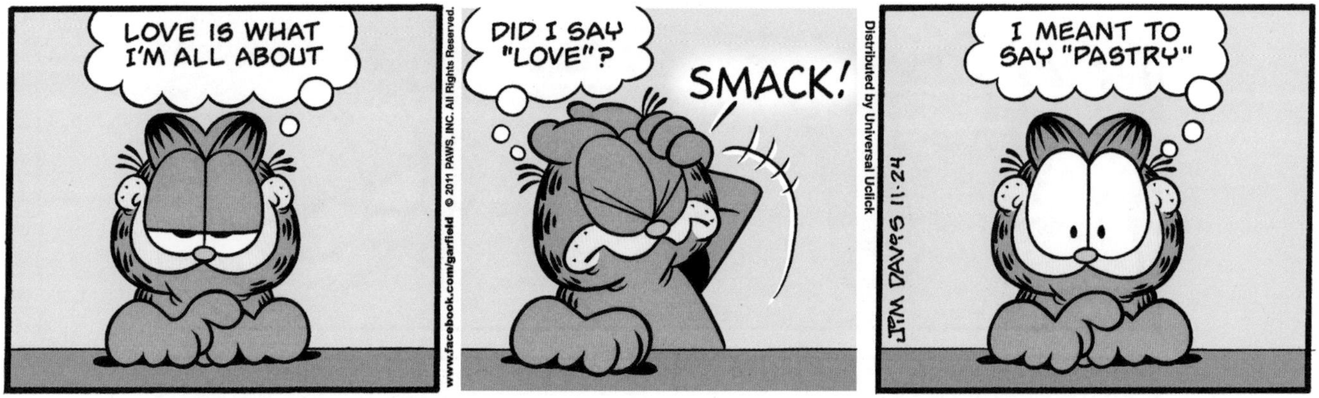
LOVE IS WHAT I'M ALL ABOUT
www.facebook.com/garfield © 2011 PAWS, INC. All Rights Reserved.
DID I SAY "LOVE"?
SMACK!
Distributed by Universal Uclick
JIM DAVIS 11-24
I MEANT TO SAY "PASTRY"

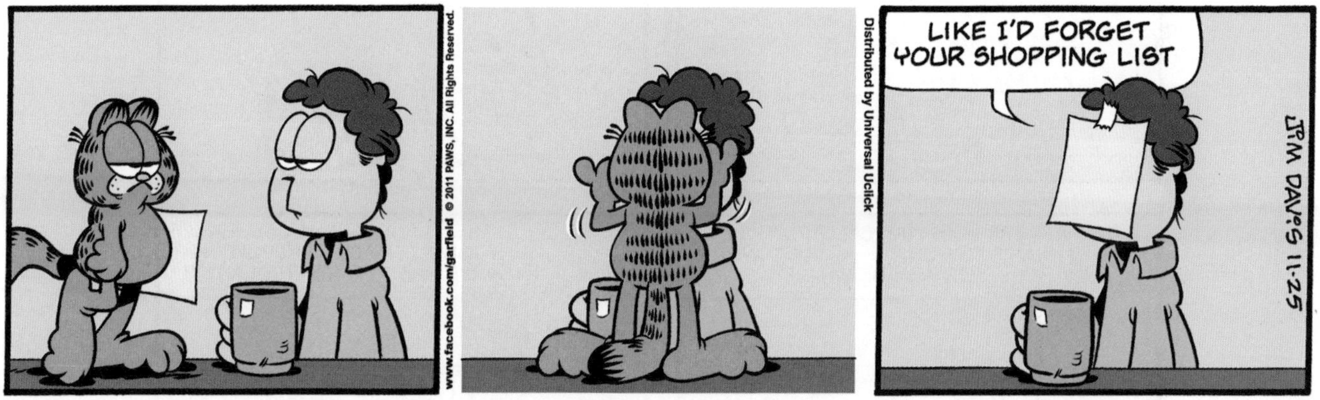
www.facebook.com/garfield © 2011 PAWS, INC. All Rights Reserved.
Distributed by Universal Uclick
LIKE I'D FORGET YOUR SHOPPING LIST
JIM DAVIS 11-25

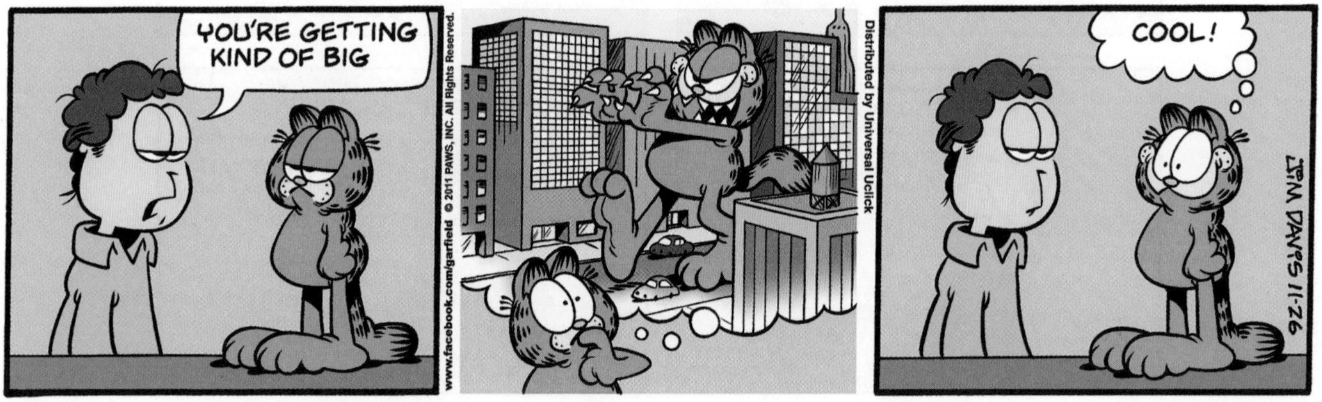
YOU'RE GETTING KIND OF BIG
www.facebook.com/garfield © 2011 PAWS, INC. All Rights Reserved.
Distributed by Universal Uclick
COOL!
JIM DAVIS 11-26

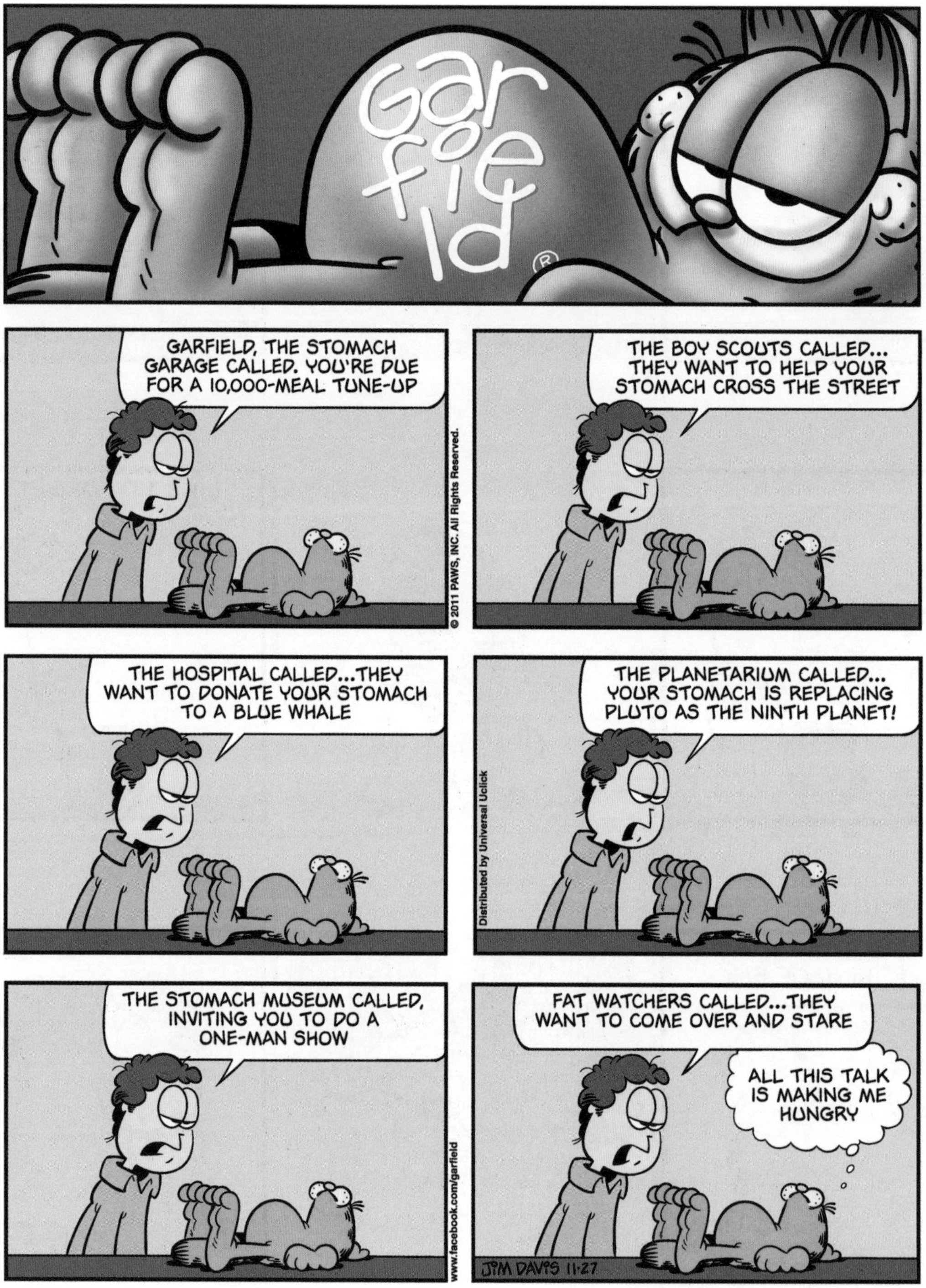
GARFIELD
GARFIELD, THE STOMACH GARAGE CALLED. YOU'RE DUE FOR A 10,000-MEAL TUNE-UP
© 2011 PAWS, INC. All Rights Reserved.
THE BOY SCOUTS CALLED... THEY WANT TO HELP YOUR STOMACH CROSS THE STREET
THE HOSPITAL CALLED...THEY WANT TO DONATE YOUR STOMACH TO A BLUE WHALE
Distributed by Universal Uclick
THE PLANETARIUM CALLED... YOUR STOMACH IS REPLACING PLUTO AS THE NINTH PLANET!
THE STOMACH MUSEUM CALLED, INVITING YOU TO DO A ONE-MAN SHOW
www.facebook.com/garfield
FAT WATCHERS CALLED...THEY WANT TO COME OVER AND STARE
ALL THIS TALK IS MAKING ME HUNGRY
JIM DAVIS 11-27

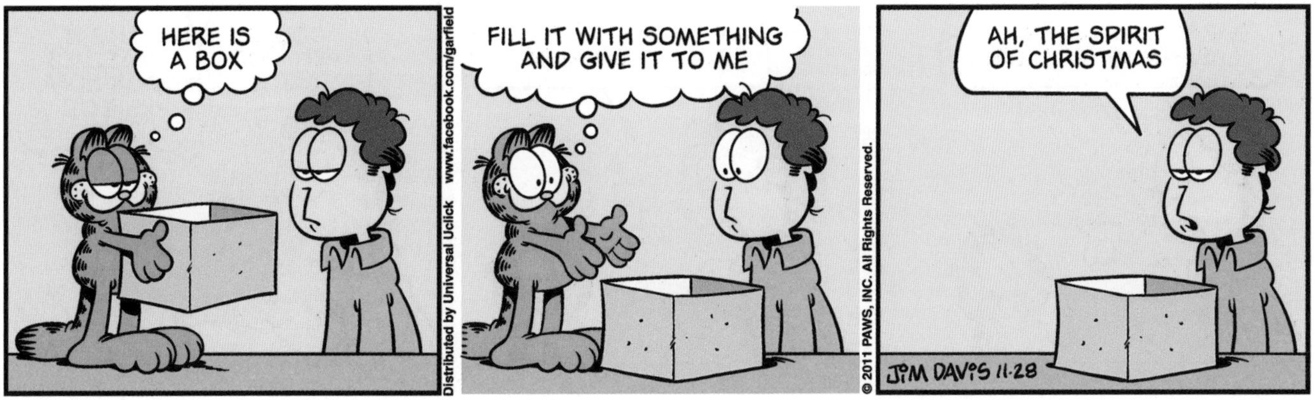
HERE IS A BOX
Distributed by Universal Uclick www.facebook.com/garfield
FILL IT WITH SOMETHING AND GIVE IT TO ME
© 2011 PAWS, INC. All Rights Reserved.
AH, THE SPIRIT OF CHRISTMAS
JIM DAVIS 11-28

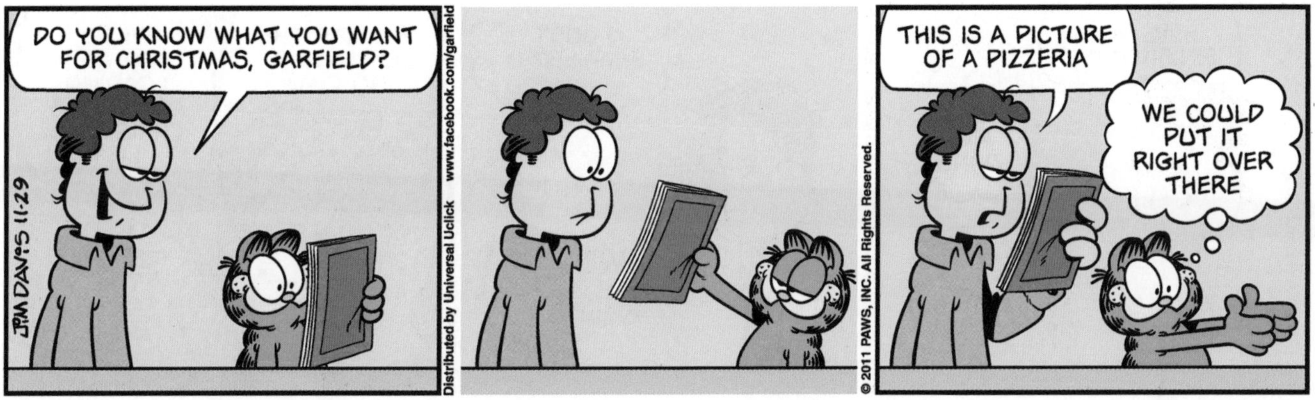
DO YOU KNOW WHAT YOU WANT FOR CHRISTMAS, GARFIELD?
JIM DAVIS 11-29
Distributed by Universal Uclick www.facebook.com/garfield
© 2011 PAWS, INC. All Rights Reserved.
THIS IS A PICTURE OF A PIZZERIA
WE COULD PUT IT RIGHT OVER THERE

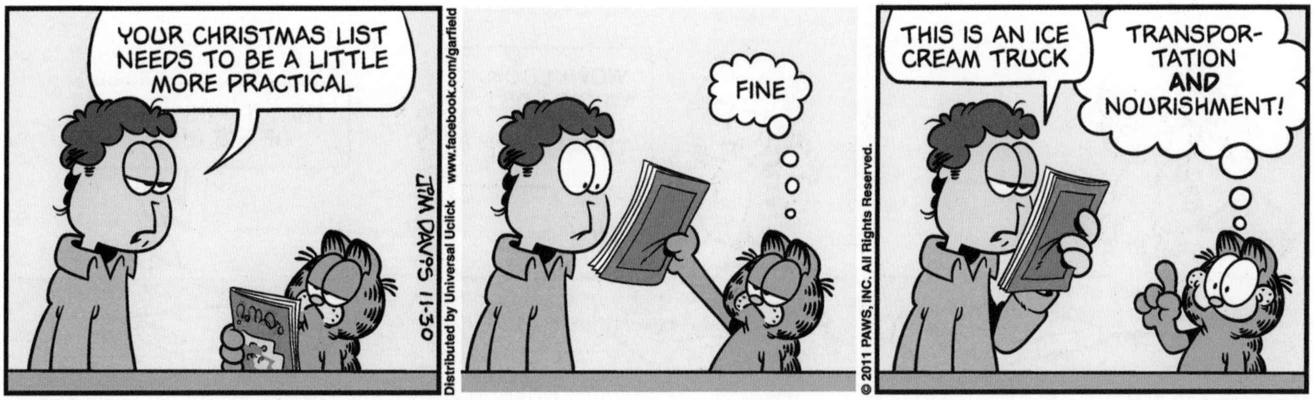
YOUR CHRISTMAS LIST NEEDS TO BE A LITTLE MORE PRACTICAL
JIM DAVIS 11-30
Distributed by Universal Uclick www.facebook.com/garfield
FINE
© 2011 PAWS, INC. All Rights Reserved.
THIS IS AN ICE CREAM TRUCK
TRANSPOR-TATION **AND** NOURISHMENT!

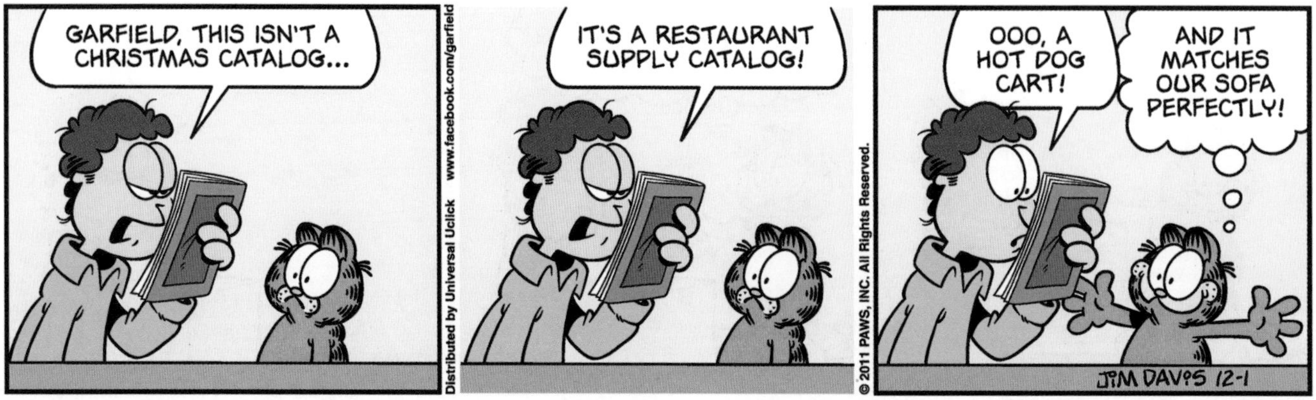
GARFIELD, THIS ISN'T A CHRISTMAS CATALOG...
IT'S A RESTAURANT SUPPLY CATALOG!
OOO, A HOT DOG CART!
AND IT MATCHES OUR SOFA PERFECTLY!
JIM DAVIS 12-1
Distributed by Universal Uclick www.facebook.com/garfield
© 2011 PAWS, INC. All Rights Reserved.

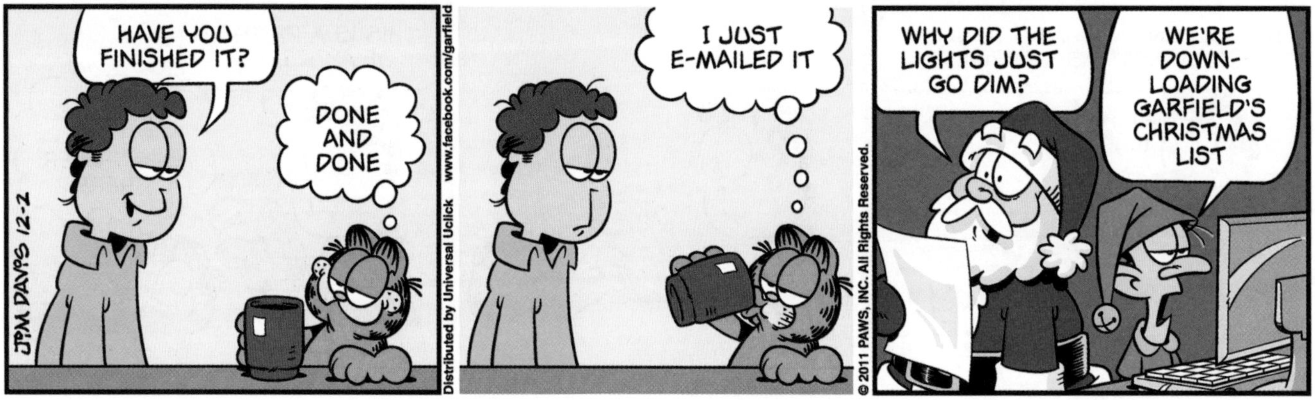
HAVE YOU FINISHED IT?
DONE AND DONE
I JUST E-MAILED IT
WHY DID THE LIGHTS JUST GO DIM?
WE'RE DOWN-LOADING GARFIELD'S CHRISTMAS LIST
JIM DAVIS 12-2
Distributed by Universal Uclick www.facebook.com/garfield
© 2011 PAWS, INC. All Rights Reserved.

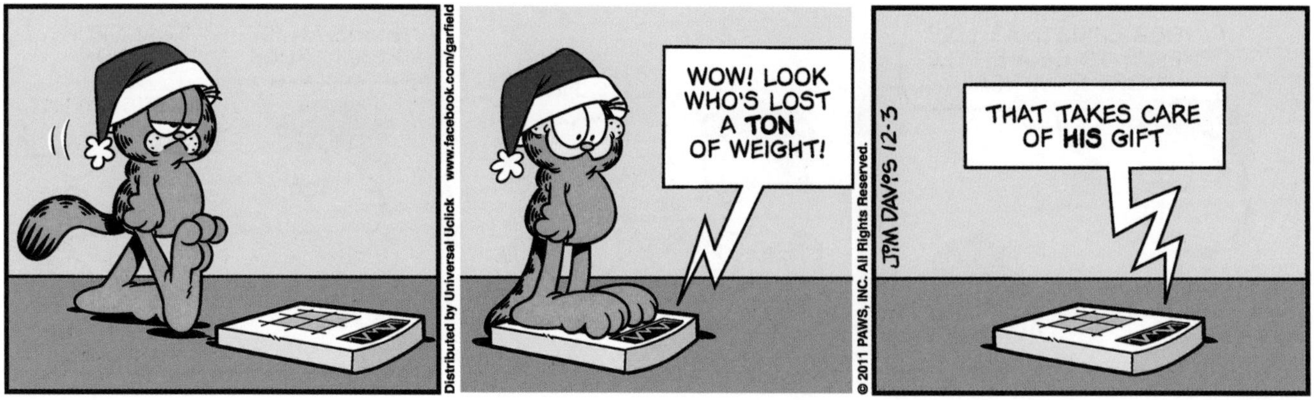
WOW! LOOK WHO'S LOST A **TON** OF WEIGHT!
THAT TAKES CARE OF **HIS** GIFT
JIM DAVIS 12-3
Distributed by Universal Uclick www.facebook.com/garfield
© 2011 PAWS, INC. All Rights Reserved.

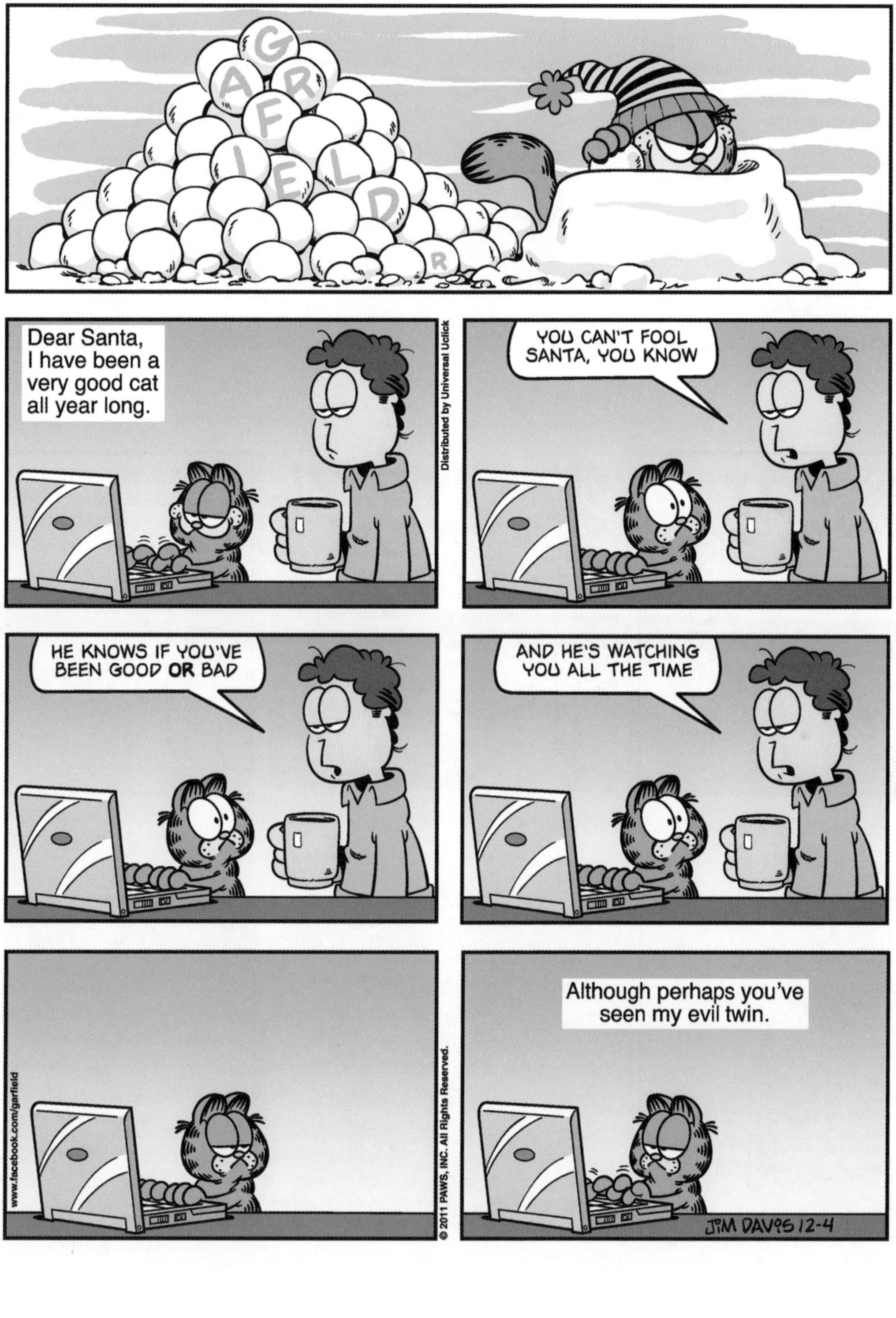
GARFIELD
R
Dear Santa, I have been a very good cat all year long.
Distributed by Universal Uclick
YOU CAN'T FOOL SANTA, YOU KNOW
HE KNOWS IF YOU'VE BEEN GOOD **OR** BAD
AND HE'S WATCHING YOU ALL THE TIME
www.facebook.com/garfield
© 2011 PAWS, INC. All Rights Reserved.
Although perhaps you've seen my evil twin.
JIM DAVIS 12-4

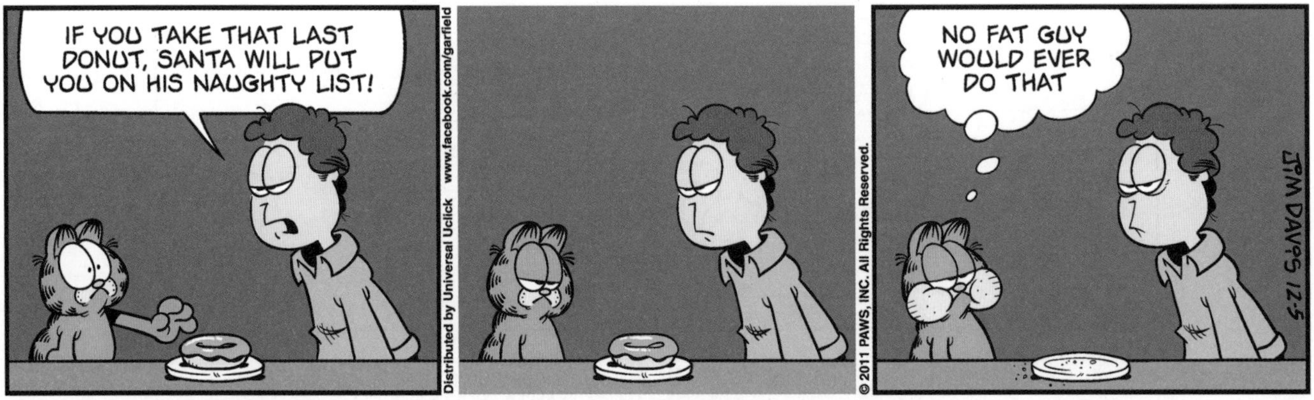
IF YOU TAKE THAT LAST DONUT, SANTA WILL PUT YOU ON HIS NAUGHTY LIST!
Distributed by Universal Uclick www.facebook.com/garfield
© 2011 PAWS, INC. All Rights Reserved.
NO FAT GUY WOULD EVER DO THAT
JIM DAVIS 12-5

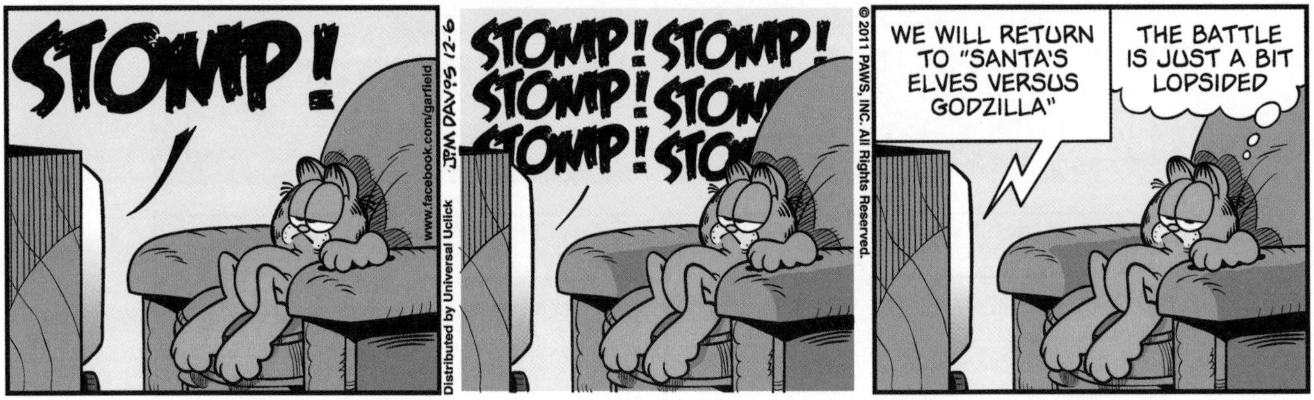
STOMP!
JIM DAVIS 12-6
Distributed by Universal Uclick www.facebook.com/garfield
STOMP! STOMP! STOMP! STOMP! STOMP!
© 2011 PAWS, INC. All Rights Reserved.
WE WILL RETURN TO "SANTA'S ELVES VERSUS GODZILLA"
THE BATTLE IS JUST A BIT LOPSIDED

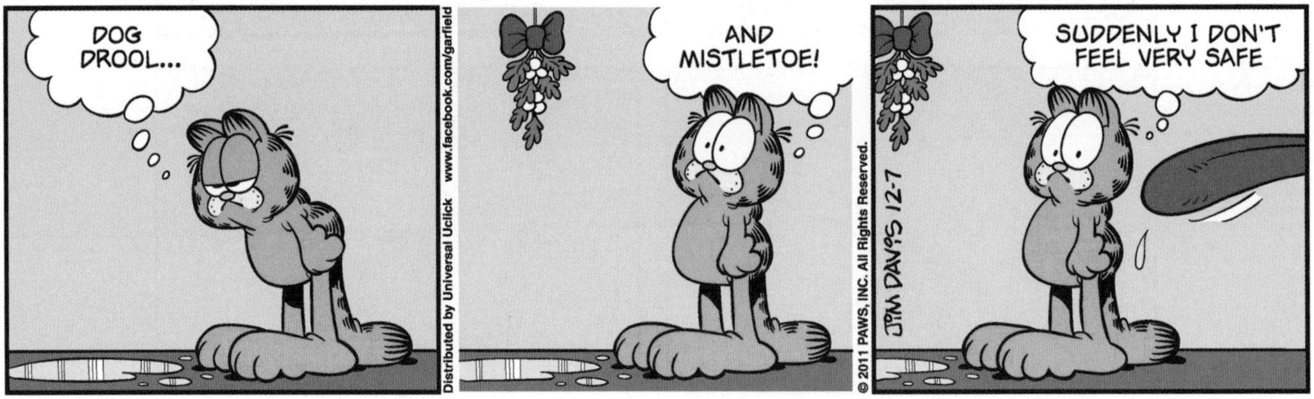
DOG DROOL...
Distributed by Universal Uclick www.facebook.com/garfield
AND MISTLETOE!
© 2011 PAWS, INC. All Rights Reserved.
JIM DAVIS 12-7
SUDDENLY I DON'T FEEL VERY SAFE

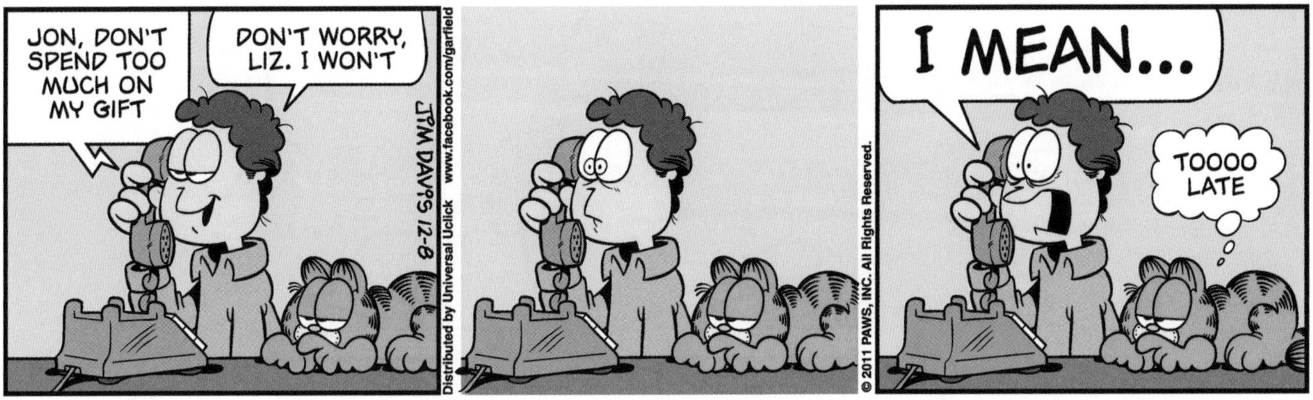
JON, DON'T SPEND TOO MUCH ON MY GIFT
DON'T WORRY, LIZ. I WON'T
I MEAN...
TOOOO LATE

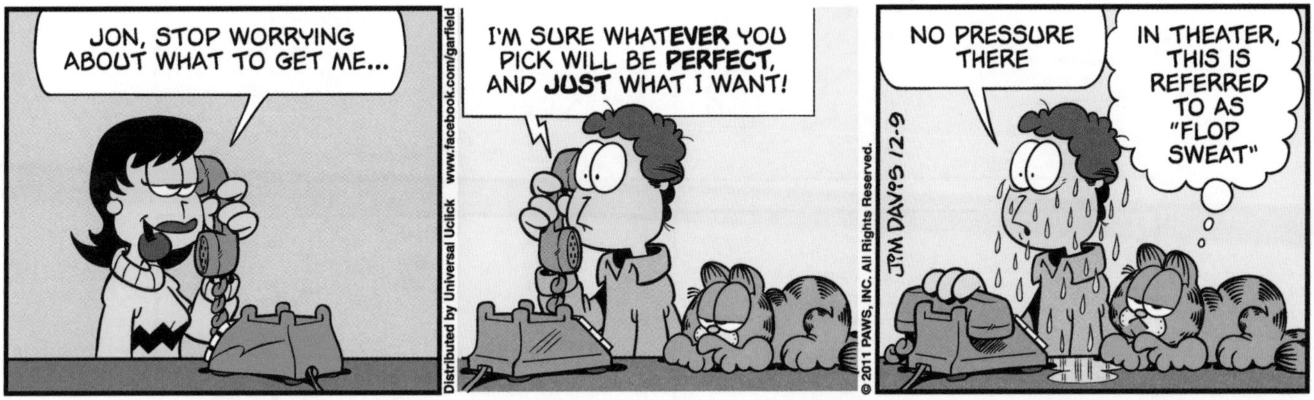
JON, STOP WORRYING ABOUT WHAT TO GET ME...
I'M SURE WHATEVER YOU PICK WILL BE PERFECT, AND JUST WHAT I WANT!
NO PRESSURE THERE
IN THEATER, THIS IS REFERRED TO AS "FLOP SWEAT"

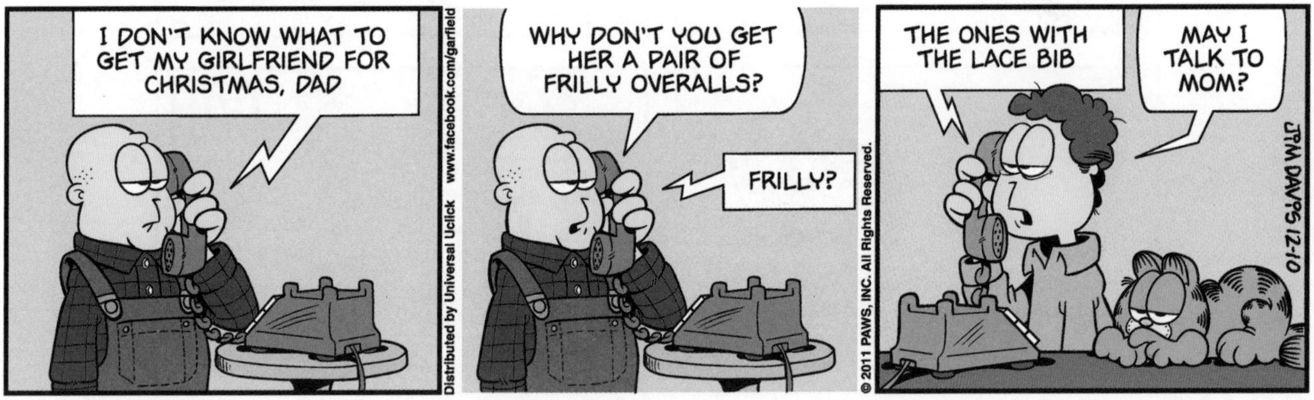
I DON'T KNOW WHAT TO GET MY GIRLFRIEND FOR CHRISTMAS, DAD
WHY DON'T YOU GET HER A PAIR OF FRILLY OVERALLS?
FRILLY?
THE ONES WITH THE LACE BIB
MAY I TALK TO MOM?

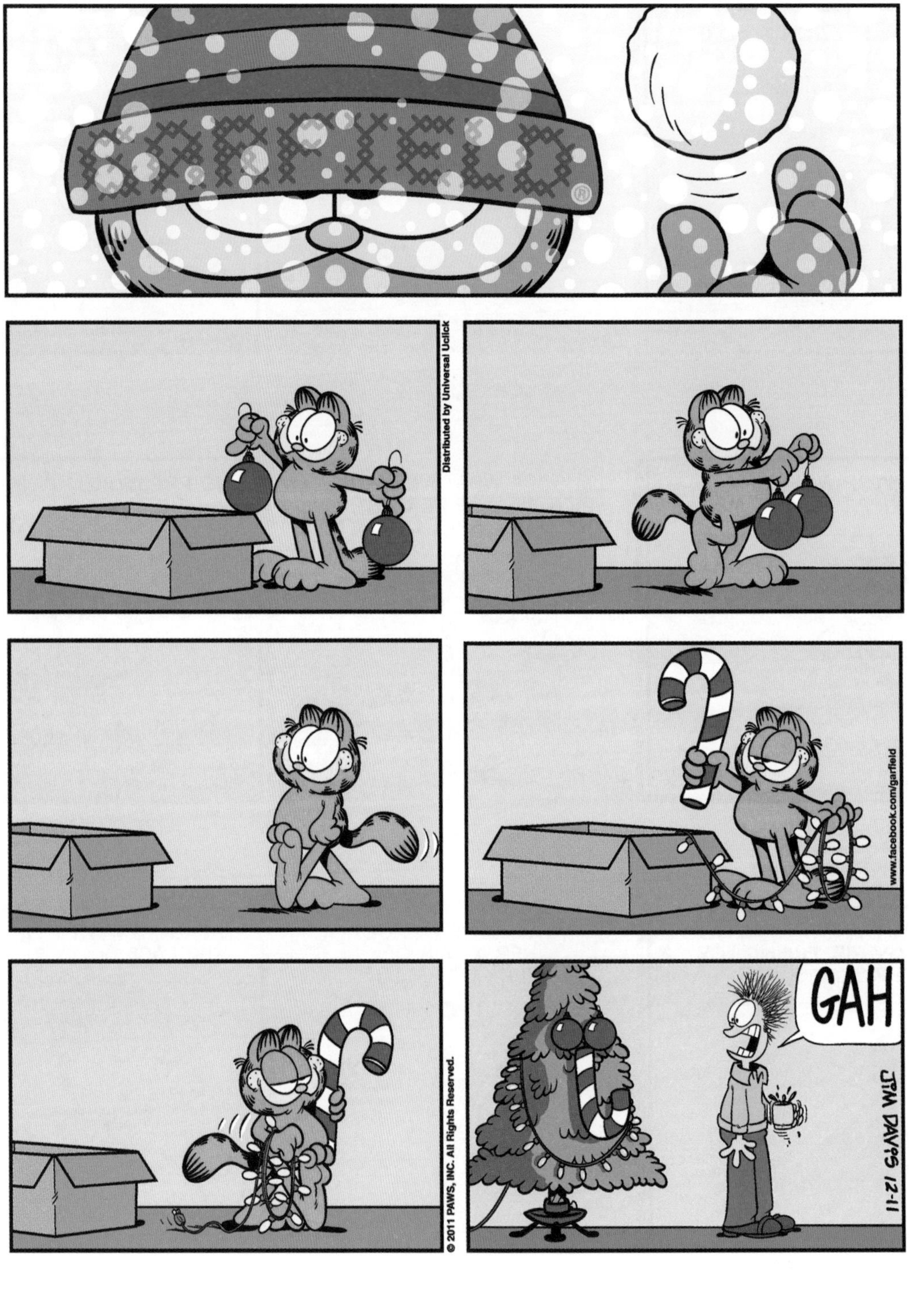
GARFIELD
Distributed by Universal Uclick
www.facebook.com/garfield
© 2011 PAWS, INC. All Rights Reserved.
GAH
JIM DAVIS 12-11

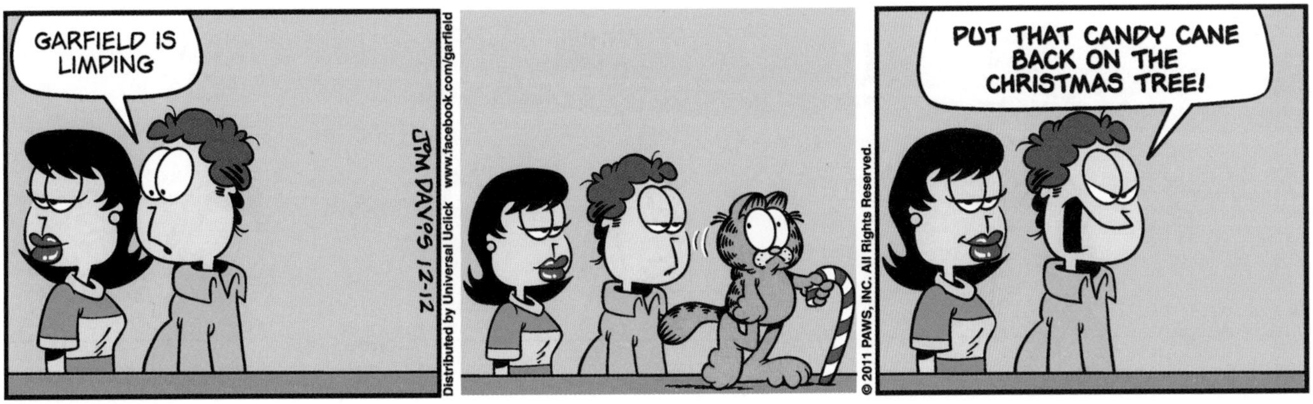
GARFIELD IS LIMPING
JIM DAVIS 12-12
Distributed by Universal Uclick www.facebook.com/garfield
© 2011 PAWS, INC. All Rights Reserved.
PUT THAT CANDY CANE BACK ON THE CHRISTMAS TREE!

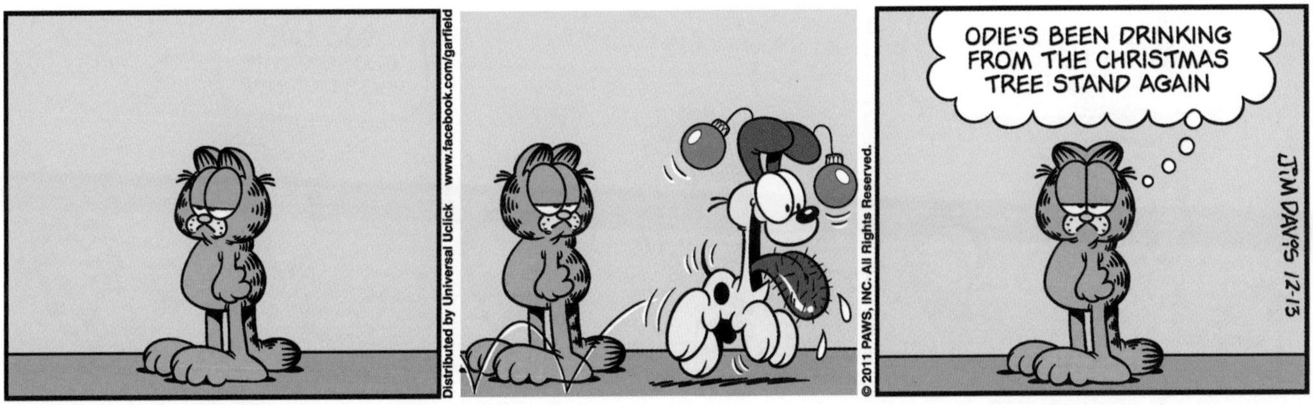
Distributed by Universal Uclick www.facebook.com/garfield
© 2011 PAWS, INC. All Rights Reserved.
ODIE'S BEEN DRINKING FROM THE CHRISTMAS TREE STAND AGAIN
JIM DAVIS 12-13

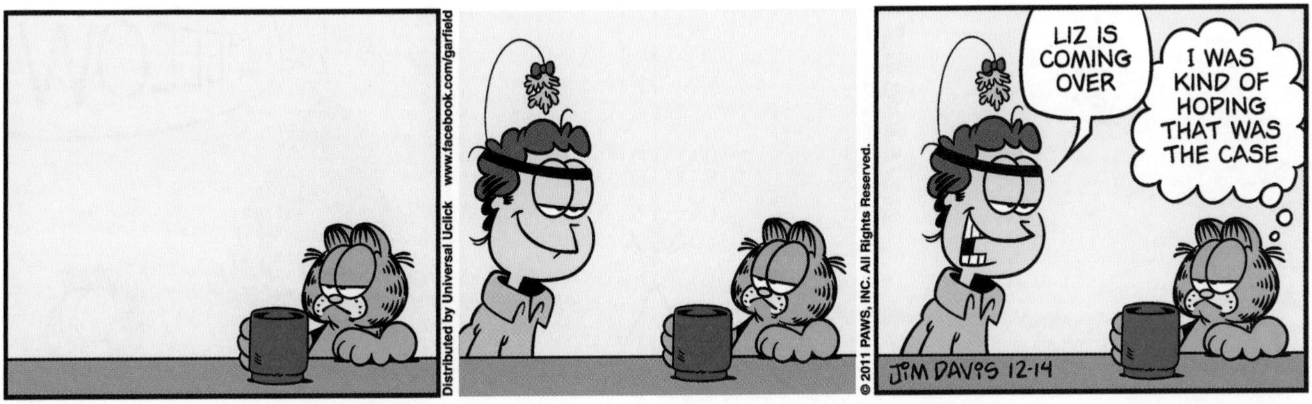
Distributed by Universal Uclick www.facebook.com/garfield
© 2011 PAWS, INC. All Rights Reserved.
LIZ IS COMING OVER
I WAS KIND OF HOPING THAT WAS THE CASE
JIM DAVIS 12-14

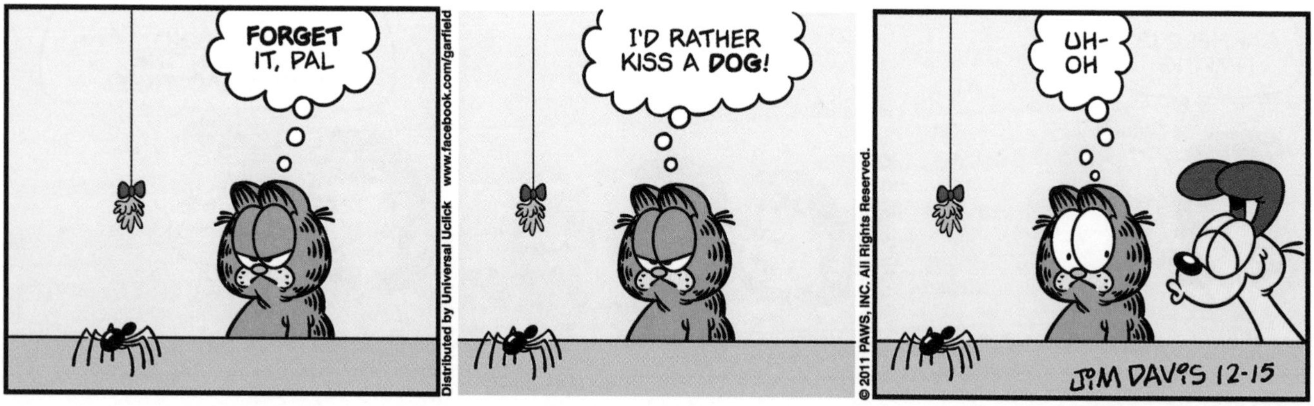
FORGET IT, PAL
I'D RATHER KISS A DOG!
UH-OH
JIM DAVIS 12-15

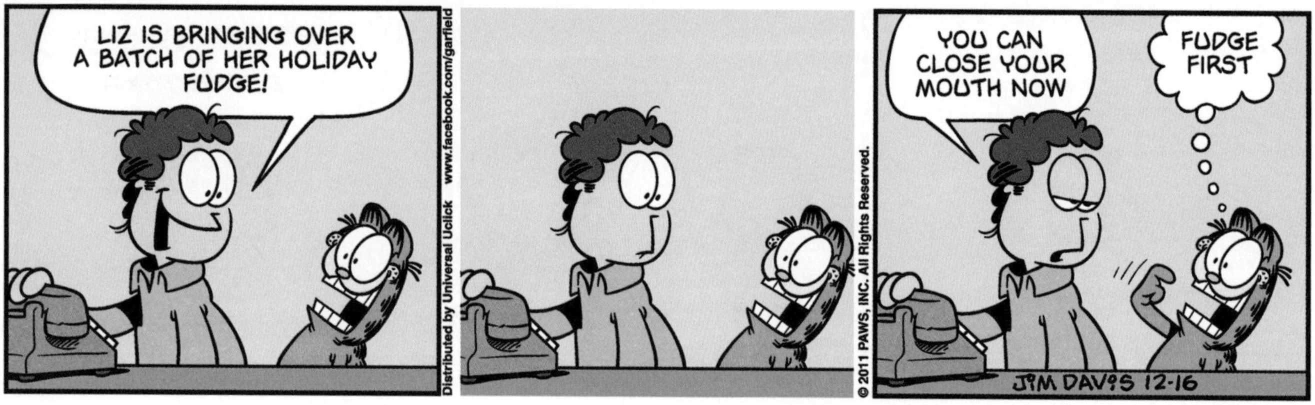
LIZ IS BRINGING OVER A BATCH OF HER HOLIDAY FUDGE!
YOU CAN CLOSE YOUR MOUTH NOW
FUDGE FIRST
JIM DAVIS 12-16

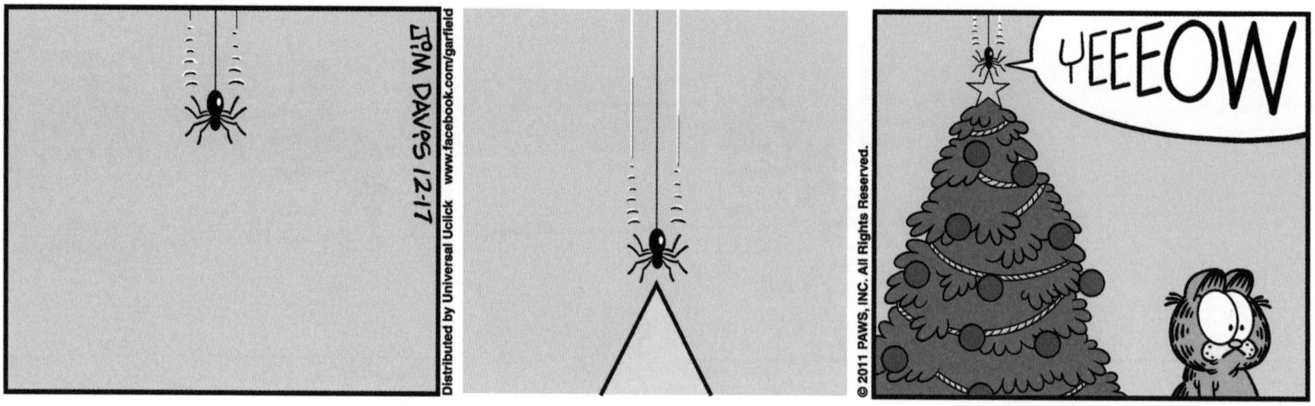
JIM DAVIS 12-17
YEEEOW

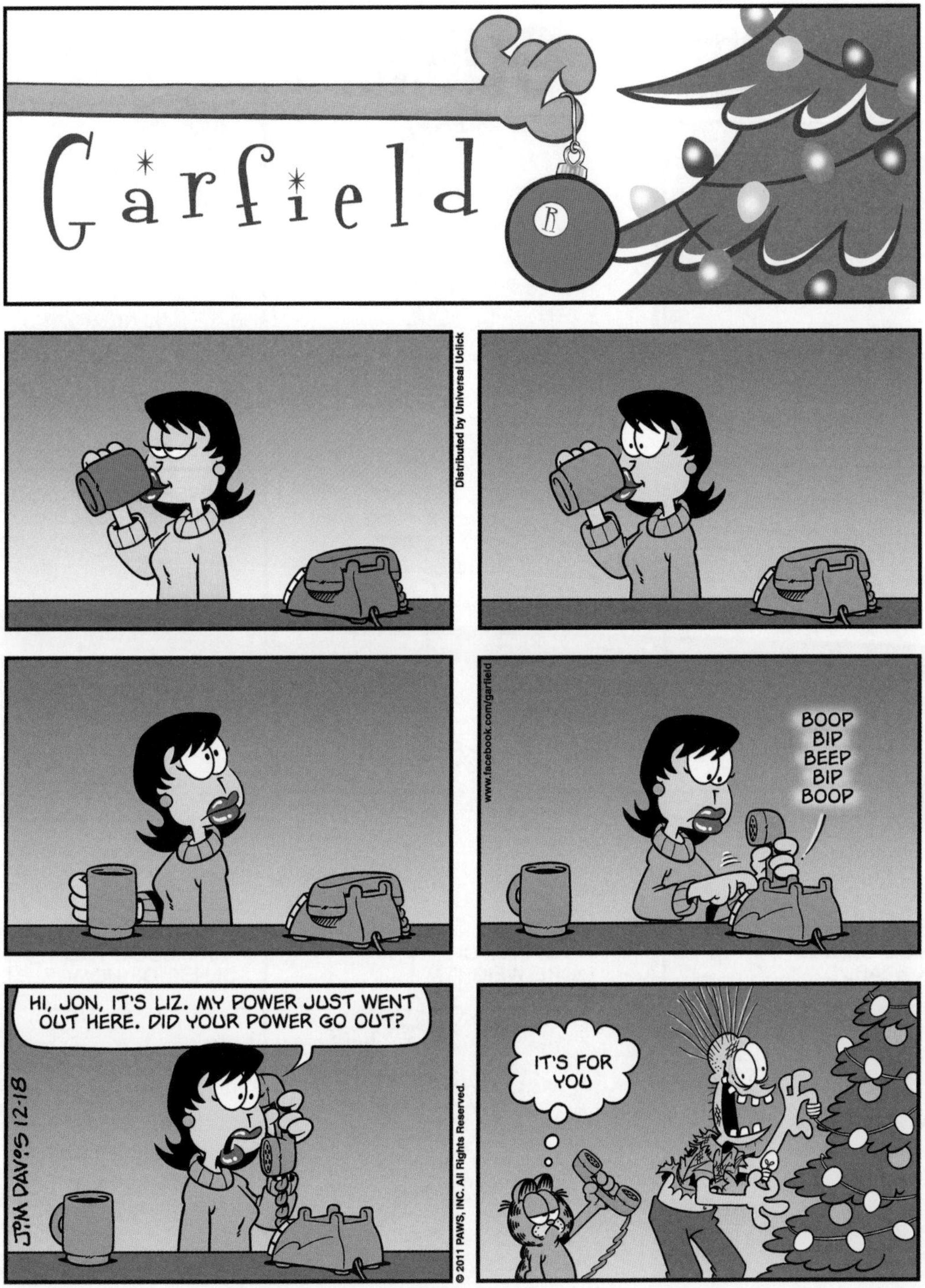
Garfield
Distributed by Universal Uclick
www.facebook.com/garfield
BOOP BIP BEEP BIP BOOP
HI, JON, IT'S LIZ. MY POWER JUST WENT OUT HERE. DID YOUR POWER GO OUT?
JPM DAVIS 12-18
© 2011 PAWS, INC. All Rights Reserved.
IT'S FOR YOU

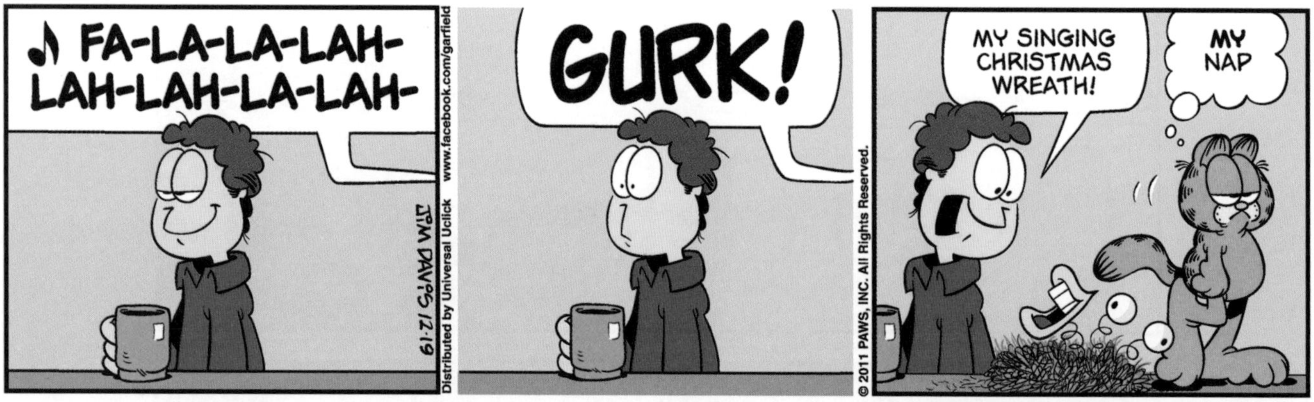
♪ FA-LA-LA-LAH-LAH-LAH-LA-LAH-
JIM DAVIS 12-19
Distributed by Universal Uclick www.facebook.com/garfield
GURK!
© 2011 PAWS, INC. All Rights Reserved.
MY SINGING CHRISTMAS WREATH!
MY NAP

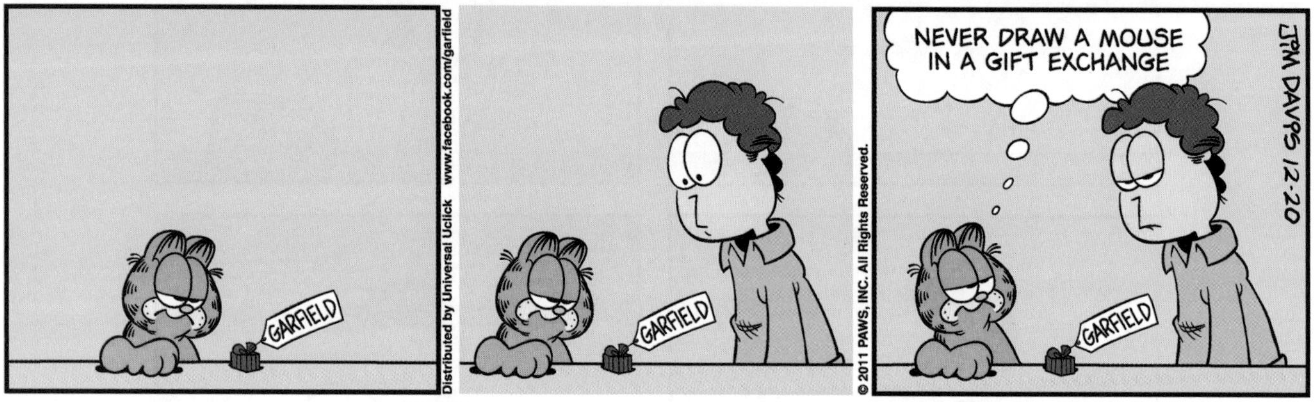
GARFIELD
Distributed by Universal Uclick www.facebook.com/garfield
GARFIELD
© 2011 PAWS, INC. All Rights Reserved.
NEVER DRAW A MOUSE IN A GIFT EXCHANGE
GARFIELD
JIM DAVIS 12-20

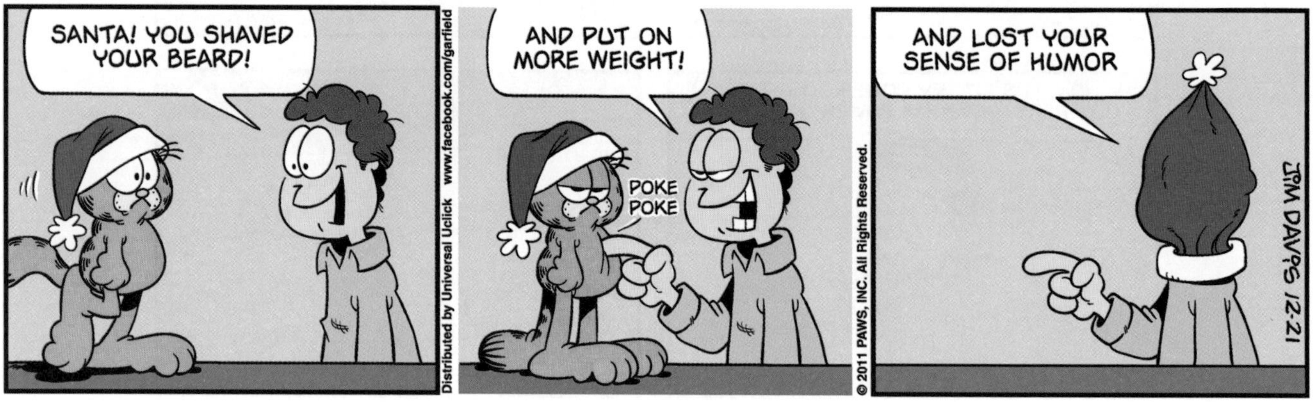
SANTA! YOU SHAVED YOUR BEARD!
Distributed by Universal Uclick www.facebook.com/garfield
AND PUT ON MORE WEIGHT!
POKE POKE
© 2011 PAWS, INC. All Rights Reserved.
AND LOST YOUR SENSE OF HUMOR
JIM DAVIS 12-21

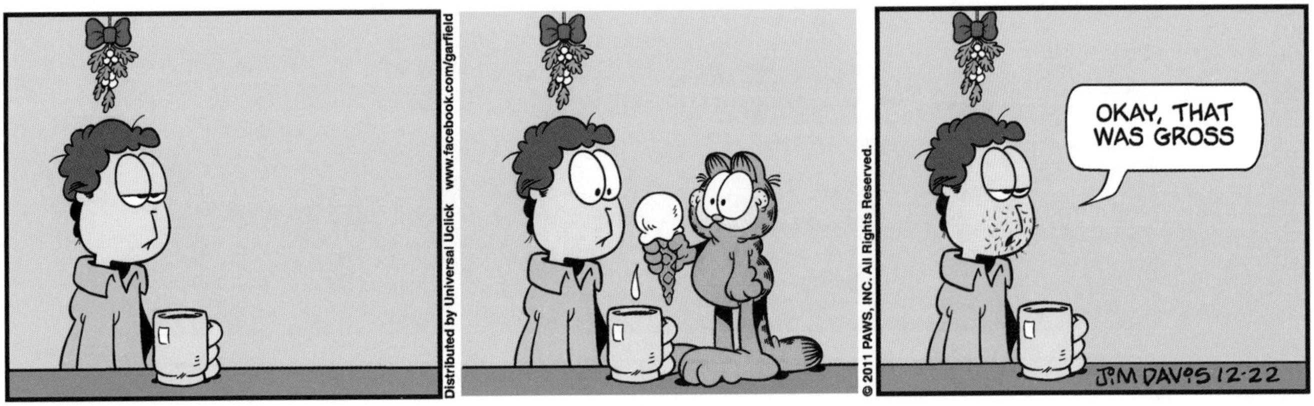
Distributed by Universal Uclick www.facebook.com/garfield
© 2011 PAWS, INC. All Rights Reserved.
OKAY, THAT WAS GROSS
JIM DAVIS 12-22

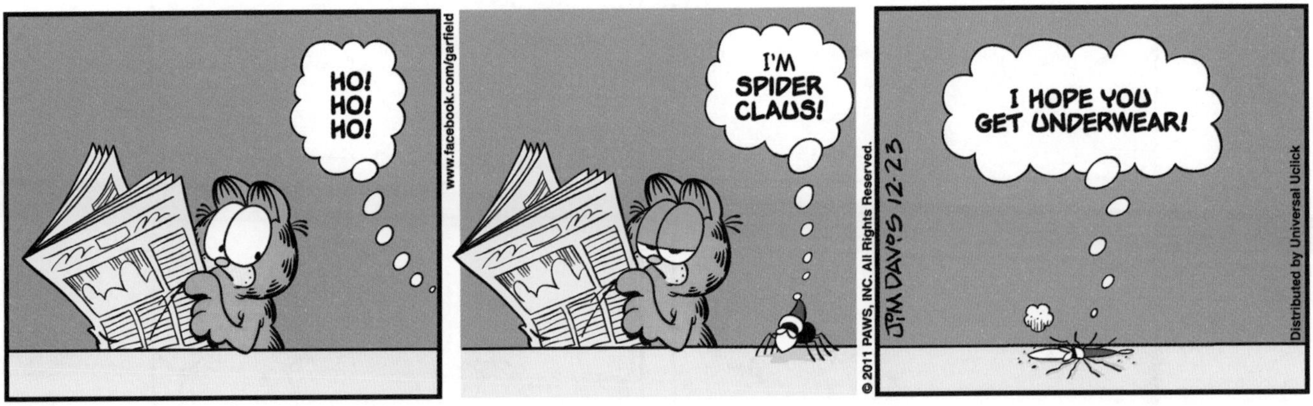
HO! HO! HO!
www.facebook.com/garfield
I'M SPIDER CLAUS!
© 2011 PAWS, INC. All Rights Reserved.
JIM DAVIS 12-23
I HOPE YOU GET UNDERWEAR!
Distributed by Universal Uclick

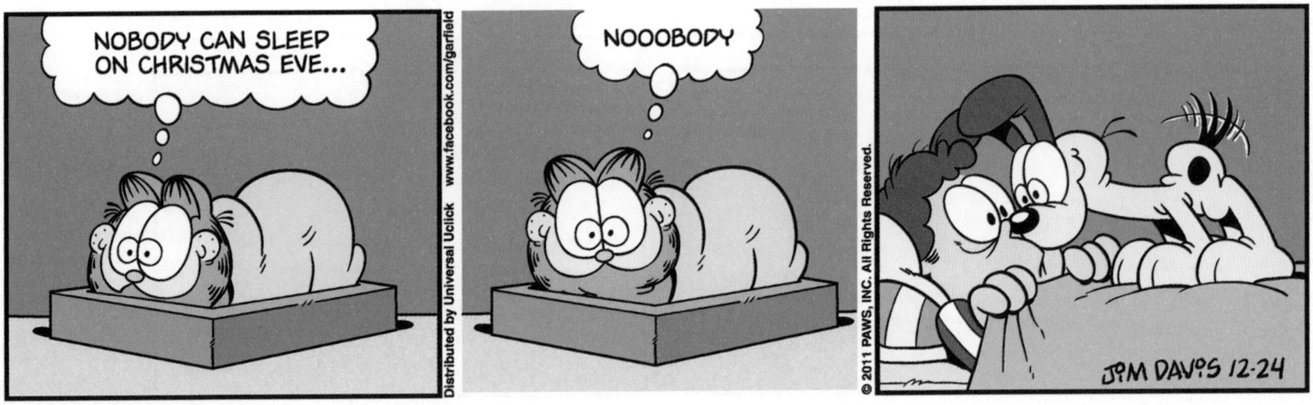
NOBODY CAN SLEEP ON CHRISTMAS EVE...
Distributed by Universal Uclick www.facebook.com/garfield
NOOOBODY
© 2011 PAWS, INC. All Rights Reserved.
JIM DAVIS 12-24

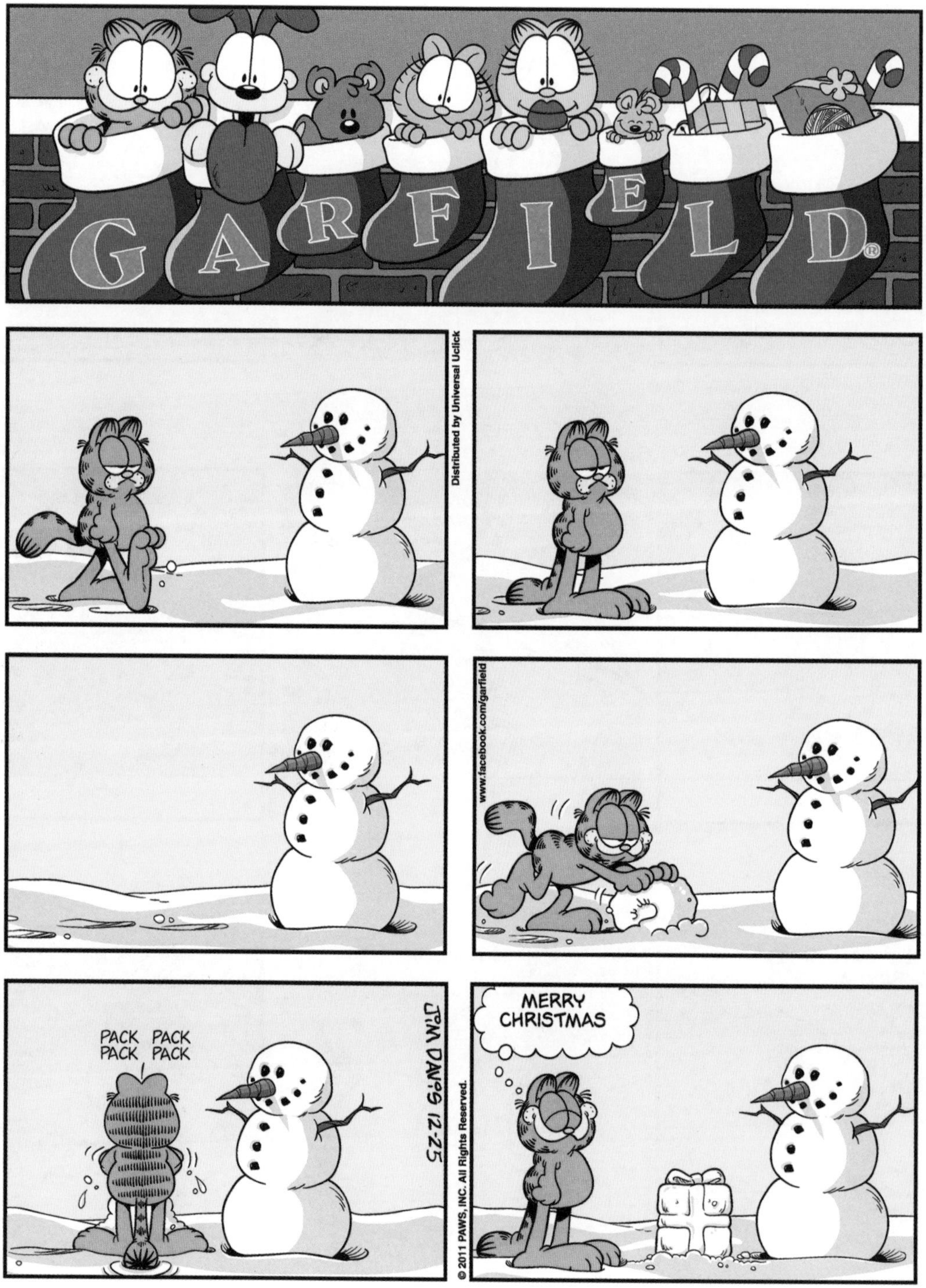
GARFIELD®
Distributed by Universal Uclick
www.facebook.com/garfield
PACK PACK
PACK PACK
JPM DAVIS 12-25
© 2011 PAWS, INC. All Rights Reserved.
MERRY CHRISTMAS

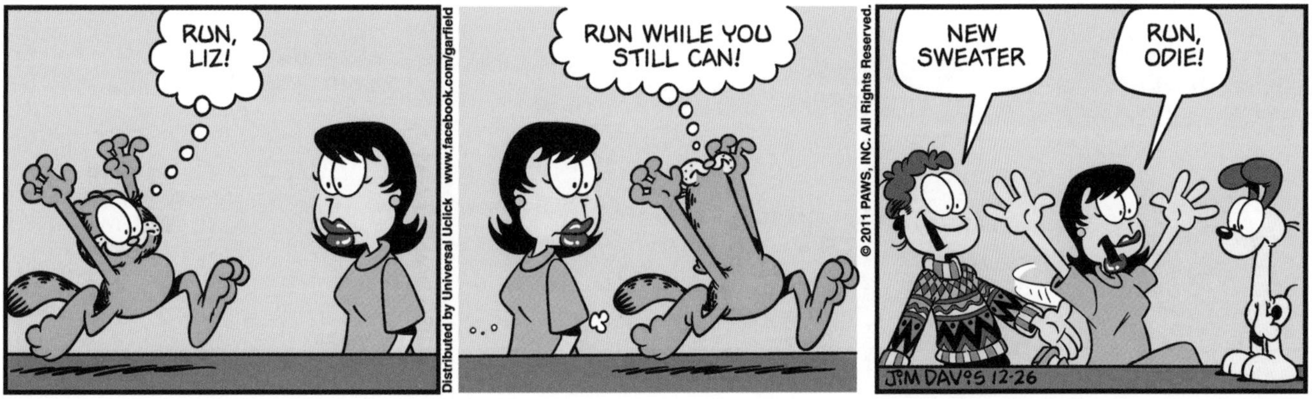
RUN, LIZ!
RUN WHILE YOU STILL CAN!
NEW SWEATER
RUN, ODIE!
JIM DAVIS 12-26
Distributed by Universal Uclick www.facebook.com/garfield
© 2011 PAWS, INC. All Rights Reserved.

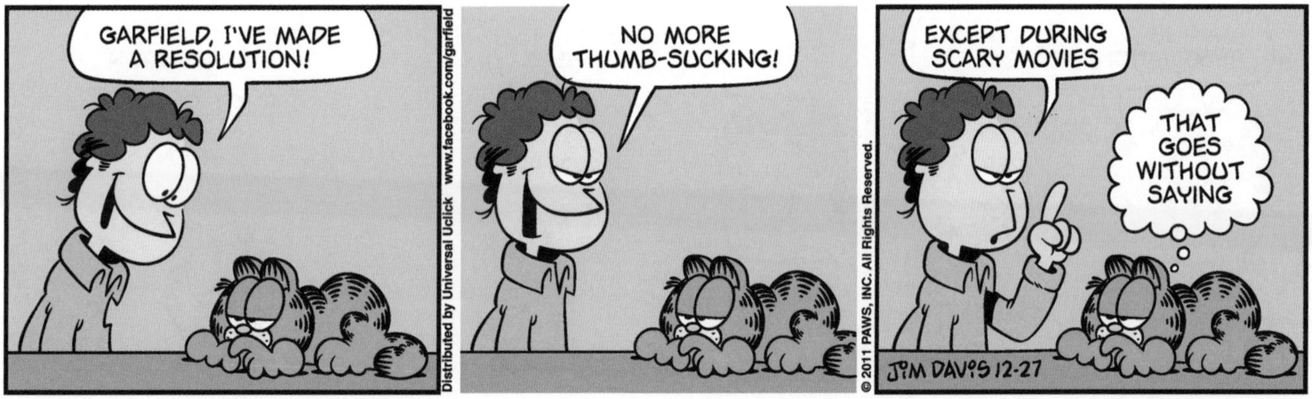
GARFIELD, I'VE MADE A RESOLUTION!
NO MORE THUMB-SUCKING!
EXCEPT DURING SCARY MOVIES
THAT GOES WITHOUT SAYING
JIM DAVIS 12-27
Distributed by Universal Uclick www.facebook.com/garfield
© 2011 PAWS, INC. All Rights Reserved.

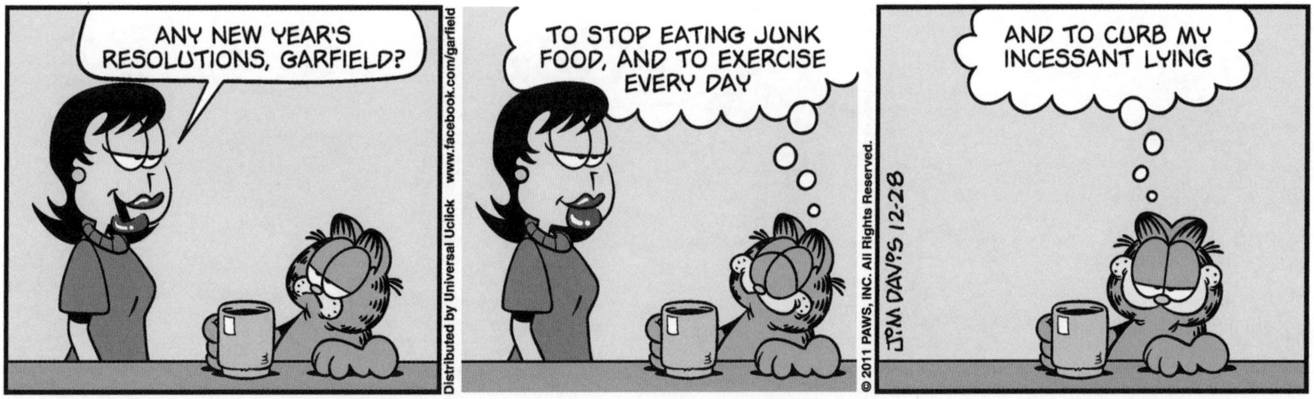
ANY NEW YEAR'S RESOLUTIONS, GARFIELD?
TO STOP EATING JUNK FOOD, AND TO EXERCISE EVERY DAY
AND TO CURB MY INCESSANT LYING
JIM DAVIS 12-28
Distributed by Universal Uclick www.facebook.com/garfield
© 2011 PAWS, INC. All Rights Reserved.

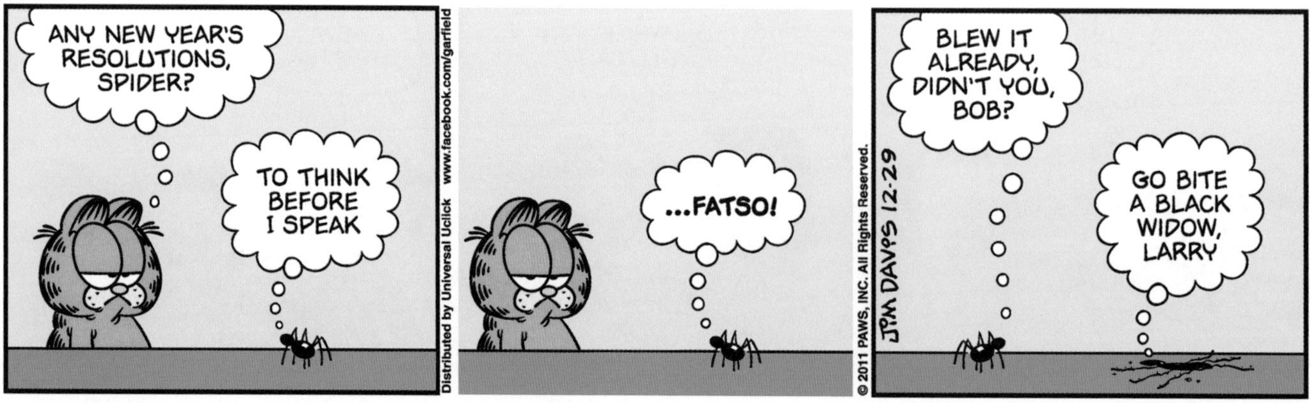
ANY NEW YEAR'S RESOLUTIONS, SPIDER?
TO THINK BEFORE I SPEAK
Distributed by Universal Uclick www.facebook.com/garfield
...FATSO!
© 2011 PAWS, INC. All Rights Reserved.
JIM DAVIS 12-29
BLEW IT ALREADY, DIDN'T YOU, BOB?
GO BITE A BLACK WIDOW, LARRY

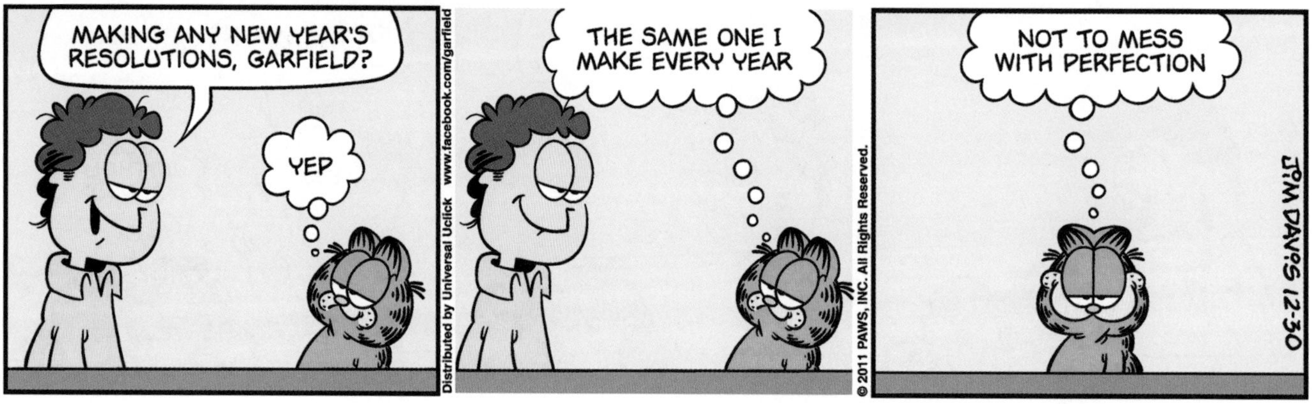
MAKING ANY NEW YEAR'S RESOLUTIONS, GARFIELD?
YEP
Distributed by Universal Uclick www.facebook.com/garfield
THE SAME ONE I MAKE EVERY YEAR
© 2011 PAWS, INC. All Rights Reserved.
NOT TO MESS WITH PERFECTION
JIM DAVIS 12-30

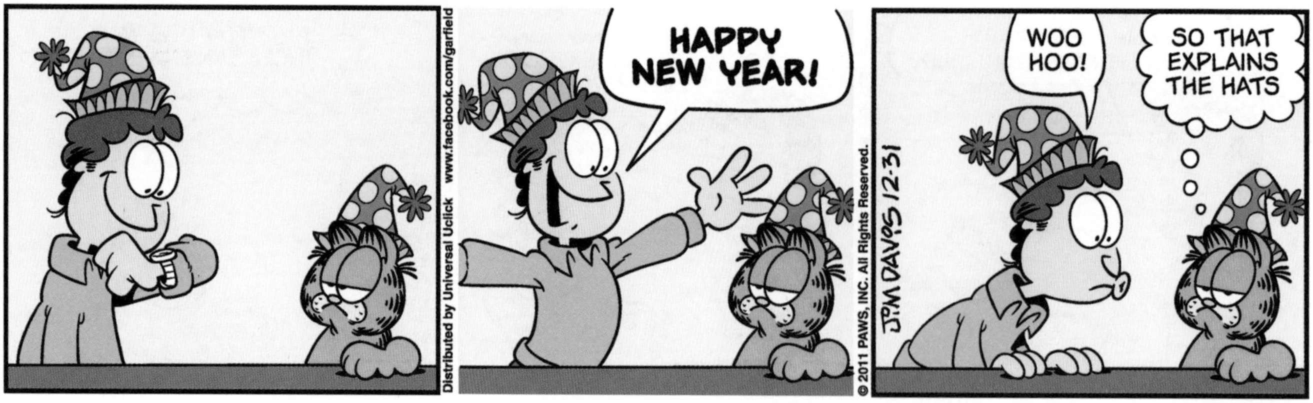
Distributed by Universal Uclick www.facebook.com/garfield
HAPPY NEW YEAR!
JIM DAVIS 12-31
© 2011 PAWS, INC. All Rights Reserved.
WOO HOO!
SO THAT EXPLAINS THE HATS

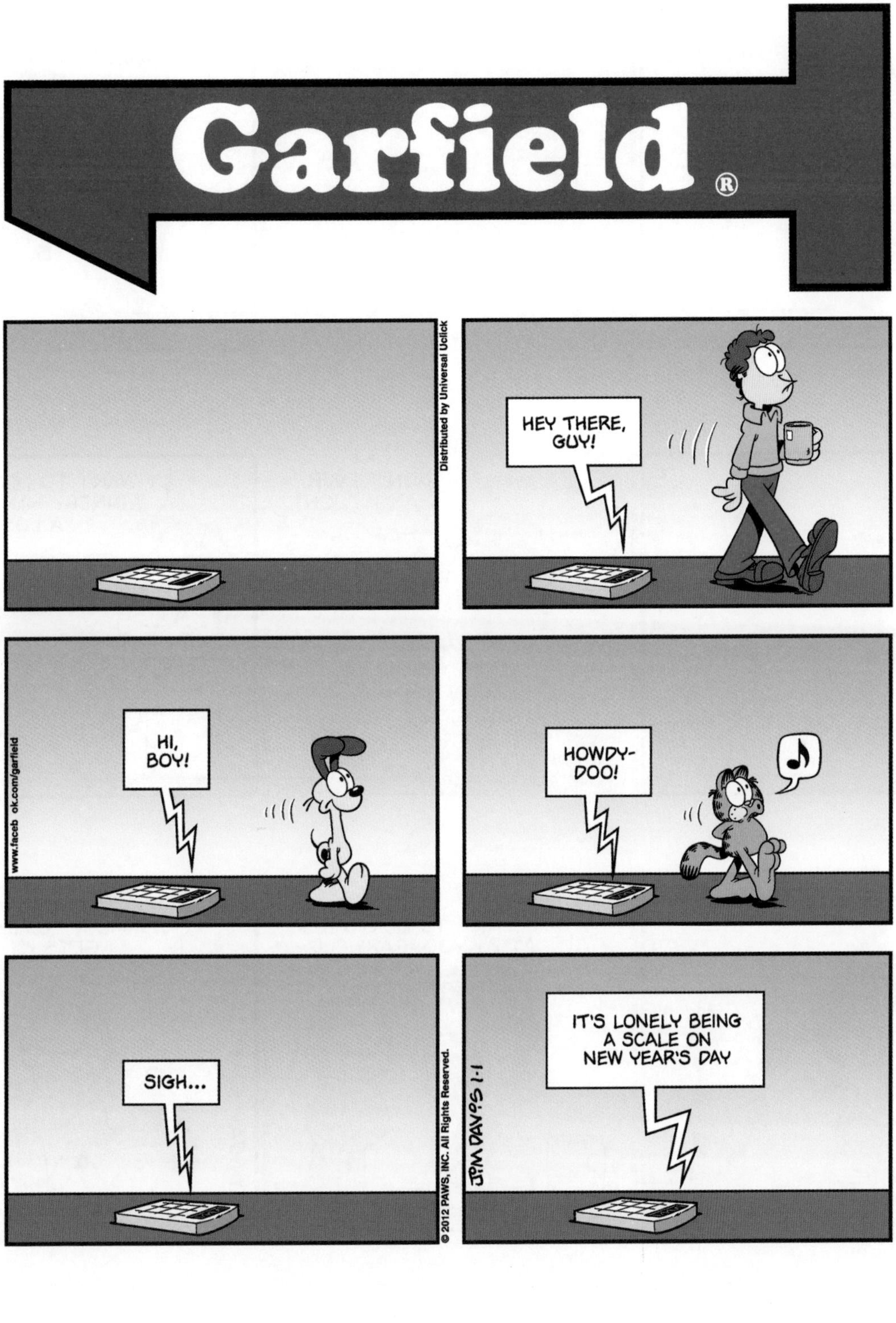
Garfield®
HEY THERE, GUY!
HI, BOY!
HOWDY-DOO!
SIGH...
IT'S LONELY BEING A SCALE ON NEW YEAR'S DAY
Distributed by Universal Uclick
www.facebook.com/garfield
© 2012 PAWS, INC. All Rights Reserved.
JPM DAVIS 1-1

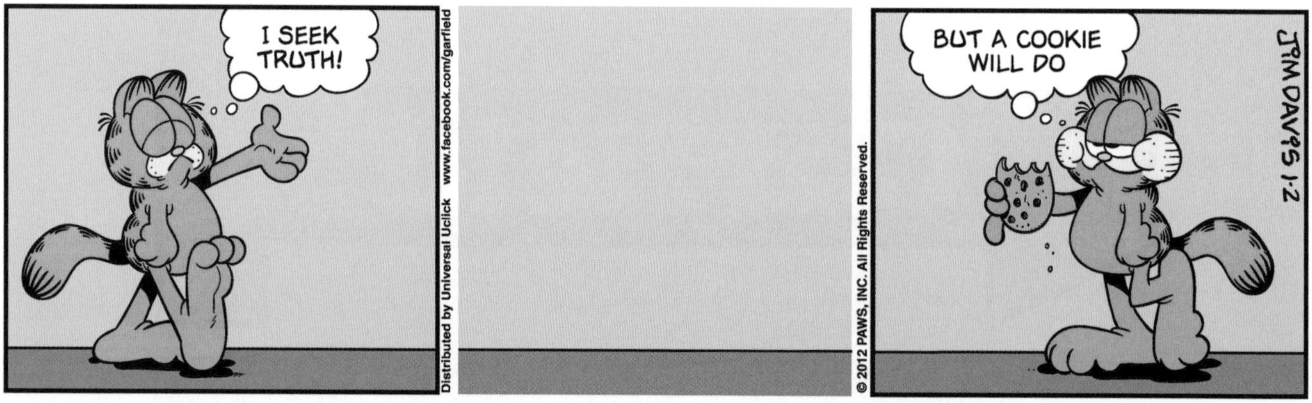
I SEEK TRUTH!
Distributed by Universal Uclick www.facebook.com/garfield
© 2012 PAWS, INC. All Rights Reserved.
BUT A COOKIE WILL DO
JPM DAVPS 1-2

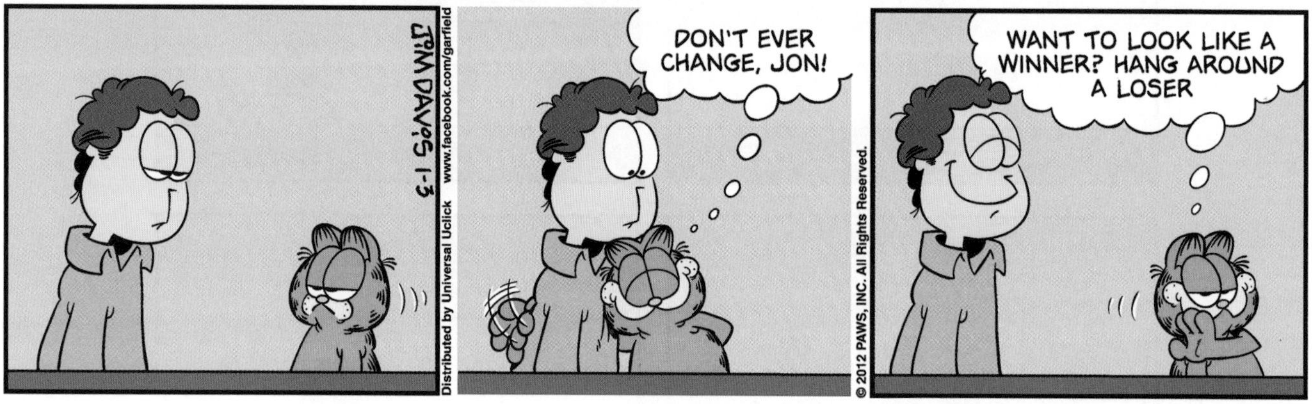
JPM DAVPS 1-3
Distributed by Universal Uclick www.facebook.com/garfield
DON'T EVER CHANGE, JON!
© 2012 PAWS, INC. All Rights Reserved.
WANT TO LOOK LIKE A WINNER? HANG AROUND A LOSER

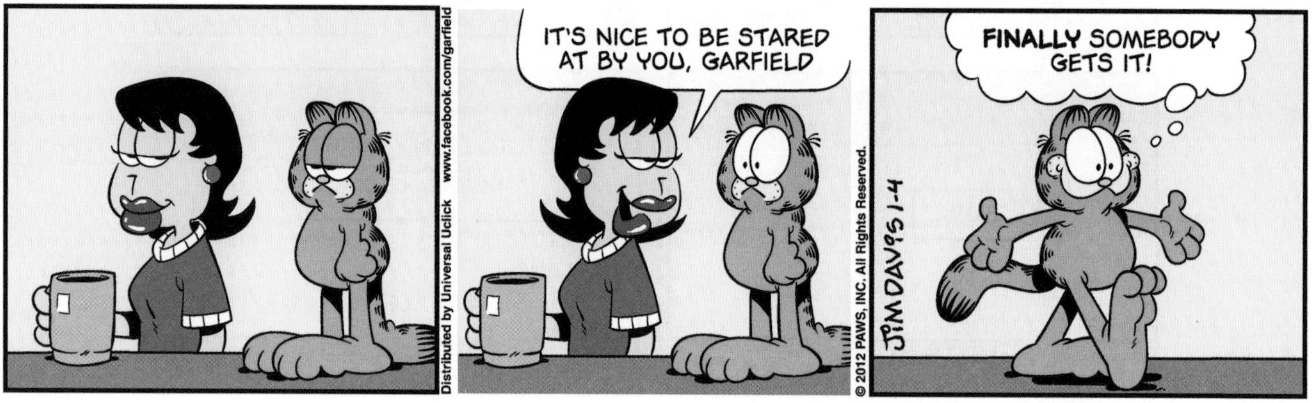
Distributed by Universal Uclick www.facebook.com/garfield
IT'S NICE TO BE STARED AT BY YOU, GARFIELD
© 2012 PAWS, INC. All Rights Reserved.
JPM DAVPS 1-4
FINALLY SOMEBODY GETS IT!

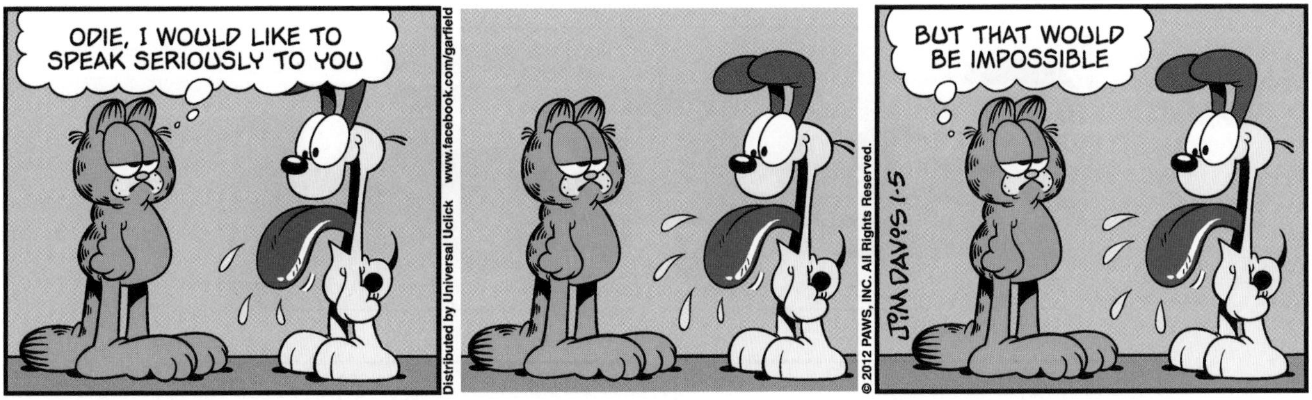
ODIE, I WOULD LIKE TO SPEAK SERIOUSLY TO YOU
BUT THAT WOULD BE IMPOSSIBLE
Distributed by Universal Uclick www.facebook.com/garfield
© 2012 PAWS, INC. All Rights Reserved.
JIM DAVIS 1-5

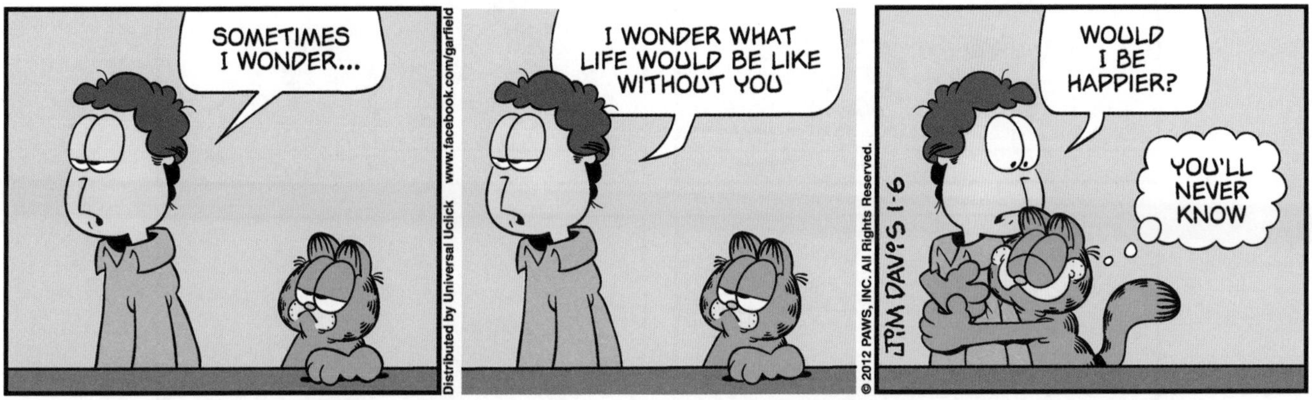
SOMETIMES I WONDER...
I WONDER WHAT LIFE WOULD BE LIKE WITHOUT YOU
WOULD I BE HAPPIER?
YOU'LL NEVER KNOW
Distributed by Universal Uclick www.facebook.com/garfield
© 2012 PAWS, INC. All Rights Reserved.
JIM DAVIS 1-6

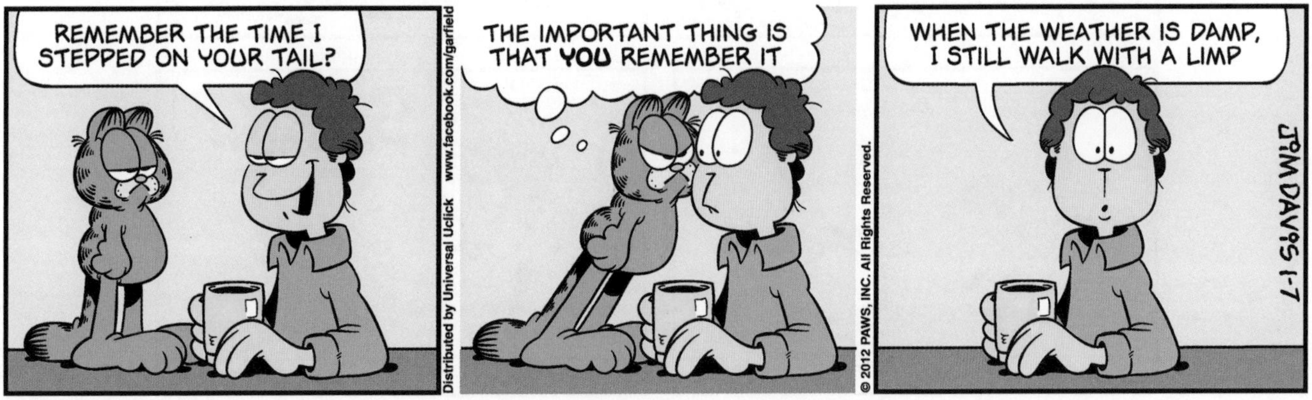
REMEMBER THE TIME I STEPPED ON YOUR TAIL?
THE IMPORTANT THING IS THAT **YOU** REMEMBER IT
WHEN THE WEATHER IS DAMP, I STILL WALK WITH A LIMP
Distributed by Universal Uclick www.facebook.com/garfield
© 2012 PAWS, INC. All Rights Reserved.
JIM DAVIS 1-7

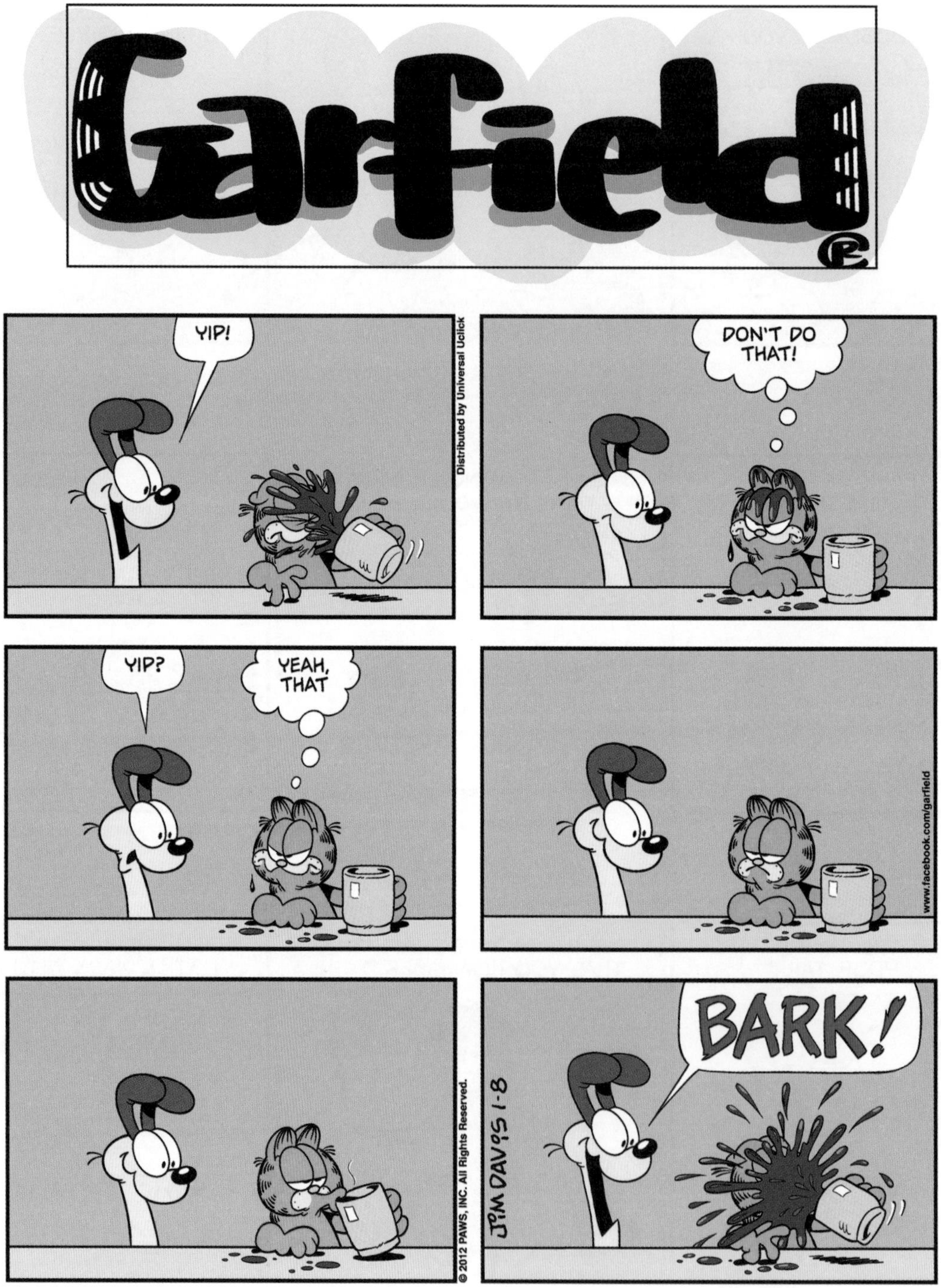

Garfield
YIP!
Distributed by Universal Uclick
DON'T DO THAT!
YIP?
YEAH, THAT
www.facebook.com/garfield
© 2012 PAWS, INC. All Rights Reserved.
JIM DAVIS 1-8
BARK!

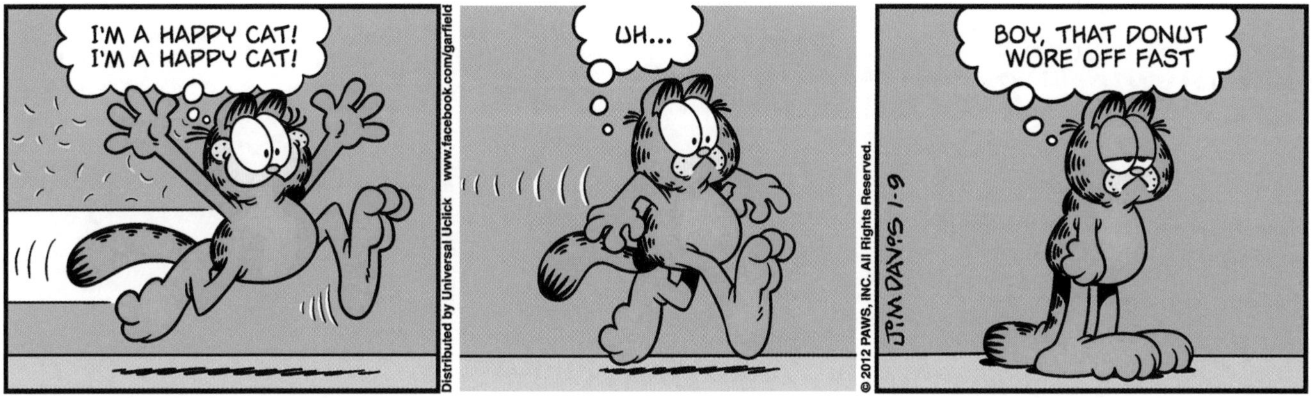
I'M A HAPPY CAT!
I'M A HAPPY CAT!
UH...
BOY, THAT DONUT WORE OFF FAST
Distributed by Universal Uclick www.facebook.com/garfield
© 2012 PAWS, INC. All Rights Reserved.
JIM DAVIS 1-9

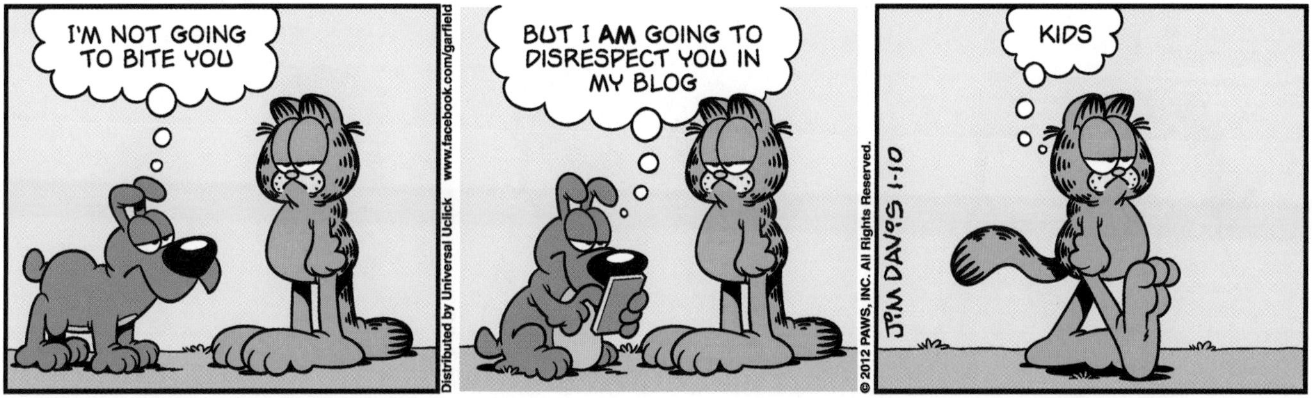
I'M NOT GOING TO BITE YOU
BUT I AM GOING TO DISRESPECT YOU IN MY BLOG
KIDS
Distributed by Universal Uclick www.facebook.com/garfield
© 2012 PAWS, INC. All Rights Reserved.
JIM DAVIS 1-10

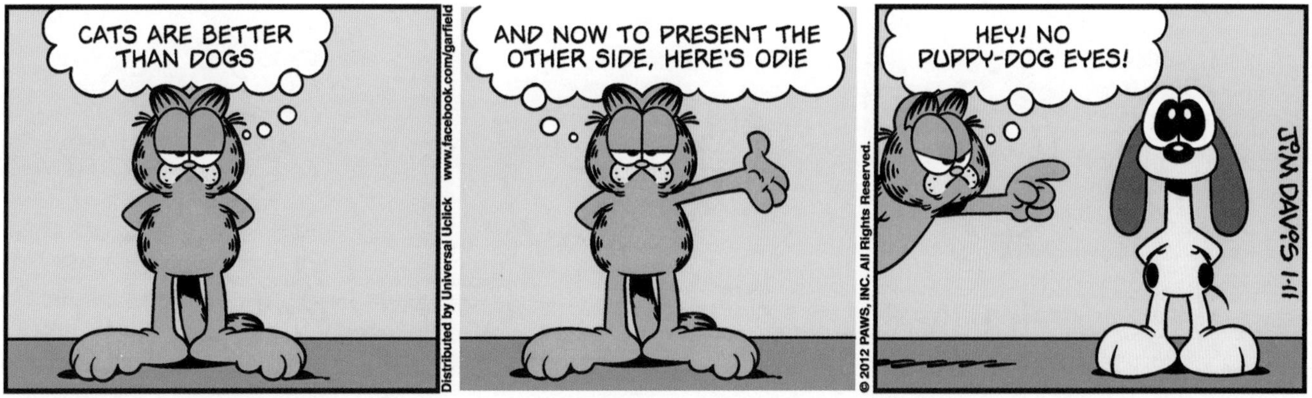
CATS ARE BETTER THAN DOGS
AND NOW TO PRESENT THE OTHER SIDE, HERE'S ODIE
HEY! NO PUPPY-DOG EYES!
Distributed by Universal Uclick www.facebook.com/garfield
© 2012 PAWS, INC. All Rights Reserved.
JIM DAVIS 1-11

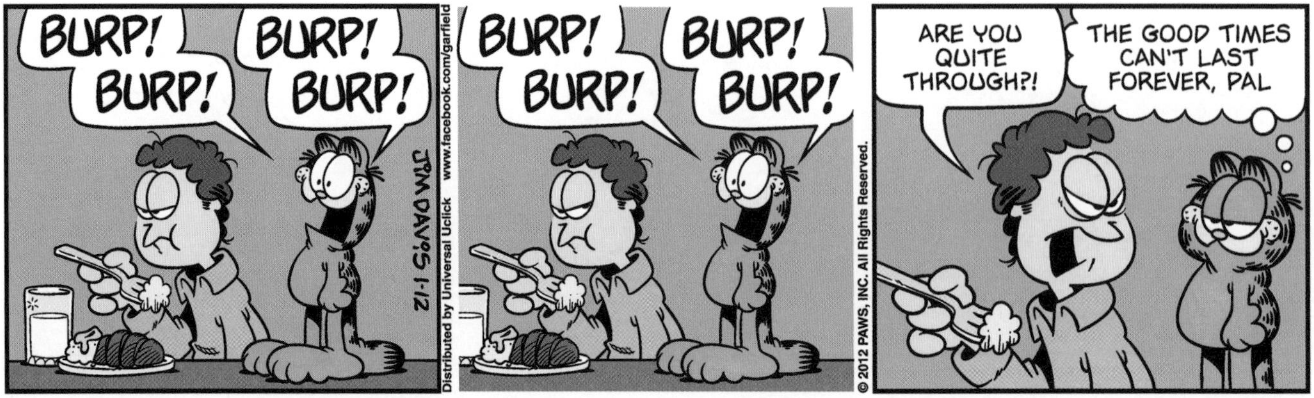
BURP! BURP!
BURP! BURP!
JIM DAVIS 1-12
Distributed by Universal Uclick www.facebook.com/garfield
BURP! BURP!
BURP! BURP!
© 2012 PAWS, INC. All Rights Reserved.
ARE YOU QUITE THROUGH?!
THE GOOD TIMES CAN'T LAST FOREVER, PAL

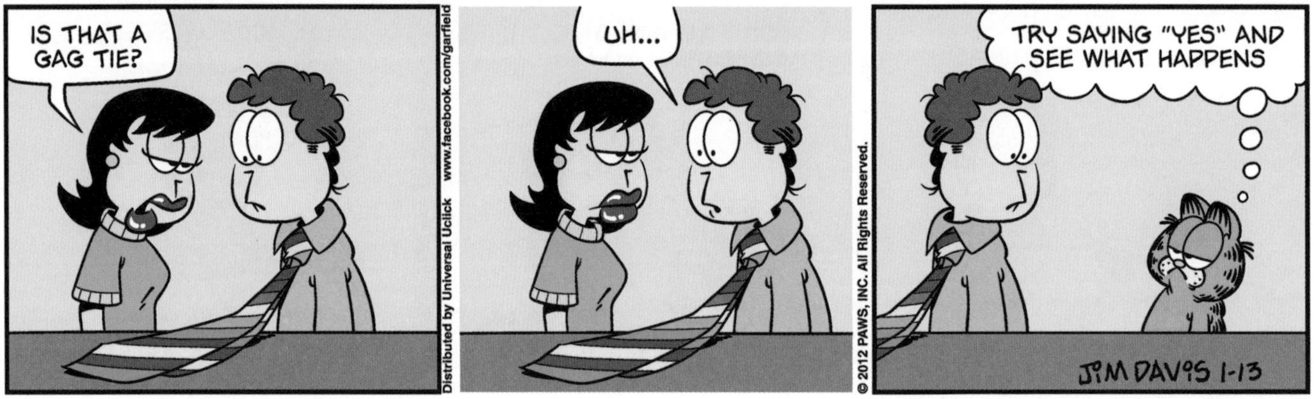
IS THAT A GAG TIE?
Distributed by Universal Uclick www.facebook.com/garfield
UH...
© 2012 PAWS, INC. All Rights Reserved.
TRY SAYING "YES" AND SEE WHAT HAPPENS
JIM DAVIS 1-13

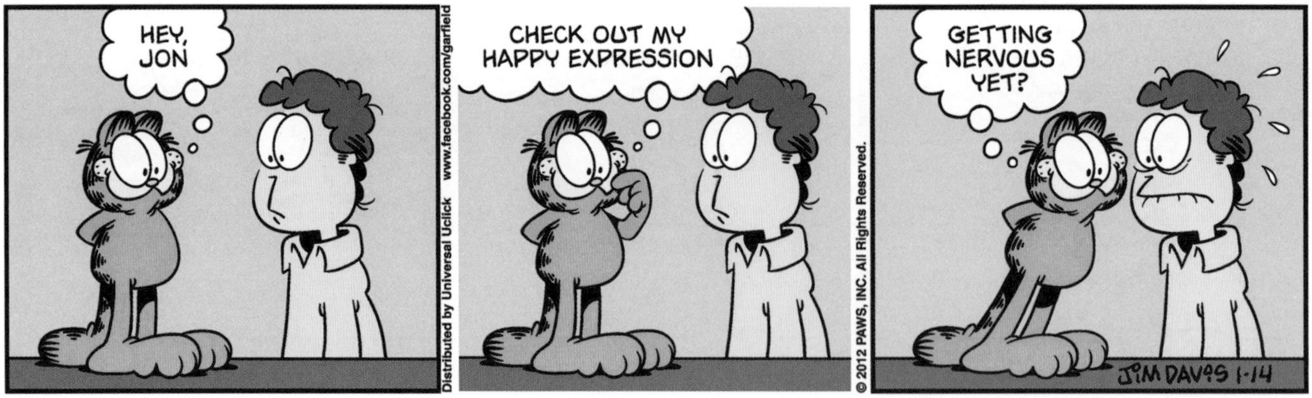
HEY, JON
Distributed by Universal Uclick www.facebook.com/garfield
CHECK OUT MY HAPPY EXPRESSION
© 2012 PAWS, INC. All Rights Reserved.
GETTING NERVOUS YET?
JIM DAVIS 1-14

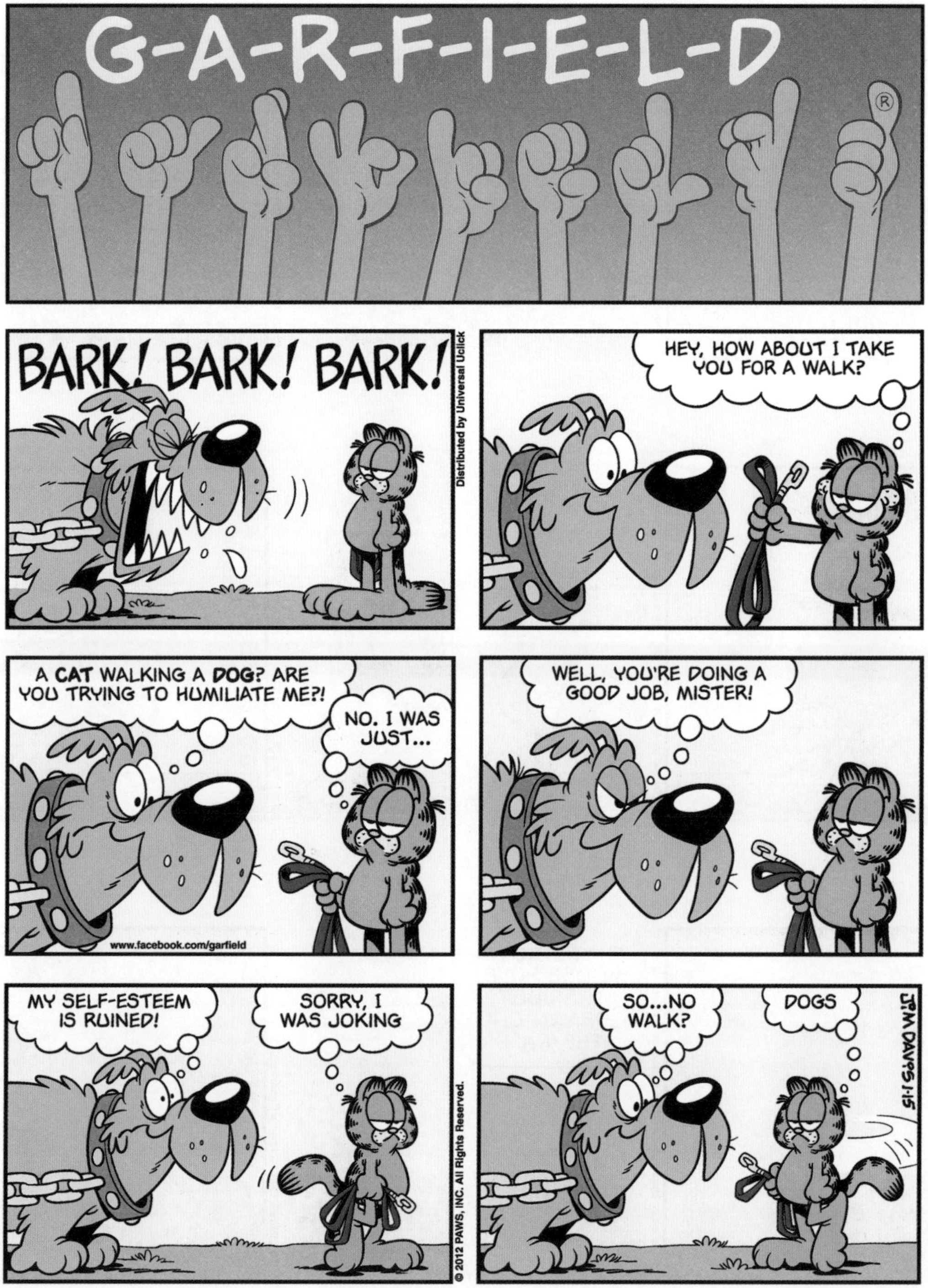
G-A-R-F-I-E-L-D
BARK! BARK! BARK!
Distributed by Universal Uclick
HEY, HOW ABOUT I TAKE YOU FOR A WALK?
A CAT WALKING A DOG? ARE YOU TRYING TO HUMILIATE ME?!
NO. I WAS JUST...
www.facebook.com/garfield
WELL, YOU'RE DOING A GOOD JOB, MISTER!
MY SELF-ESTEEM IS RUINED!
SORRY, I WAS JOKING
© 2012 PAWS, INC. All Rights Reserved.
SO...NO WALK?
DOGS

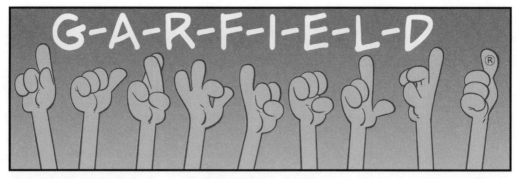

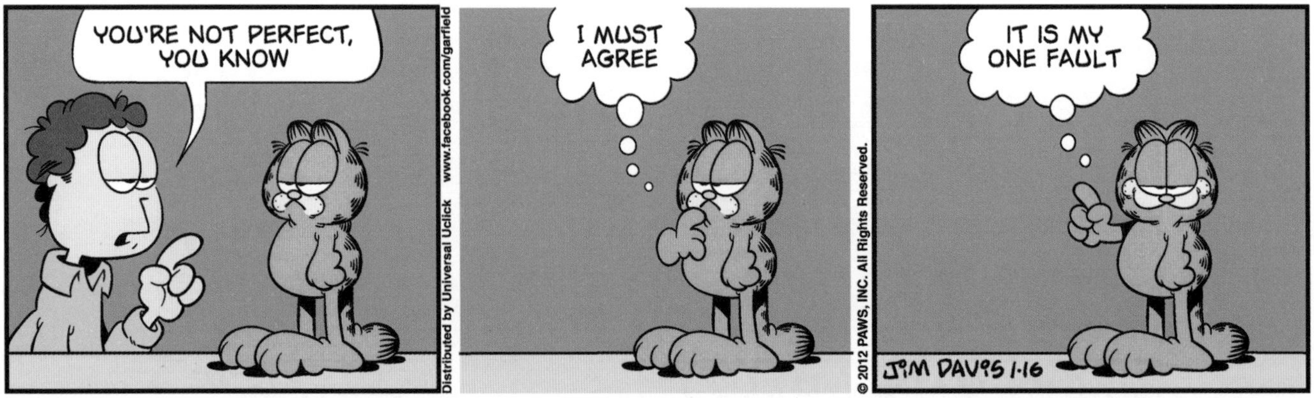
YOU'RE NOT PERFECT, YOU KNOW
Distributed by Universal Uclick www.facebook.com/garfield
I MUST AGREE
© 2012 PAWS, INC. All Rights Reserved.
IT IS MY ONE FAULT
JIM DAVIS 1-16

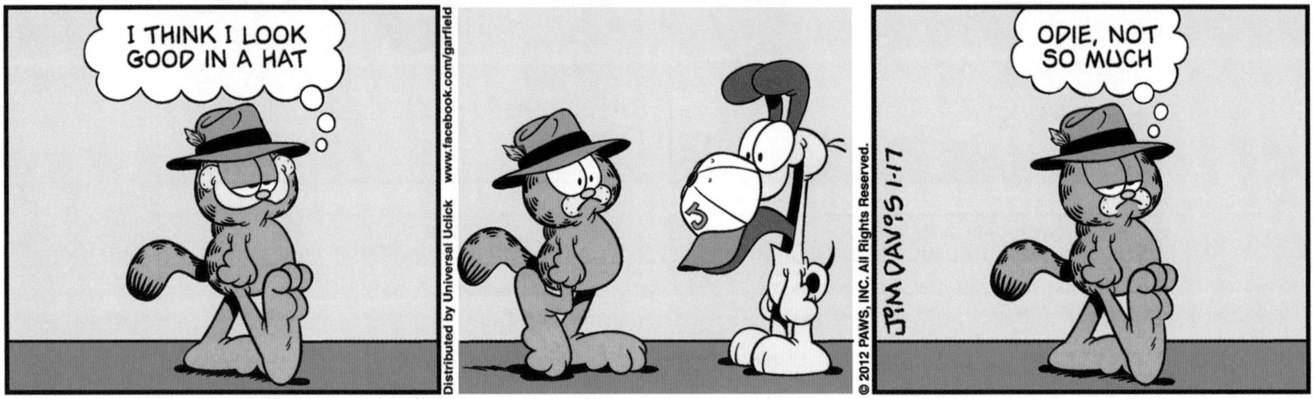
I THINK I LOOK GOOD IN A HAT
Distributed by Universal Uclick www.facebook.com/garfield
5
© 2012 PAWS, INC. All Rights Reserved.
JIM DAVIS 1-17
ODIE, NOT SO MUCH

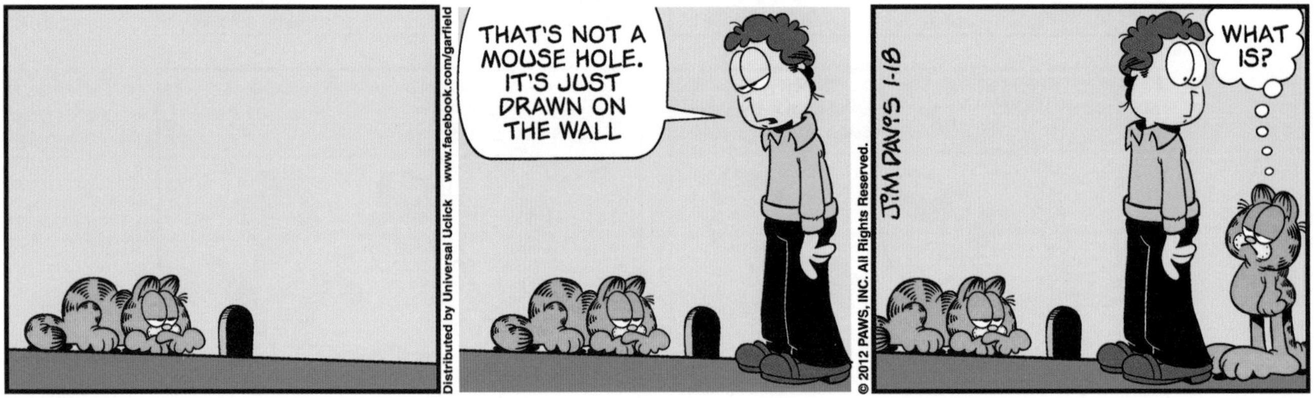
Distributed by Universal Uclick www.facebook.com/garfield
THAT'S NOT A MOUSE HOLE. IT'S JUST DRAWN ON THE WALL
© 2012 PAWS, INC. All Rights Reserved.
JIM DAVIS 1-18
WHAT IS?

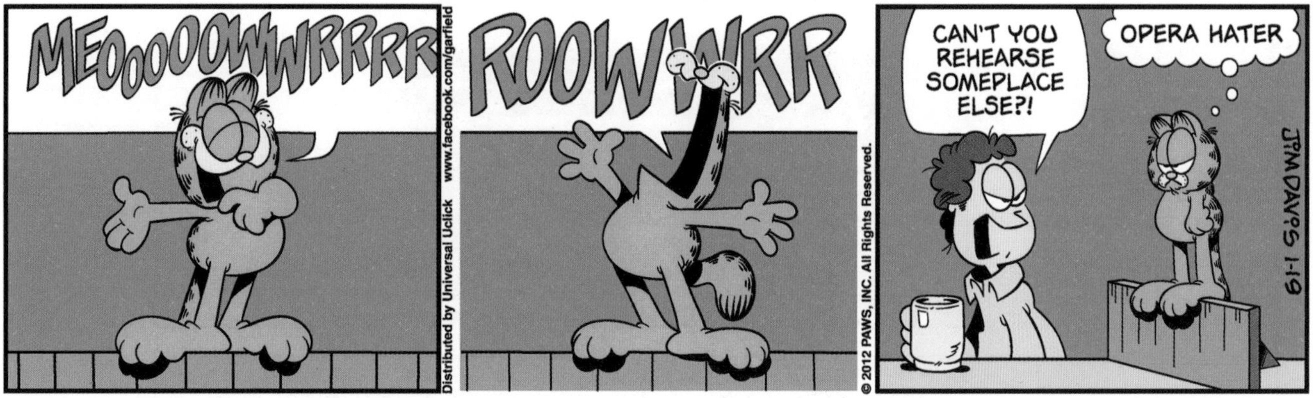
MEOOOOOWWRRRRR
Distributed by Universal Uclick www.facebook.com/garfield
ROOWWRR
© 2012 PAWS, INC. All Rights Reserved.
CAN'T YOU REHEARSE SOMEPLACE ELSE?!
OPERA HATER
JPM DAVPS 1-19

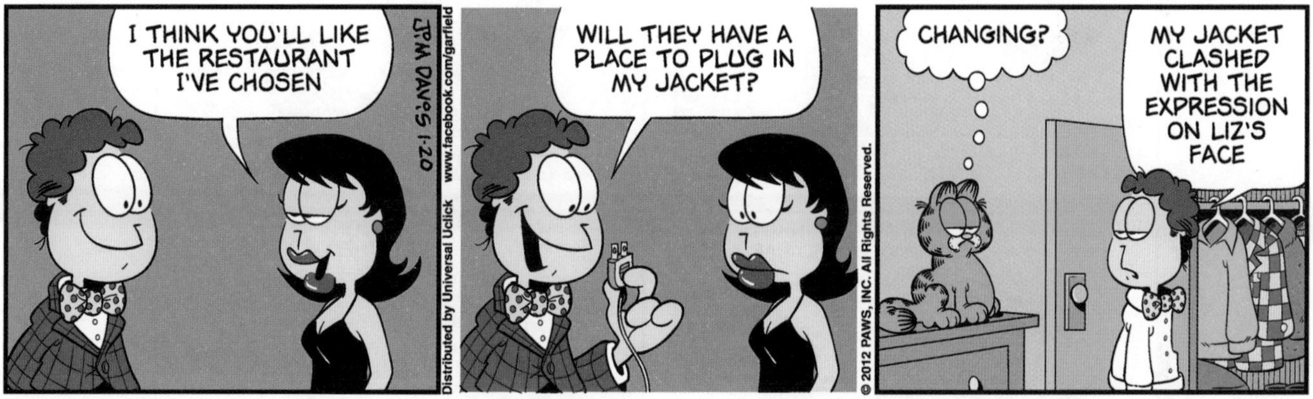
I THINK YOU'LL LIKE THE RESTAURANT I'VE CHOSEN
JPM DAVPS 1-20
Distributed by Universal Uclick www.facebook.com/garfield
WILL THEY HAVE A PLACE TO PLUG IN MY JACKET?
© 2012 PAWS, INC. All Rights Reserved.
CHANGING?
MY JACKET CLASHED WITH THE EXPRESSION ON LIZ'S FACE

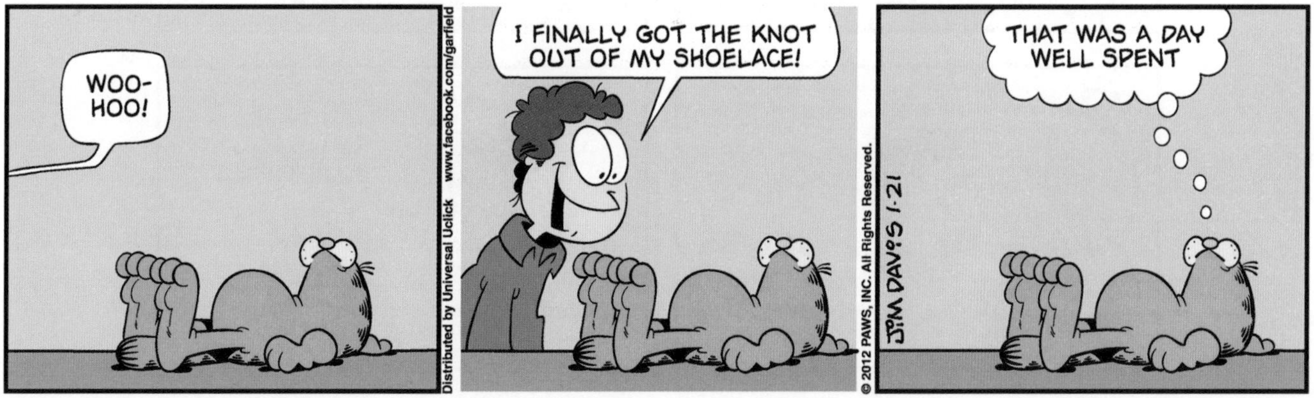
WOO-HOO!
Distributed by Universal Uclick www.facebook.com/garfield
I FINALLY GOT THE KNOT OUT OF MY SHOELACE!
© 2012 PAWS, INC. All Rights Reserved.
JPM DAVPS 1-21
THAT WAS A DAY WELL SPENT

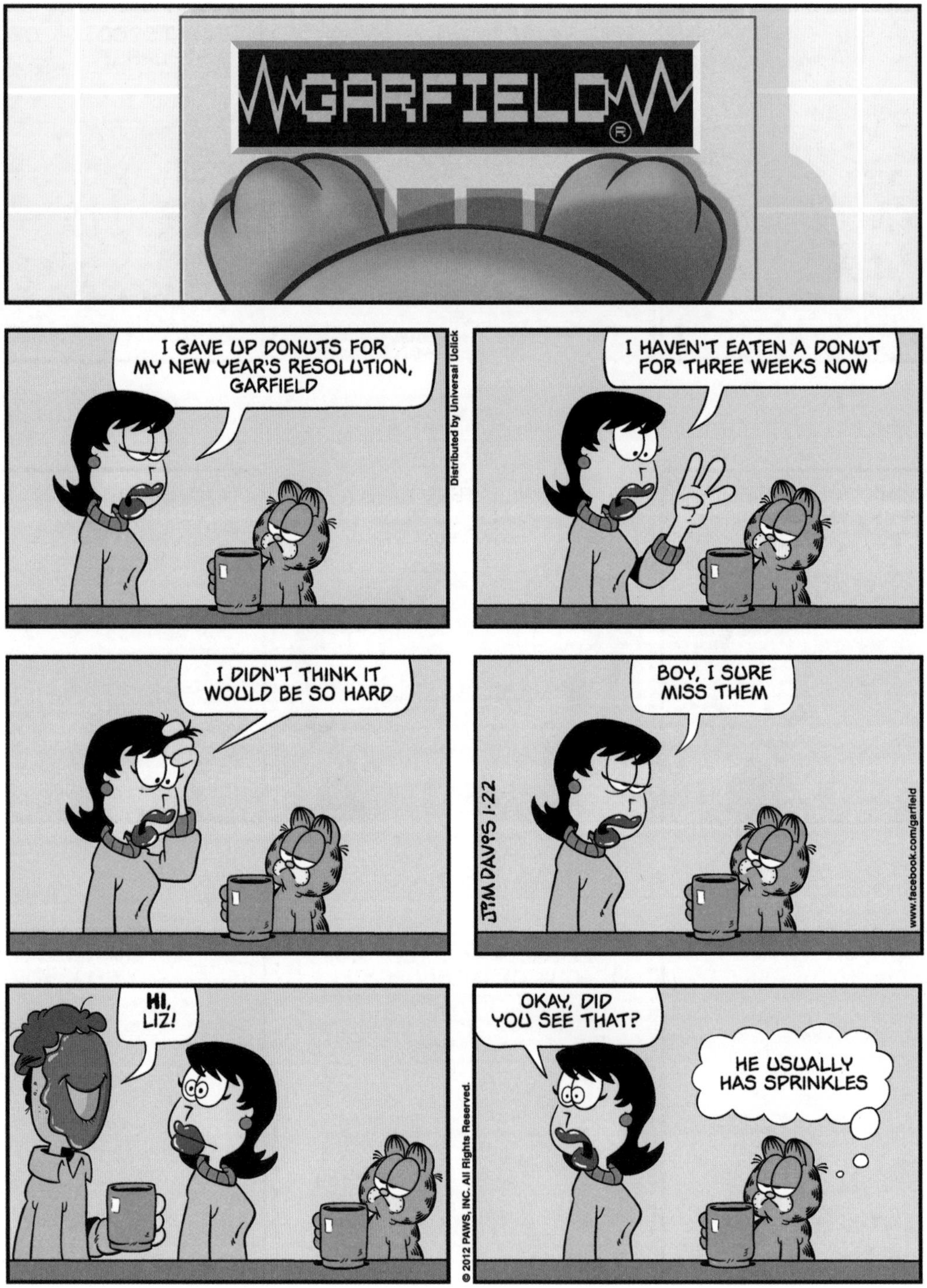
GARFIELD
I GAVE UP DONUTS FOR MY NEW YEAR'S RESOLUTION, GARFIELD
Distributed by Universal Uclick
I HAVEN'T EATEN A DONUT FOR THREE WEEKS NOW
I DIDN'T THINK IT WOULD BE SO HARD
JPM DAVPS 1-22
BOY, I SURE MISS THEM
www.facebook.com/garfield
HI, LIZ!
© 2012 PAWS, INC. All Rights Reserved.
OKAY, DID YOU SEE THAT?
HE USUALLY HAS SPRINKLES

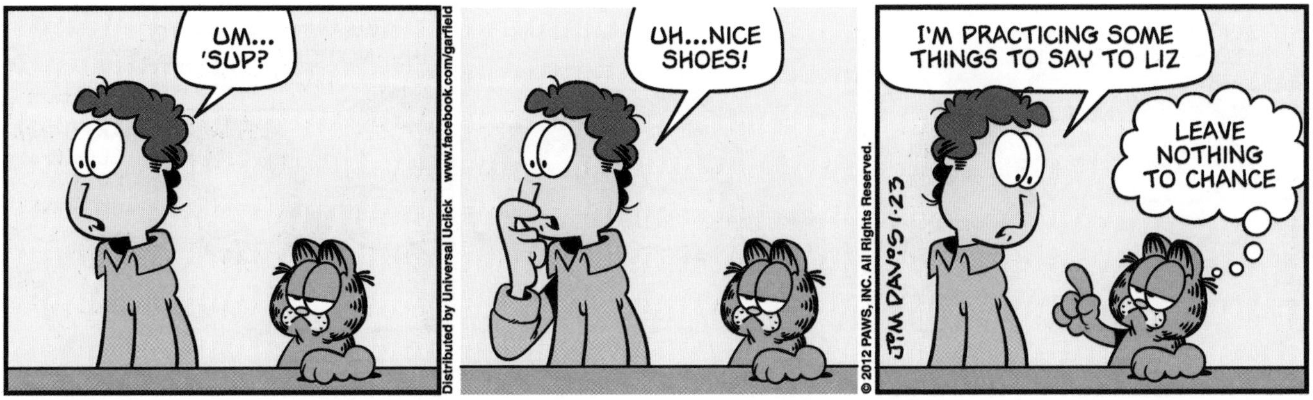
UM...
'SUP?
UH...NICE
SHOES!
I'M PRACTICING SOME
THINGS TO SAY TO LIZ
LEAVE
NOTHING
TO CHANCE

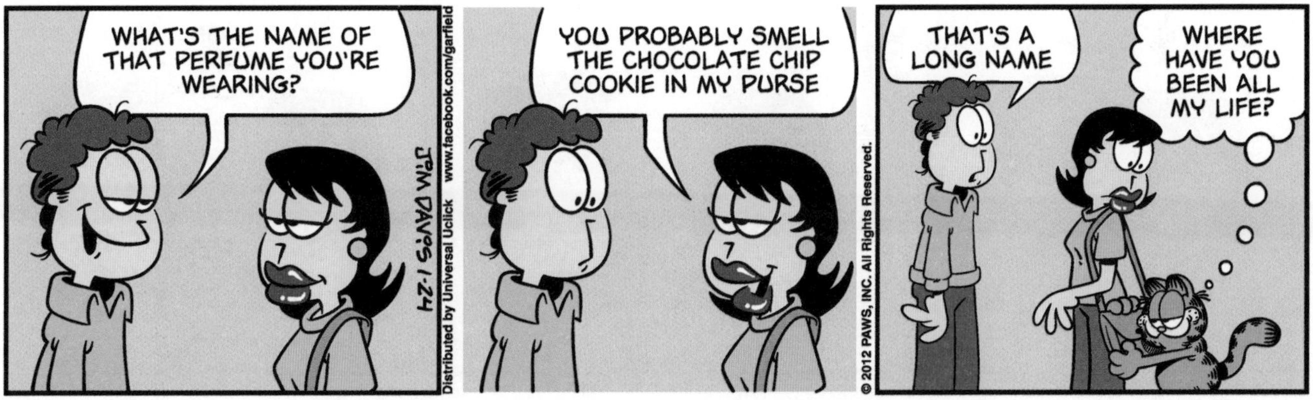
WHAT'S THE NAME OF
THAT PERFUME YOU'RE
WEARING?
YOU PROBABLY SMELL
THE CHOCOLATE CHIP
COOKIE IN MY PURSE
THAT'S A
LONG NAME
WHERE
HAVE YOU
BEEN ALL
MY LIFE?

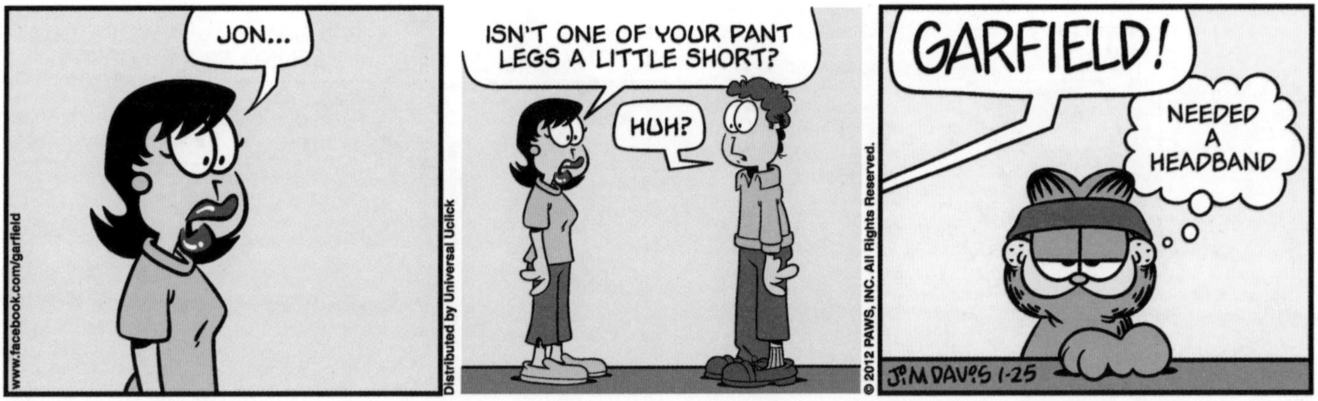
JON...
ISN'T ONE OF YOUR PANT
LEGS A LITTLE SHORT?
HUH?
GARFIELD!
NEEDED
A
HEADBAND

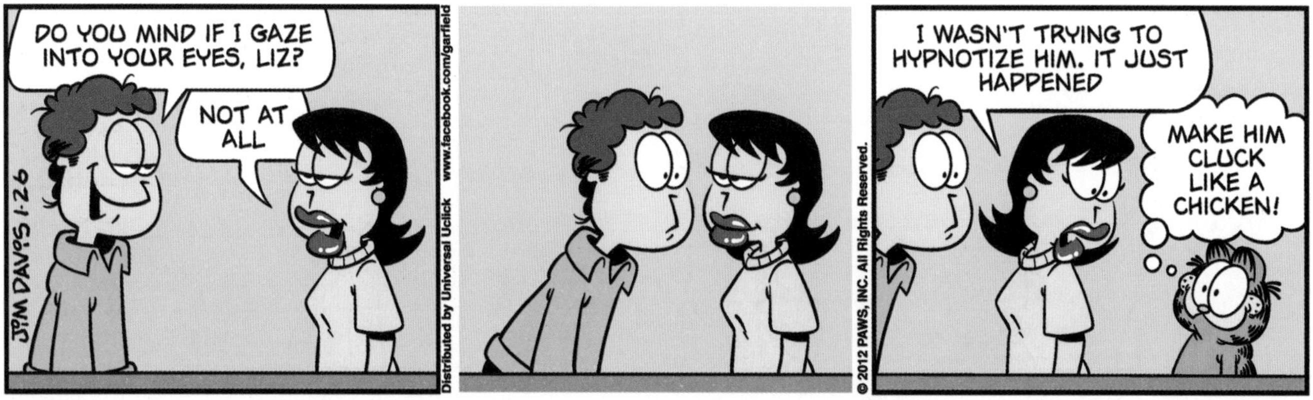
DO YOU MIND IF I GAZE INTO YOUR EYES, LIZ?
NOT AT ALL
JIM DAVIS 1-26
Distributed by Universal Uclick www.facebook.com/garfield
© 2012 PAWS, INC. All Rights Reserved.
I WASN'T TRYING TO HYPNOTIZE HIM. IT JUST HAPPENED
MAKE HIM CLUCK LIKE A CHICKEN!

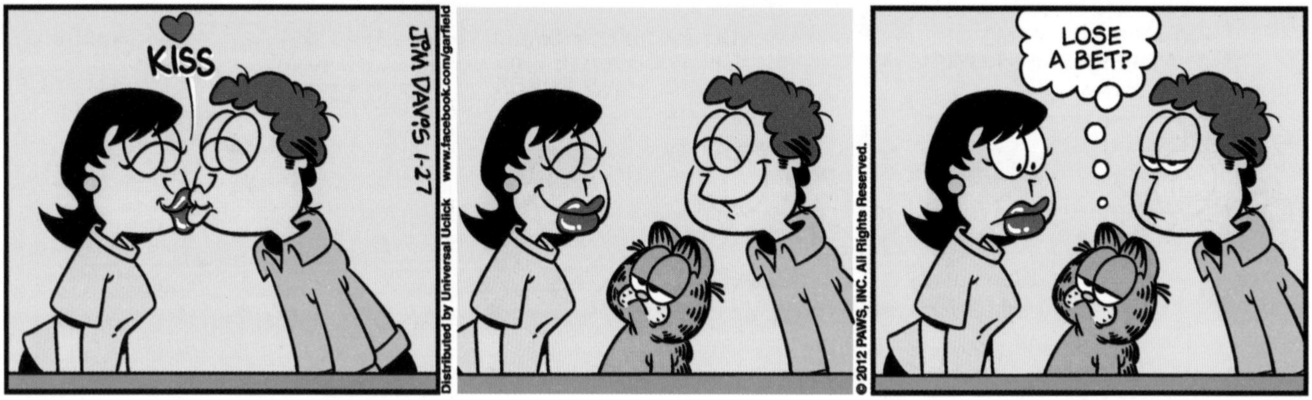
KISS
JIM DAVIS 1-27
Distributed by Universal Uclick www.facebook.com/garfield
© 2012 PAWS, INC. All Rights Reserved.
LOSE A BET?

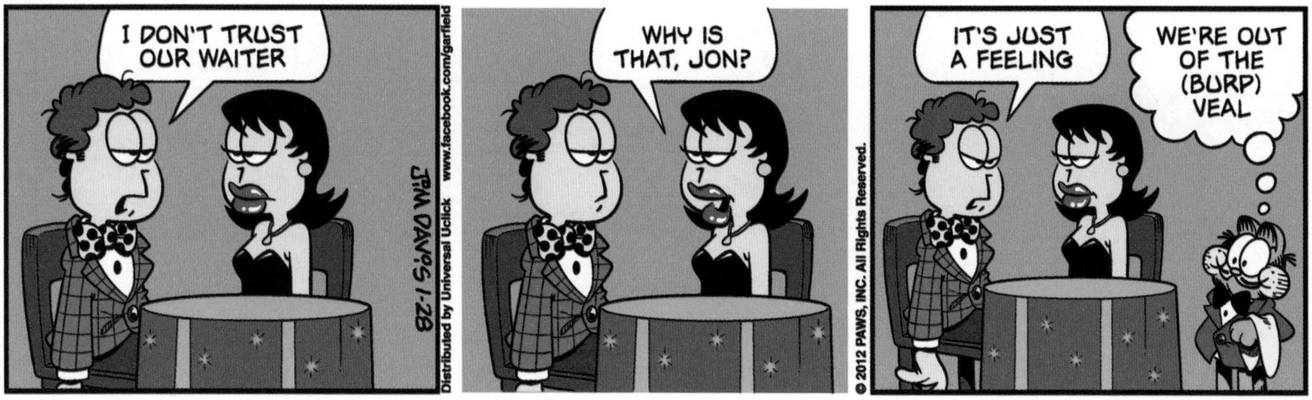
I DON'T TRUST OUR WAITER
JIM DAVIS 1-28
Distributed by Universal Uclick www.facebook.com/garfield
WHY IS THAT, JON?
© 2012 PAWS, INC. All Rights Reserved.
IT'S JUST A FEELING
WE'RE OUT OF THE (BURP) VEAL

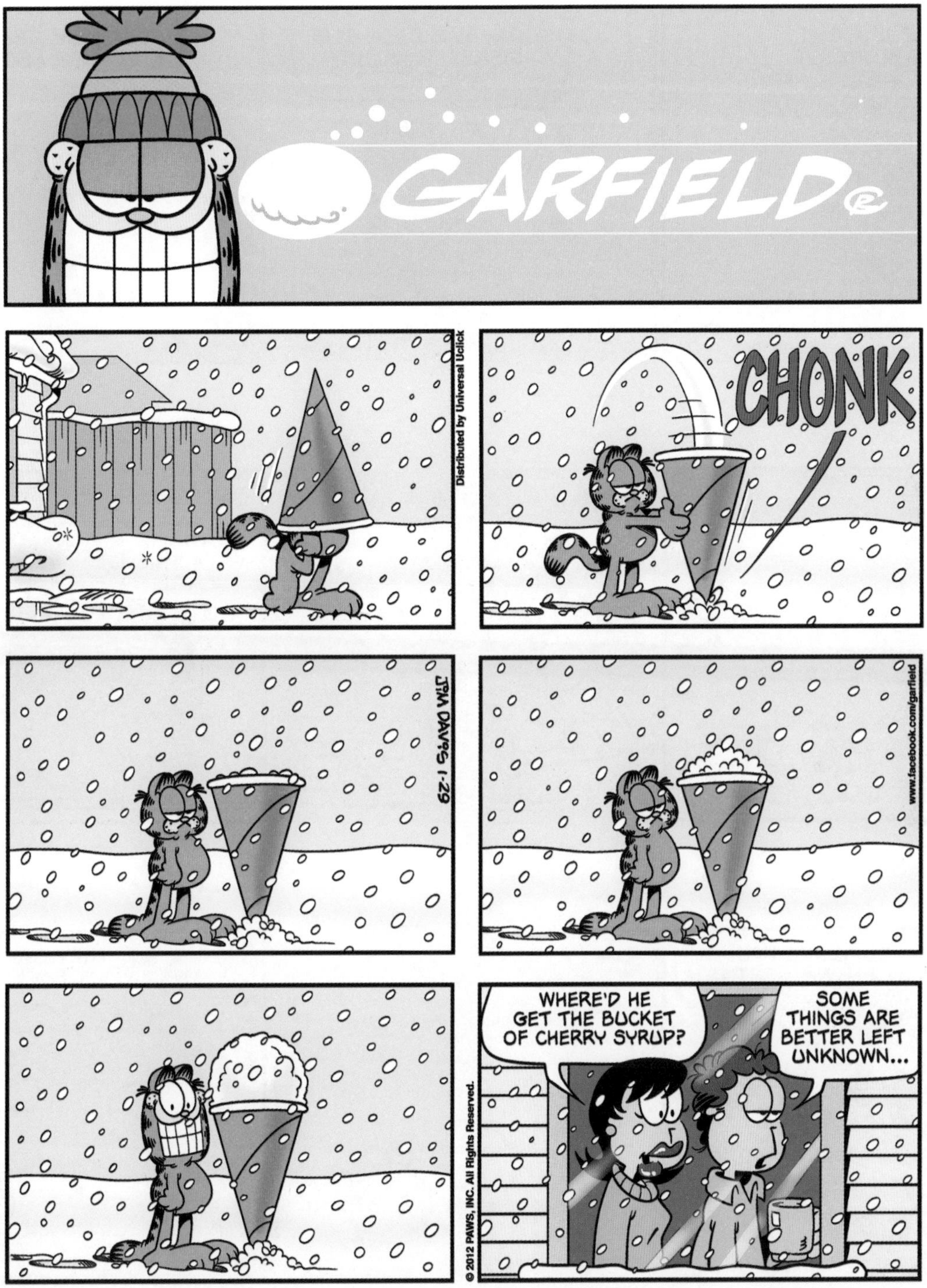
GARFIELD®
Distributed by Universal Uclick
CHONK
JPM DAVPS 1-29
www.facebook.com/garfield
© 2012 PAWS, INC. All Rights Reserved.
WHERE'D HE GET THE BUCKET OF CHERRY SYRUP?
SOME THINGS ARE BETTER LEFT UNKNOWN...

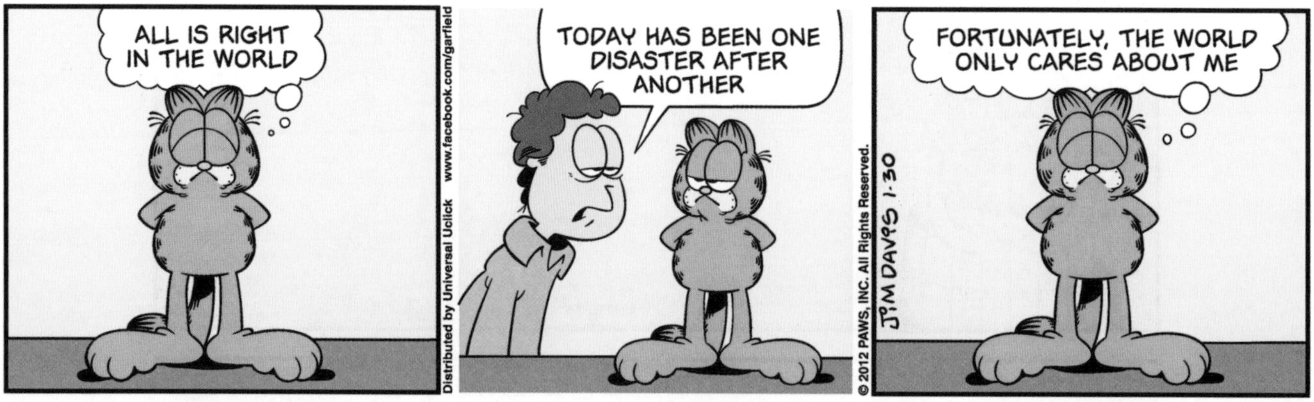
ALL IS RIGHT IN THE WORLD
Distributed by Universal Uclick www.facebook.com/garfield
TODAY HAS BEEN ONE DISASTER AFTER ANOTHER
© 2012 PAWS, INC. All Rights Reserved.
JIM DAVIS 1·30
FORTUNATELY, THE WORLD ONLY CARES ABOUT ME

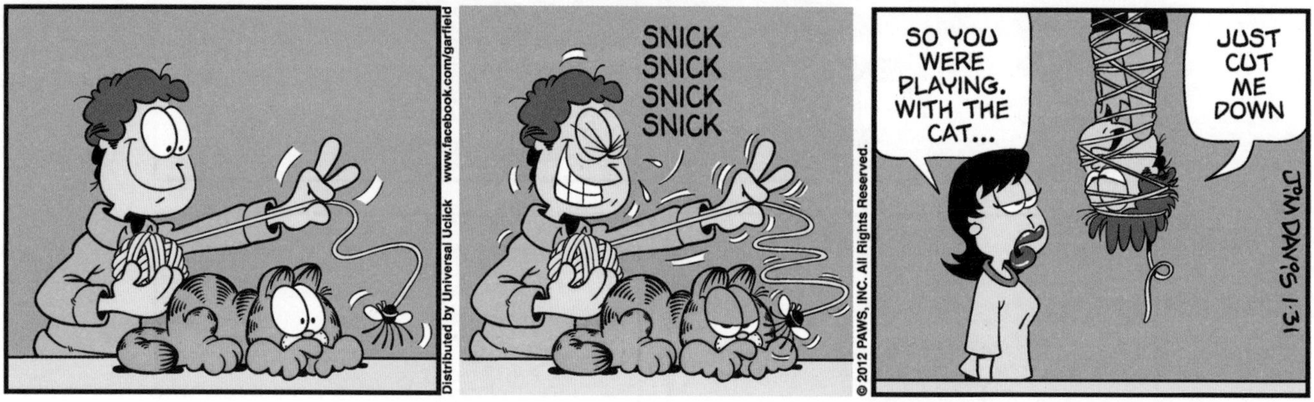
Distributed by Universal Uclick www.facebook.com/garfield
SNICK
SNICK
SNICK
SNICK
© 2012 PAWS, INC. All Rights Reserved.
SO YOU WERE PLAYING. WITH THE CAT...
JUST CUT ME DOWN
JIM DAVIS 1·31

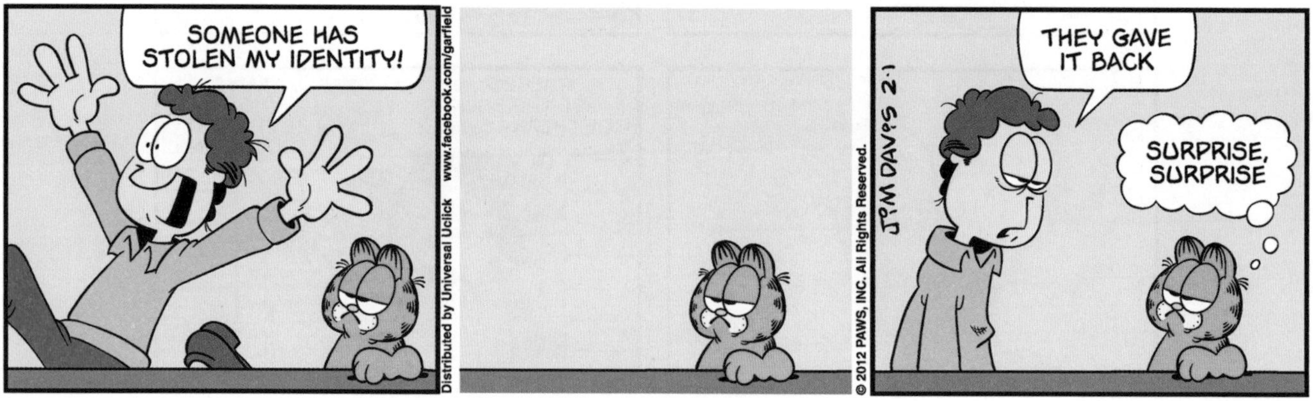
SOMEONE HAS STOLEN MY IDENTITY!
Distributed by Universal Uclick www.facebook.com/garfield
© 2012 PAWS, INC. All Rights Reserved.
JIM DAVIS 2·1
THEY GAVE IT BACK
SURPRISE, SURPRISE

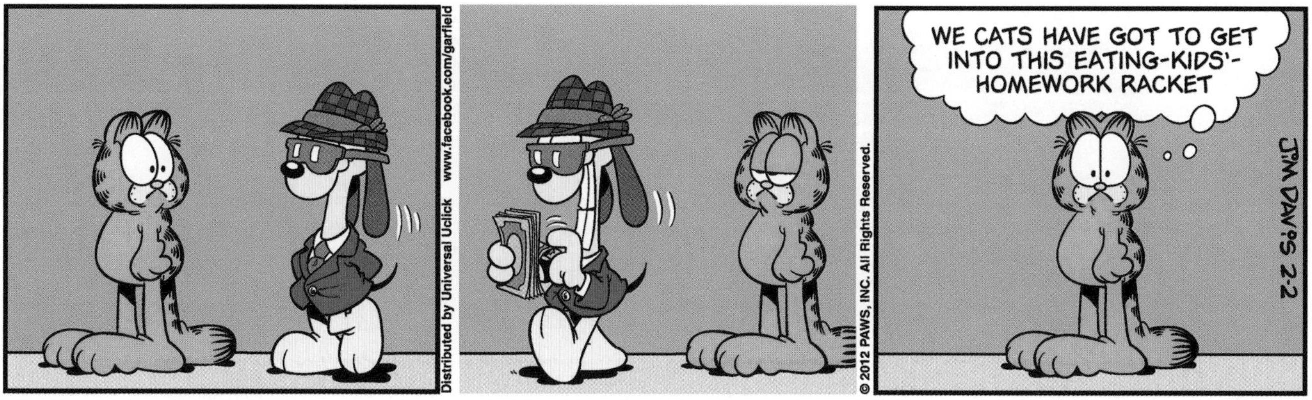
Distributed by Universal Uclick www.facebook.com/garfield
© 2012 PAWS, INC. All Rights Reserved.
WE CATS HAVE GOT TO GET INTO THIS EATING-KIDS'-HOMEWORK RACKET
JIM DAVIS 2-2

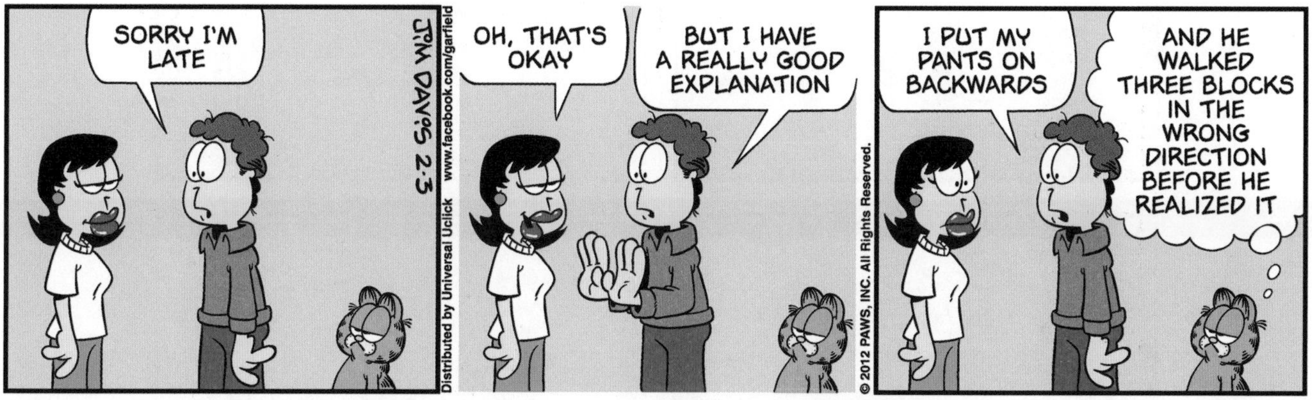
SORRY I'M LATE
JIM DAVIS 2-3
Distributed by Universal Uclick www.facebook.com/garfield
OH, THAT'S OKAY
BUT I HAVE A REALLY GOOD EXPLANATION
© 2012 PAWS, INC. All Rights Reserved.
I PUT MY PANTS ON BACKWARDS
AND HE WALKED THREE BLOCKS IN THE WRONG DIRECTION BEFORE HE REALIZED IT

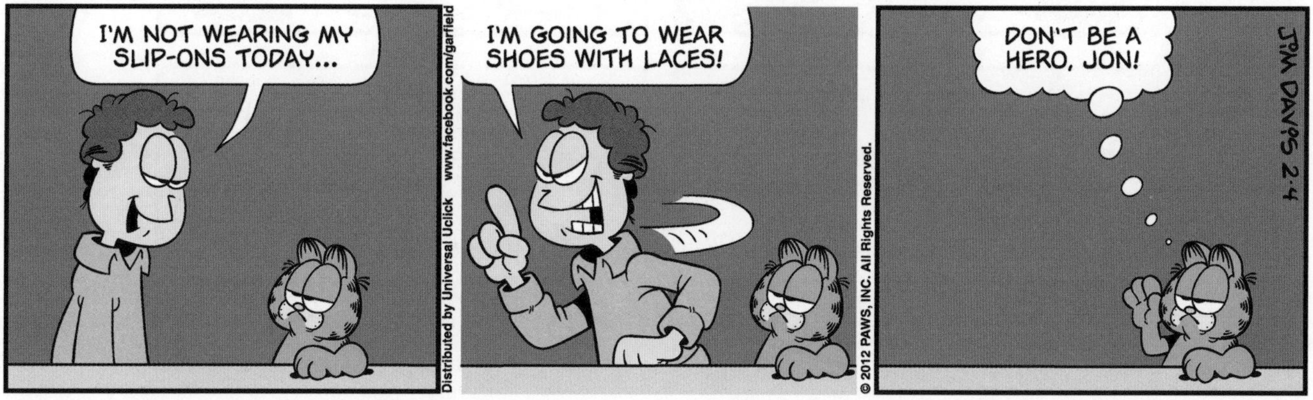
I'M NOT WEARING MY SLIP-ONS TODAY...
Distributed by Universal Uclick www.facebook.com/garfield
I'M GOING TO WEAR SHOES WITH LACES!
© 2012 PAWS, INC. All Rights Reserved.
DON'T BE A HERO, JON!
JIM DAVIS 2-4

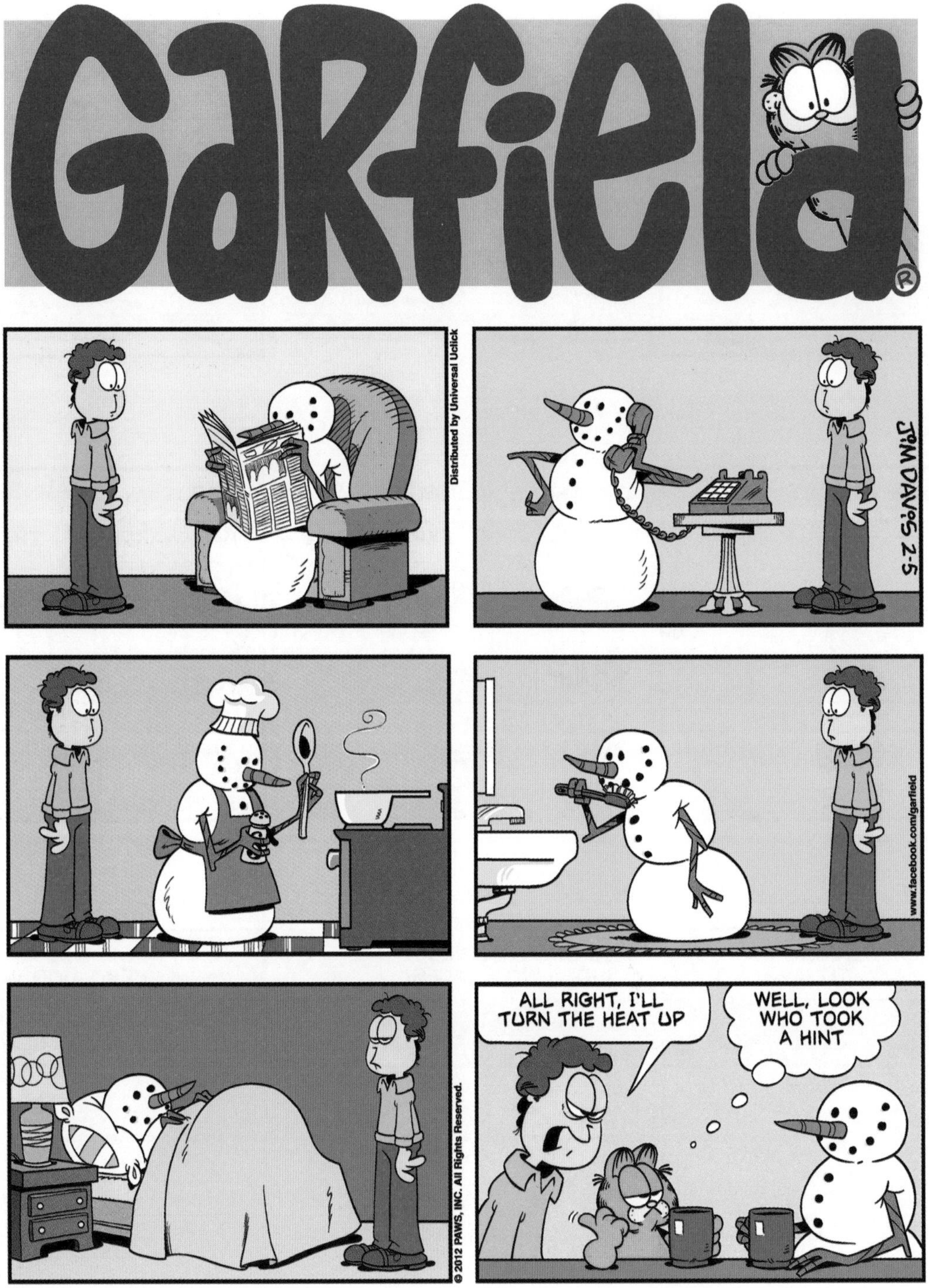
Garfield®
Distributed by Universal Uclick
JIM DAVIS 2-5
www.facebook.com/garfield
© 2012 PAWS, INC. All Rights Reserved.
ALL RIGHT, I'LL TURN THE HEAT UP
WELL, LOOK WHO TOOK A HINT

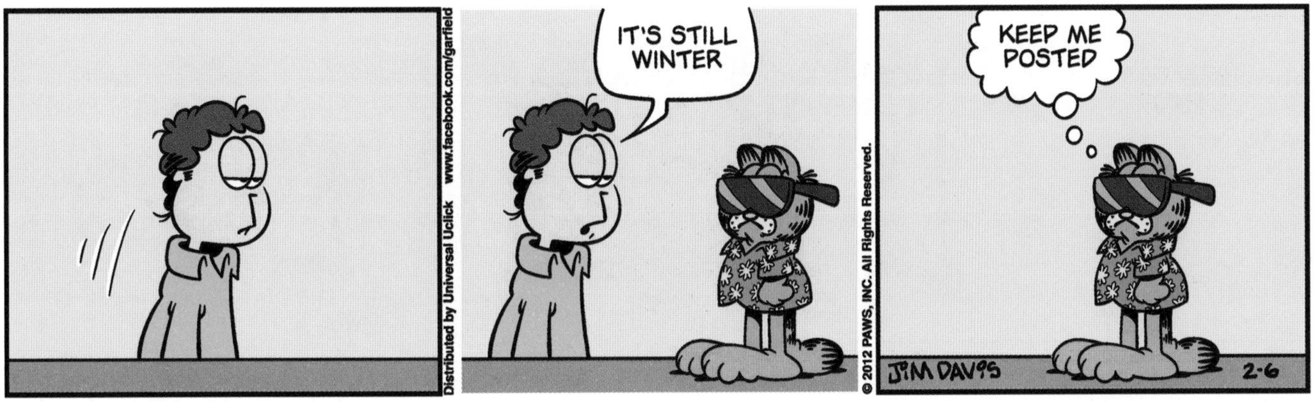
Distributed by Universal Uclick www.facebook.com/garfield
IT'S STILL WINTER
© 2012 PAWS, INC. All Rights Reserved.
KEEP ME POSTED
JIM DAVIS 2-6

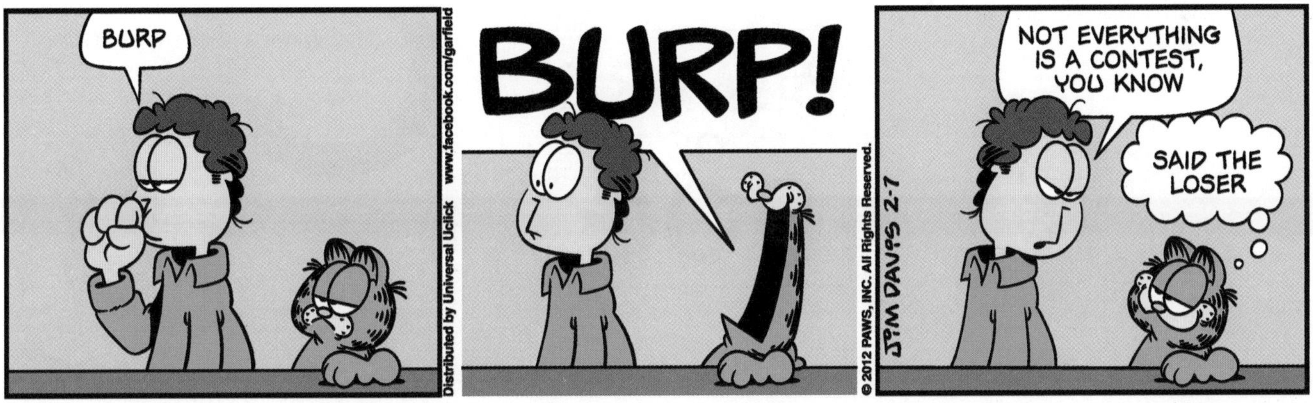
BURP
Distributed by Universal Uclick www.facebook.com/garfield
BURP!
© 2012 PAWS, INC. All Rights Reserved.
JIM DAVIS 2-7
NOT EVERYTHING IS A CONTEST, YOU KNOW
SAID THE LOSER

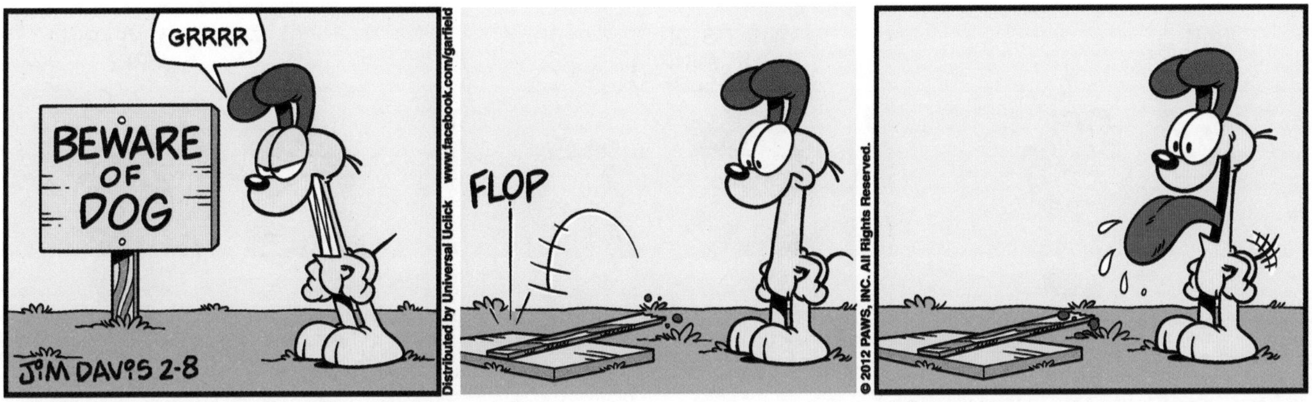
GRRRR
BEWARE OF DOG
JIM DAVIS 2-8
Distributed by Universal Uclick www.facebook.com/garfield
FLOP
© 2012 PAWS, INC. All Rights Reserved.

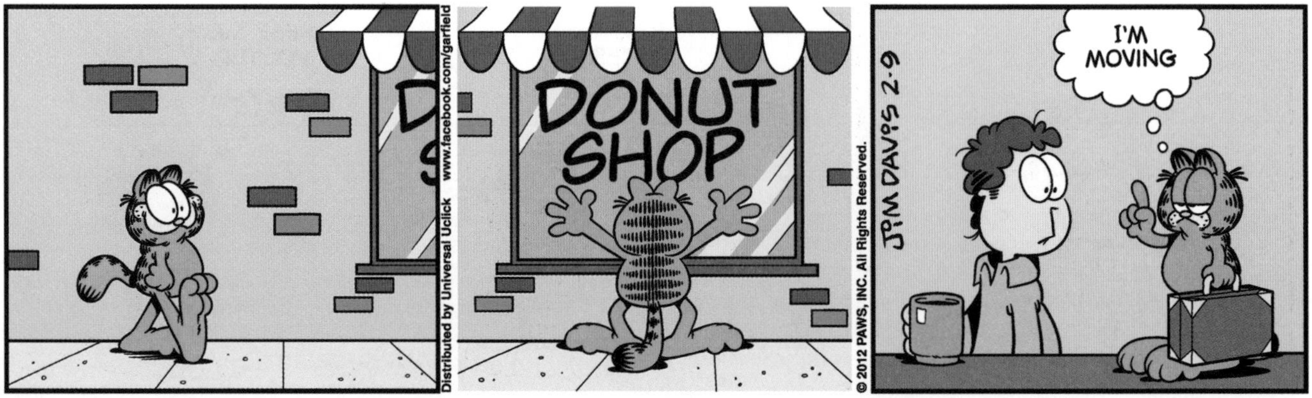
D
S
Distributed by Universal Uclick www.facebook.com/garfield
DONUT
SHOP
© 2012 PAWS, INC. All Rights Reserved.
JIM DAVIS 2-9
I'M
MOVING

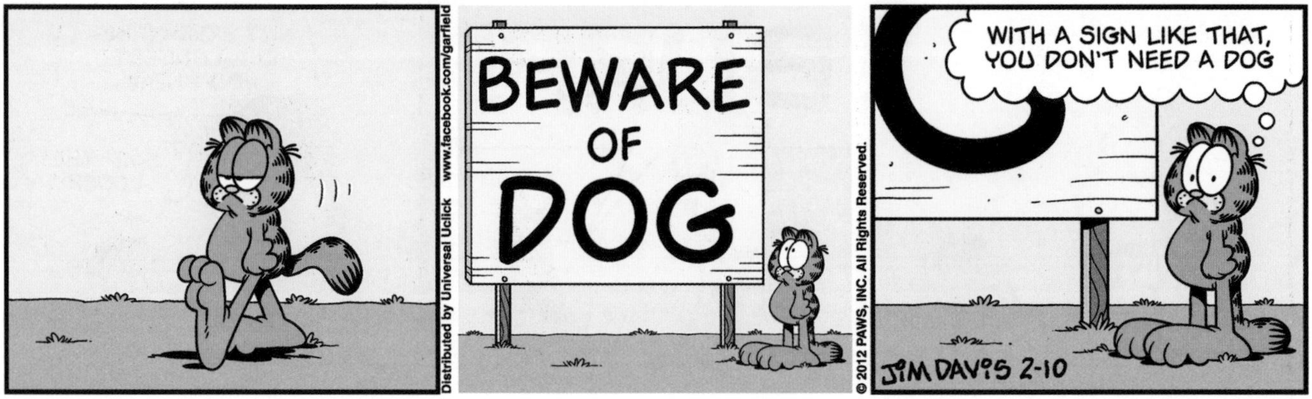
Distributed by Universal Uclick www.facebook.com/garfield
BEWARE
OF
DOG
© 2012 PAWS, INC. All Rights Reserved.
WITH A SIGN LIKE THAT, YOU DON'T NEED A DOG
JIM DAVIS 2-10

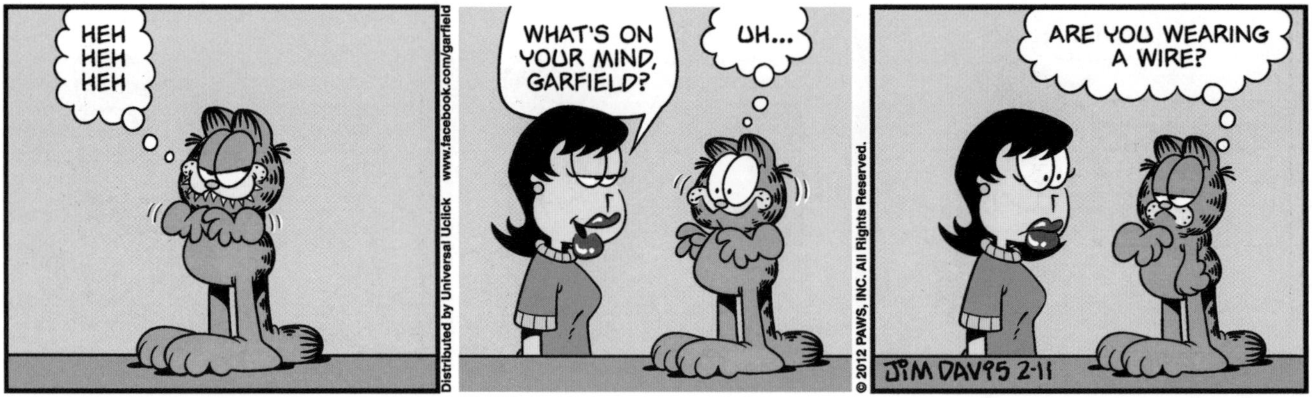
HEH
HEH
HEH
Distributed by Universal Uclick www.facebook.com/garfield
WHAT'S ON YOUR MIND, GARFIELD?
UH...
© 2012 PAWS, INC. All Rights Reserved.
ARE YOU WEARING A WIRE?
JIM DAVIS 2-11

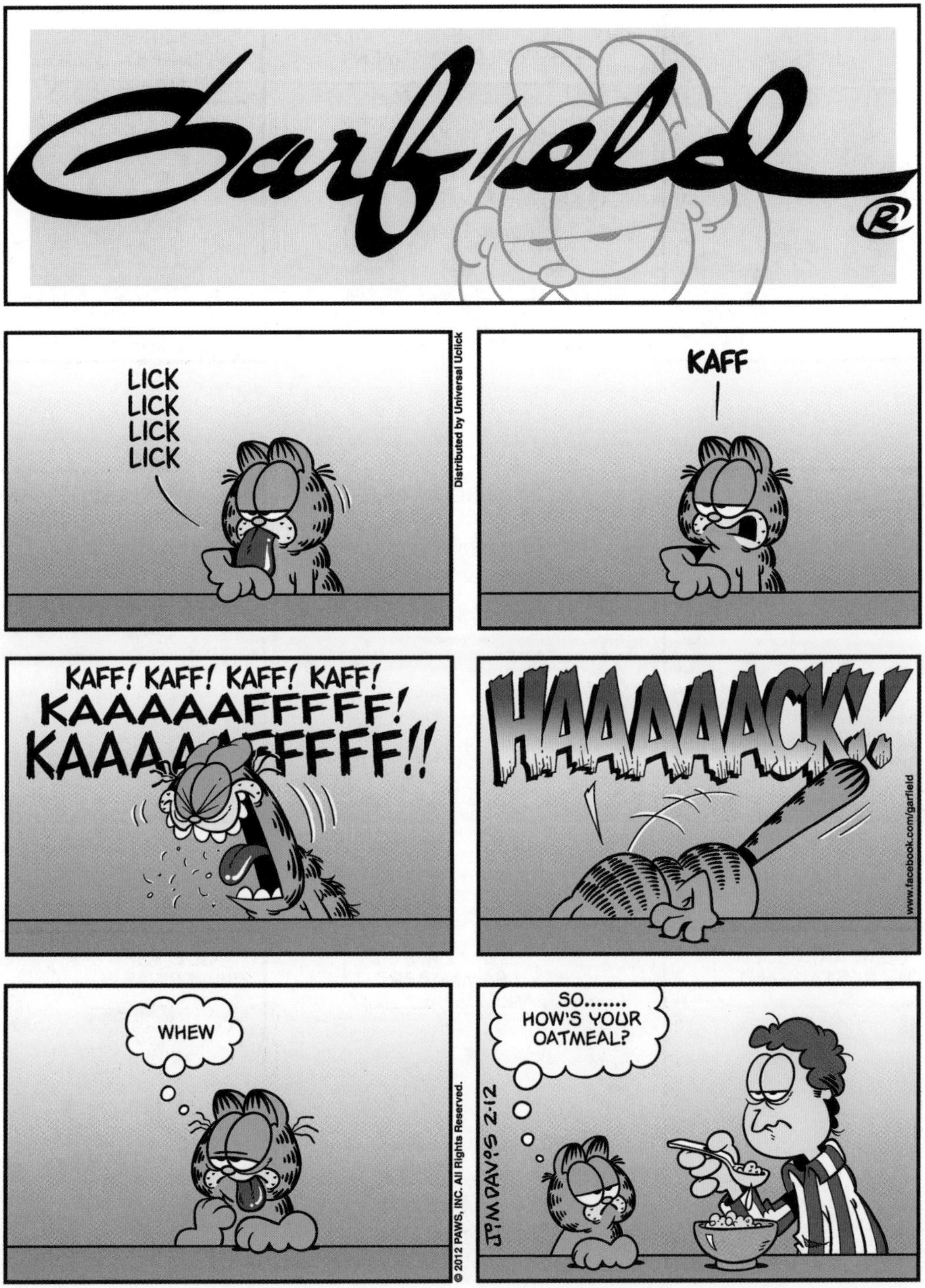
Garfield
LICK LICK LICK LICK
Distributed by Universal Uclick
KAFF
KAFF! KAFF! KAFF! KAFF!
KAAAAAFFFFF!
KAAAAAFFFFF!!
HAAAAACK!!
www.facebook.com/garfield
WHEW
© 2012 PAWS, INC. All Rights Reserved.
JIM DAVIS 2-12
SO....... HOW'S YOUR OATMEAL?

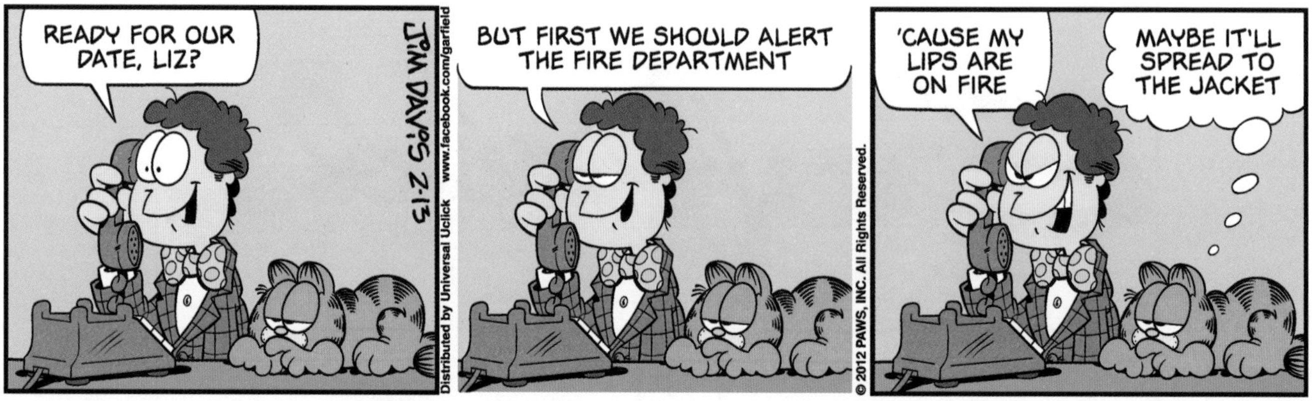
READY FOR OUR DATE, LIZ?
JIM DAVIS 2-13
Distributed by Universal Uclick www.facebook.com/garfield
BUT FIRST WE SHOULD ALERT THE FIRE DEPARTMENT
© 2012 PAWS, INC. All Rights Reserved.
'CAUSE MY LIPS ARE ON FIRE
MAYBE IT'LL SPREAD TO THE JACKET

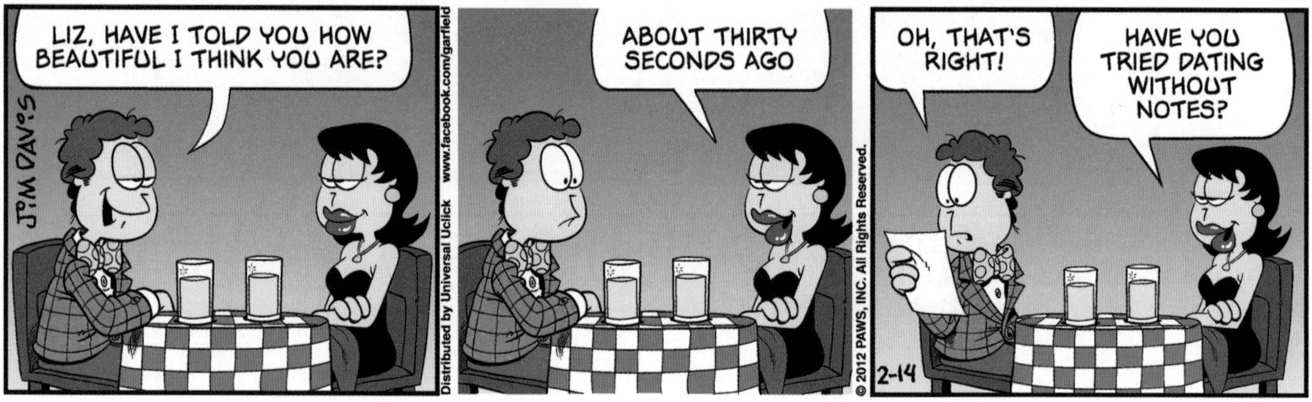
LIZ, HAVE I TOLD YOU HOW BEAUTIFUL I THINK YOU ARE?
JIM DAVIS
Distributed by Universal Uclick www.facebook.com/garfield
ABOUT THIRTY SECONDS AGO
© 2012 PAWS, INC. All Rights Reserved.
OH, THAT'S RIGHT!
HAVE YOU TRIED DATING WITHOUT NOTES?
2-14

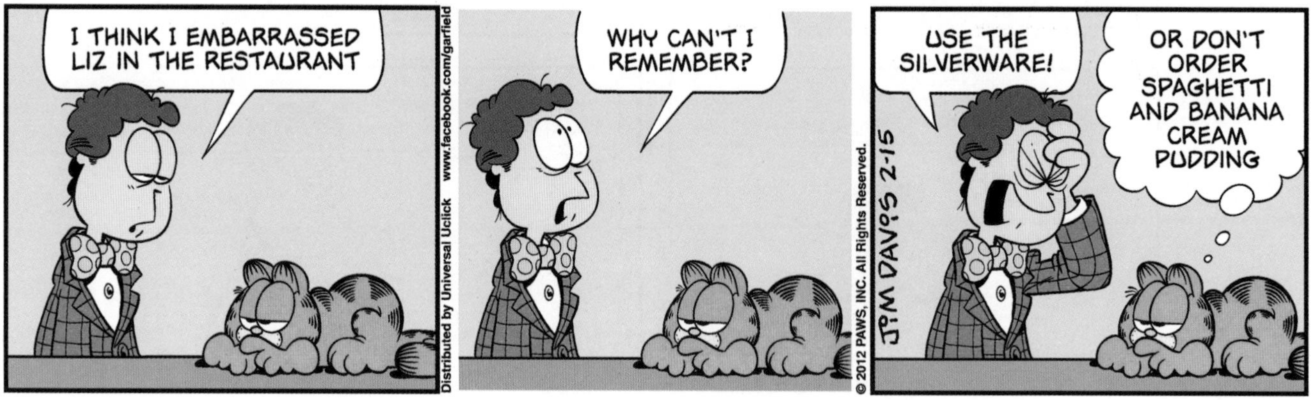
I THINK I EMBARRASSED LIZ IN THE RESTAURANT
Distributed by Universal Uclick www.facebook.com/garfield
WHY CAN'T I REMEMBER?
© 2012 PAWS, INC. All Rights Reserved.
JIM DAVIS 2-15
USE THE SILVERWARE!
OR DON'T ORDER SPAGHETTI AND BANANA CREAM PUDDING

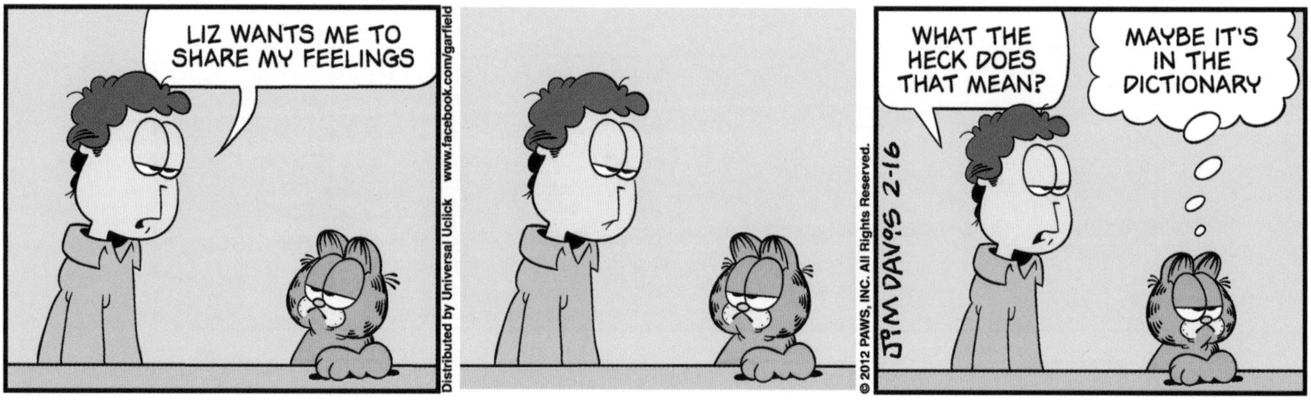
LIZ WANTS ME TO SHARE MY FEELINGS
Distributed by Universal Uclick www.facebook.com/garfield
© 2012 PAWS, INC. All Rights Reserved.
JIM DAVIS 2-16
WHAT THE HECK DOES THAT MEAN?
MAYBE IT'S IN THE DICTIONARY

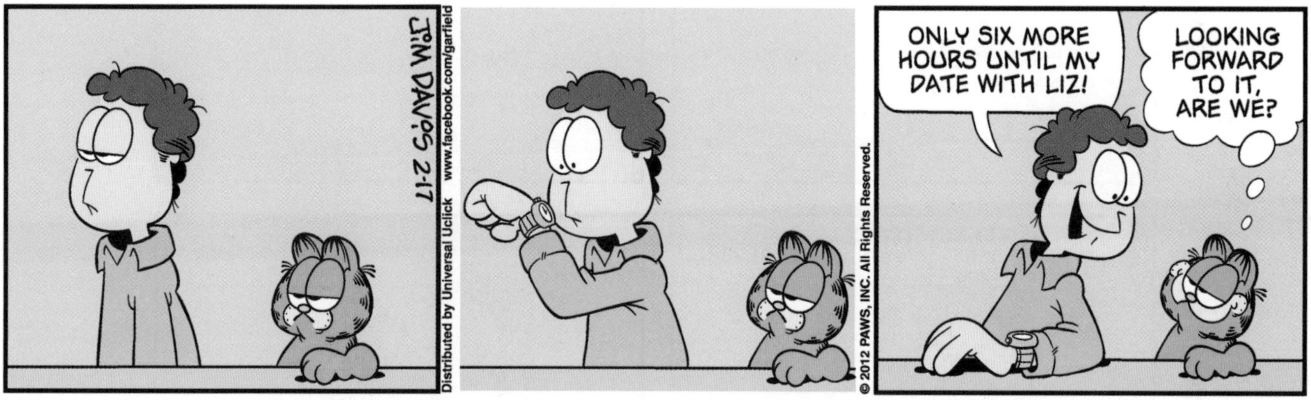
JIM DAVIS 2-17
Distributed by Universal Uclick www.facebook.com/garfield
© 2012 PAWS, INC. All Rights Reserved.
ONLY SIX MORE HOURS UNTIL MY DATE WITH LIZ!
LOOKING FORWARD TO IT, ARE WE?

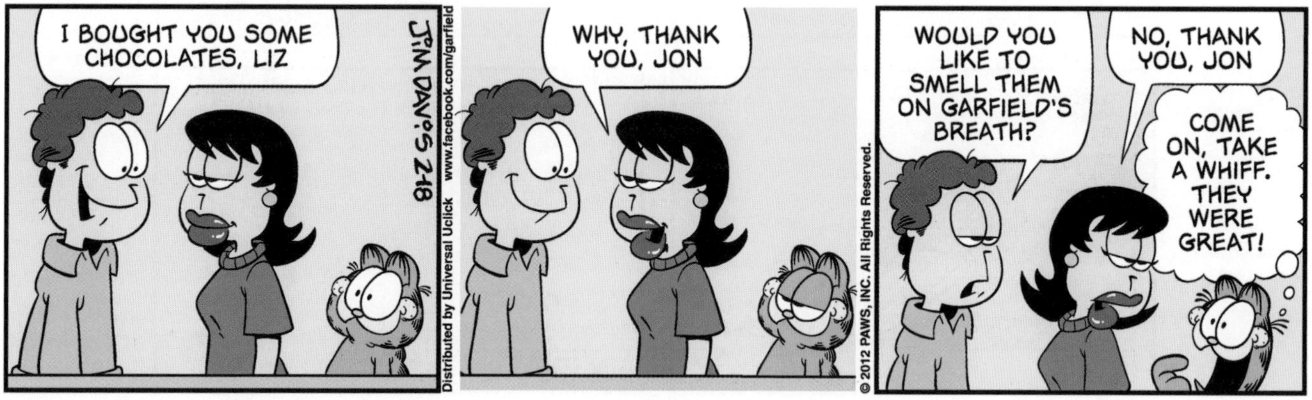
I BOUGHT YOU SOME CHOCOLATES, LIZ
JIM DAVIS 2-18
Distributed by Universal Uclick www.facebook.com/garfield
WHY, THANK YOU, JON
© 2012 PAWS, INC. All Rights Reserved.
WOULD YOU LIKE TO SMELL THEM ON GARFIELD'S BREATH?
NO, THANK YOU, JON
COME ON, TAKE A WHIFF. THEY WERE GREAT!

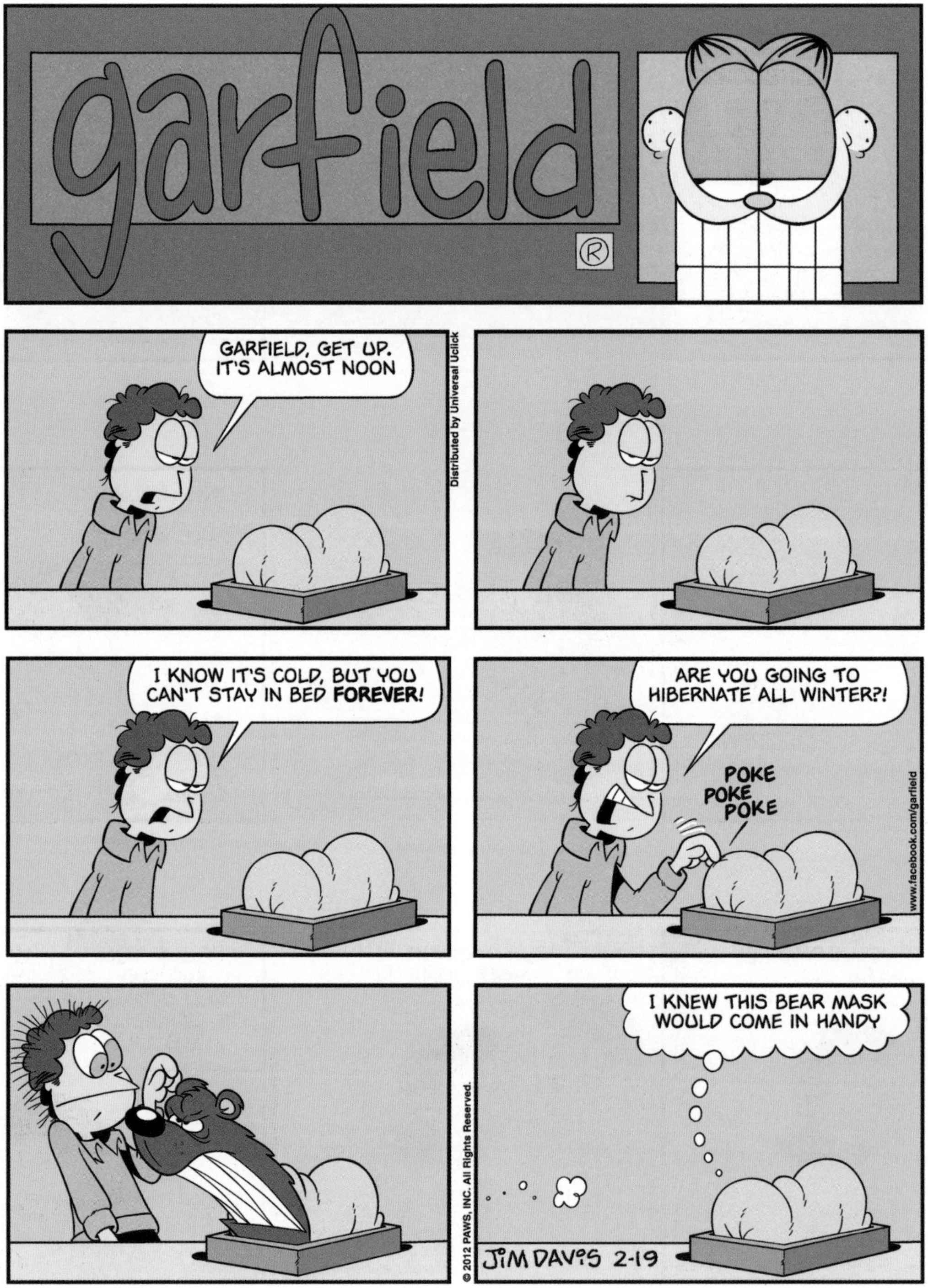
garfield
GARFIELD, GET UP. IT'S ALMOST NOON
Distributed by Universal Uclick
I KNOW IT'S COLD, BUT YOU CAN'T STAY IN BED **FOREVER**!
ARE YOU GOING TO HIBERNATE ALL WINTER?!
POKE POKE POKE
www.facebook.com/garfield
© 2012 PAWS, INC. All Rights Reserved.
I KNEW THIS BEAR MASK WOULD COME IN HANDY
JIM DAVIS 2-19

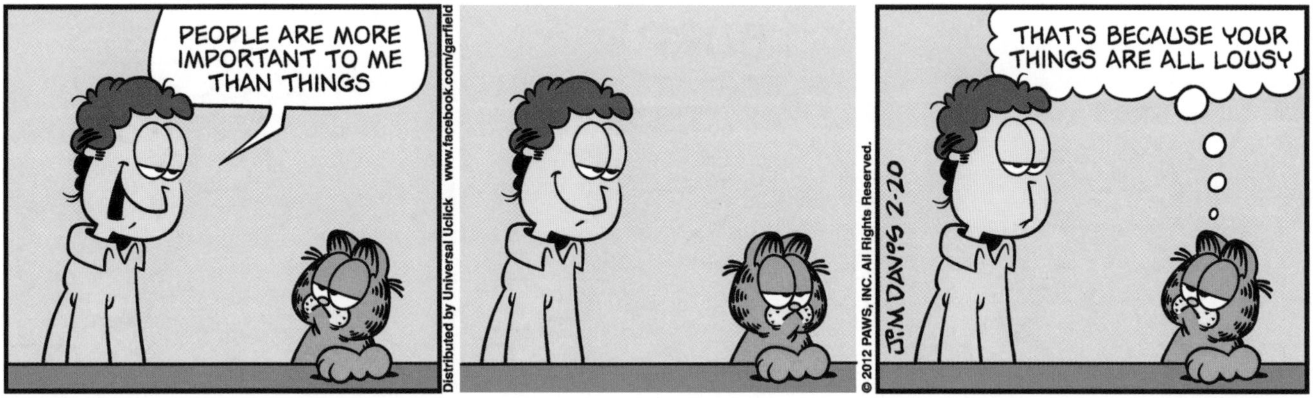
PEOPLE ARE MORE IMPORTANT TO ME THAN THINGS
Distributed by Universal Uclick www.facebook.com/garfield
© 2012 PAWS, INC. All Rights Reserved.
JPM DAVPS 2-20
THAT'S BECAUSE YOUR THINGS ARE ALL LOUSY

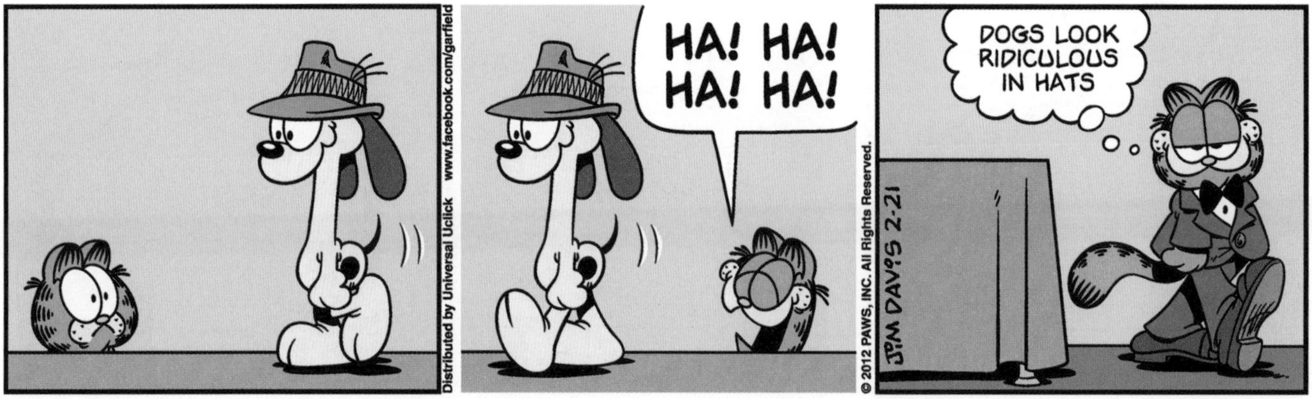
Distributed by Universal Uclick www.facebook.com/garfield
HA! HA! HA! HA!
© 2012 PAWS, INC. All Rights Reserved.
JPM DAVPS 2-21
DOGS LOOK RIDICULOUS IN HATS

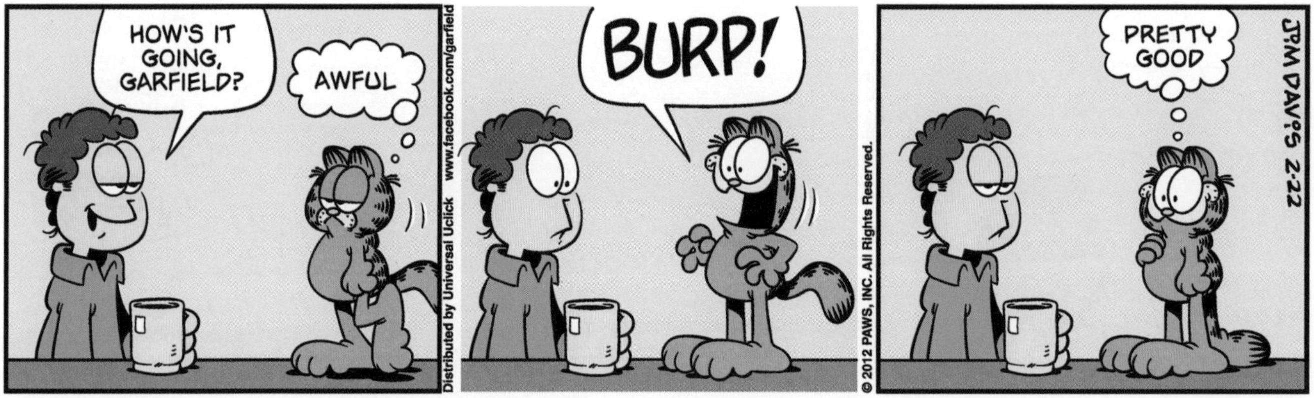
HOW'S IT GOING, GARFIELD?
AWFUL
Distributed by Universal Uclick www.facebook.com/garfield
BURP!
© 2012 PAWS, INC. All Rights Reserved.
PRETTY GOOD
JPM DAVPS 2-22

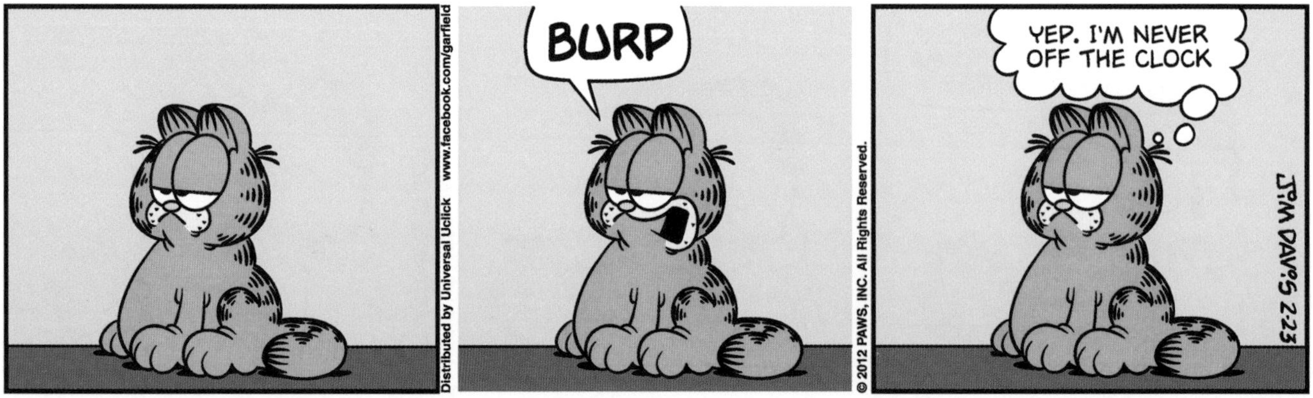
BURP
YEP. I'M NEVER OFF THE CLOCK
Distributed by Universal Uclick www.facebook.com/garfield
© 2012 PAWS, INC. All Rights Reserved.
JIM DAVIS 2·23

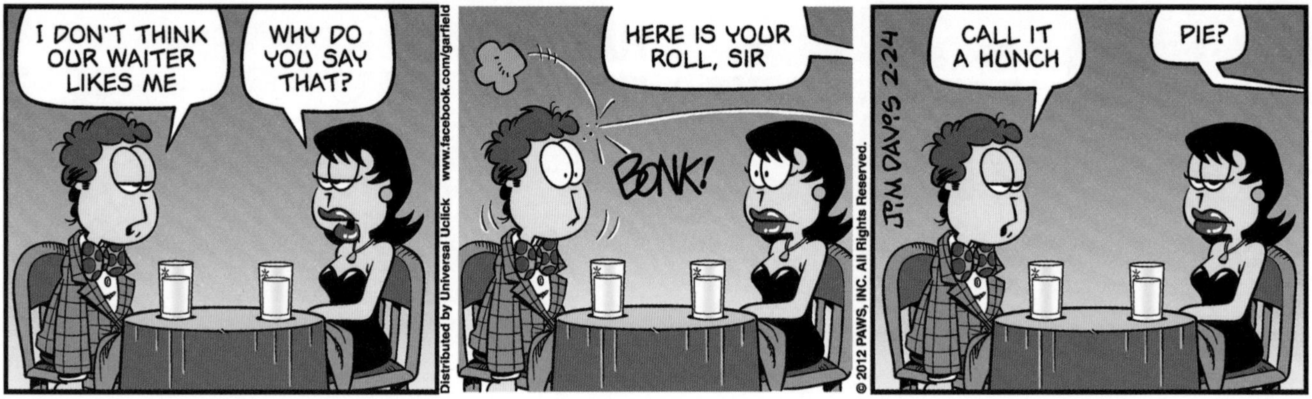
I DON'T THINK OUR WAITER LIKES ME
WHY DO YOU SAY THAT?
HERE IS YOUR ROLL, SIR
BONK!
CALL IT A HUNCH
PIE?
Distributed by Universal Uclick www.facebook.com/garfield
© 2012 PAWS, INC. All Rights Reserved.
JIM DAVIS 2·24

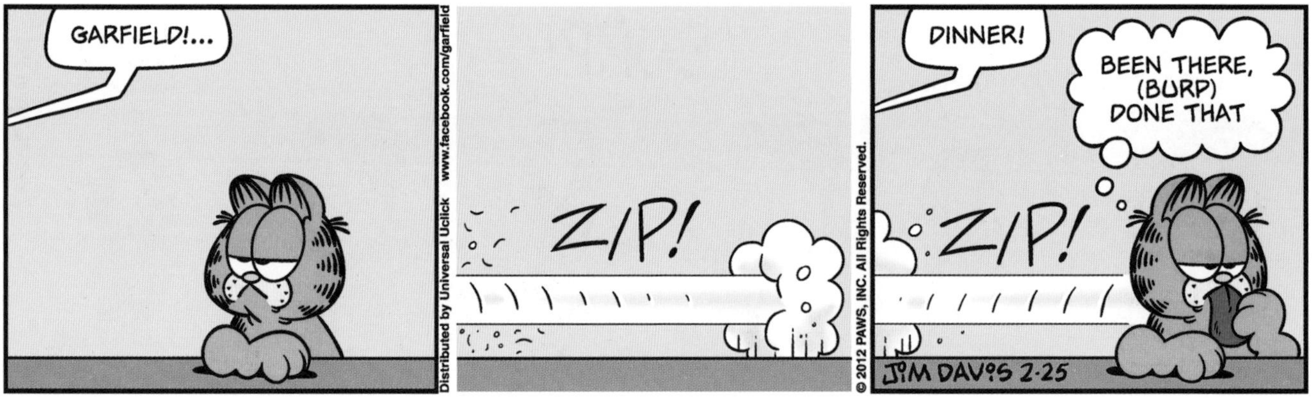
GARFIELD!...
ZIP!
DINNER!
ZIP!
BEEN THERE, (BURP) DONE THAT
Distributed by Universal Uclick www.facebook.com/garfield
© 2012 PAWS, INC. All Rights Reserved.
JIM DAVIS 2·25

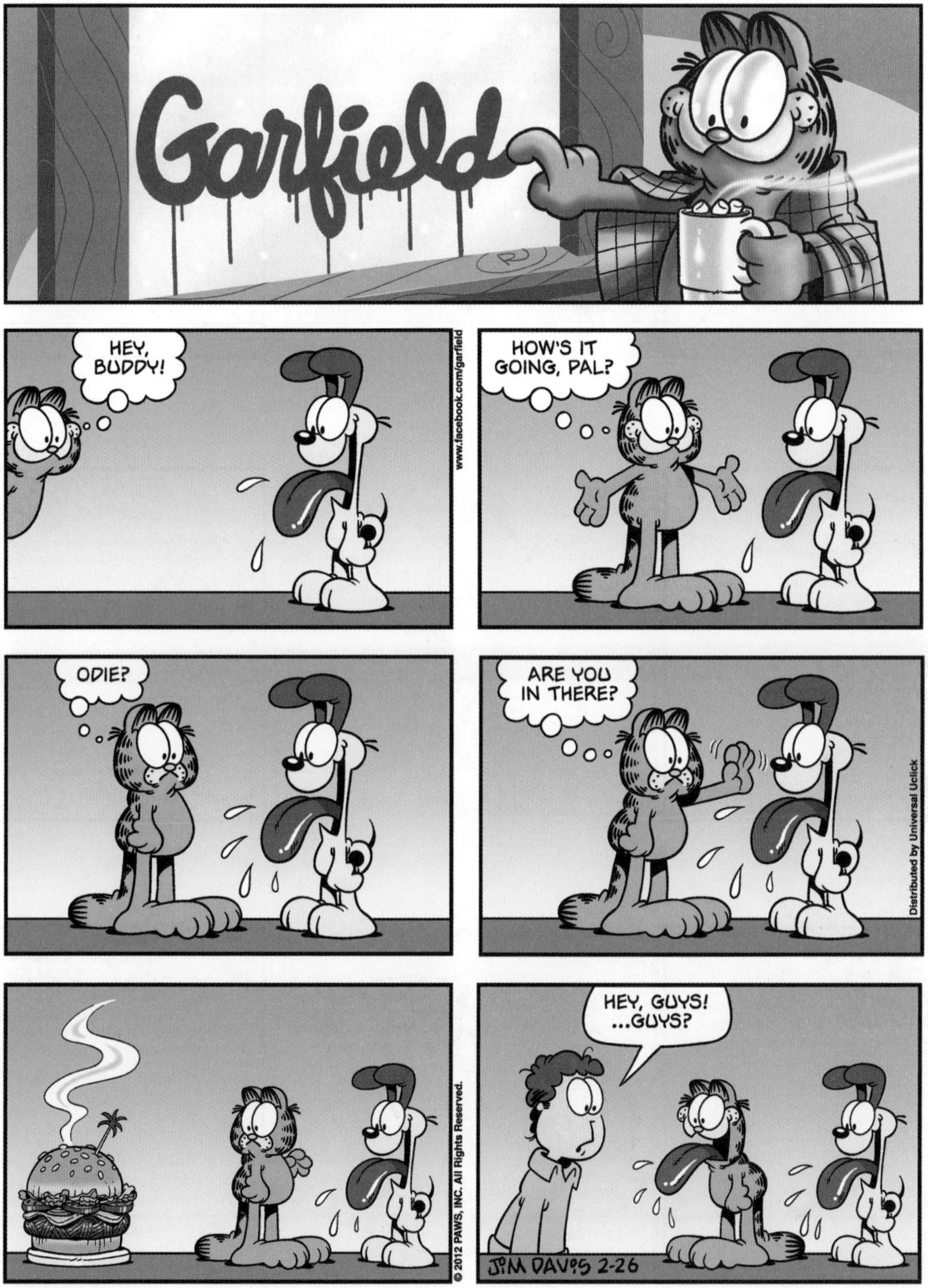
Garfield
HEY, BUDDY!
HOW'S IT GOING, PAL?
ODIE?
ARE YOU IN THERE?
HEY, GUYS! ...GUYS?
JIM DAVIS 2-26
www.facebook.com/garfield
Distributed by Universal Uclick
© 2012 PAWS, INC. All Rights Reserved.

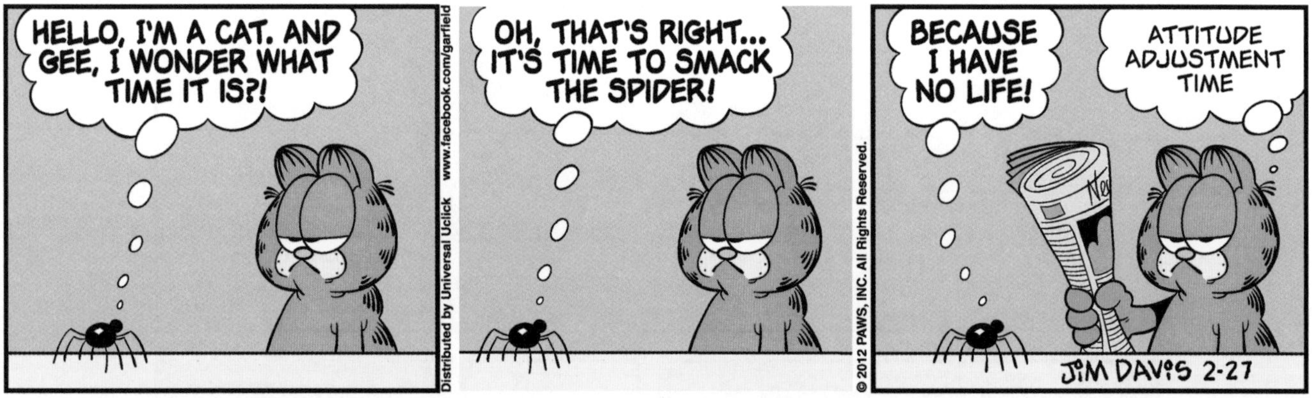
HELLO, I'M A CAT. AND GEE, I WONDER WHAT TIME IT IS?!
OH, THAT'S RIGHT... IT'S TIME TO SMACK THE SPIDER!
BECAUSE I HAVE NO LIFE!
ATTITUDE ADJUSTMENT TIME
JIM DAVIS 2-27
Distributed by Universal Uclick www.facebook.com/garfield
© 2012 PAWS, INC. All Rights Reserved.

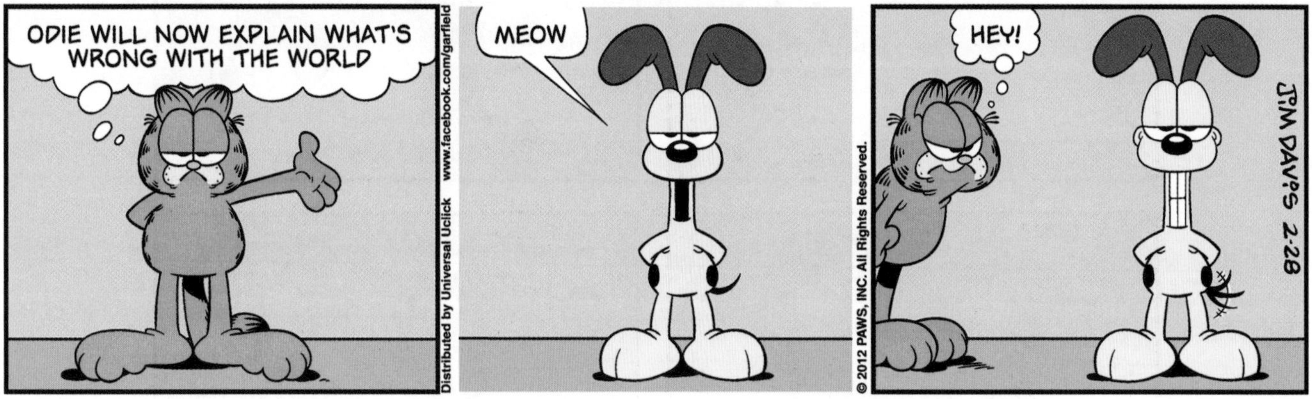
ODIE WILL NOW EXPLAIN WHAT'S WRONG WITH THE WORLD
MEOW
HEY!
JIM DAVIS 2-28
Distributed by Universal Uclick www.facebook.com/garfield
© 2012 PAWS, INC. All Rights Reserved.

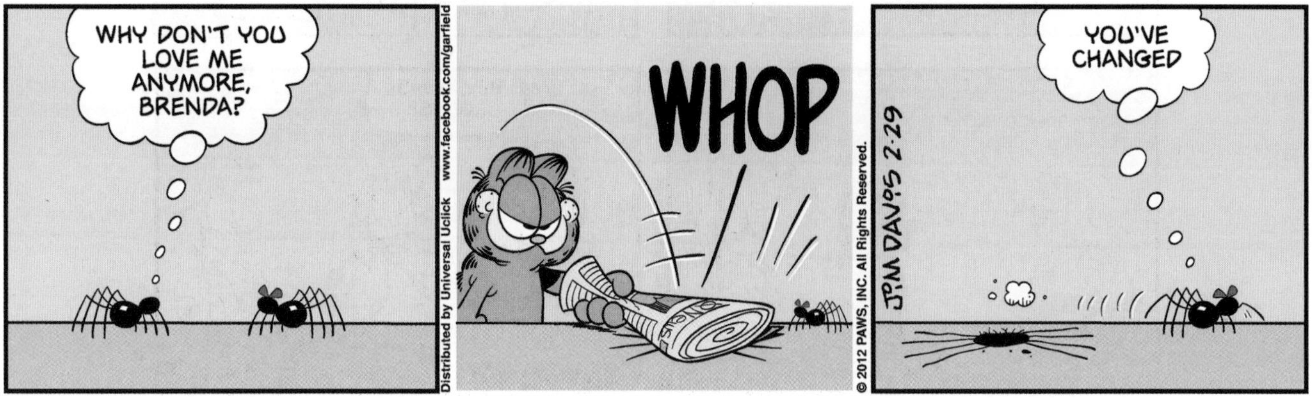
WHY DON'T YOU LOVE ME ANYMORE, BRENDA?
WHOP
YOU'VE CHANGED
JIM DAVIS 2-29
Distributed by Universal Uclick www.facebook.com/garfield
© 2012 PAWS, INC. All Rights Reserved.

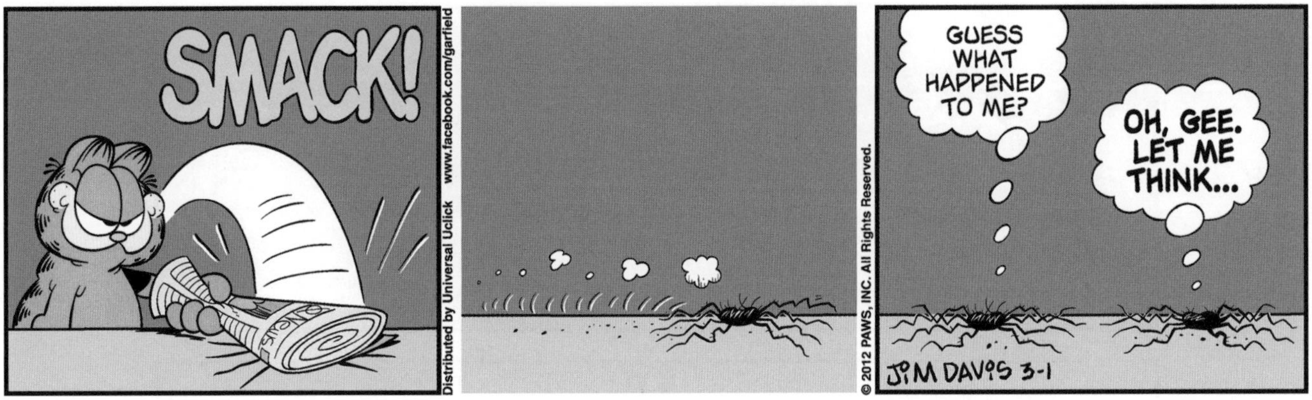
SMACK!
Distributed by Universal Uclick www.facebook.com/garfield
GUESS WHAT HAPPENED TO ME?
OH, GEE. LET ME THINK...
© 2012 PAWS, INC. All Rights Reserved.
JIM DAVIS 3-1

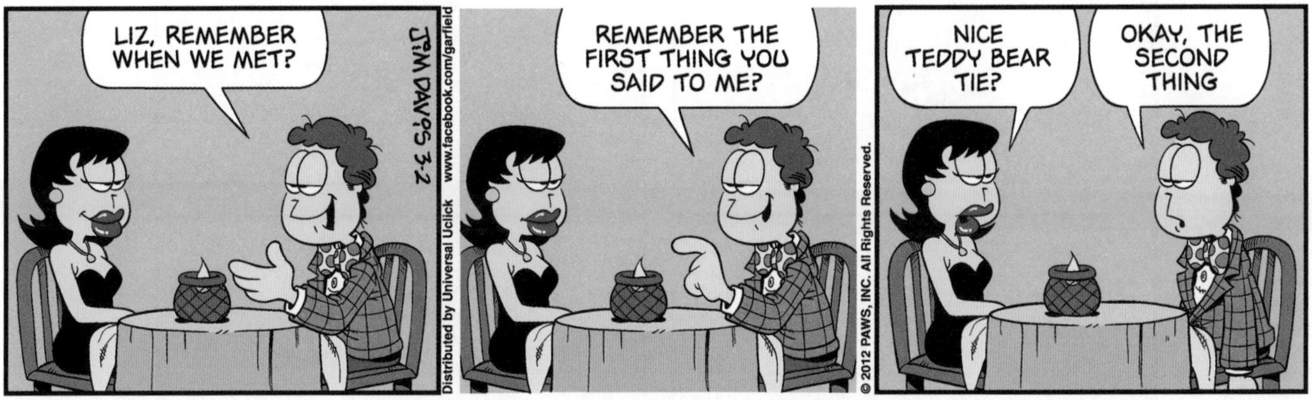
LIZ, REMEMBER WHEN WE MET?
JIM DAVIS 3-2
Distributed by Universal Uclick www.facebook.com/garfield
REMEMBER THE FIRST THING YOU SAID TO ME?
© 2012 PAWS, INC. All Rights Reserved.
NICE TEDDY BEAR TIE?
OKAY, THE SECOND THING

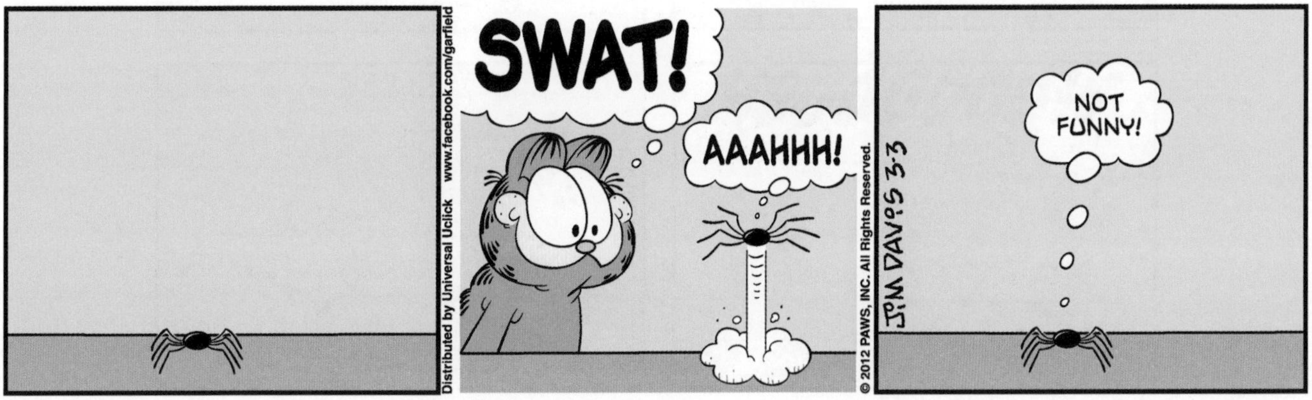
Distributed by Universal Uclick www.facebook.com/garfield
SWAT!
AAAHHH!
© 2012 PAWS, INC. All Rights Reserved.
JIM DAVIS 3-3
NOT FUNNY!

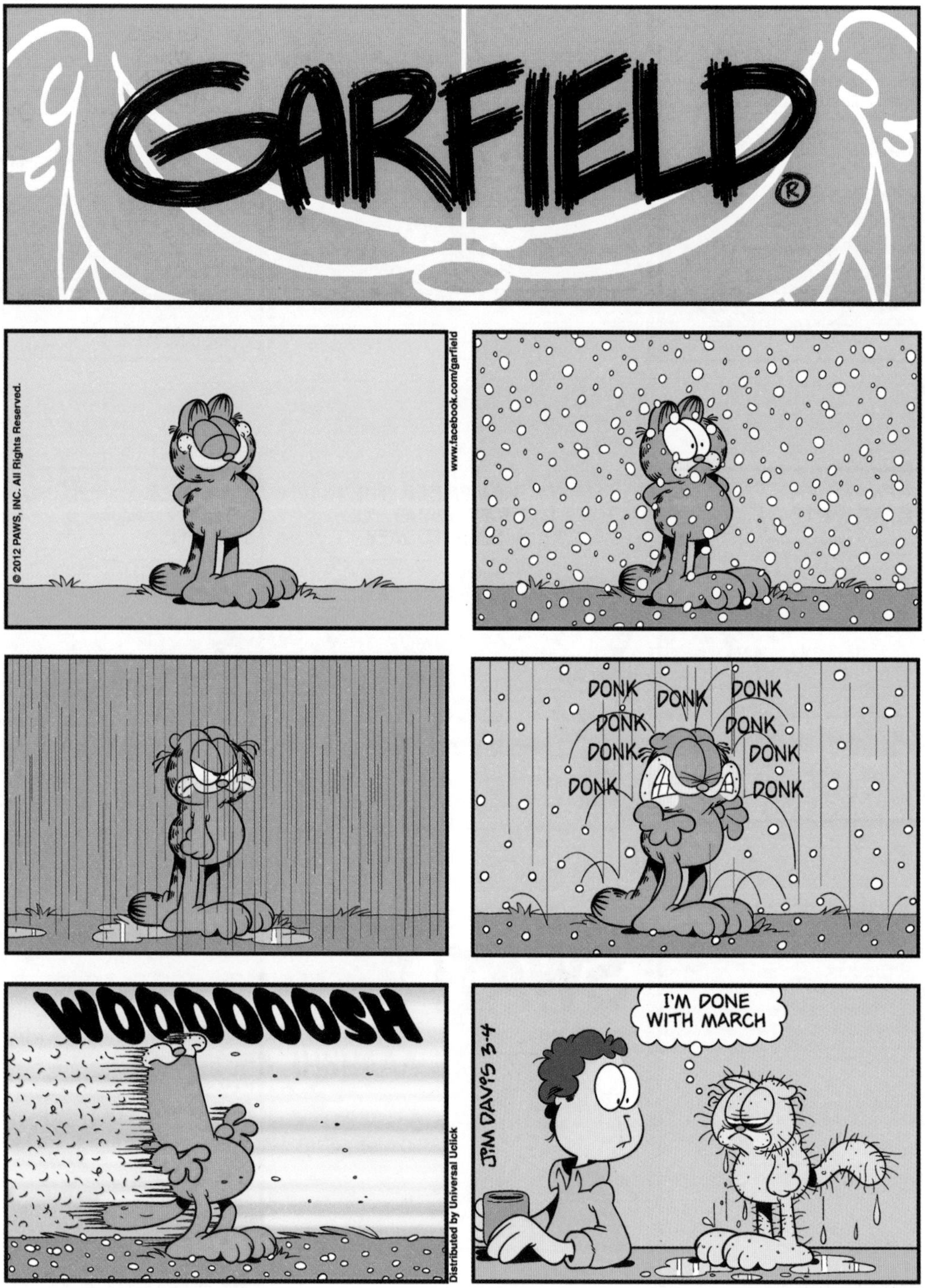
GARFIELD®
© 2012 PAWS, INC. All Rights Reserved.
www.facebook.com/garfield
DONK
DONK
DONK
DONK
DONK
DONK
DONK
DONK
DONK
WOOOOOOSH
Distributed by Universal Uclick
JPM DAVIS 3-4
I'M DONE WITH MARCH

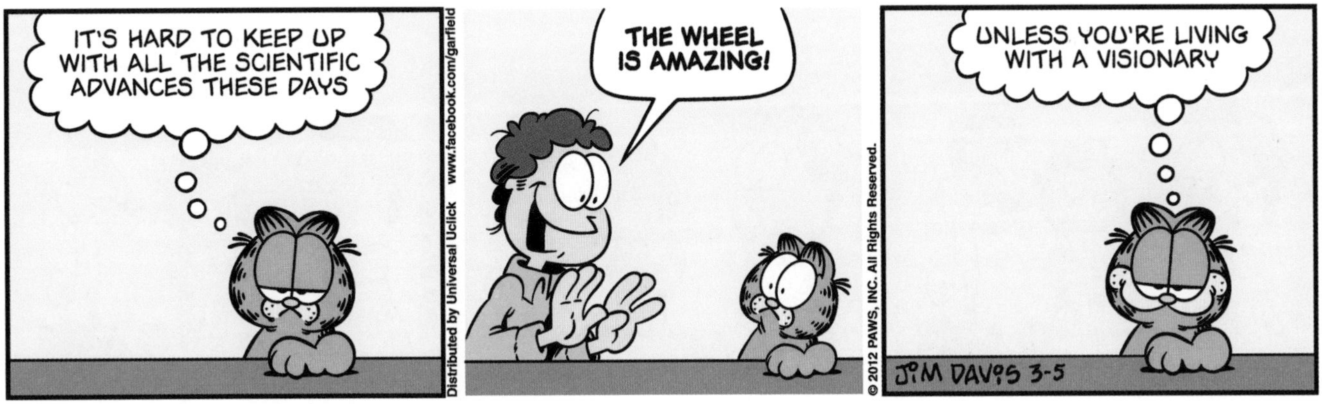
IT'S HARD TO KEEP UP WITH ALL THE SCIENTIFIC ADVANCES THESE DAYS
Distributed by Universal Uclick www.facebook.com/garfield
THE WHEEL IS AMAZING!
© 2012 PAWS, INC. All Rights Reserved.
UNLESS YOU'RE LIVING WITH A VISIONARY
JIM DAVIS 3-5

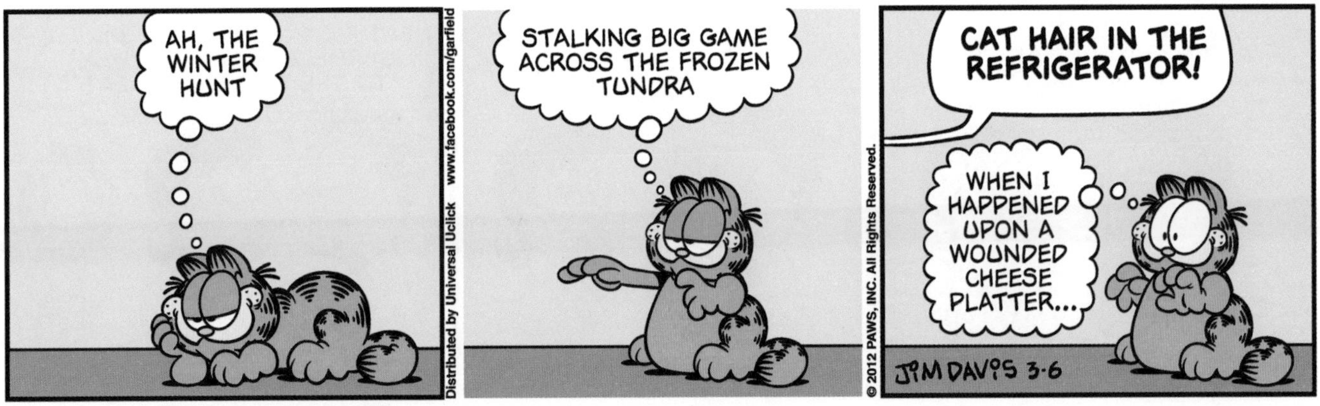
AH, THE WINTER HUNT
Distributed by Universal Uclick www.facebook.com/garfield
STALKING BIG GAME ACROSS THE FROZEN TUNDRA
© 2012 PAWS, INC. All Rights Reserved.
CAT HAIR IN THE REFRIGERATOR!
WHEN I HAPPENED UPON A WOUNDED CHEESE PLATTER...
JIM DAVIS 3-6

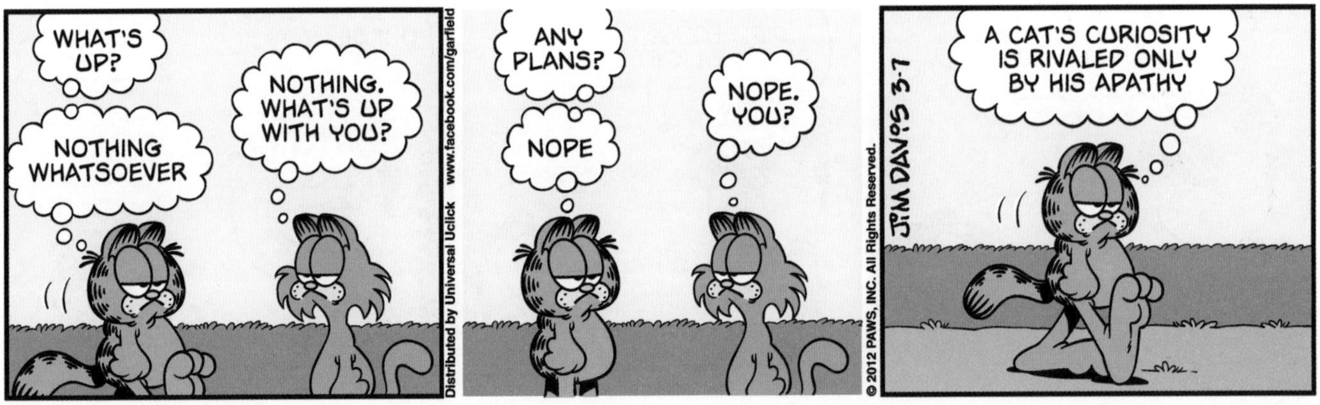
WHAT'S UP?
NOTHING. WHAT'S UP WITH YOU?
NOTHING WHATSOEVER
Distributed by Universal Uclick www.facebook.com/garfield
ANY PLANS?
NOPE. YOU?
NOPE
© 2012 PAWS, INC. All Rights Reserved.
JIM DAVIS 3-7
A CAT'S CURIOSITY IS RIVALED ONLY BY HIS APATHY

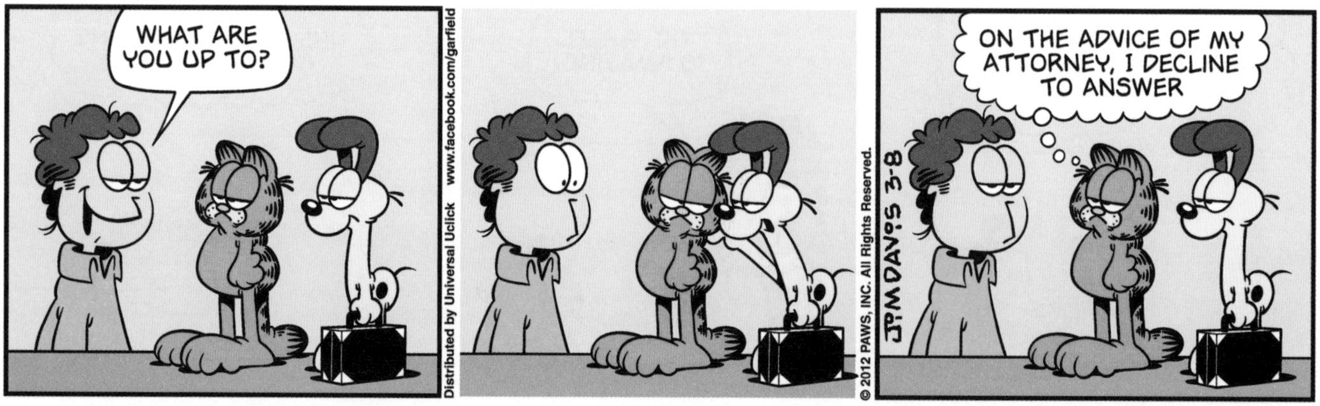
WHAT ARE YOU UP TO?
Distributed by Universal Uclick www.facebook.com/garfield
© 2012 PAWS, INC. All Rights Reserved.
JIM DAVIS 3-8
ON THE ADVICE OF MY ATTORNEY, I DECLINE TO ANSWER

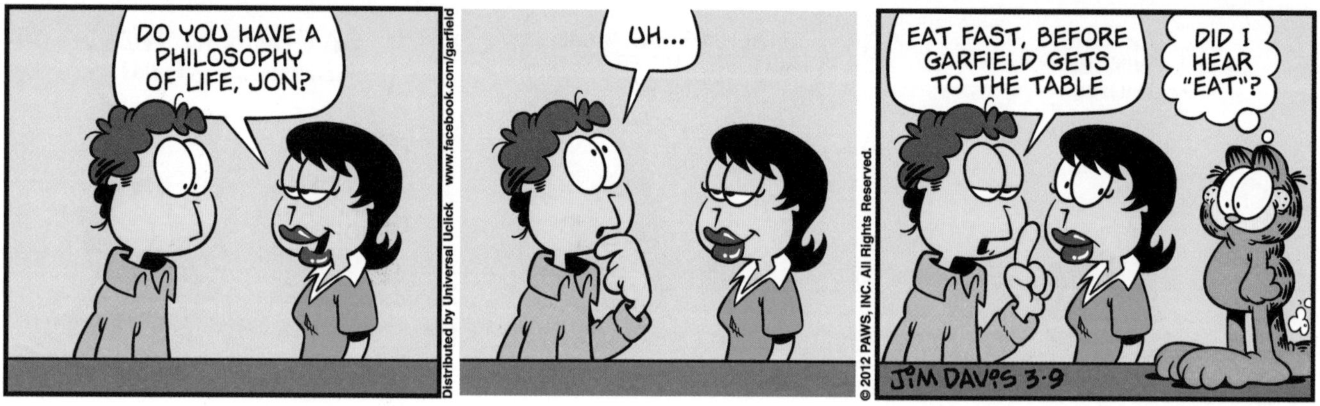
DO YOU HAVE A PHILOSOPHY OF LIFE, JON?
Distributed by Universal Uclick www.facebook.com/garfield
UH...
© 2012 PAWS, INC. All Rights Reserved.
EAT FAST, BEFORE GARFIELD GETS TO THE TABLE
DID I HEAR "EAT"?
JIM DAVIS 3-9

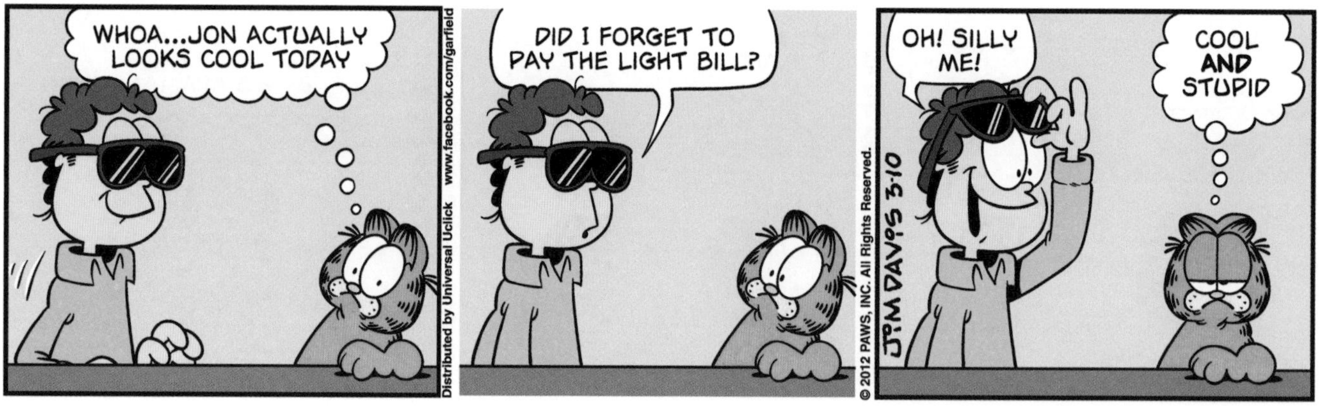
WHOA...JON ACTUALLY LOOKS COOL TODAY
Distributed by Universal Uclick www.facebook.com/garfield
DID I FORGET TO PAY THE LIGHT BILL?
© 2012 PAWS, INC. All Rights Reserved.
JIM DAVIS 3-10
OH! SILLY ME!
COOL **AND** STUPID

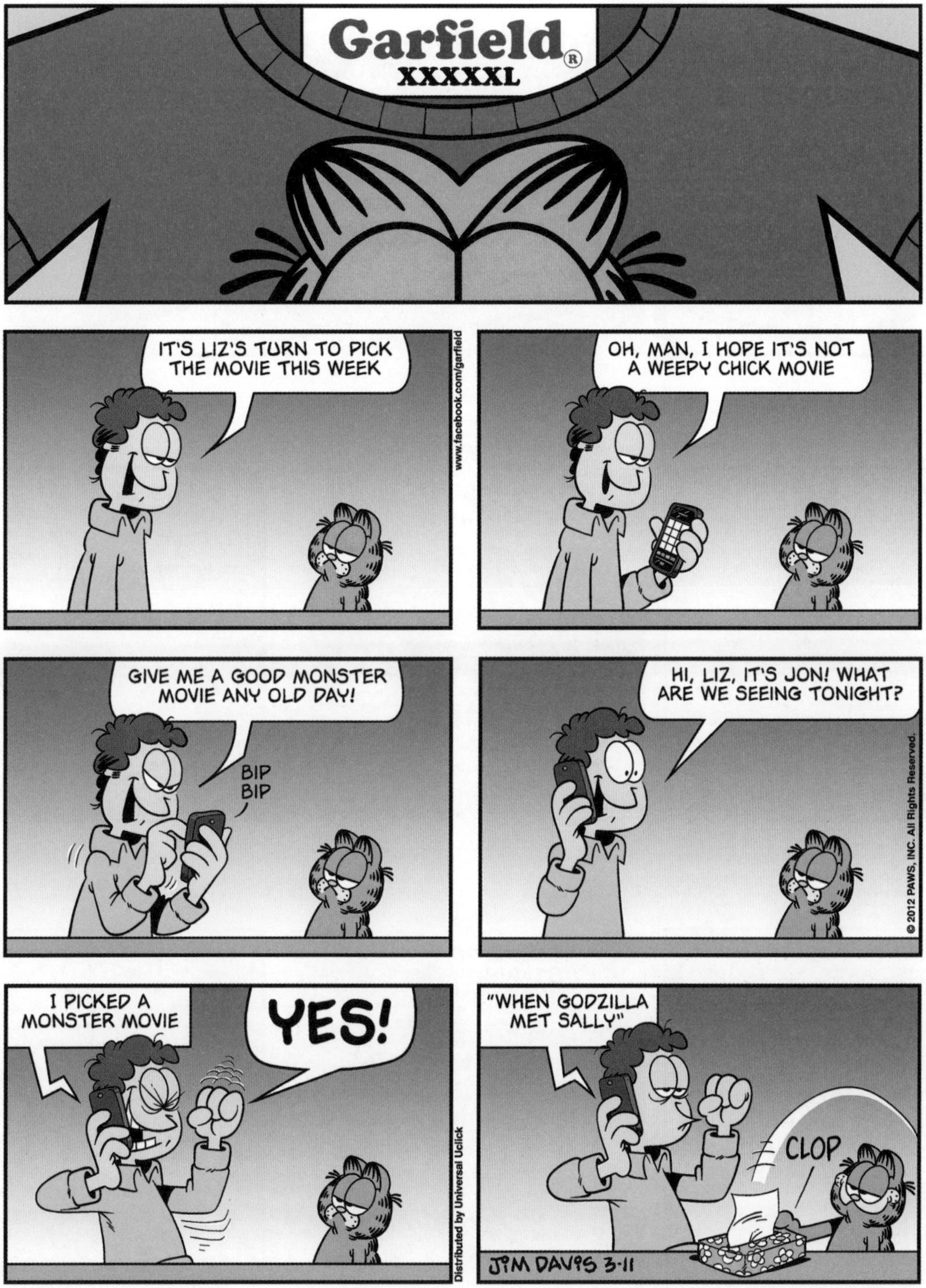
Garfield®
XXXXXL
IT'S LIZ'S TURN TO PICK THE MOVIE THIS WEEK
www.facebook.com/garfield
OH, MAN, I HOPE IT'S NOT A WEEPY CHICK MOVIE
GIVE ME A GOOD MONSTER MOVIE ANY OLD DAY!
BIP BIP
HI, LIZ, IT'S JON! WHAT ARE WE SEEING TONIGHT?
© 2012 PAWS, INC. All Rights Reserved.
I PICKED A MONSTER MOVIE
YES!
Distributed by Universal Uclick
"WHEN GODZILLA MET SALLY"
CLOP
JIM DAVIS 3-11

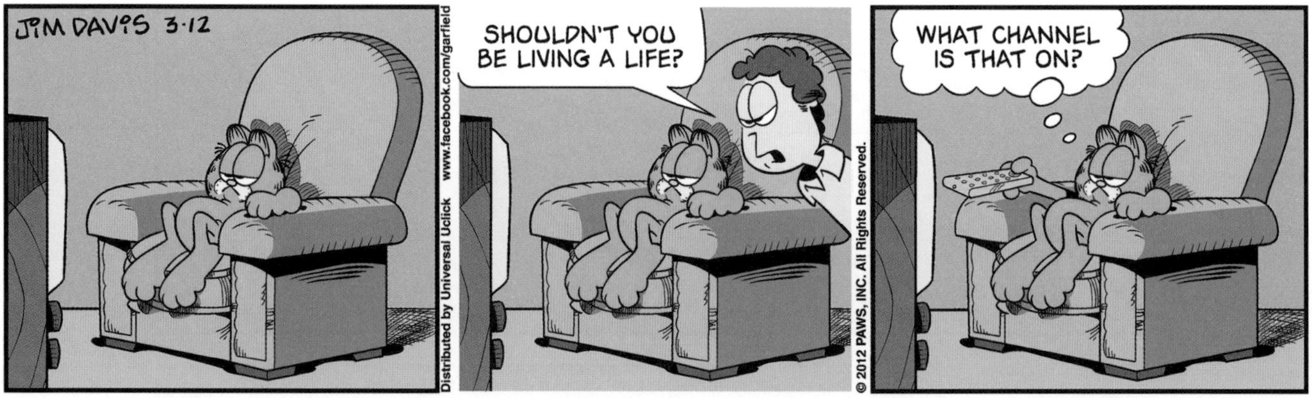
JIM DAVIS 3-12
Distributed by Universal Uclick www.facebook.com/garfield
SHOULDN'T YOU BE LIVING A LIFE?
© 2012 PAWS, INC. All Rights Reserved.
WHAT CHANNEL IS THAT ON?

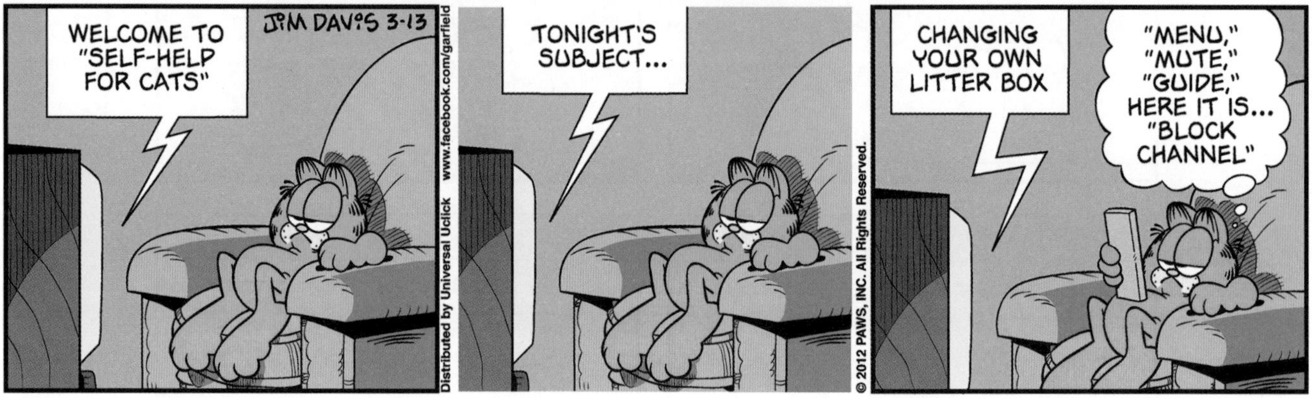
WELCOME TO "SELF-HELP FOR CATS"
JIM DAVIS 3-13
Distributed by Universal Uclick www.facebook.com/garfield
TONIGHT'S SUBJECT...
© 2012 PAWS, INC. All Rights Reserved.
CHANGING YOUR OWN LITTER BOX
"MENU," "MUTE," "GUIDE," HERE IT IS... "BLOCK CHANNEL"

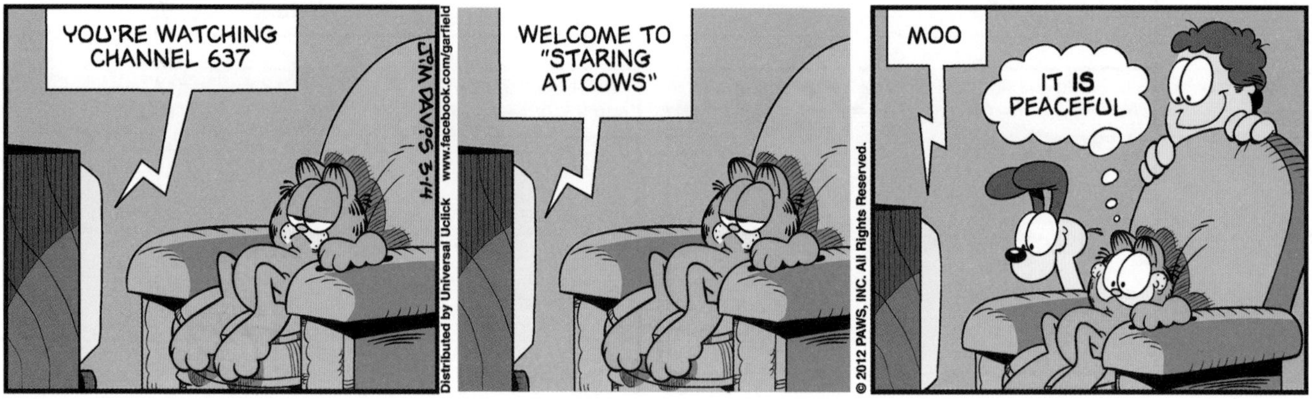
YOU'RE WATCHING CHANNEL 637
JIM DAVIS 3-14
Distributed by Universal Uclick www.facebook.com/garfield
WELCOME TO "STARING AT COWS"
© 2012 PAWS, INC. All Rights Reserved.
MOO
IT **IS** PEACEFUL

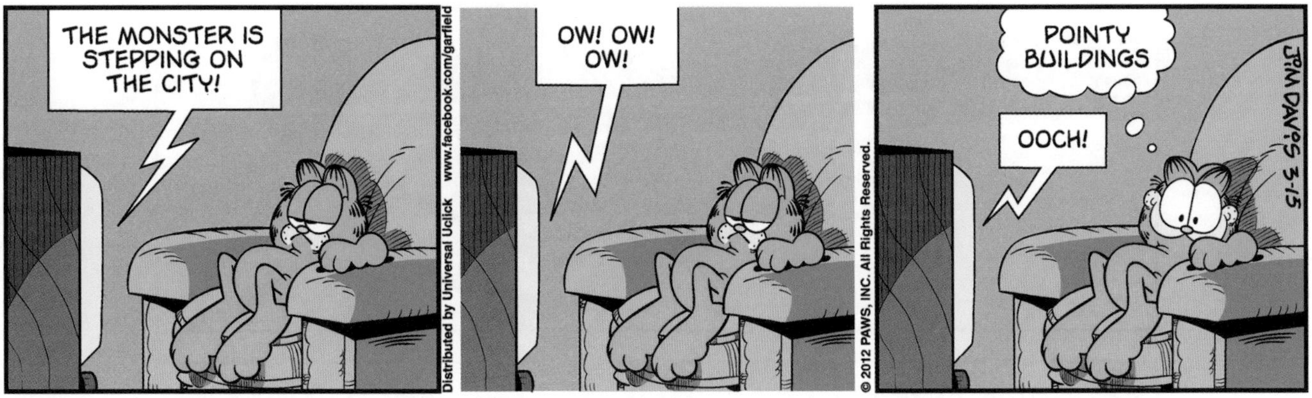
THE MONSTER IS STEPPING ON THE CITY!
Distributed by Universal Uclick www.facebook.com/garfield
OW! OW! OW!
© 2012 PAWS, INC. All Rights Reserved.
POINTY BUILDINGS
OOCH!
JIM DAVIS 3-15

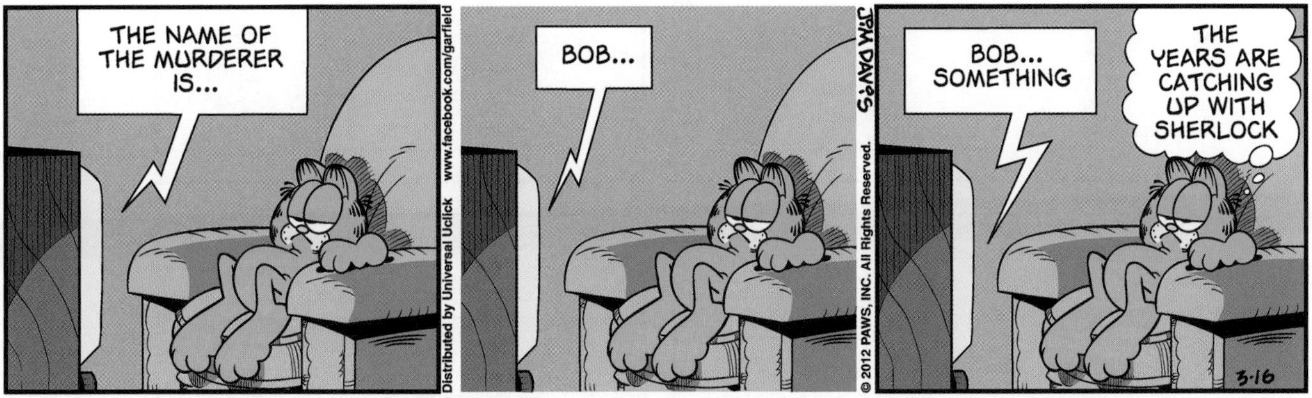
THE NAME OF THE MURDERER IS...
Distributed by Universal Uclick www.facebook.com/garfield
BOB...
JIM DAVIS
© 2012 PAWS, INC. All Rights Reserved.
BOB... SOMETHING
THE YEARS ARE CATCHING UP WITH SHERLOCK
3-16

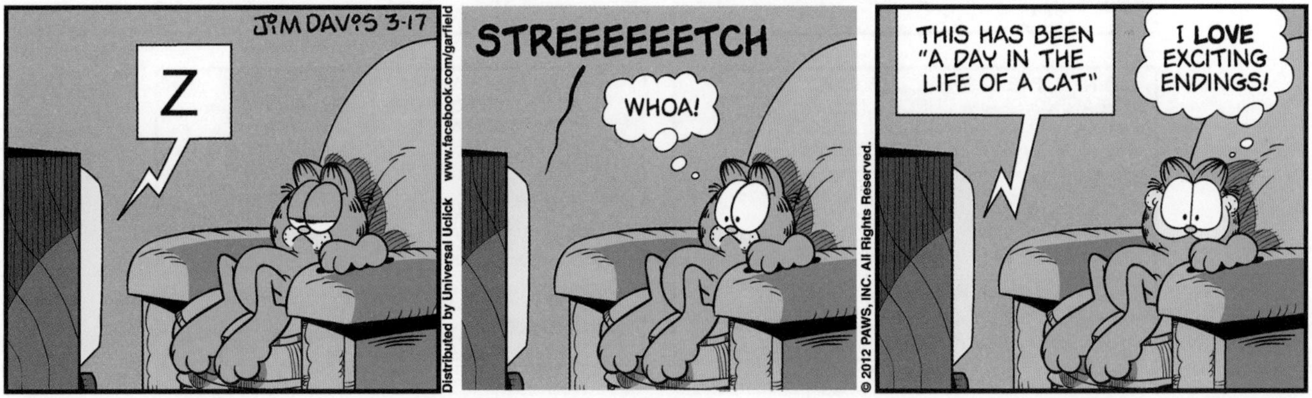
JIM DAVIS 3-17
Z
Distributed by Universal Uclick www.facebook.com/garfield
STREEEEEETCH
WHOA!
© 2012 PAWS, INC. All Rights Reserved.
THIS HAS BEEN "A DAY IN THE LIFE OF A CAT"
I **LOVE** EXCITING ENDINGS!

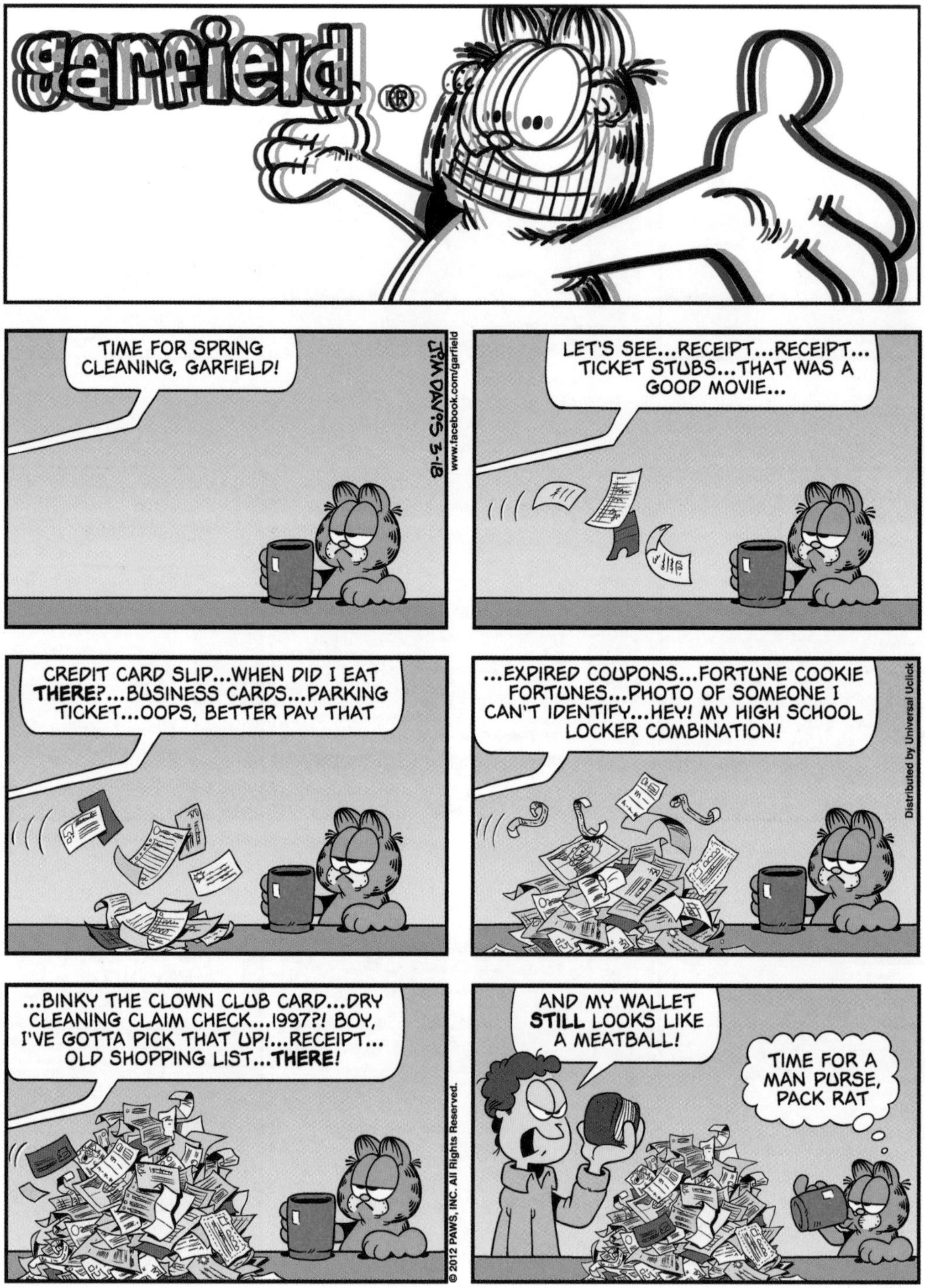
garfield ®
TIME FOR SPRING CLEANING, GARFIELD!
JIM DAVIS 3-18
www.facebook.com/garfield
LET'S SEE...RECEIPT...RECEIPT... TICKET STUBS...THAT WAS A GOOD MOVIE...
CREDIT CARD SLIP...WHEN DID I EAT THERE?...BUSINESS CARDS...PARKING TICKET...OOPS, BETTER PAY THAT
...EXPIRED COUPONS...FORTUNE COOKIE FORTUNES...PHOTO OF SOMEONE I CAN'T IDENTIFY...HEY! MY HIGH SCHOOL LOCKER COMBINATION!
Distributed by Universal Uclick
...BINKY THE CLOWN CLUB CARD...DRY CLEANING CLAIM CHECK...1997?! BOY, I'VE GOTTA PICK THAT UP!...RECEIPT... OLD SHOPPING LIST...THERE!
© 2012 PAWS, INC. All Rights Reserved.
AND MY WALLET STILL LOOKS LIKE A MEATBALL!
TIME FOR A MAN PURSE, PACK RAT

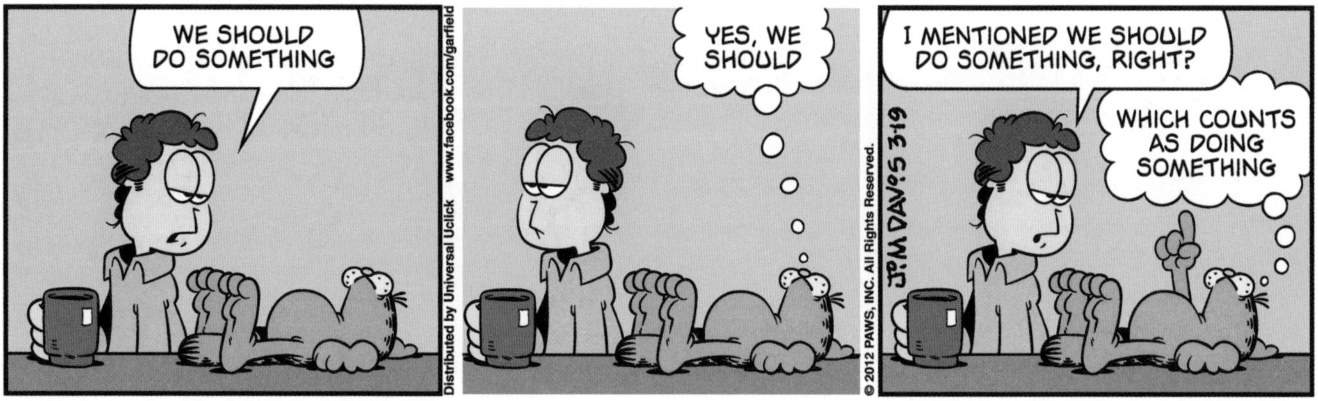
WE SHOULD DO SOMETHING
Distributed by Universal Uclick www.facebook.com/garfield
YES, WE SHOULD
© 2012 PAWS, INC. All Rights Reserved.
JIM DAVIS 3-19
I MENTIONED WE SHOULD DO SOMETHING, RIGHT?
WHICH COUNTS AS DOING SOMETHING

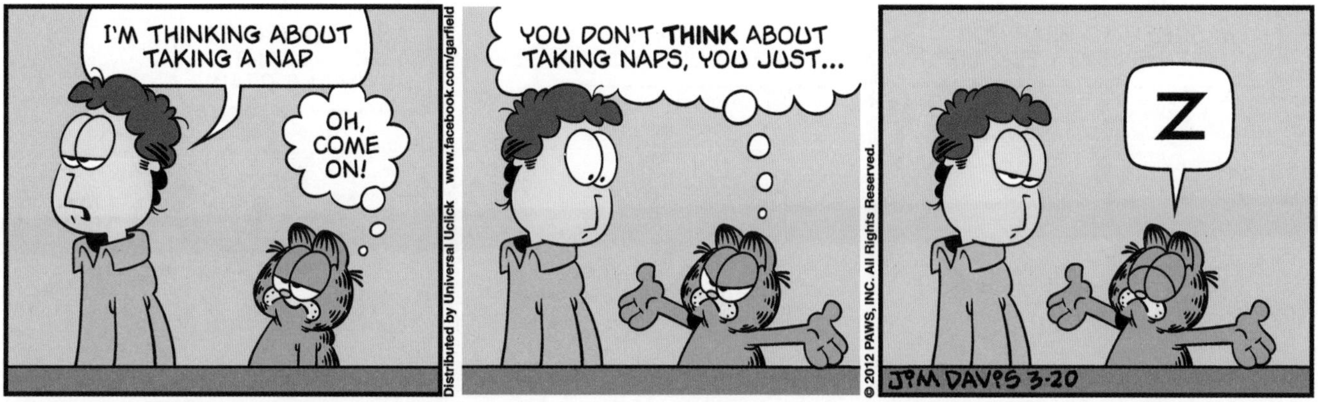
I'M THINKING ABOUT TAKING A NAP
OH, COME ON!
Distributed by Universal Uclick www.facebook.com/garfield
YOU DON'T **THINK** ABOUT TAKING NAPS, YOU JUST...
© 2012 PAWS, INC. All Rights Reserved.
Z
JIM DAVIS 3-20

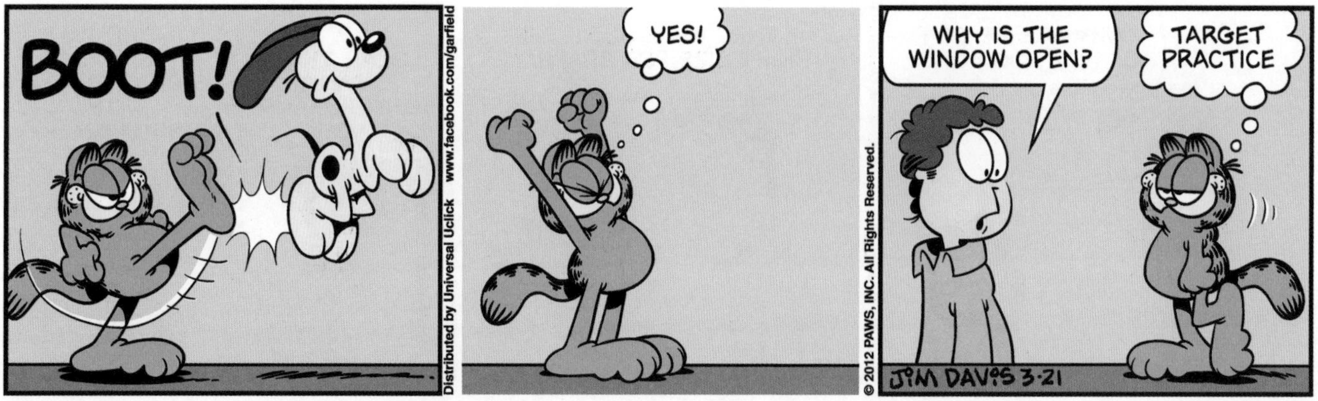
BOOT!
Distributed by Universal Uclick www.facebook.com/garfield
YES!
© 2012 PAWS, INC. All Rights Reserved.
WHY IS THE WINDOW OPEN?
TARGET PRACTICE
JIM DAVIS 3-21

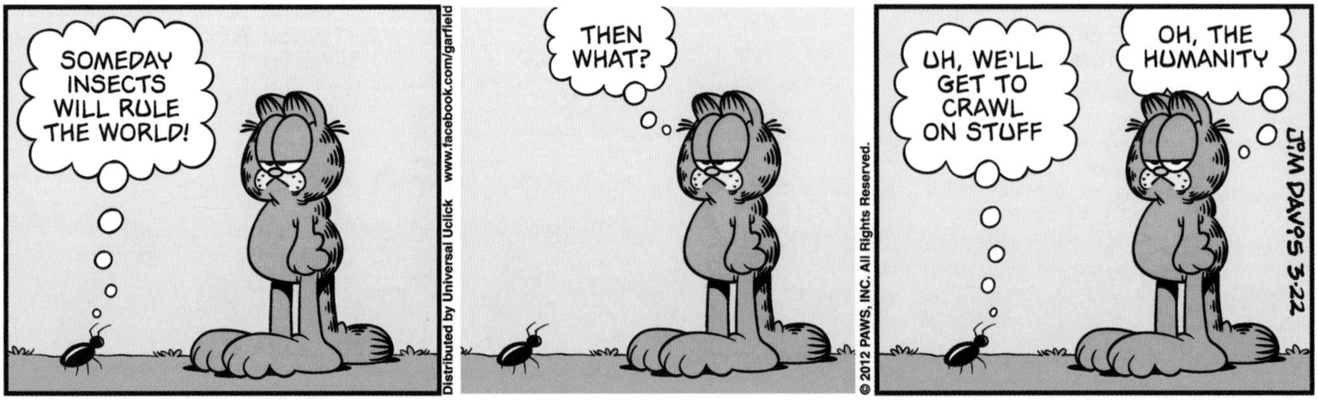
SOMEDAY INSECTS WILL RULE THE WORLD!
Distributed by Universal Uclick www.facebook.com/garfield
THEN WHAT?
© 2012 PAWS, INC. All Rights Reserved.
UH, WE'LL GET TO CRAWL ON STUFF
OH, THE HUMANITY
JIM DAVIS 3-22

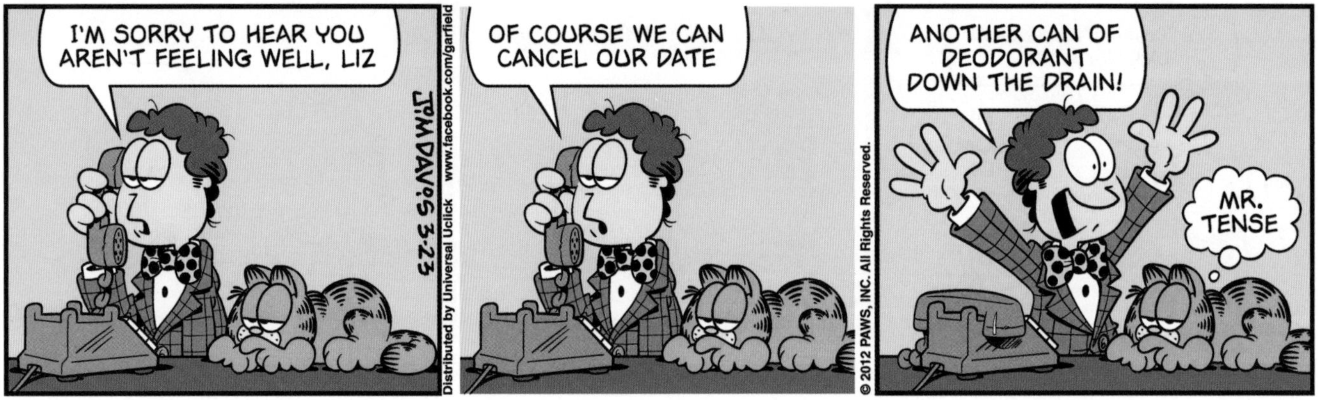
I'M SORRY TO HEAR YOU AREN'T FEELING WELL, LIZ
JIM DAVIS 3-23
Distributed by Universal Uclick www.facebook.com/garfield
OF COURSE WE CAN CANCEL OUR DATE
© 2012 PAWS, INC. All Rights Reserved.
ANOTHER CAN OF DEODORANT DOWN THE DRAIN!
MR. TENSE

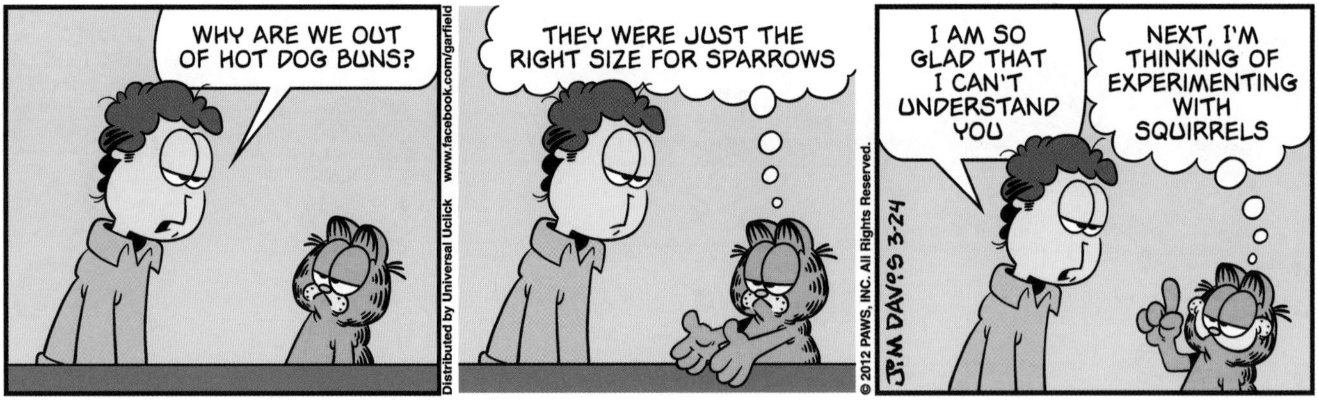
WHY ARE WE OUT OF HOT DOG BUNS?
Distributed by Universal Uclick www.facebook.com/garfield
THEY WERE JUST THE RIGHT SIZE FOR SPARROWS
© 2012 PAWS, INC. All Rights Reserved.
JIM DAVIS 3-24
I AM SO GLAD THAT I CAN'T UNDERSTAND YOU
NEXT, I'M THINKING OF EXPERIMENTING WITH SQUIRRELS

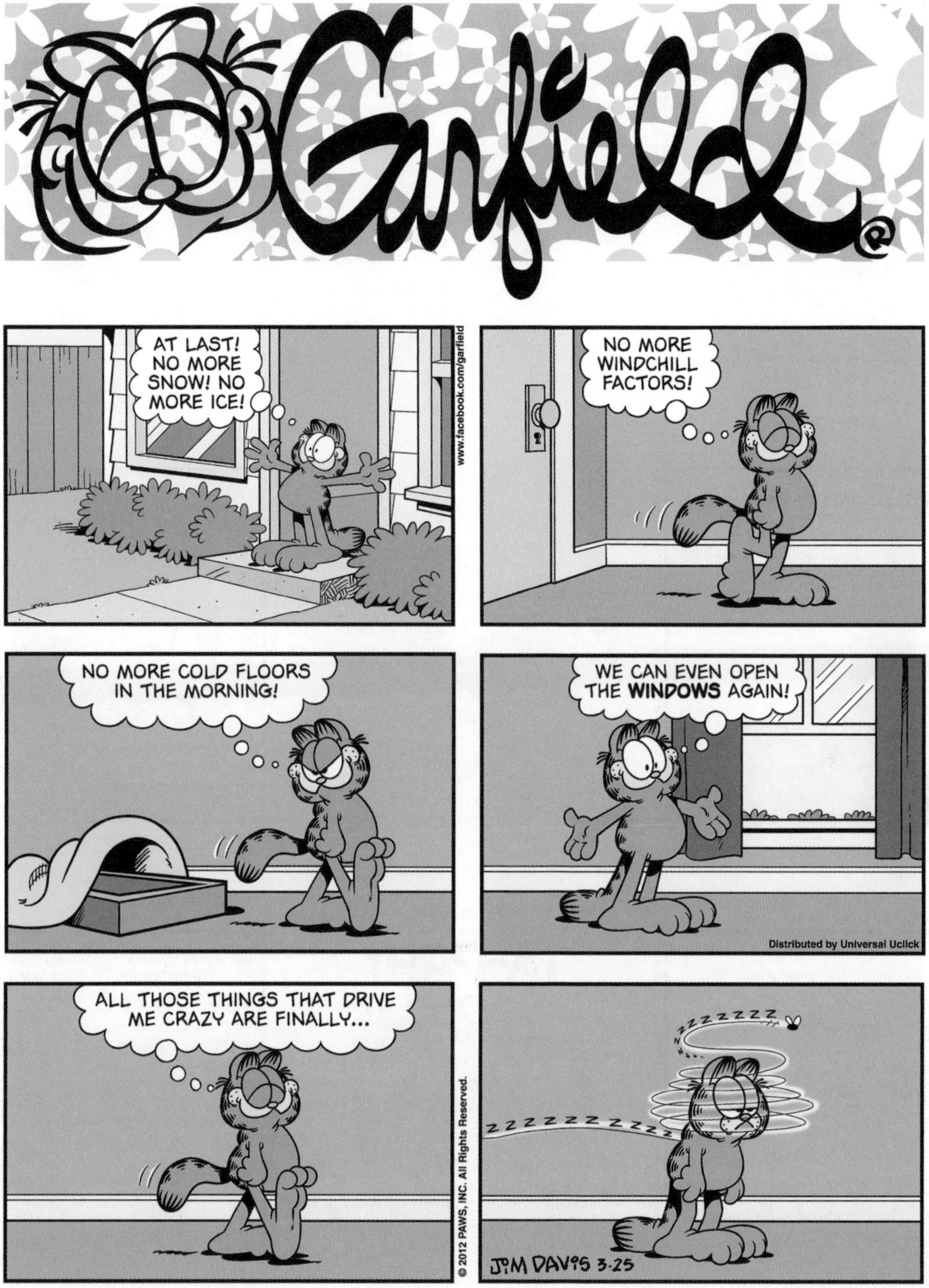
Garfield
www.facebook.com/garfield
AT LAST! NO MORE SNOW! NO MORE ICE!
NO MORE WINDCHILL FACTORS!
NO MORE COLD FLOORS IN THE MORNING!
WE CAN EVEN OPEN THE **WINDOWS** AGAIN!
Distributed by Universal Uclick
ALL THOSE THINGS THAT DRIVE ME CRAZY ARE FINALLY...
© 2012 PAWS, INC. All Rights Reserved.
ZZZZZZZ
ZZZZZZZZZZZ
JIM DAVIS 3-25

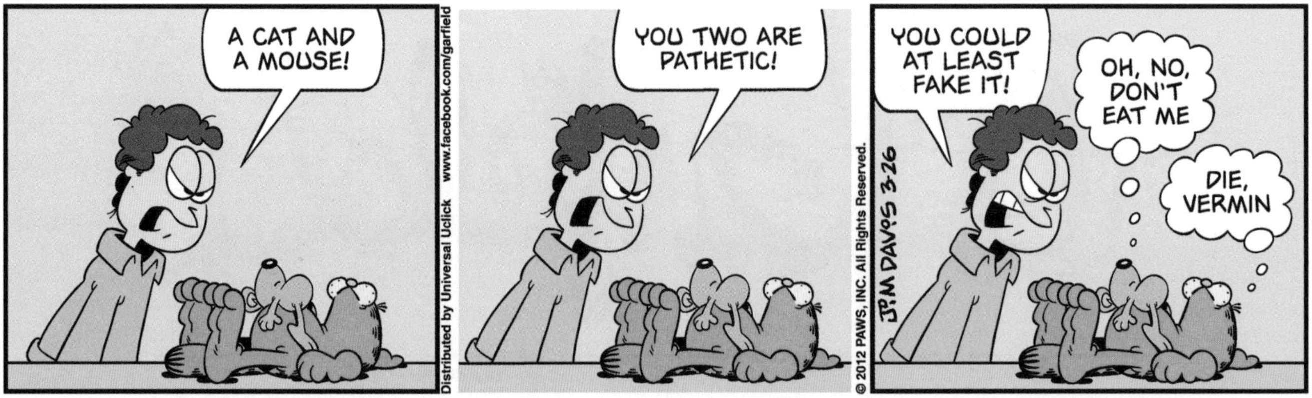
A CAT AND A MOUSE!
Distributed by Universal Uclick www.facebook.com/garfield
YOU TWO ARE PATHETIC!
© 2012 PAWS, INC. All Rights Reserved.
JPM DAVIS 3-26
YOU COULD AT LEAST FAKE IT!
OH, NO, DON'T EAT ME
DIE, VERMIN

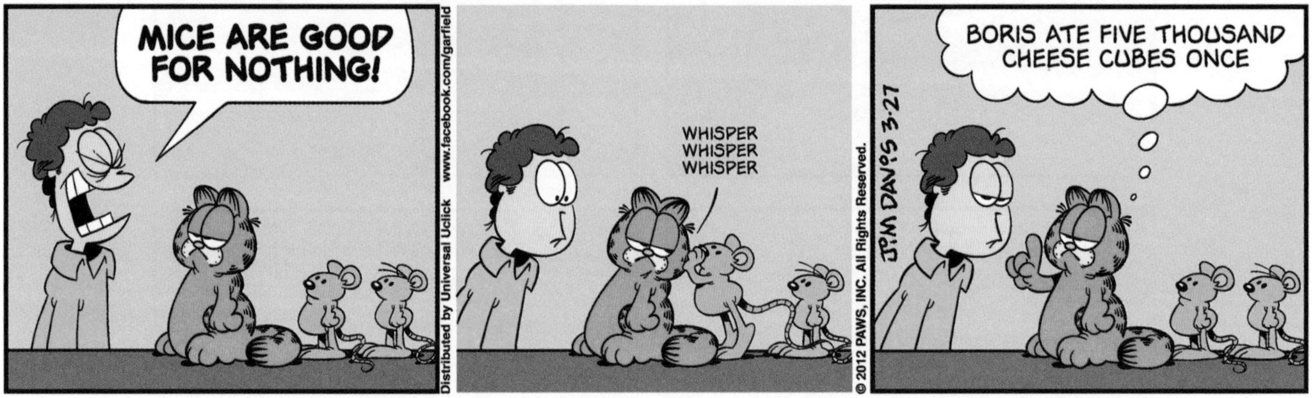
MICE ARE GOOD FOR NOTHING!
Distributed by Universal Uclick www.facebook.com/garfield
WHISPER WHISPER WHISPER
© 2012 PAWS, INC. All Rights Reserved.
JPM DAVIS 3-27
BORIS ATE FIVE THOUSAND CHEESE CUBES ONCE

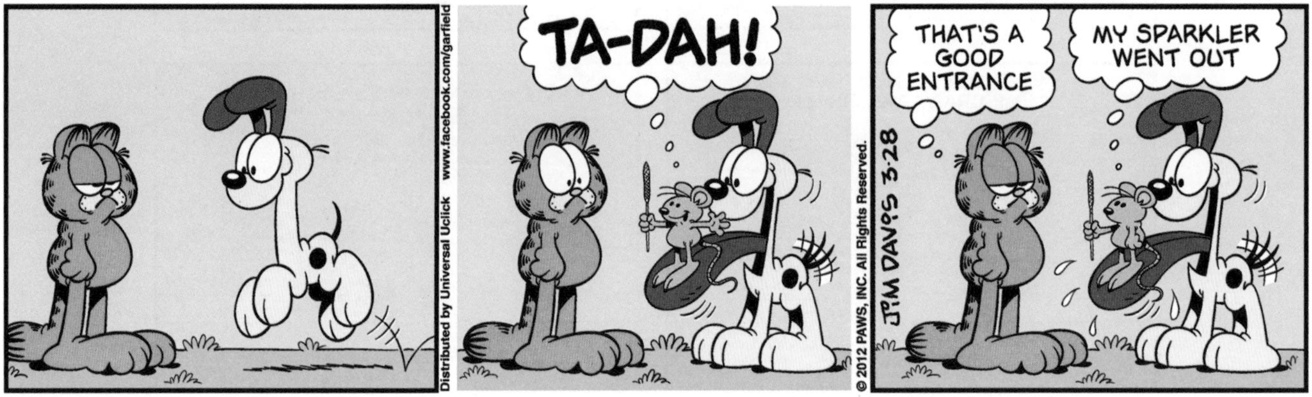
Distributed by Universal Uclick www.facebook.com/garfield
TA-DAH!
© 2012 PAWS, INC. All Rights Reserved.
JPM DAVIS 3-28
THAT'S A GOOD ENTRANCE
MY SPARKLER WENT OUT

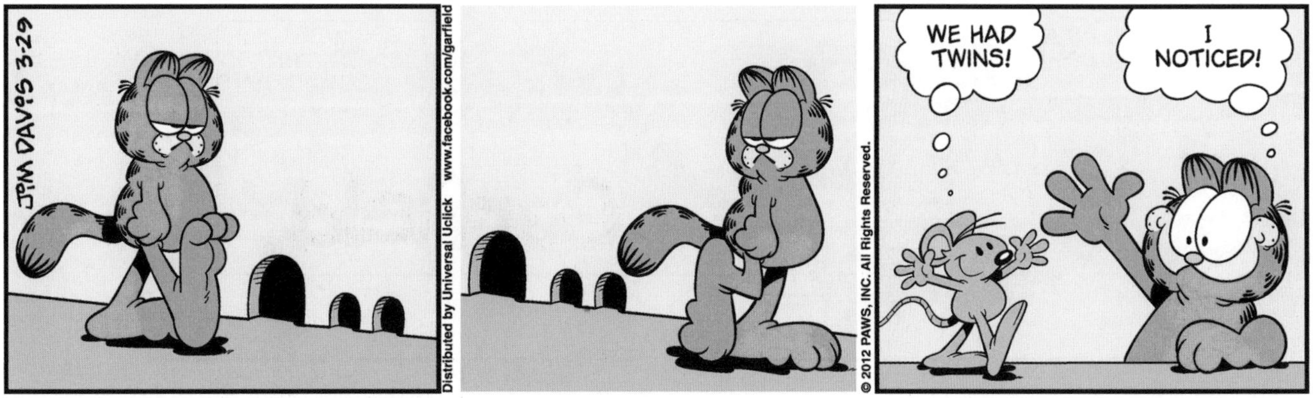
JIM DAVIS 3-29
Distributed by Universal Uclick www.facebook.com/garfield
© 2012 PAWS, INC. All Rights Reserved.
WE HAD TWINS!
I NOTICED!

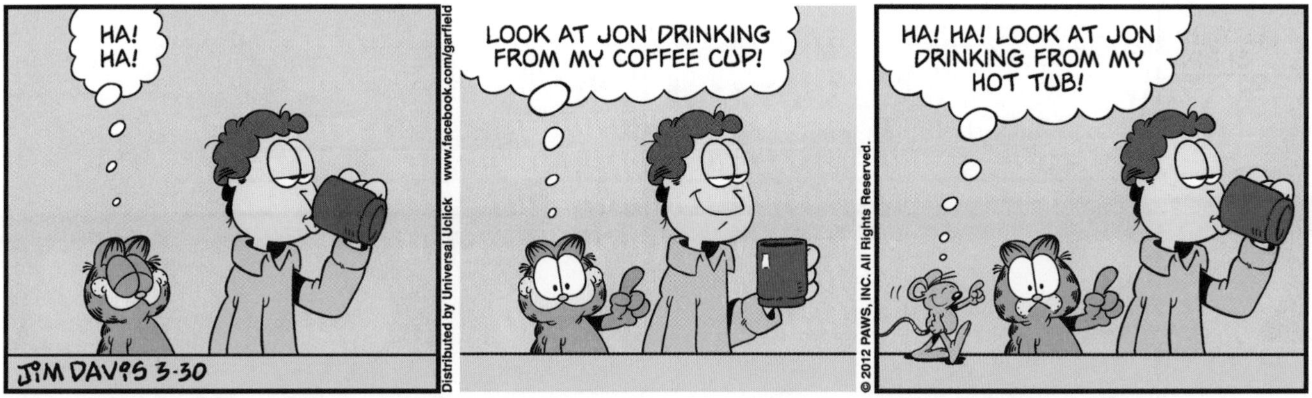
HA! HA!
JIM DAVIS 3-30
Distributed by Universal Uclick www.facebook.com/garfield
LOOK AT JON DRINKING FROM MY COFFEE CUP!
© 2012 PAWS, INC. All Rights Reserved.
HA! HA! LOOK AT JON DRINKING FROM MY HOT TUB!

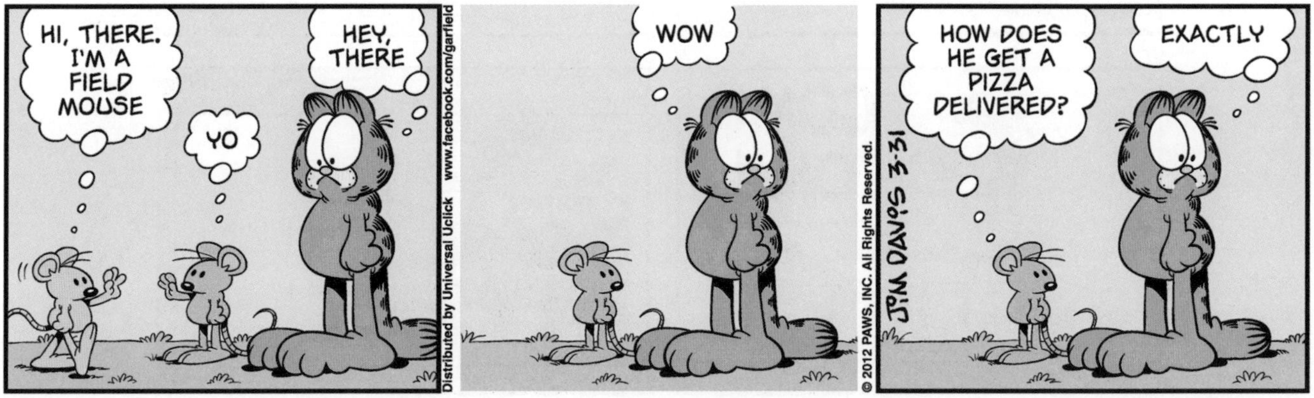
HI, THERE. I'M A FIELD MOUSE
YO
HEY, THERE
Distributed by Universal Uclick www.facebook.com/garfield
WOW
© 2012 PAWS, INC. All Rights Reserved.
JIM DAVIS 3-31
HOW DOES HE GET A PIZZA DELIVERED?
EXACTLY

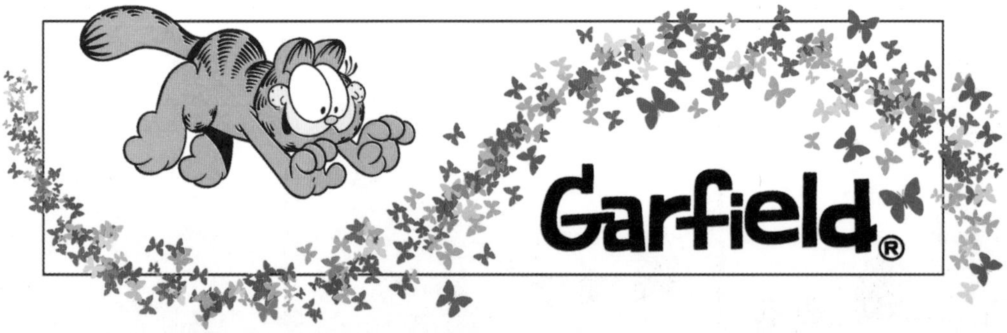
Garfield®

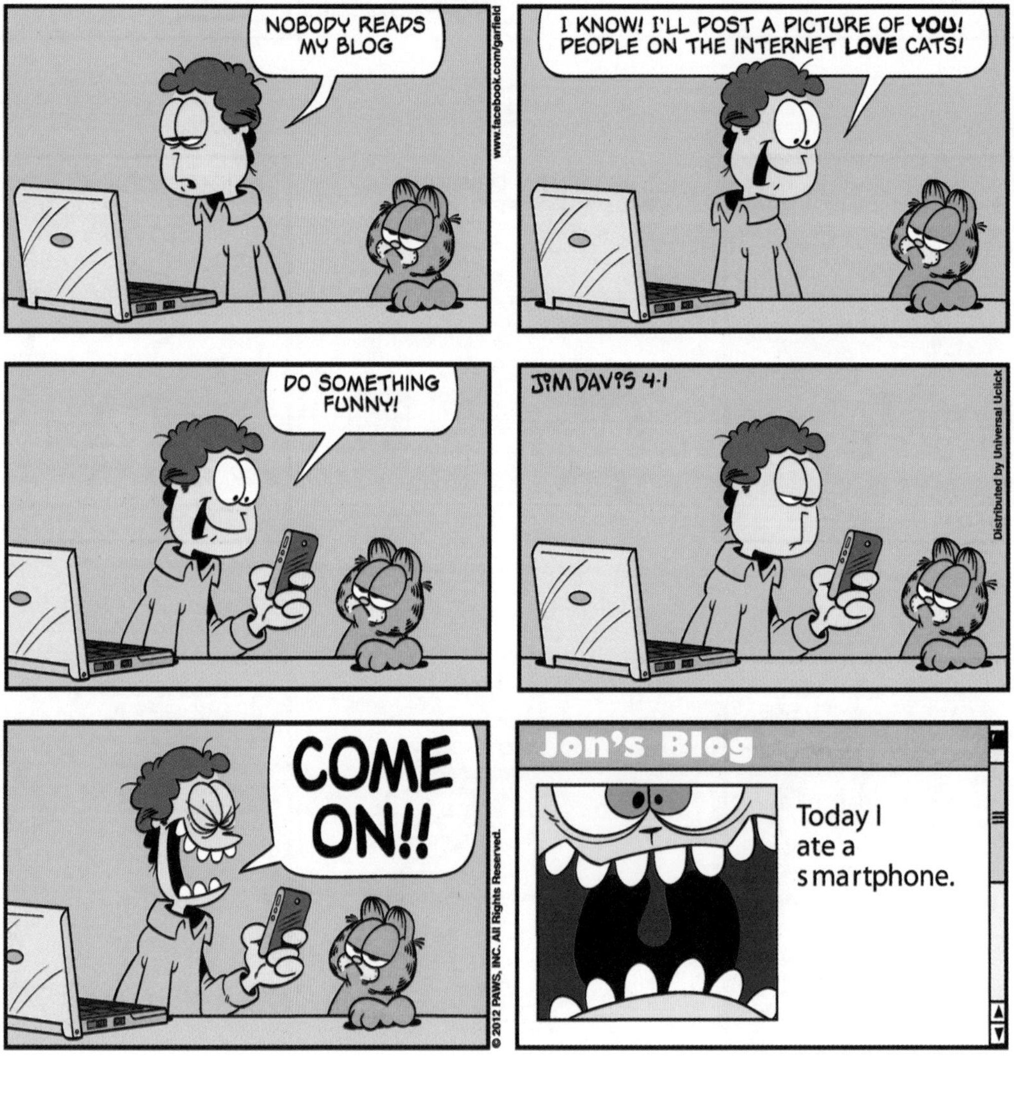
NOBODY READS MY BLOG
www.facebook.com/garfield
I KNOW! I'LL POST A PICTURE OF **YOU**! PEOPLE ON THE INTERNET **LOVE** CATS!
DO SOMETHING FUNNY!
JIM DAVIS 4-1
Distributed by Universal Uclick
COME ON!!
© 2012 PAWS, INC. All Rights Reserved.
Jon's Blog
Today I ate a smartphone.

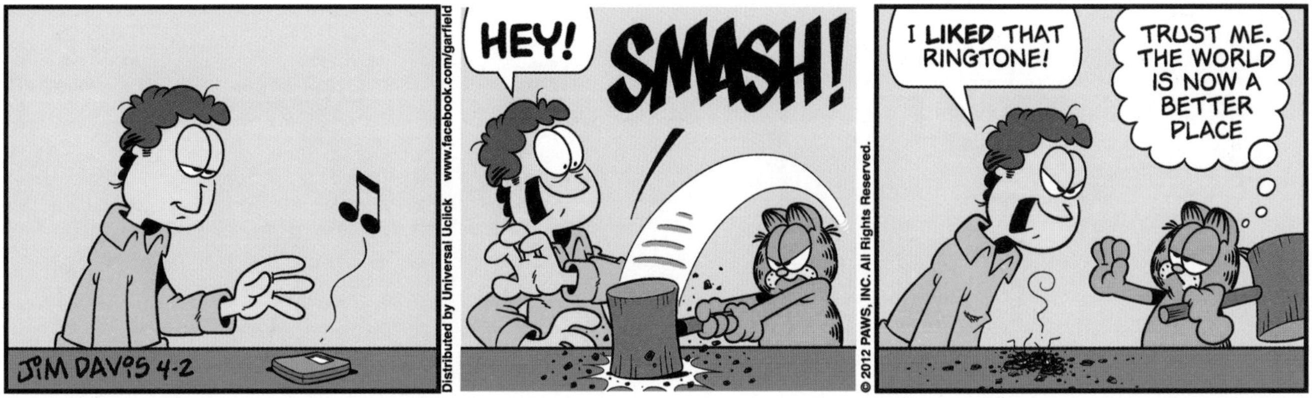
JIM DAVIS 4-2
Distributed by Universal Uclick www.facebook.com/garfield
HEY!
SMASH!
© 2012 PAWS, INC. All Rights Reserved.
I LIKED THAT RINGTONE!
TRUST ME. THE WORLD IS NOW A BETTER PLACE

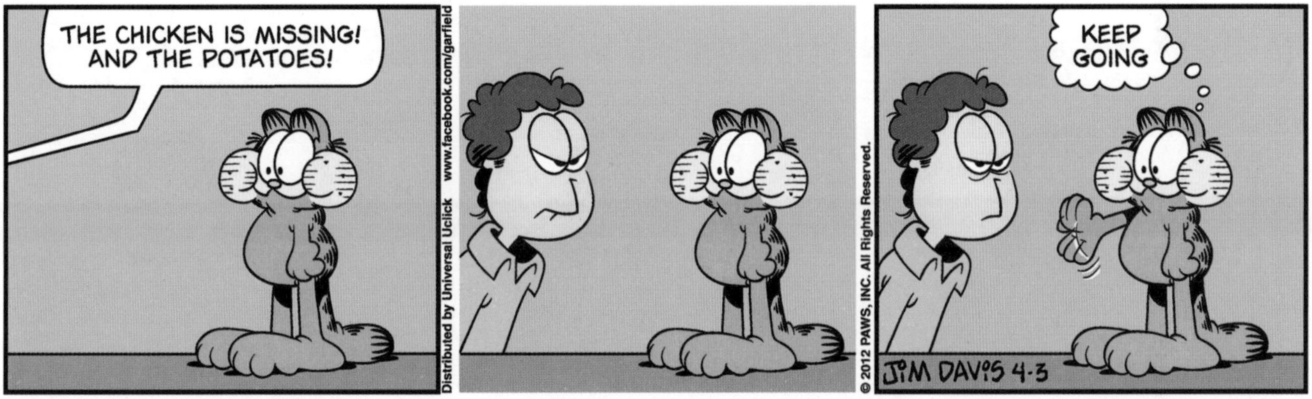
THE CHICKEN IS MISSING! AND THE POTATOES!
Distributed by Universal Uclick www.facebook.com/garfield
© 2012 PAWS, INC. All Rights Reserved.
KEEP GOING
JIM DAVIS 4-3

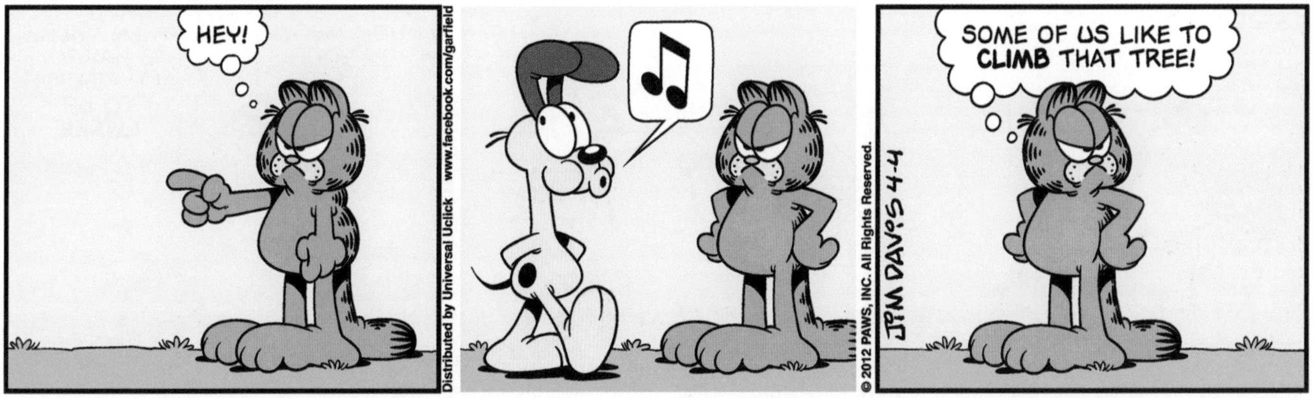
HEY!
Distributed by Universal Uclick www.facebook.com/garfield
© 2012 PAWS, INC. All Rights Reserved.
JIM DAVIS 4-4
SOME OF US LIKE TO CLIMB THAT TREE!

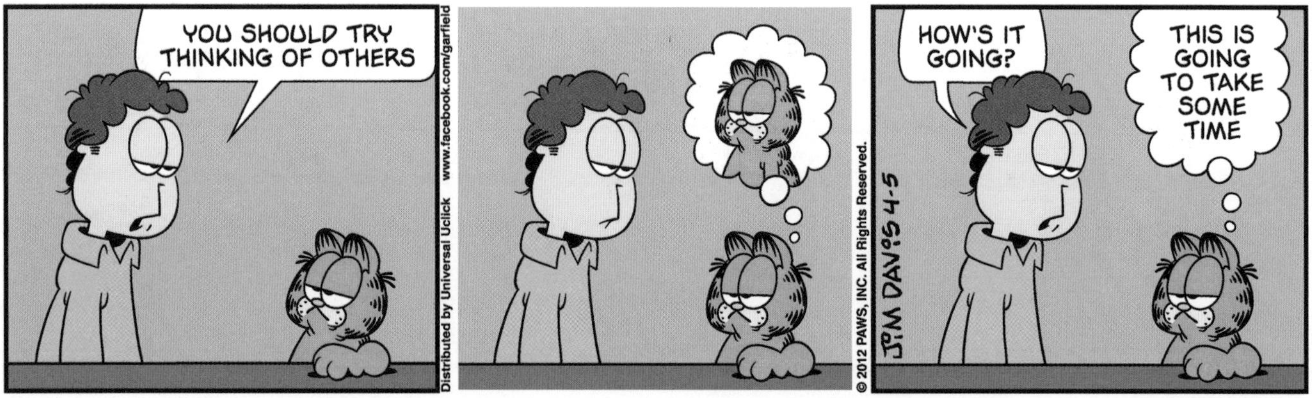
YOU SHOULD TRY THINKING OF OTHERS
Distributed by Universal Uclick www.facebook.com/garfield
© 2012 PAWS, INC. All Rights Reserved.
JIM DAVIS 4-5
HOW'S IT GOING?
THIS IS GOING TO TAKE SOME TIME

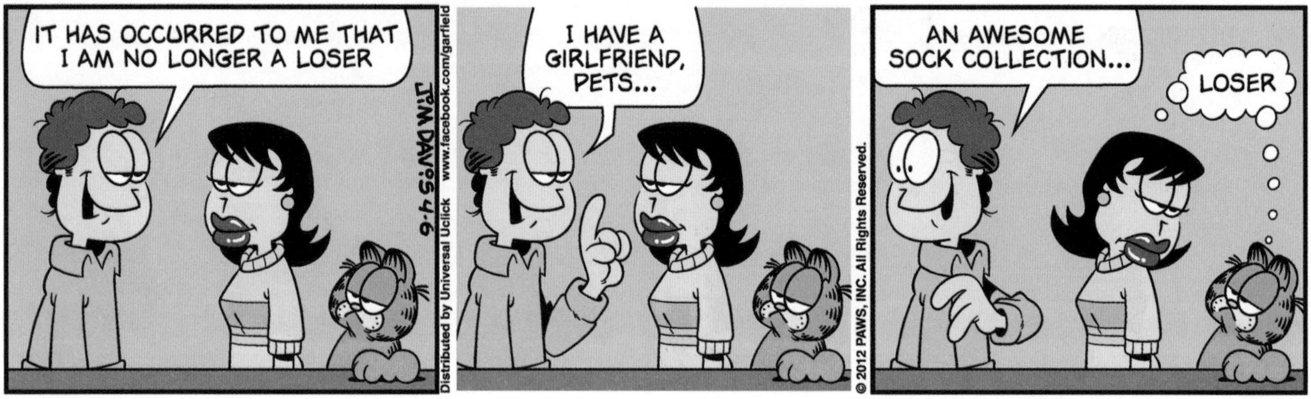
IT HAS OCCURRED TO ME THAT I AM NO LONGER A LOSER
JIM DAVIS 4-6
Distributed by Universal Uclick www.facebook.com/garfield
I HAVE A GIRLFRIEND, PETS...
© 2012 PAWS, INC. All Rights Reserved.
AN AWESOME SOCK COLLECTION...
LOSER

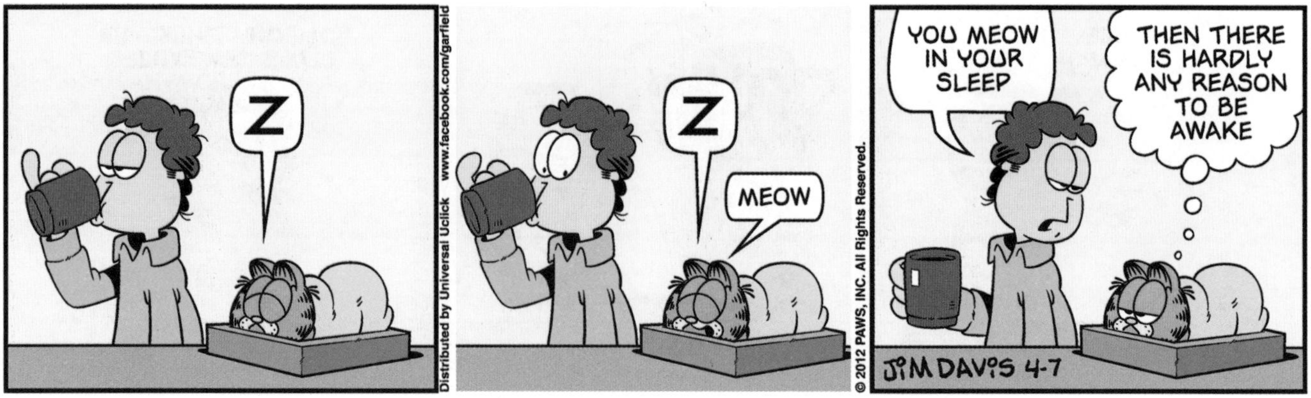
Z
Distributed by Universal Uclick www.facebook.com/garfield
Z
MEOW
© 2012 PAWS, INC. All Rights Reserved.
YOU MEOW IN YOUR SLEEP
THEN THERE IS HARDLY ANY REASON TO BE AWAKE
JIM DAVIS 4-7

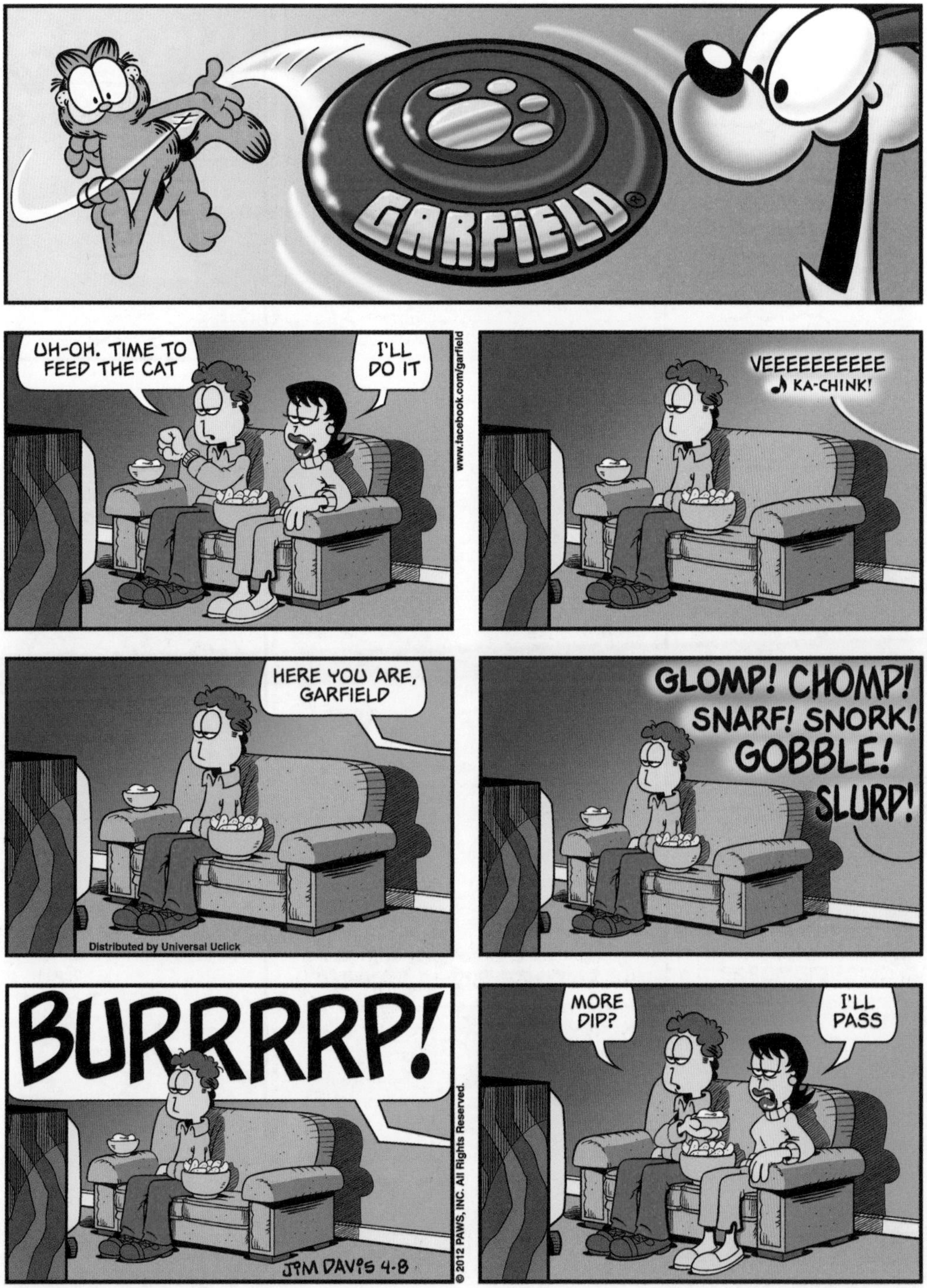
GARFIELD®
UH-OH. TIME TO FEED THE CAT
I'LL DO IT
www.facebook.com/garfield
VEEEEEEEEEE
KA-CHINK!
HERE YOU ARE, GARFIELD
Distributed by Universal Uclick
GLOMP! CHOMP!
SNARF! SNORK!
GOBBLE!
SLURP!
BURRRRP!
JIM DAVIS 4-8
© 2012 PAWS, INC. All Rights Reserved.
MORE DIP?
I'LL PASS

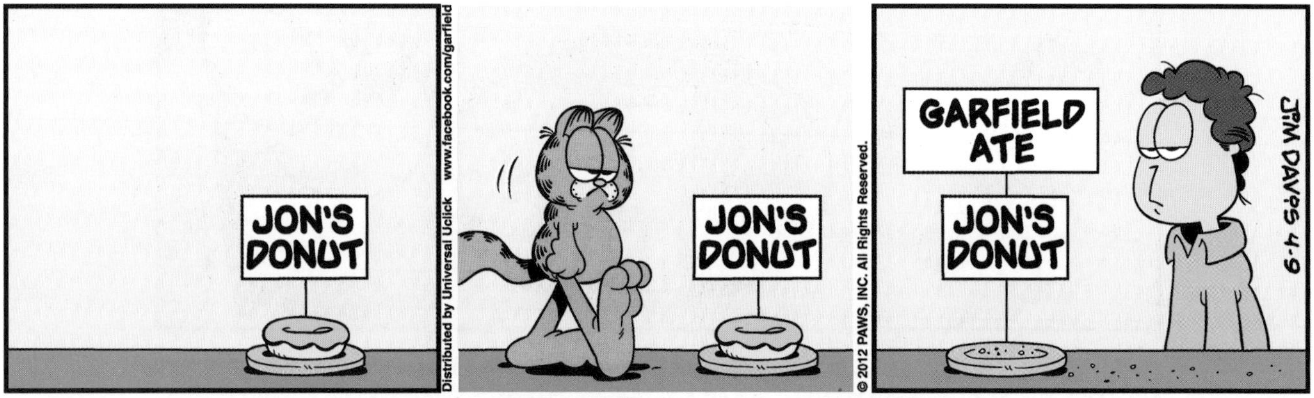
JON'S DONUT
Distributed by Universal Uclick www.facebook.com/garfield
JON'S DONUT
© 2012 PAWS, INC. All Rights Reserved.
GARFIELD ATE
JON'S DONUT
JIM DAVIS 4-9

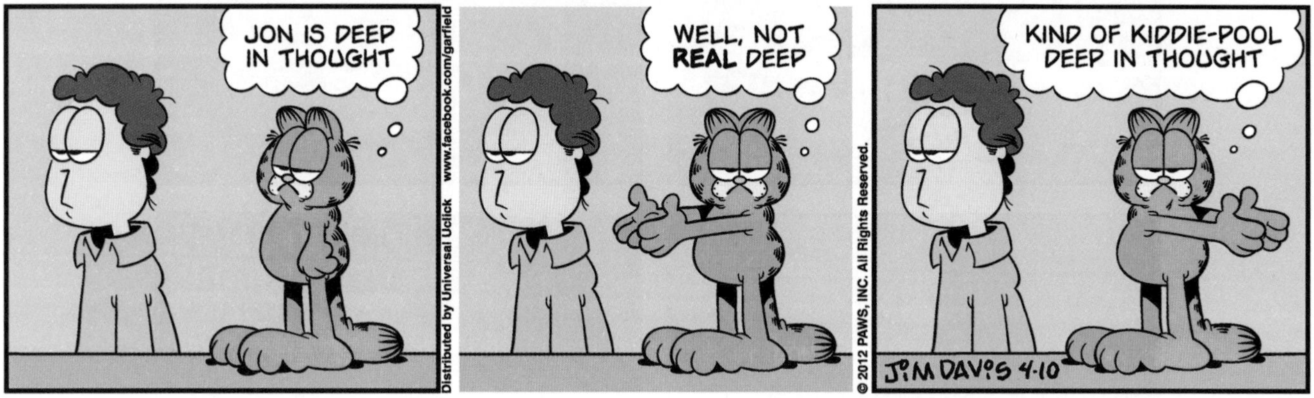
JON IS DEEP IN THOUGHT
Distributed by Universal Uclick www.facebook.com/garfield
WELL, NOT REAL DEEP
© 2012 PAWS, INC. All Rights Reserved.
KIND OF KIDDIE-POOL DEEP IN THOUGHT
JIM DAVIS 4-10

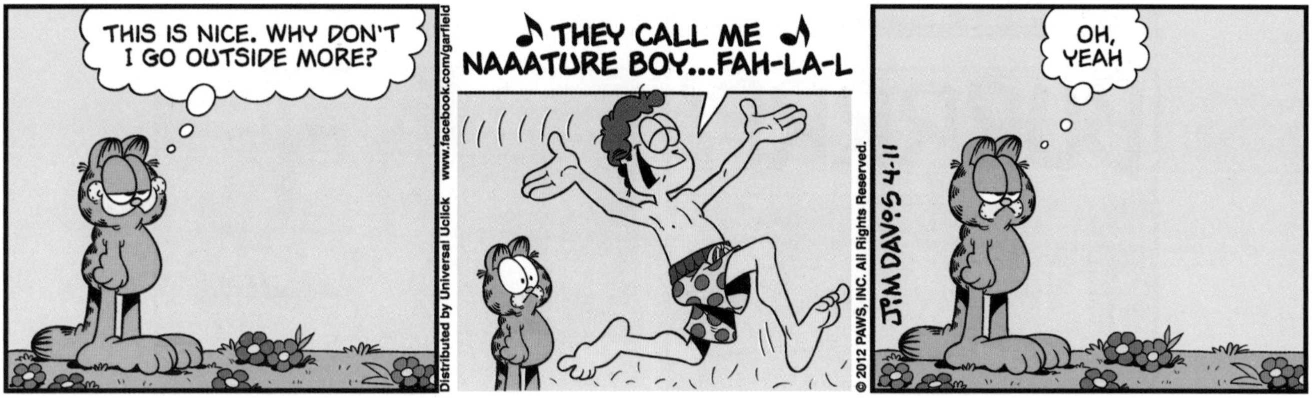
THIS IS NICE. WHY DON'T I GO OUTSIDE MORE?
Distributed by Universal Uclick www.facebook.com/garfield
♪ THEY CALL ME ♪ NAAATURE BOY...FAH-LA-L
© 2012 PAWS, INC. All Rights Reserved.
JIM DAVIS 4-11
OH, YEAH

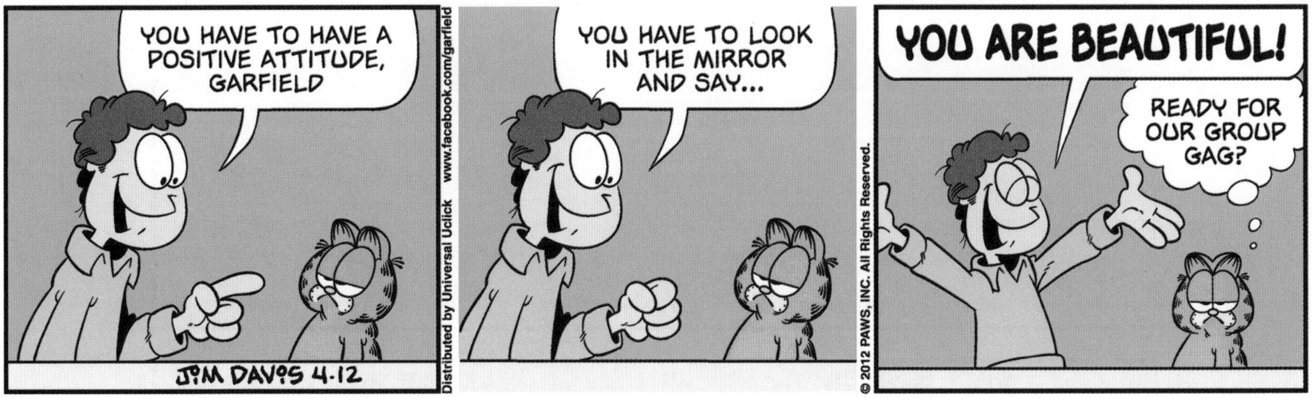
YOU HAVE TO HAVE A POSITIVE ATTITUDE, GARFIELD
JIM DAVIS 4-12
Distributed by Universal Uclick www.facebook.com/garfield
YOU HAVE TO LOOK IN THE MIRROR AND SAY...
© 2012 PAWS, INC. All Rights Reserved.
YOU ARE BEAUTIFUL!
READY FOR OUR GROUP GAG?

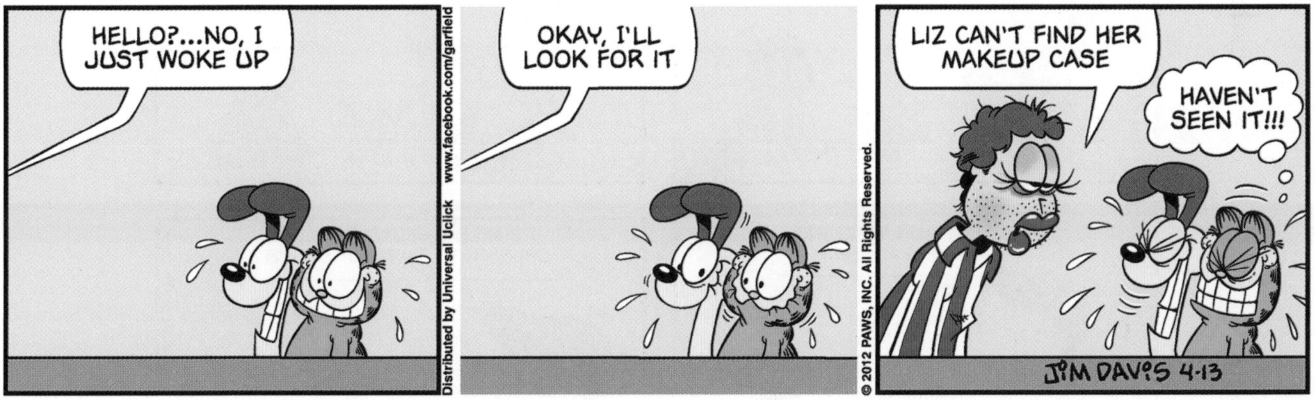
HELLO?...NO, I JUST WOKE UP
Distributed by Universal Uclick www.facebook.com/garfield
OKAY, I'LL LOOK FOR IT
© 2012 PAWS, INC. All Rights Reserved.
LIZ CAN'T FIND HER MAKEUP CASE
HAVEN'T SEEN IT!!!
JIM DAVIS 4-13

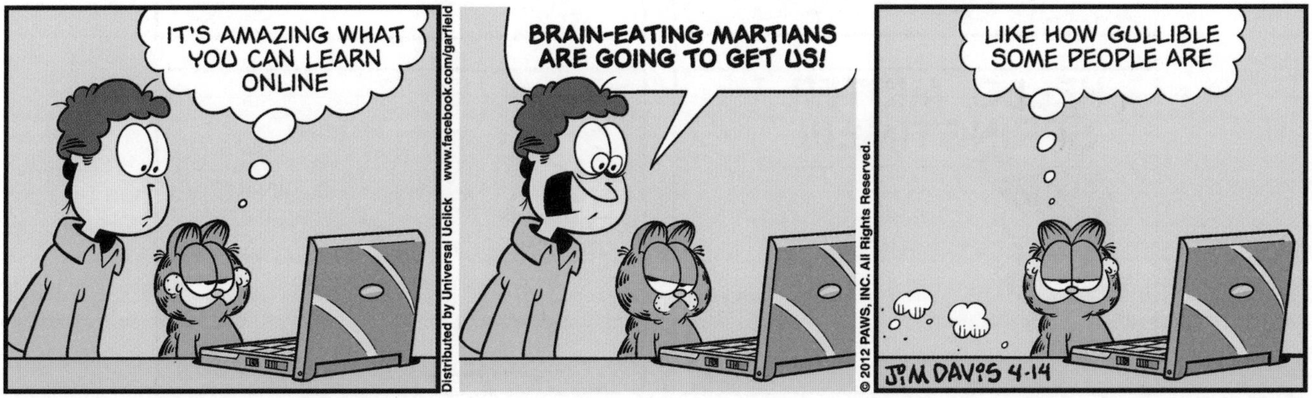
IT'S AMAZING WHAT YOU CAN LEARN ONLINE
Distributed by Universal Uclick www.facebook.com/garfield
BRAIN-EATING MARTIANS ARE GOING TO GET US!
© 2012 PAWS, INC. All Rights Reserved.
LIKE HOW GULLIBLE SOME PEOPLE ARE
JIM DAVIS 4-14

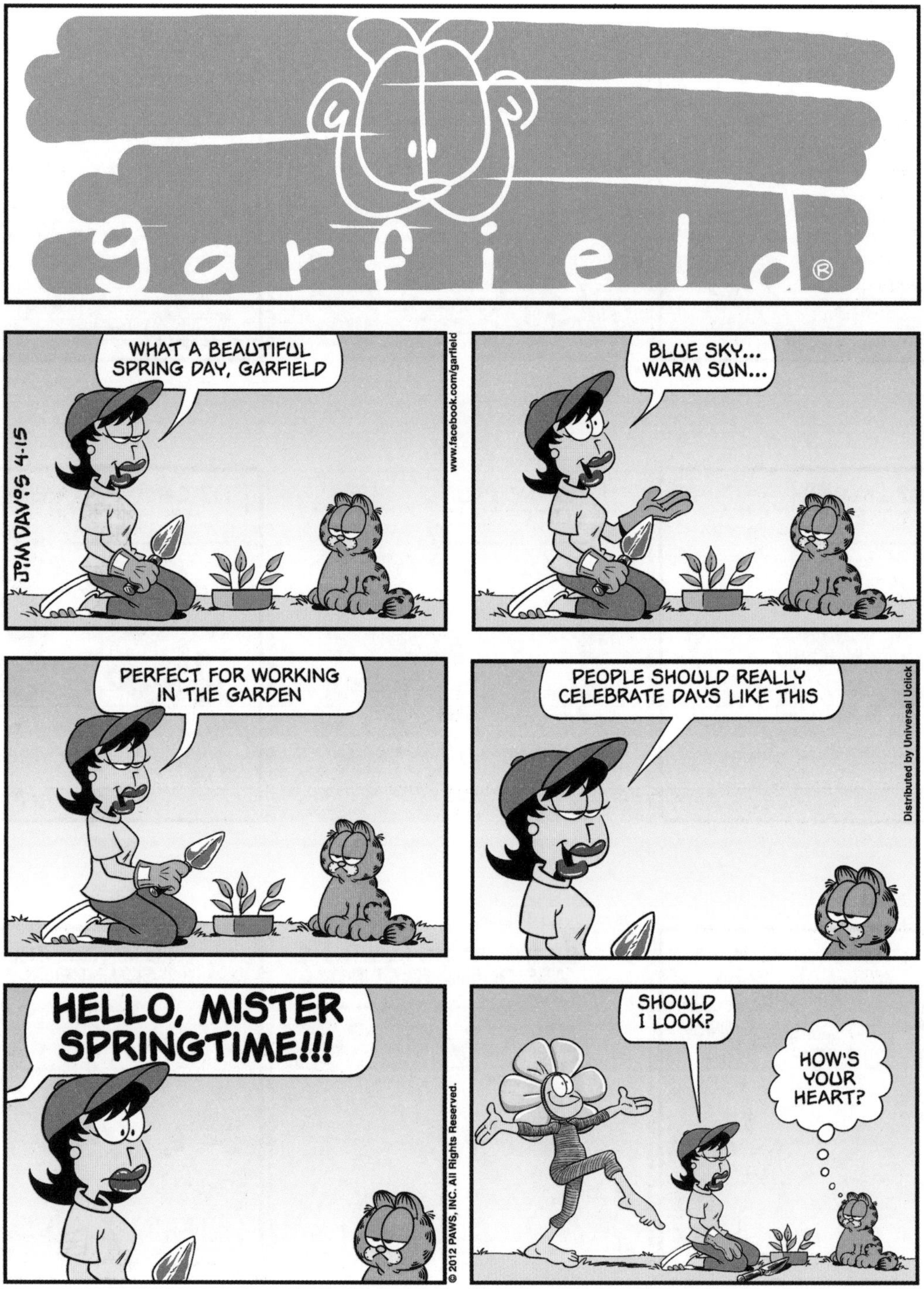
garfield®
JPM DAVIS 4-15
www.facebook.com/garfield
WHAT A BEAUTIFUL SPRING DAY, GARFIELD
BLUE SKY... WARM SUN...
PERFECT FOR WORKING IN THE GARDEN
PEOPLE SHOULD REALLY CELEBRATE DAYS LIKE THIS
Distributed by Universal Uclick
HELLO, MISTER SPRINGTIME!!!
© 2012 PAWS, INC. All Rights Reserved.
SHOULD I LOOK?
HOW'S YOUR HEART?

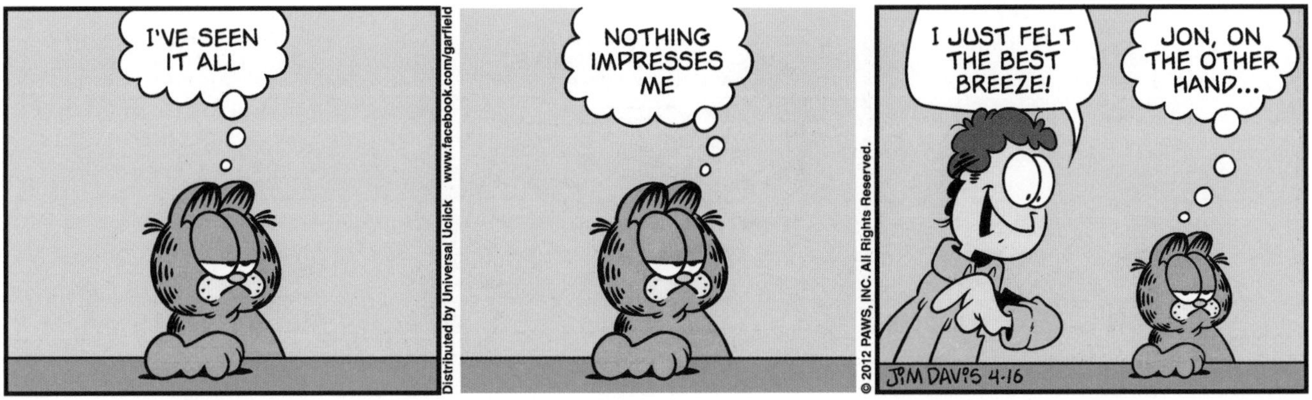
I'VE SEEN IT ALL
Distributed by Universal Uclick www.facebook.com/garfield
NOTHING IMPRESSES ME
© 2012 PAWS, INC. All Rights Reserved.
I JUST FELT THE BEST BREEZE!
JON, ON THE OTHER HAND...
JIM DAVIS 4-16

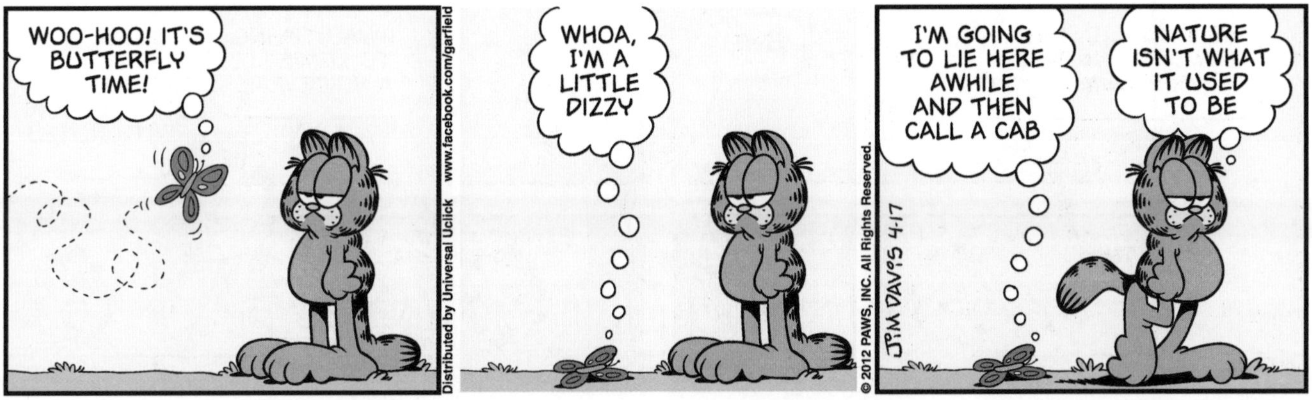
WOO-HOO! IT'S BUTTERFLY TIME!
Distributed by Universal Uclick www.facebook.com/garfield
WHOA, I'M A LITTLE DIZZY
© 2012 PAWS, INC. All Rights Reserved.
I'M GOING TO LIE HERE AWHILE AND THEN CALL A CAB
NATURE ISN'T WHAT IT USED TO BE
JIM DAVIS 4-17

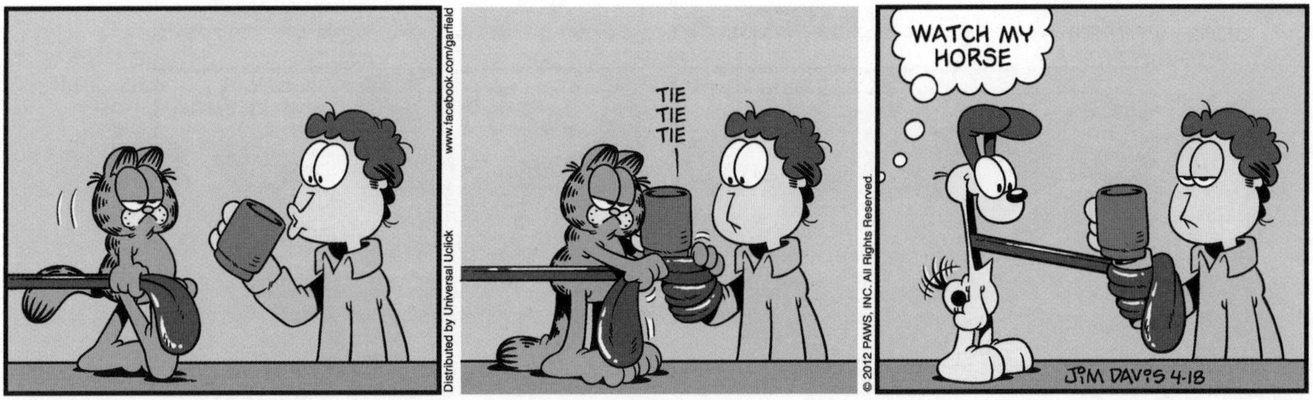
Distributed by Universal Uclick www.facebook.com/garfield
TIE TIE TIE
© 2012 PAWS, INC. All Rights Reserved.
WATCH MY HORSE
JIM DAVIS 4-18

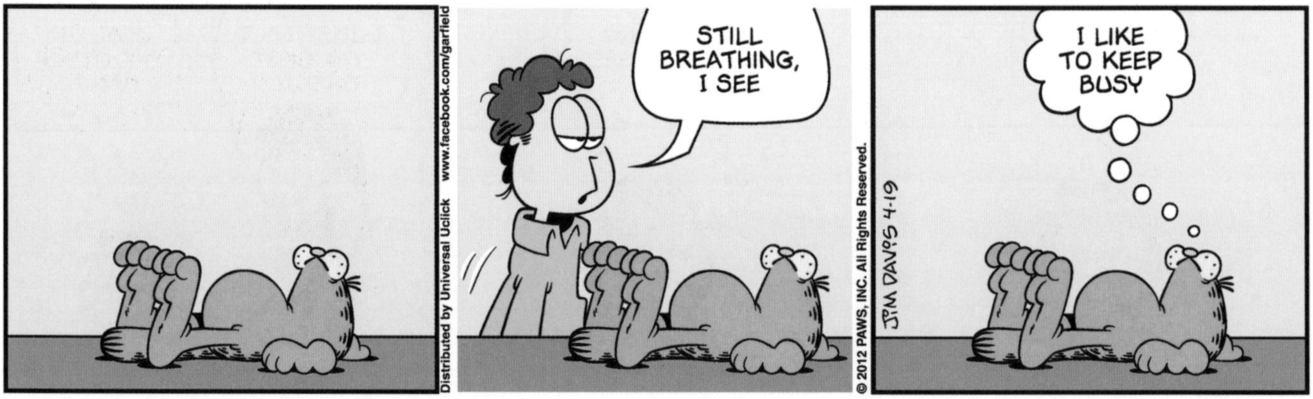
STILL BREATHING, I SEE
I LIKE TO KEEP BUSY
Distributed by Universal Uclick www.facebook.com/garfield
© 2012 PAWS, INC. All Rights Reserved.
JPM DAVPS 4·19

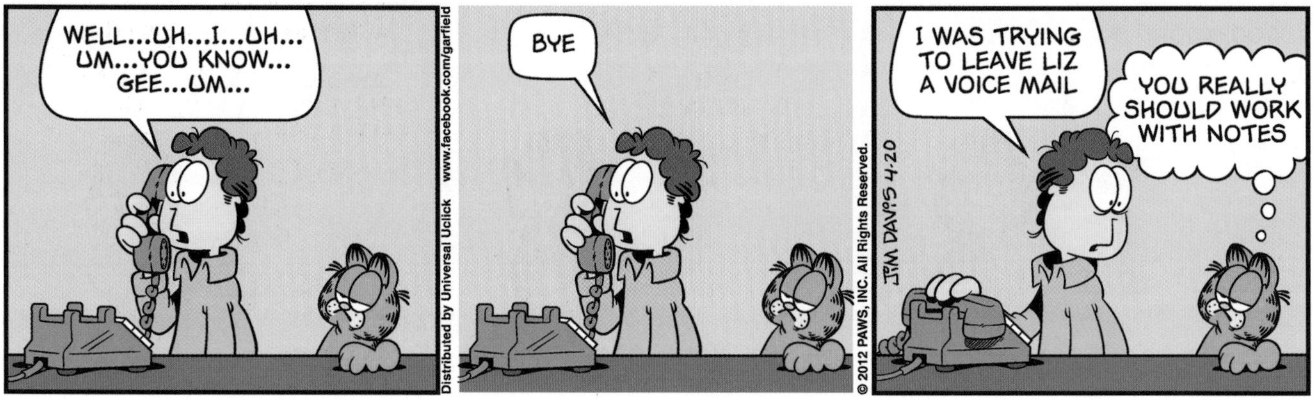
WELL...UH...I...UH... UM...YOU KNOW... GEE...UM...
BYE
I WAS TRYING TO LEAVE LIZ A VOICE MAIL
YOU REALLY SHOULD WORK WITH NOTES
Distributed by Universal Uclick www.facebook.com/garfield
© 2012 PAWS, INC. All Rights Reserved.
JPM DAVPS 4·20

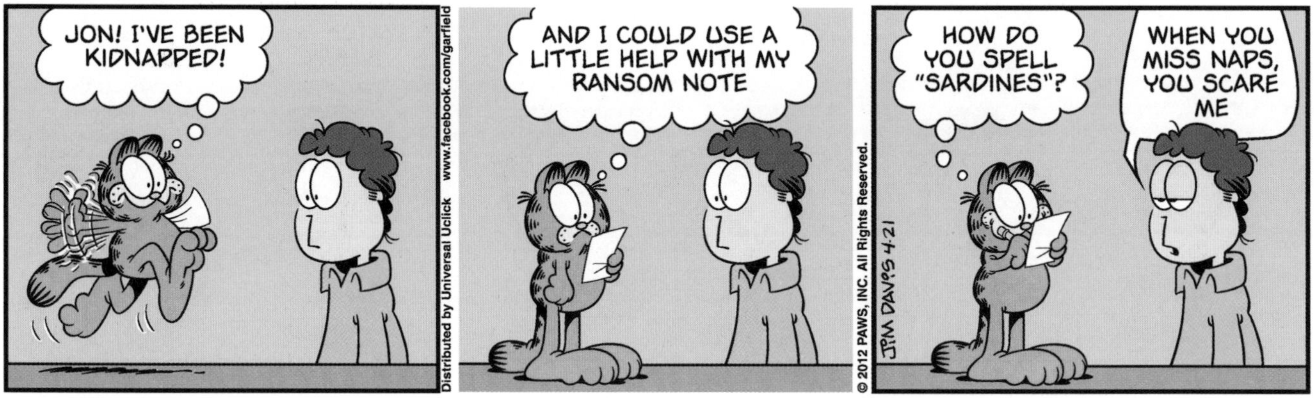
JON! I'VE BEEN KIDNAPPED!
AND I COULD USE A LITTLE HELP WITH MY RANSOM NOTE
HOW DO YOU SPELL "SARDINES"?
WHEN YOU MISS NAPS, YOU SCARE ME
Distributed by Universal Uclick www.facebook.com/garfield
© 2012 PAWS, INC. All Rights Reserved.
JPM DAVPS 4·21

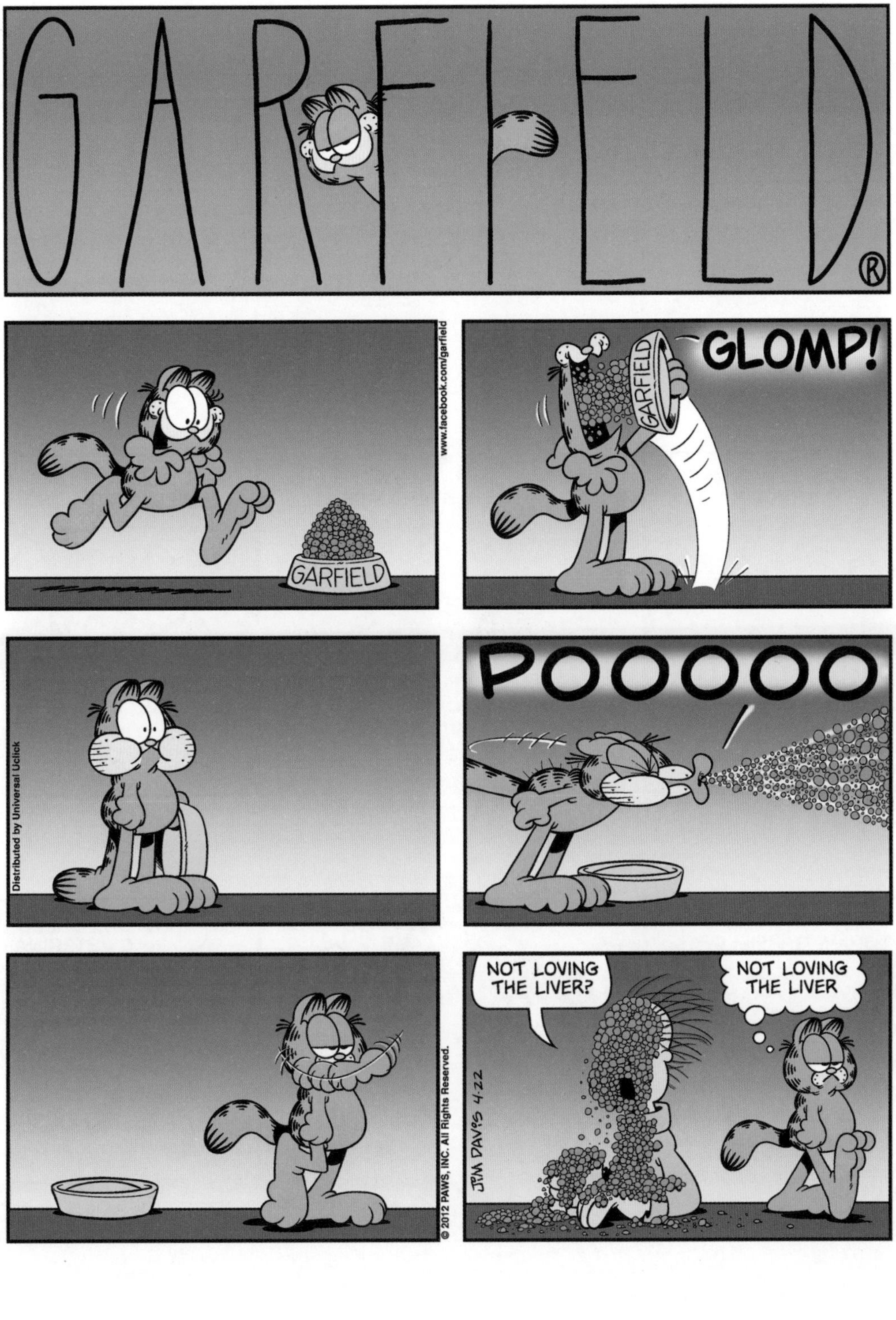
GARFIELD®
www.facebook.com/garfield
GARFIELD
GLOMP!
GARFIELD
Distributed by Universal Uclick
POOOOO
© 2012 PAWS, INC. All Rights Reserved.
JPM DAVPS 4-22
NOT LOVING THE LIVER?
NOT LOVING THE LIVER

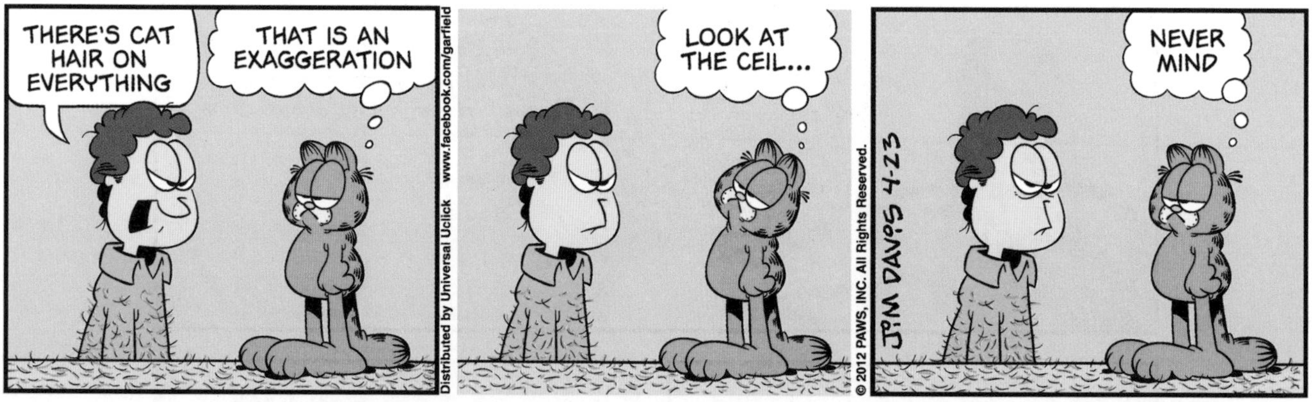
THERE'S CAT HAIR ON EVERYTHING
THAT IS AN EXAGGERATION
LOOK AT THE CEIL...
NEVER MIND
Distributed by Universal Uclick www.facebook.com/garfield
© 2012 PAWS, INC. All Rights Reserved.
JIM DAVIS 4-23

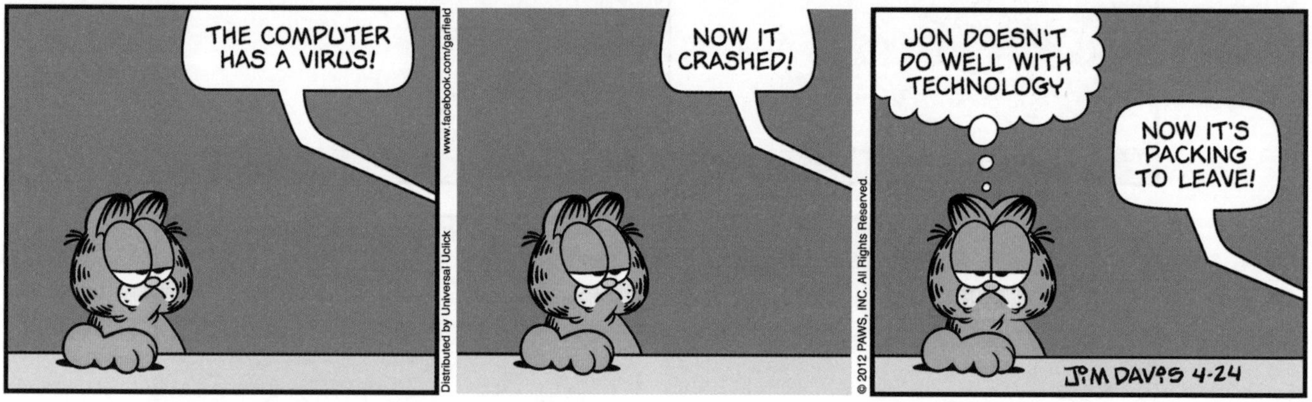
THE COMPUTER HAS A VIRUS!
NOW IT CRASHED!
JON DOESN'T DO WELL WITH TECHNOLOGY
NOW IT'S PACKING TO LEAVE!
Distributed by Universal Uclick www.facebook.com/garfield
© 2012 PAWS, INC. All Rights Reserved.
JIM DAVIS 4-24

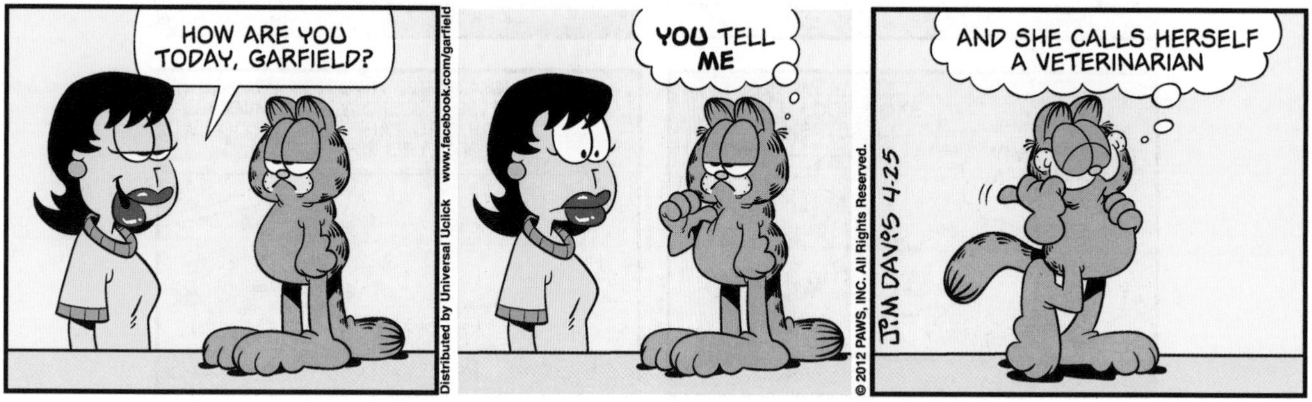
HOW ARE YOU TODAY, GARFIELD?
YOU TELL ME
AND SHE CALLS HERSELF A VETERINARIAN
Distributed by Universal Uclick www.facebook.com/garfield
© 2012 PAWS, INC. All Rights Reserved.
JIM DAVIS 4-25

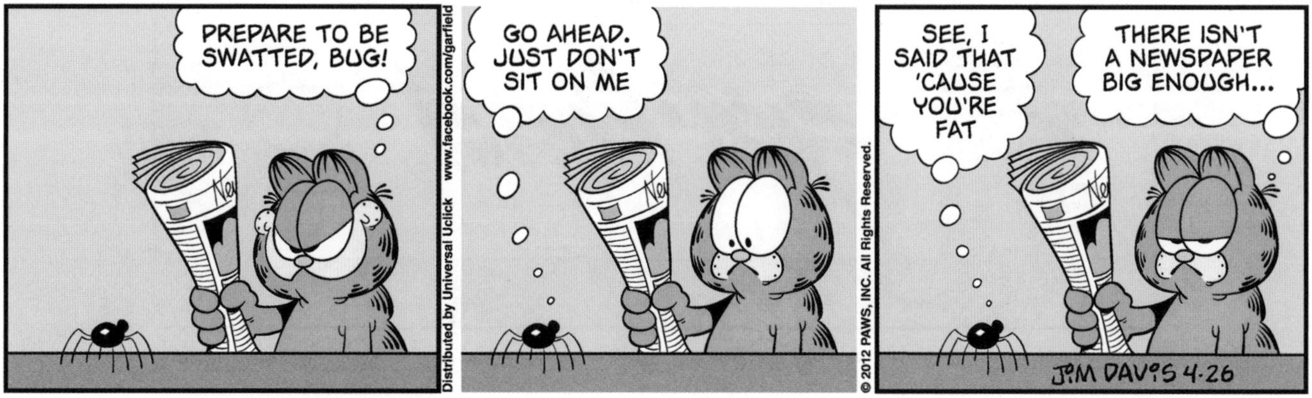
PREPARE TO BE SWATTED, BUG!
Distributed by Universal Uclick www.facebook.com/garfield
GO AHEAD. JUST DON'T SIT ON ME
© 2012 PAWS, INC. All Rights Reserved.
SEE, I SAID THAT 'CAUSE YOU'RE FAT
THERE ISN'T A NEWSPAPER BIG ENOUGH...
JIM DAVIS 4-26

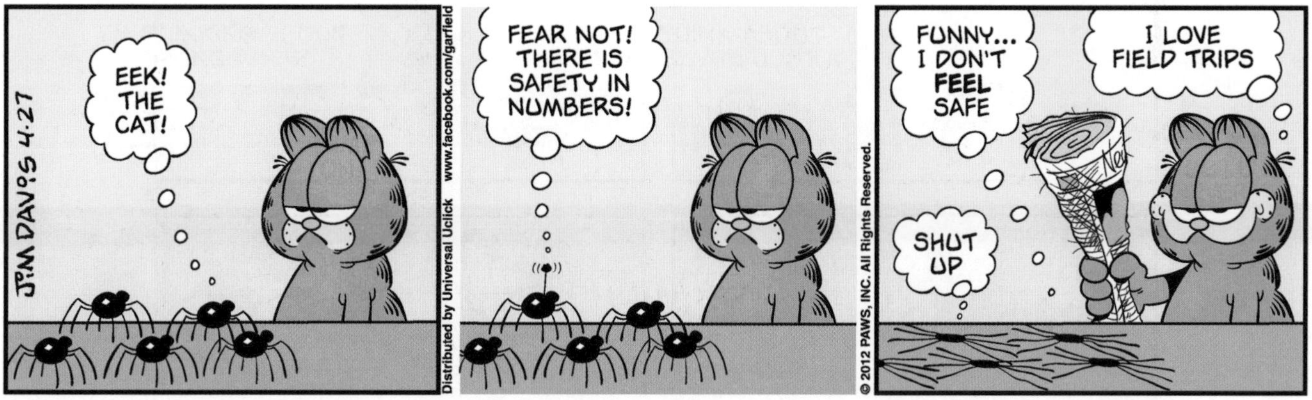
JIM DAVIS 4-27
EEK! THE CAT!
Distributed by Universal Uclick www.facebook.com/garfield
FEAR NOT! THERE IS SAFETY IN NUMBERS!
© 2012 PAWS, INC. All Rights Reserved.
FUNNY... I DON'T **FEEL** SAFE
SHUT UP
I LOVE FIELD TRIPS

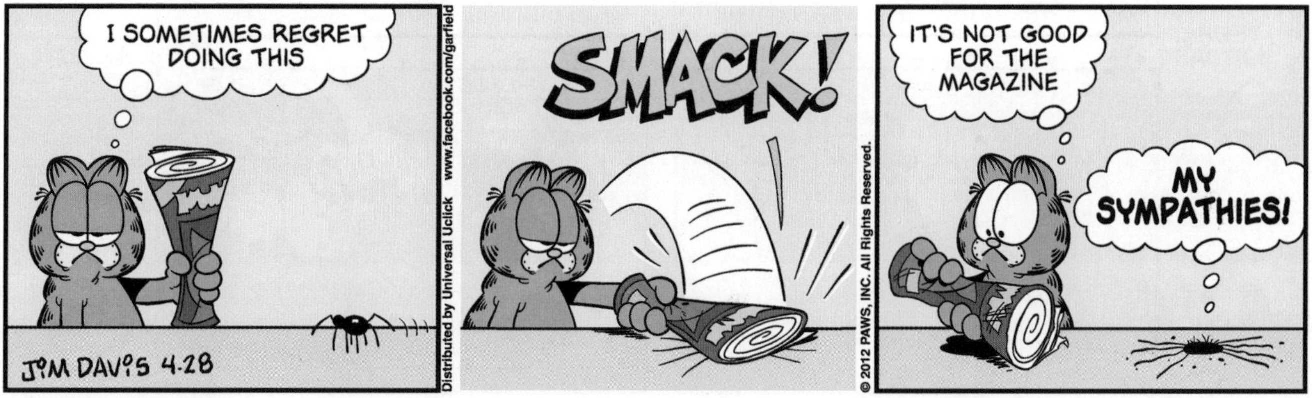
I SOMETIMES REGRET DOING THIS
JIM DAVIS 4-28
Distributed by Universal Uclick www.facebook.com/garfield
SMACK!
© 2012 PAWS, INC. All Rights Reserved.
IT'S NOT GOOD FOR THE MAGAZINE
MY SYMPATHIES!

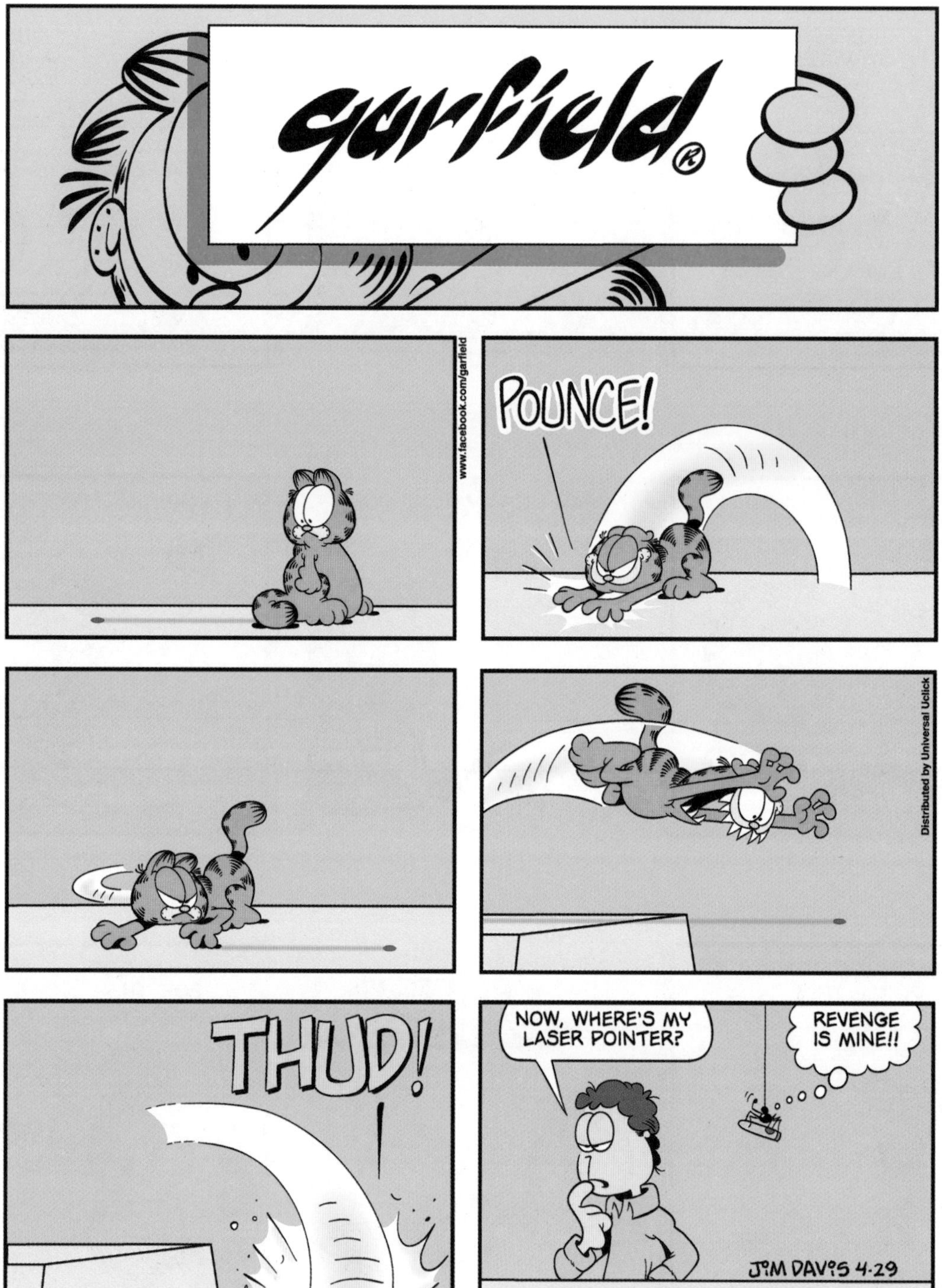
garfield®
www.facebook.com/garfield
POUNCE!
Distributed by Universal Uclick
THUD!
NOW, WHERE'S MY LASER POINTER?
REVENGE IS MINE!!
JIM DAVIS 4-29
© 2012 PAWS, INC. All Rights Reserved.

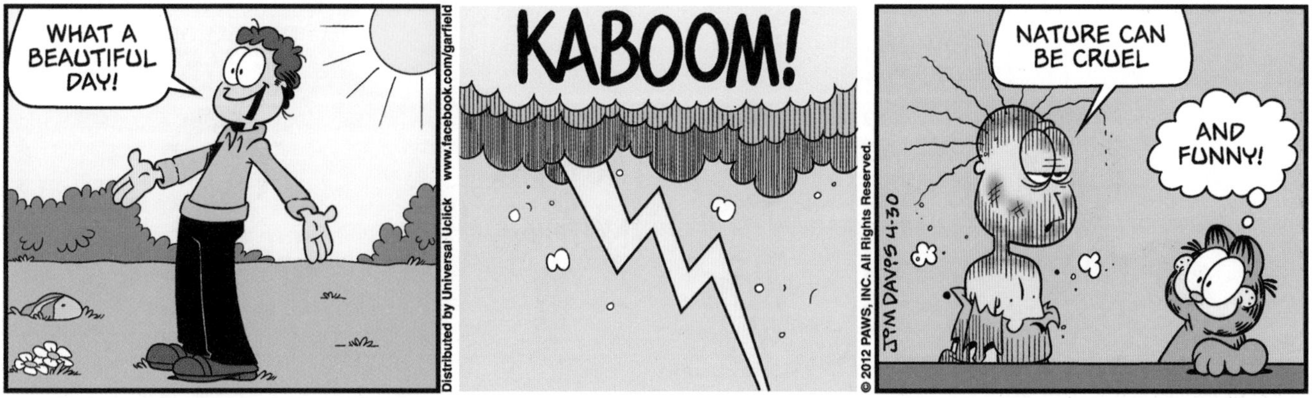
WHAT A BEAUTIFUL DAY!
Distributed by Universal Uclick www.facebook.com/garfield
KABOOM!
© 2012 PAWS, INC. All Rights Reserved.
JIM DAVIS 4-30
NATURE CAN BE CRUEL
AND FUNNY!

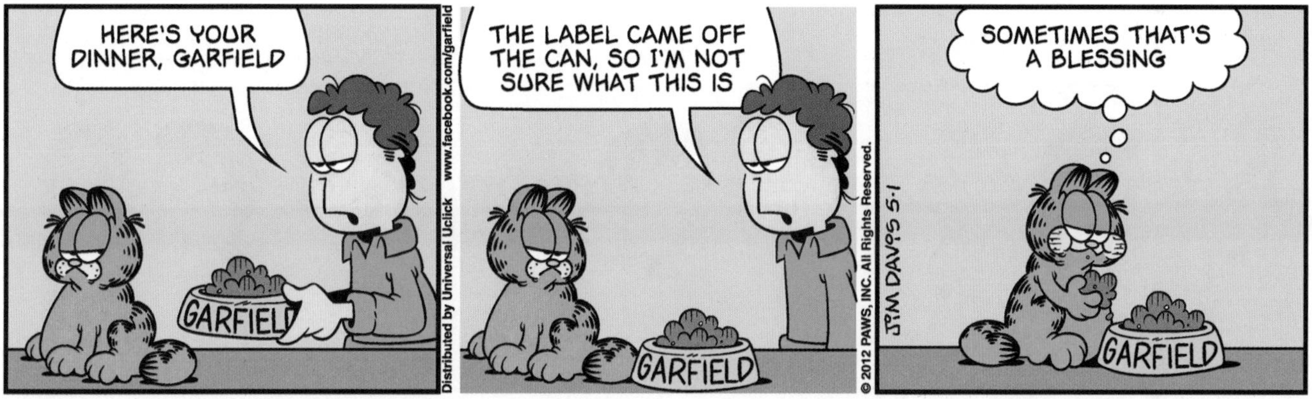
HERE'S YOUR DINNER, GARFIELD
GARFIELD
Distributed by Universal Uclick www.facebook.com/garfield
THE LABEL CAME OFF THE CAN, SO I'M NOT SURE WHAT THIS IS
GARFIELD
© 2012 PAWS, INC. All Rights Reserved.
JIM DAVIS 5-1
SOMETIMES THAT'S A BLESSING
GARFIELD

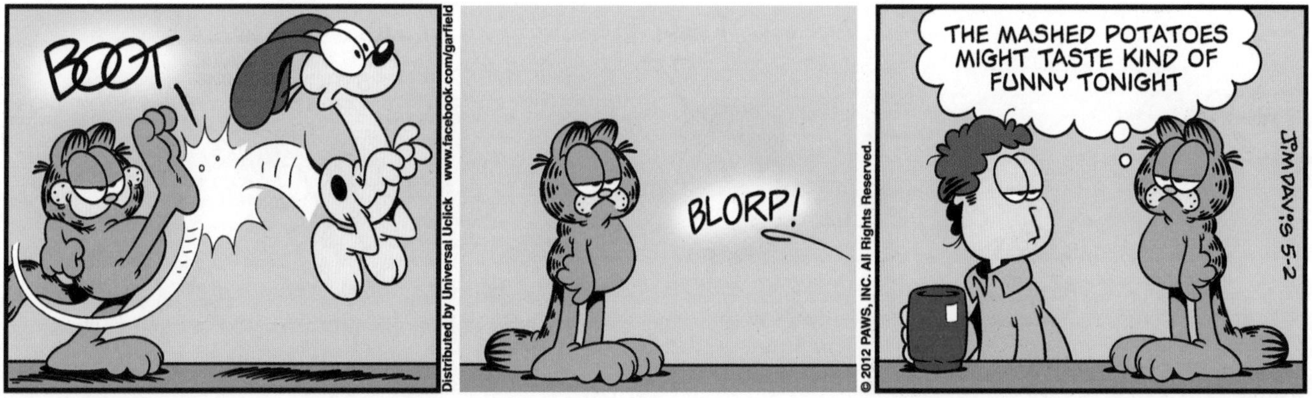
BOOT!
Distributed by Universal Uclick www.facebook.com/garfield
BLORP!
© 2012 PAWS, INC. All Rights Reserved.
THE MASHED POTATOES MIGHT TASTE KIND OF FUNNY TONIGHT
JIM DAVIS 5-2

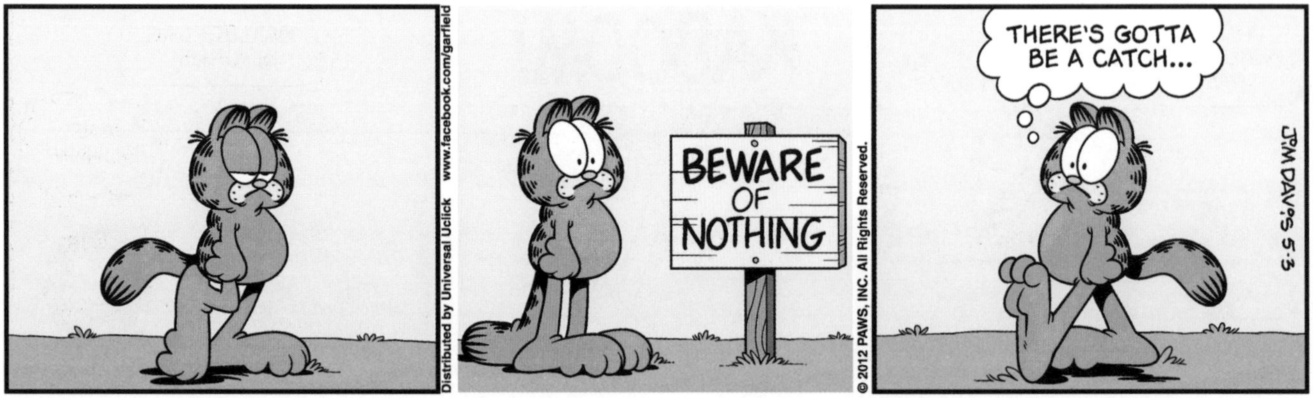
Distributed by Universal Uclick www.facebook.com/garfield
BEWARE OF NOTHING
© 2012 PAWS, INC. All Rights Reserved.
THERE'S GOTTA BE A CATCH...
JIM DAVIS 5-3

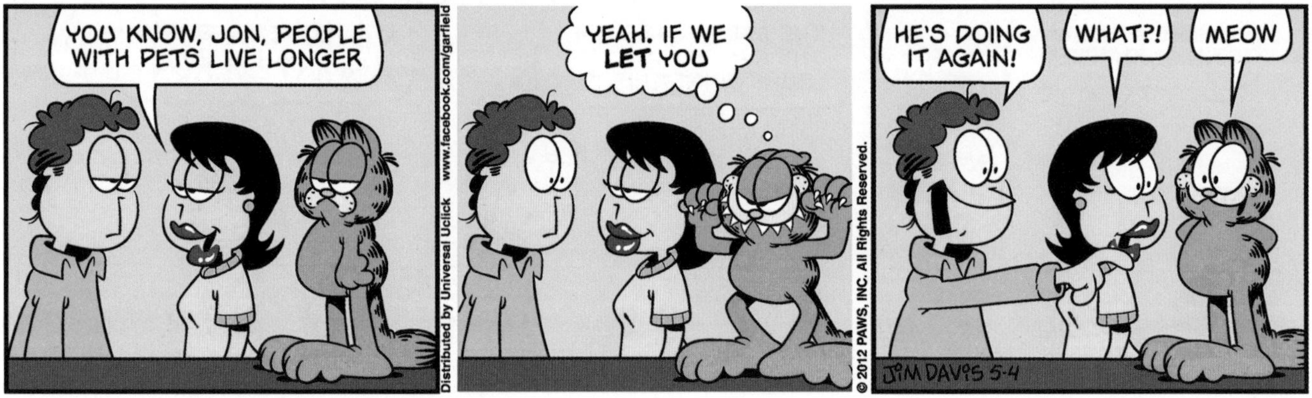
YOU KNOW, JON, PEOPLE WITH PETS LIVE LONGER
Distributed by Universal Uclick www.facebook.com/garfield
YEAH. IF WE **LET** YOU
© 2012 PAWS, INC. All Rights Reserved.
HE'S DOING IT AGAIN!
WHAT?!
MEOW
JIM DAVIS 5-4

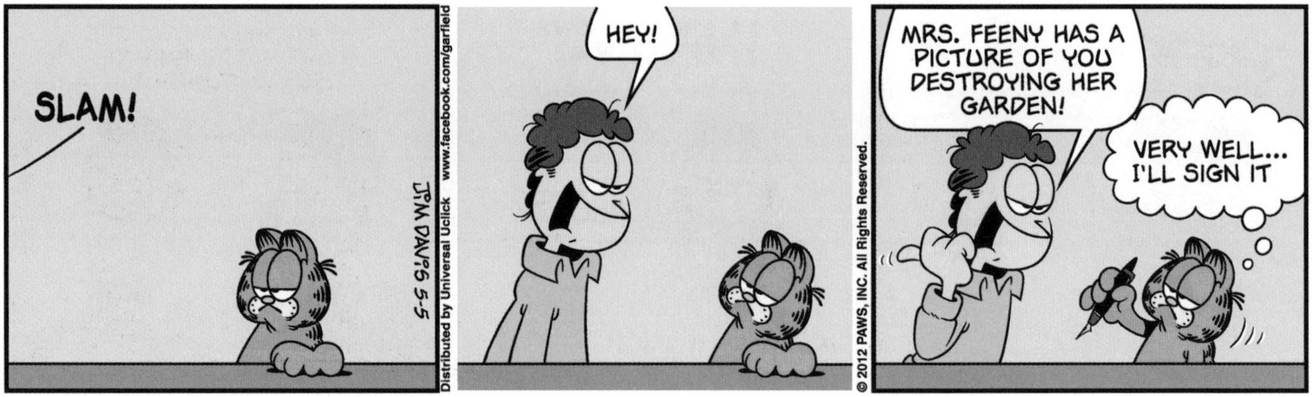
SLAM!
JIM DAVIS 5-5
Distributed by Universal Uclick www.facebook.com/garfield
HEY!
© 2012 PAWS, INC. All Rights Reserved.
MRS. FEENY HAS A PICTURE OF YOU DESTROYING HER GARDEN!
VERY WELL... I'LL SIGN IT

MORE OODLES OF DOODLES

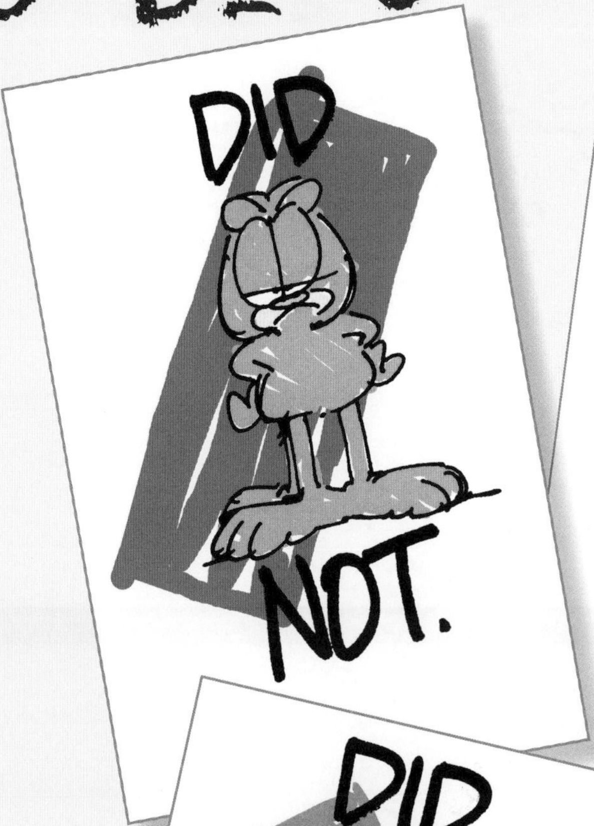
DID
NOT.

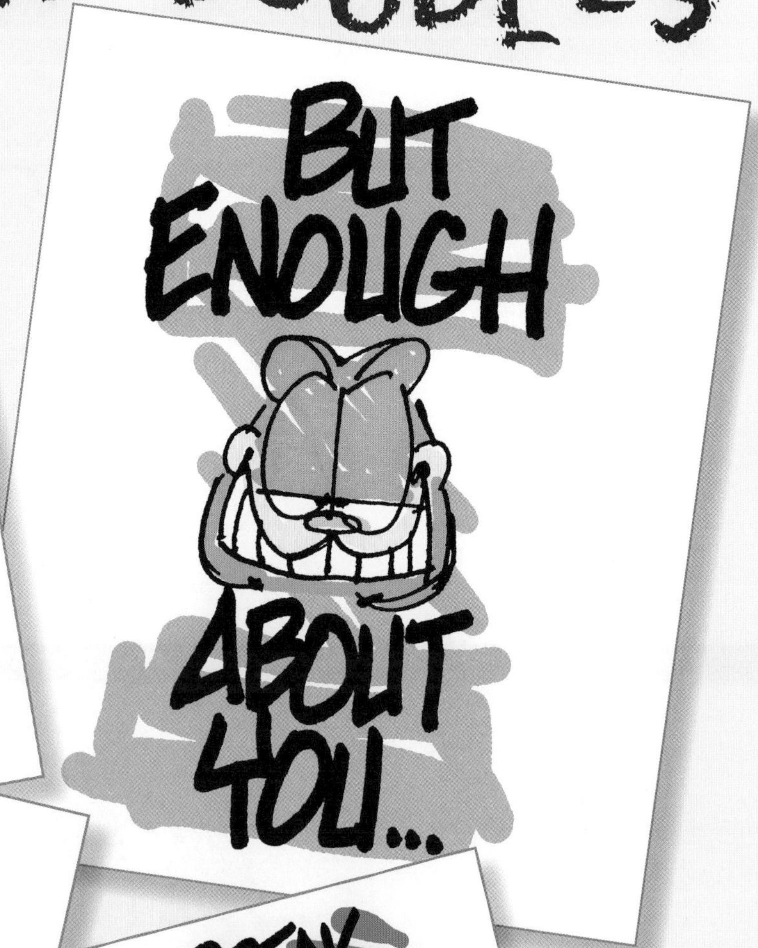
BUT ENOUGH
ABOUT YOU...

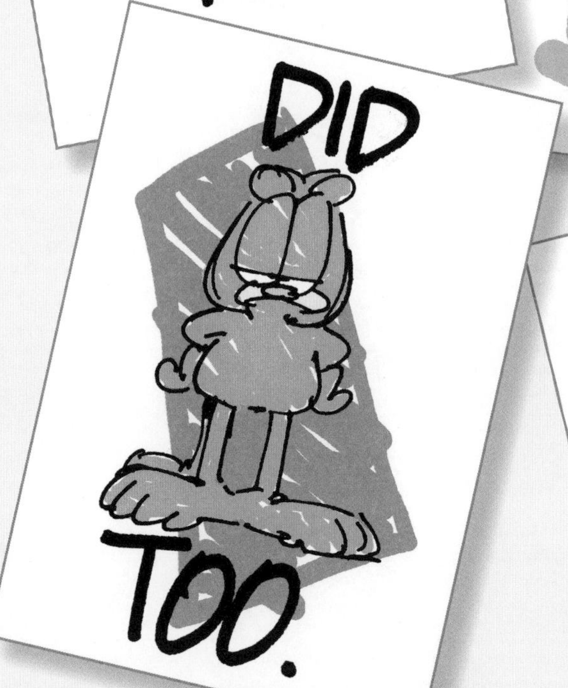
DID
TOO.

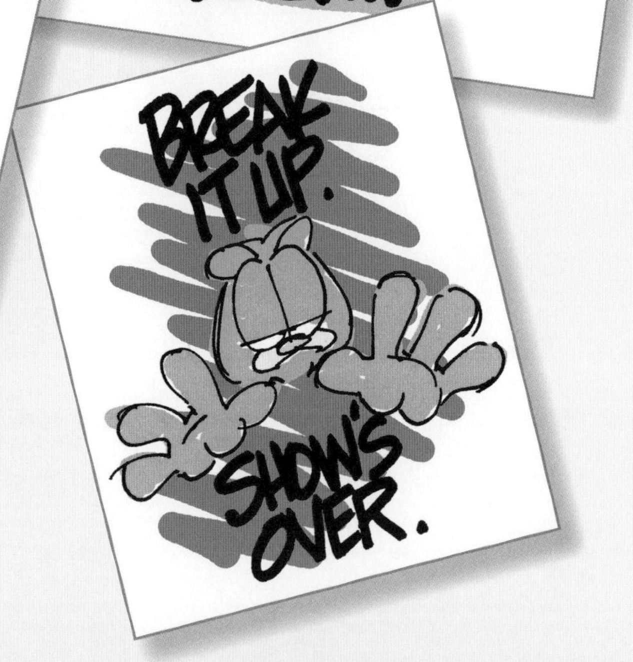
BREAK IT UP.
SHOW'S OVER.

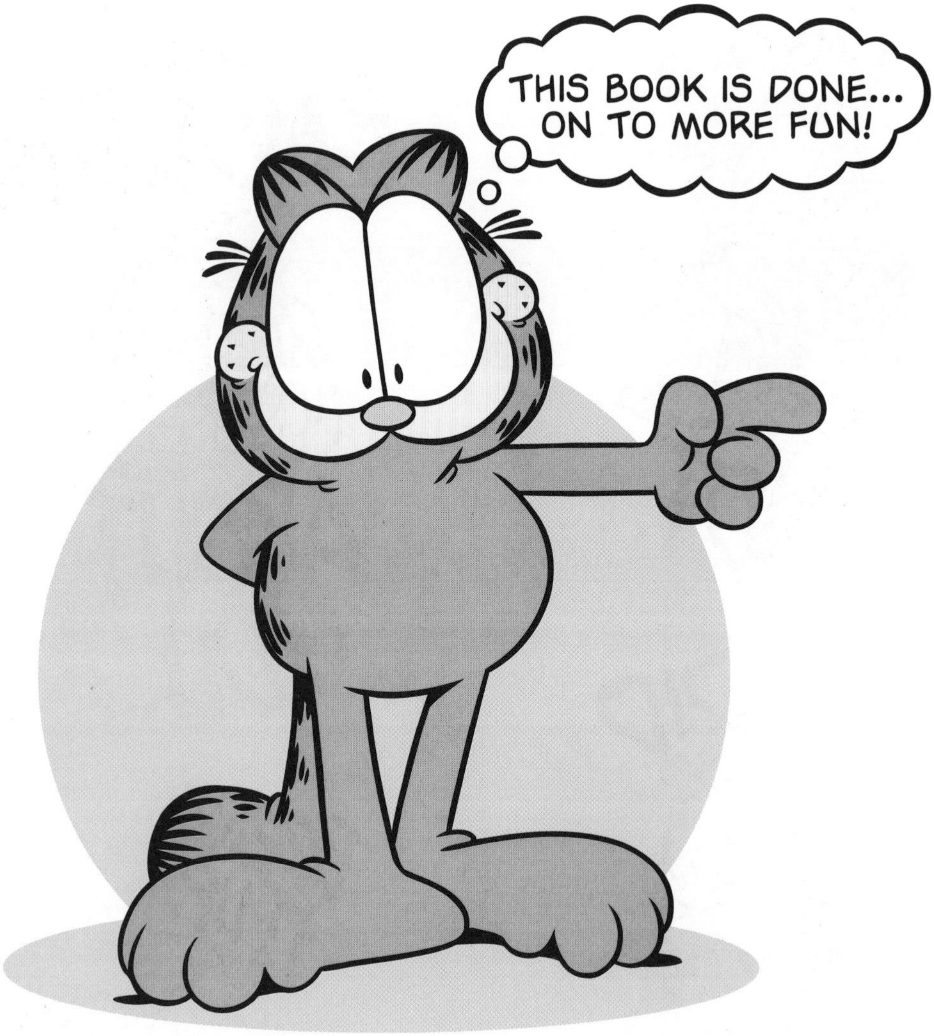
THIS BOOK IS DONE...
ON TO MORE FUN!

Garfield
THE BIG CHEESE

BY JIM DAVIS

Ballantine Books ● New York

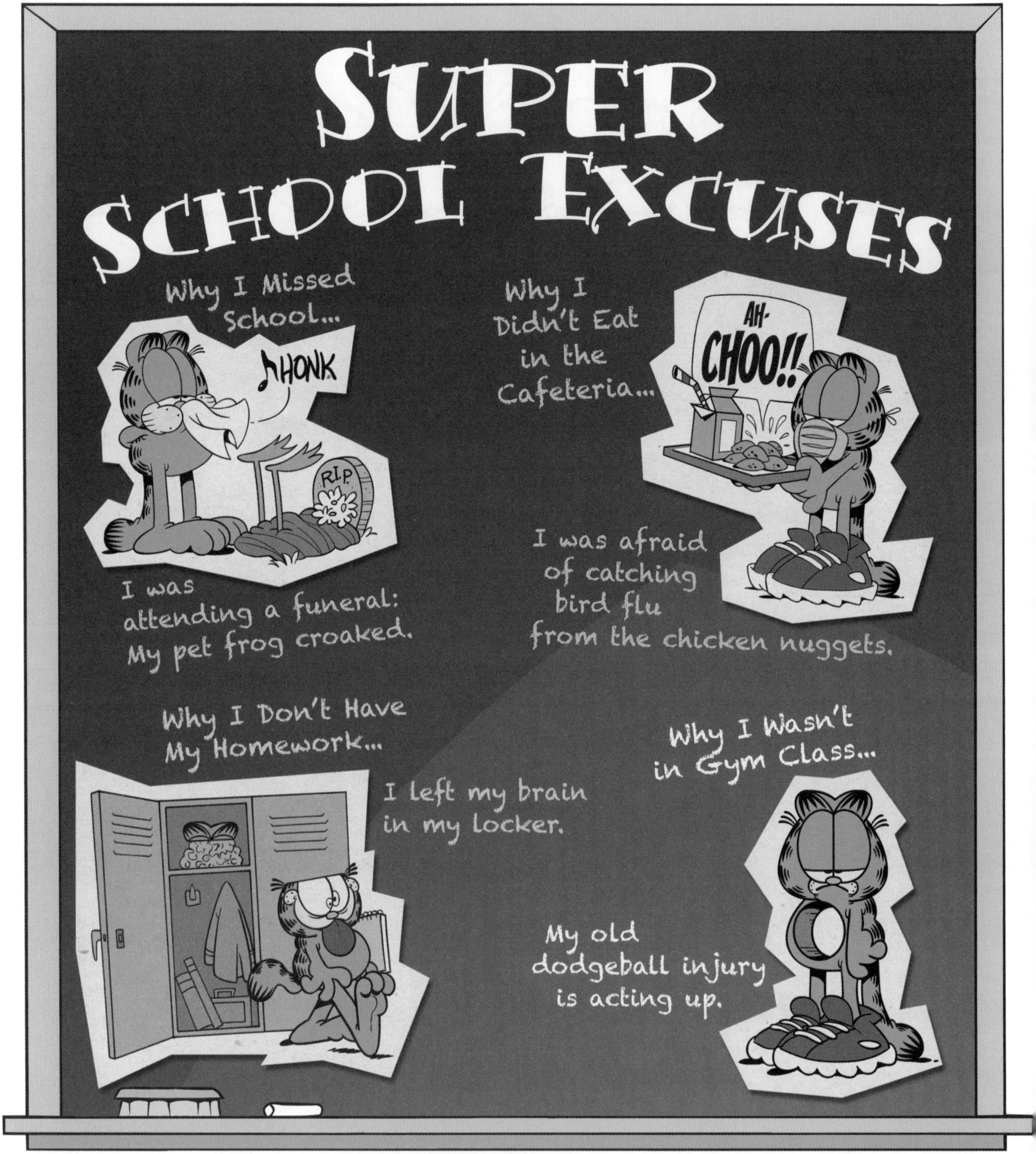
SUPER SCHOOL EXCUSES
Why I Missed School...
HONK
R.I.P.
I was attending a funeral: My pet frog croaked.
Why I Didn't Eat in the Cafeteria...
AH-CHOO!!
I was afraid of catching bird flu from the chicken nuggets.
Why I Don't Have My Homework...
I left my brain in my locker.
Why I Wasn't in Gym Class...
My old dodgeball injury is acting up.

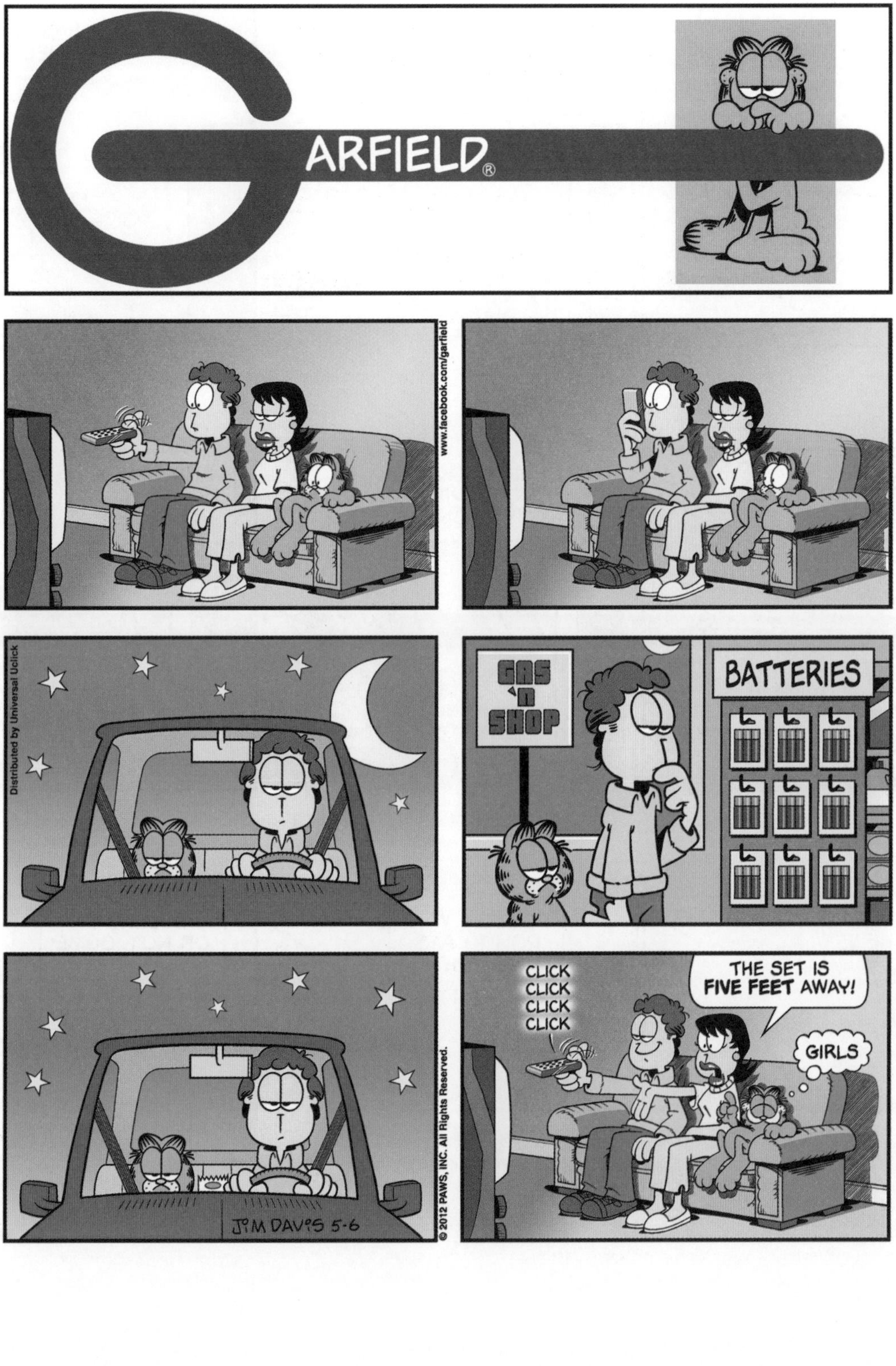
GARFIELD®
www.facebook.com/garfield
Distributed by Universal Uclick
GAS 'N SHOP
BATTERIES
CLICK CLICK CLICK CLICK
THE SET IS FIVE FEET AWAY!
GIRLS
JIM DAVIS 5-6
© 2012 PAWS, INC. All Rights Reserved.

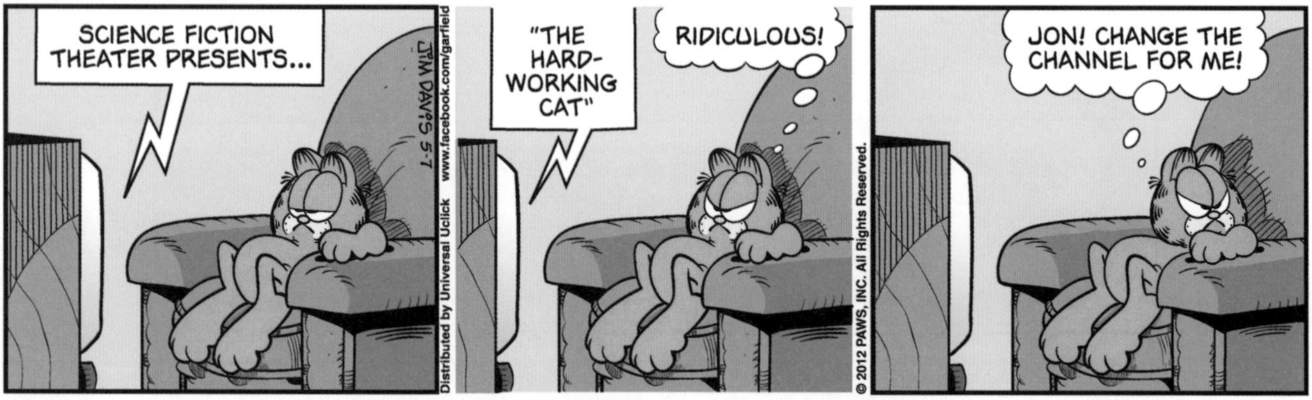
SCIENCE FICTION THEATER PRESENTS...
JIM DAVIS 5-7
Distributed by Universal Uclick www.facebook.com/garfield
"THE HARD-WORKING CAT"
RIDICULOUS!
© 2012 PAWS, INC. All Rights Reserved.
JON! CHANGE THE CHANNEL FOR ME!

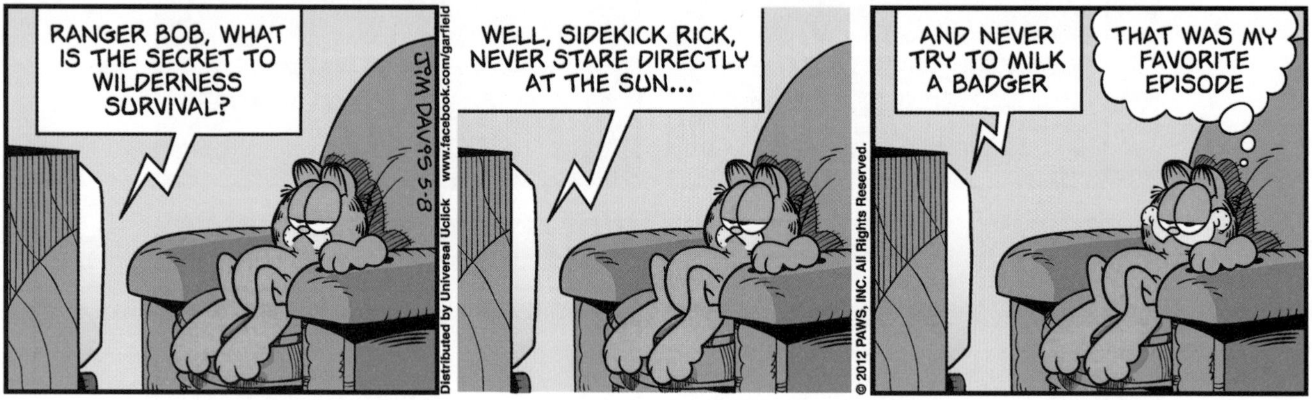
RANGER BOB, WHAT IS THE SECRET TO WILDERNESS SURVIVAL?
JIM DAVIS 5-8
Distributed by Universal Uclick www.facebook.com/garfield
WELL, SIDEKICK RICK, NEVER STARE DIRECTLY AT THE SUN...
© 2012 PAWS, INC. All Rights Reserved.
AND NEVER TRY TO MILK A BADGER
THAT WAS MY FAVORITE EPISODE

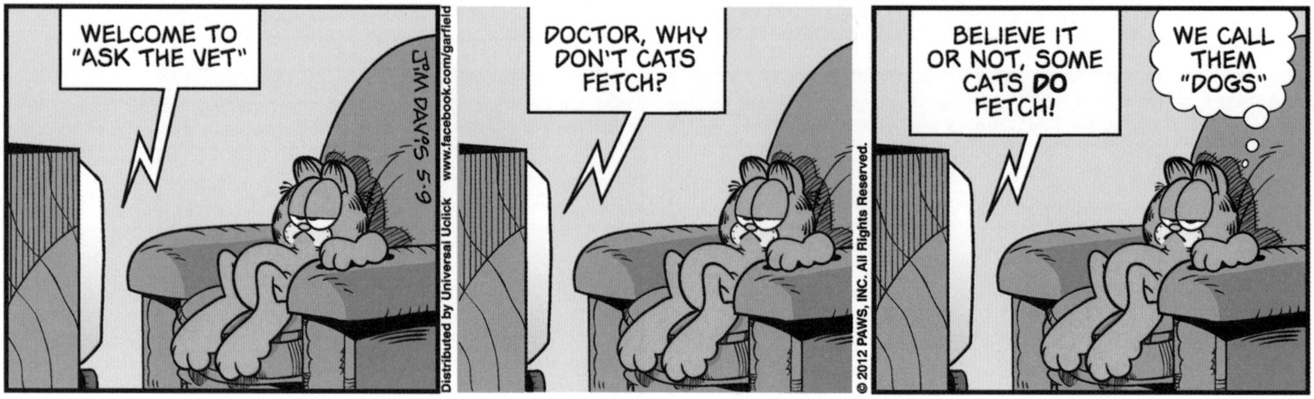
WELCOME TO "ASK THE VET"
JIM DAVIS 5-9
Distributed by Universal Uclick www.facebook.com/garfield
DOCTOR, WHY DON'T CATS FETCH?
© 2012 PAWS, INC. All Rights Reserved.
BELIEVE IT OR NOT, SOME CATS **DO** FETCH!
WE CALL THEM "DOGS"

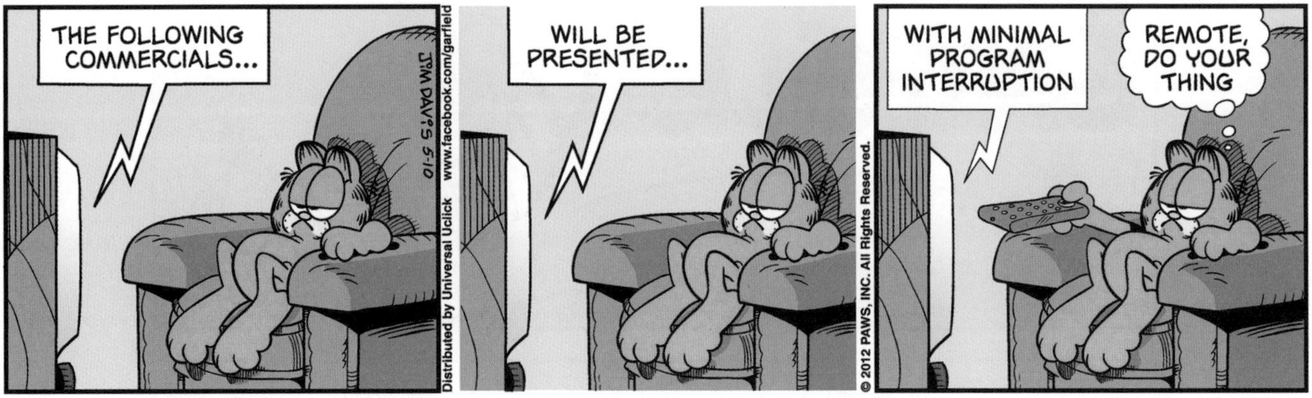
THE FOLLOWING COMMERCIALS...
JIM DAVIS 5-10
WILL BE PRESENTED...
WITH MINIMAL PROGRAM INTERRUPTION
REMOTE, DO YOUR THING
Distributed by Universal Uclick www.facebook.com/garfield
© 2012 PAWS, INC. All Rights Reserved.

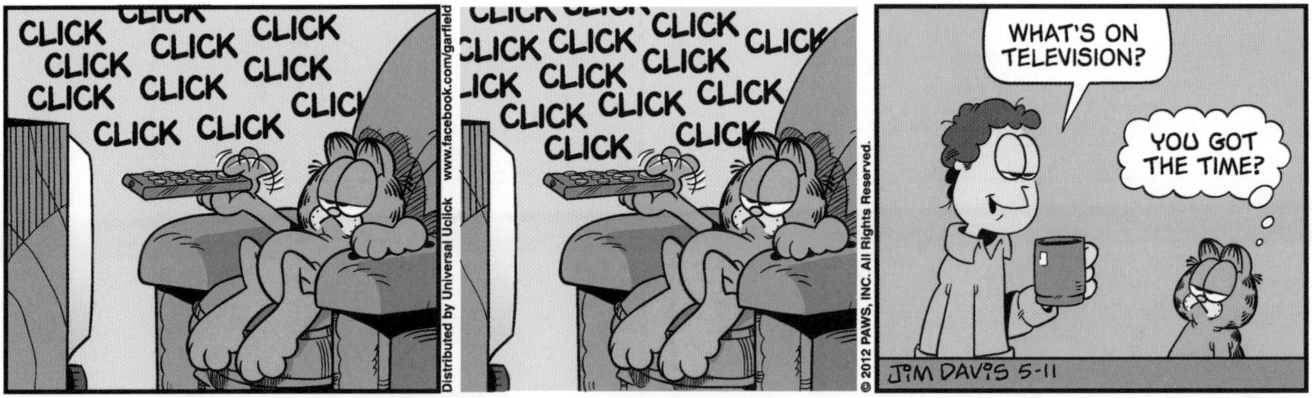
CLICK CLICK CLICK CLICK CLICK CLICK CLICK CLICK CLICK CLICK CLICK
CLICK CLICK CLICK CLICK CLICK CLICK CLICK CLICK CLICK
WHAT'S ON TELEVISION?
YOU GOT THE TIME?
JIM DAVIS 5-11
Distributed by Universal Uclick www.facebook.com/garfield
© 2012 PAWS, INC. All Rights Reserved.

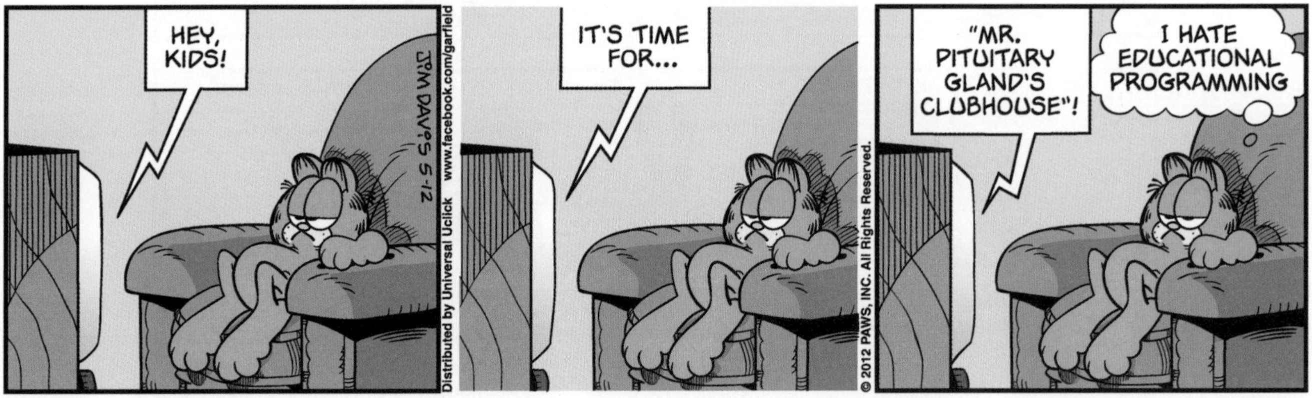
HEY, KIDS!
JIM DAVIS 5-12
IT'S TIME FOR...
"MR. PITUITARY GLAND'S CLUBHOUSE"!
I HATE EDUCATIONAL PROGRAMMING
Distributed by Universal Uclick www.facebook.com/garfield
© 2012 PAWS, INC. All Rights Reserved.

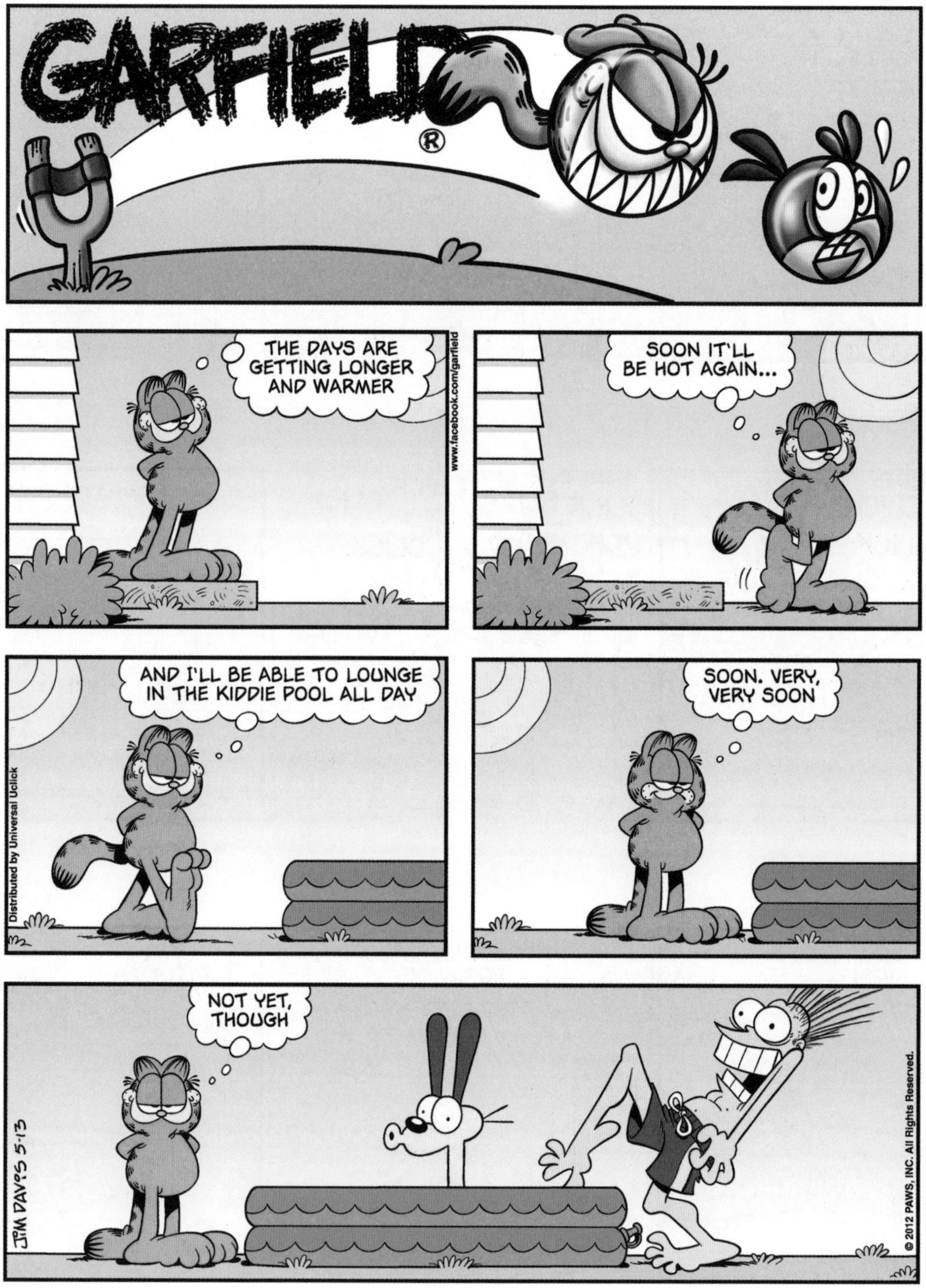
GARFIELD®
www.facebook.com/garfield
THE DAYS ARE GETTING LONGER AND WARMER
SOON IT'LL BE HOT AGAIN...
Distributed by Universal Uclick
AND I'LL BE ABLE TO LOUNGE IN THE KIDDIE POOL ALL DAY
SOON. VERY, VERY SOON
NOT YET, THOUGH
JPM DAV?S 5-13
© 2012 PAWS, INC. All Rights Reserved.

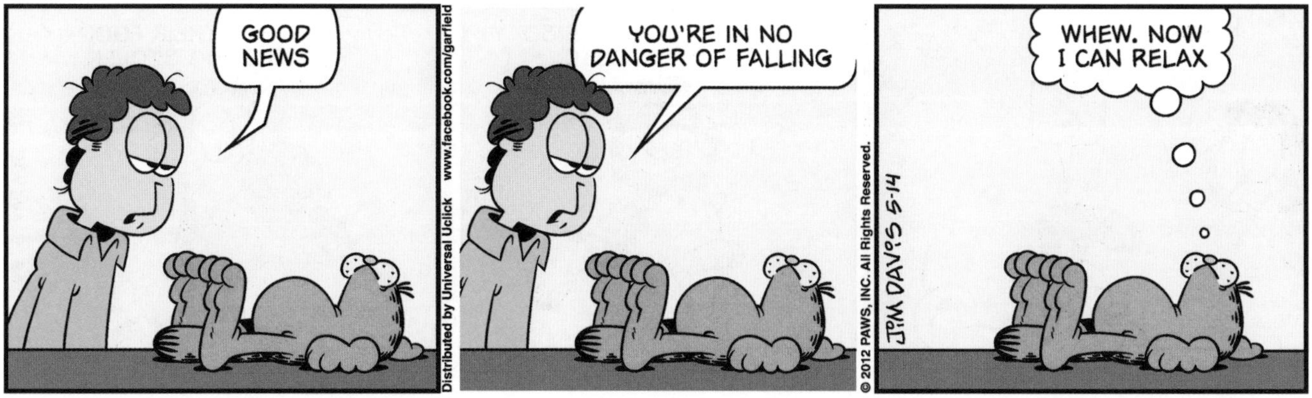
GOOD NEWS
YOU'RE IN NO DANGER OF FALLING
WHEW. NOW I CAN RELAX
JIM DAVIS 5-14

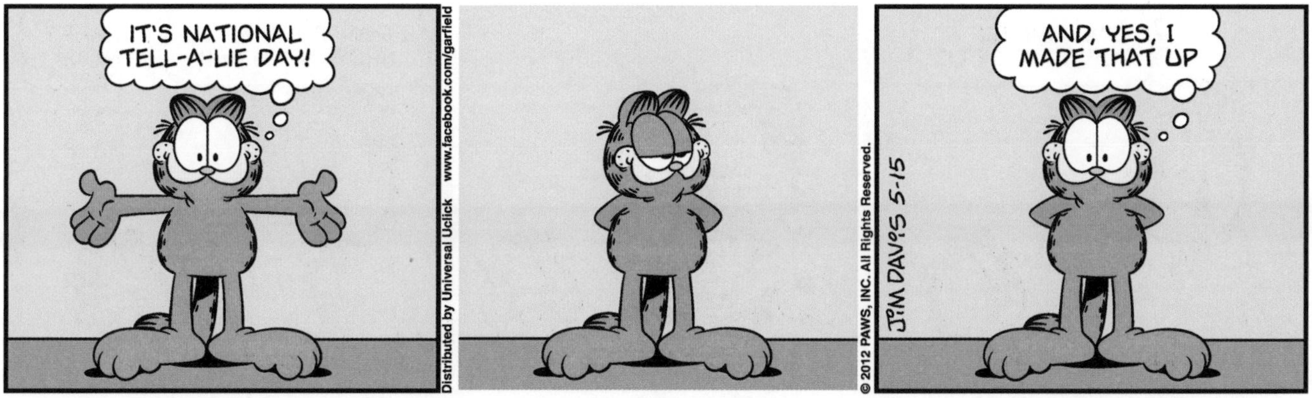
IT'S NATIONAL TELL-A-LIE DAY!
AND, YES, I MADE THAT UP
JIM DAVIS 5-15

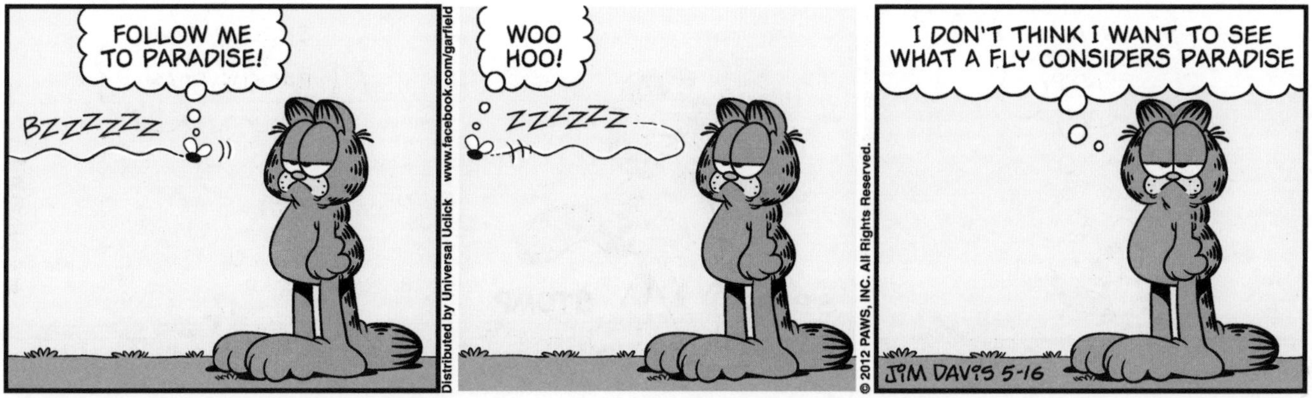
FOLLOW ME TO PARADISE!
BZZZZZZ
WOO HOO!
ZZZZZZ
I DON'T THINK I WANT TO SEE WHAT A FLY CONSIDERS PARADISE
JIM DAVIS 5-16

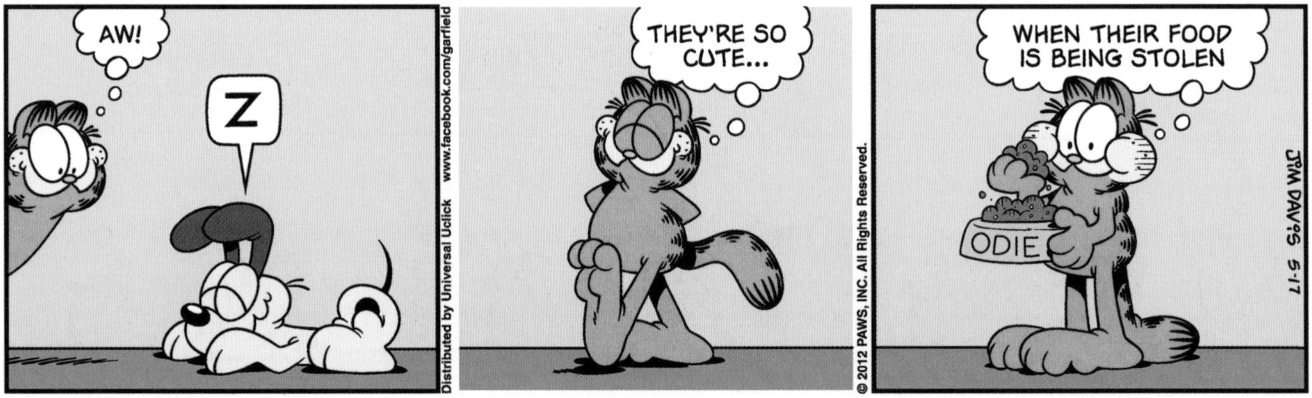
AW!
Z
THEY'RE SO CUTE...
WHEN THEIR FOOD IS BEING STOLEN
ODIE
JIM DAVIS 5-17
Distributed by Universal Uclick www.facebook.com/garfield
© 2012 PAWS, INC. All Rights Reserved.

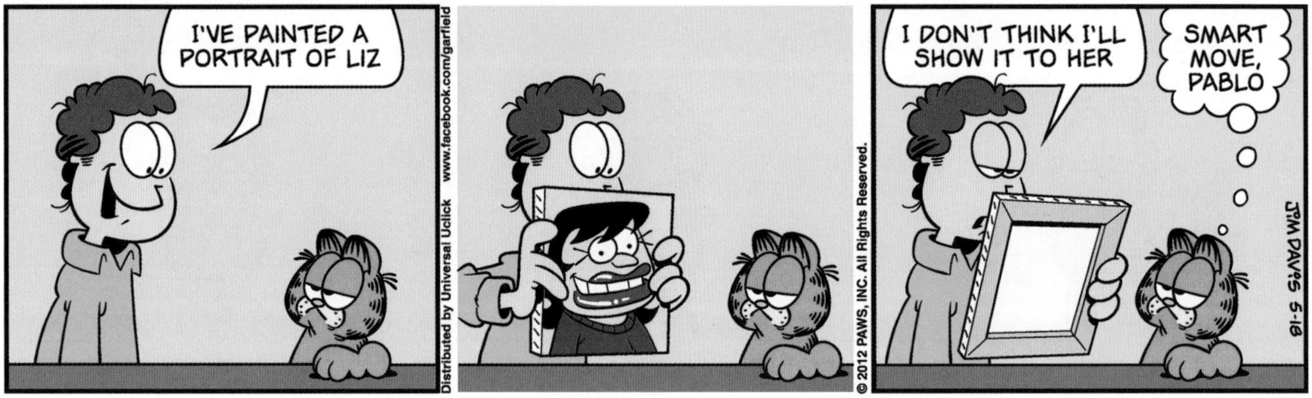
I'VE PAINTED A PORTRAIT OF LIZ
I DON'T THINK I'LL SHOW IT TO HER
SMART MOVE, PABLO
JIM DAVIS 5-18
Distributed by Universal Uclick www.facebook.com/garfield
© 2012 PAWS, INC. All Rights Reserved.

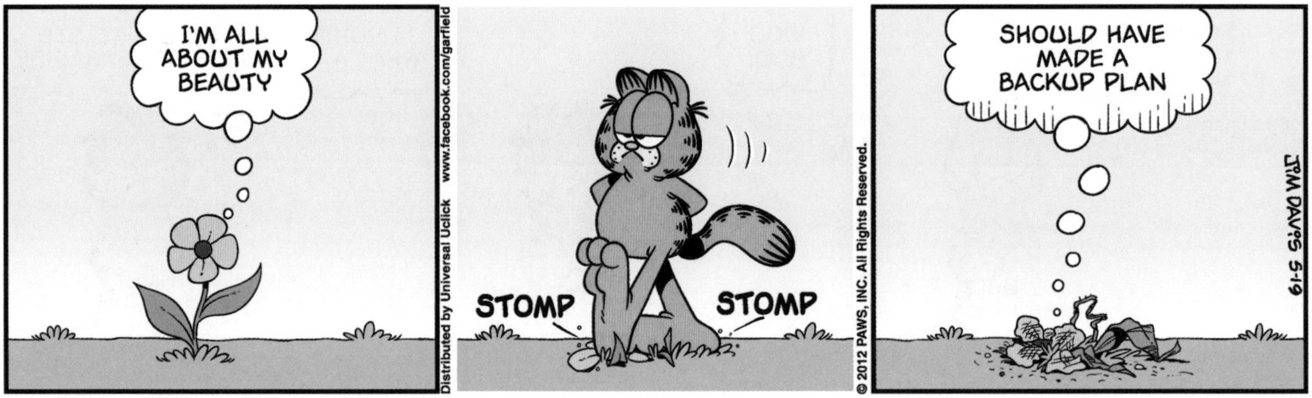
I'M ALL ABOUT MY BEAUTY
STOMP
STOMP
SHOULD HAVE MADE A BACKUP PLAN
JIM DAVIS 5-19
Distributed by Universal Uclick www.facebook.com/garfield
© 2012 PAWS, INC. All Rights Reserved.

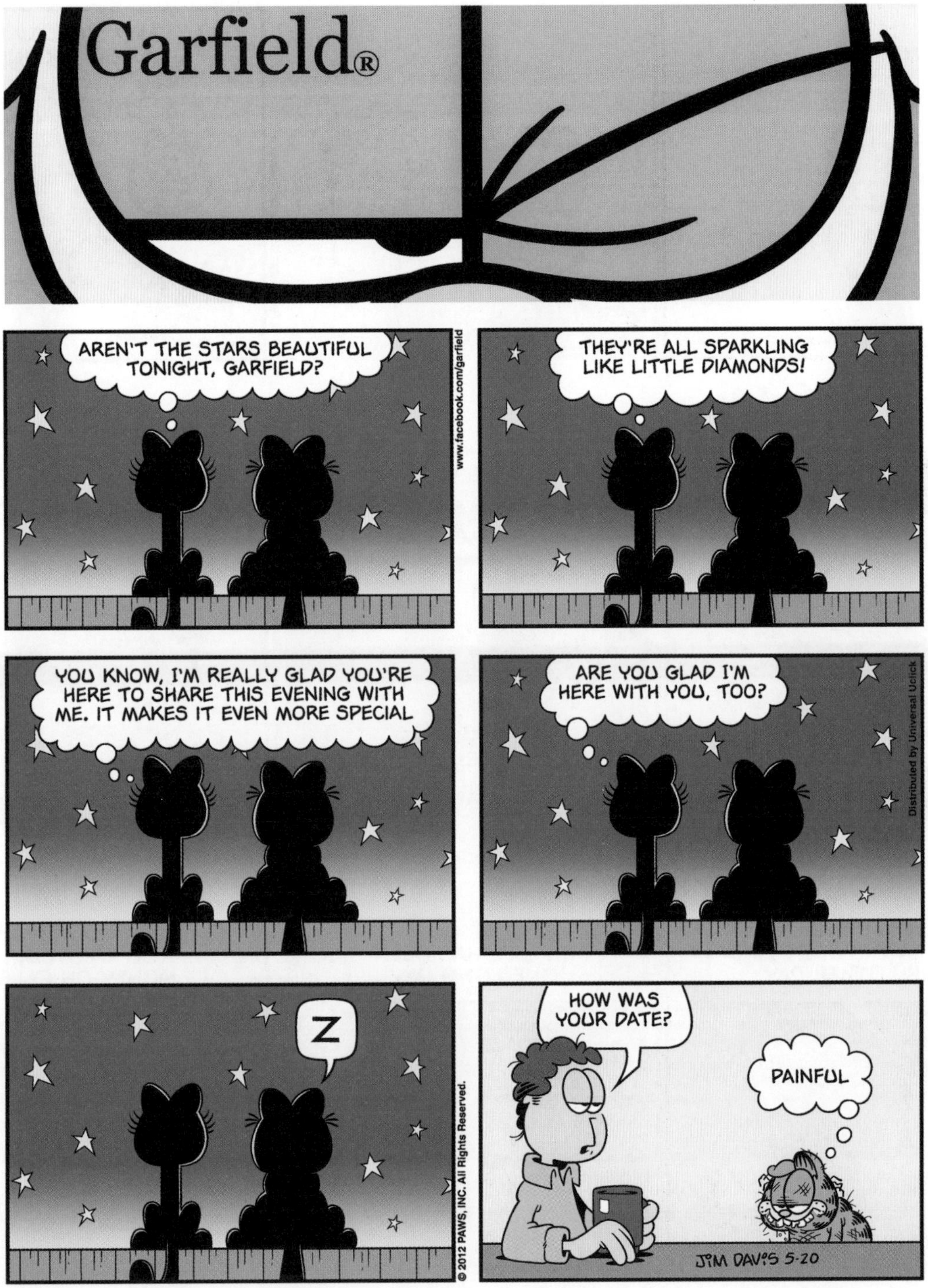
Garfield®
AREN'T THE STARS BEAUTIFUL TONIGHT, GARFIELD?
www.facebook.com/garfield
THEY'RE ALL SPARKLING LIKE LITTLE DIAMONDS!
YOU KNOW, I'M REALLY GLAD YOU'RE HERE TO SHARE THIS EVENING WITH ME. IT MAKES IT EVEN MORE SPECIAL
ARE YOU GLAD I'M HERE WITH YOU, TOO?
Distributed by Universal Uclick
Z
© 2012 PAWS, INC. All Rights Reserved.
HOW WAS YOUR DATE?
PAINFUL
JIM DAVIS 5-20

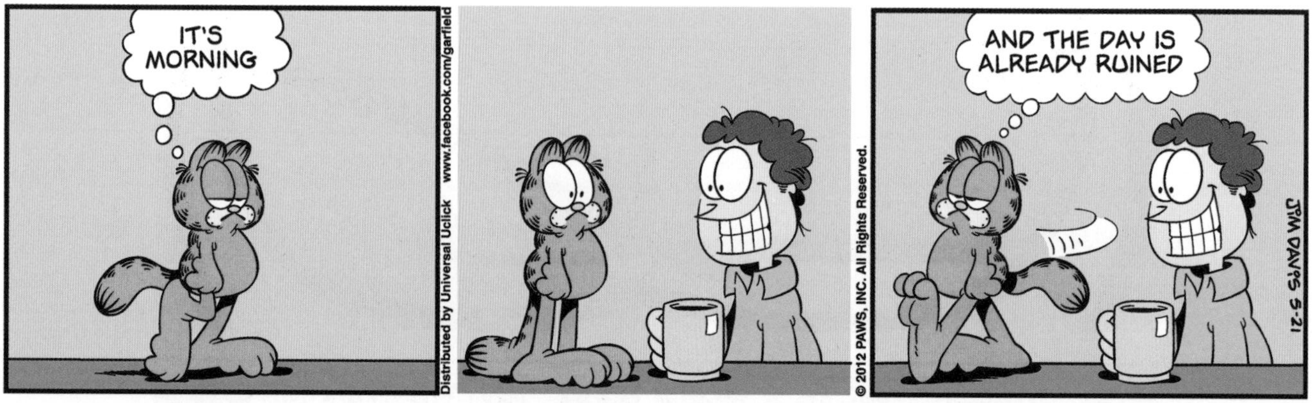
IT'S MORNING
AND THE DAY IS ALREADY RUINED
JIM DAVIS 5-21
Distributed by Universal Uclick www.facebook.com/garfield
© 2012 PAWS, INC. All Rights Reserved.

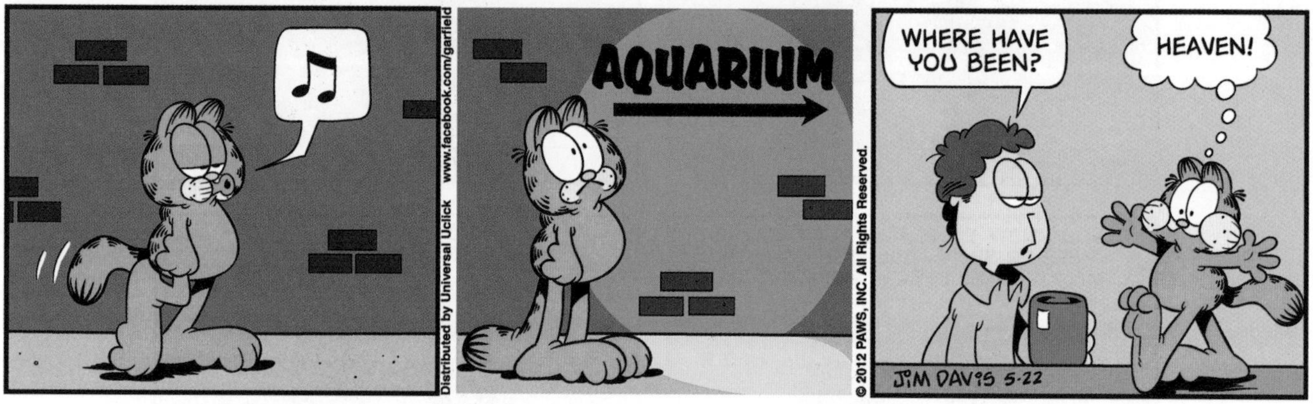
AQUARIUM
WHERE HAVE YOU BEEN?
HEAVEN!
JIM DAVIS 5-22
Distributed by Universal Uclick www.facebook.com/garfield
© 2012 PAWS, INC. All Rights Reserved.

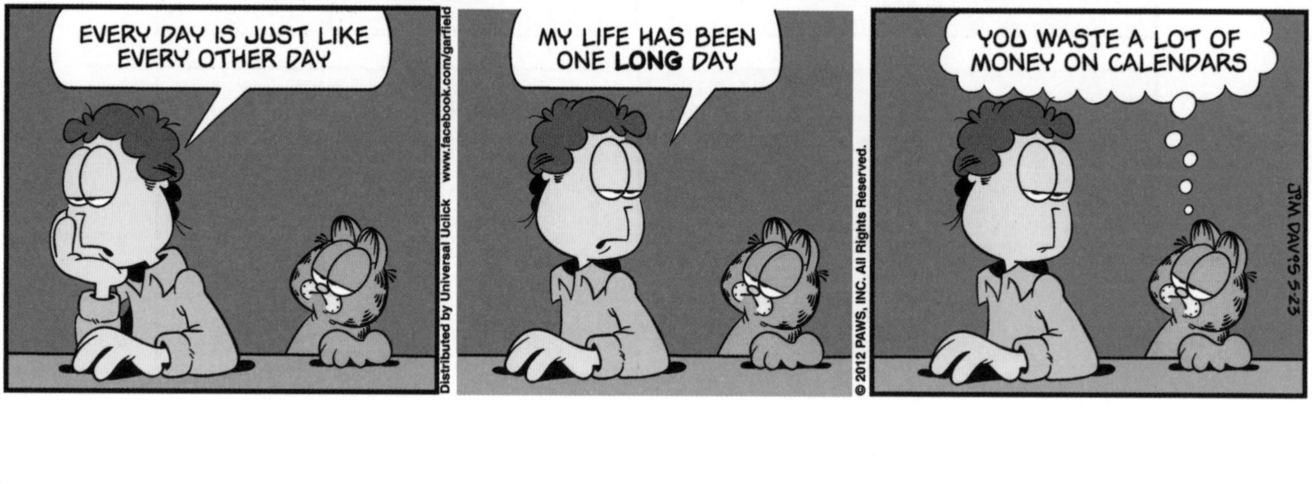
EVERY DAY IS JUST LIKE EVERY OTHER DAY
MY LIFE HAS BEEN ONE **LONG** DAY
YOU WASTE A LOT OF MONEY ON CALENDARS
JIM DAVIS 5-23
Distributed by Universal Uclick www.facebook.com/garfield
© 2012 PAWS, INC. All Rights Reserved.

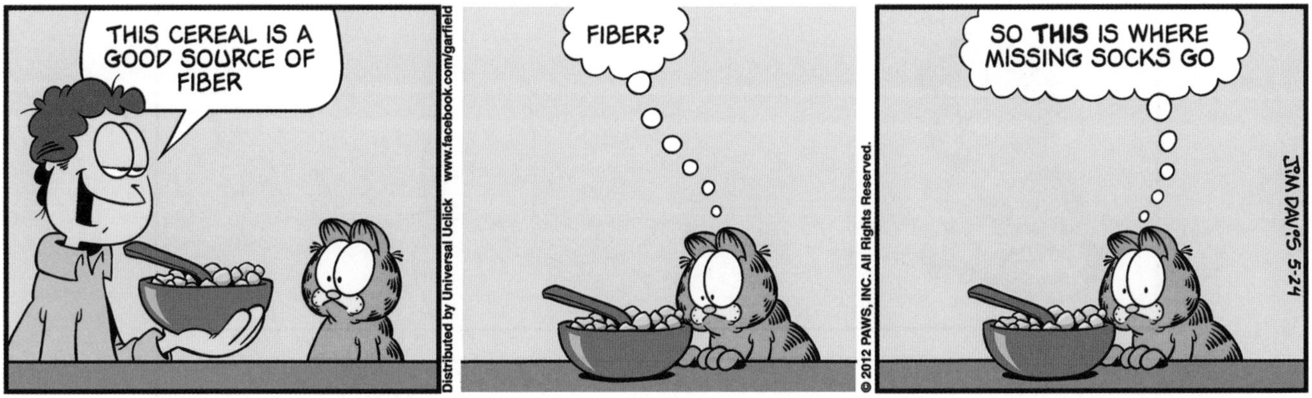
THIS CEREAL IS A GOOD SOURCE OF FIBER
FIBER?
SO THIS IS WHERE MISSING SOCKS GO
JIM DAVIS 5-24
Distributed by Universal Uclick www.facebook.com/garfield
© 2012 PAWS, INC. All Rights Reserved.

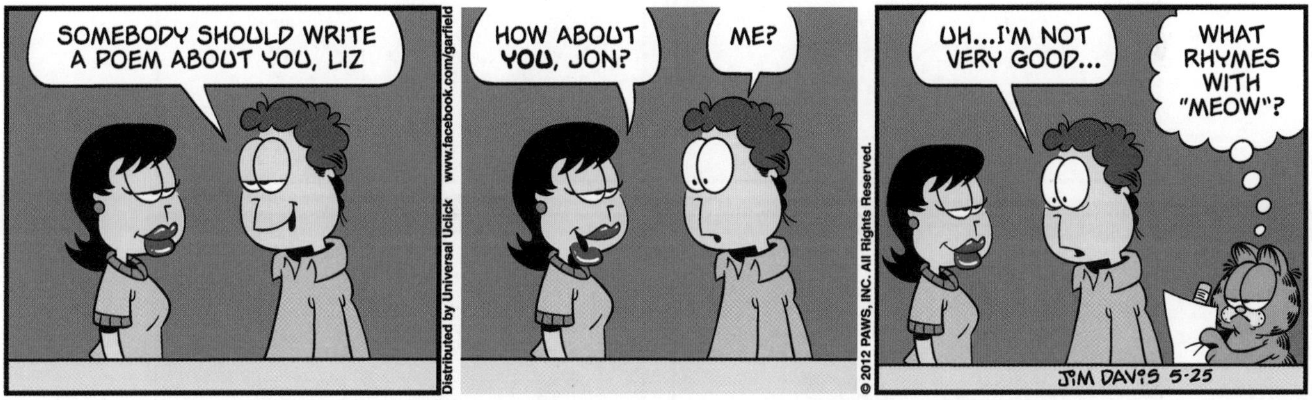
SOMEBODY SHOULD WRITE A POEM ABOUT YOU, LIZ
HOW ABOUT YOU, JON?
ME?
UH...I'M NOT VERY GOOD...
WHAT RHYMES WITH "MEOW"?
JIM DAVIS 5-25
Distributed by Universal Uclick www.facebook.com/garfield
© 2012 PAWS, INC. All Rights Reserved.

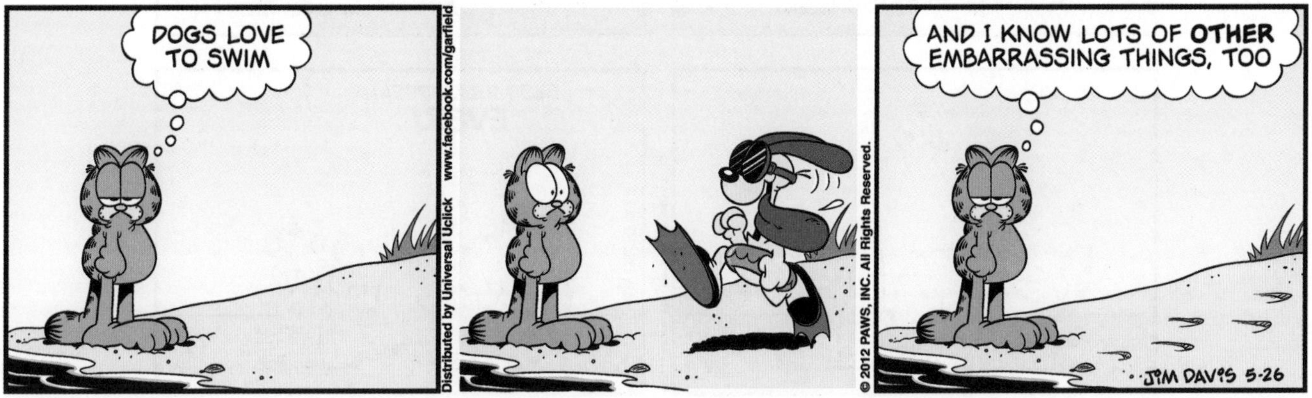
DOGS LOVE TO SWIM
AND I KNOW LOTS OF OTHER EMBARRASSING THINGS, TOO
JIM DAVIS 5-26
Distributed by Universal Uclick www.facebook.com/garfield
© 2012 PAWS, INC. All Rights Reserved.

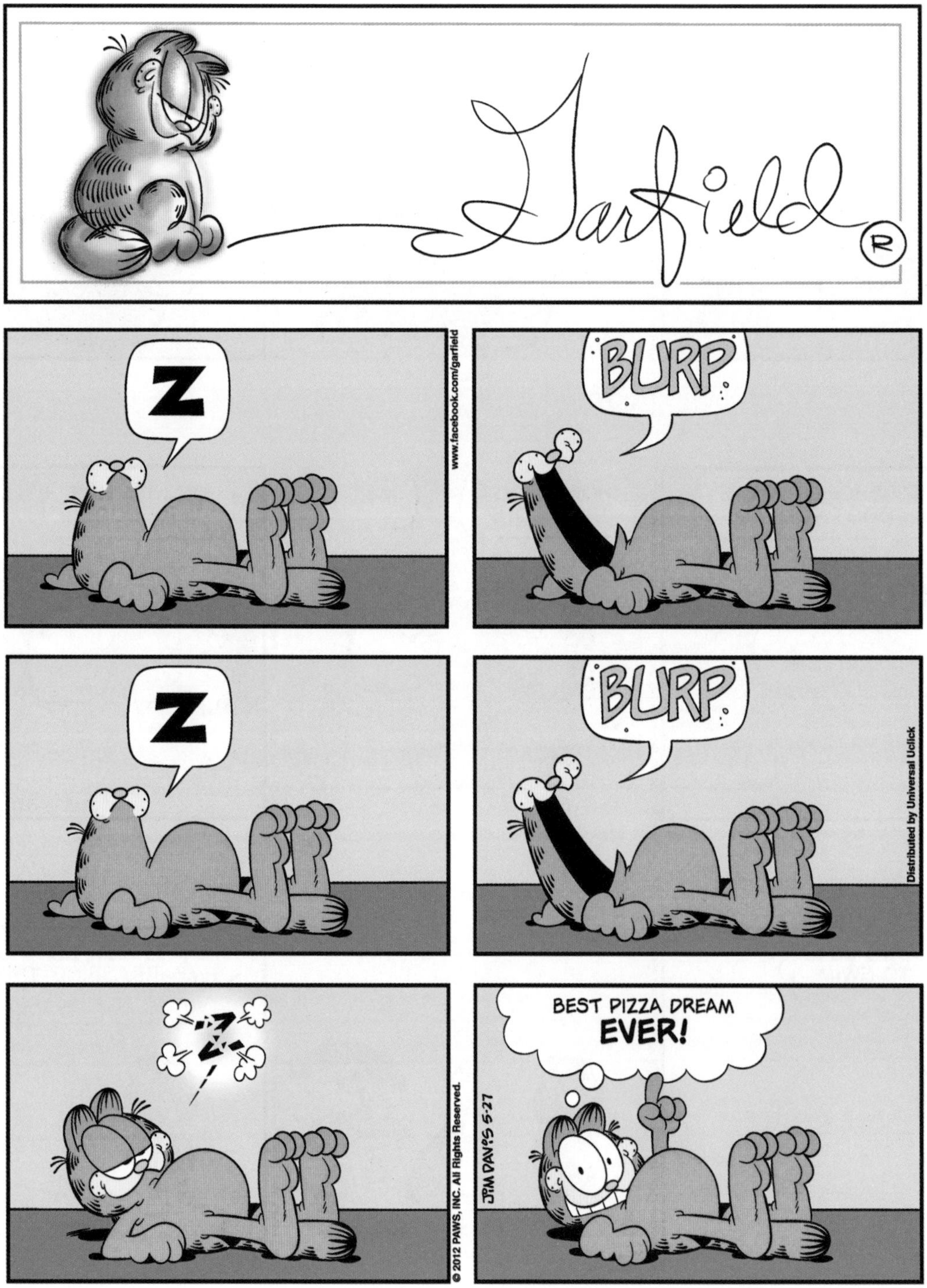
Garfield ®
Z
BURP
Z
BURP
BEST PIZZA DREAM
EVER!
www.facebook.com/garfield
Distributed by Universal Uclick
© 2012 PAWS, INC. All Rights Reserved.
JPM DAVPS 5-27

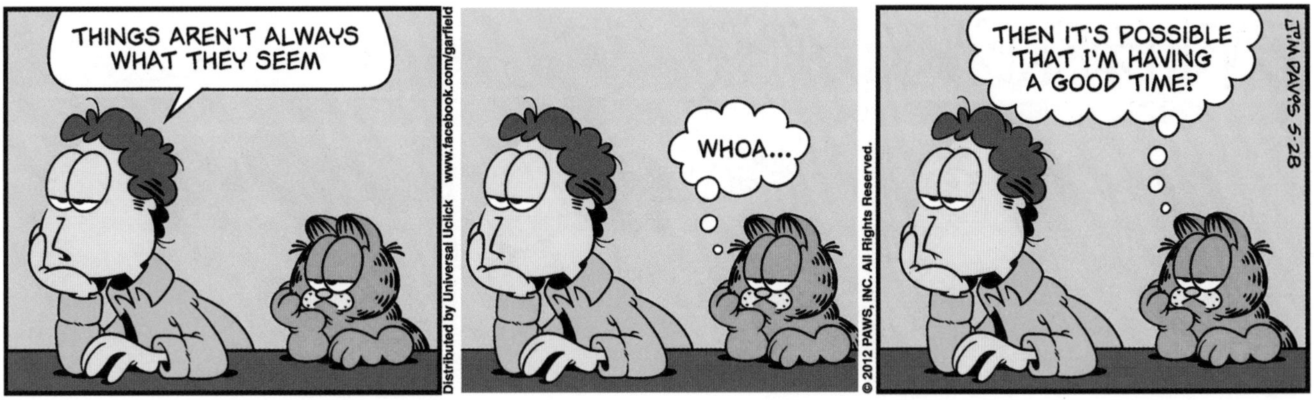
THINGS AREN'T ALWAYS WHAT THEY SEEM
WHOA...
THEN IT'S POSSIBLE THAT I'M HAVING A GOOD TIME?
JIM DAVIS 5-28
Distributed by Universal Uclick www.facebook.com/garfield
© 2012 PAWS, INC. All Rights Reserved.

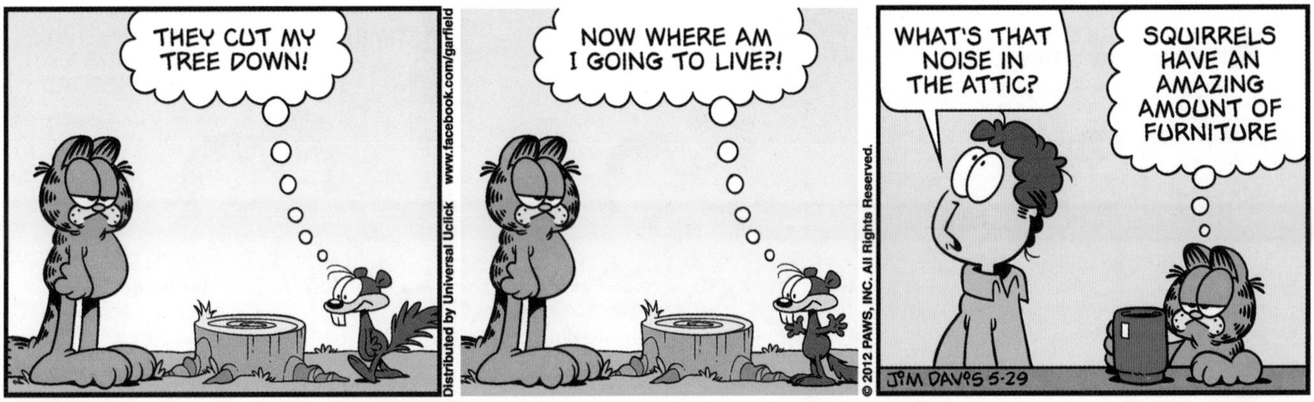
THEY CUT MY TREE DOWN!
NOW WHERE AM I GOING TO LIVE?!
WHAT'S THAT NOISE IN THE ATTIC?
SQUIRRELS HAVE AN AMAZING AMOUNT OF FURNITURE
JIM DAVIS 5-29
Distributed by Universal Uclick www.facebook.com/garfield
© 2012 PAWS, INC. All Rights Reserved.

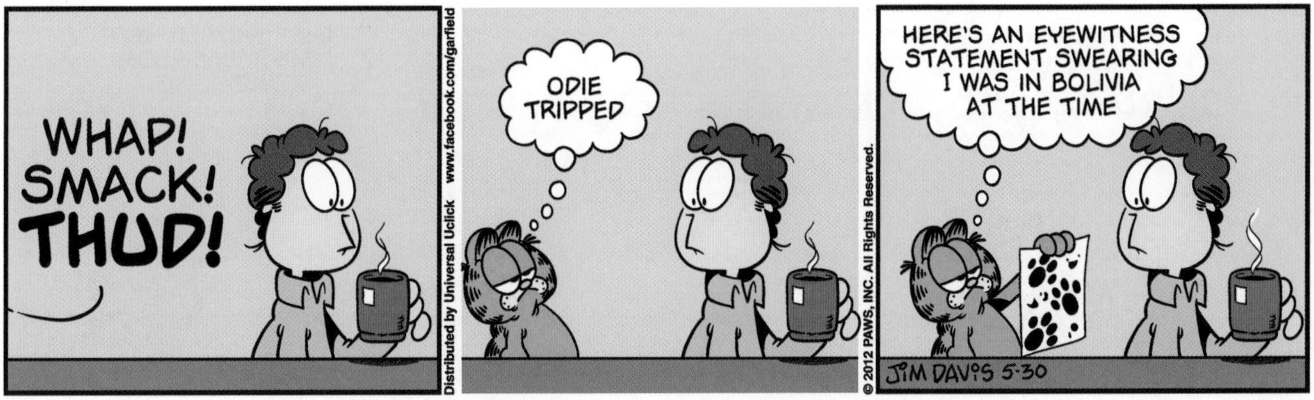
WHAP! SMACK! THUD!
ODIE TRIPPED
HERE'S AN EYEWITNESS STATEMENT SWEARING I WAS IN BOLIVIA AT THE TIME
JIM DAVIS 5-30
Distributed by Universal Uclick www.facebook.com/garfield
© 2012 PAWS, INC. All Rights Reserved.

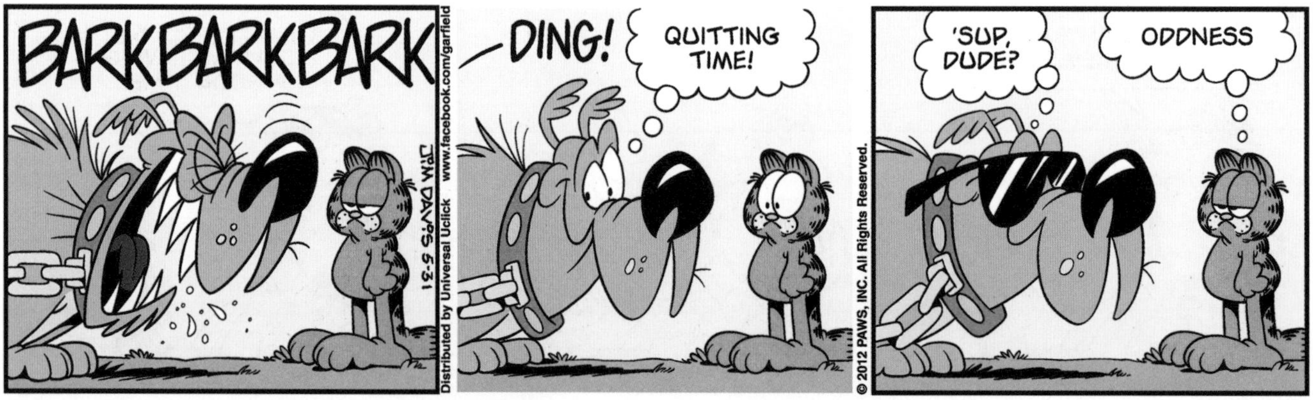
BARKBARKBARK
JIM DAVIS 5-31
Distributed by Universal Uclick www.facebook.com/garfield
—DING!
QUITTING TIME!
© 2012 PAWS, INC. All Rights Reserved.
'SUP, DUDE?
ODDNESS

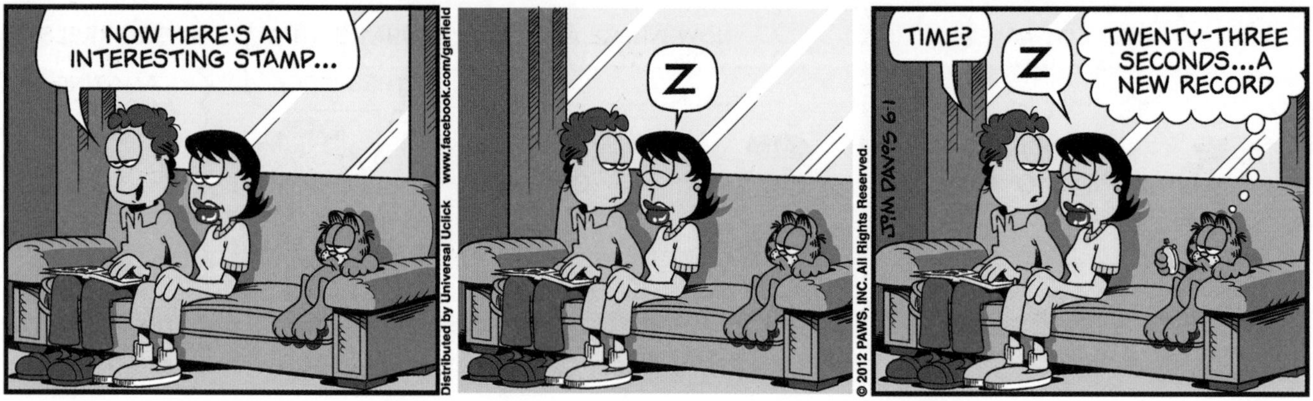
NOW HERE'S AN INTERESTING STAMP...
Distributed by Universal Uclick www.facebook.com/garfield
Z
© 2012 PAWS, INC. All Rights Reserved.
JIM DAVIS 6-1
TIME?
Z
TWENTY-THREE SECONDS...A NEW RECORD

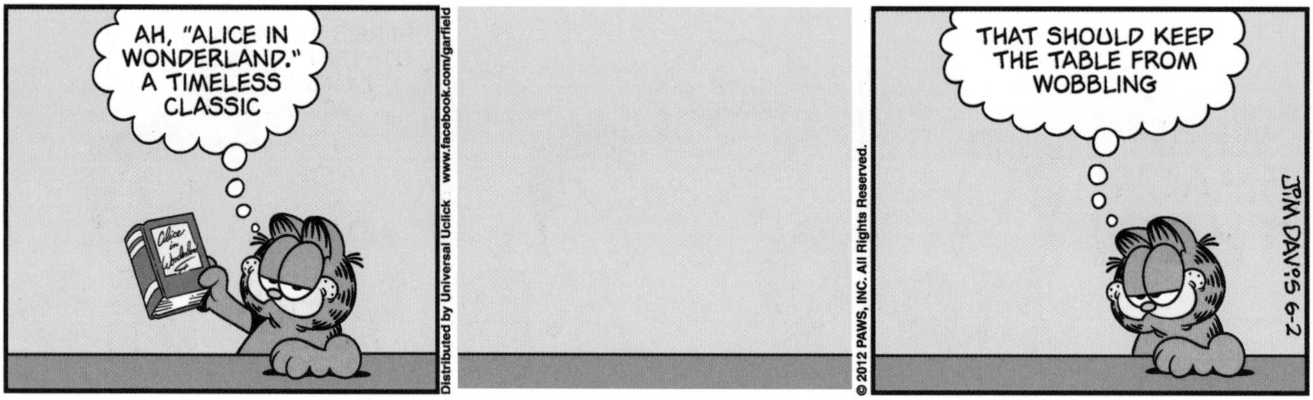
AH, "ALICE IN WONDERLAND." A TIMELESS CLASSIC
Distributed by Universal Uclick www.facebook.com/garfield
© 2012 PAWS, INC. All Rights Reserved.
THAT SHOULD KEEP THE TABLE FROM WOBBLING
JIM DAVIS 6-2

GARFIELD®

STOP IT, ODIE!
www.facebook.com/garfield
MAN, THAT CREEPS ME OUT
Distributed by Universal Uclick
SNICK!
JIM DAVIS 6-3
I HATE HIS "LIZARD" DAYS
© 2012 PAWS, INC. All Rights Reserved.

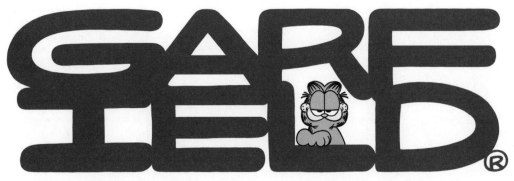

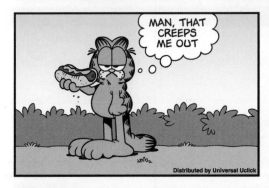

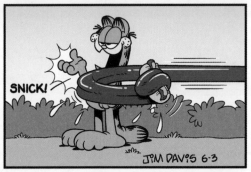

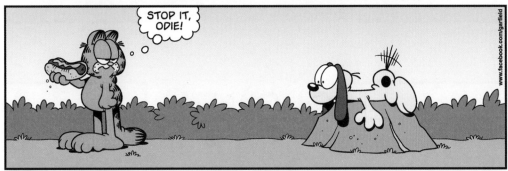

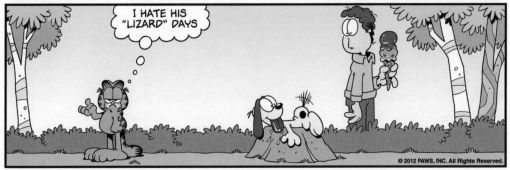

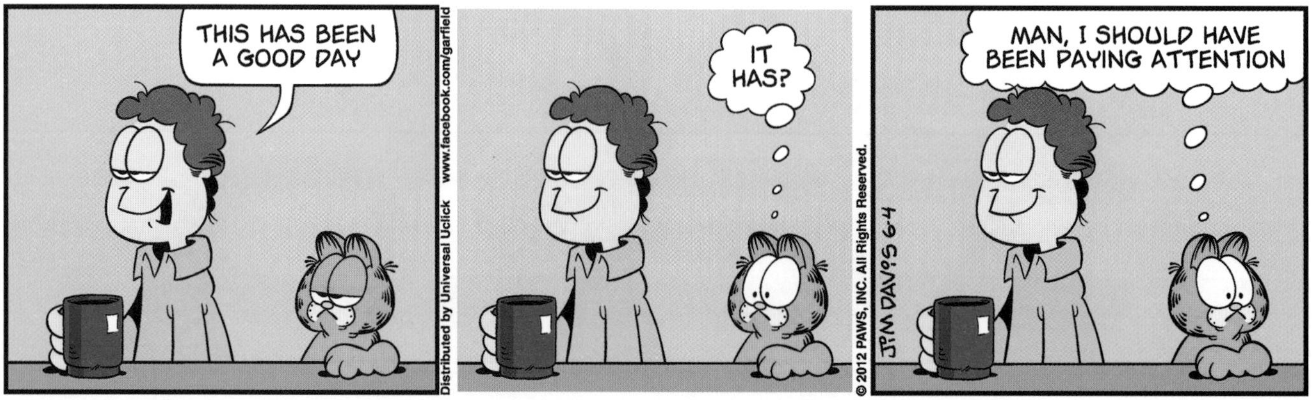
THIS HAS BEEN A GOOD DAY
IT HAS?
MAN, I SHOULD HAVE BEEN PAYING ATTENTION
Distributed by Universal Uclick www.facebook.com/garfield
© 2012 PAWS, INC. All Rights Reserved.

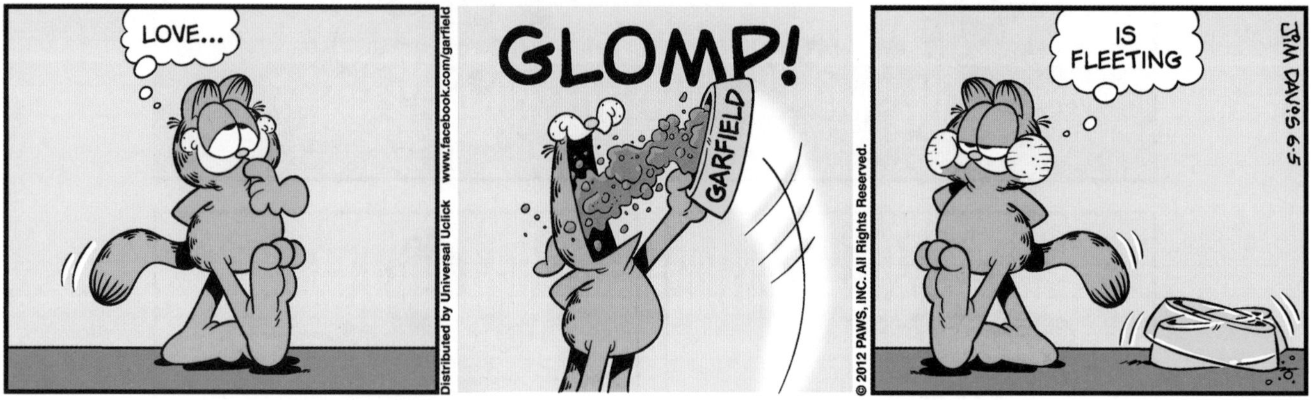
LOVE...
GLOMP!
GARFIELD
IS FLEETING
Distributed by Universal Uclick www.facebook.com/garfield
© 2012 PAWS, INC. All Rights Reserved.

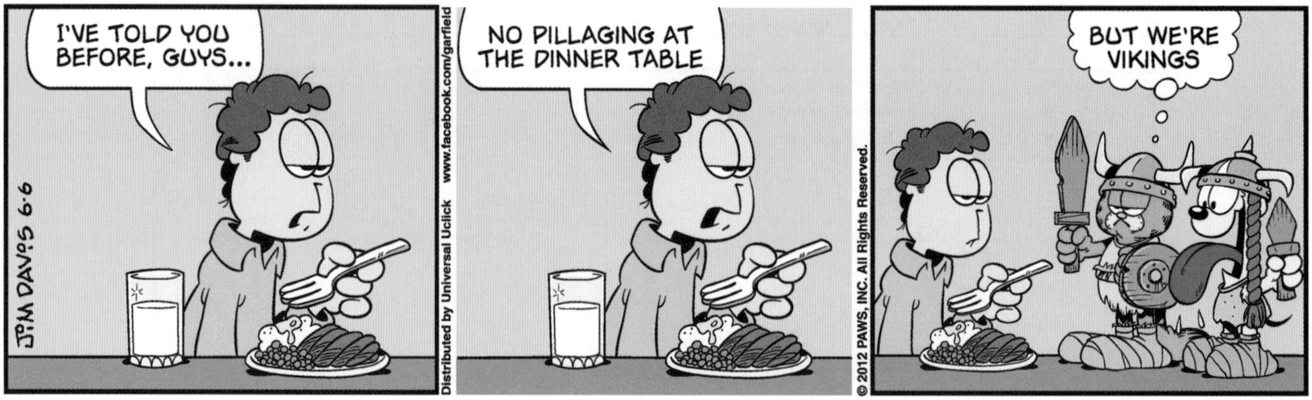
I'VE TOLD YOU BEFORE, GUYS...
NO PILLAGING AT THE DINNER TABLE
BUT WE'RE VIKINGS
Distributed by Universal Uclick www.facebook.com/garfield
© 2012 PAWS, INC. All Rights Reserved.

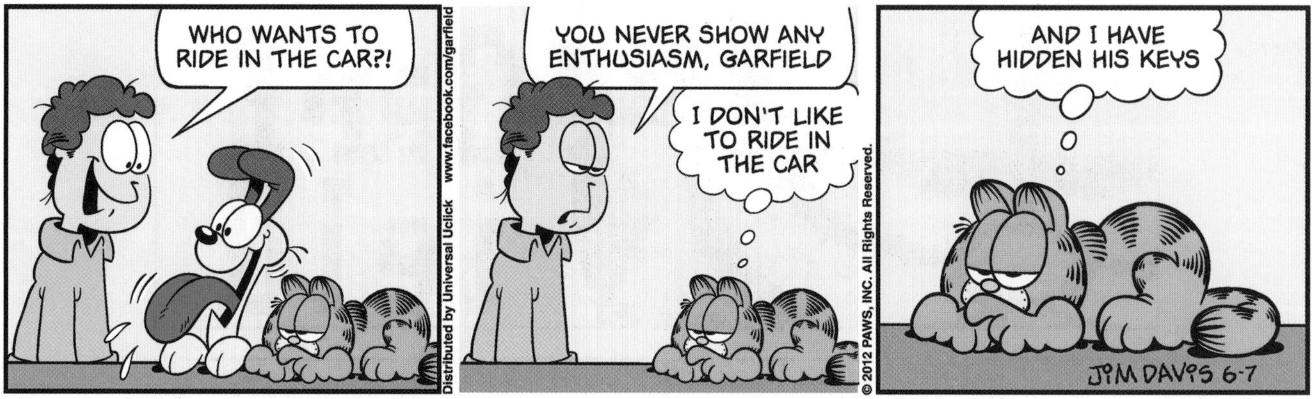
WHO WANTS TO RIDE IN THE CAR?!
Distributed by Universal Uclick www.facebook.com/garfield
YOU NEVER SHOW ANY ENTHUSIASM, GARFIELD
I DON'T LIKE TO RIDE IN THE CAR
© 2012 PAWS, INC. All Rights Reserved.
AND I HAVE HIDDEN HIS KEYS
JIM DAVIS 6-7

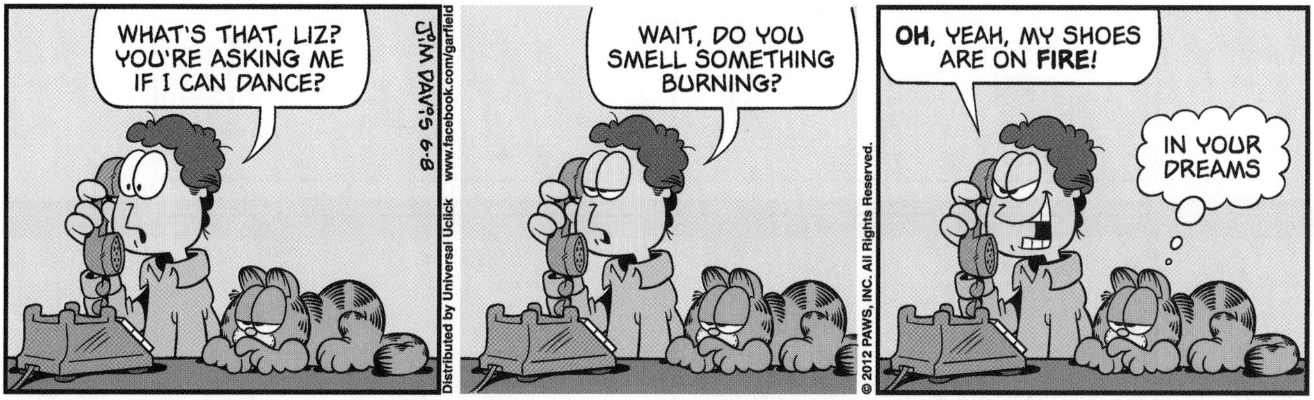
WHAT'S THAT, LIZ? YOU'RE ASKING ME IF I CAN DANCE?
JIM DAVIS 6-8
Distributed by Universal Uclick www.facebook.com/garfield
WAIT, DO YOU SMELL SOMETHING BURNING?
© 2012 PAWS, INC. All Rights Reserved.
OH, YEAH, MY SHOES ARE ON FIRE!
IN YOUR DREAMS

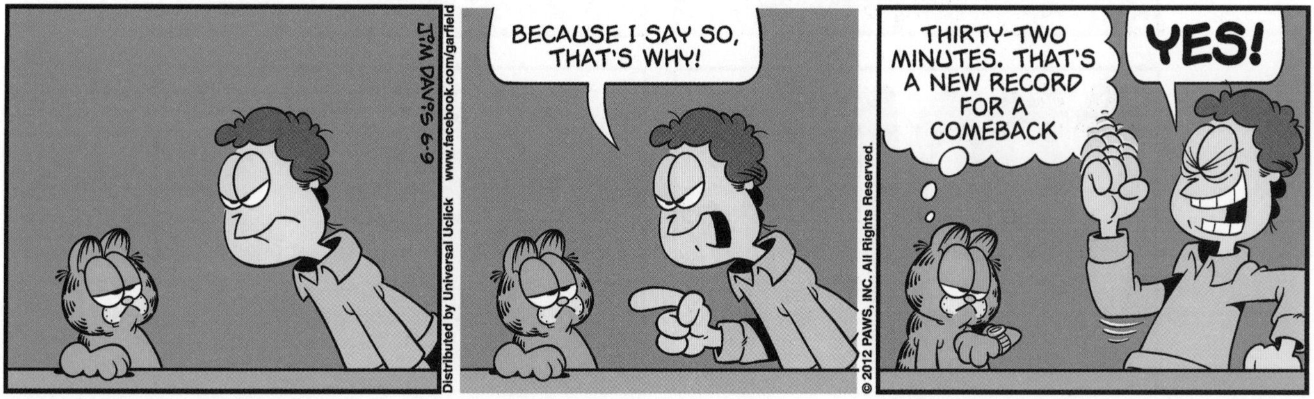
JIM DAVIS 6-9
Distributed by Universal Uclick www.facebook.com/garfield
BECAUSE I SAY SO, THAT'S WHY!
© 2012 PAWS, INC. All Rights Reserved.
THIRTY-TWO MINUTES. THAT'S A NEW RECORD FOR A COMEBACK
YES!

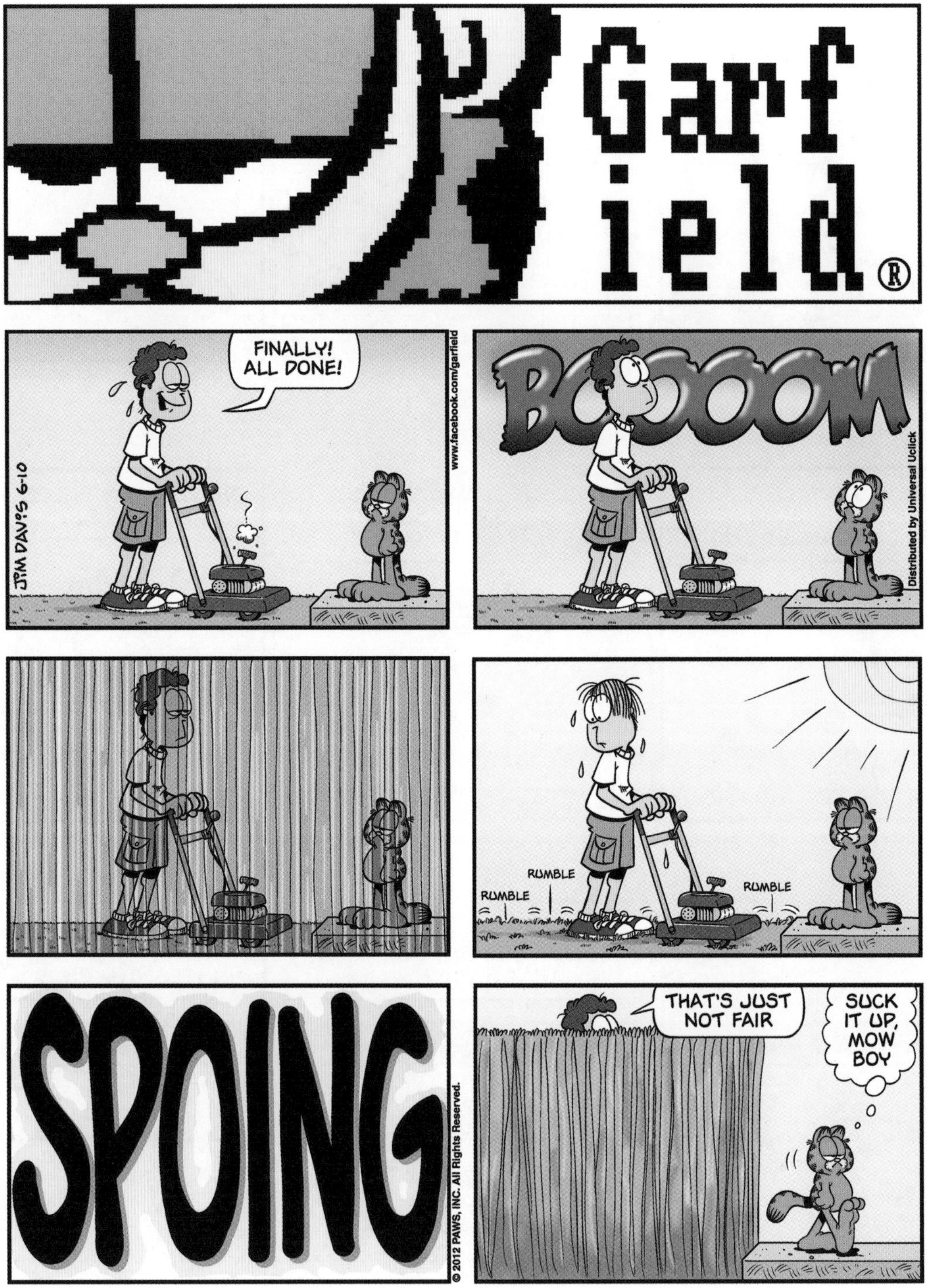
Garfield®
FINALLY! ALL DONE!
JIM DAVIS 6-10
www.facebook.com/garfield
BOOOOOM
Distributed by Universal Uclick
RUMBLE
RUMBLE
RUMBLE
SPOING
© 2012 PAWS, INC. All Rights Reserved.
THAT'S JUST NOT FAIR
SUCK IT UP, MOW BOY

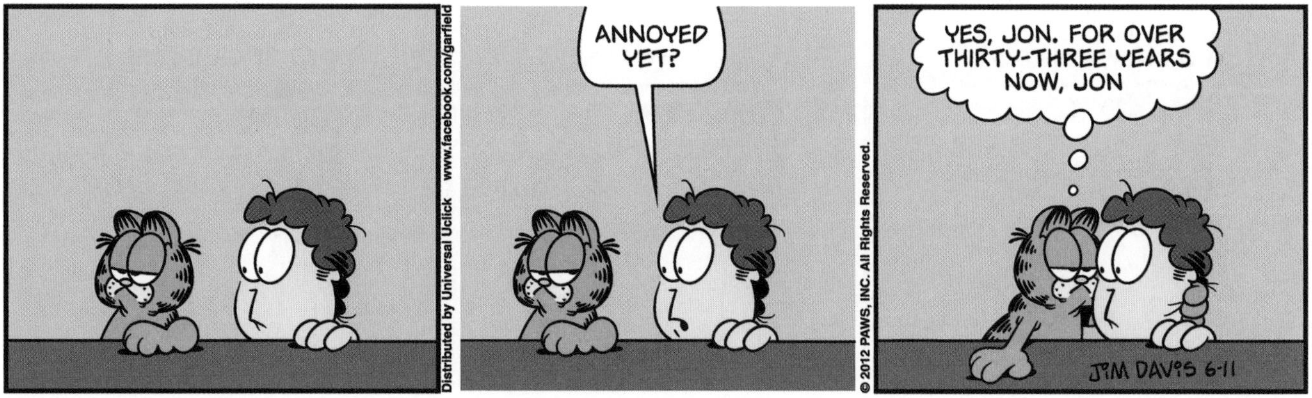
Distributed by Universal Uclick www.facebook.com/garfield
ANNOYED YET?
© 2012 PAWS, INC. All Rights Reserved.
YES, JON. FOR OVER THIRTY-THREE YEARS NOW, JON
JIM DAVIS 6-11

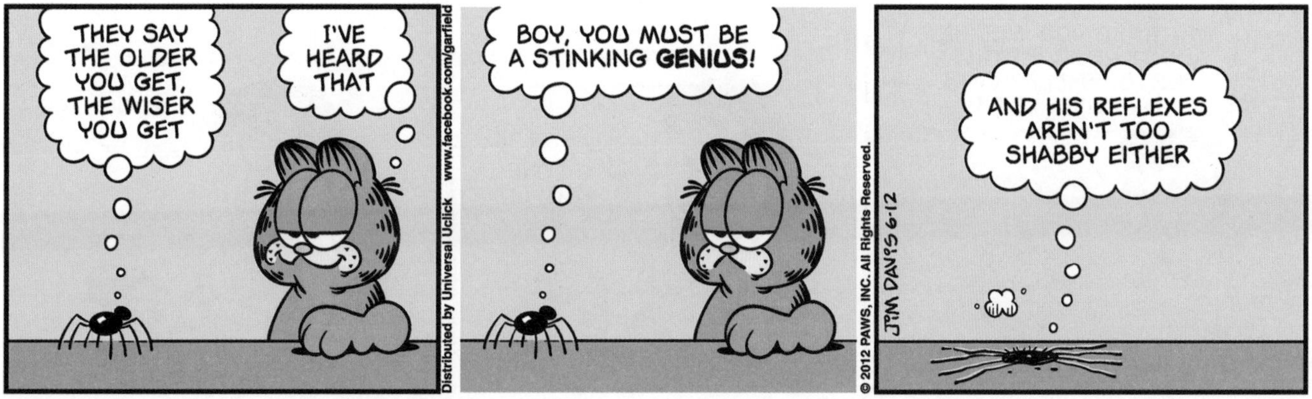
THEY SAY THE OLDER YOU GET, THE WISER YOU GET
I'VE HEARD THAT
Distributed by Universal Uclick www.facebook.com/garfield
BOY, YOU MUST BE A STINKING **GENIUS**!
© 2012 PAWS, INC. All Rights Reserved.
JIM DAVIS 6-12
AND HIS REFLEXES AREN'T TOO SHABBY EITHER

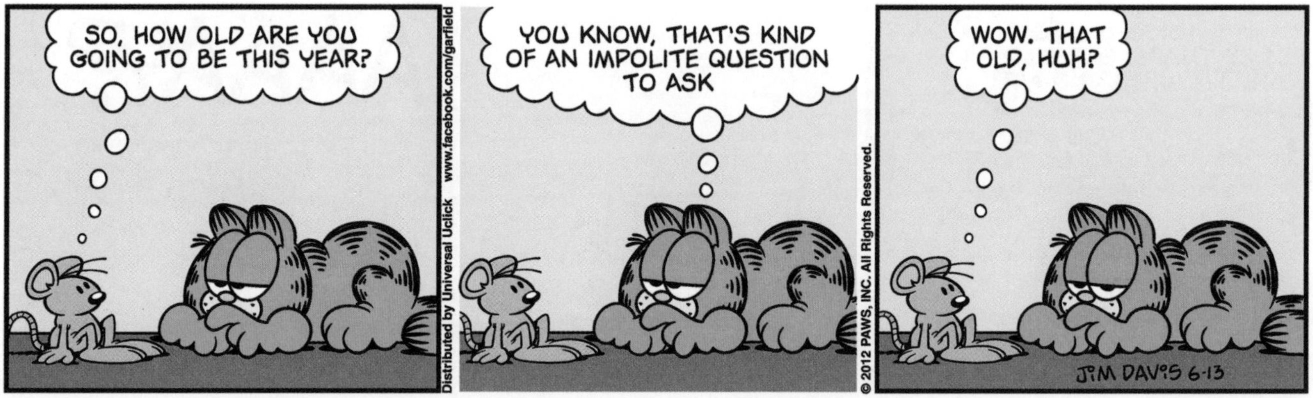
SO, HOW OLD ARE YOU GOING TO BE THIS YEAR?
Distributed by Universal Uclick www.facebook.com/garfield
YOU KNOW, THAT'S KIND OF AN IMPOLITE QUESTION TO ASK
© 2012 PAWS, INC. All Rights Reserved.
WOW. THAT OLD, HUH?
JIM DAVIS 6-13

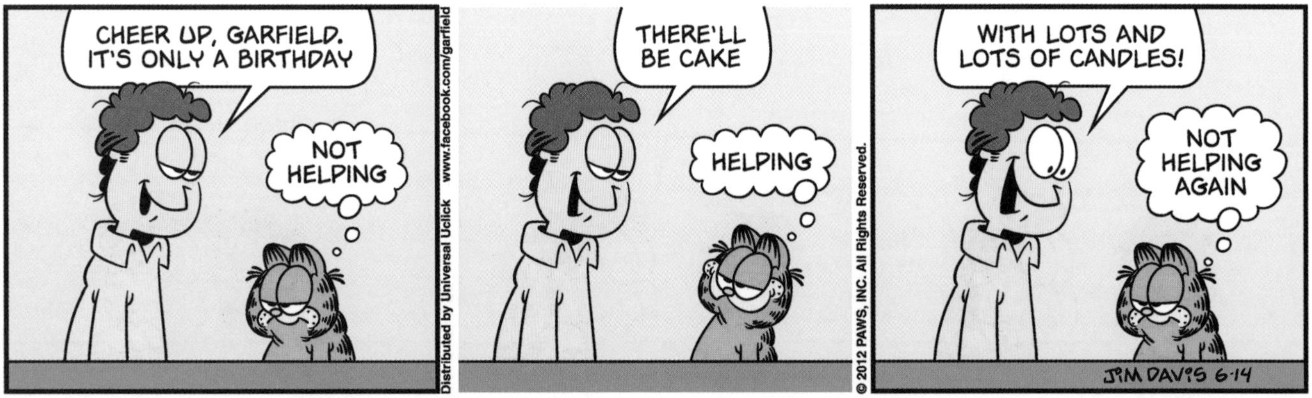
CHEER UP, GARFIELD. IT'S ONLY A BIRTHDAY
NOT HELPING
THERE'LL BE CAKE
HELPING
WITH LOTS AND LOTS OF CANDLES!
NOT HELPING AGAIN
JIM DAVIS 6-14
Distributed by Universal Uclick www.facebook.com/garfield
© 2012 PAWS, INC. All Rights Reserved.

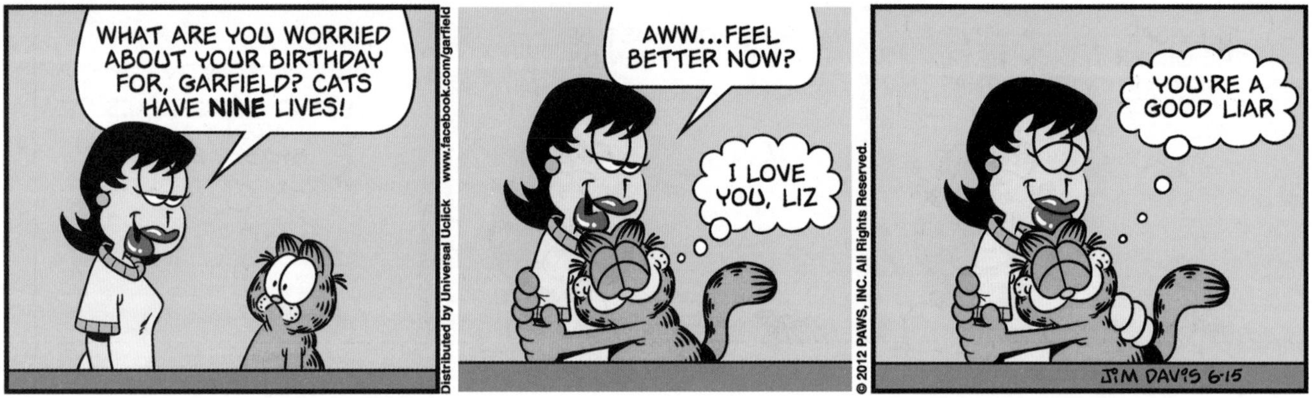
WHAT ARE YOU WORRIED ABOUT YOUR BIRTHDAY FOR, GARFIELD? CATS HAVE NINE LIVES!
AWW...FEEL BETTER NOW?
I LOVE YOU, LIZ
YOU'RE A GOOD LIAR
JIM DAVIS 6-15
Distributed by Universal Uclick www.facebook.com/garfield
© 2012 PAWS, INC. All Rights Reserved.

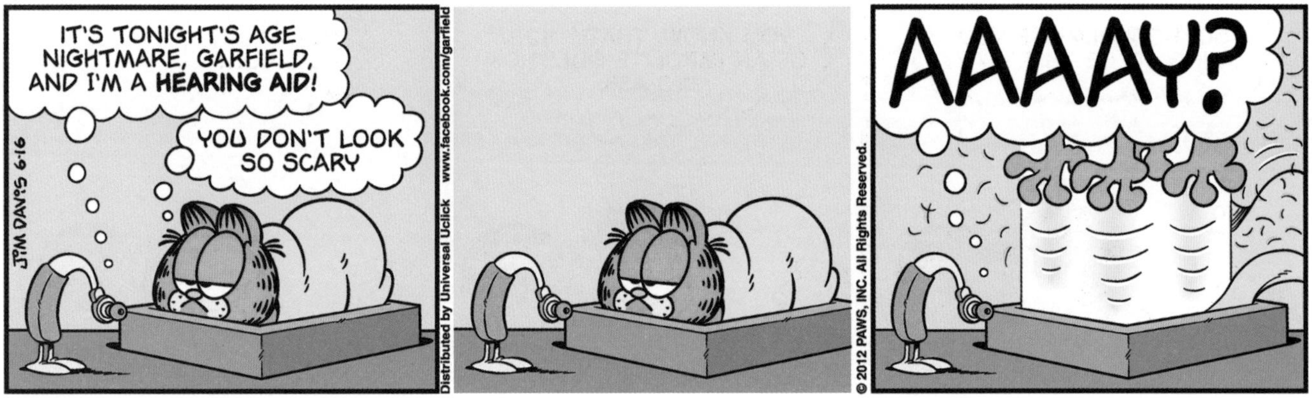
IT'S TONIGHT'S AGE NIGHTMARE, GARFIELD, AND I'M A HEARING AID!
YOU DON'T LOOK SO SCARY
AAAAY?
JIM DAVIS 6-16
Distributed by Universal Uclick www.facebook.com/garfield
© 2012 PAWS, INC. All Rights Reserved.

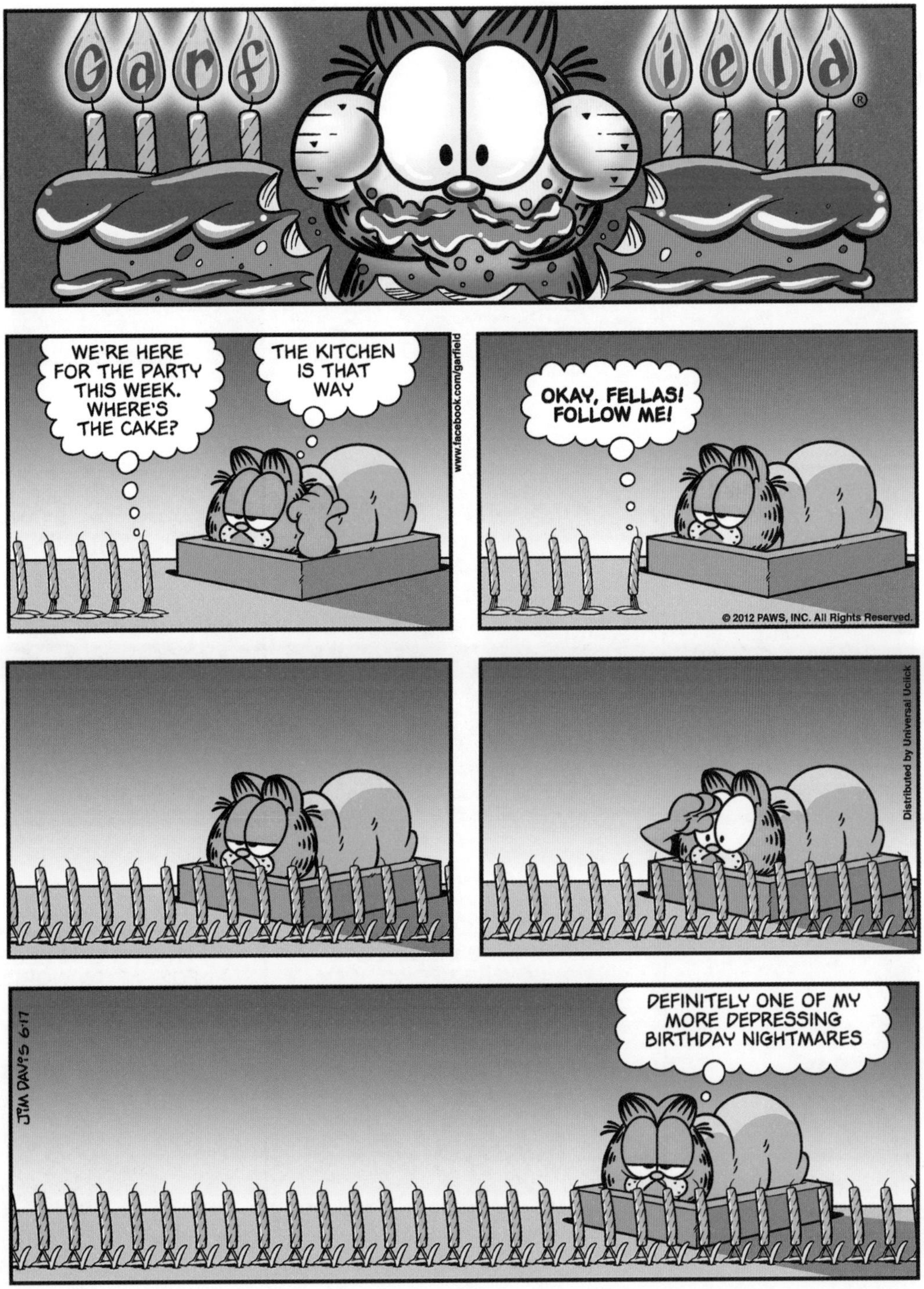
Garfield®
WE'RE HERE FOR THE PARTY THIS WEEK. WHERE'S THE CAKE?
THE KITCHEN IS THAT WAY
www.facebook.com/garfield
OKAY, FELLAS! FOLLOW ME!
© 2012 PAWS, INC. All Rights Reserved.
Distributed by Universal Uclick
JIM DAVIS 6·17
DEFINITELY ONE OF MY MORE DEPRESSING BIRTHDAY NIGHTMARES

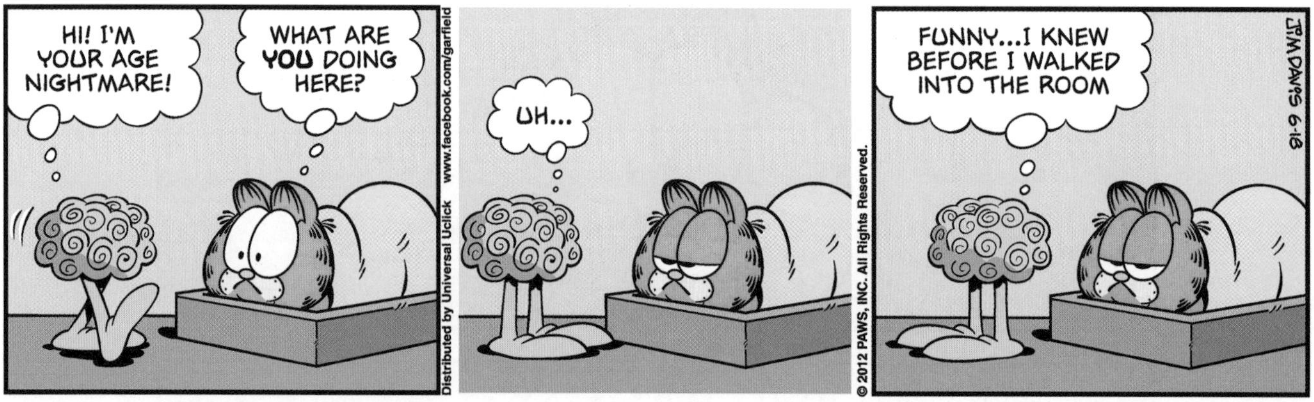
HI! I'M YOUR AGE NIGHTMARE!
WHAT ARE YOU DOING HERE?
Distributed by Universal Uclick www.facebook.com/garfield
UH...
© 2012 PAWS, INC. All Rights Reserved.
FUNNY...I KNEW BEFORE I WALKED INTO THE ROOM
JIM DAVIS 6-18

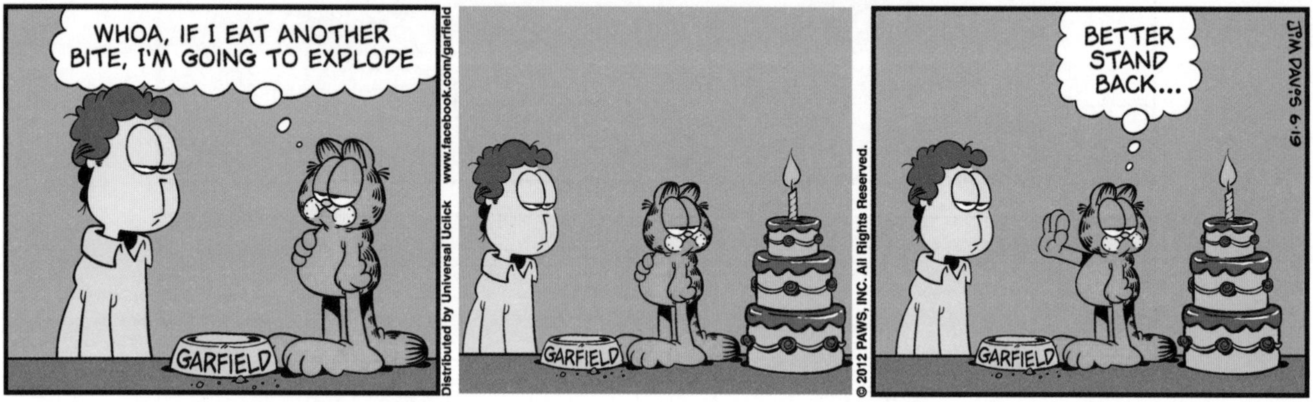
WHOA, IF I EAT ANOTHER BITE, I'M GOING TO EXPLODE
GARFIELD
Distributed by Universal Uclick www.facebook.com/garfield
GARFIELD
© 2012 PAWS, INC. All Rights Reserved.
BETTER STAND BACK...
GARFIELD
JIM DAVIS 6-19

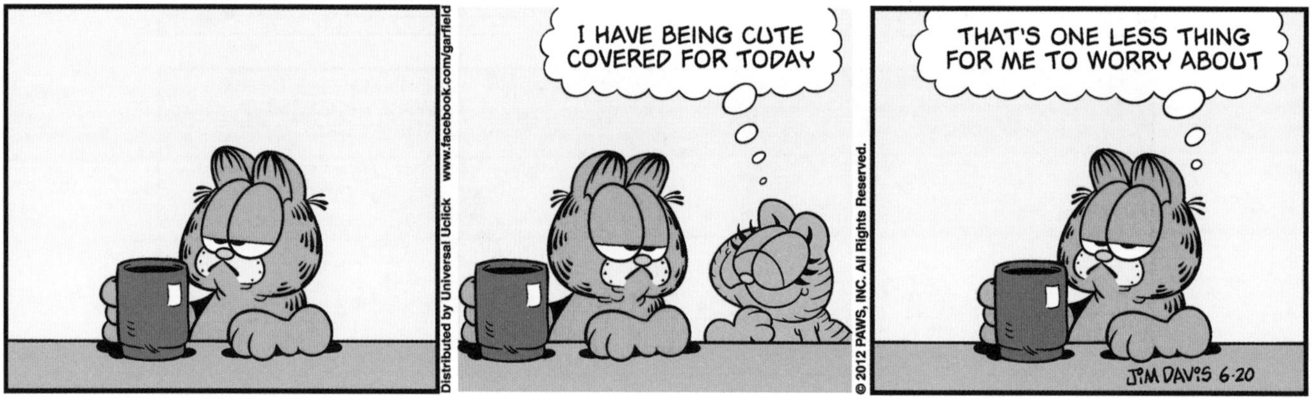
Distributed by Universal Uclick www.facebook.com/garfield
I HAVE BEING CUTE COVERED FOR TODAY
© 2012 PAWS, INC. All Rights Reserved.
THAT'S ONE LESS THING FOR ME TO WORRY ABOUT
JIM DAVIS 6-20

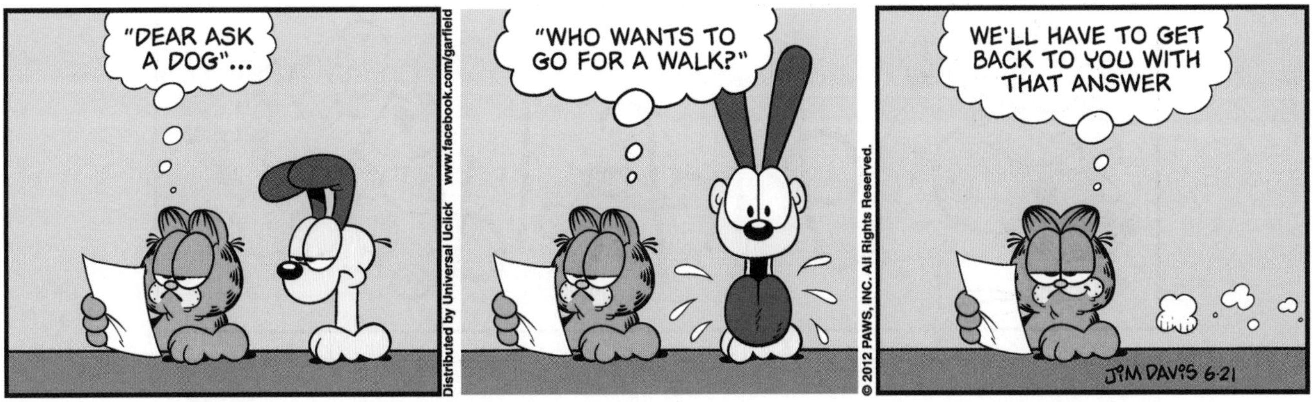
"DEAR ASK A DOG"...
Distributed by Universal Uclick www.facebook.com/garfield
"WHO WANTS TO GO FOR A WALK?"
© 2012 PAWS, INC. All Rights Reserved.
WE'LL HAVE TO GET BACK TO YOU WITH THAT ANSWER
JIM DAVIS 6-21

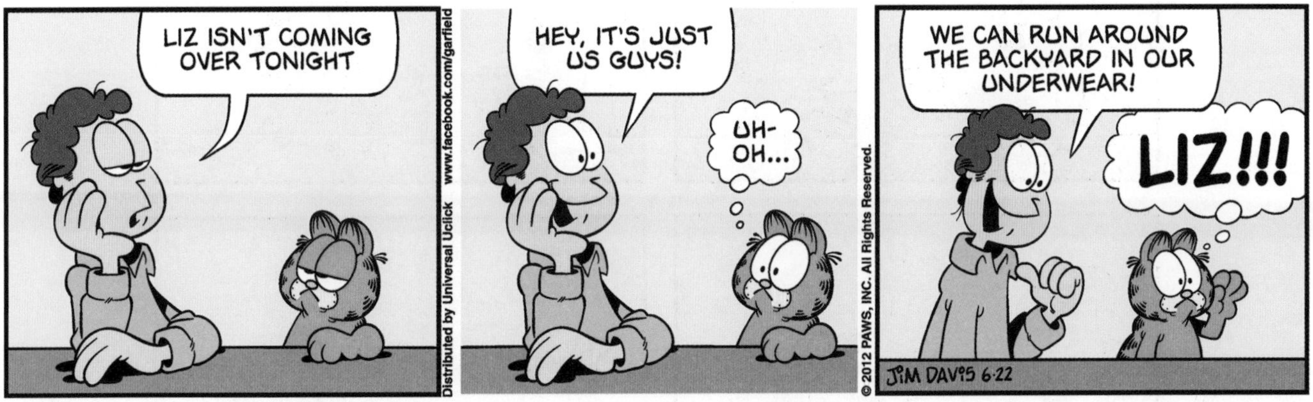
LIZ ISN'T COMING OVER TONIGHT
Distributed by Universal Uclick www.facebook.com/garfield
HEY, IT'S JUST US GUYS!
UH-OH...
© 2012 PAWS, INC. All Rights Reserved.
WE CAN RUN AROUND THE BACKYARD IN OUR UNDERWEAR!
LIZ!!!
JIM DAVIS 6-22

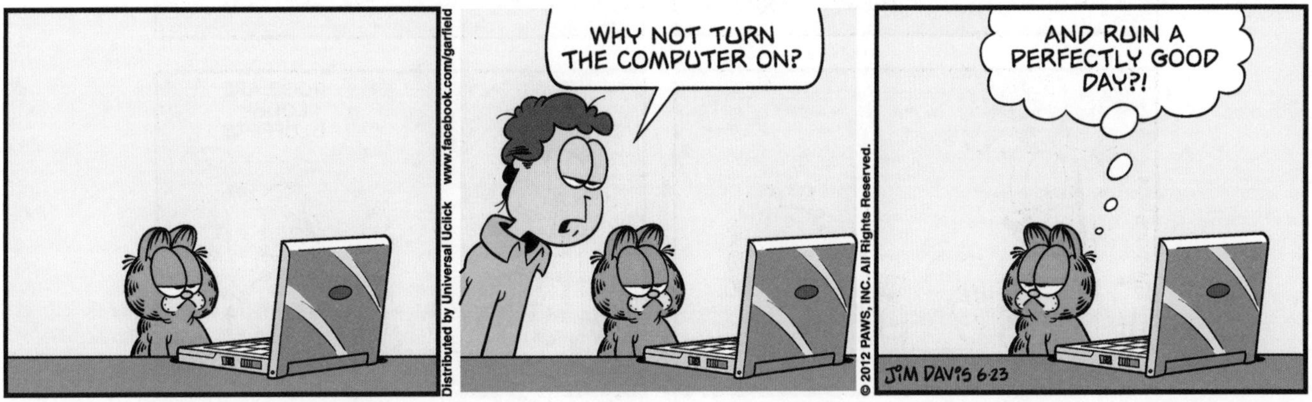
Distributed by Universal Uclick www.facebook.com/garfield
WHY NOT TURN THE COMPUTER ON?
© 2012 PAWS, INC. All Rights Reserved.
AND RUIN A PERFECTLY GOOD DAY?!
JIM DAVIS 6-23

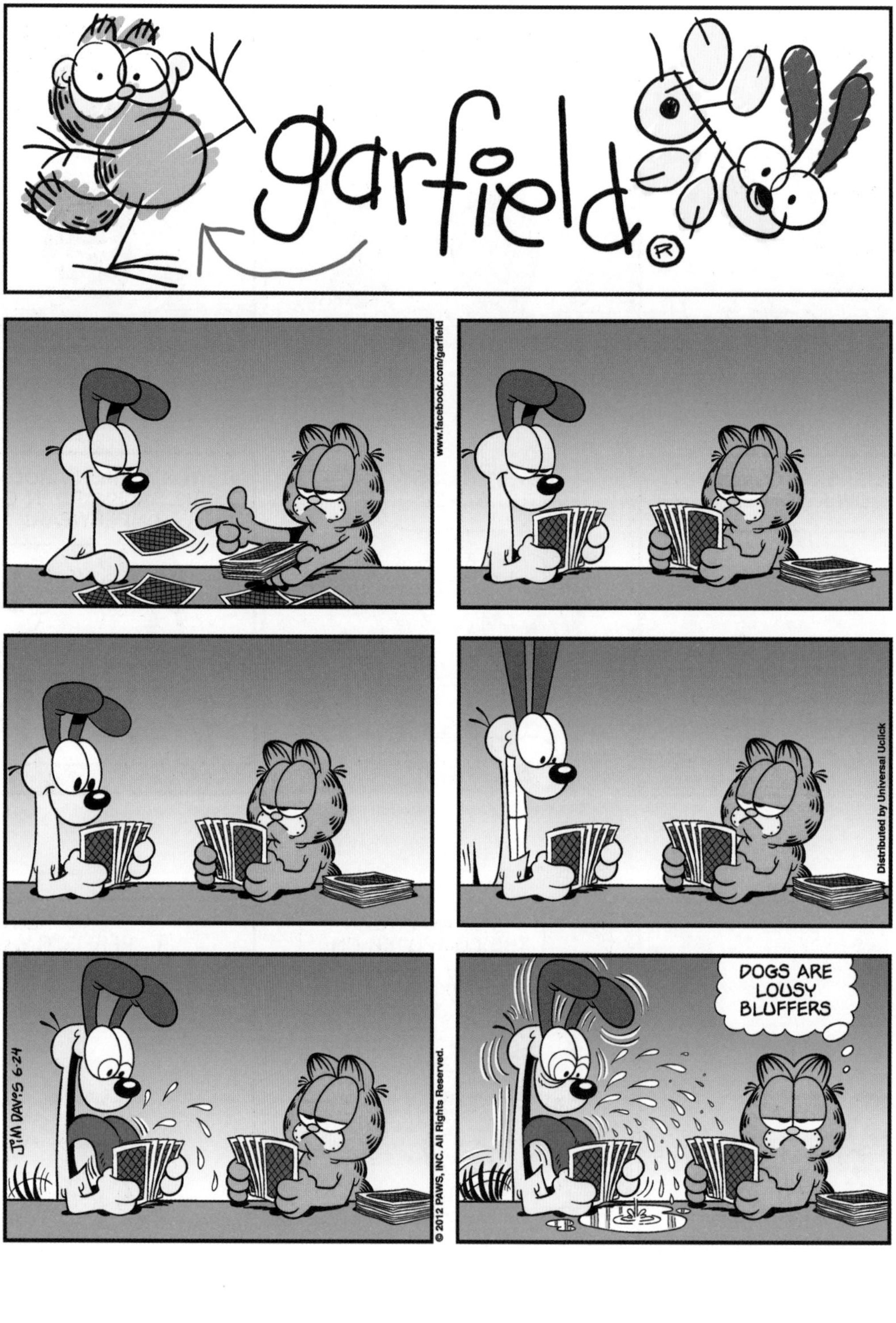
garfield®
www.facebook.com/garfield
Distributed by Universal Uclick
JIM DAVIS 6-24
© 2012 PAWS, INC. All Rights Reserved.
DOGS ARE LOUSY BLUFFERS

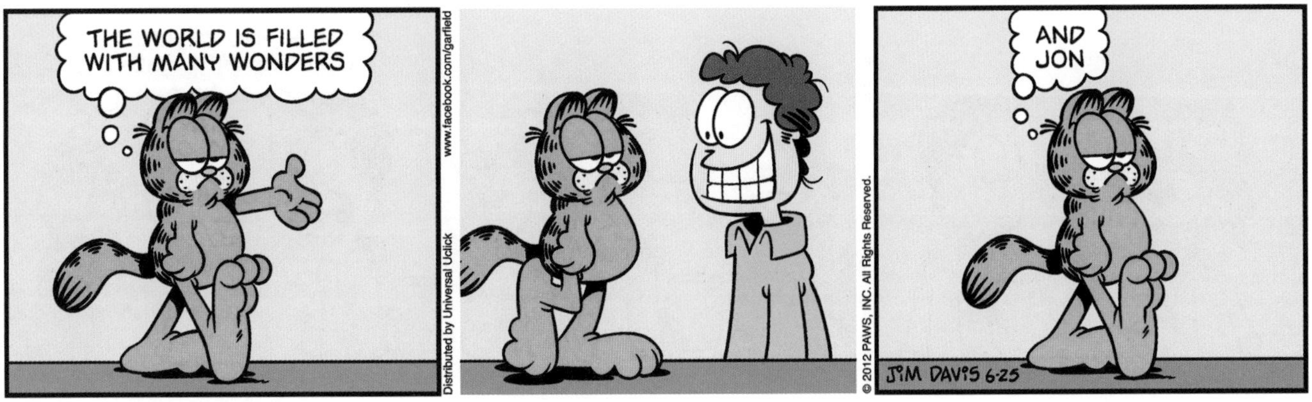
THE WORLD IS FILLED WITH MANY WONDERS
AND JON
Distributed by Universal Uclick www.facebook.com/garfield
© 2012 PAWS, INC. All Rights Reserved.
JIM DAVIS 6-25

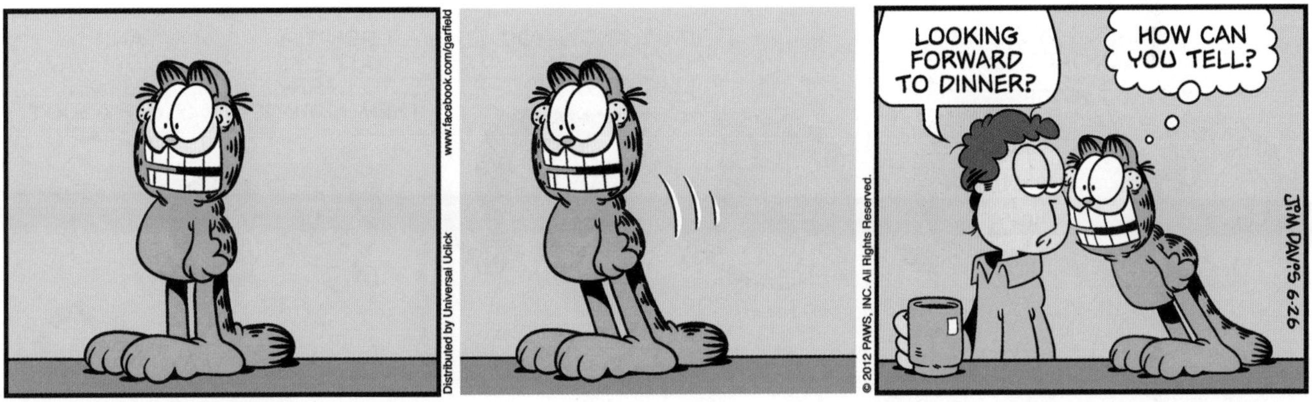
Distributed by Universal Uclick www.facebook.com/garfield
© 2012 PAWS, INC. All Rights Reserved.
LOOKING FORWARD TO DINNER?
HOW CAN YOU TELL?
JIM DAVIS 6-26

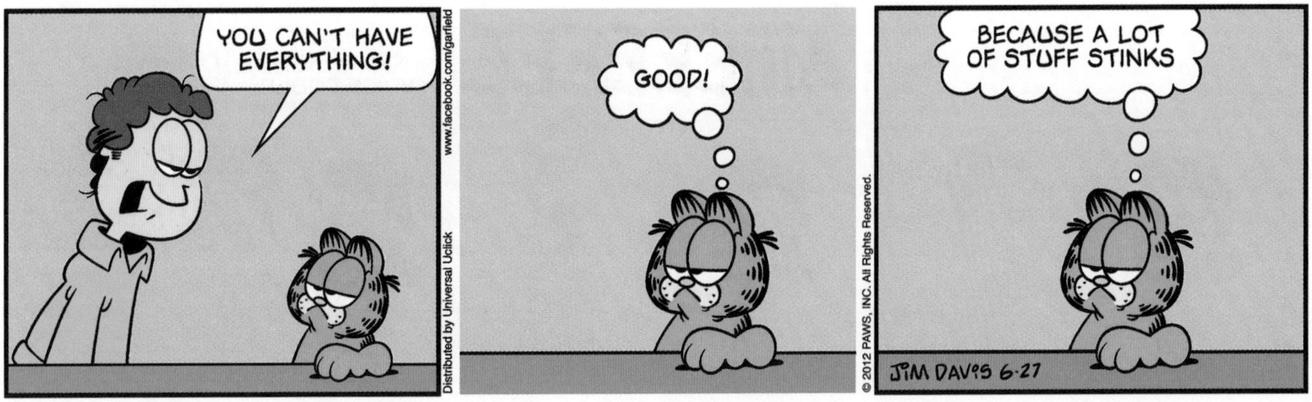
YOU CAN'T HAVE EVERYTHING!
Distributed by Universal Uclick www.facebook.com/garfield
GOOD!
© 2012 PAWS, INC. All Rights Reserved.
BECAUSE A LOT OF STUFF STINKS
JIM DAVIS 6-27

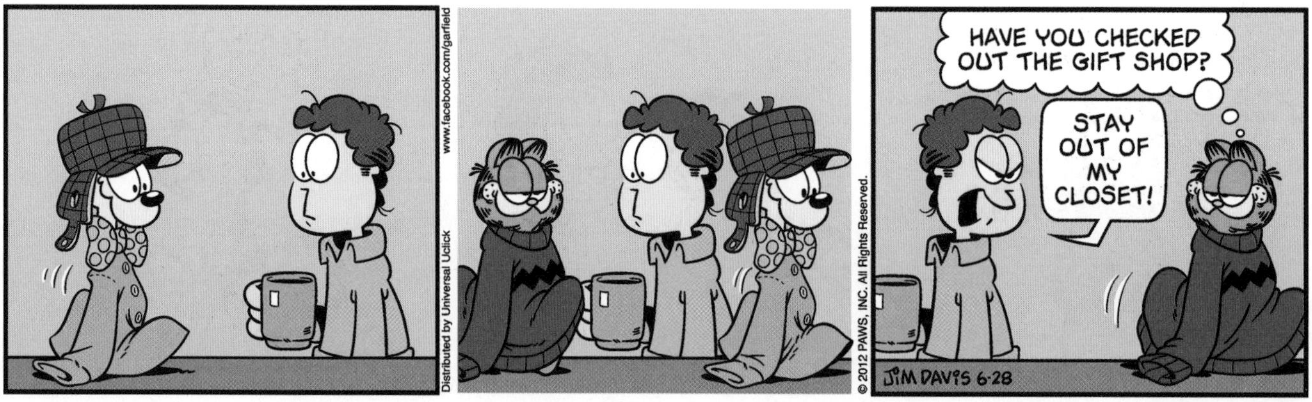
HAVE YOU CHECKED OUT THE GIFT SHOP?
STAY OUT OF MY CLOSET!
JIM DAVIS 6-28
www.facebook.com/garfield
Distributed by Universal Uclick
© 2012 PAWS, INC. All Rights Reserved.

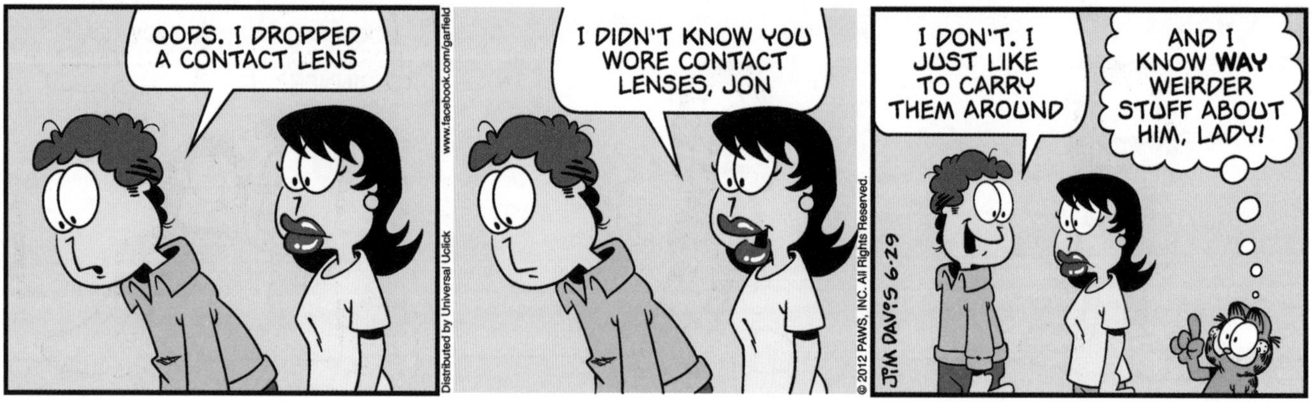
OOPS. I DROPPED A CONTACT LENS
I DIDN'T KNOW YOU WORE CONTACT LENSES, JON
I DON'T. I JUST LIKE TO CARRY THEM AROUND
AND I KNOW **WAY** WEIRDER STUFF ABOUT HIM, LADY!
JIM DAVIS 6-29
www.facebook.com/garfield
Distributed by Universal Uclick
© 2012 PAWS, INC. All Rights Reserved.

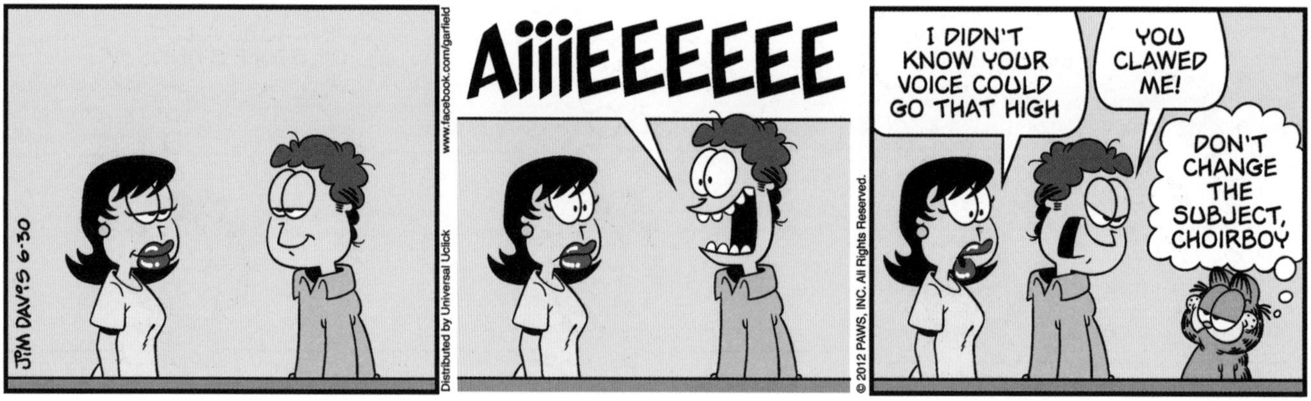
JIM DAVIS 6-30
AiiiEEEEEE
I DIDN'T KNOW YOUR VOICE COULD GO THAT HIGH
YOU CLAWED ME!
DON'T CHANGE THE SUBJECT, CHOIRBOY
www.facebook.com/garfield
Distributed by Universal Uclick
© 2012 PAWS, INC. All Rights Reserved.

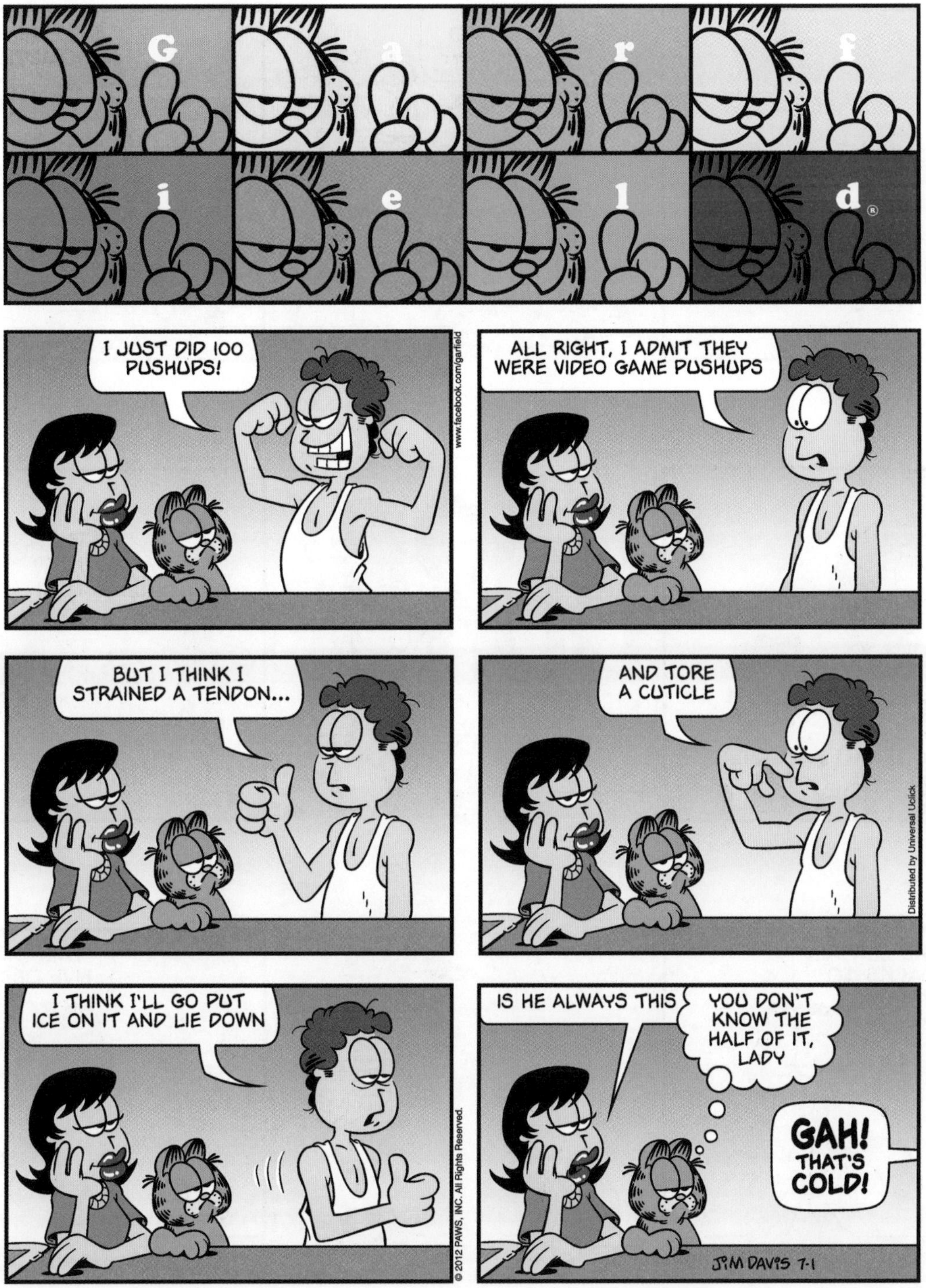
Garfield®
I JUST DID 100 PUSHUPS!
www.facebook.com/garfield
ALL RIGHT, I ADMIT THEY WERE VIDEO GAME PUSHUPS
BUT I THINK I STRAINED A TENDON...
AND TORE A CUTICLE
Distributed by Universal Uclick
I THINK I'LL GO PUT ICE ON IT AND LIE DOWN
© 2012 PAWS, INC. All Rights Reserved.
IS HE ALWAYS THIS
YOU DON'T KNOW THE HALF OF IT, LADY
GAH! THAT'S COLD!
JIM DAVIS 7-1

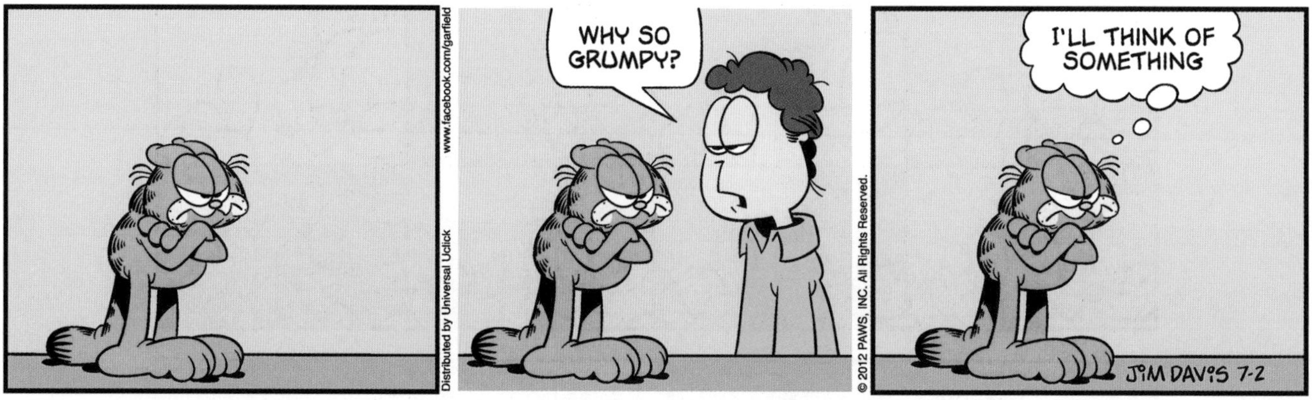
Distributed by Universal Uclick
www.facebook.com/garfield
WHY SO GRUMPY?
© 2012 PAWS, INC. All Rights Reserved.
I'LL THINK OF SOMETHING
JIM DAVIS 7-2

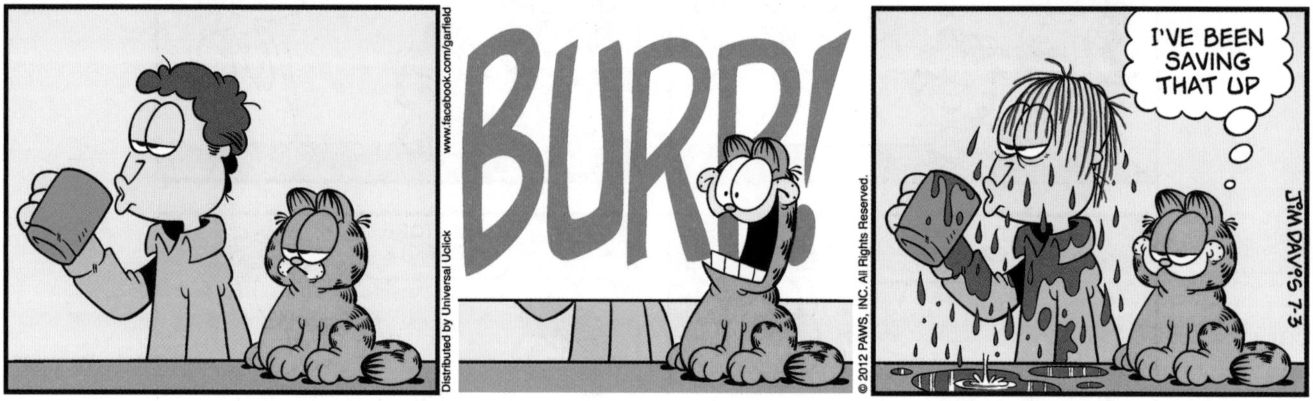
Distributed by Universal Uclick
www.facebook.com/garfield
BURP!
© 2012 PAWS, INC. All Rights Reserved.
I'VE BEEN SAVING THAT UP
JIM DAVIS 7-3

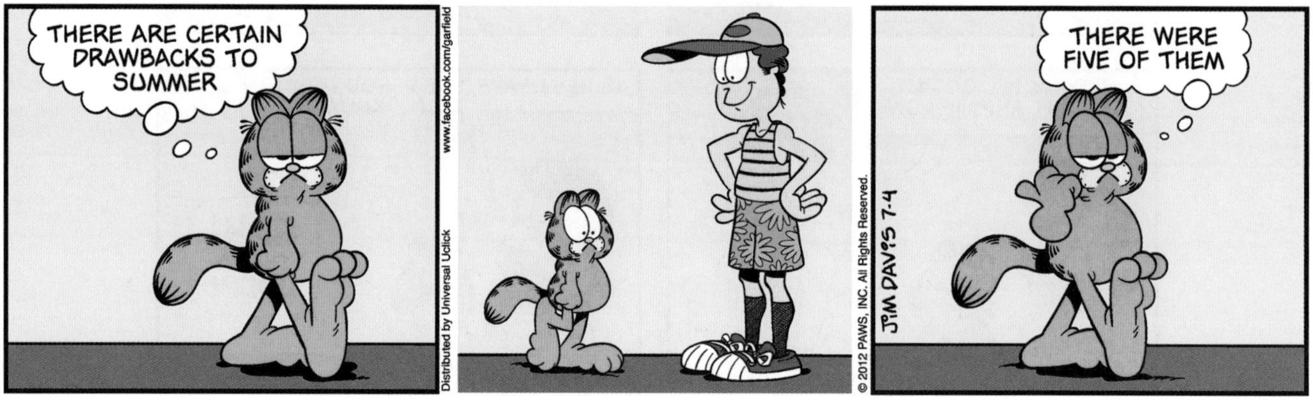
THERE ARE CERTAIN DRAWBACKS TO SUMMER
Distributed by Universal Uclick
www.facebook.com/garfield
© 2012 PAWS, INC. All Rights Reserved.
JIM DAVIS 7-4
THERE WERE FIVE OF THEM

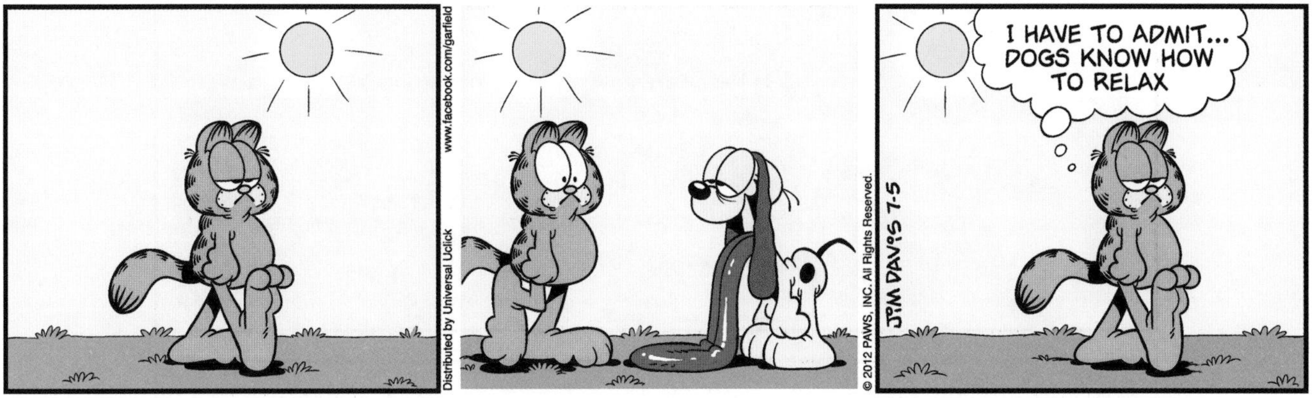
Distributed by Universal Uclick www.facebook.com/garfield
© 2012 PAWS, INC. All Rights Reserved.
JIM DAVIS 7-5
I HAVE TO ADMIT... DOGS KNOW HOW TO RELAX

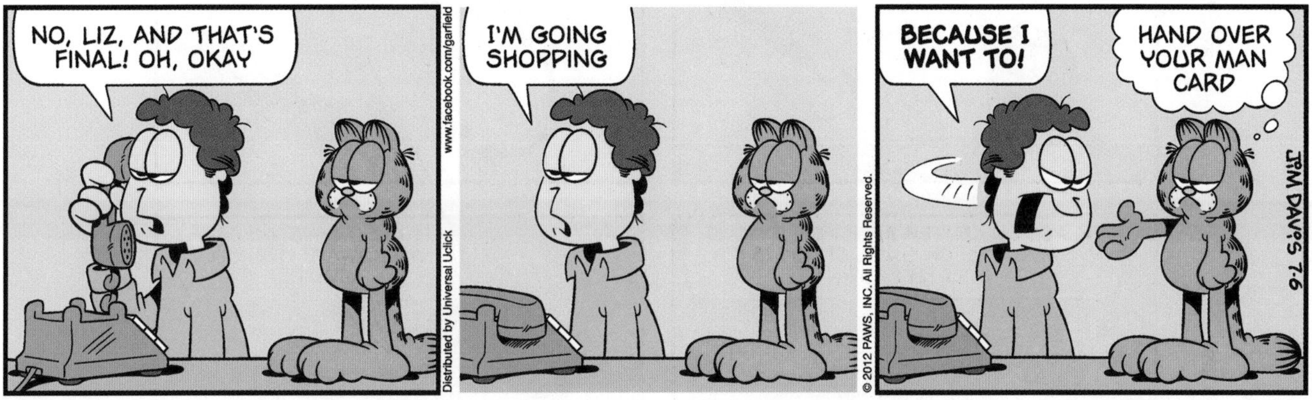
NO, LIZ, AND THAT'S FINAL! OH, OKAY
Distributed by Universal Uclick www.facebook.com/garfield
I'M GOING SHOPPING
© 2012 PAWS, INC. All Rights Reserved.
BECAUSE I WANT TO!
HAND OVER YOUR MAN CARD
JIM DAVIS 7-6

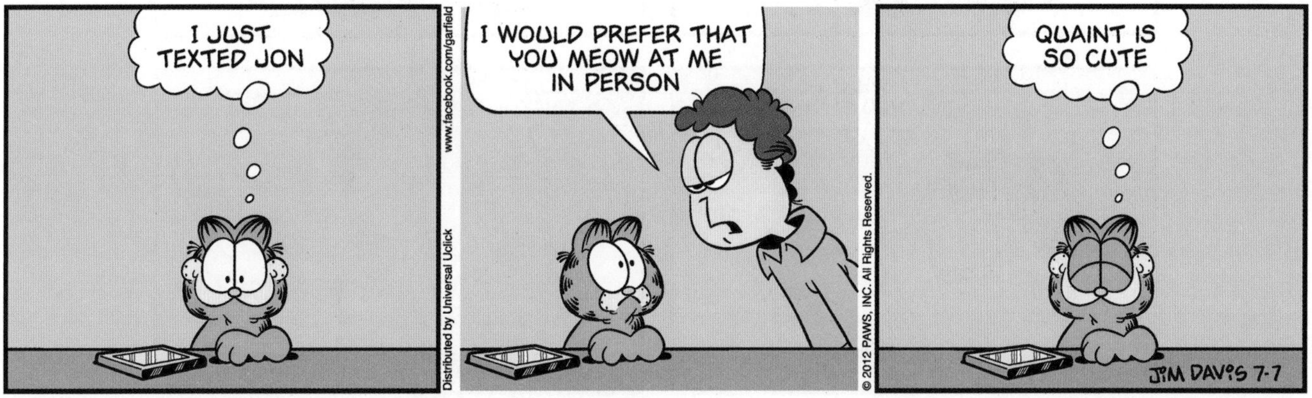
I JUST TEXTED JON
Distributed by Universal Uclick www.facebook.com/garfield
I WOULD PREFER THAT YOU MEOW AT ME IN PERSON
© 2012 PAWS, INC. All Rights Reserved.
QUAINT IS SO CUTE
JIM DAVIS 7-7

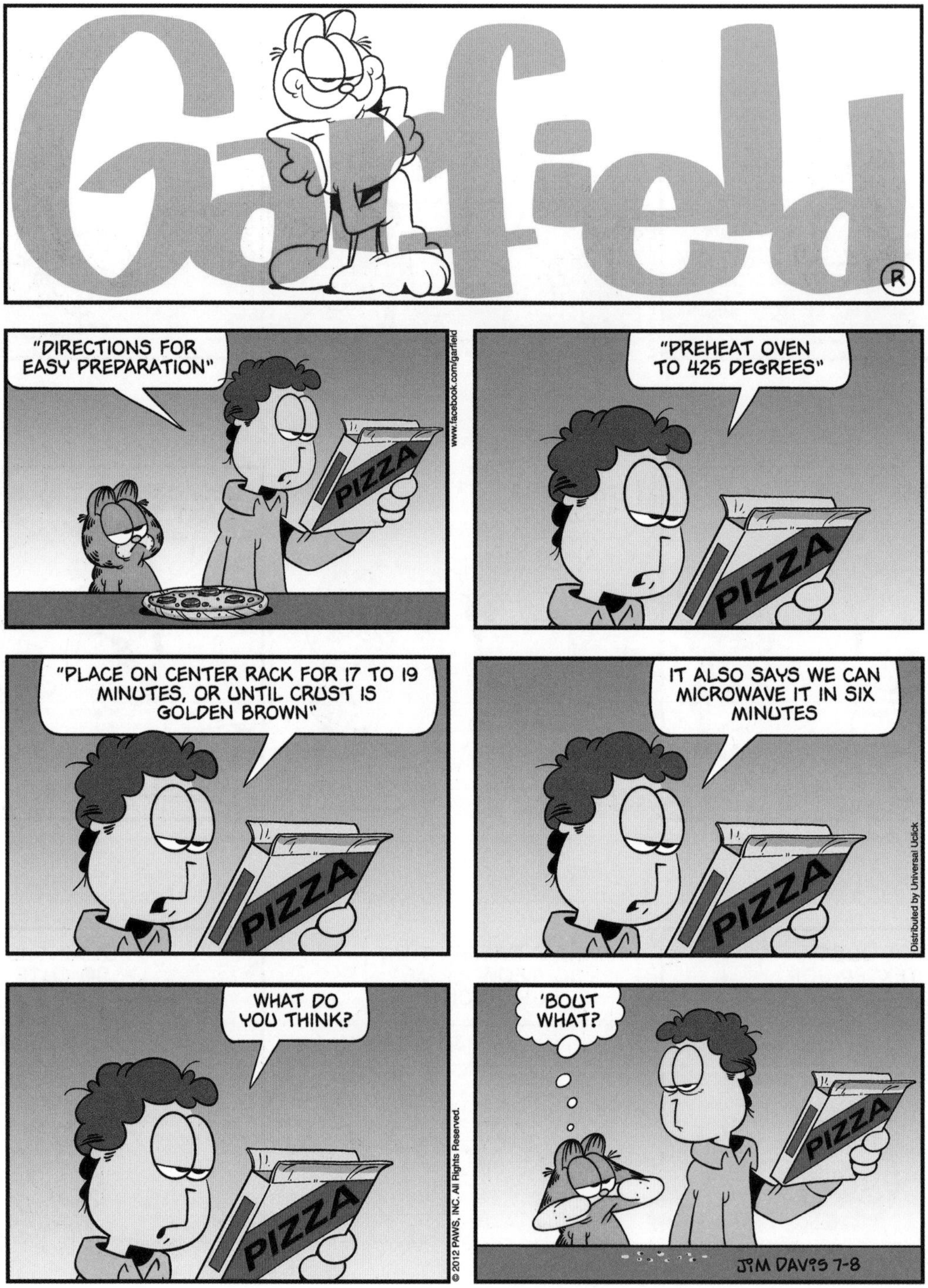
Garfield
"DIRECTIONS FOR EASY PREPARATION"
www.facebook.com/garfield
PIZZA
"PREHEAT OVEN TO 425 DEGREES"
"PLACE ON CENTER RACK FOR 17 TO 19 MINUTES, OR UNTIL CRUST IS GOLDEN BROWN"
IT ALSO SAYS WE CAN MICROWAVE IT IN SIX MINUTES
Distributed by Universal Uclick
WHAT DO YOU THINK?
© 2012 PAWS, INC. All Rights Reserved.
'BOUT WHAT?
JIM DAVIS 7-8

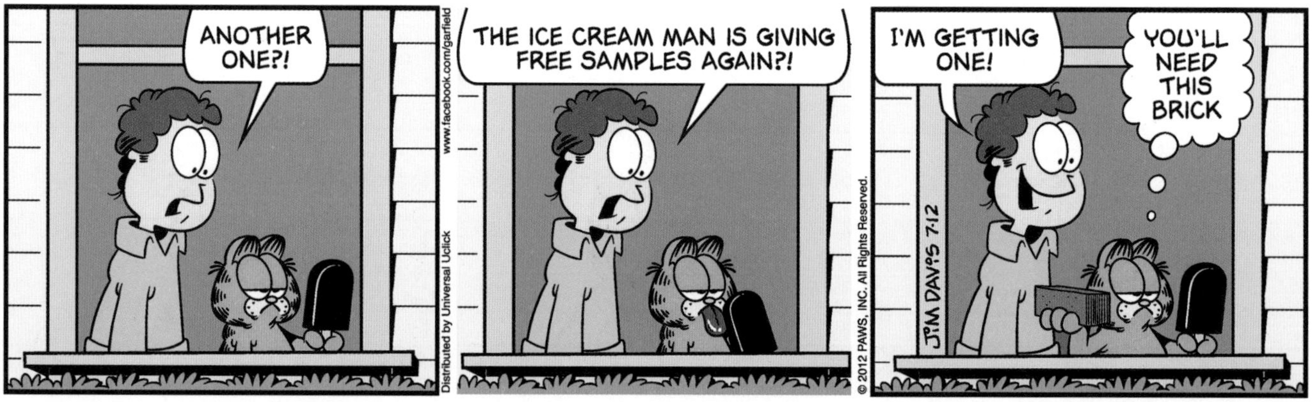
ANOTHER ONE?!
Distributed by Universal Uclick www.facebook.com/garfield
THE ICE CREAM MAN IS GIVING FREE SAMPLES AGAIN?!
© 2012 PAWS, INC. All Rights Reserved.
I'M GETTING ONE!
YOU'LL NEED THIS BRICK
JIM DAVIS 7-12

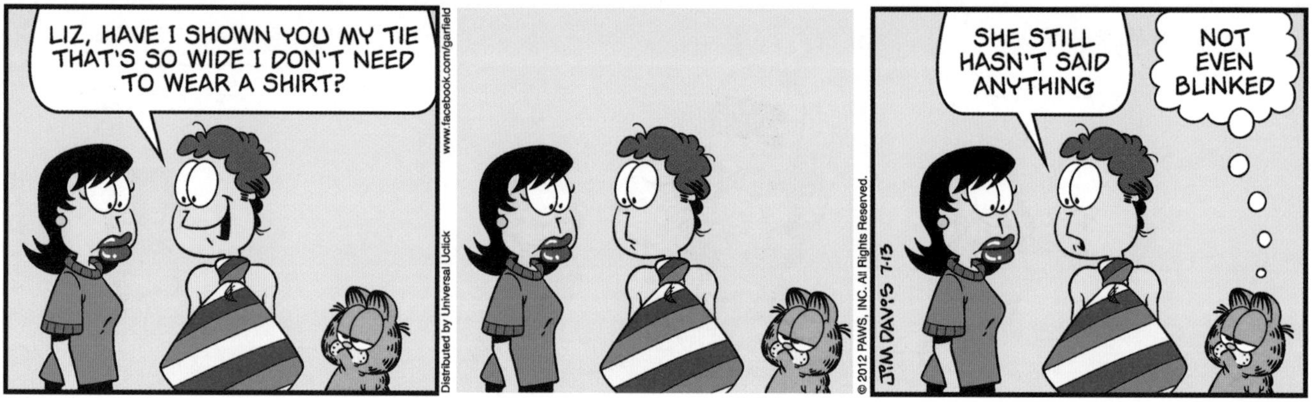
LIZ, HAVE I SHOWN YOU MY TIE THAT'S SO WIDE I DON'T NEED TO WEAR A SHIRT?
Distributed by Universal Uclick www.facebook.com/garfield
© 2012 PAWS, INC. All Rights Reserved.
SHE STILL HASN'T SAID ANYTHING
NOT EVEN BLINKED
JIM DAVIS 7-13

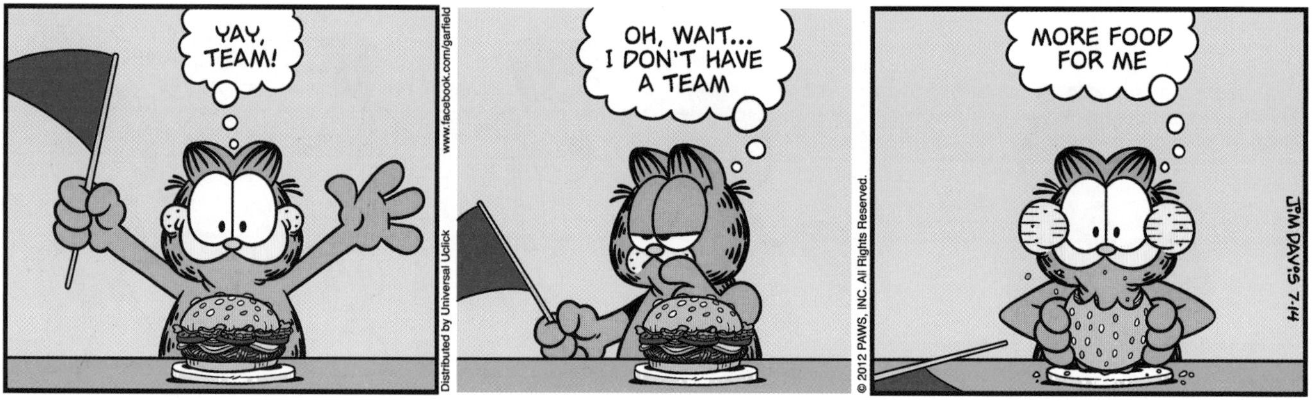
YAY, TEAM!
Distributed by Universal Uclick www.facebook.com/garfield
OH, WAIT... I DON'T HAVE A TEAM
© 2012 PAWS, INC. All Rights Reserved.
MORE FOOD FOR ME
JIM DAVIS 7-14

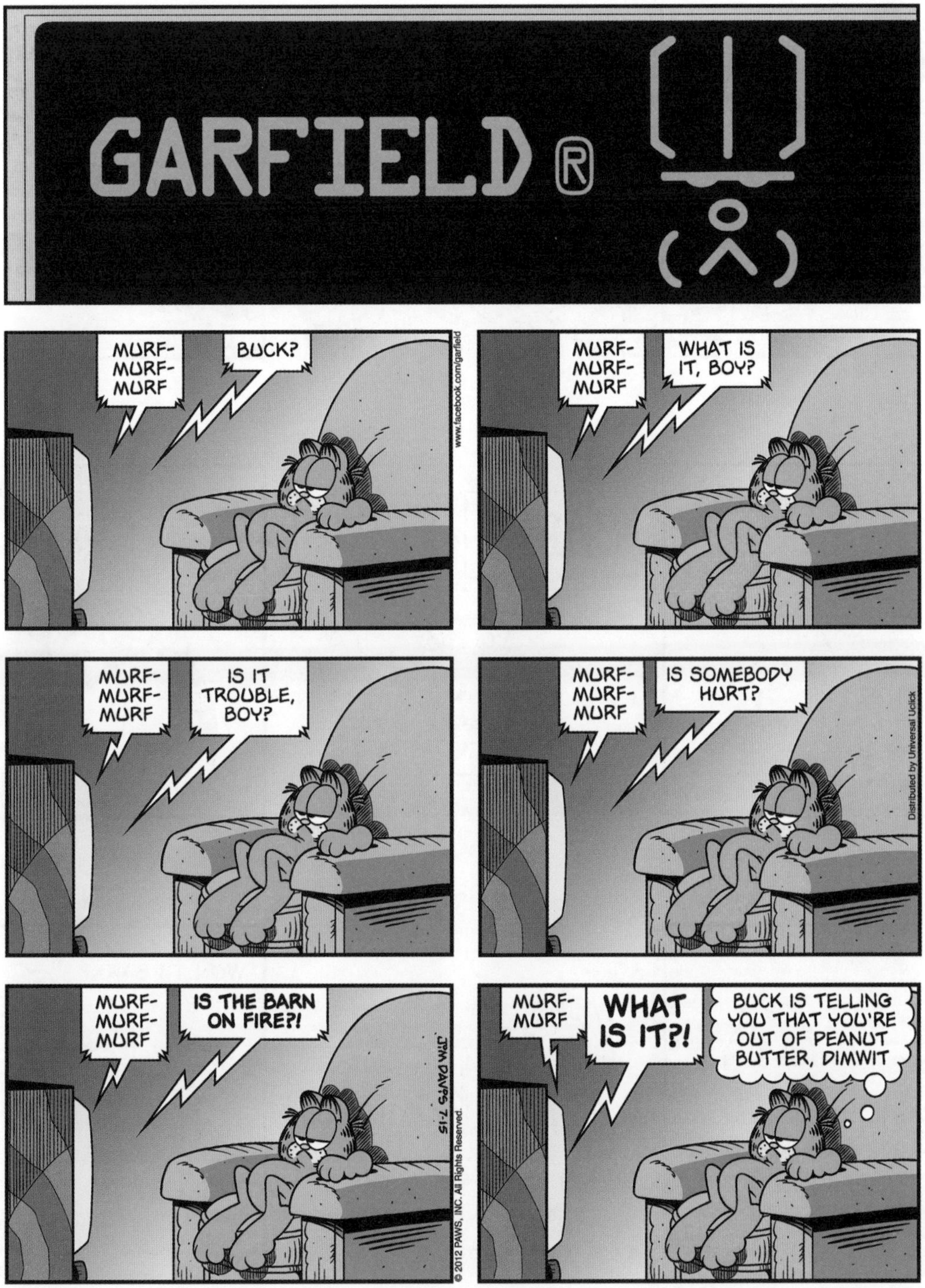
GARFIELD ®
MURF-MURF-MURF
BUCK?
www.facebook.com/garfield
MURF-MURF-MURF
WHAT IS IT, BOY?
MURF-MURF-MURF
IS IT TROUBLE, BOY?
MURF-MURF-MURF
IS SOMEBODY HURT?
Distributed by Universal Uclick
MURF-MURF-MURF
IS THE BARN ON FIRE?!
JIM DAVIS 7-15
© 2012 PAWS, INC. All Rights Reserved.
MURF-MURF
WHAT IS IT?!
BUCK IS TELLING YOU THAT YOU'RE OUT OF PEANUT BUTTER, DIMWIT

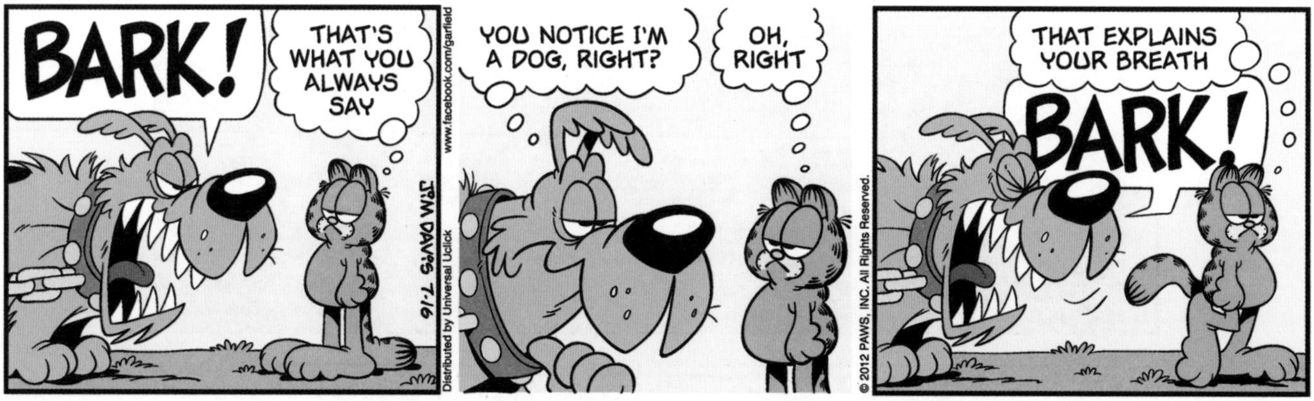
BARK!
THAT'S WHAT YOU ALWAYS SAY
JIM DAVIS 7-16
www.facebook.com/garfield
Distributed by Universal Uclick
YOU NOTICE I'M A DOG, RIGHT?
OH, RIGHT
© 2012 PAWS, INC. All Rights Reserved.
THAT EXPLAINS YOUR BREATH
BARK!

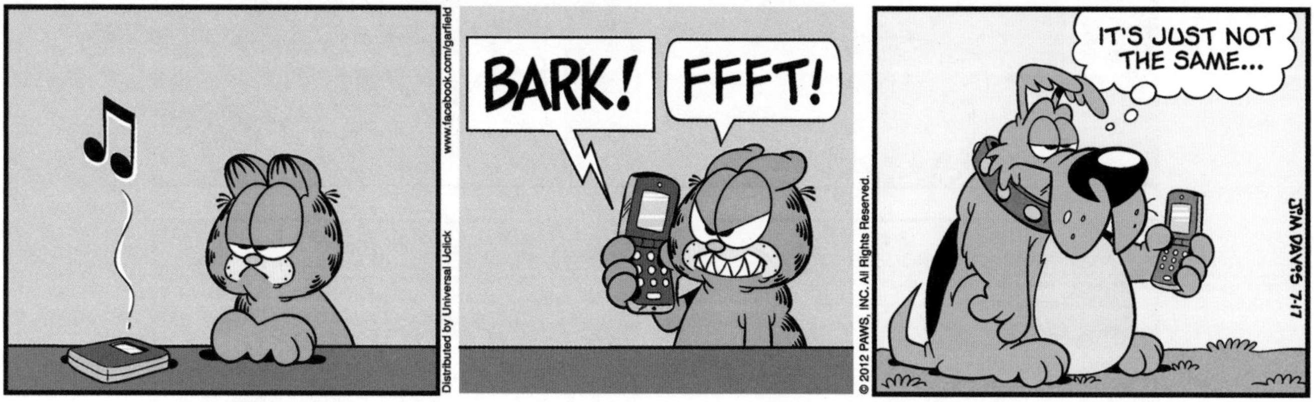
www.facebook.com/garfield
Distributed by Universal Uclick
BARK!
FFFT!
© 2012 PAWS, INC. All Rights Reserved.
IT'S JUST NOT THE SAME...
JIM DAVIS 7-17

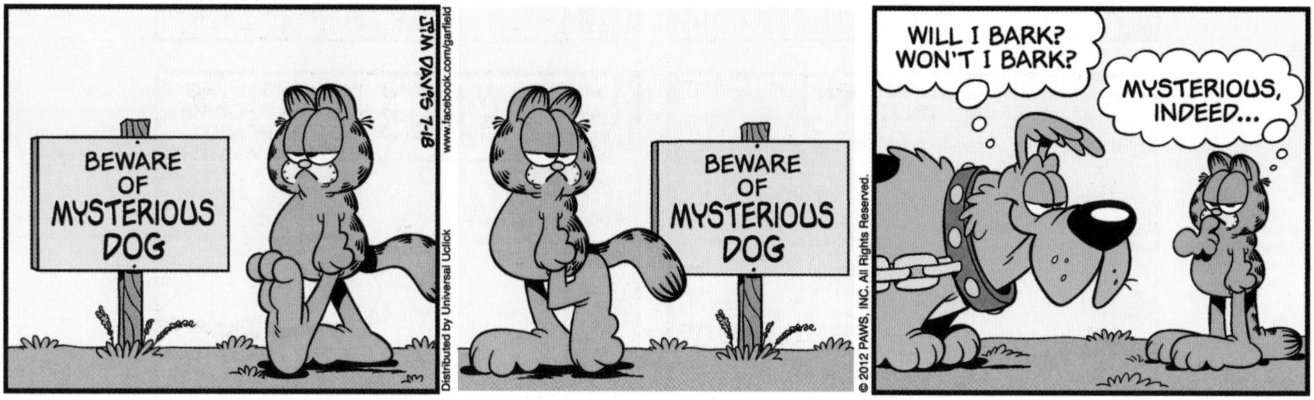
BEWARE OF MYSTERIOUS DOG
JIM DAVIS 7-18
www.facebook.com/garfield
Distributed by Universal Uclick
BEWARE OF MYSTERIOUS DOG
© 2012 PAWS, INC. All Rights Reserved.
WILL I BARK? WON'T I BARK?
MYSTERIOUS, INDEED...

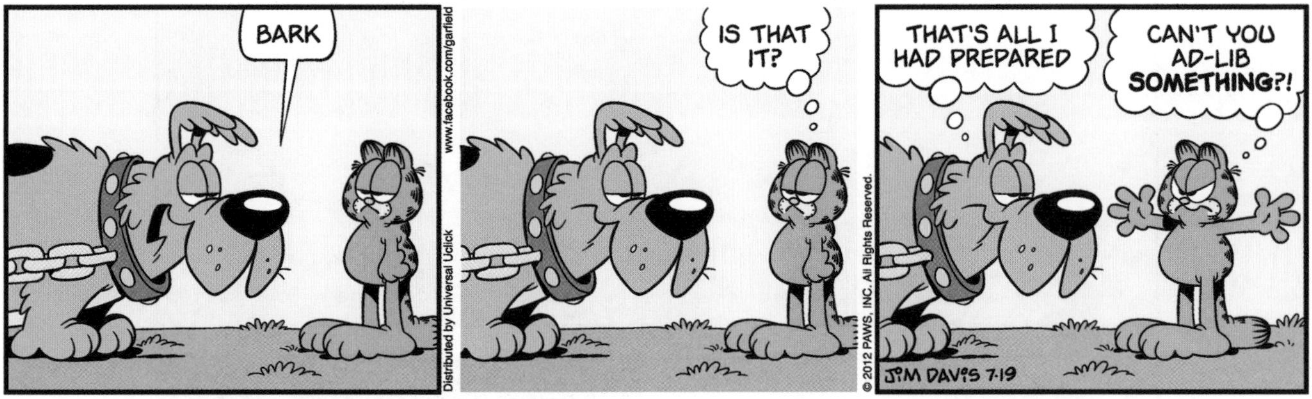
BARK
IS THAT IT?
THAT'S ALL I HAD PREPARED
CAN'T YOU AD-LIB **SOMETHING**?!
Distributed by Universal Uclick
www.facebook.com/garfield
© 2012 PAWS, INC. All Rights Reserved.
JIM DAVIS 7-19

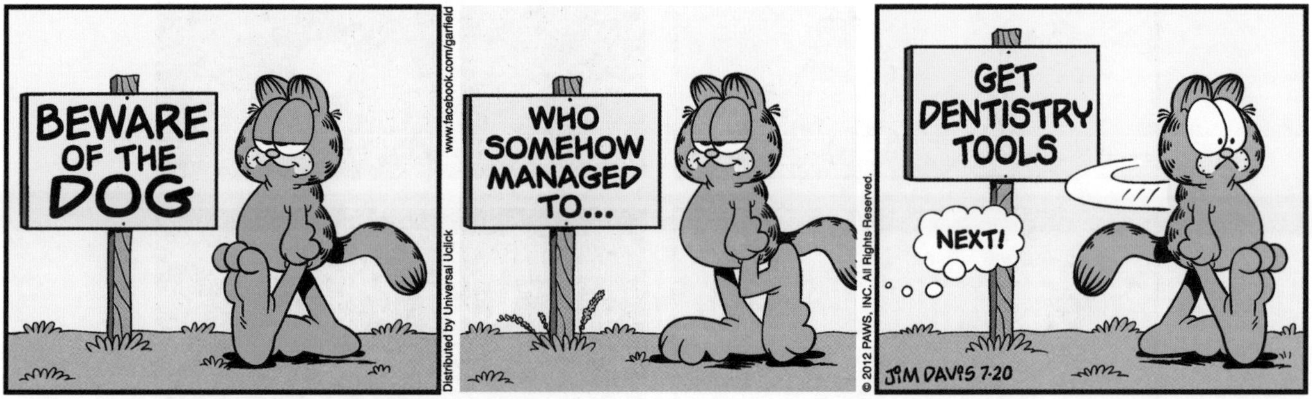
BEWARE OF THE DOG
WHO SOMEHOW MANAGED TO...
GET DENTISTRY TOOLS
NEXT!
Distributed by Universal Uclick
www.facebook.com/garfield
© 2012 PAWS, INC. All Rights Reserved.
JIM DAVIS 7-20

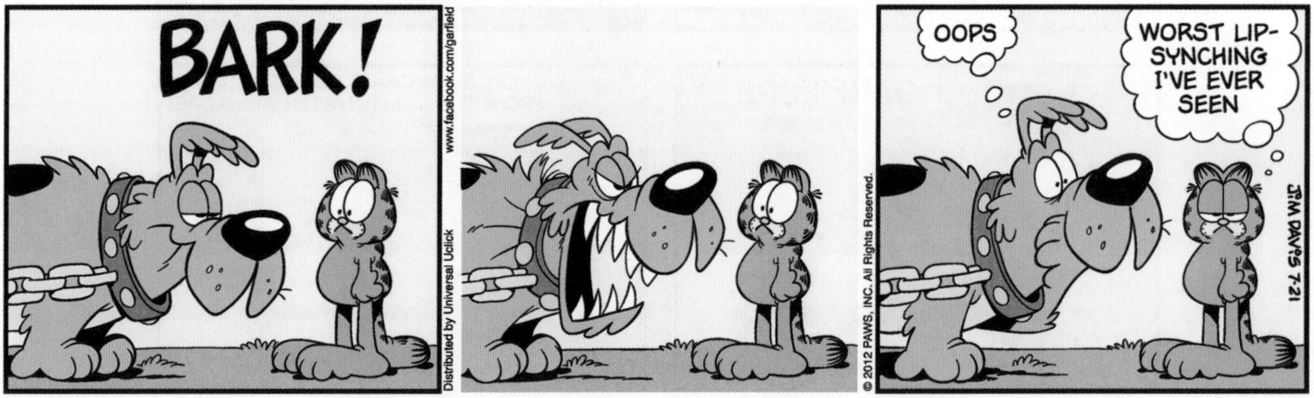
BARK!
OOPS
WORST LIP-SYNCHING I'VE EVER SEEN
Distributed by Universal Uclick
www.facebook.com/garfield
© 2012 PAWS, INC. All Rights Reserved.
JIM DAVIS 7-21

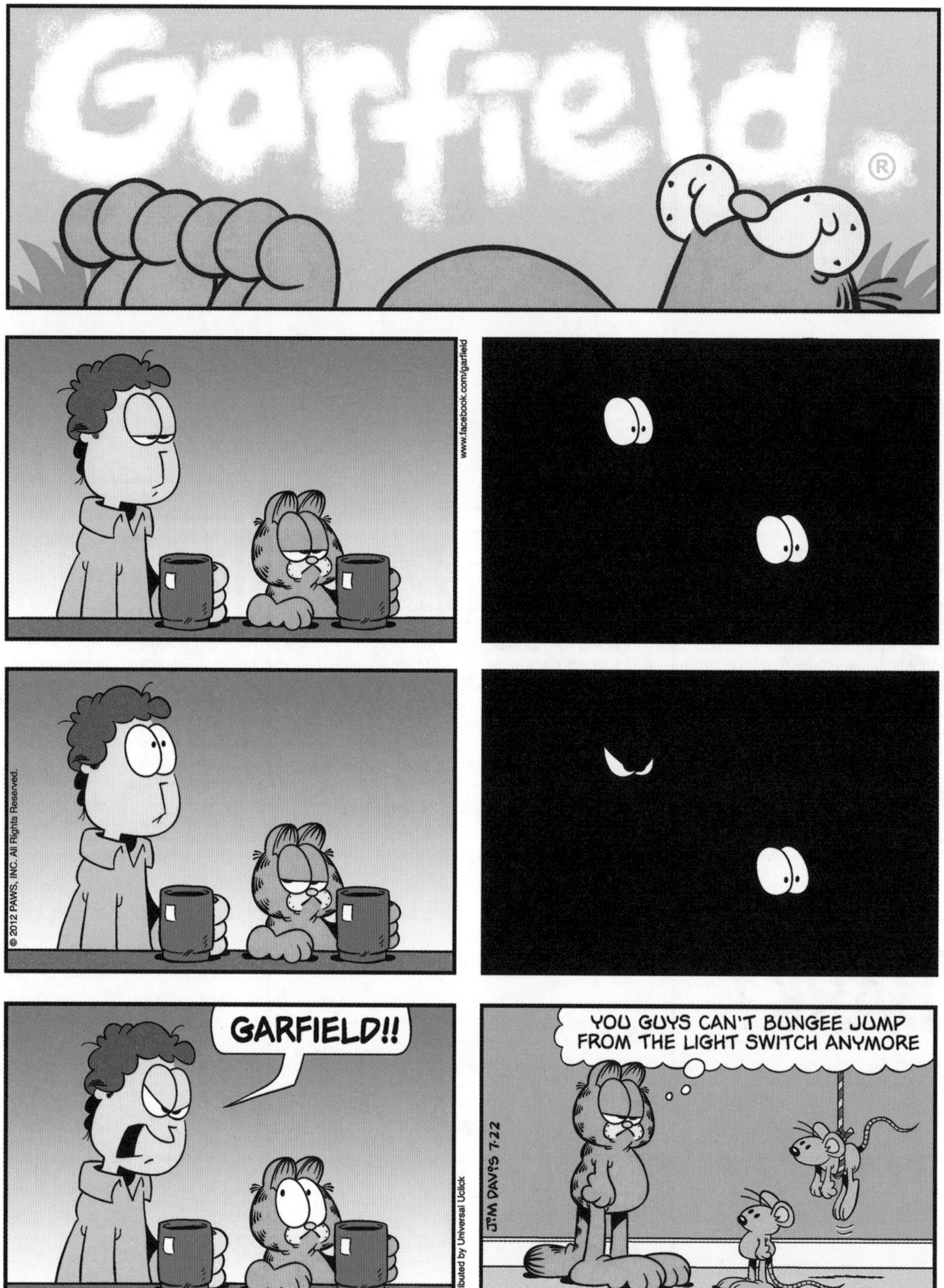
Garfield®
www.facebook.com/garfield
© 2012 PAWS, INC. All Rights Reserved.
GARFIELD!!
Distributed by Universal Uclick
YOU GUYS CAN'T BUNGEE JUMP FROM THE LIGHT SWITCH ANYMORE
JIM DAVIS 7-22

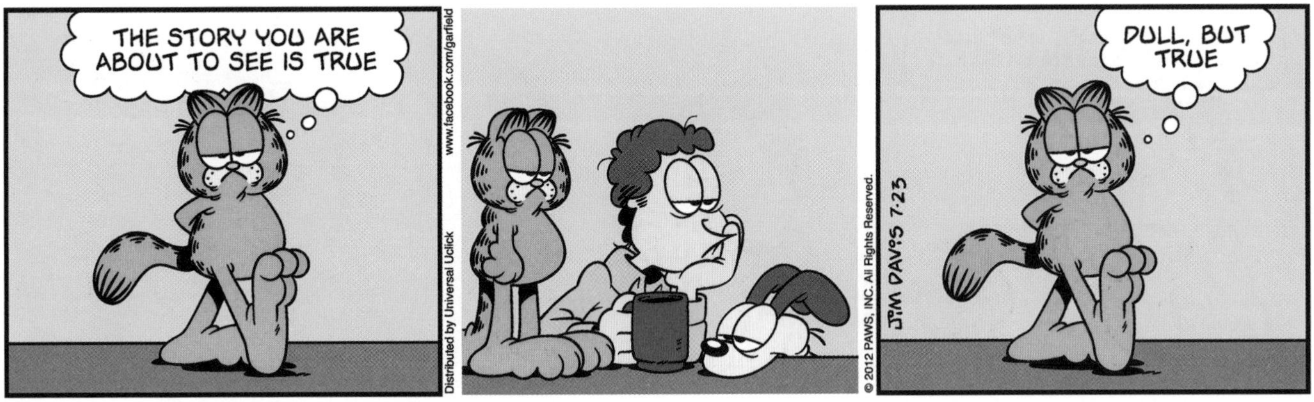
THE STORY YOU ARE ABOUT TO SEE IS TRUE
DULL, BUT TRUE
Distributed by Universal Uclick www.facebook.com/garfield
© 2012 PAWS, INC. All Rights Reserved.
JIM DAVIS 7-23

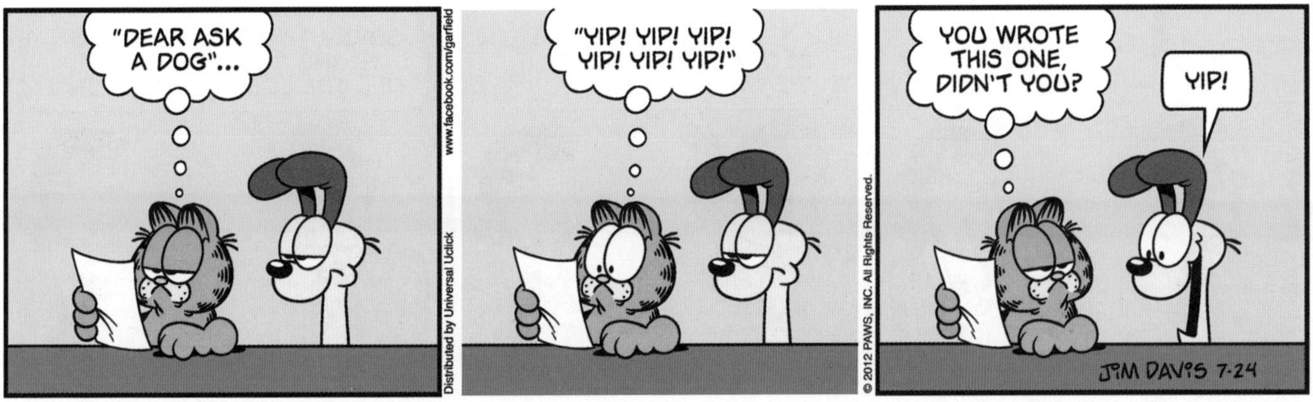
"DEAR ASK A DOG"...
"YIP! YIP! YIP! YIP! YIP! YIP!"
YOU WROTE THIS ONE, DIDN'T YOU?
YIP!
Distributed by Universal Uclick www.facebook.com/garfield
© 2012 PAWS, INC. All Rights Reserved.
JIM DAVIS 7-24

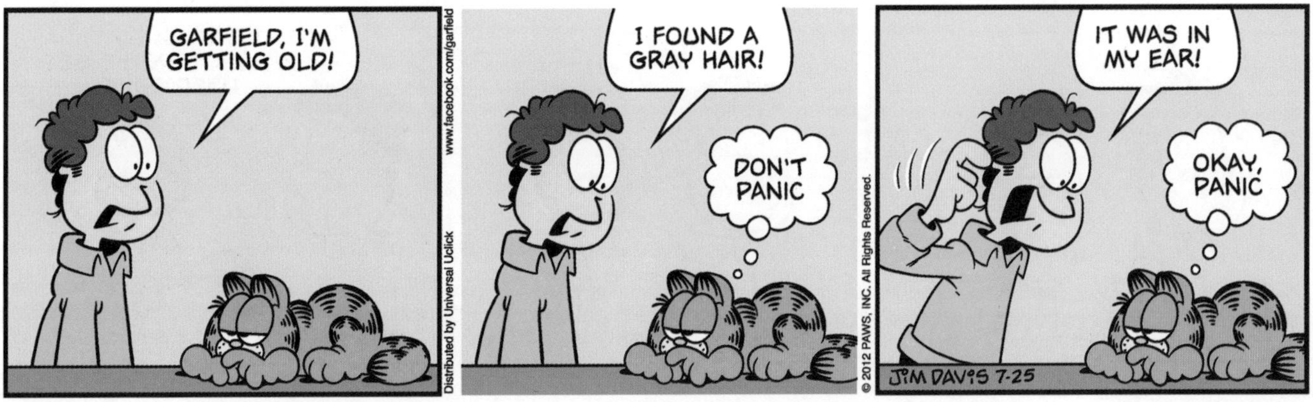
GARFIELD, I'M GETTING OLD!
I FOUND A GRAY HAIR!
DON'T PANIC
IT WAS IN MY EAR!
OKAY, PANIC
Distributed by Universal Uclick www.facebook.com/garfield
© 2012 PAWS, INC. All Rights Reserved.
JIM DAVIS 7-25

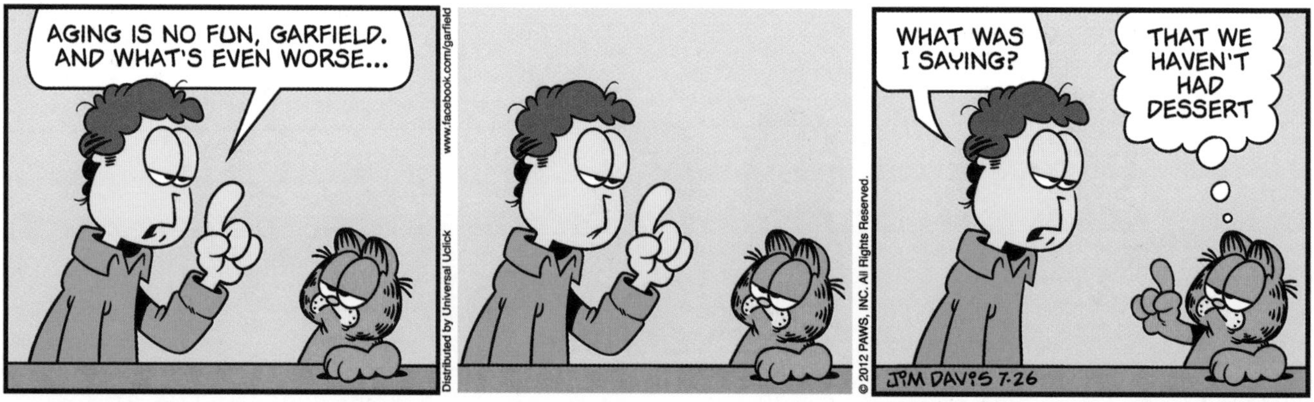
AGING IS NO FUN, GARFIELD. AND WHAT'S EVEN WORSE...
WHAT WAS I SAYING?
THAT WE HAVEN'T HAD DESSERT
JIM DAVIS 7-26
Distributed by Universal Uclick www.facebook.com/garfield
© 2012 PAWS, INC. All Rights Reserved.

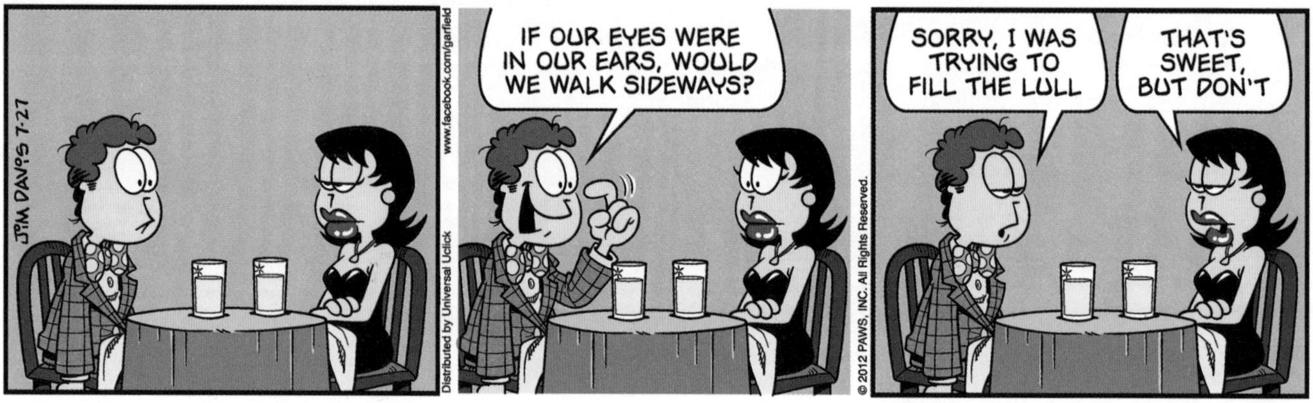
JIM DAVIS 7-27
IF OUR EYES WERE IN OUR EARS, WOULD WE WALK SIDEWAYS?
SORRY, I WAS TRYING TO FILL THE LULL
THAT'S SWEET, BUT DON'T
Distributed by Universal Uclick www.facebook.com/garfield
© 2012 PAWS, INC. All Rights Reserved.

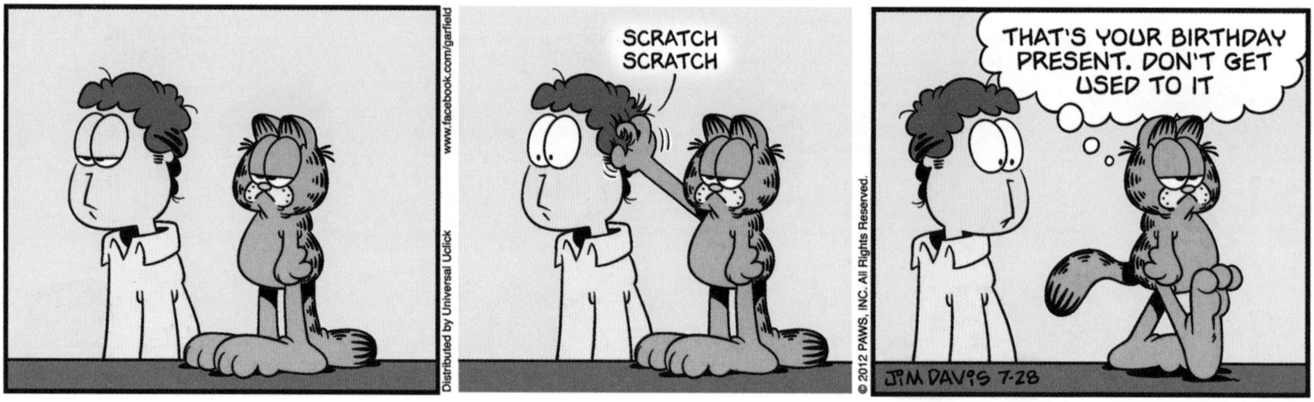
SCRATCH SCRATCH
THAT'S YOUR BIRTHDAY PRESENT. DON'T GET USED TO IT
JIM DAVIS 7-28
Distributed by Universal Uclick www.facebook.com/garfield
© 2012 PAWS, INC. All Rights Reserved.

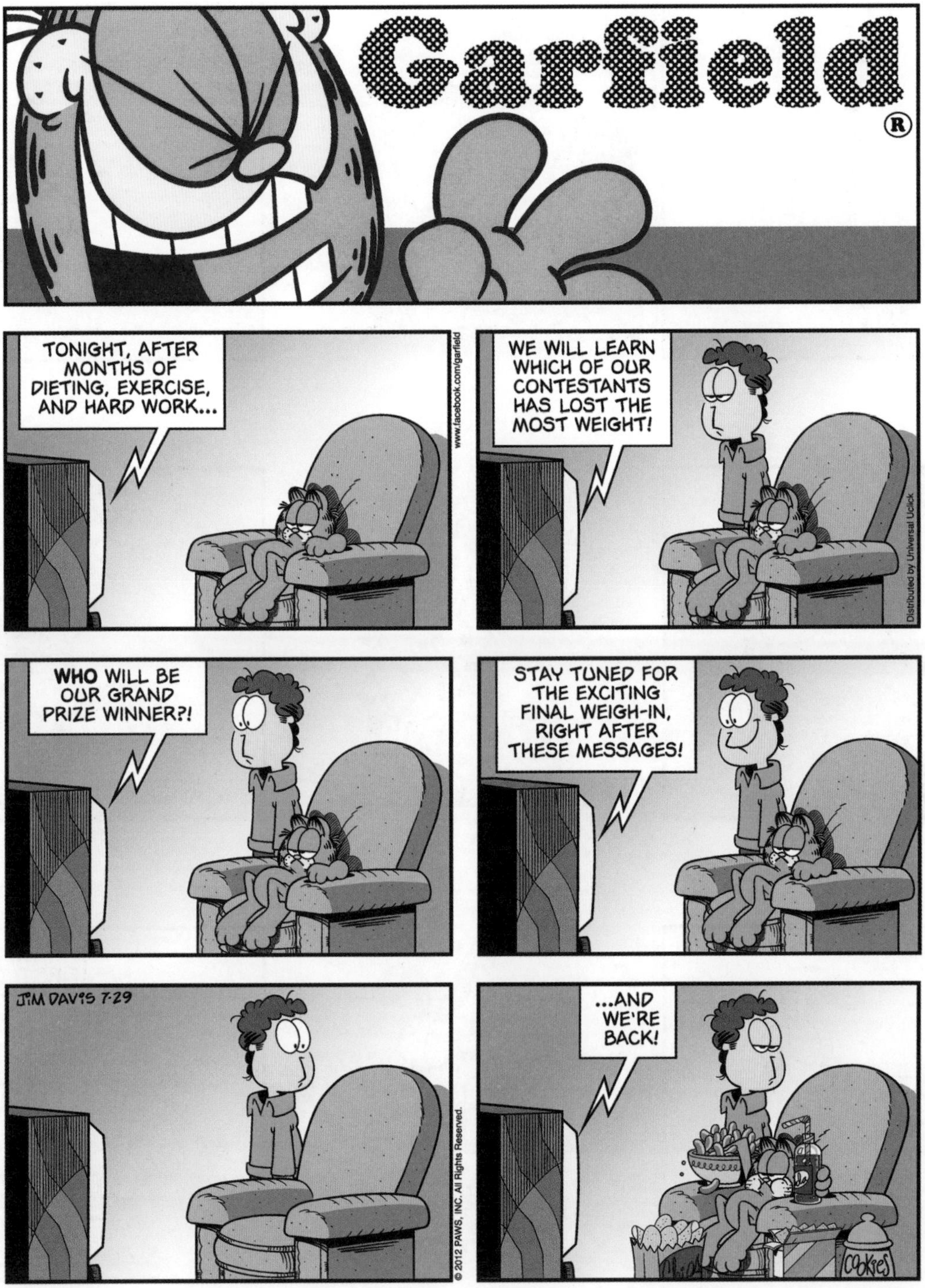
Garfield®
TONIGHT, AFTER MONTHS OF DIETING, EXERCISE, AND HARD WORK...
www.facebook.com/garfield
WE WILL LEARN WHICH OF OUR CONTESTANTS HAS LOST THE MOST WEIGHT!
Distributed by Universal Uclick
WHO WILL BE OUR GRAND PRIZE WINNER?!
STAY TUNED FOR THE EXCITING FINAL WEIGH-IN, RIGHT AFTER THESE MESSAGES!
JIM DAVIS 7-29
© 2012 PAWS, INC. All Rights Reserved.
...AND WE'RE BACK!
COOKIES

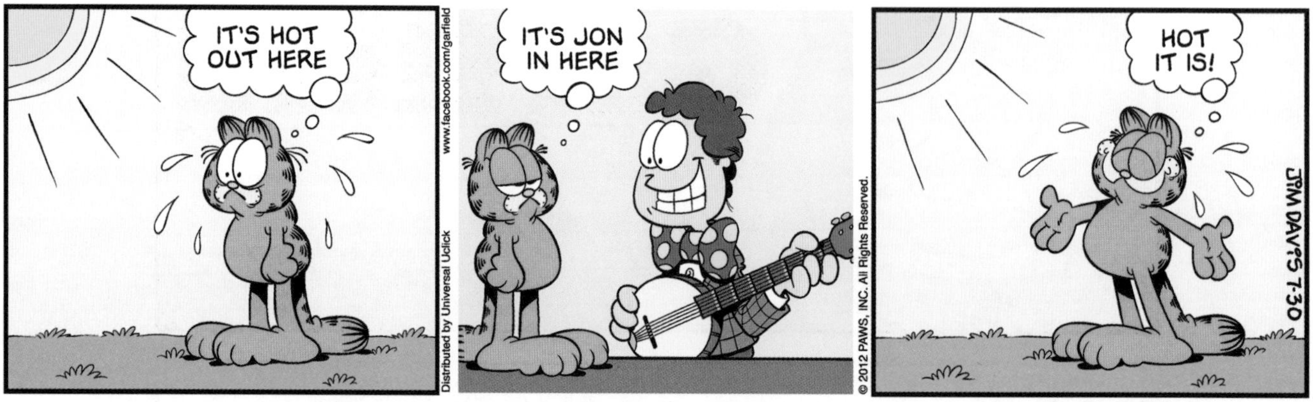
IT'S HOT OUT HERE
Distributed by Universal Uclick www.facebook.com/garfield
IT'S JON IN HERE
© 2012 PAWS, INC. All Rights Reserved.
HOT IT IS!
JIM DAVIS 7-30

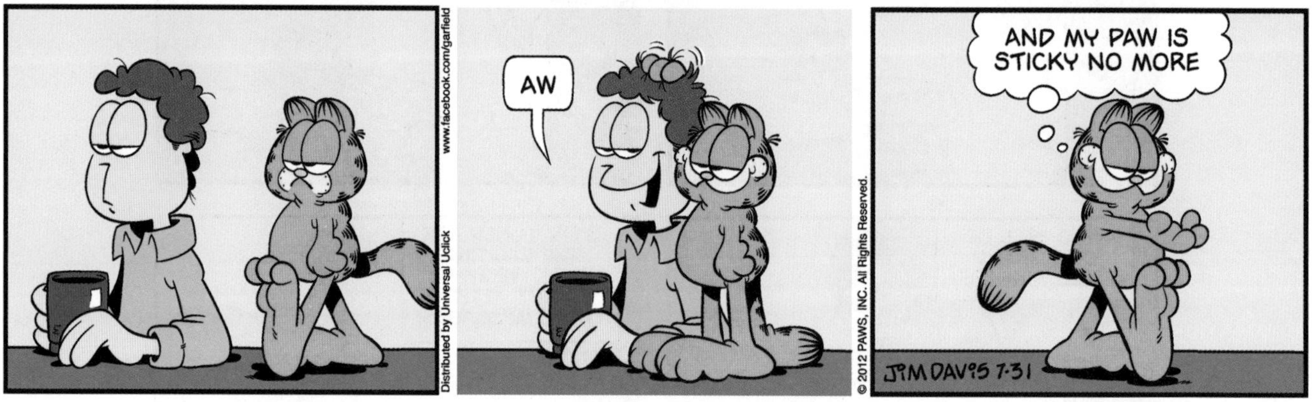
Distributed by Universal Uclick www.facebook.com/garfield
AW
© 2012 PAWS, INC. All Rights Reserved.
AND MY PAW IS STICKY NO MORE
JIM DAVIS 7-31

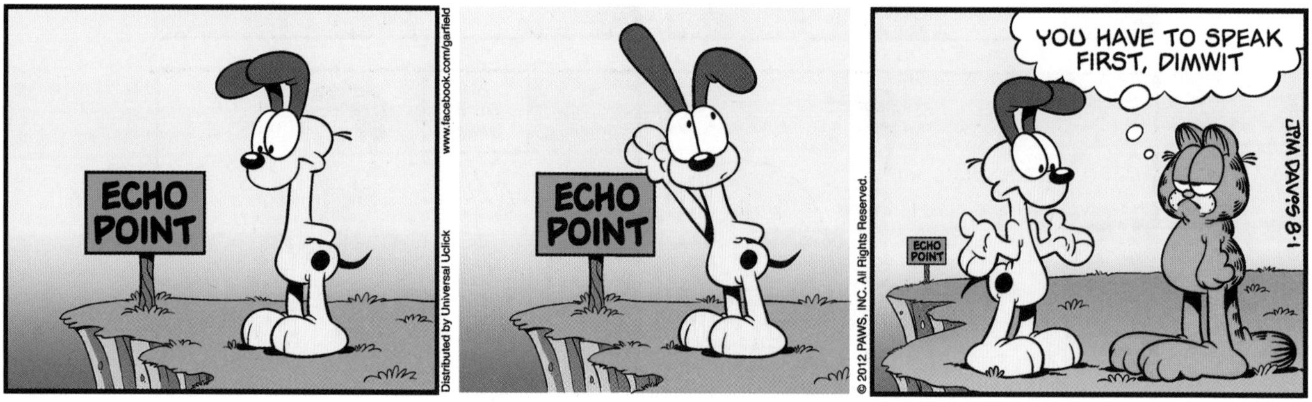
ECHO POINT
Distributed by Universal Uclick www.facebook.com/garfield
ECHO POINT
© 2012 PAWS, INC. All Rights Reserved.
YOU HAVE TO SPEAK FIRST, DIMWIT
ECHO POINT
JIM DAVIS 8-1

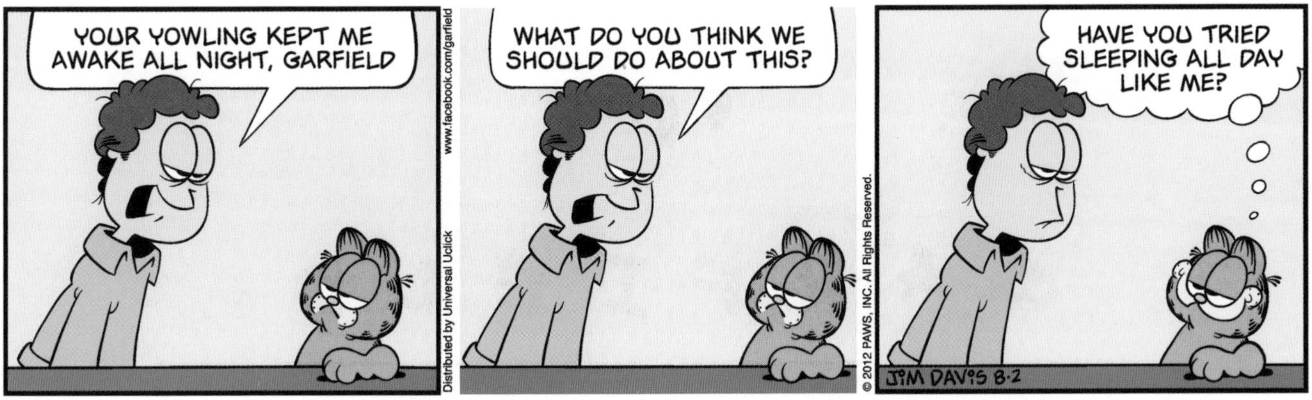
YOUR YOWLING KEPT ME AWAKE ALL NIGHT, GARFIELD
www.facebook.com/garfield
Distributed by Universal Uclick
WHAT DO YOU THINK WE SHOULD DO ABOUT THIS?
© 2012 PAWS, INC. All Rights Reserved.
HAVE YOU TRIED SLEEPING ALL DAY LIKE ME?
JIM DAVIS 8-2

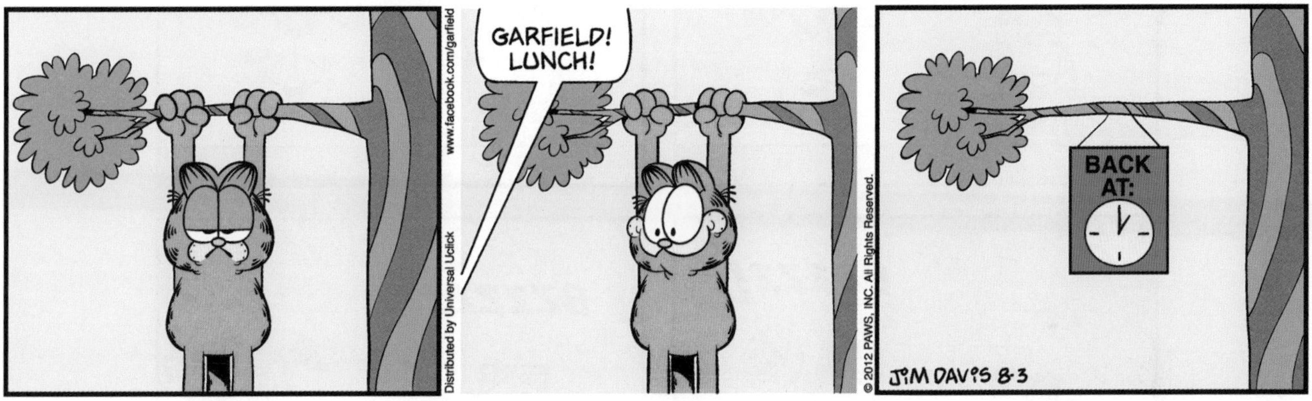
www.facebook.com/garfield
Distributed by Universal Uclick
GARFIELD! LUNCH!
© 2012 PAWS, INC. All Rights Reserved.
BACK AT:
JIM DAVIS 8-3

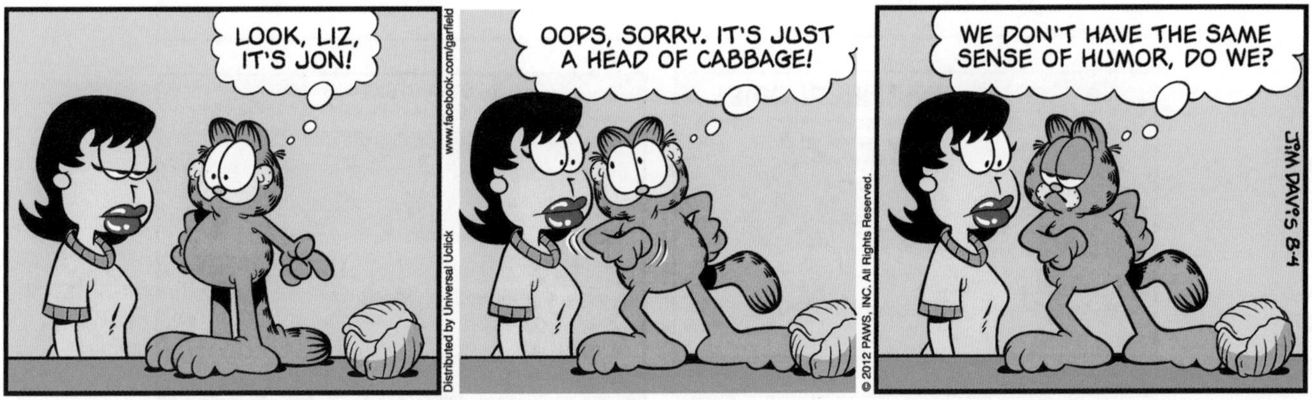
LOOK, LIZ, IT'S JON!
www.facebook.com/garfield
Distributed by Universal Uclick
OOPS, SORRY. IT'S JUST A HEAD OF CABBAGE!
© 2012 PAWS, INC. All Rights Reserved.
WE DON'T HAVE THE SAME SENSE OF HUMOR, DO WE?
JIM DAVIS 8-4

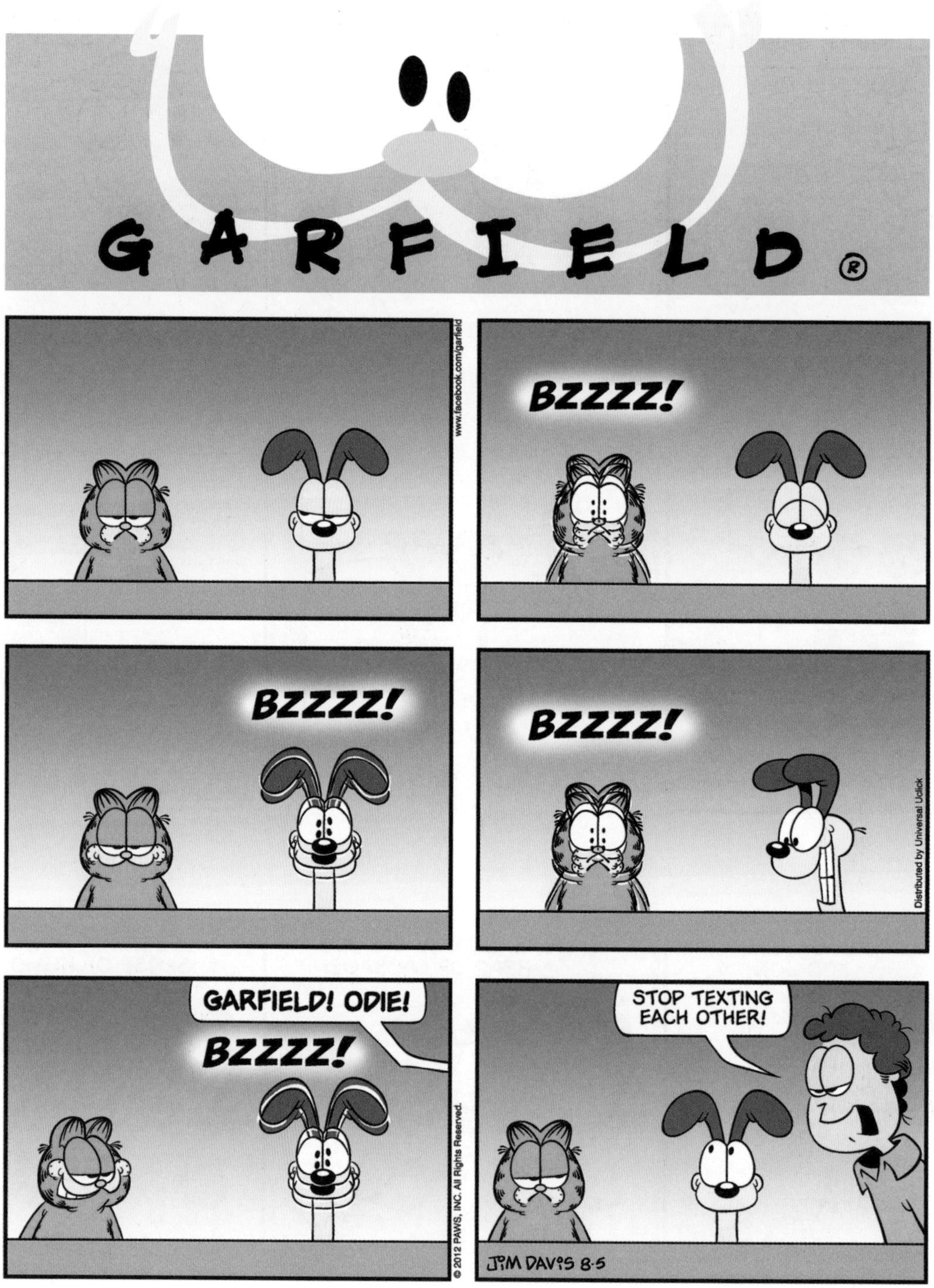
GARFIELD®
www.facebook.com/garfield
BZZZZ!
BZZZZ!
BZZZZ!
Distributed by Universal Uclick
GARFIELD! ODIE!
BZZZZ!
© 2012 PAWS, INC. All Rights Reserved.
STOP TEXTING EACH OTHER!
JIM DAVIS 8-5

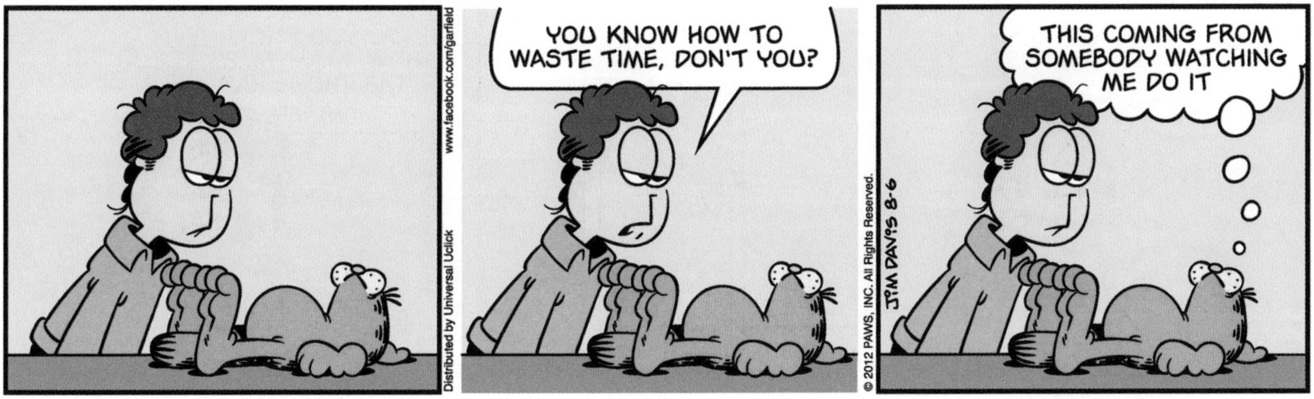
Distributed by Universal Uclick
www.facebook.com/garfield
YOU KNOW HOW TO WASTE TIME, DON'T YOU?
© 2012 PAWS, INC. All Rights Reserved.
JIM DAVIS 8-6
THIS COMING FROM SOMEBODY WATCHING ME DO IT

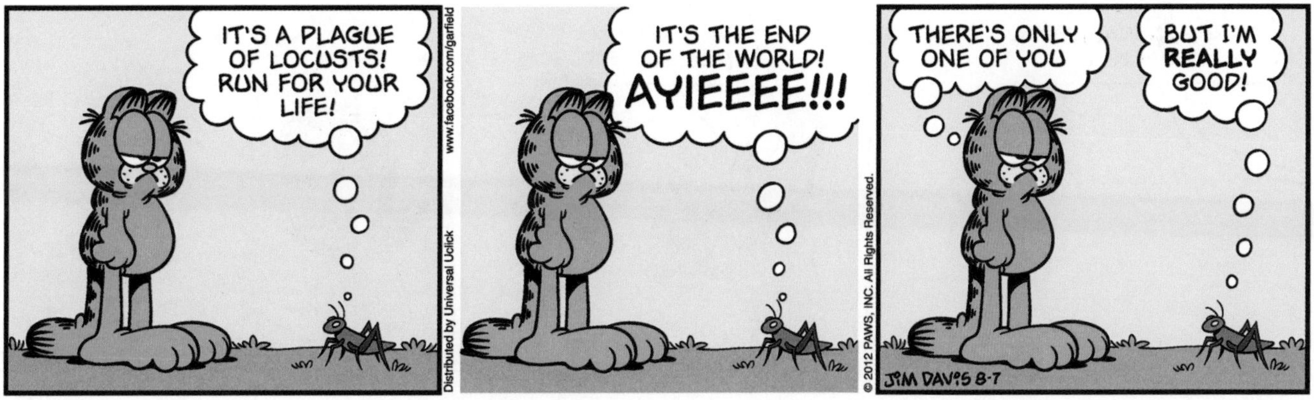
IT'S A PLAGUE OF LOCUSTS! RUN FOR YOUR LIFE!
Distributed by Universal Uclick
www.facebook.com/garfield
IT'S THE END OF THE WORLD! AYIEEEEE!!!
© 2012 PAWS, INC. All Rights Reserved.
THERE'S ONLY ONE OF YOU
BUT I'M **REALLY** GOOD!
JIM DAVIS 8-7

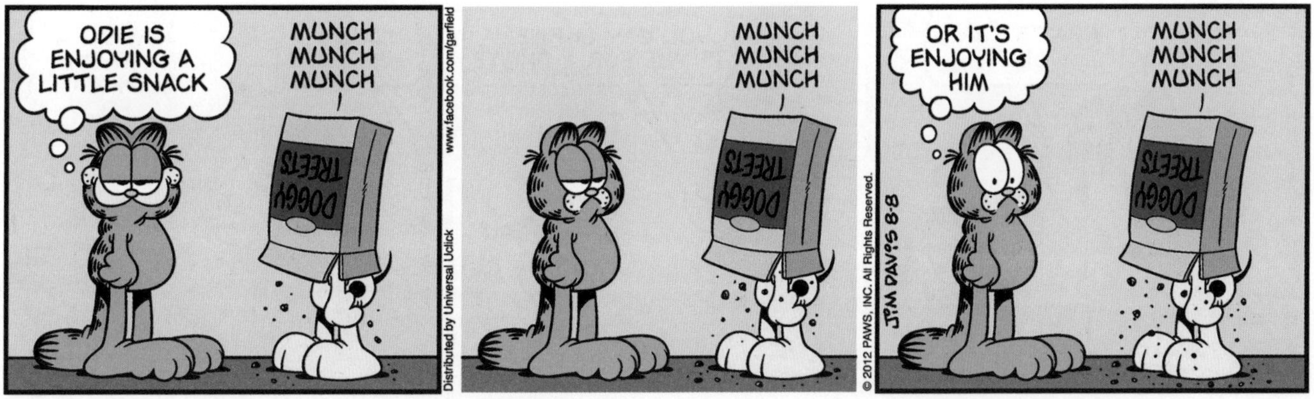
ODIE IS ENJOYING A LITTLE SNACK
MUNCH MUNCH MUNCH
DOGGY TREATS
Distributed by Universal Uclick
www.facebook.com/garfield
MUNCH MUNCH MUNCH
DOGGY TREATS
© 2012 PAWS, INC. All Rights Reserved.
JIM DAVIS 8-8
OR IT'S ENJOYING HIM
MUNCH MUNCH MUNCH
DOGGY TREATS

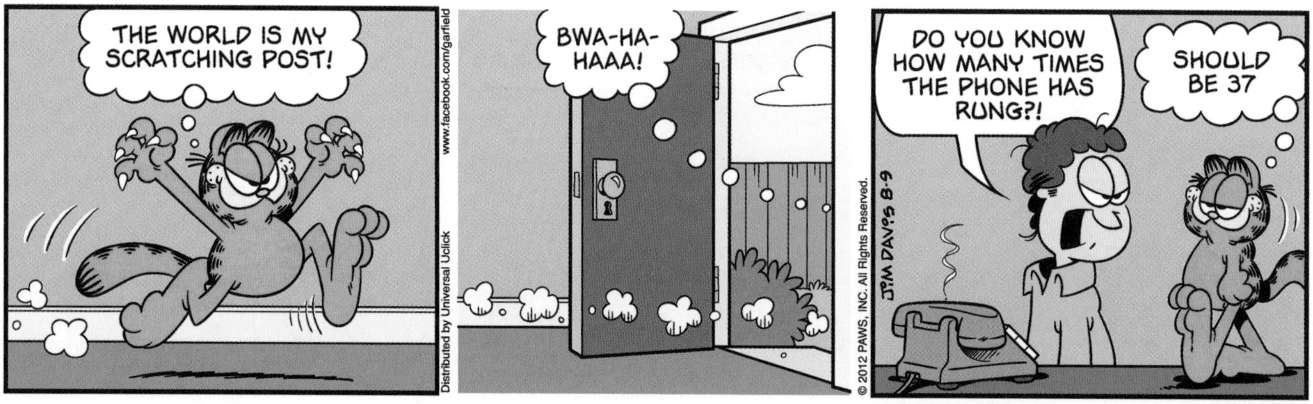
THE WORLD IS MY SCRATCHING POST!
Distributed by Universal Uclick
www.facebook.com/garfield
BWA-HA-HAAA!
© 2012 PAWS, INC. All Rights Reserved.
JIM DAVIS 8-9
DO YOU KNOW HOW MANY TIMES THE PHONE HAS RUNG?!
SHOULD BE 37

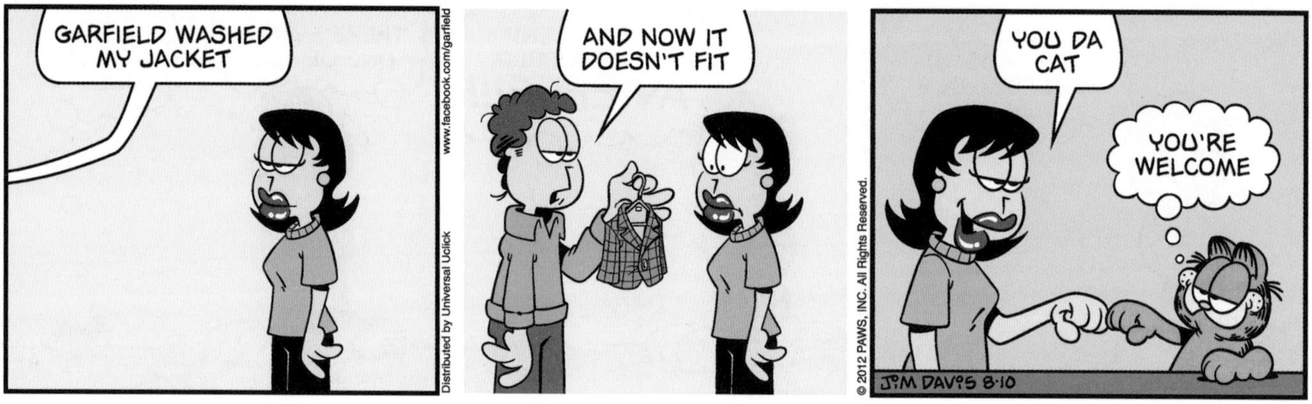
GARFIELD WASHED MY JACKET
Distributed by Universal Uclick
www.facebook.com/garfield
AND NOW IT DOESN'T FIT
© 2012 PAWS, INC. All Rights Reserved.
YOU DA CAT
YOU'RE WELCOME
JIM DAVIS 8-10

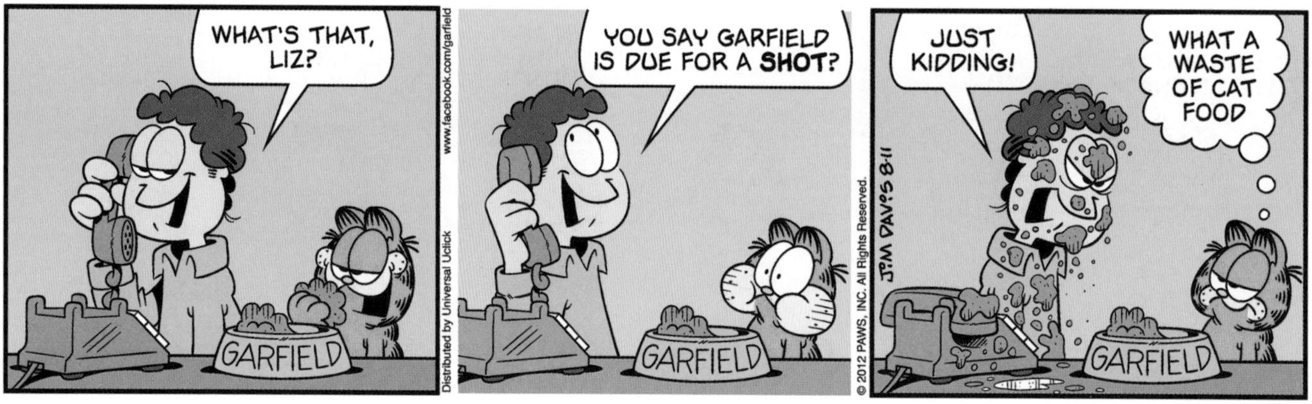
WHAT'S THAT, LIZ?
GARFIELD
Distributed by Universal Uclick
www.facebook.com/garfield
YOU SAY GARFIELD IS DUE FOR A **SHOT**?
GARFIELD
© 2012 PAWS, INC. All Rights Reserved.
JIM DAVIS 8-11
JUST KIDDING!
WHAT A WASTE OF CAT FOOD
GARFIELD

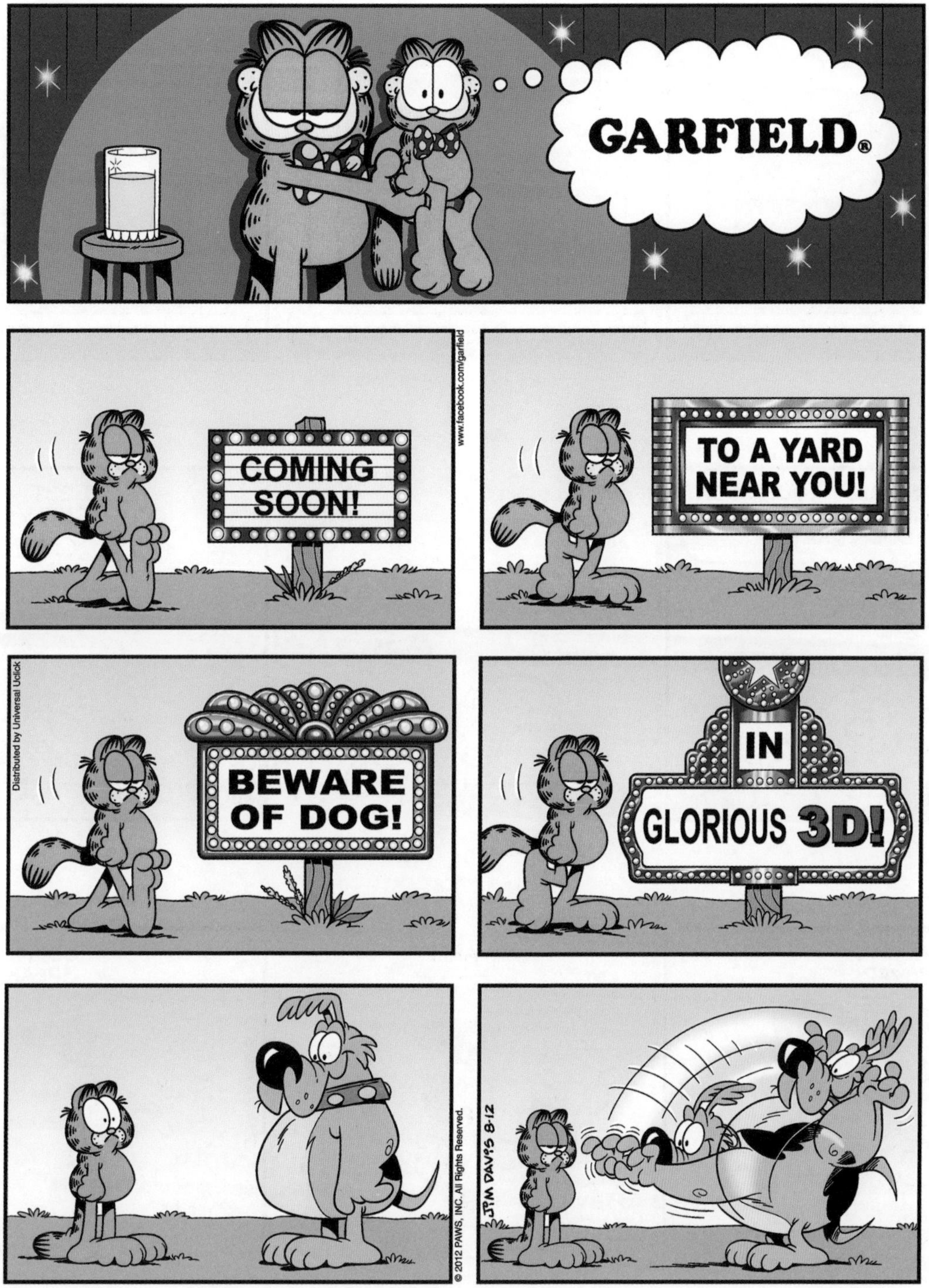
GARFIELD®
COMING SOON!
www.facebook.com/garfield
TO A YARD NEAR YOU!
Distributed by Universal Uclick
BEWARE OF DOG!
IN
GLORIOUS 3D!
© 2012 PAWS, INC. All Rights Reserved.
JPM DAVIS 8-12

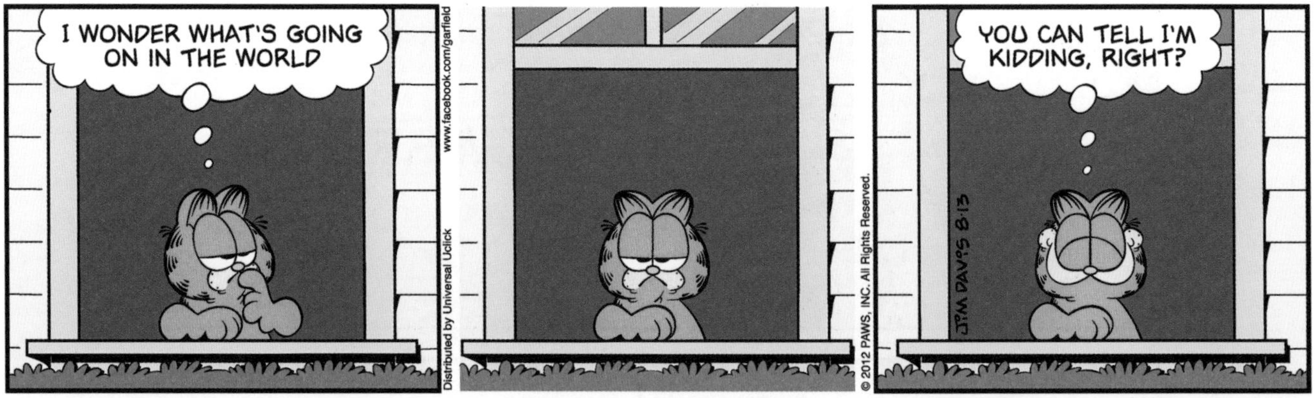
I WONDER WHAT'S GOING ON IN THE WORLD
YOU CAN TELL I'M KIDDING, RIGHT?
JIM DAVIS 8·13
Distributed by Universal Uclick www.facebook.com/garfield
© 2012 PAWS, INC. All Rights Reserved.

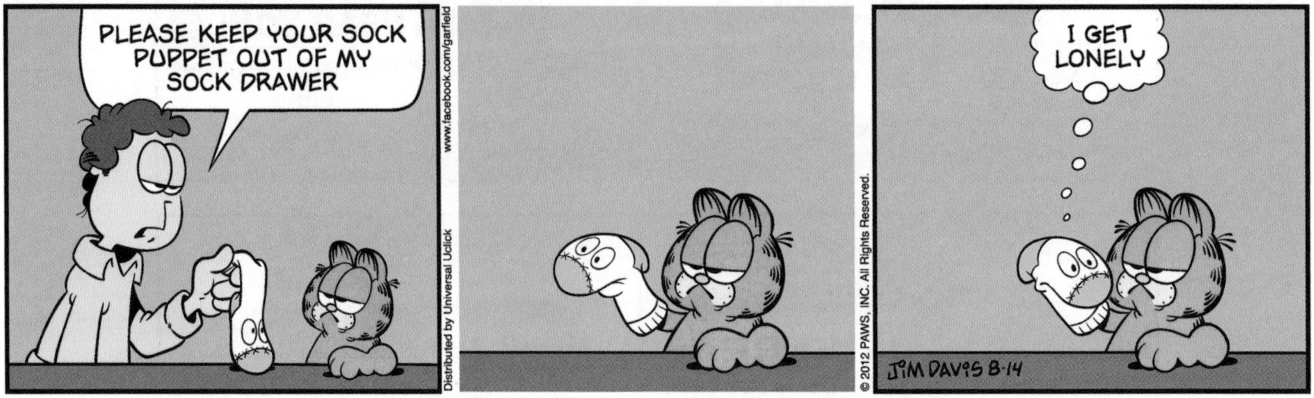
PLEASE KEEP YOUR SOCK PUPPET OUT OF MY SOCK DRAWER
I GET LONELY
JIM DAVIS 8·14
Distributed by Universal Uclick www.facebook.com/garfield
© 2012 PAWS, INC. All Rights Reserved.

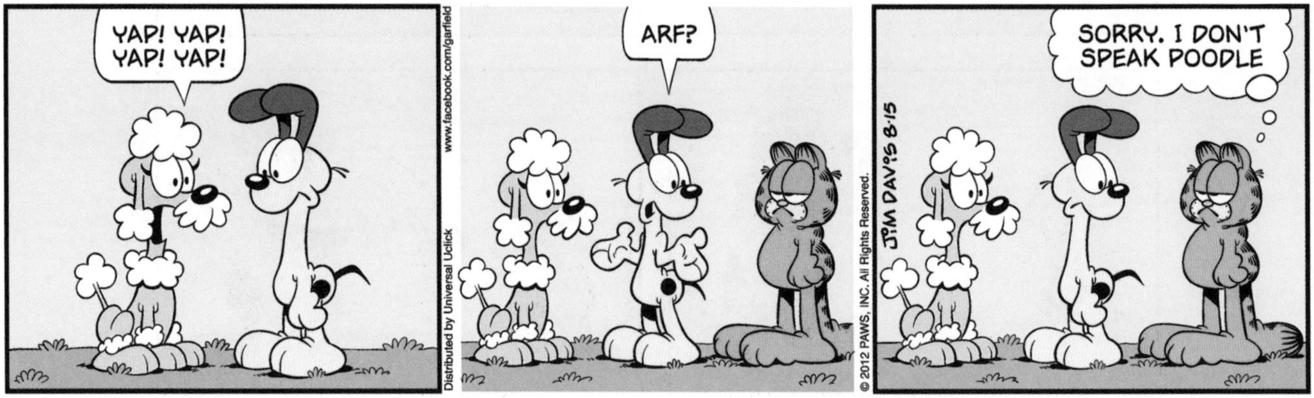
YAP! YAP! YAP! YAP!
ARF?
SORRY. I DON'T SPEAK POODLE
JIM DAVIS 8·15
Distributed by Universal Uclick www.facebook.com/garfield
© 2012 PAWS, INC. All Rights Reserved.

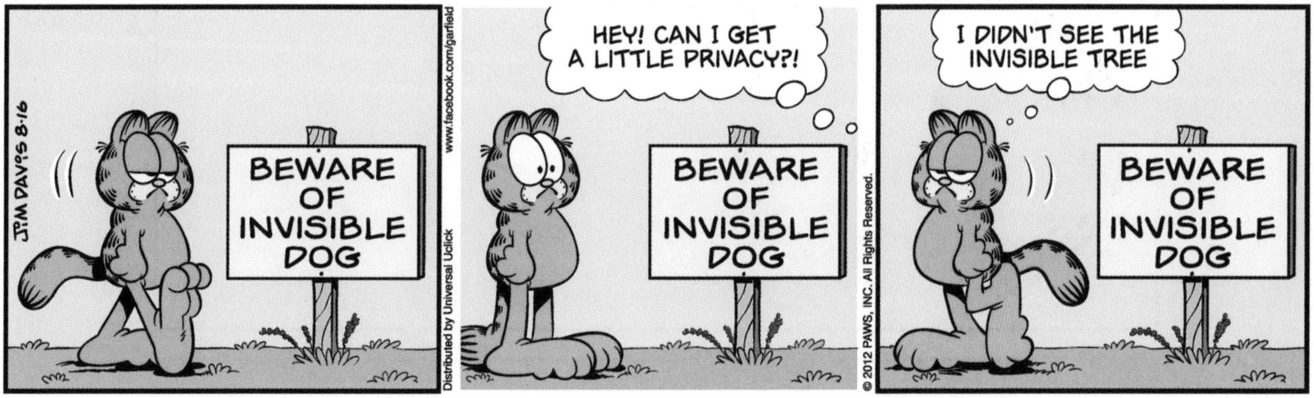
JIM DAVIS 8-16
BEWARE OF INVISIBLE DOG
Distributed by Universal Uclick
www.facebook.com/garfield
HEY! CAN I GET A LITTLE PRIVACY?!
BEWARE OF INVISIBLE DOG
© 2012 PAWS, INC. All Rights Reserved.
I DIDN'T SEE THE INVISIBLE TREE
BEWARE OF INVISIBLE DOG

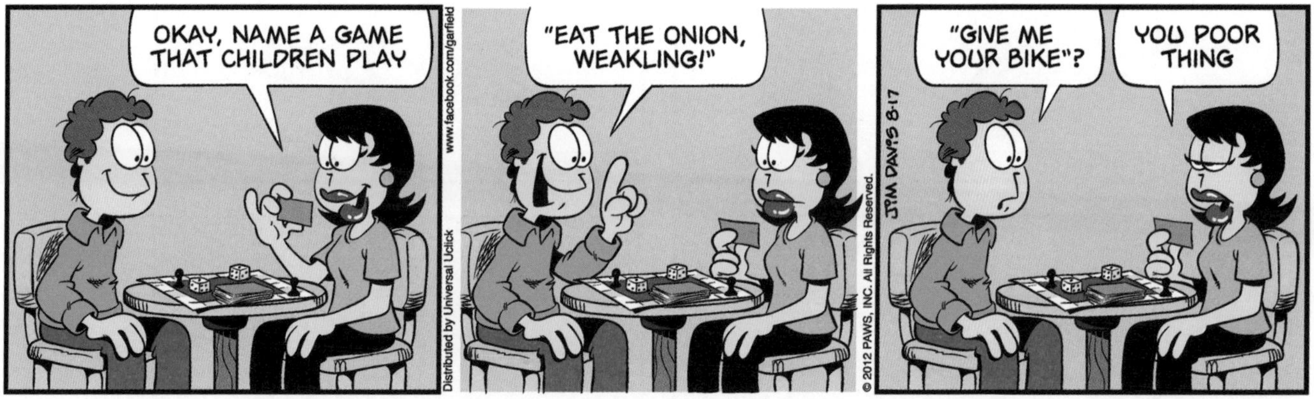
OKAY, NAME A GAME THAT CHILDREN PLAY
Distributed by Universal Uclick
www.facebook.com/garfield
"EAT THE ONION, WEAKLING!"
© 2012 PAWS, INC. All Rights Reserved.
"GIVE ME YOUR BIKE"?
YOU POOR THING
JIM DAVIS 8-17

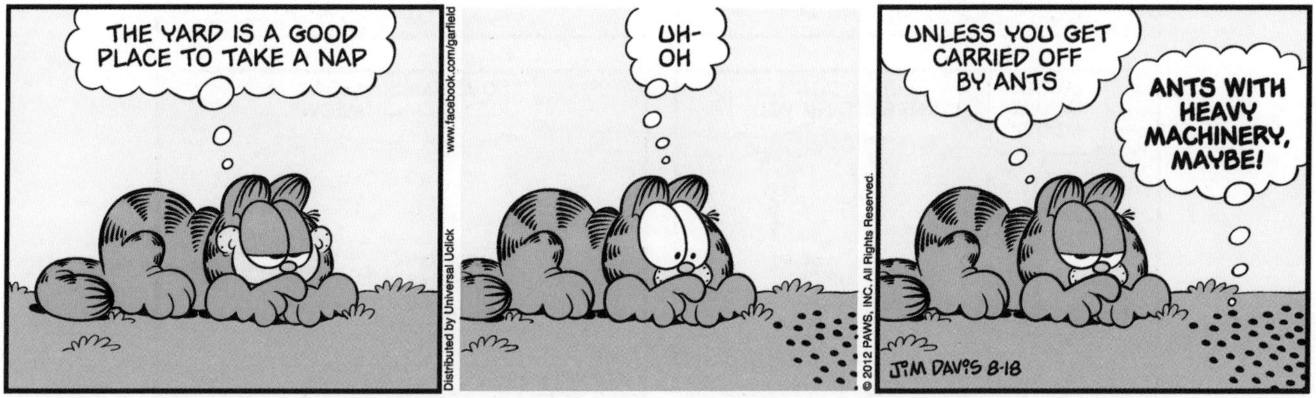
THE YARD IS A GOOD PLACE TO TAKE A NAP
Distributed by Universal Uclick
www.facebook.com/garfield
UH-OH
© 2012 PAWS, INC. All Rights Reserved.
UNLESS YOU GET CARRIED OFF BY ANTS
ANTS WITH HEAVY MACHINERY, MAYBE!
JIM DAVIS 8-18

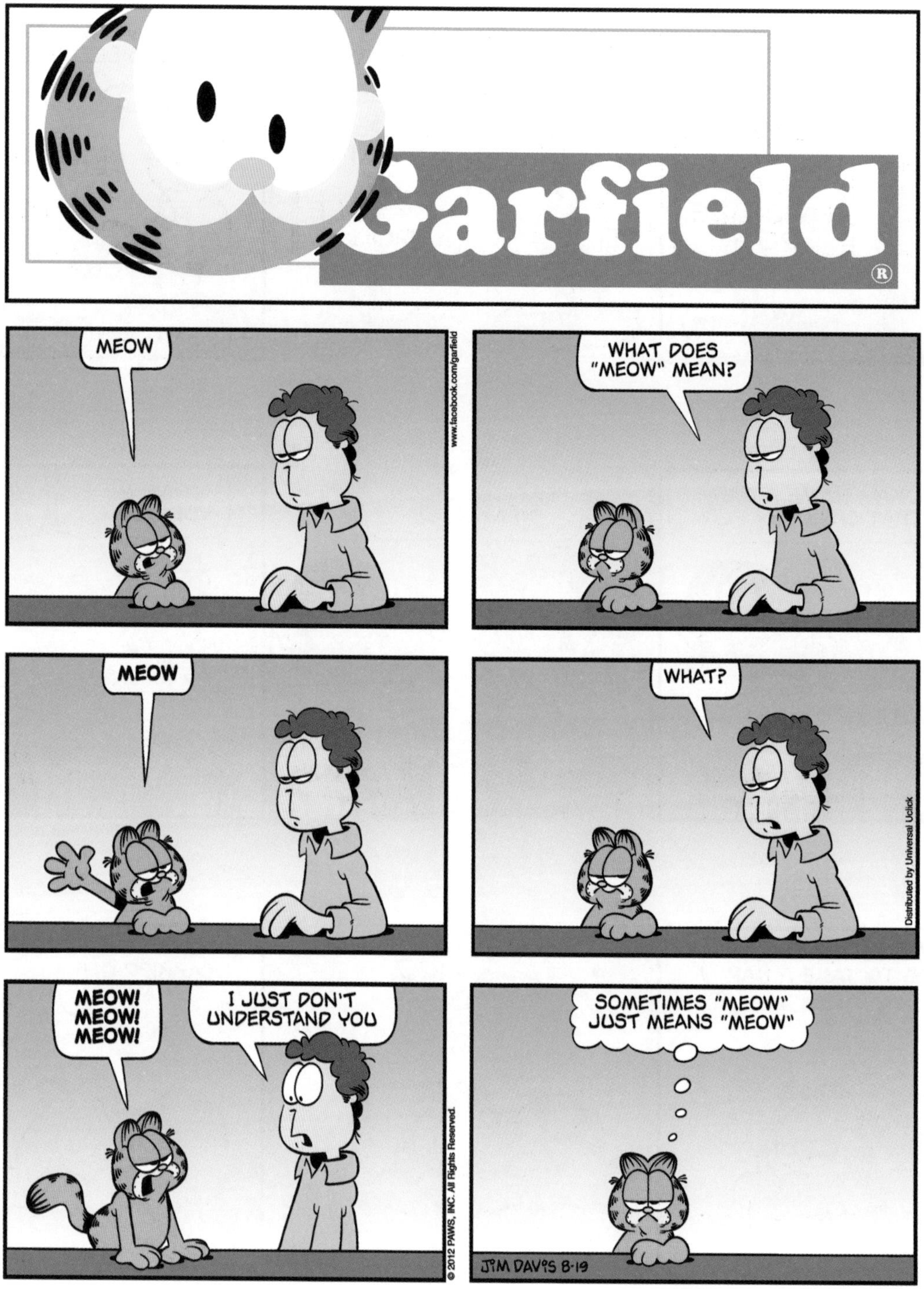
Garfield®
MEOW
www.facebook.com/garfield
WHAT DOES "MEOW" MEAN?
MEOW
WHAT?
Distributed by Universal Uclick
MEOW! MEOW! MEOW!
I JUST DON'T UNDERSTAND YOU
© 2012 PAWS, INC. All Rights Reserved.
SOMETIMES "MEOW" JUST MEANS "MEOW"
JIM DAVIS 8-19

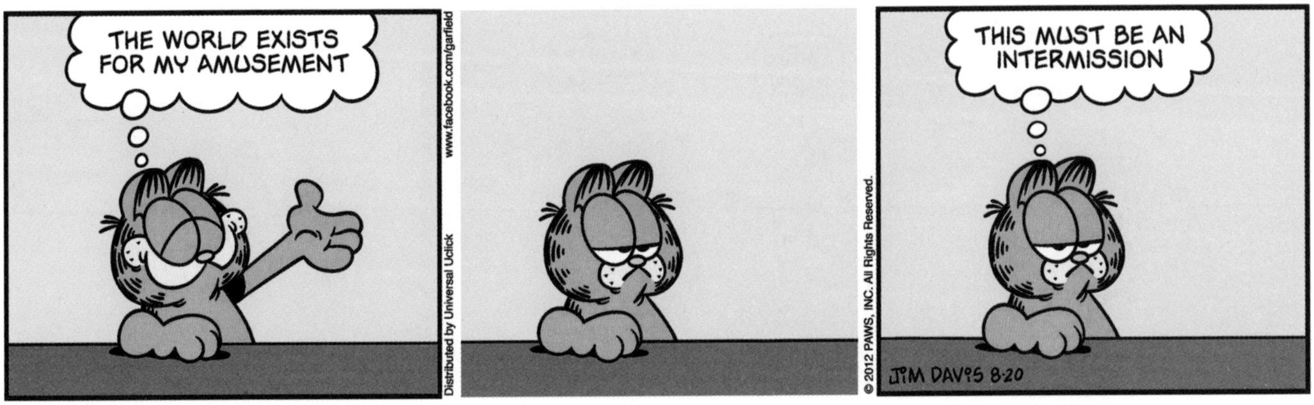
THE WORLD EXISTS FOR MY AMUSEMENT
Distributed by Universal Uclick
www.facebook.com/garfield
THIS MUST BE AN INTERMISSION
© 2012 PAWS, INC. All Rights Reserved.
JIM DAVIS 8-20

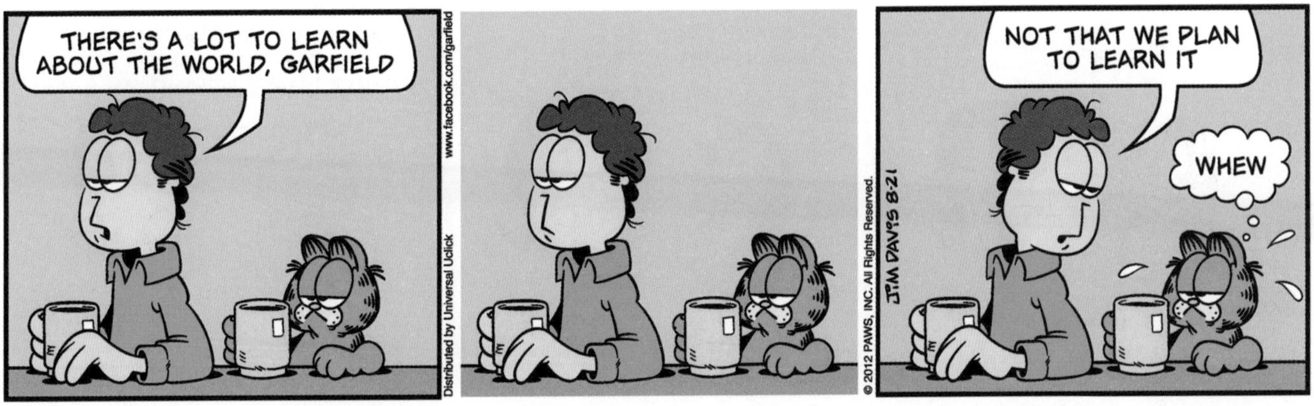
THERE'S A LOT TO LEARN ABOUT THE WORLD, GARFIELD
Distributed by Universal Uclick
www.facebook.com/garfield
© 2012 PAWS, INC. All Rights Reserved.
JIM DAVIS 8-21
NOT THAT WE PLAN TO LEARN IT
WHEW

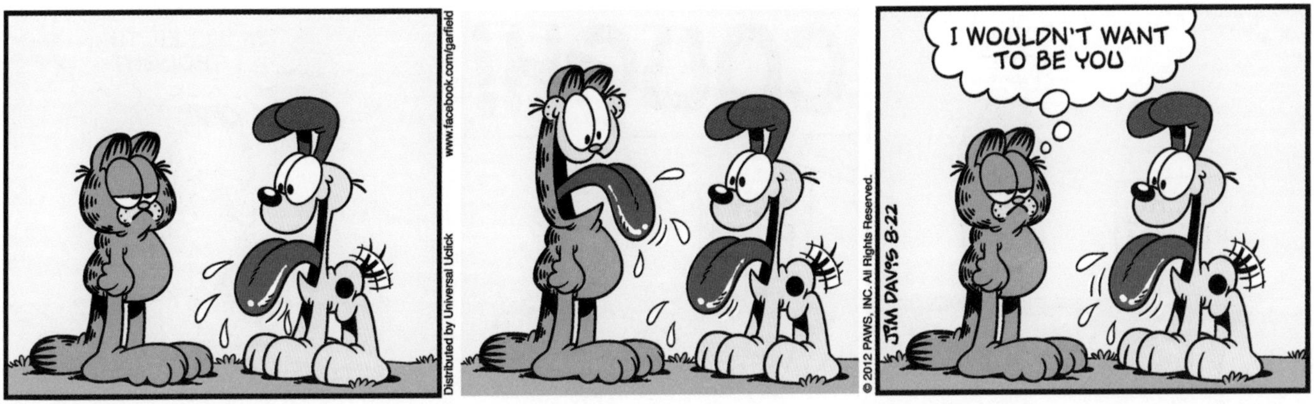
Distributed by Universal Uclick
www.facebook.com/garfield
© 2012 PAWS, INC. All Rights Reserved.
JIM DAVIS 8-22
I WOULDN'T WANT TO BE YOU

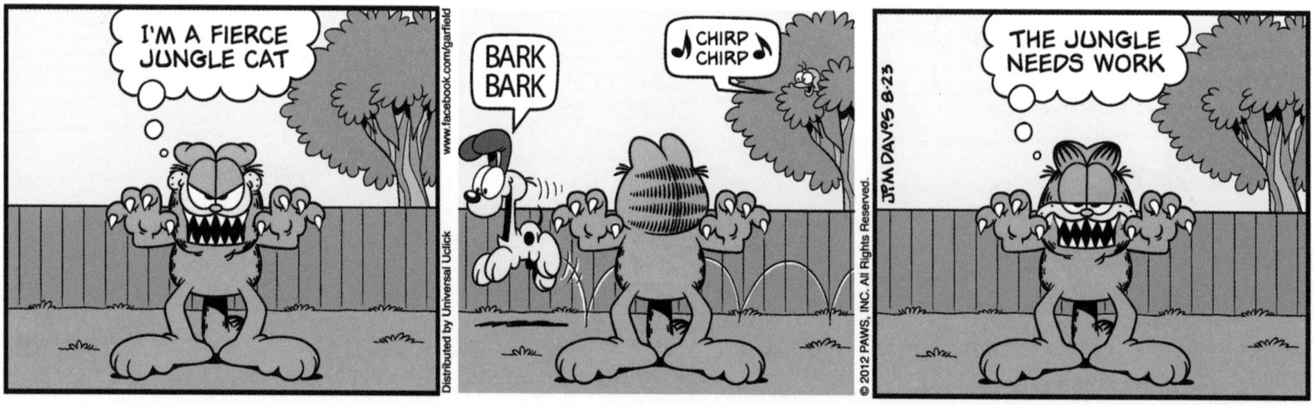
I'M A FIERCE JUNGLE CAT
Distributed by Universal Uclick www.facebook.com/garfield
BARK BARK
CHIRP CHIRP
© 2012 PAWS, INC. All Rights Reserved.
JIM DAVIS 8-23
THE JUNGLE NEEDS WORK

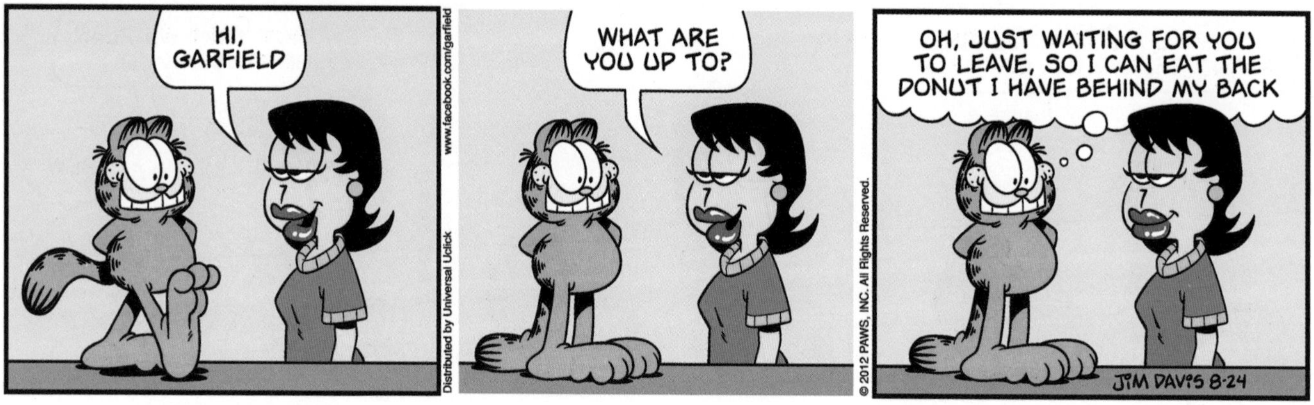
HI, GARFIELD
Distributed by Universal Uclick www.facebook.com/garfield
WHAT ARE YOU UP TO?
© 2012 PAWS, INC. All Rights Reserved.
OH, JUST WAITING FOR YOU TO LEAVE, SO I CAN EAT THE DONUT I HAVE BEHIND MY BACK
JIM DAVIS 8-24

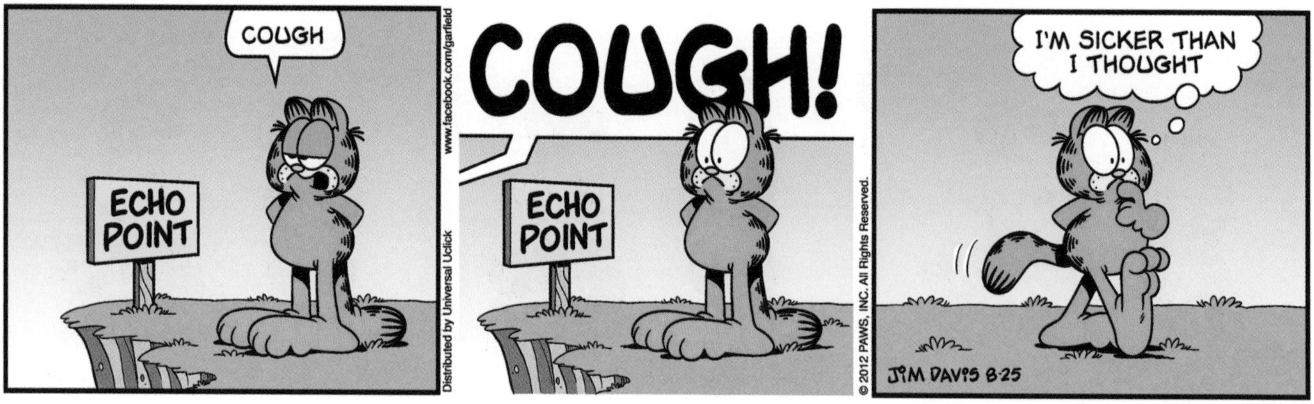
COUGH
ECHO POINT
Distributed by Universal Uclick www.facebook.com/garfield
COUGH!
ECHO POINT
© 2012 PAWS, INC. All Rights Reserved.
I'M SICKER THAN I THOUGHT
JIM DAVIS 8-25

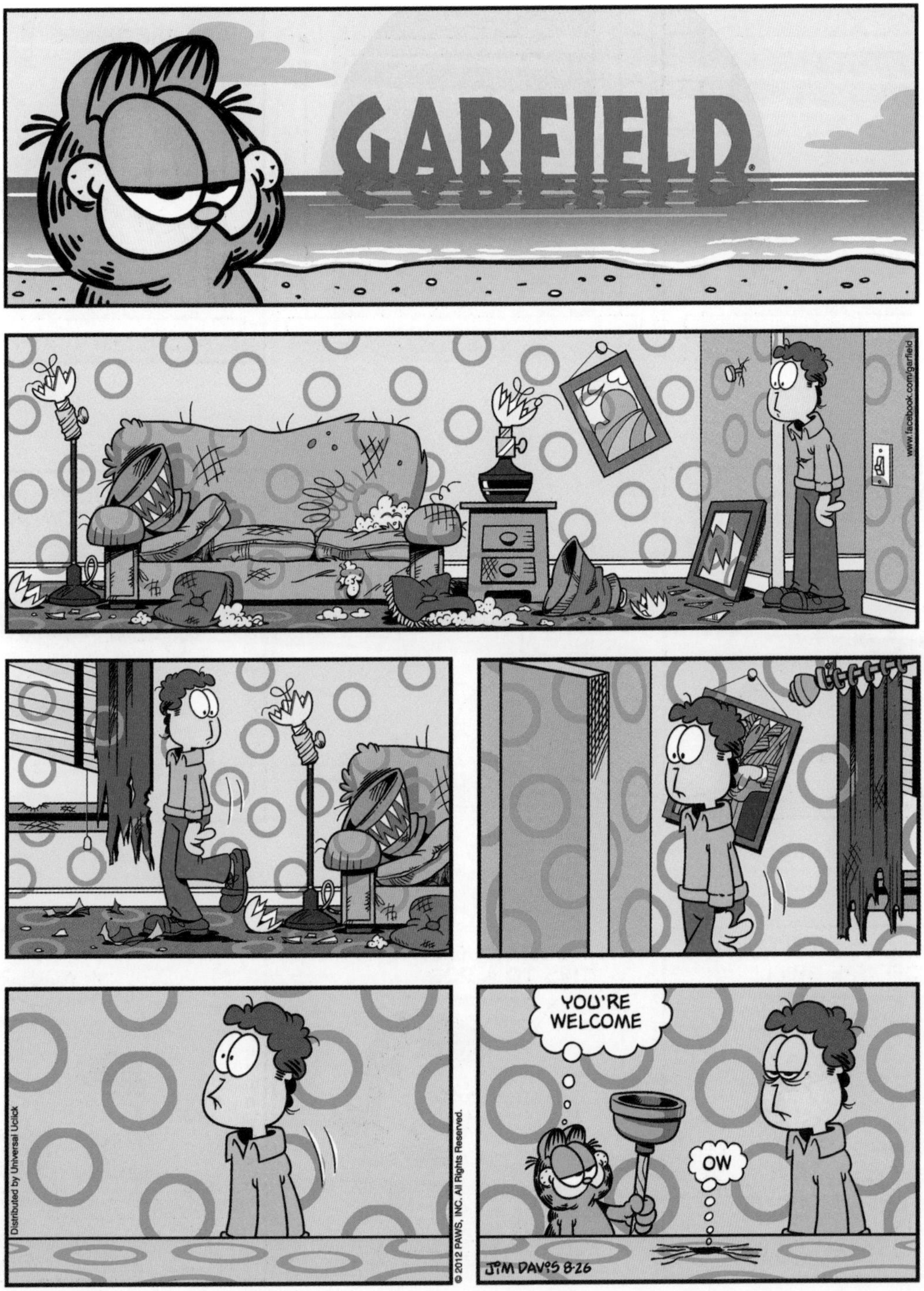
GARFIELD
www.facebook.com/garfield
Distributed by Universal Uclick
© 2012 PAWS, INC. All Rights Reserved.
YOU'RE WELCOME
OW
JIM DAVIS 8-26

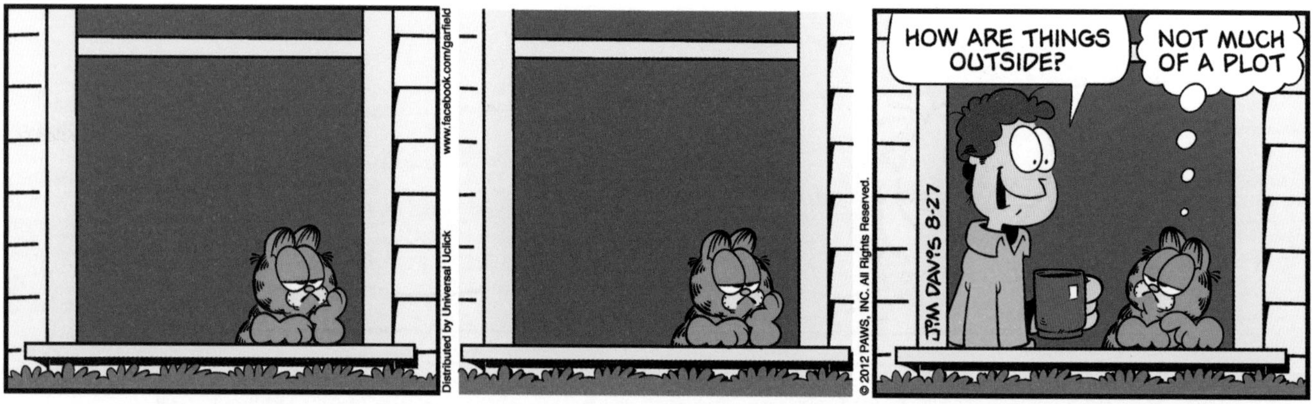
Distributed by Universal Uclick
www.facebook.com/garfield
© 2012 PAWS, INC. All Rights Reserved.
JIM DAVIS 8-27
HOW ARE THINGS OUTSIDE?
NOT MUCH OF A PLOT

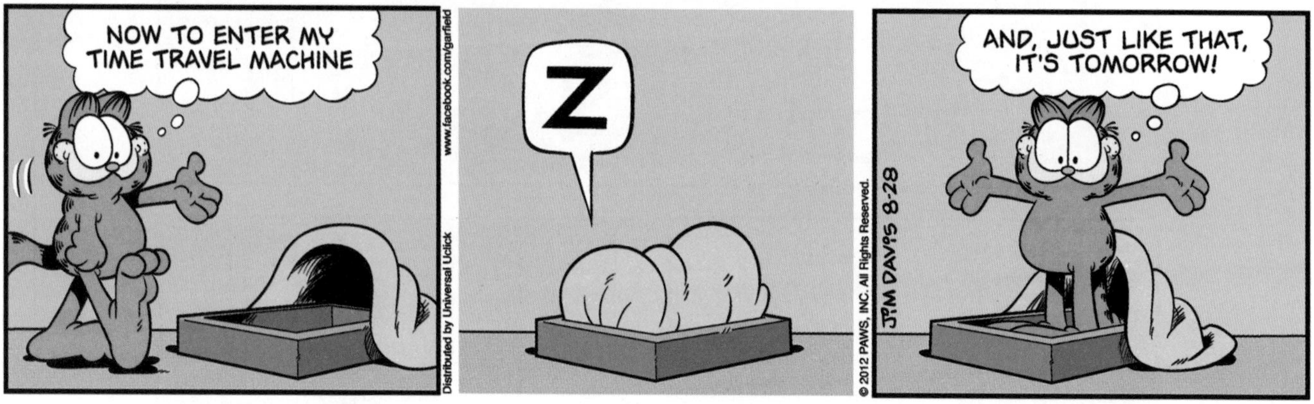
NOW TO ENTER MY TIME TRAVEL MACHINE
Distributed by Universal Uclick
www.facebook.com/garfield
Z
© 2012 PAWS, INC. All Rights Reserved.
JIM DAVIS 8-28
AND, JUST LIKE THAT, IT'S TOMORROW!

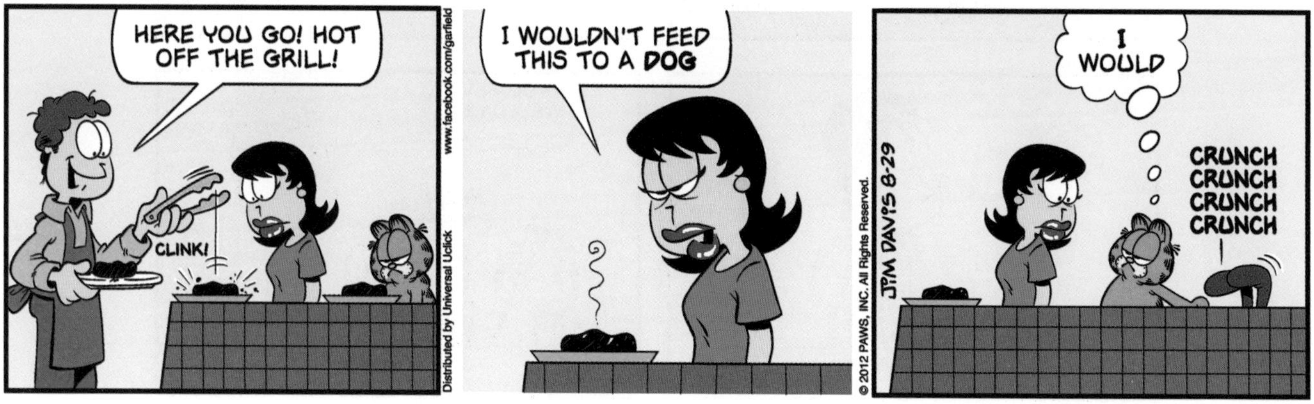
HERE YOU GO! HOT OFF THE GRILL!
CLINK!
Distributed by Universal Uclick
www.facebook.com/garfield
I WOULDN'T FEED THIS TO A DOG
© 2012 PAWS, INC. All Rights Reserved.
JIM DAVIS 8-29
I WOULD
CRUNCH
CRUNCH
CRUNCH
CRUNCH

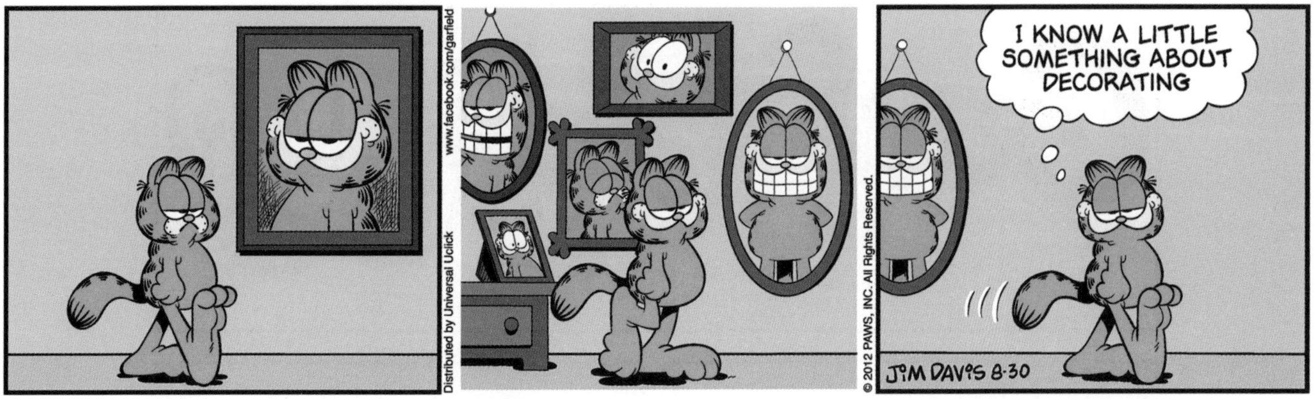
Distributed by Universal Uclick
www.facebook.com/garfield
© 2012 PAWS, INC. All Rights Reserved.
I KNOW A LITTLE SOMETHING ABOUT DECORATING
JIM DAVIS 8-30

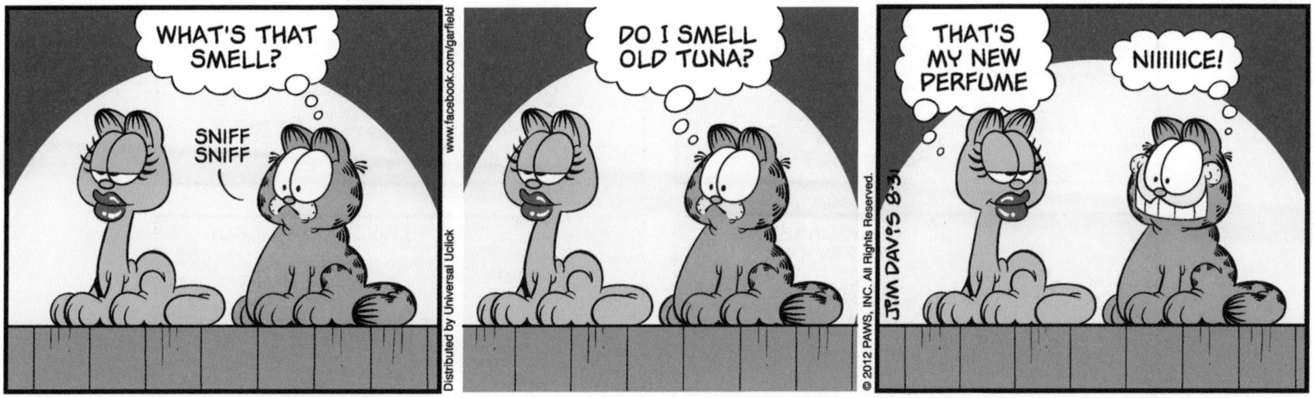
WHAT'S THAT SMELL?
SNIFF SNIFF
Distributed by Universal Uclick
www.facebook.com/garfield
DO I SMELL OLD TUNA?
© 2012 PAWS, INC. All Rights Reserved.
JIM DAVIS 8-31
THAT'S MY NEW PERFUME
NIIIIIICE!

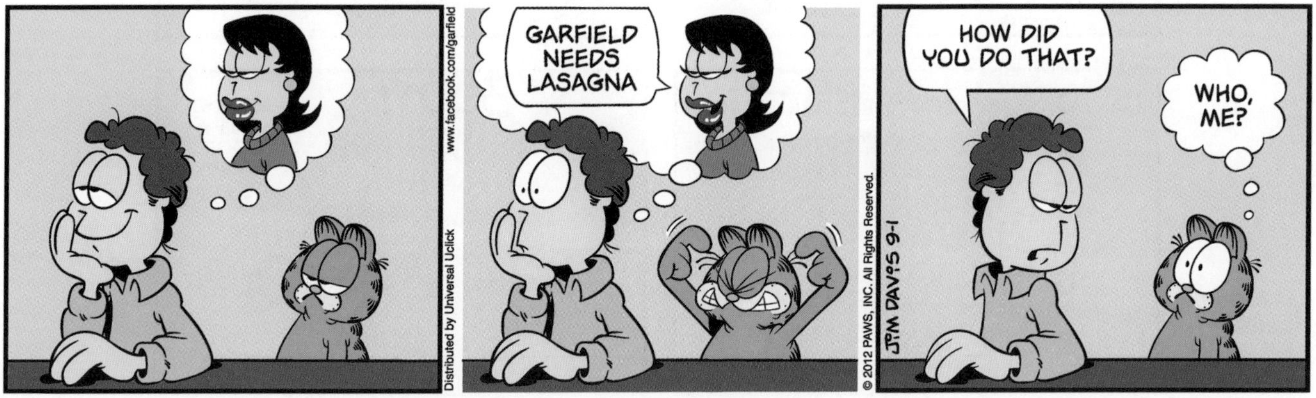
Distributed by Universal Uclick
www.facebook.com/garfield
GARFIELD NEEDS LASAGNA
© 2012 PAWS, INC. All Rights Reserved.
JIM DAVIS 9-1
HOW DID YOU DO THAT?
WHO, ME?

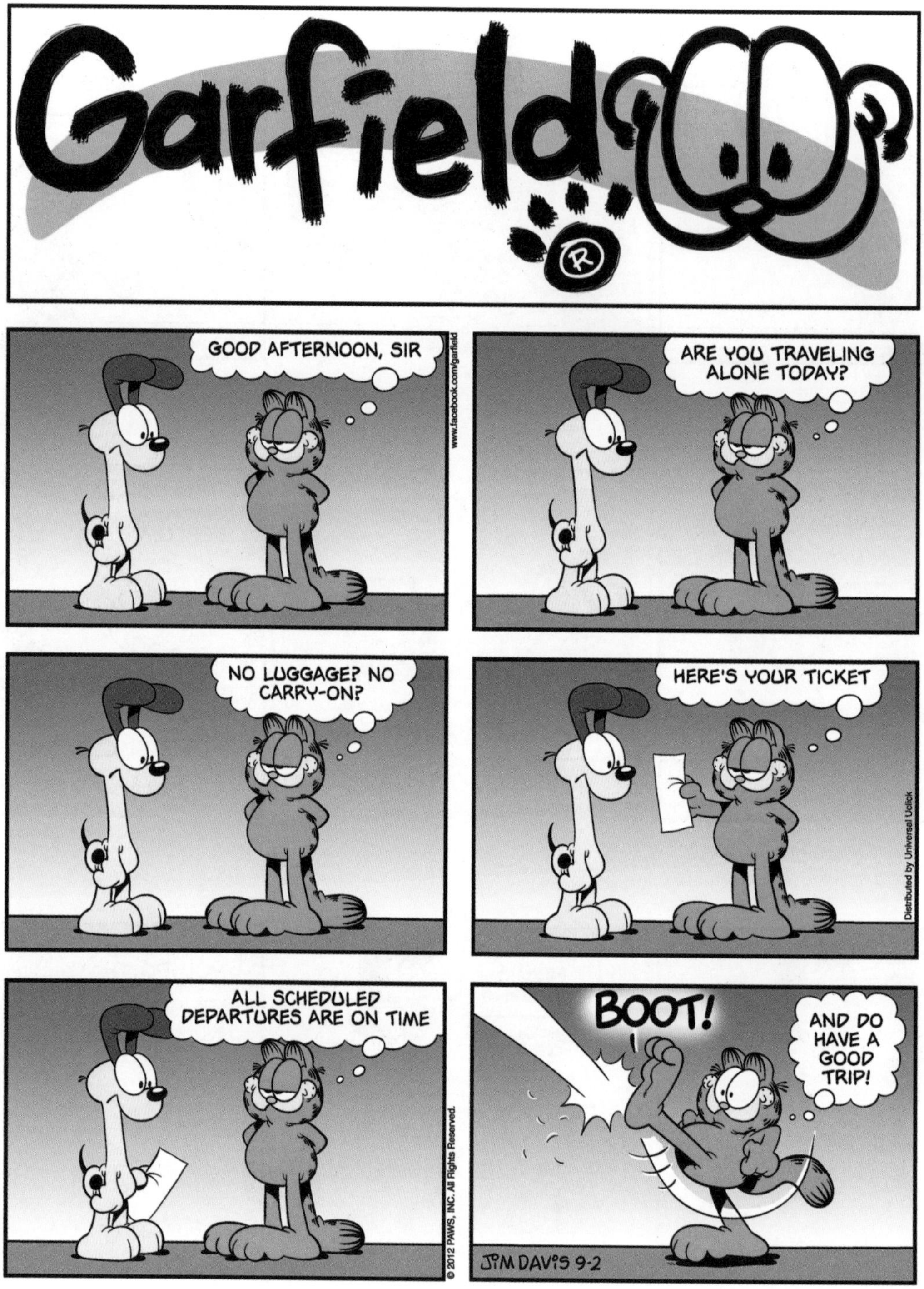
Garfield®
GOOD AFTERNOON, SIR
www.facebook.com/garfield
ARE YOU TRAVELING ALONE TODAY?
NO LUGGAGE? NO CARRY-ON?
HERE'S YOUR TICKET
Distributed by Universal Uclick
ALL SCHEDULED DEPARTURES ARE ON TIME
© 2012 PAWS, INC. All Rights Reserved.
BOOT!
AND DO HAVE A GOOD TRIP!
JIM DAVIS 9-2

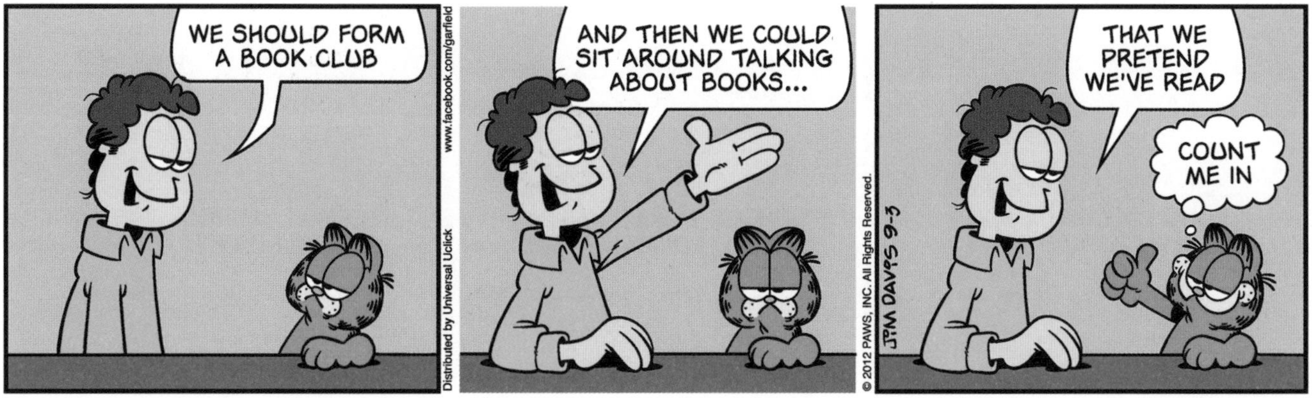
WE SHOULD FORM A BOOK CLUB
AND THEN WE COULD SIT AROUND TALKING ABOUT BOOKS...
THAT WE PRETEND WE'VE READ
COUNT ME IN
JIM DAVIS 9-3
Distributed by Universal Uclick www.facebook.com/garfield
© 2012 PAWS, INC. All Rights Reserved.

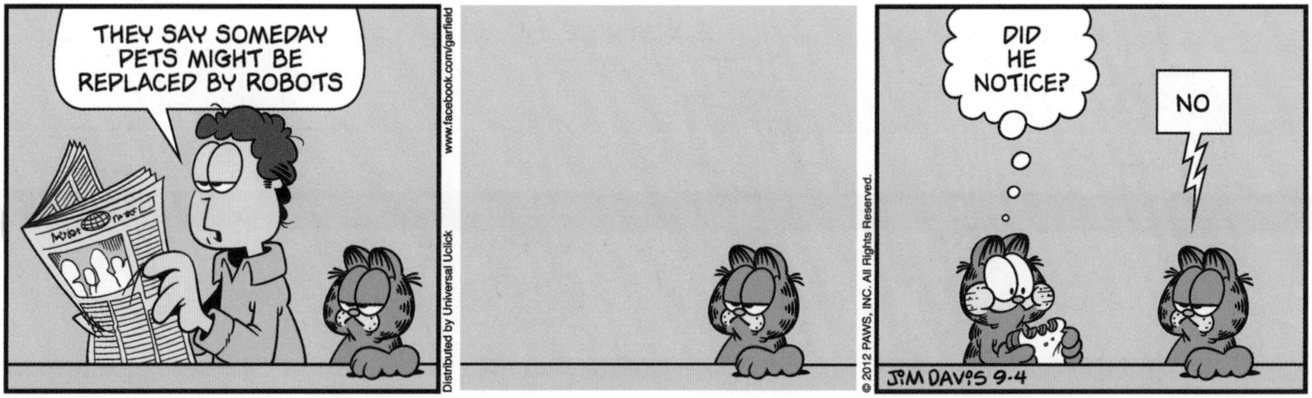
THEY SAY SOMEDAY PETS MIGHT BE REPLACED BY ROBOTS
DID HE NOTICE?
NO
JIM DAVIS 9-4
Distributed by Universal Uclick www.facebook.com/garfield
© 2012 PAWS, INC. All Rights Reserved.

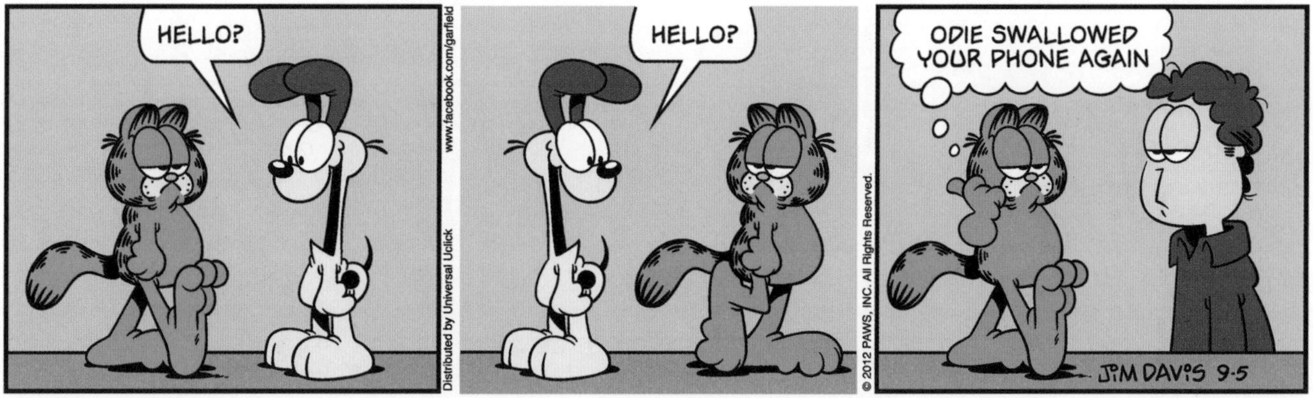
HELLO?
HELLO?
ODIE SWALLOWED YOUR PHONE AGAIN
JIM DAVIS 9-5
Distributed by Universal Uclick www.facebook.com/garfield
© 2012 PAWS, INC. All Rights Reserved.

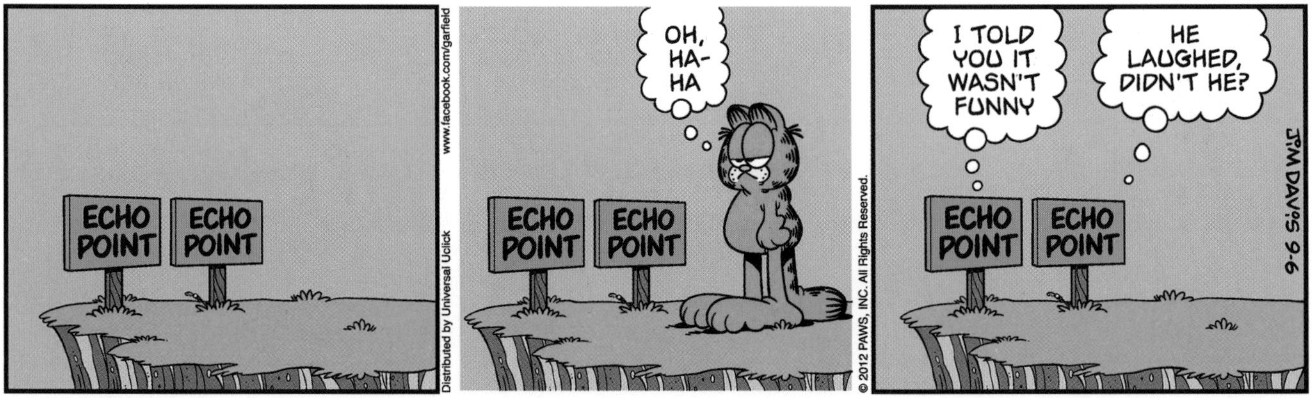
ECHO POINT
ECHO POINT
Distributed by Universal Uclick www.facebook.com/garfield
OH, HA-HA
© 2012 PAWS, INC. All Rights Reserved.
I TOLD YOU IT WASN'T FUNNY
HE LAUGHED, DIDN'T HE?
JIM DAVIS 9-6

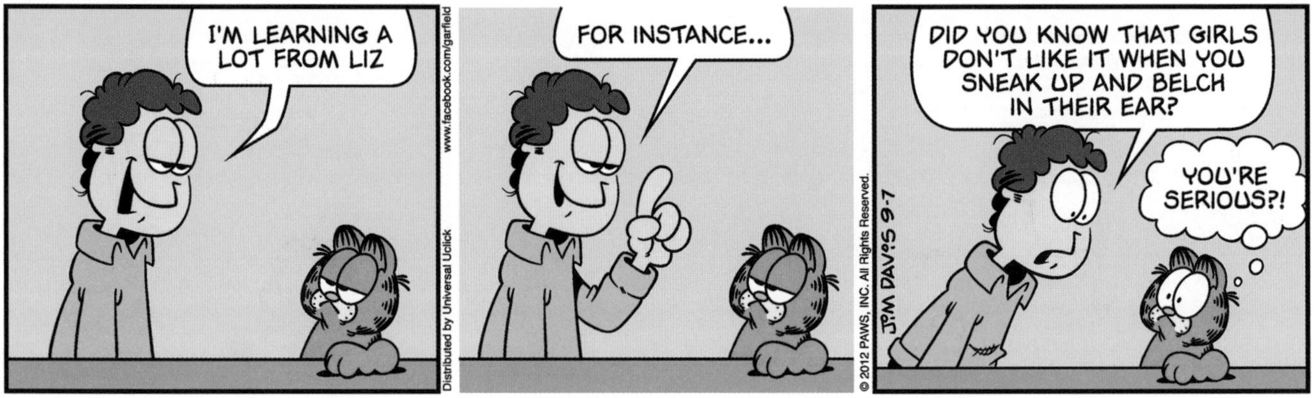
I'M LEARNING A LOT FROM LIZ
Distributed by Universal Uclick www.facebook.com/garfield
FOR INSTANCE...
© 2012 PAWS, INC. All Rights Reserved.
JIM DAVIS 9-7
DID YOU KNOW THAT GIRLS DON'T LIKE IT WHEN YOU SNEAK UP AND BELCH IN THEIR EAR?
YOU'RE SERIOUS?!

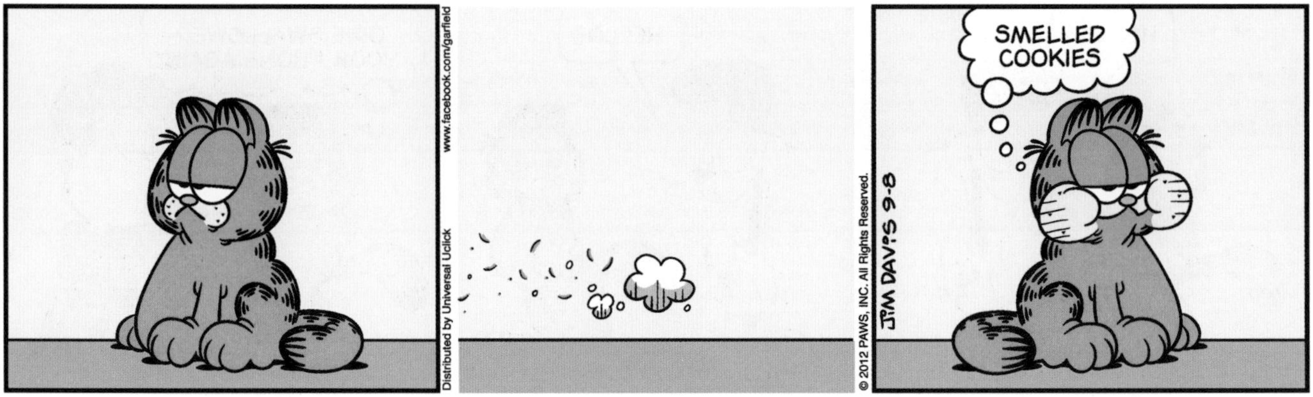
Distributed by Universal Uclick www.facebook.com/garfield
© 2012 PAWS, INC. All Rights Reserved.
JIM DAVIS 9-8
SMELLED COOKIES

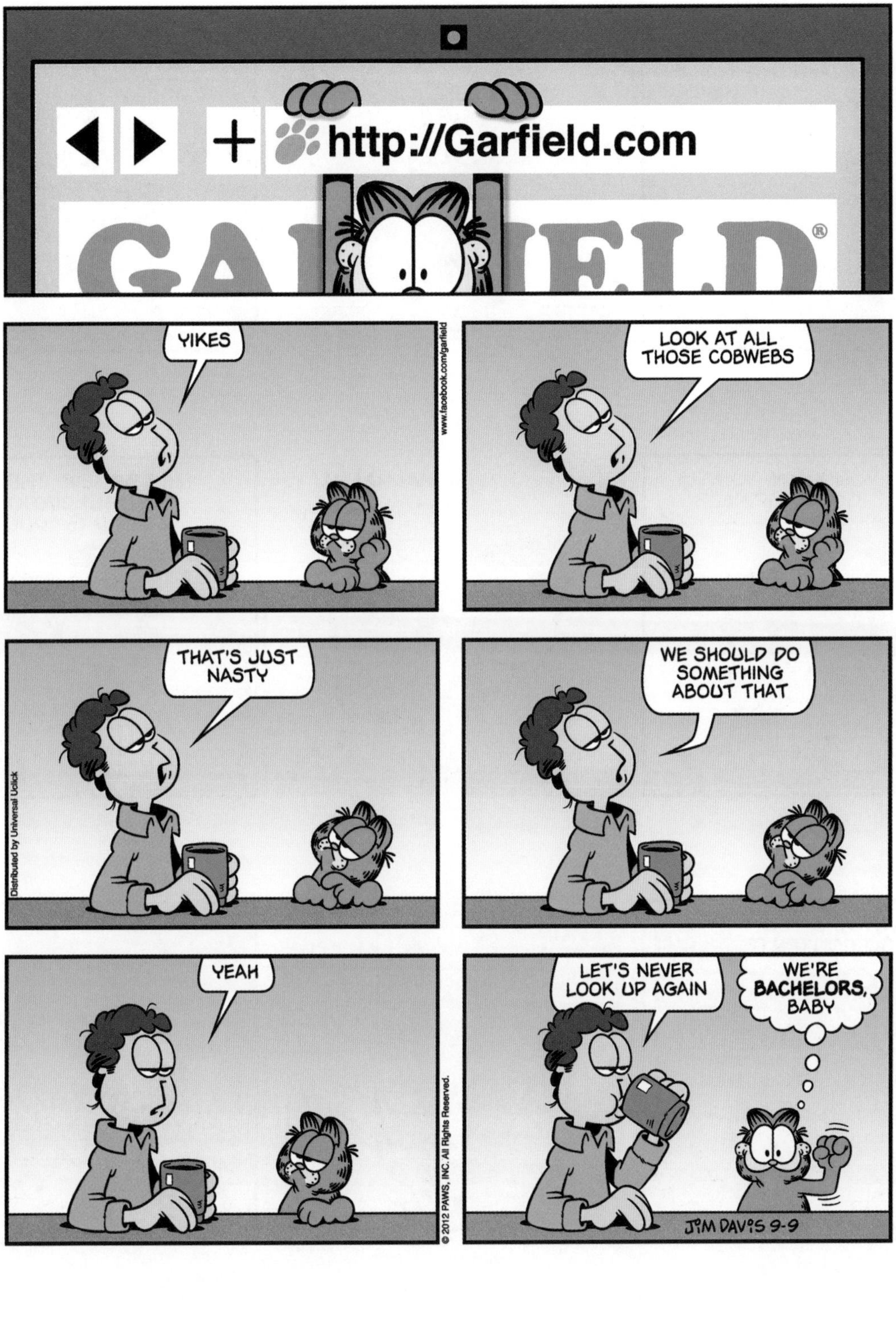
http://Garfield.com
GARFIELD®
YIKES
www.facebook.com/garfield
LOOK AT ALL THOSE COBWEBS
THAT'S JUST NASTY
Distributed by Universal Uclick
WE SHOULD DO SOMETHING ABOUT THAT
YEAH
© 2012 PAWS, INC. All Rights Reserved.
LET'S NEVER LOOK UP AGAIN
WE'RE **BACHELORS,** BABY
JIM DAVIS 9-9

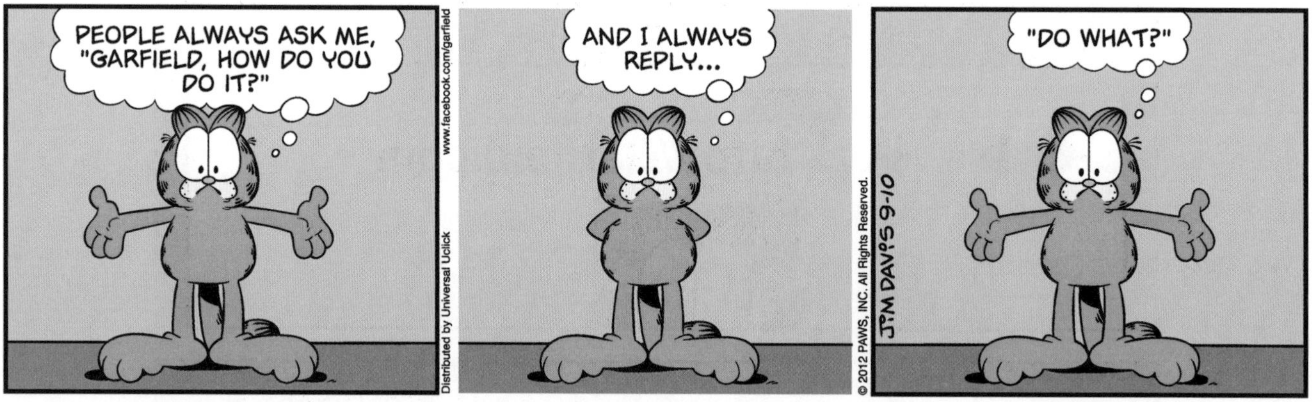
PEOPLE ALWAYS ASK ME, "GARFIELD, HOW DO YOU DO IT?"
AND I ALWAYS REPLY...
"DO WHAT?"
JIM DAVIS 9-10
Distributed by Universal Uclick www.facebook.com/garfield
© 2012 PAWS, INC. All Rights Reserved.

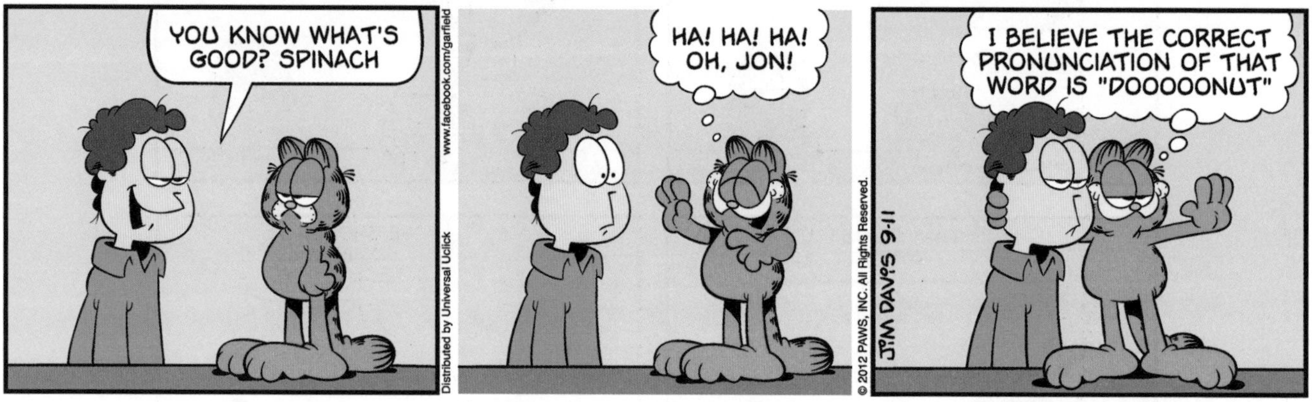
YOU KNOW WHAT'S GOOD? SPINACH
HA! HA! HA! OH, JON!
I BELIEVE THE CORRECT PRONUNCIATION OF THAT WORD IS "DOOOOONUT"
JIM DAVIS 9-11
Distributed by Universal Uclick www.facebook.com/garfield
© 2012 PAWS, INC. All Rights Reserved.

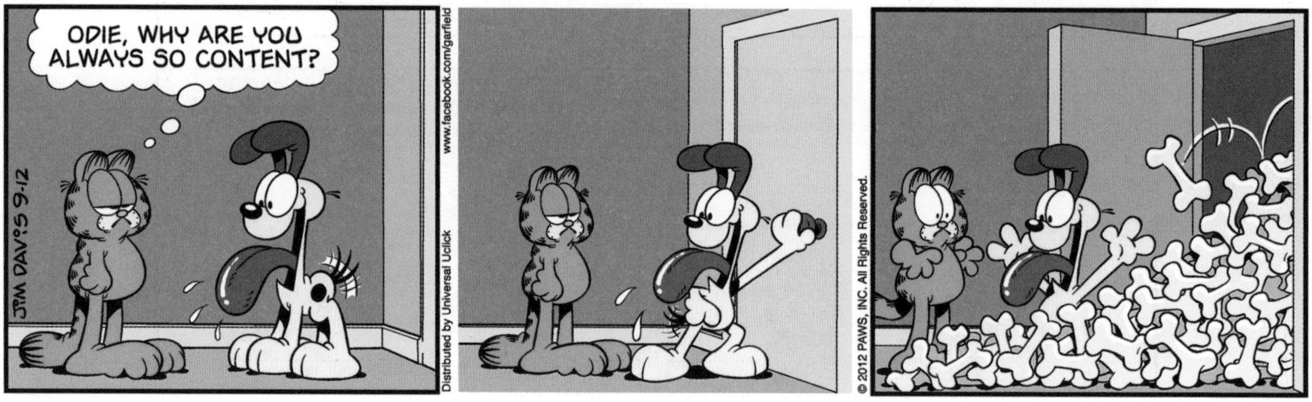
ODIE, WHY ARE YOU ALWAYS SO CONTENT?
JIM DAVIS 9-12
Distributed by Universal Uclick www.facebook.com/garfield
© 2012 PAWS, INC. All Rights Reserved.

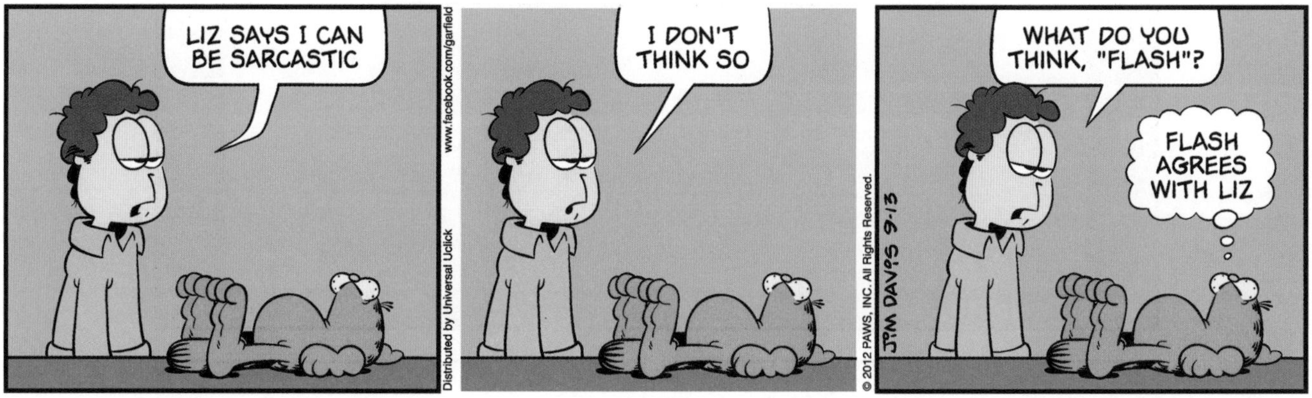
LIZ SAYS I CAN BE SARCASTIC
I DON'T THINK SO
WHAT DO YOU THINK, "FLASH"?
FLASH AGREES WITH LIZ
Distributed by Universal Uclick
www.facebook.com/garfield
© 2012 PAWS, INC. All Rights Reserved.
JIM DAVIS 9-13

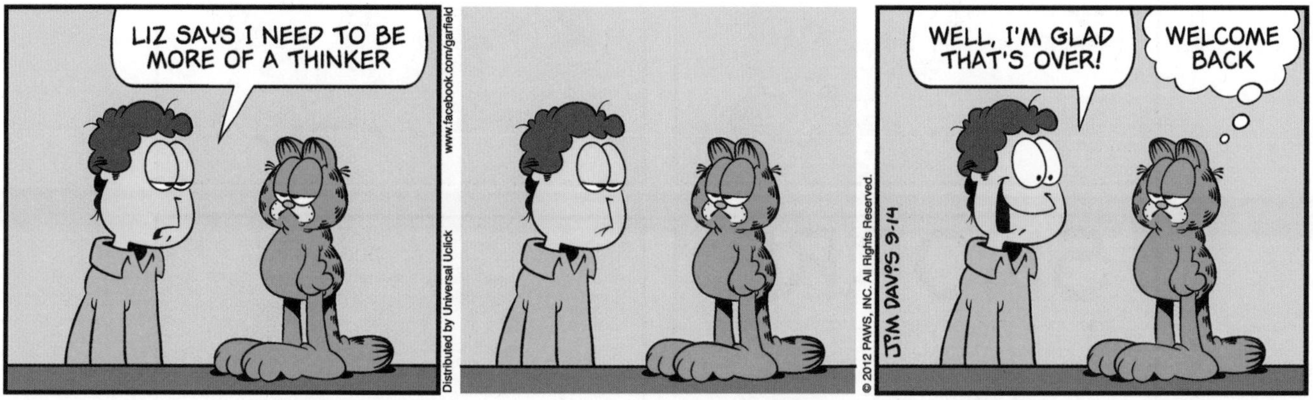
LIZ SAYS I NEED TO BE MORE OF A THINKER
WELL, I'M GLAD THAT'S OVER!
WELCOME BACK
Distributed by Universal Uclick
www.facebook.com/garfield
© 2012 PAWS, INC. All Rights Reserved.
JIM DAVIS 9-14

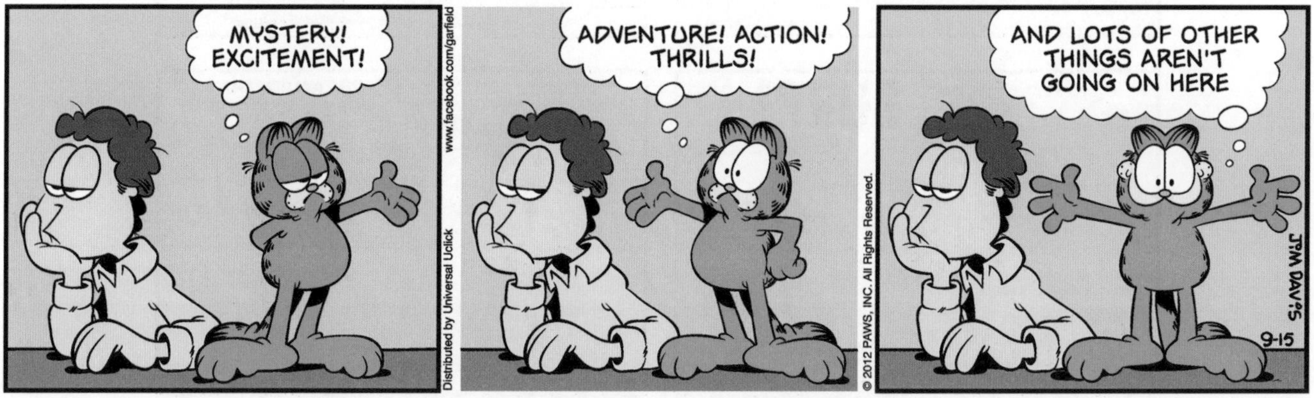
MYSTERY! EXCITEMENT!
ADVENTURE! ACTION! THRILLS!
AND LOTS OF OTHER THINGS AREN'T GOING ON HERE
Distributed by Universal Uclick
www.facebook.com/garfield
© 2012 PAWS, INC. All Rights Reserved.
JIM DAVIS
9-15

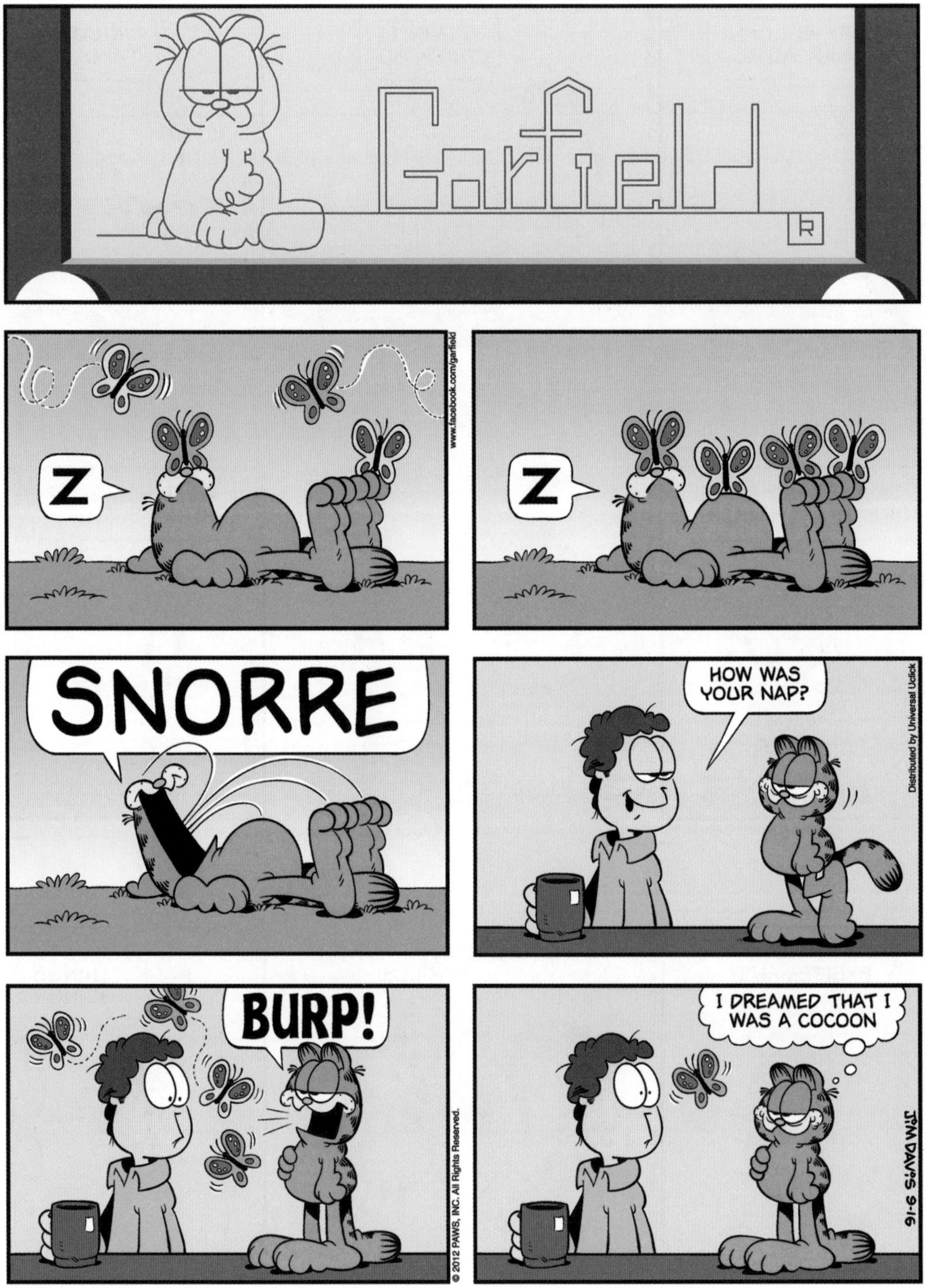
Garfield
www.facebook.com/garfield
Z
Z
SNORRE
HOW WAS YOUR NAP?
Distributed by Universal Uclick
BURP!
© 2012 PAWS, INC. All Rights Reserved.
I DREAMED THAT I WAS A COCOON
JPM DAVIS 9-16

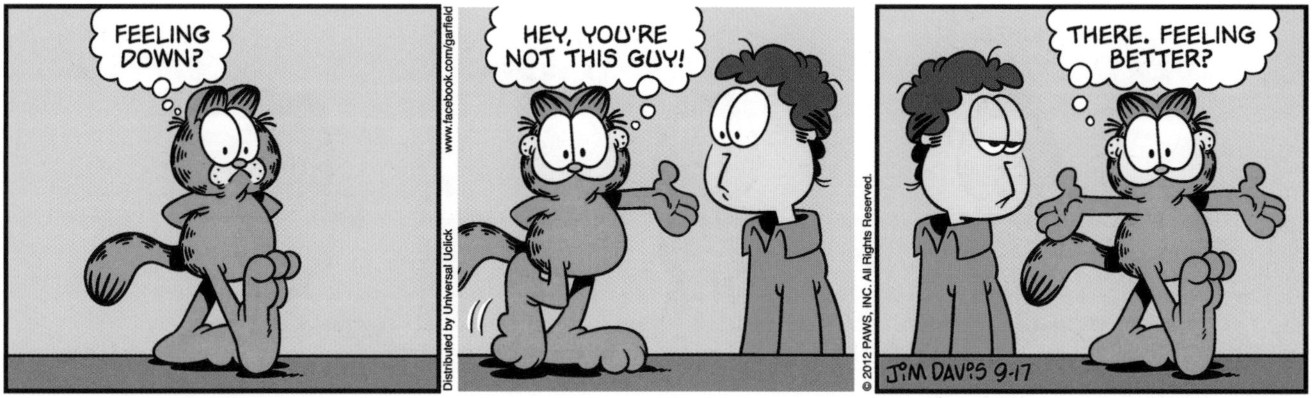
FEELING DOWN?
HEY, YOU'RE NOT THIS GUY!
THERE. FEELING BETTER?
Distributed by Universal Uclick www.facebook.com/garfield
© 2012 PAWS, INC. All Rights Reserved.
JIM DAVIS 9-17

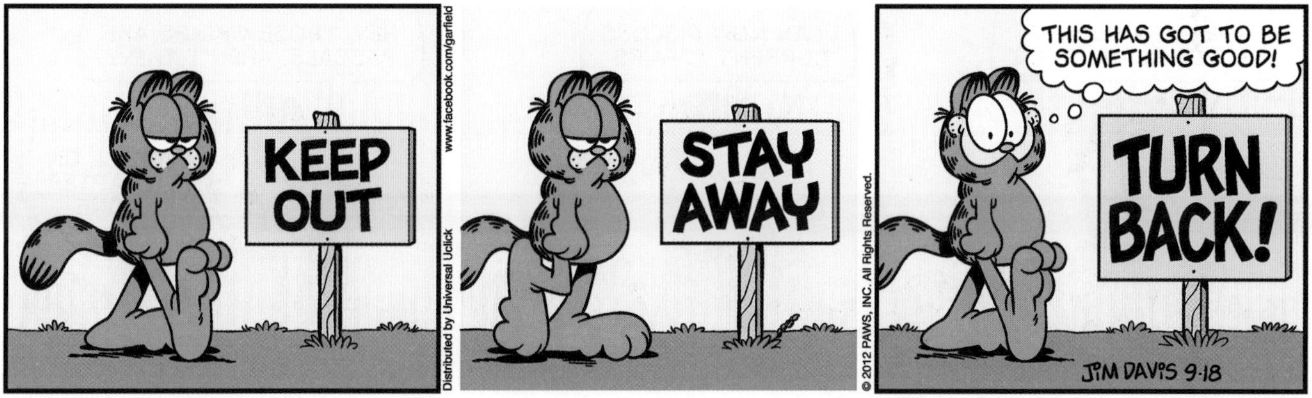
KEEP OUT
STAY AWAY
THIS HAS GOT TO BE SOMETHING GOOD!
TURN BACK!
Distributed by Universal Uclick www.facebook.com/garfield
© 2012 PAWS, INC. All Rights Reserved.
JIM DAVIS 9-18

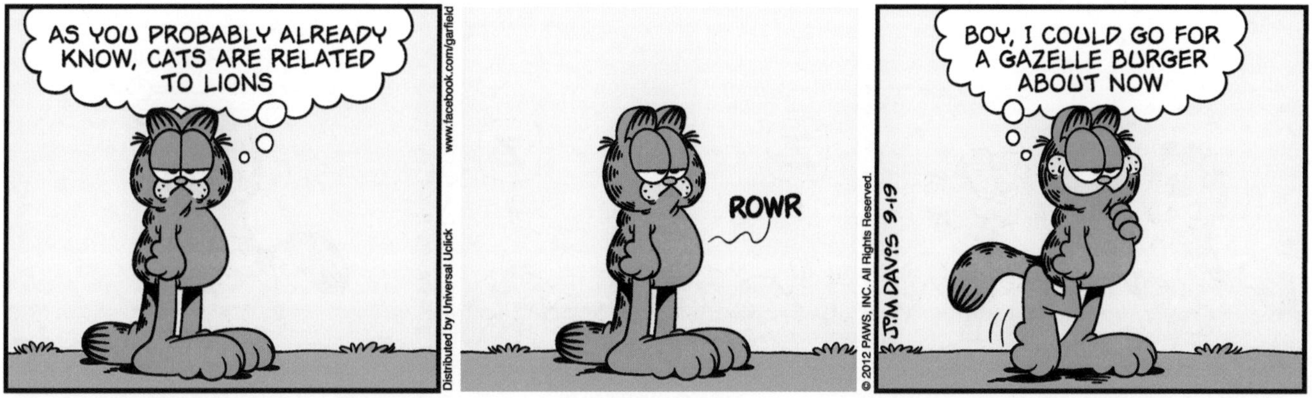
AS YOU PROBABLY ALREADY KNOW, CATS ARE RELATED TO LIONS
ROWR
BOY, I COULD GO FOR A GAZELLE BURGER ABOUT NOW
Distributed by Universal Uclick www.facebook.com/garfield
© 2012 PAWS, INC. All Rights Reserved.
JIM DAVIS 9-19

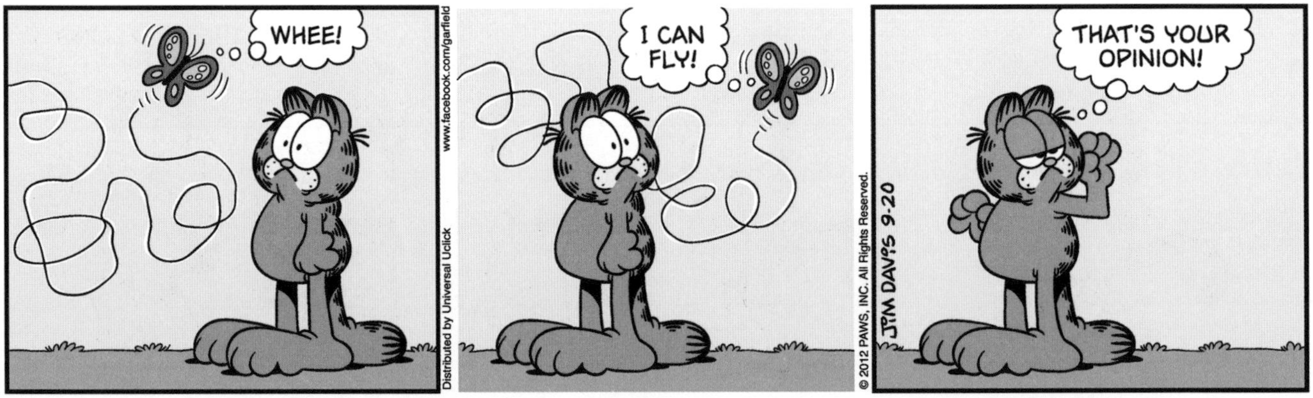
WHEE!
www.facebook.com/garfield
Distributed by Universal Uclick
I CAN FLY!
© 2012 PAWS, INC. All Rights Reserved.
JIM DAVIS 9-20
THAT'S YOUR OPINION!

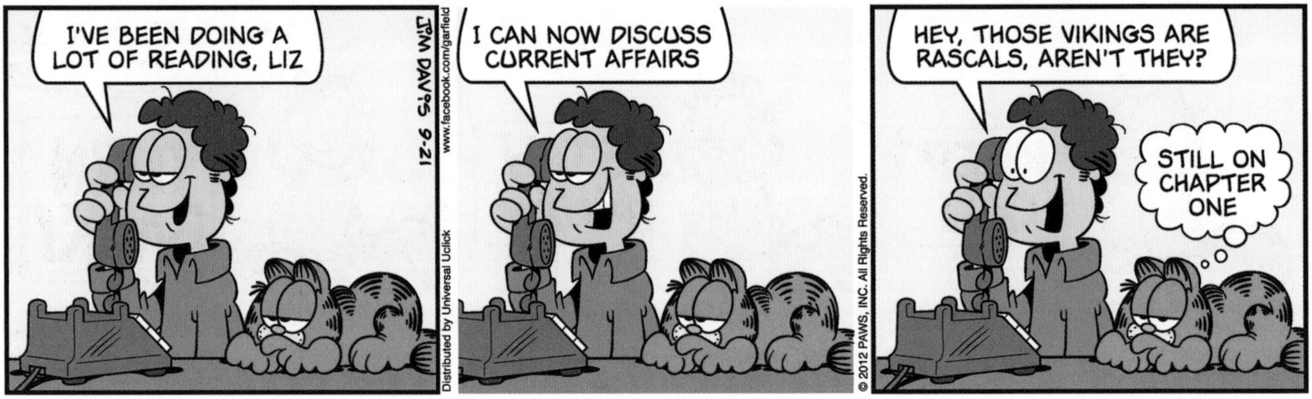
I'VE BEEN DOING A LOT OF READING, LIZ
JIM DAVIS 9-21
www.facebook.com/garfield
Distributed by Universal Uclick
I CAN NOW DISCUSS CURRENT AFFAIRS
© 2012 PAWS, INC. All Rights Reserved.
HEY, THOSE VIKINGS ARE RASCALS, AREN'T THEY?
STILL ON CHAPTER ONE

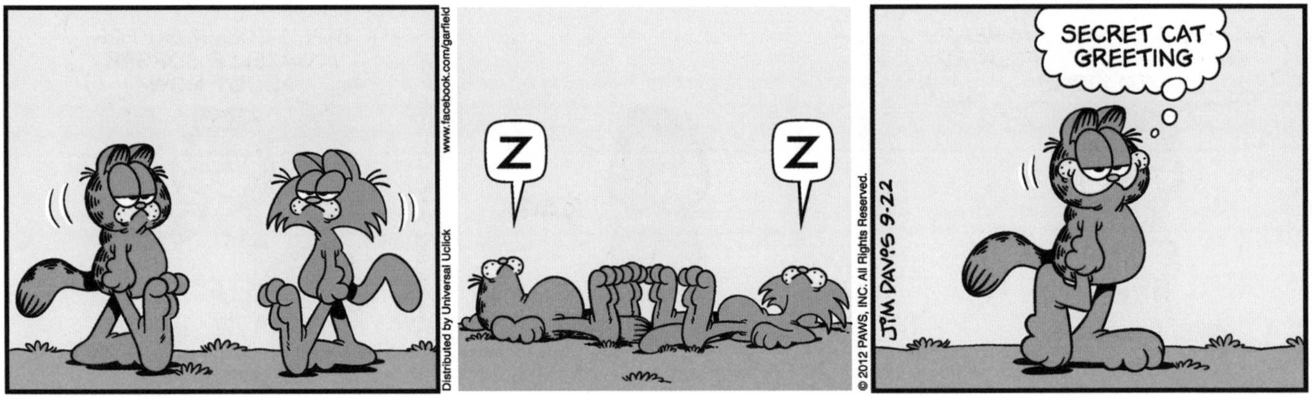
www.facebook.com/garfield
Distributed by Universal Uclick
Z
Z
© 2012 PAWS, INC. All Rights Reserved.
JIM DAVIS 9-22
SECRET CAT GREETING

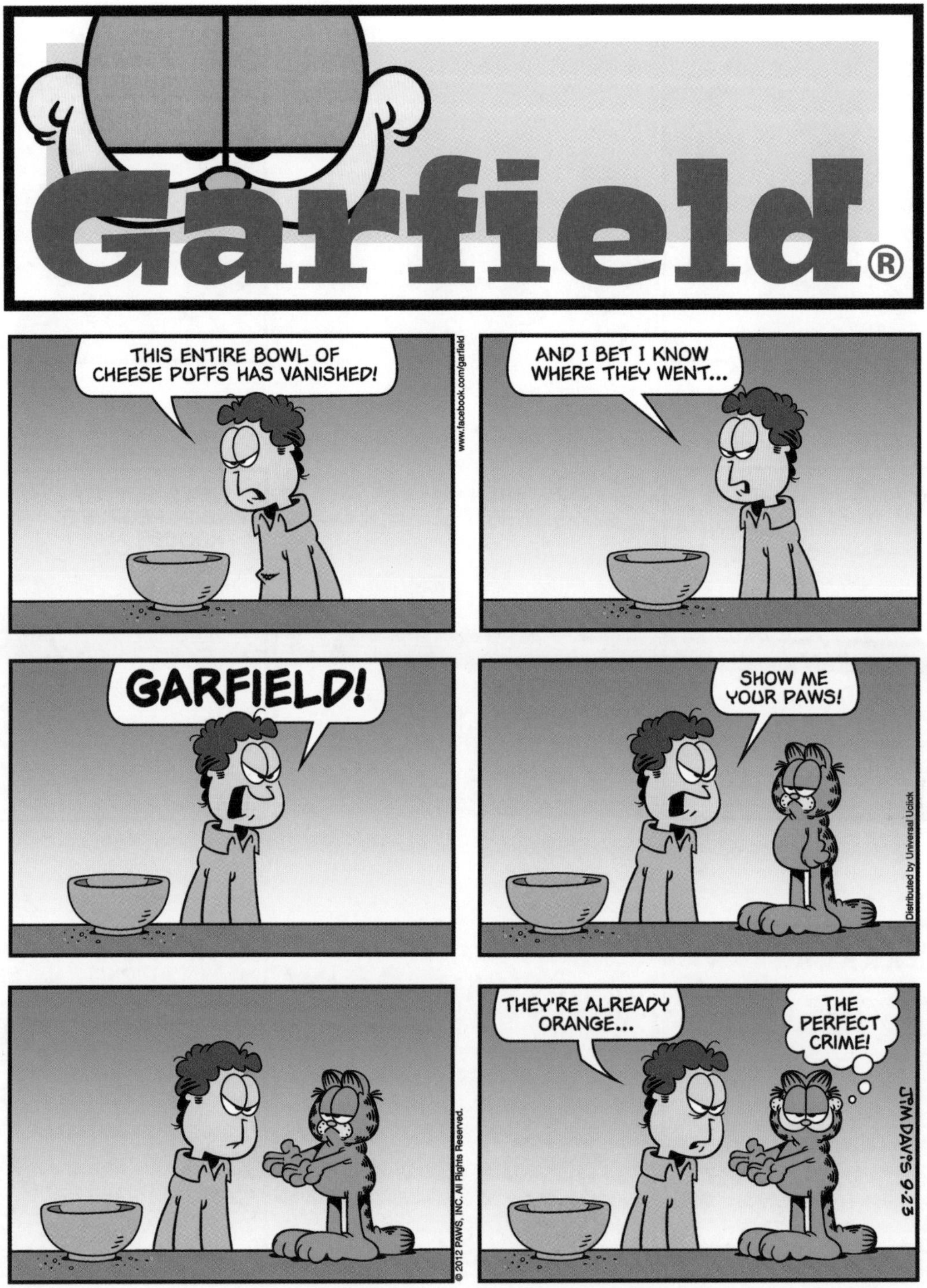
Garfield®
THIS ENTIRE BOWL OF CHEESE PUFFS HAS VANISHED!
www.facebook.com/garfield
AND I BET I KNOW WHERE THEY WENT...
GARFIELD!
SHOW ME YOUR PAWS!
Distributed by Universal Uclick
© 2012 PAWS, INC. All Rights Reserved.
THEY'RE ALREADY ORANGE...
THE PERFECT CRIME!
JIM DAVIS 9-23

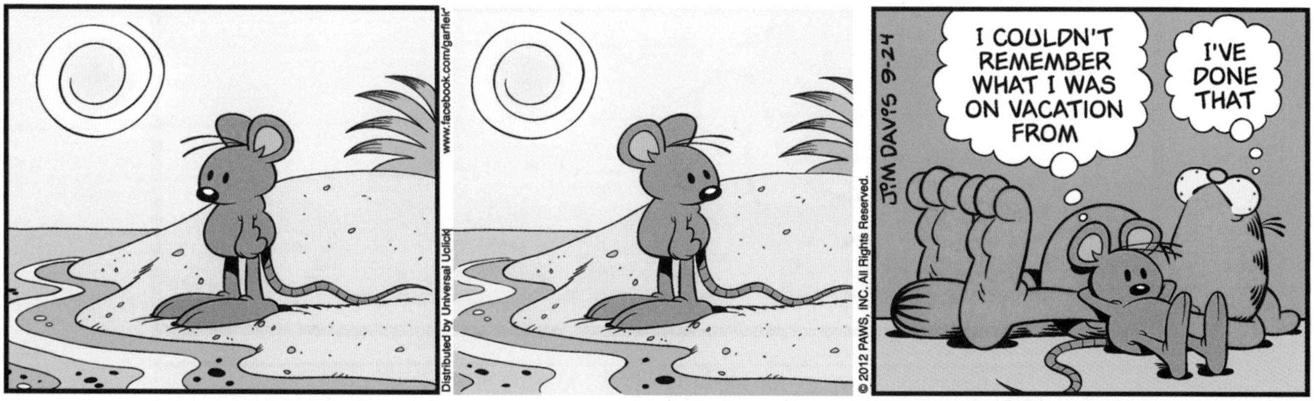
www.facebook.com/garfield
Distributed by Universal Uclick
© 2012 PAWS, INC. All Rights Reserved.
JIM DAVIS 9-24
I COULDN'T REMEMBER WHAT I WAS ON VACATION FROM
I'VE DONE THAT

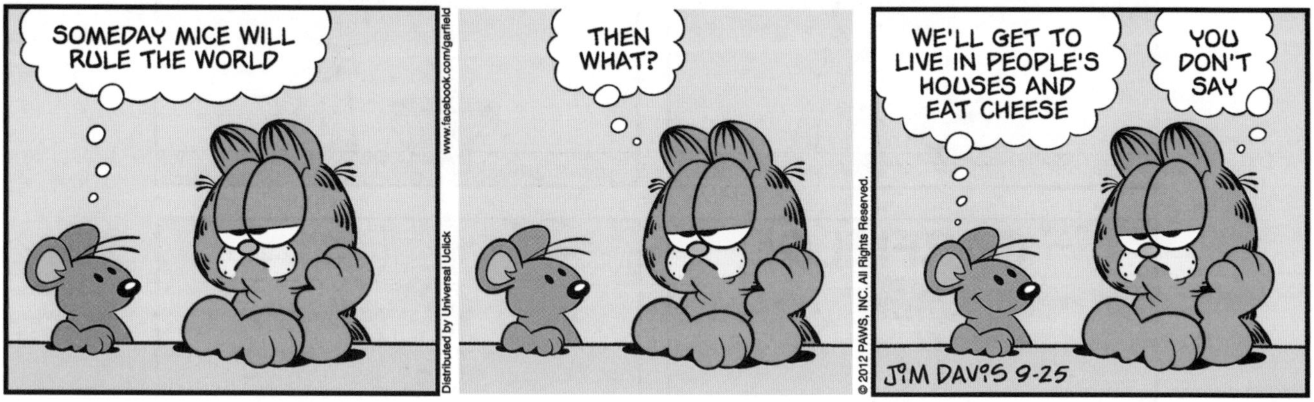
SOMEDAY MICE WILL RULE THE WORLD
www.facebook.com/garfield
Distributed by Universal Uclick
THEN WHAT?
© 2012 PAWS, INC. All Rights Reserved.
WE'LL GET TO LIVE IN PEOPLE'S HOUSES AND EAT CHEESE
YOU DON'T SAY
JIM DAVIS 9-25

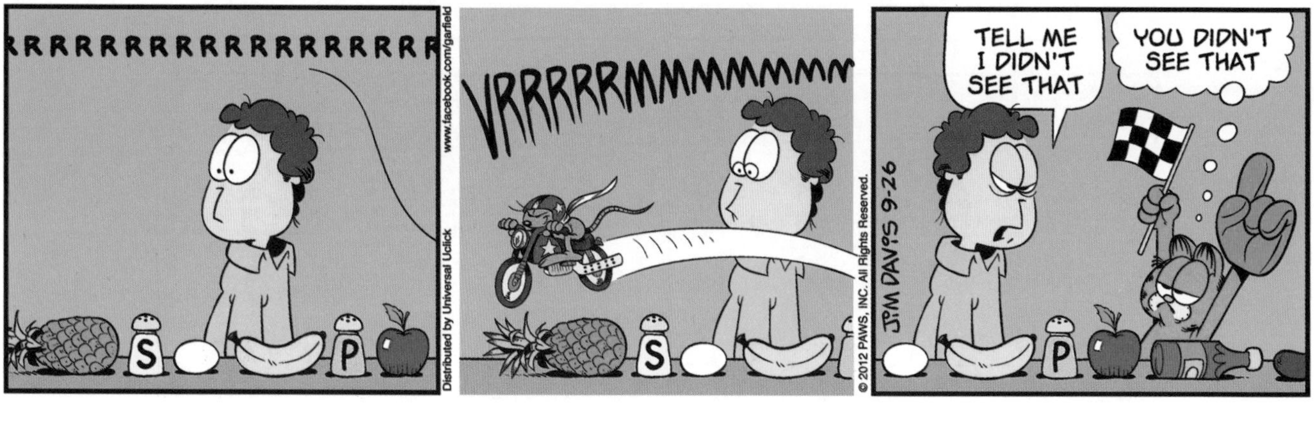
RRRRRRRRRRRRRRRRRRRR
www.facebook.com/garfield
Distributed by Universal Uclick
VRRRRRMMMMMMM
© 2012 PAWS, INC. All Rights Reserved.
JIM DAVIS 9-26
TELL ME I DIDN'T SEE THAT
YOU DIDN'T SEE THAT

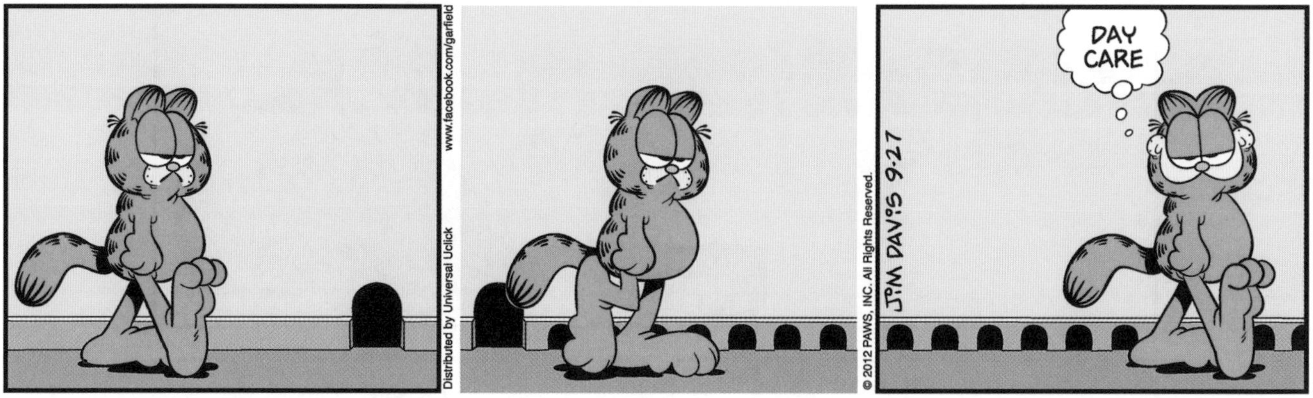
Distributed by Universal Uclick
www.facebook.com/garfield
© 2012 PAWS, INC. All Rights Reserved.
JIM DAVIS 9-27
DAY CARE

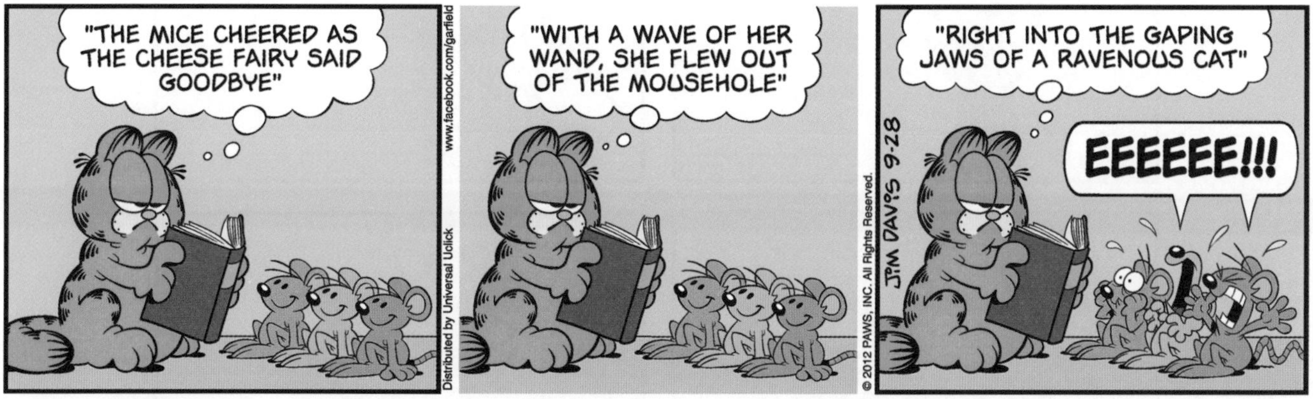
"THE MICE CHEERED AS THE CHEESE FAIRY SAID GOODBYE"
Distributed by Universal Uclick
www.facebook.com/garfield
"WITH A WAVE OF HER WAND, SHE FLEW OUT OF THE MOUSEHOLE"
© 2012 PAWS, INC. All Rights Reserved.
JIM DAVIS 9-28
"RIGHT INTO THE GAPING JAWS OF A RAVENOUS CAT"
EEEEEE!!!

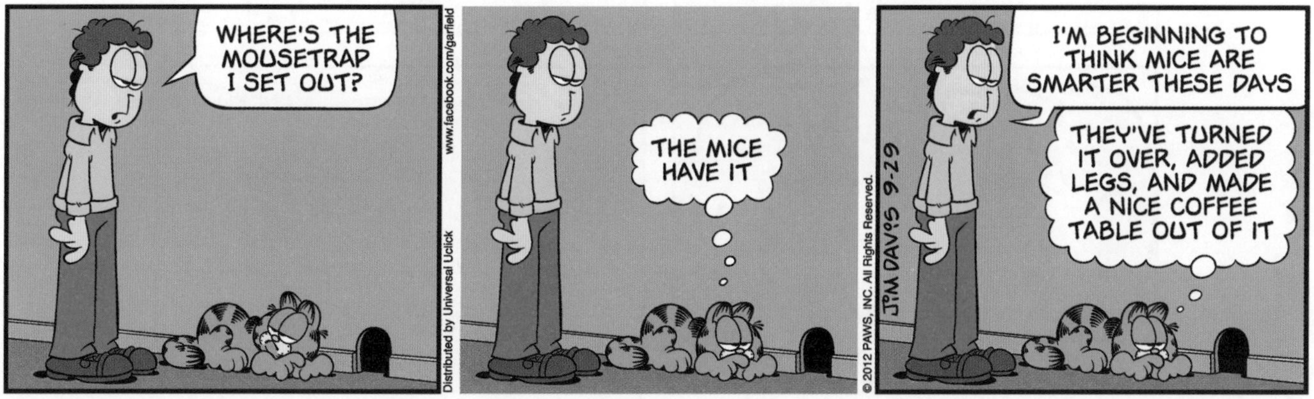
WHERE'S THE MOUSETRAP I SET OUT?
Distributed by Universal Uclick
www.facebook.com/garfield
THE MICE HAVE IT
© 2012 PAWS, INC. All Rights Reserved.
JIM DAVIS 9-29
I'M BEGINNING TO THINK MICE ARE SMARTER THESE DAYS
THEY'VE TURNED IT OVER, ADDED LEGS, AND MADE A NICE COFFEE TABLE OUT OF IT

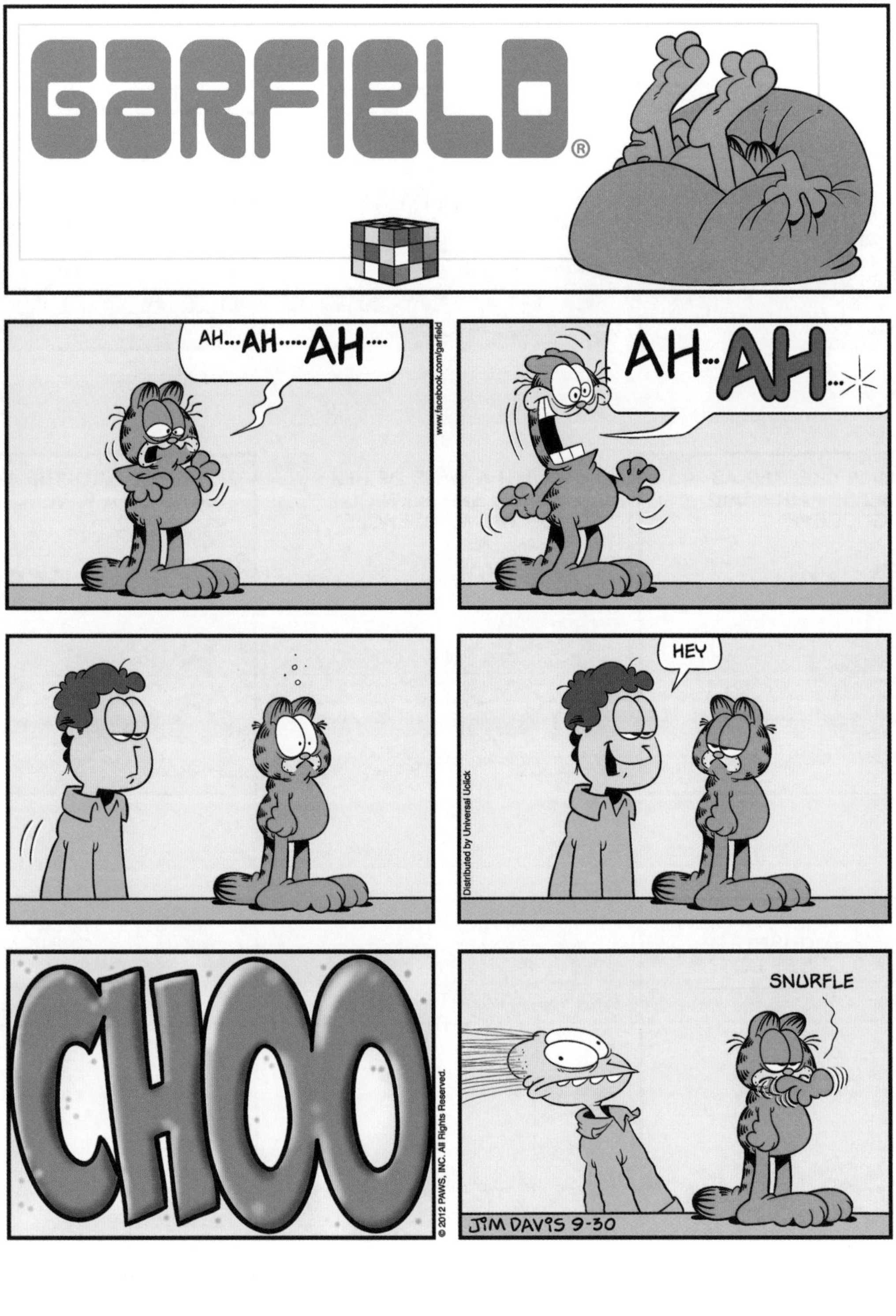
GARFIELD®
AH....AH.....AH....
www.facebook.com/garfield
AH...AH...
Distributed by Universal Uclick
HEY
CHOO
© 2012 PAWS, INC. All Rights Reserved.
SNURFLE
JIM DAVIS 9-30

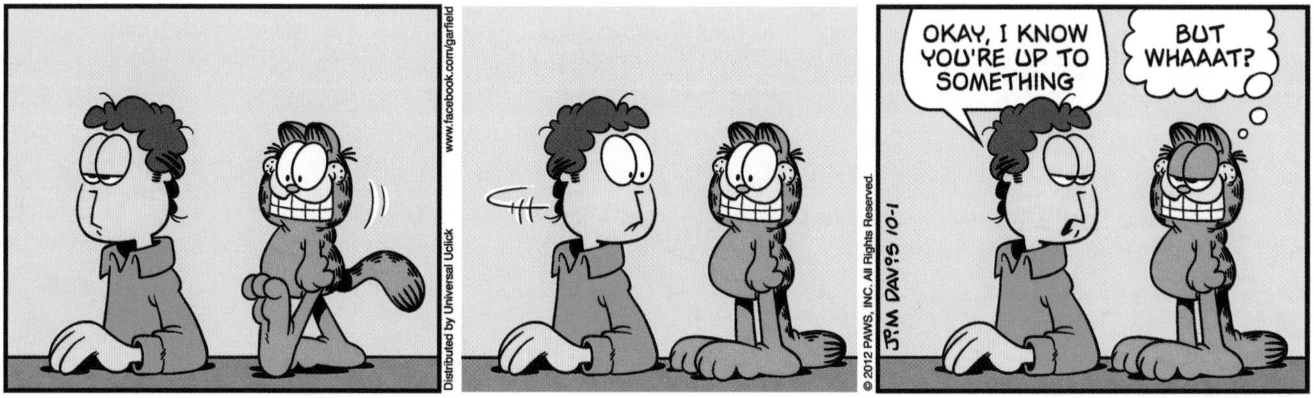
Distributed by Universal Uclick
www.facebook.com/garfield
© 2012 PAWS, INC. All Rights Reserved.
JIM DAVIS 10-1
OKAY, I KNOW YOU'RE UP TO SOMETHING
BUT WHAAAT?

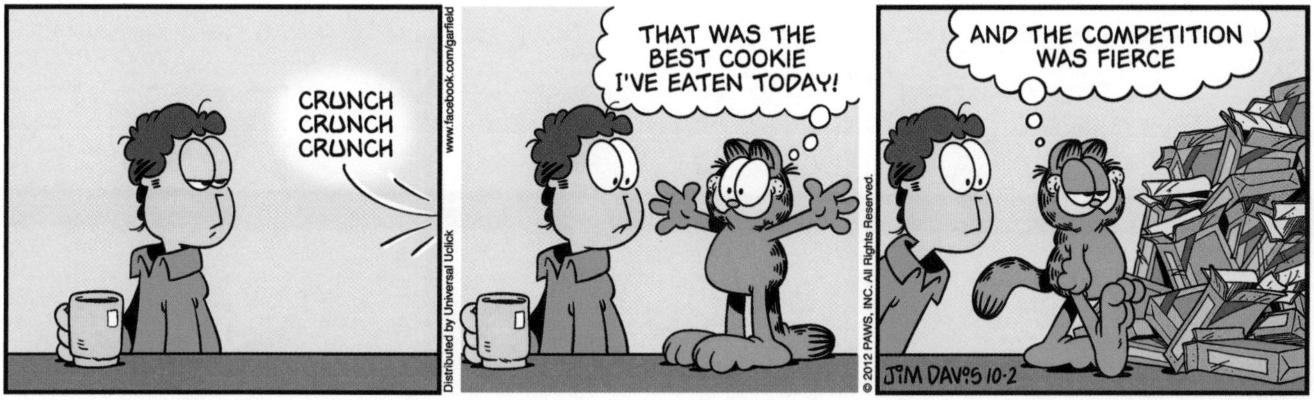
CRUNCH CRUNCH CRUNCH
Distributed by Universal Uclick
www.facebook.com/garfield
THAT WAS THE BEST COOKIE I'VE EATEN TODAY!
© 2012 PAWS, INC. All Rights Reserved.
AND THE COMPETITION WAS FIERCE
JIM DAVIS 10-2

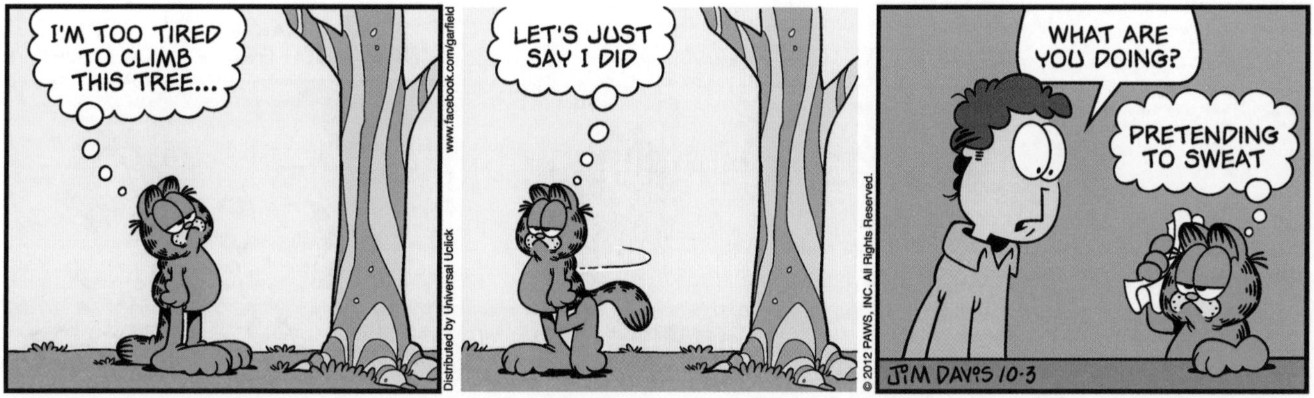
I'M TOO TIRED TO CLIMB THIS TREE...
Distributed by Universal Uclick
www.facebook.com/garfield
LET'S JUST SAY I DID
© 2012 PAWS, INC. All Rights Reserved.
WHAT ARE YOU DOING?
PRETENDING TO SWEAT
JIM DAVIS 10-3

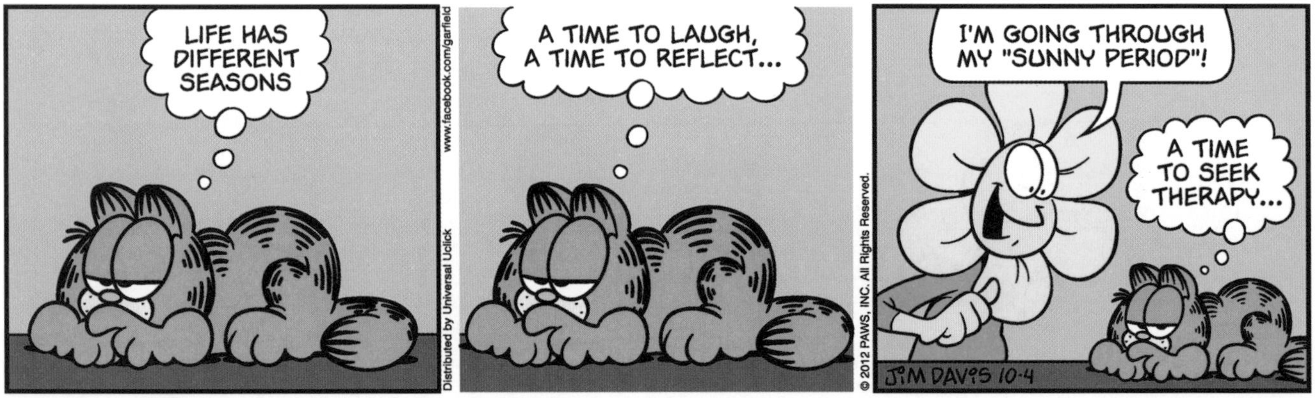
LIFE HAS DIFFERENT SEASONS
A TIME TO LAUGH, A TIME TO REFLECT...
I'M GOING THROUGH MY "SUNNY PERIOD"!
A TIME TO SEEK THERAPY...
JIM DAVIS 10-4
Distributed by Universal Uclick www.facebook.com/garfield
© 2012 PAWS, INC. All Rights Reserved.

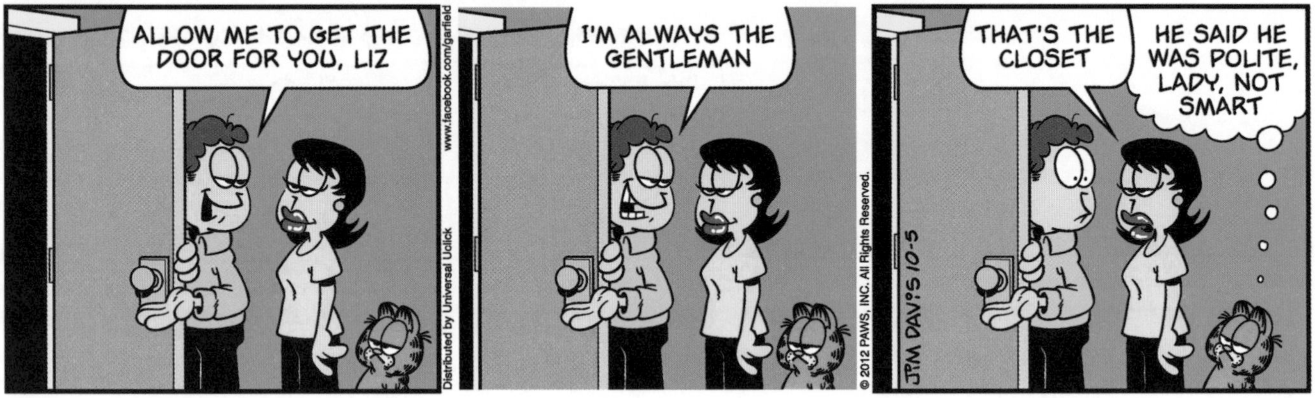
ALLOW ME TO GET THE DOOR FOR YOU, LIZ
I'M ALWAYS THE GENTLEMAN
THAT'S THE CLOSET
HE SAID HE WAS POLITE, LADY, NOT SMART
JIM DAVIS 10-5
Distributed by Universal Uclick www.facebook.com/garfield
© 2012 PAWS, INC. All Rights Reserved.

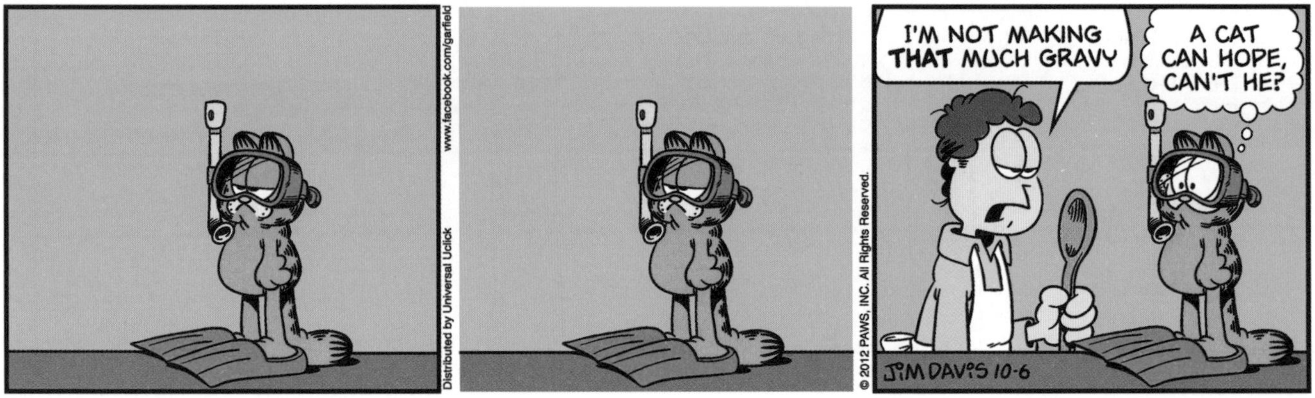
I'M NOT MAKING **THAT** MUCH GRAVY
A CAT CAN HOPE, CAN'T HE?
JIM DAVIS 10-6
Distributed by Universal Uclick www.facebook.com/garfield
© 2012 PAWS, INC. All Rights Reserved.

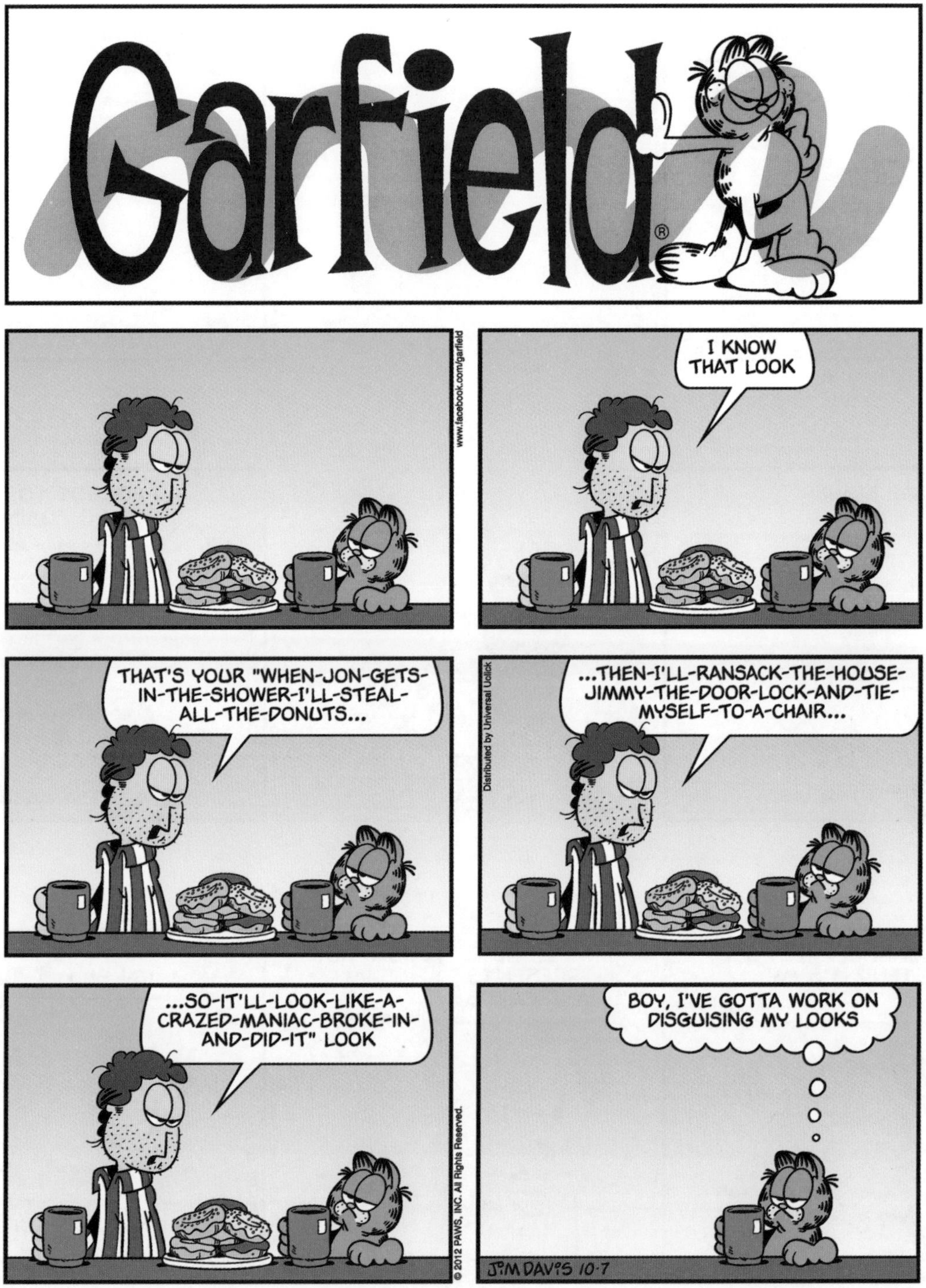
Garfield
www.facebook.com/garfield
I KNOW THAT LOOK
THAT'S YOUR "WHEN-JON-GETS-IN-THE-SHOWER-I'LL-STEAL-ALL-THE-DONUTS...
Distributed by Universal Uclick
...THEN-I'LL-RANSACK-THE-HOUSE-JIMMY-THE-DOOR-LOCK-AND-TIE-MYSELF-TO-A-CHAIR...
...SO-IT'LL-LOOK-LIKE-A-CRAZED-MANIAC-BROKE-IN-AND-DID-IT" LOOK
© 2012 PAWS, INC. All Rights Reserved.
BOY, I'VE GOTTA WORK ON DISGUISING MY LOOKS
JIM DAVIS 10·7

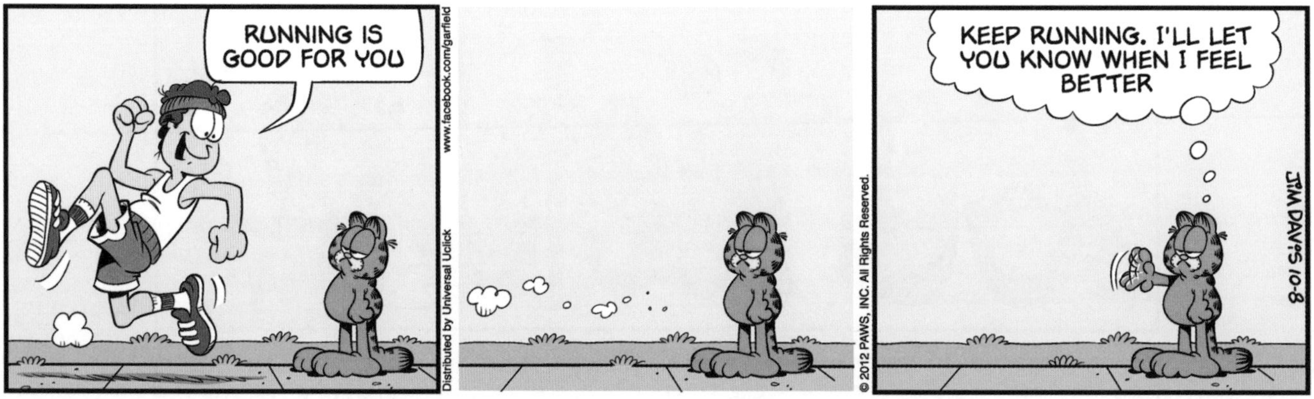
RUNNING IS GOOD FOR YOU
KEEP RUNNING. I'LL LET YOU KNOW WHEN I FEEL BETTER
JIM DAVIS 10-8
Distributed by Universal Uclick www.facebook.com/garfield
© 2012 PAWS, INC. All Rights Reserved.

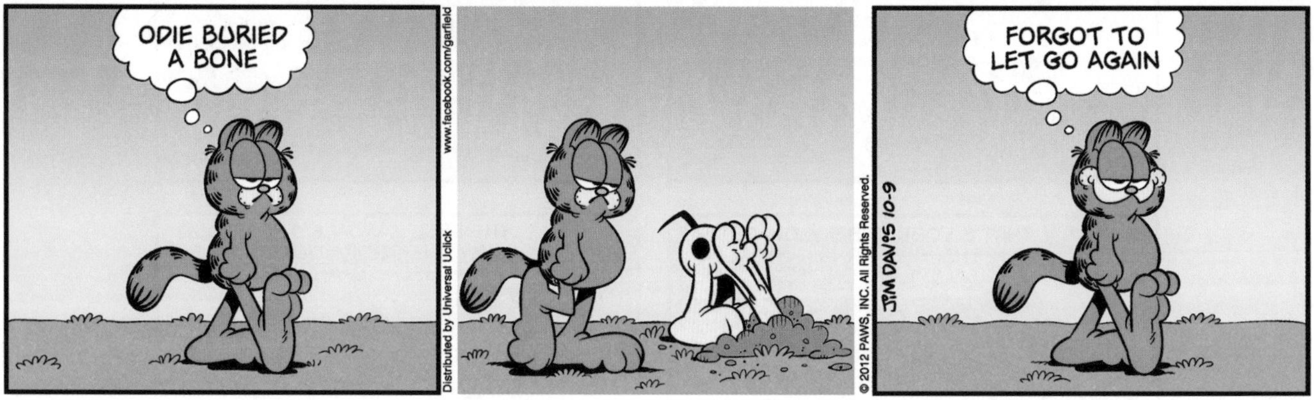
ODIE BURIED A BONE
FORGOT TO LET GO AGAIN
JIM DAVIS 10-9
Distributed by Universal Uclick www.facebook.com/garfield
© 2012 PAWS, INC. All Rights Reserved.

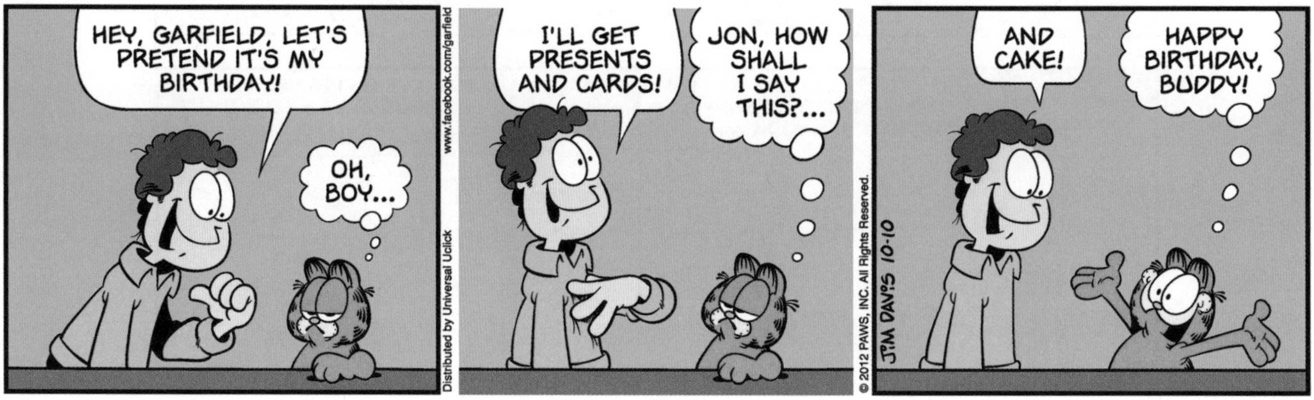
HEY, GARFIELD, LET'S PRETEND IT'S MY BIRTHDAY!
OH, BOY...
I'LL GET PRESENTS AND CARDS!
JON, HOW SHALL I SAY THIS?...
AND CAKE!
HAPPY BIRTHDAY, BUDDY!
JIM DAVIS 10-10
Distributed by Universal Uclick www.facebook.com/garfield
© 2012 PAWS, INC. All Rights Reserved.

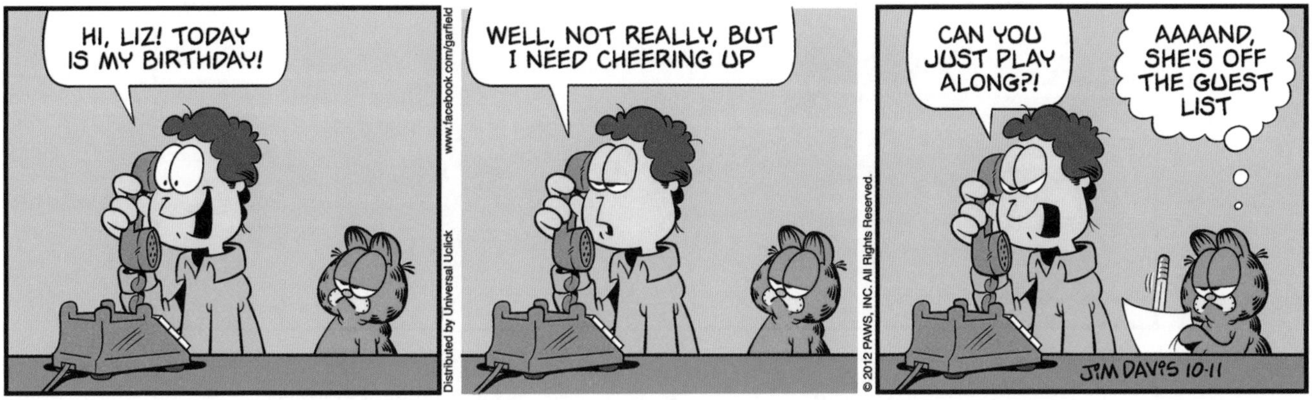
HI, LIZ! TODAY IS MY BIRTHDAY!
WELL, NOT REALLY, BUT I NEED CHEERING UP
CAN YOU JUST PLAY ALONG?!
AAAAND, SHE'S OFF THE GUEST LIST
JIM DAVIS 10-11
Distributed by Universal Uclick www.facebook.com/garfield
© 2012 PAWS, INC. All Rights Reserved.

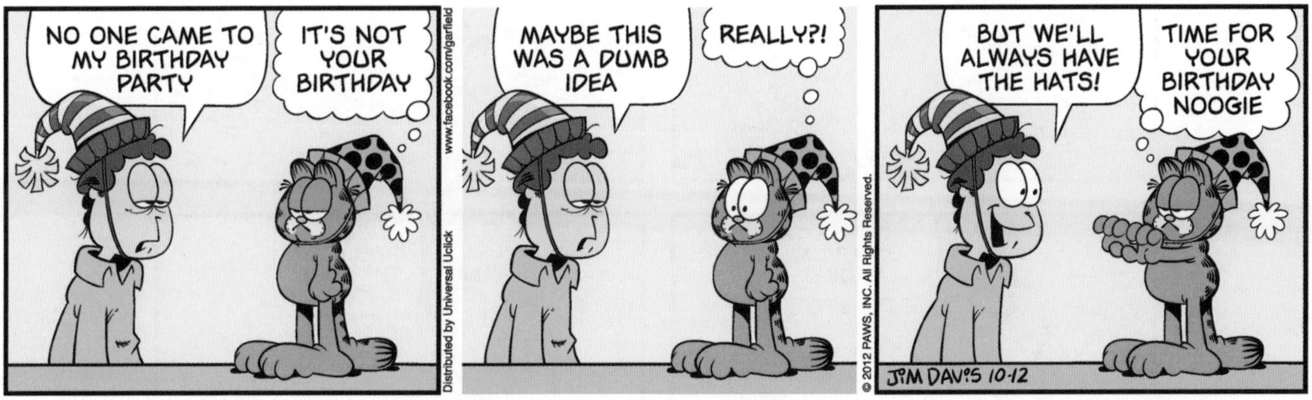
NO ONE CAME TO MY BIRTHDAY PARTY
IT'S NOT YOUR BIRTHDAY
MAYBE THIS WAS A DUMB IDEA
REALLY?!
BUT WE'LL ALWAYS HAVE THE HATS!
TIME FOR YOUR BIRTHDAY NOOGIE
JIM DAVIS 10-12
Distributed by Universal Uclick www.facebook.com/garfield
© 2012 PAWS, INC. All Rights Reserved.

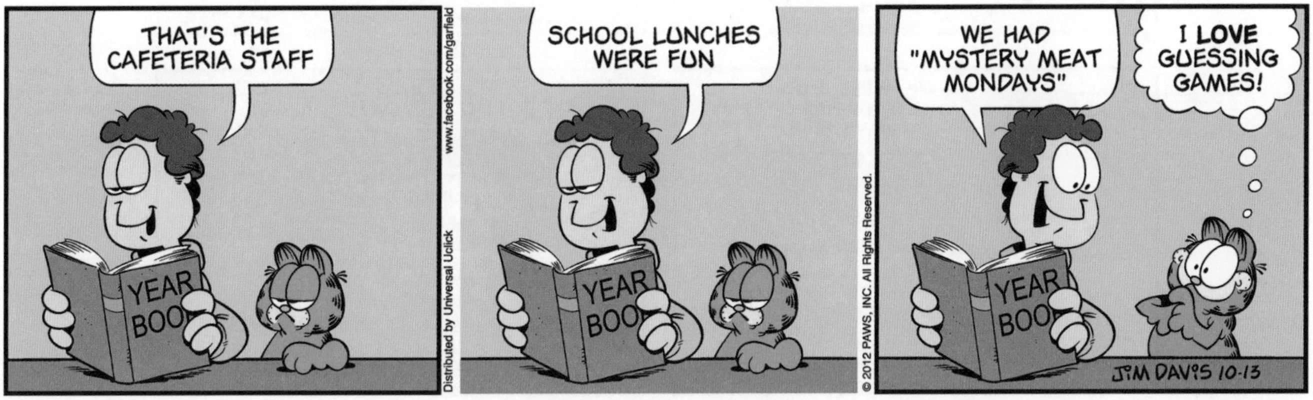
THAT'S THE CAFETERIA STAFF
YEAR BOO
SCHOOL LUNCHES WERE FUN
WE HAD "MYSTERY MEAT MONDAYS"
I **LOVE** GUESSING GAMES!
JIM DAVIS 10-13
Distributed by Universal Uclick www.facebook.com/garfield
© 2012 PAWS, INC. All Rights Reserved.

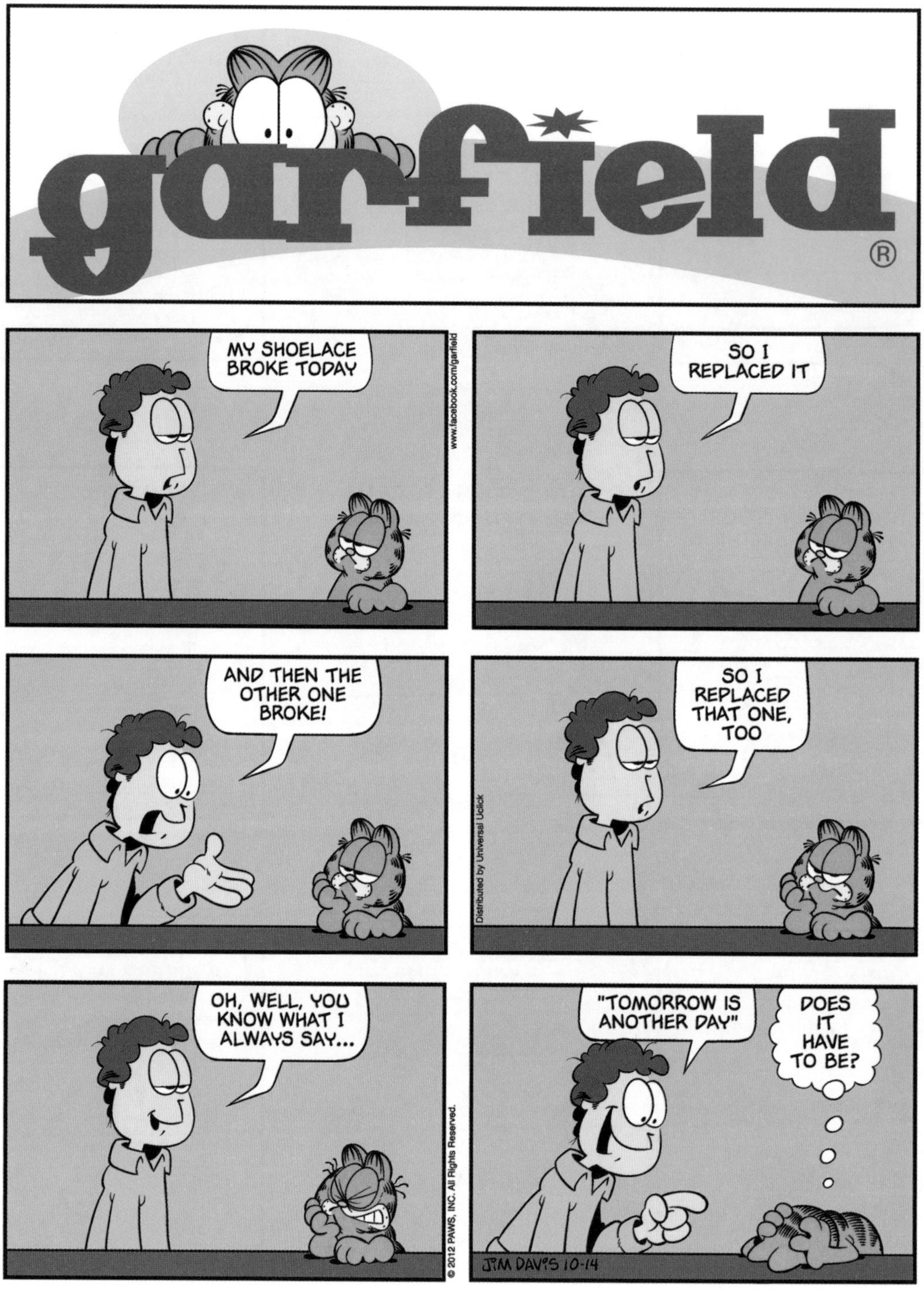
garfield
MY SHOELACE BROKE TODAY
www.facebook.com/garfield
SO I REPLACED IT
AND THEN THE OTHER ONE BROKE!
Distributed by Universal Uclick
SO I REPLACED THAT ONE, TOO
OH, WELL, YOU KNOW WHAT I ALWAYS SAY...
© 2012 PAWS, INC. All Rights Reserved.
"TOMORROW IS ANOTHER DAY"
DOES IT HAVE TO BE?
JIM DAVIS 10-14

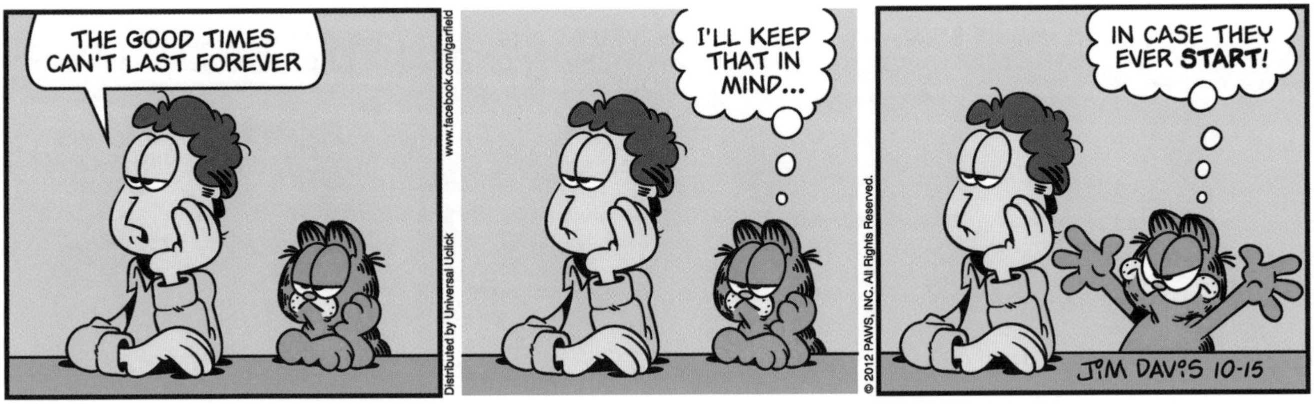
THE GOOD TIMES CAN'T LAST FOREVER
I'LL KEEP THAT IN MIND...
IN CASE THEY EVER **START**!
JIM DAVIS 10-15
www.facebook.com/garfield
Distributed by Universal Uclick
© 2012 PAWS, INC. All Rights Reserved.

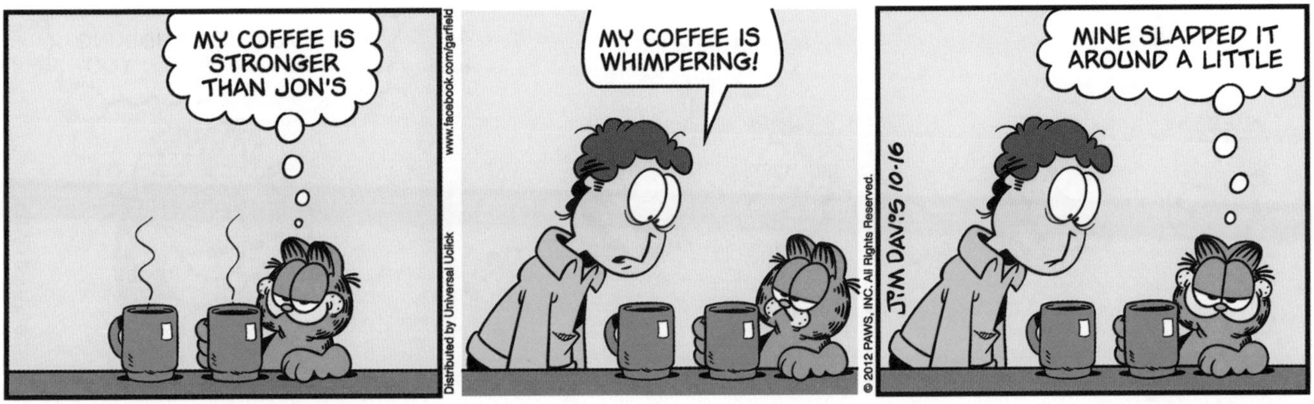
MY COFFEE IS STRONGER THAN JON'S
MY COFFEE IS WHIMPERING!
MINE SLAPPED IT AROUND A LITTLE
JIM DAVIS 10-16
www.facebook.com/garfield
Distributed by Universal Uclick
© 2012 PAWS, INC. All Rights Reserved.

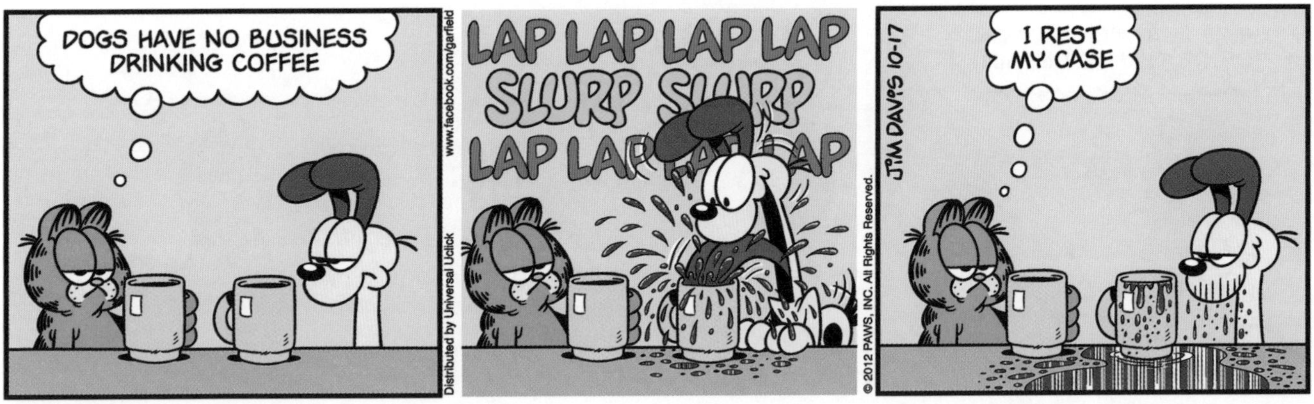
DOGS HAVE NO BUSINESS DRINKING COFFEE
LAP LAP LAP LAP
SLURP SLURP
I REST MY CASE
JIM DAVIS 10-17
www.facebook.com/garfield
Distributed by Universal Uclick
© 2012 PAWS, INC. All Rights Reserved.

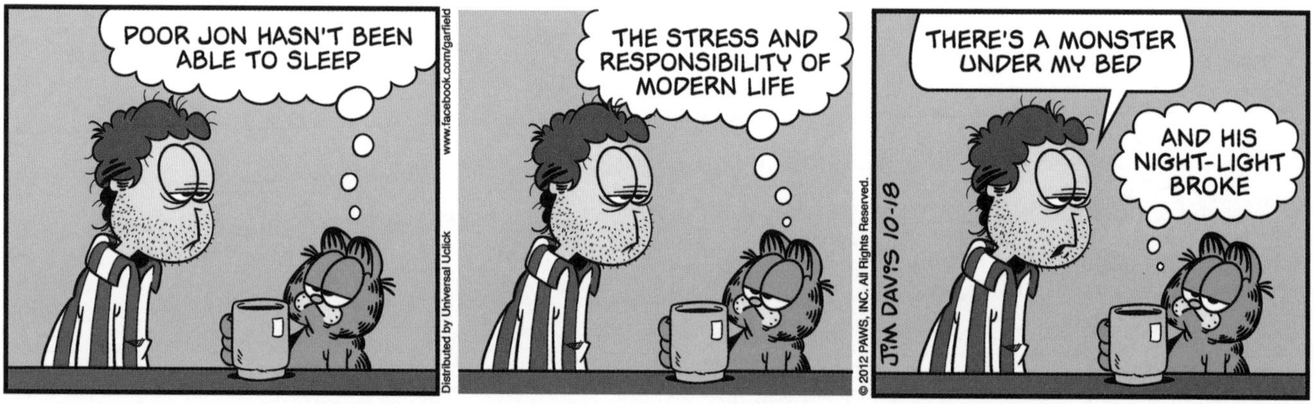
POOR JON HASN'T BEEN ABLE TO SLEEP
Distributed by Universal Uclick www.facebook.com/garfield
THE STRESS AND RESPONSIBILITY OF MODERN LIFE
© 2012 PAWS, INC. All Rights Reserved.
JIM DAVIS 10-18
THERE'S A MONSTER UNDER MY BED
AND HIS NIGHT-LIGHT BROKE

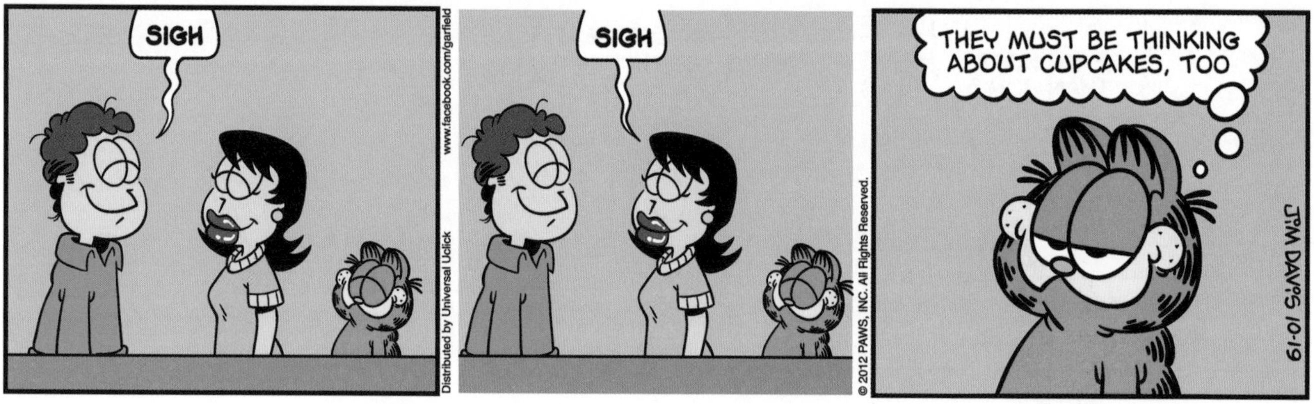
SIGH
Distributed by Universal Uclick www.facebook.com/garfield
SIGH
© 2012 PAWS, INC. All Rights Reserved.
THEY MUST BE THINKING ABOUT CUPCAKES, TOO
JIM DAVIS 10-19

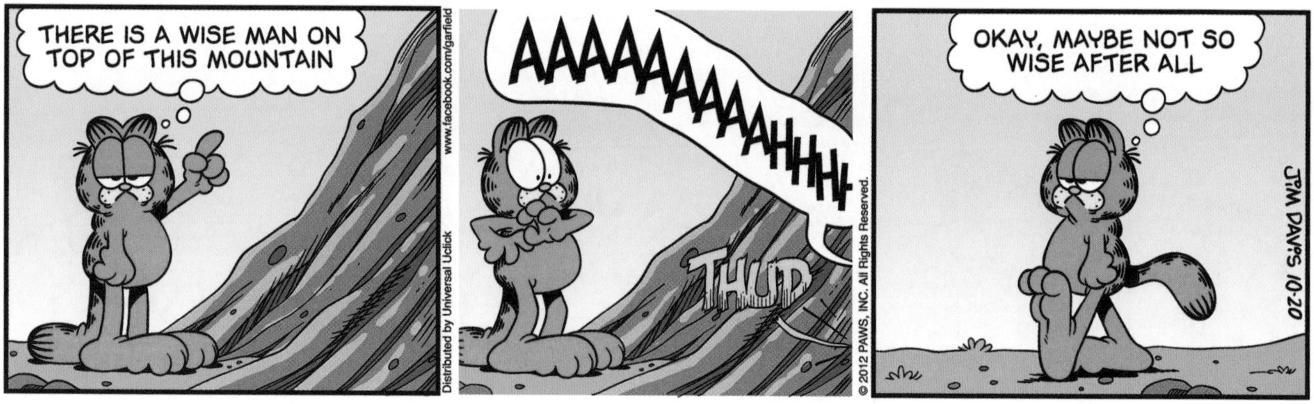
THERE IS A WISE MAN ON TOP OF THIS MOUNTAIN
Distributed by Universal Uclick www.facebook.com/garfield
AAAAAAAAAAAHHHH
THUD
© 2012 PAWS, INC. All Rights Reserved.
OKAY, MAYBE NOT SO WISE AFTER ALL
JIM DAVIS 10-20

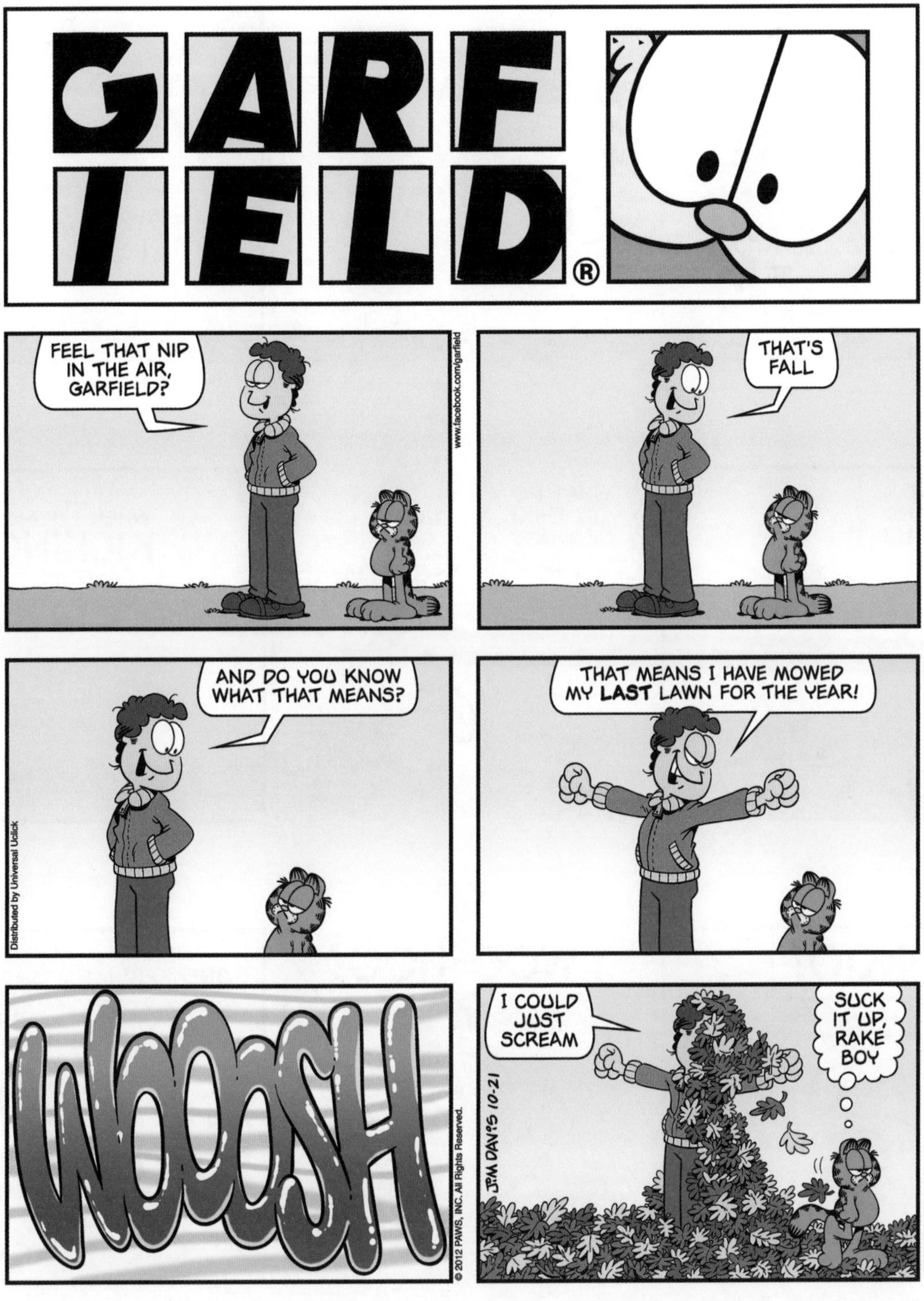
GARFIELD®
FEEL THAT NIP IN THE AIR, GARFIELD?
www.facebook.com/garfield
THAT'S FALL
AND DO YOU KNOW WHAT THAT MEANS?
Distributed by Universal Uclick
THAT MEANS I HAVE MOWED MY **LAST** LAWN FOR THE YEAR!
WOOOSH
© 2012 PAWS, INC. All Rights Reserved.
JIM DAVIS 10-21
I COULD JUST SCREAM
SUCK IT UP, RAKE BOY

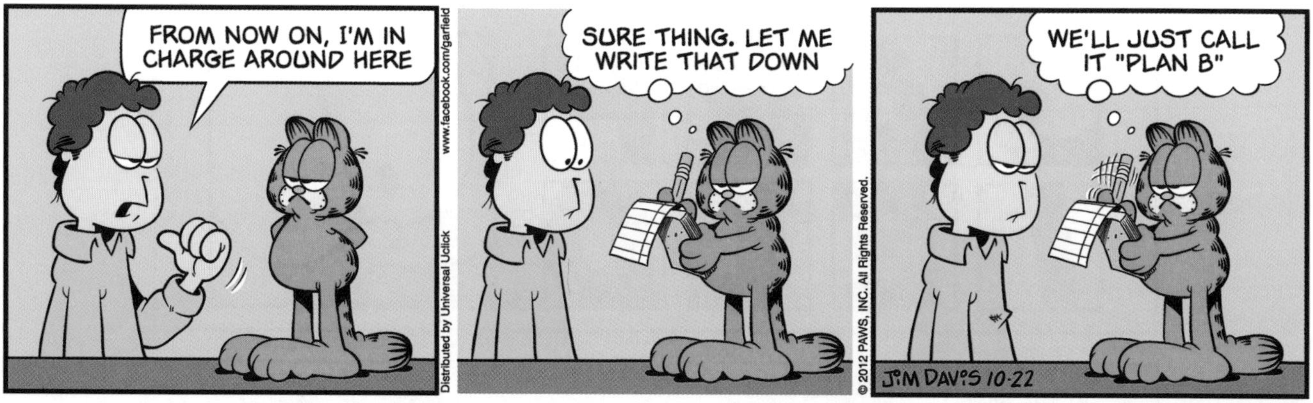
FROM NOW ON, I'M IN CHARGE AROUND HERE
www.facebook.com/garfield
Distributed by Universal Uclick
SURE THING. LET ME WRITE THAT DOWN
© 2012 PAWS, INC. All Rights Reserved.
WE'LL JUST CALL IT "PLAN B"
JIM DAVIS 10-22

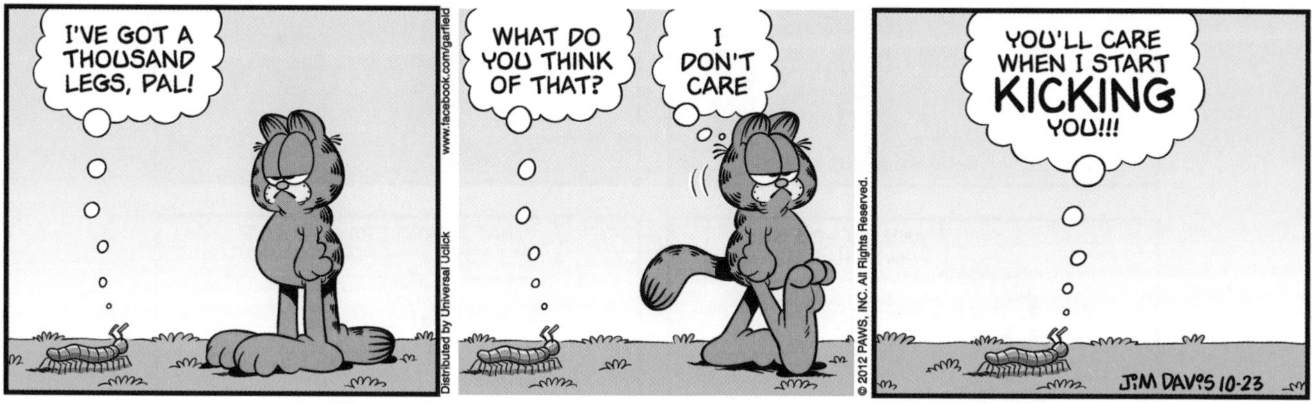
I'VE GOT A THOUSAND LEGS, PAL!
www.facebook.com/garfield
Distributed by Universal Uclick
WHAT DO YOU THINK OF THAT?
I DON'T CARE
© 2012 PAWS, INC. All Rights Reserved.
YOU'LL CARE WHEN I START KICKING YOU!!!
JIM DAVIS 10-23

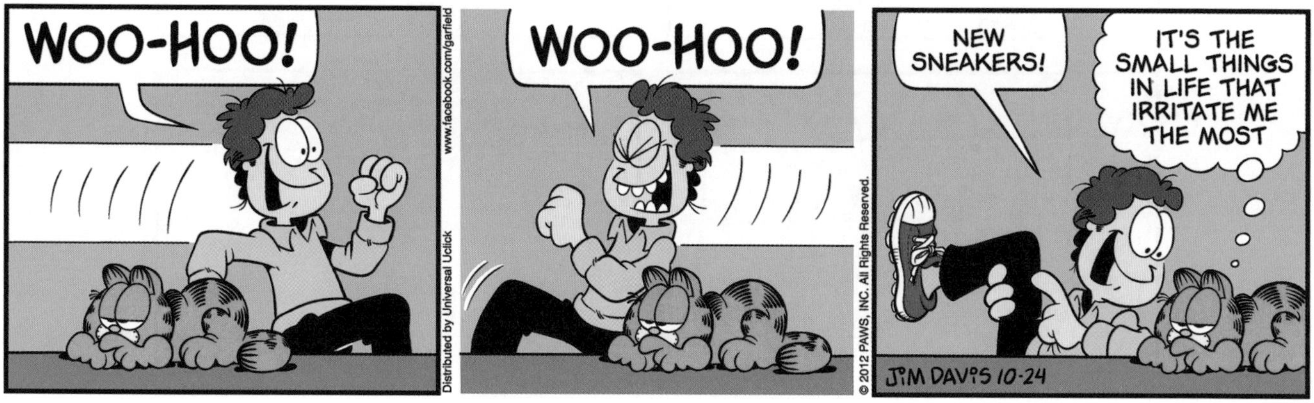
WOO-HOO!
www.facebook.com/garfield
Distributed by Universal Uclick
WOO-HOO!
© 2012 PAWS, INC. All Rights Reserved.
NEW SNEAKERS!
IT'S THE SMALL THINGS IN LIFE THAT IRRITATE ME THE MOST
JIM DAVIS 10-24

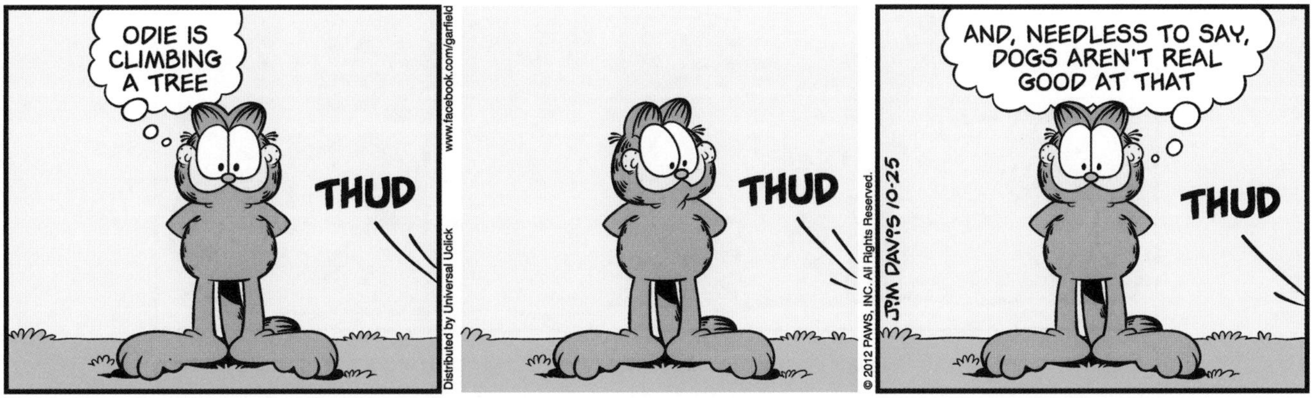
ODIE IS CLIMBING A TREE
THUD
THUD
JIM DAVIS 10-25
© 2012 PAWS, INC. All Rights Reserved.
Distributed by Universal Uclick
www.facebook.com/garfield
AND, NEEDLESS TO SAY, DOGS AREN'T REAL GOOD AT THAT
THUD

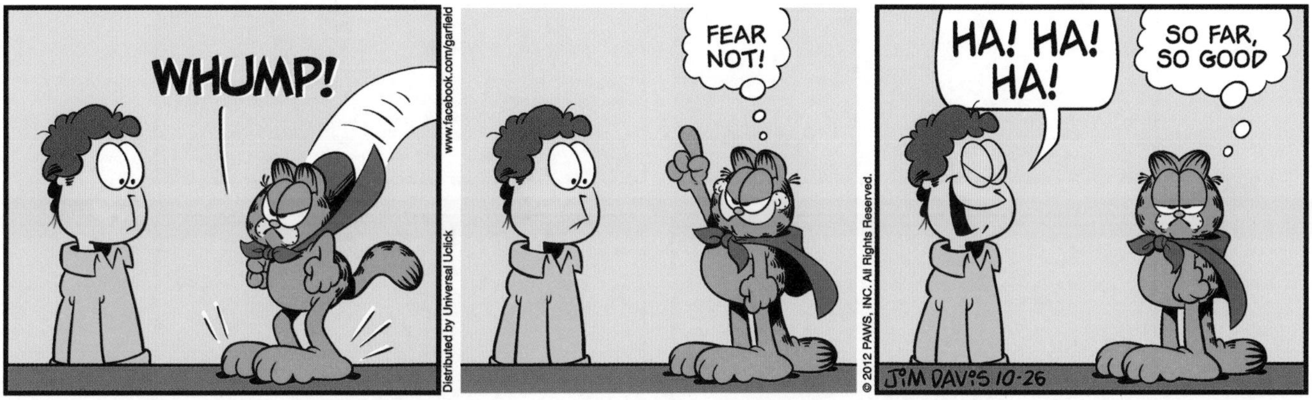
WHUMP!
Distributed by Universal Uclick
www.facebook.com/garfield
FEAR NOT!
© 2012 PAWS, INC. All Rights Reserved.
HA! HA! HA!
SO FAR, SO GOOD
JIM DAVIS 10-26

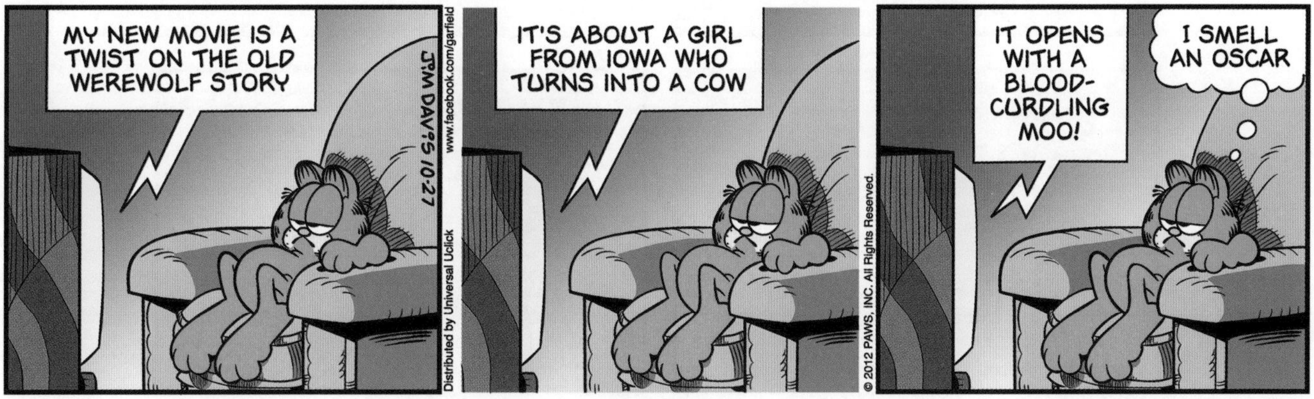
MY NEW MOVIE IS A TWIST ON THE OLD WEREWOLF STORY
JIM DAVIS 10-27
Distributed by Universal Uclick
www.facebook.com/garfield
IT'S ABOUT A GIRL FROM IOWA WHO TURNS INTO A COW
© 2012 PAWS, INC. All Rights Reserved.
IT OPENS WITH A BLOOD-CURDLING MOO!
I SMELL AN OSCAR

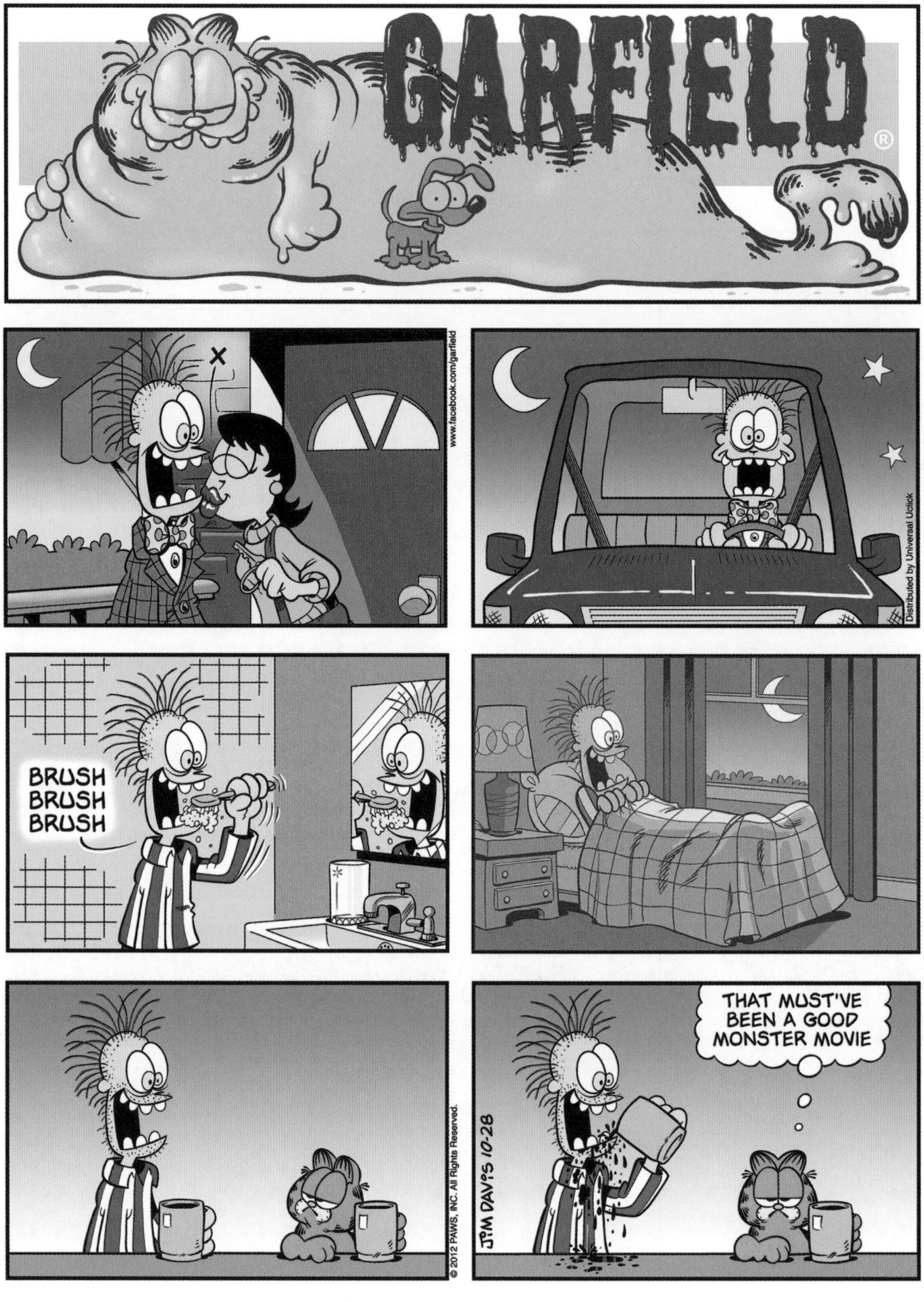
GARFIELD®
www.facebook.com/garfield
Distributed by Universal Uclick
BRUSH
BRUSH
BRUSH
© 2012 PAWS, INC. All Rights Reserved.
JIM DAVIS 10-28
THAT MUST'VE BEEN A GOOD MONSTER MOVIE

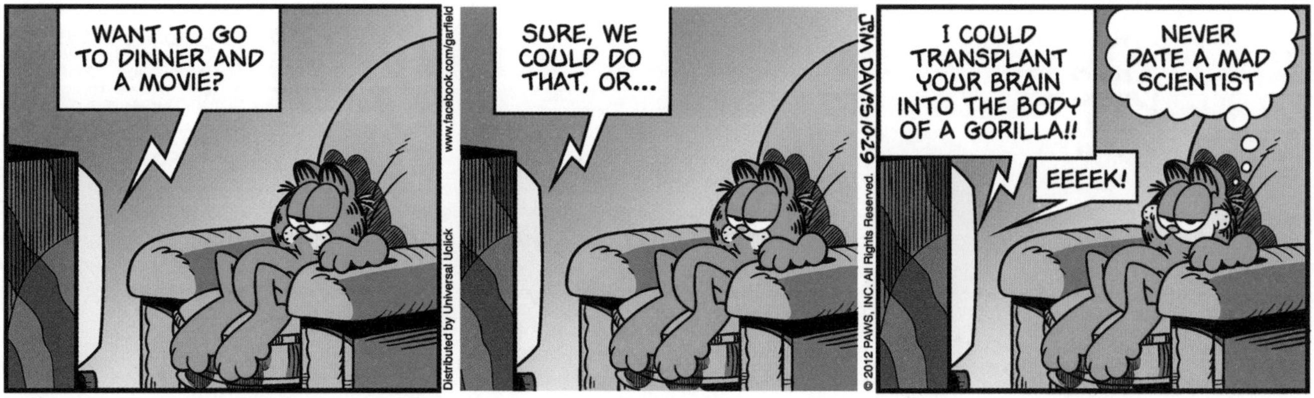
WANT TO GO TO DINNER AND A MOVIE?
SURE, WE COULD DO THAT, OR...
I COULD TRANSPLANT YOUR BRAIN INTO THE BODY OF A GORILLA!!
EEEEK!
NEVER DATE A MAD SCIENTIST
JIM DAVIS 10-29
Distributed by Universal Uclick www.facebook.com/garfield
© 2012 PAWS, INC. All Rights Reserved.

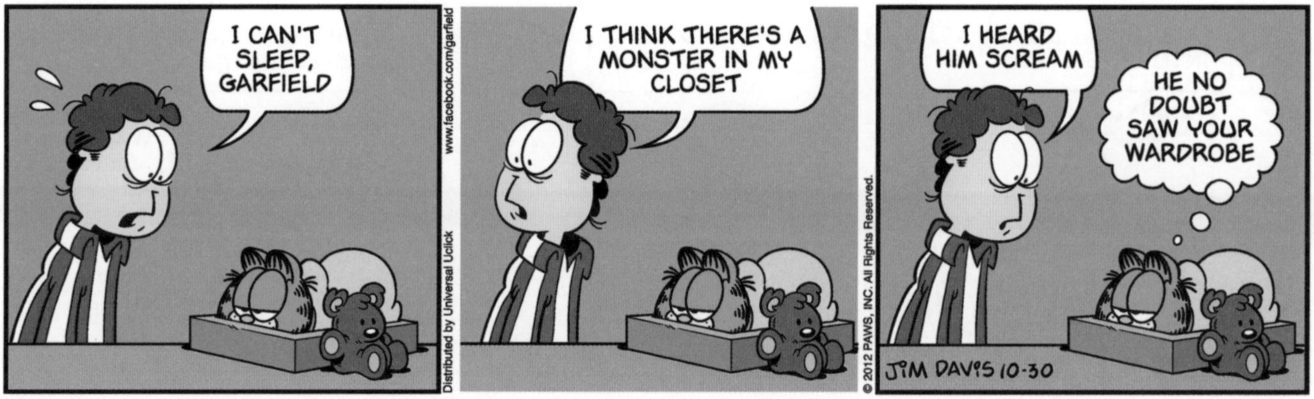
I CAN'T SLEEP, GARFIELD
I THINK THERE'S A MONSTER IN MY CLOSET
I HEARD HIM SCREAM
HE NO DOUBT SAW YOUR WARDROBE
JIM DAVIS 10-30
Distributed by Universal Uclick www.facebook.com/garfield
© 2012 PAWS, INC. All Rights Reserved.

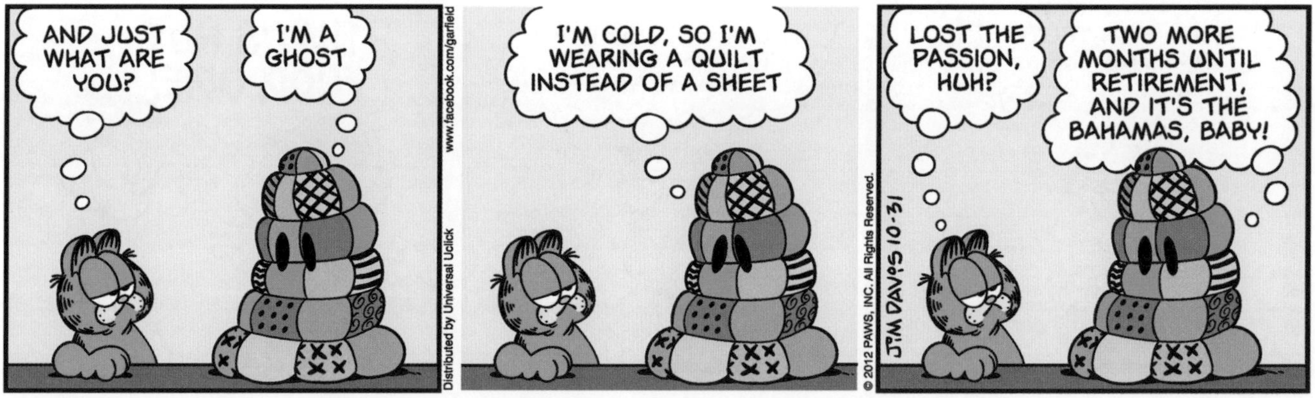
AND JUST WHAT ARE YOU?
I'M A GHOST
I'M COLD, SO I'M WEARING A QUILT INSTEAD OF A SHEET
LOST THE PASSION, HUH?
TWO MORE MONTHS UNTIL RETIREMENT, AND IT'S THE BAHAMAS, BABY!
JIM DAVIS 10-31
Distributed by Universal Uclick www.facebook.com/garfield
© 2012 PAWS, INC. All Rights Reserved.

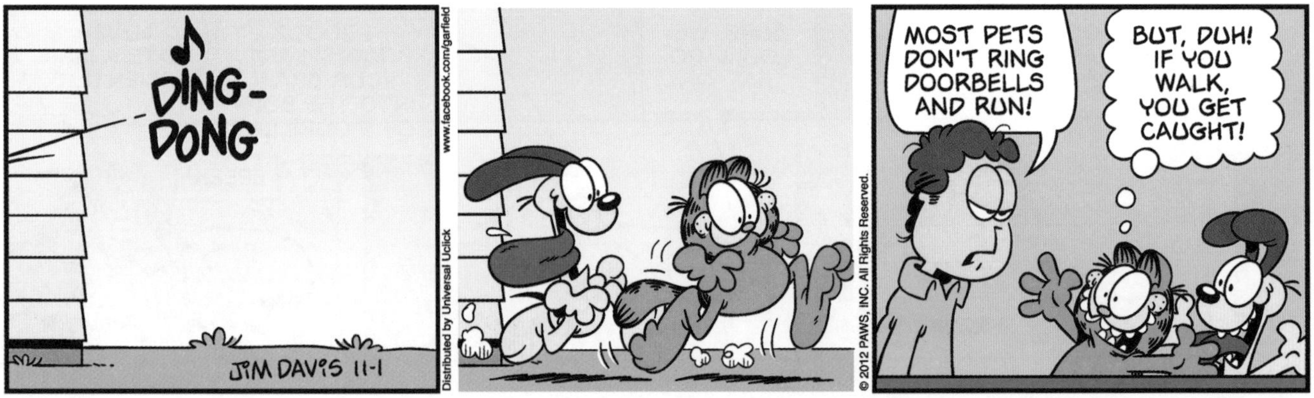

DING-DONG
JIM DAVIS 11-1
Distributed by Universal Uclick www.facebook.com/garfield
© 2012 PAWS, INC. All Rights Reserved.
MOST PETS DON'T RING DOORBELLS AND RUN!
BUT, DUH! IF YOU WALK, YOU GET CAUGHT!

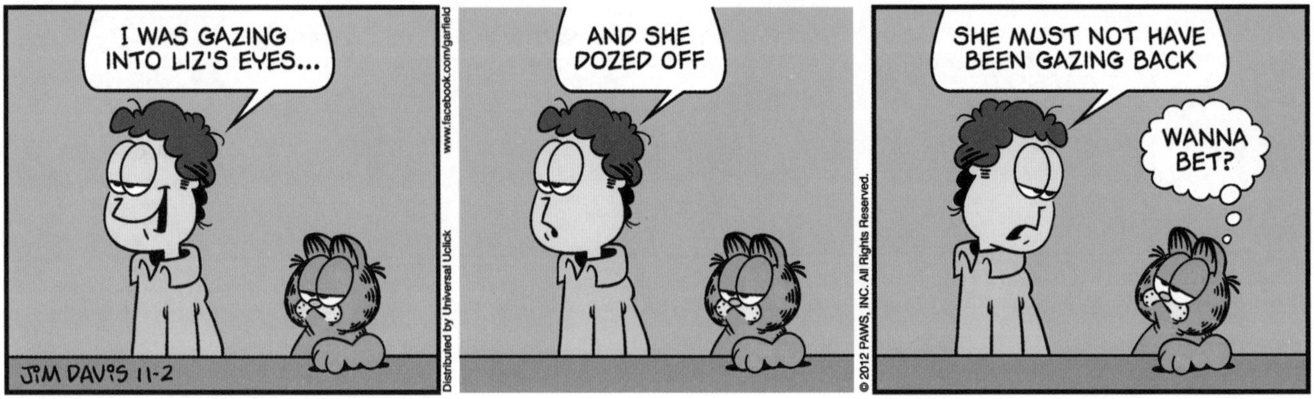

I WAS GAZING INTO LIZ'S EYES...
JIM DAVIS 11-2
Distributed by Universal Uclick www.facebook.com/garfield
AND SHE DOZED OFF
© 2012 PAWS, INC. All Rights Reserved.
SHE MUST NOT HAVE BEEN GAZING BACK
WANNA BET?

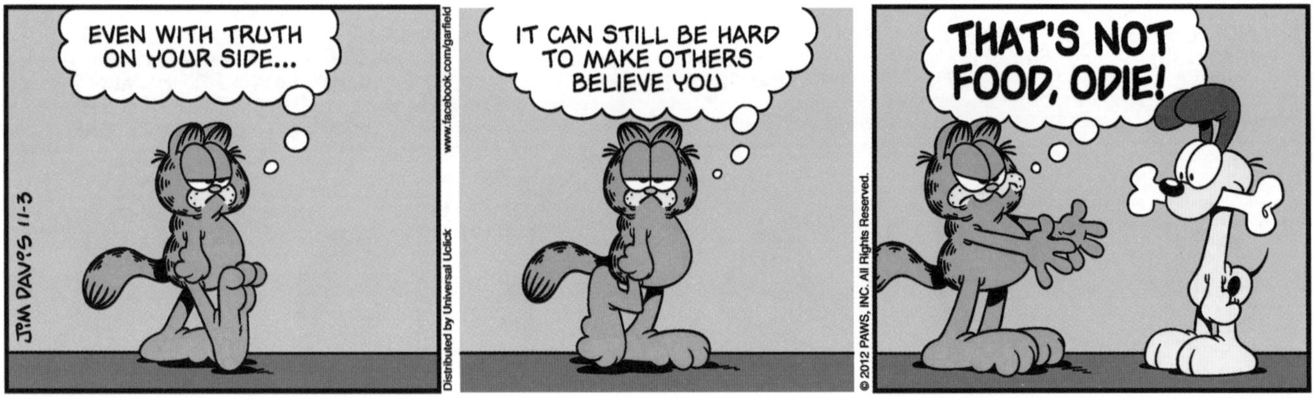

EVEN WITH TRUTH ON YOUR SIDE...
JIM DAVIS 11-3
Distributed by Universal Uclick www.facebook.com/garfield
IT CAN STILL BE HARD TO MAKE OTHERS BELIEVE YOU
© 2012 PAWS, INC. All Rights Reserved.
THAT'S NOT FOOD, ODIE!

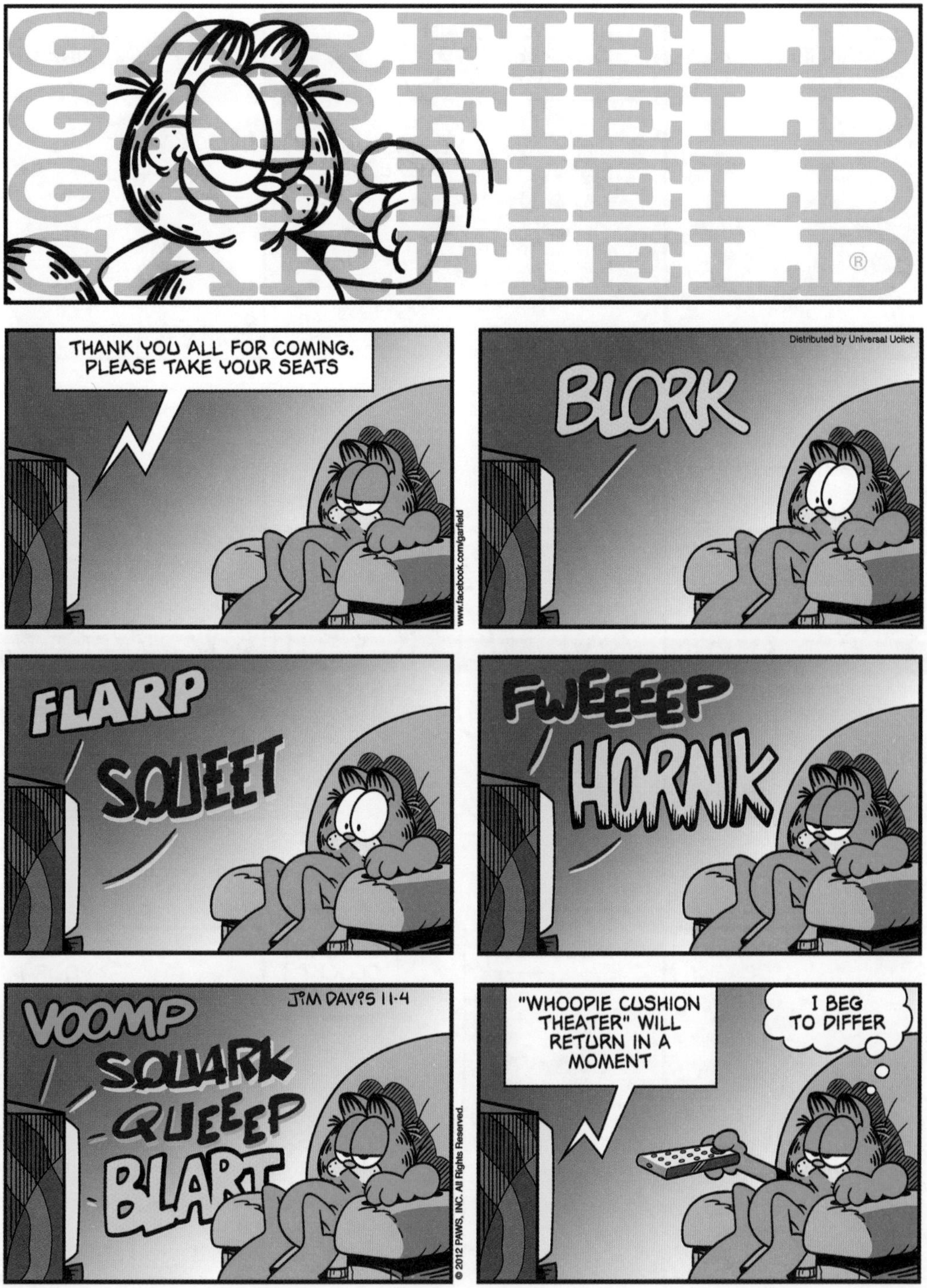
GARFIELD GARFIELD GARFIELD GARFIELD ®
THANK YOU ALL FOR COMING. PLEASE TAKE YOUR SEATS
Distributed by Universal Uclick
www.facebook.com/garfield
BLORK
FLARP
SQUEET
FWEEEEP
HORNK
JIM DAVIS 11-4
VOOMP
SQUARK
QUEEEP
BLART
© 2012 PAWS, INC. All Rights Reserved.
"WHOOPIE CUSHION THEATER" WILL RETURN IN A MOMENT
I BEG TO DIFFER

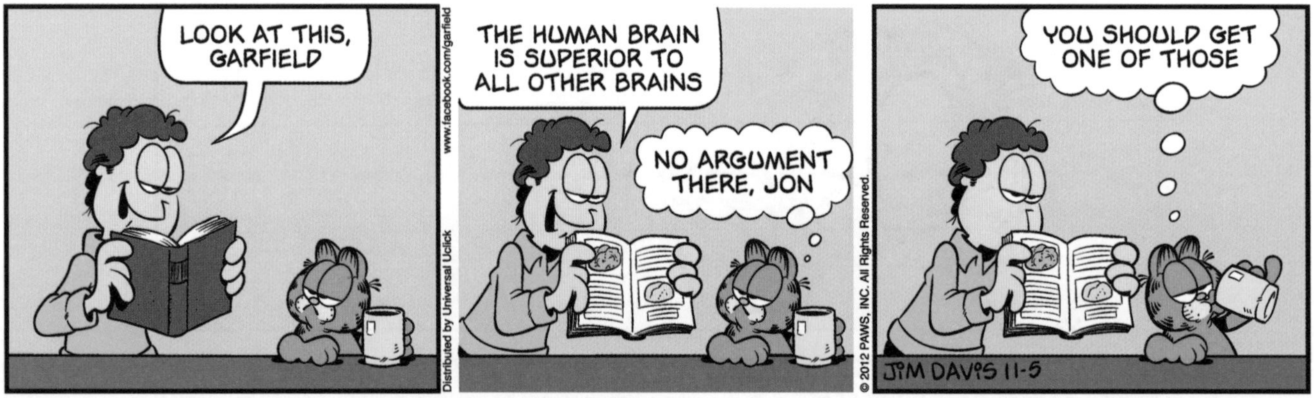
LOOK AT THIS, GARFIELD
Distributed by Universal Uclick www.facebook.com/garfield
THE HUMAN BRAIN IS SUPERIOR TO ALL OTHER BRAINS
NO ARGUMENT THERE, JON
© 2012 PAWS, INC. All Rights Reserved.
YOU SHOULD GET ONE OF THOSE
JIM DAVIS 11-5

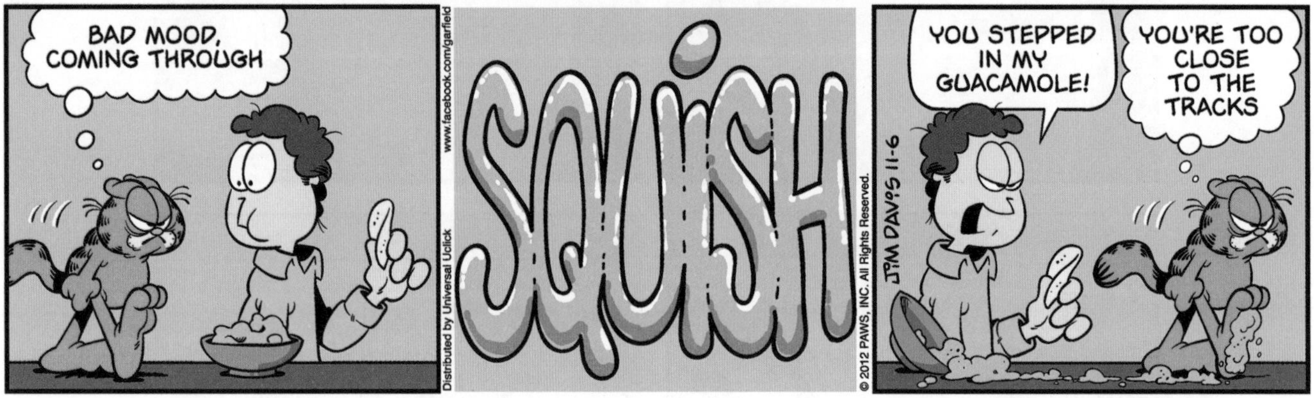
BAD MOOD, COMING THROUGH
Distributed by Universal Uclick www.facebook.com/garfield
SQUISH
© 2012 PAWS, INC. All Rights Reserved.
JIM DAVIS 11-6
YOU STEPPED IN MY GUACAMOLE!
YOU'RE TOO CLOSE TO THE TRACKS

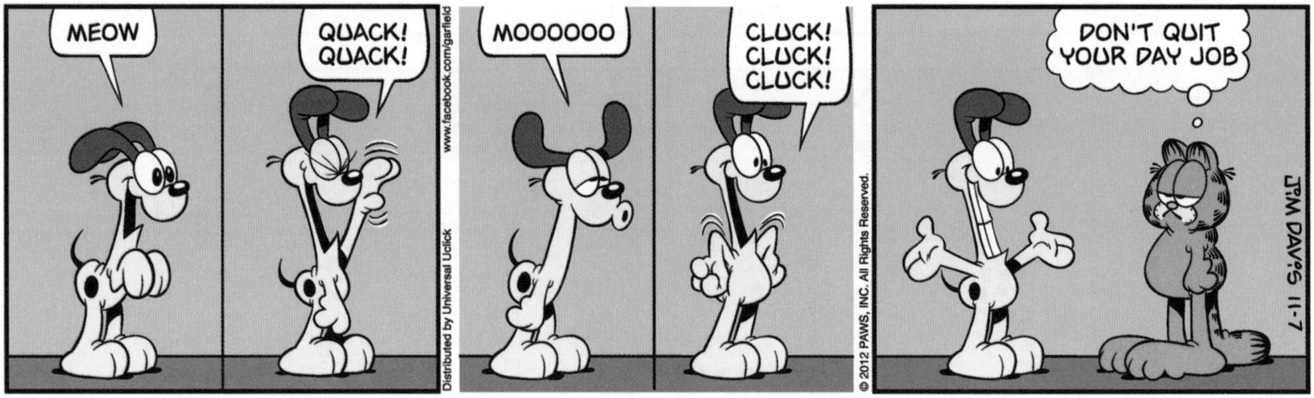
MEOW
QUACK! QUACK!
Distributed by Universal Uclick www.facebook.com/garfield
MOOOOOO
CLUCK! CLUCK! CLUCK!
© 2012 PAWS, INC. All Rights Reserved.
DON'T QUIT YOUR DAY JOB
JIM DAVIS 11-7

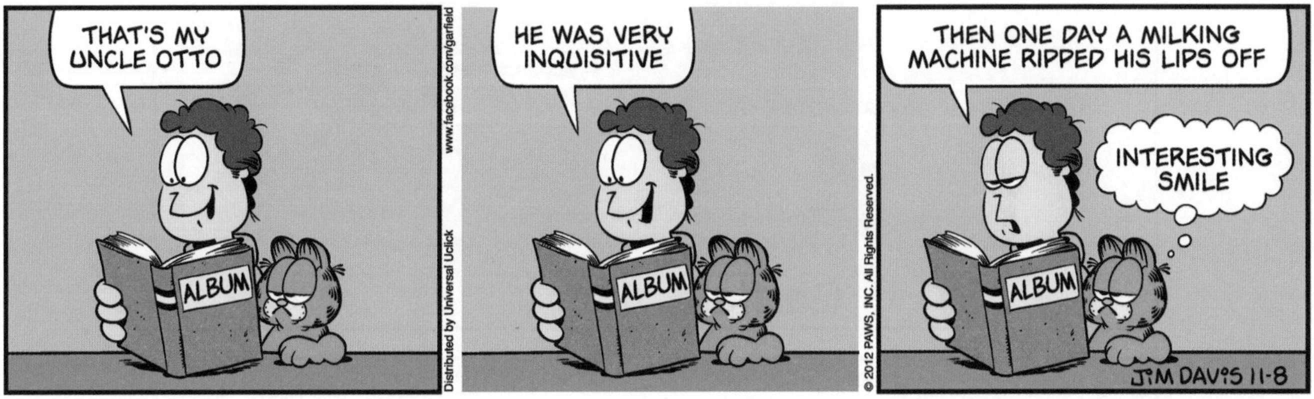
THAT'S MY UNCLE OTTO
ALBUM
www.facebook.com/garfield
Distributed by Universal Uclick
HE WAS VERY INQUISITIVE
ALBUM
© 2012 PAWS, INC. All Rights Reserved.
THEN ONE DAY A MILKING MACHINE RIPPED HIS LIPS OFF
INTERESTING SMILE
ALBUM
JIM DAVIS 11-8

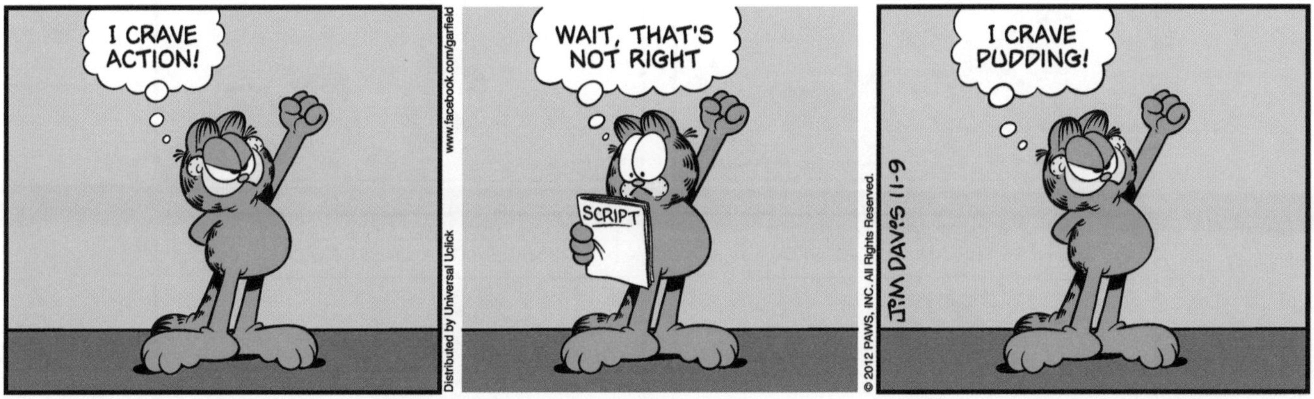
I CRAVE ACTION!
www.facebook.com/garfield
Distributed by Universal Uclick
WAIT, THAT'S NOT RIGHT
SCRIPT
JIM DAVIS 11-9
© 2012 PAWS, INC. All Rights Reserved.
I CRAVE PUDDING!

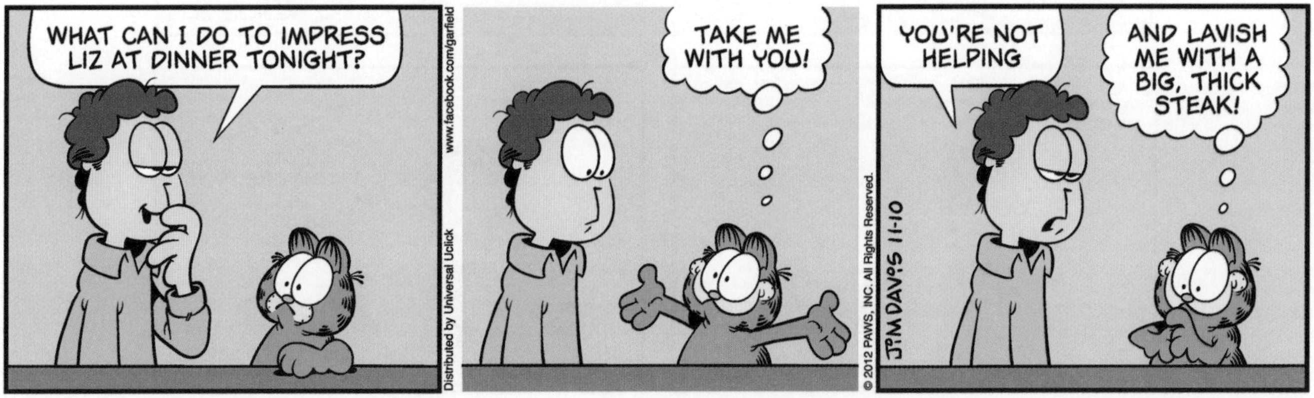
WHAT CAN I DO TO IMPRESS LIZ AT DINNER TONIGHT?
www.facebook.com/garfield
Distributed by Universal Uclick
TAKE ME WITH YOU!
JIM DAVIS 11-10
© 2012 PAWS, INC. All Rights Reserved.
YOU'RE NOT HELPING
AND LAVISH ME WITH A BIG, THICK STEAK!

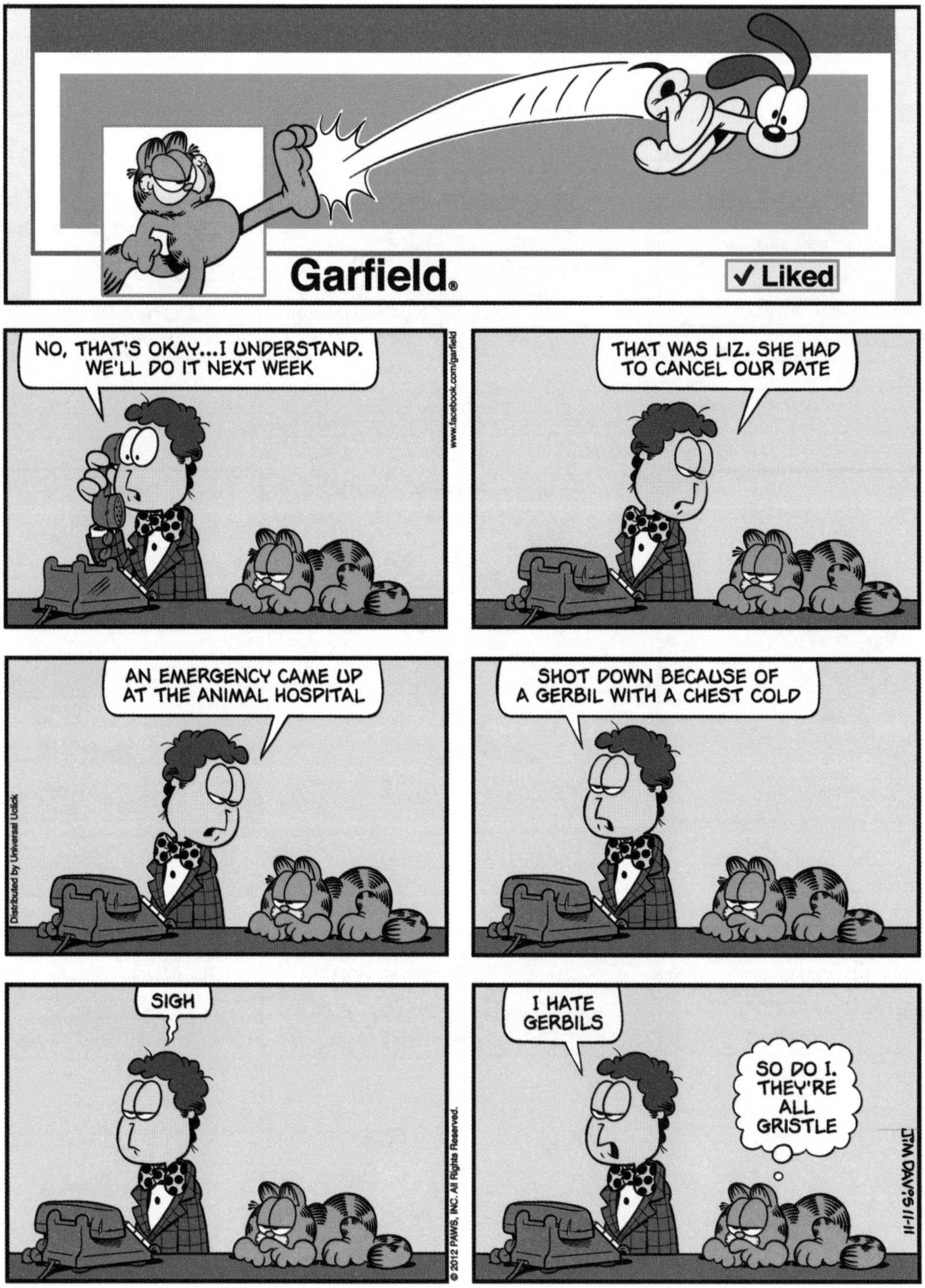
Garfield®
✓ Liked
NO, THAT'S OKAY...I UNDERSTAND. WE'LL DO IT NEXT WEEK
www.facebook.com/garfield
THAT WAS LIZ. SHE HAD TO CANCEL OUR DATE
AN EMERGENCY CAME UP AT THE ANIMAL HOSPITAL
Distributed by Universal Uclick
SHOT DOWN BECAUSE OF A GERBIL WITH A CHEST COLD
SIGH
© 2012 PAWS, INC. All Rights Reserved.
I HATE GERBILS
SO DO I. THEY'RE ALL GRISTLE
JIM DAVIS 11-11

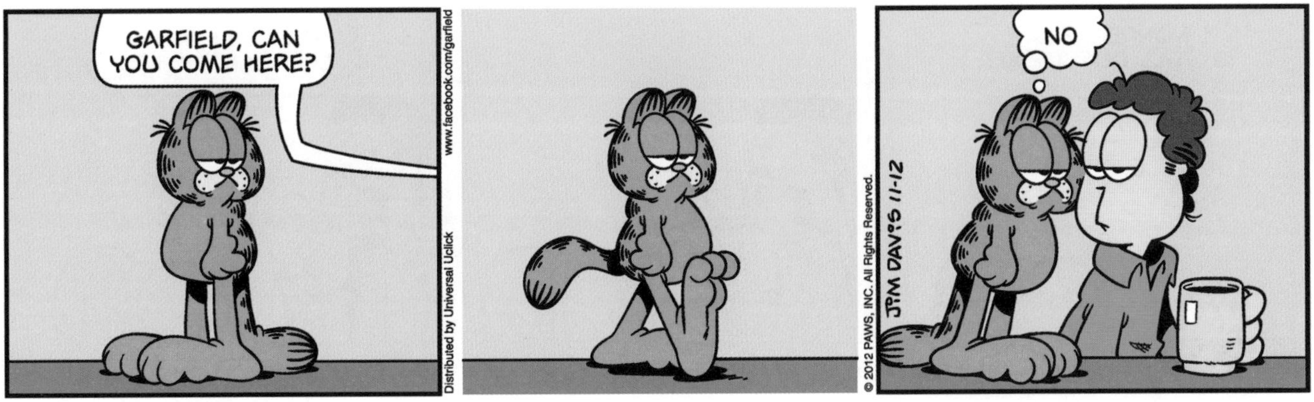
GARFIELD, CAN YOU COME HERE?
NO
JIM DAVIS 11-12
www.facebook.com/garfield
Distributed by Universal Uclick
© 2012 PAWS, INC. All Rights Reserved.

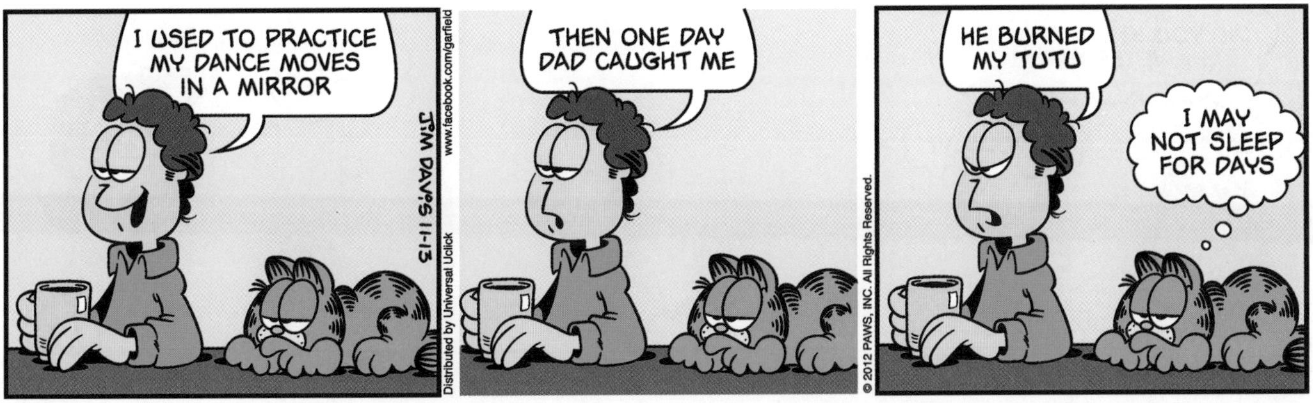
I USED TO PRACTICE MY DANCE MOVES IN A MIRROR
THEN ONE DAY DAD CAUGHT ME
HE BURNED MY TUTU
I MAY NOT SLEEP FOR DAYS
JIM DAVIS 11-13
www.facebook.com/garfield
Distributed by Universal Uclick
© 2012 PAWS, INC. All Rights Reserved.

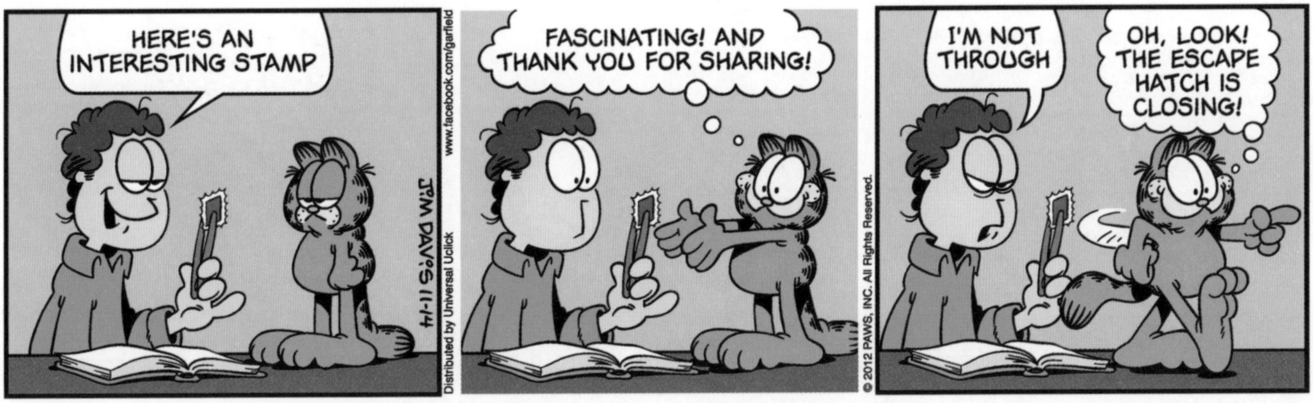
HERE'S AN INTERESTING STAMP
FASCINATING! AND THANK YOU FOR SHARING!
I'M NOT THROUGH
OH, LOOK! THE ESCAPE HATCH IS CLOSING!
JIM DAVIS 11-14
www.facebook.com/garfield
Distributed by Universal Uclick
© 2012 PAWS, INC. All Rights Reserved.

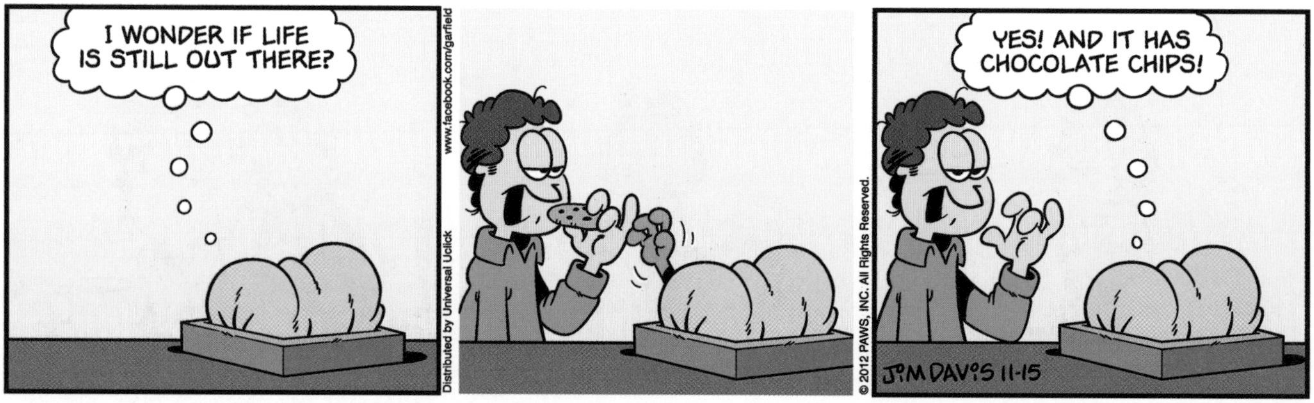
I WONDER IF LIFE IS STILL OUT THERE?
YES! AND IT HAS CHOCOLATE CHIPS!
Distributed by Universal Uclick www.facebook.com/garfield
© 2012 PAWS, INC. All Rights Reserved.
JIM DAVIS 11-15

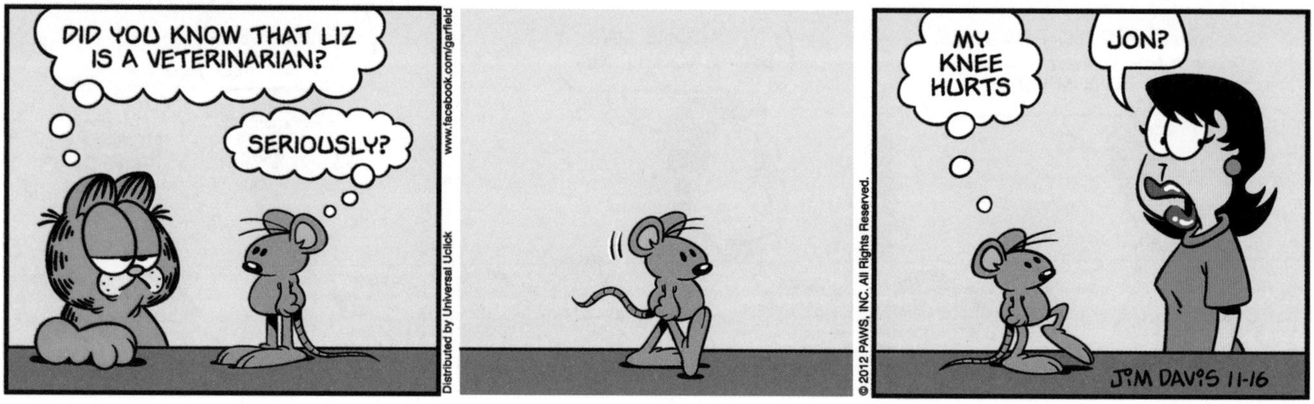
DID YOU KNOW THAT LIZ IS A VETERINARIAN?
SERIOUSLY?
MY KNEE HURTS
JON?
Distributed by Universal Uclick www.facebook.com/garfield
© 2012 PAWS, INC. All Rights Reserved.
JIM DAVIS 11-16

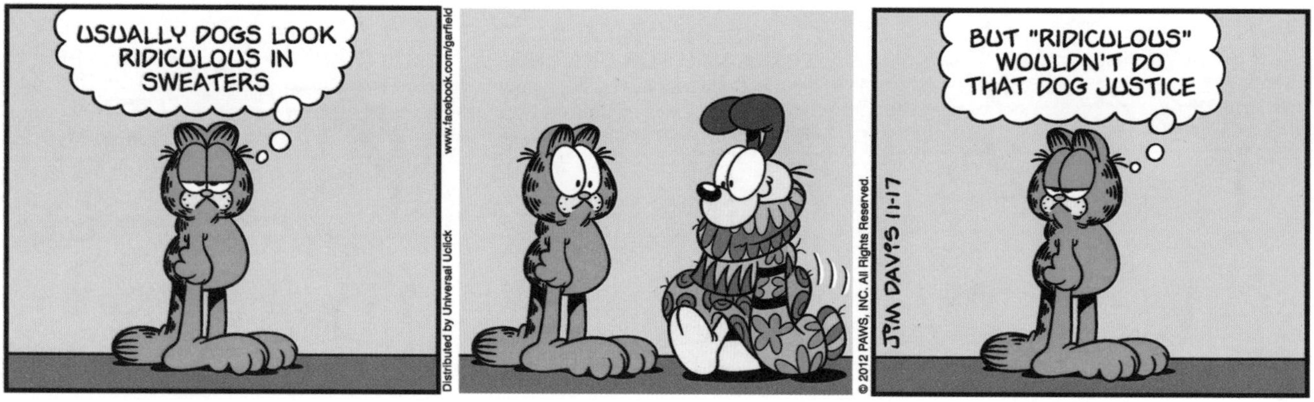
USUALLY DOGS LOOK RIDICULOUS IN SWEATERS
BUT "RIDICULOUS" WOULDN'T DO THAT DOG JUSTICE
Distributed by Universal Uclick www.facebook.com/garfield
© 2012 PAWS, INC. All Rights Reserved.
JIM DAVIS 11-17

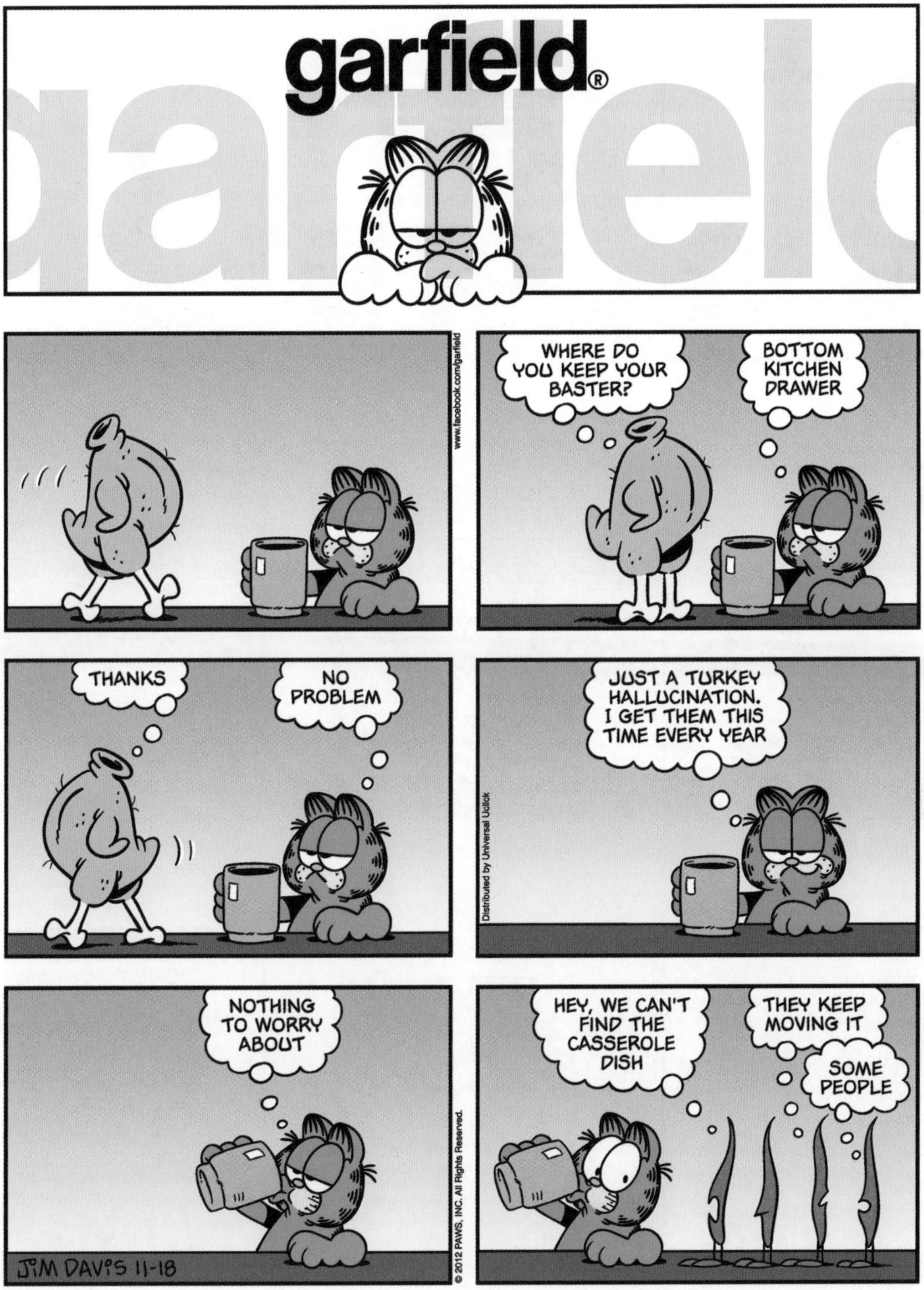
garfield®
www.facebook.com/garfield
WHERE DO YOU KEEP YOUR BASTER?
BOTTOM KITCHEN DRAWER
THANKS
NO PROBLEM
JUST A TURKEY HALLUCINATION. I GET THEM THIS TIME EVERY YEAR
Distributed by Universal Uclick
NOTHING TO WORRY ABOUT
JIM DAVIS 11-18
© 2012 PAWS, INC. All Rights Reserved.
HEY, WE CAN'T FIND THE CASSEROLE DISH
THEY KEEP MOVING IT
SOME PEOPLE

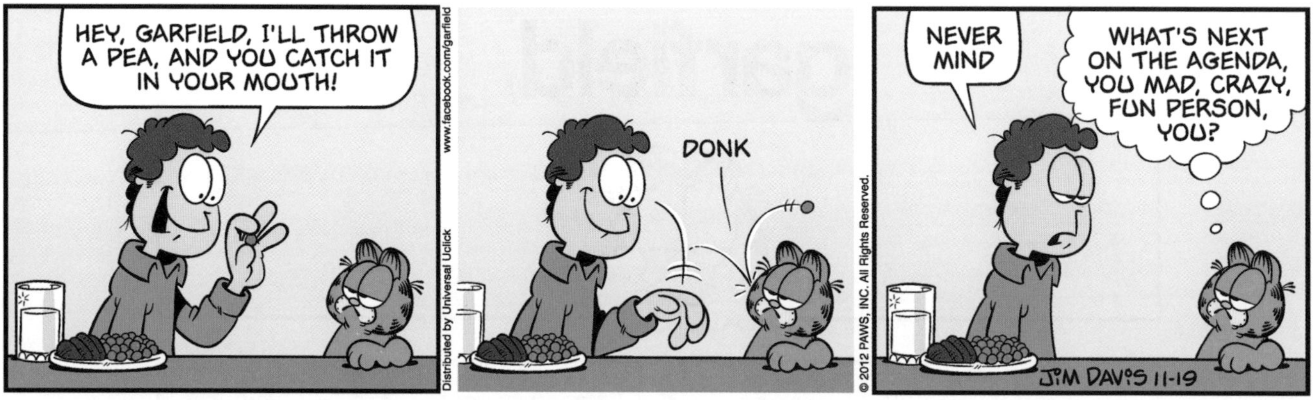
HEY, GARFIELD, I'LL THROW A PEA, AND YOU CATCH IT IN YOUR MOUTH!
DONK
NEVER MIND
WHAT'S NEXT ON THE AGENDA, YOU MAD, CRAZY, FUN PERSON, YOU?
JIM DAVIS 11-19

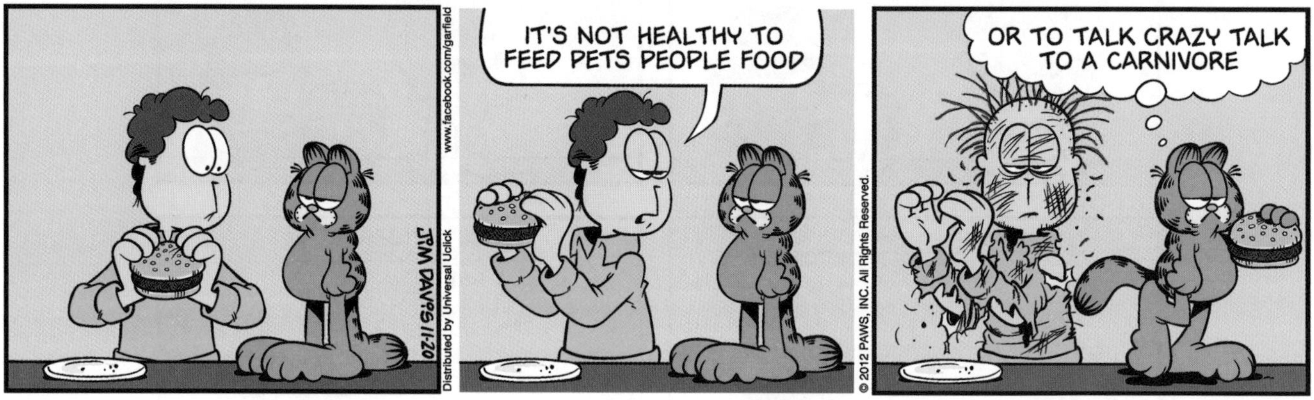
JIM DAVIS 11-20
IT'S NOT HEALTHY TO FEED PETS PEOPLE FOOD
OR TO TALK CRAZY TALK TO A CARNIVORE

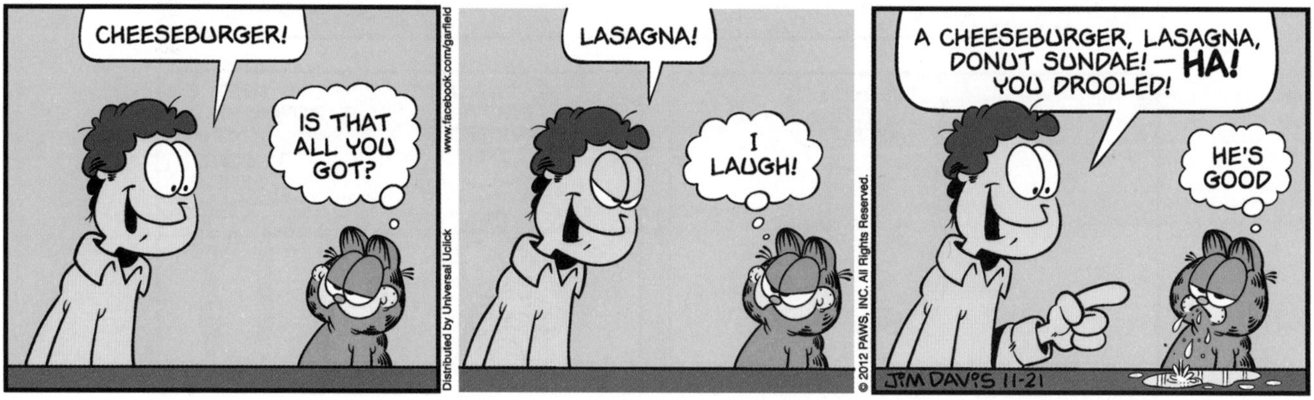
CHEESEBURGER!
IS THAT ALL YOU GOT?
LASAGNA!
I LAUGH!
A CHEESEBURGER, LASAGNA, DONUT SUNDAE! — HA! YOU DROOLED!
HE'S GOOD
JIM DAVIS 11-21

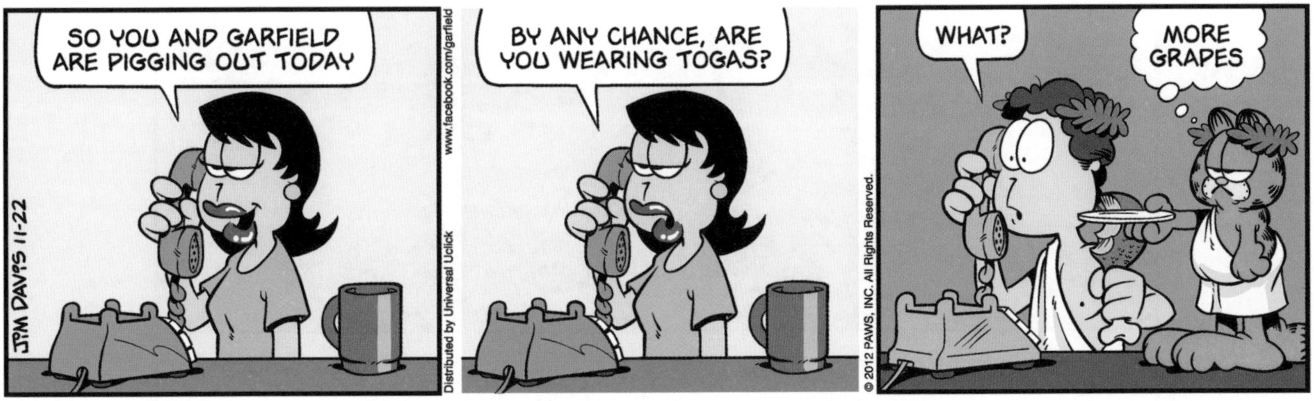
SO YOU AND GARFIELD ARE PIGGING OUT TODAY
JIM DAVIS 11-22
Distributed by Universal Uclick www.facebook.com/garfield
BY ANY CHANCE, ARE YOU WEARING TOGAS?
© 2012 PAWS, INC. All Rights Reserved.
WHAT?
MORE GRAPES

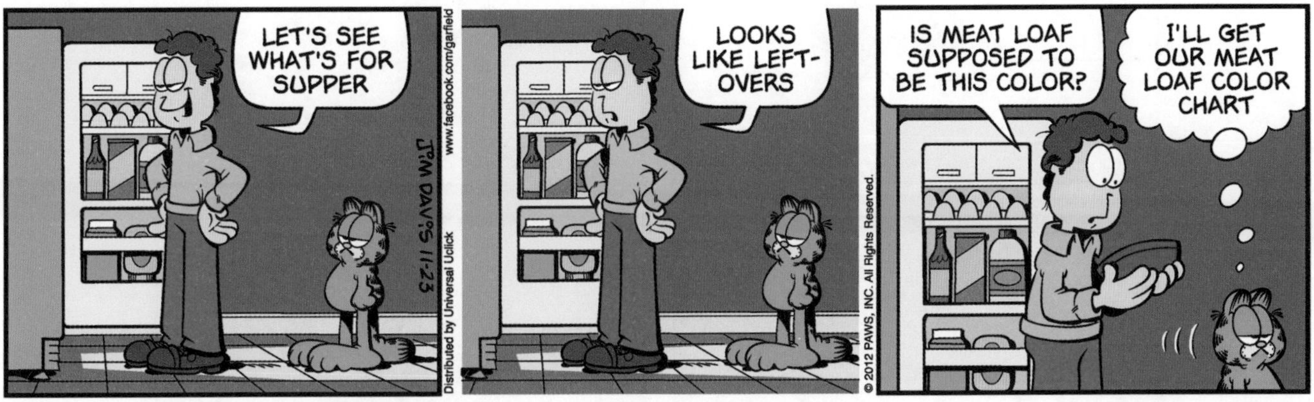
LET'S SEE WHAT'S FOR SUPPER
JIM DAVIS 11-23
Distributed by Universal Uclick www.facebook.com/garfield
LOOKS LIKE LEFT-OVERS
© 2012 PAWS, INC. All Rights Reserved.
IS MEAT LOAF SUPPOSED TO BE THIS COLOR?
I'LL GET OUR MEAT LOAF COLOR CHART

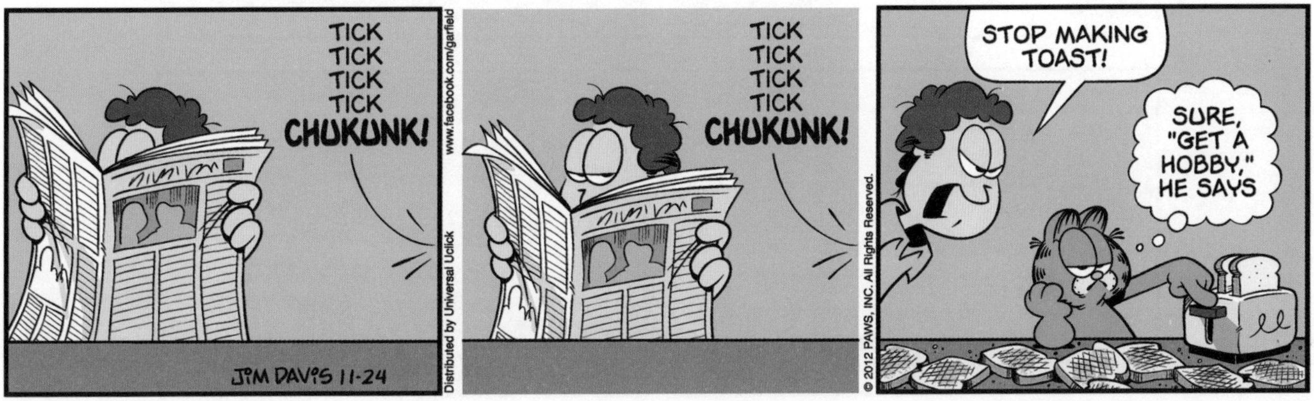
TICK TICK TICK TICK CHUKUNK!
JIM DAVIS 11-24
Distributed by Universal Uclick www.facebook.com/garfield
TICK TICK TICK TICK CHUKUNK!
© 2012 PAWS, INC. All Rights Reserved.
STOP MAKING TOAST!
SURE, "GET A HOBBY," HE SAYS

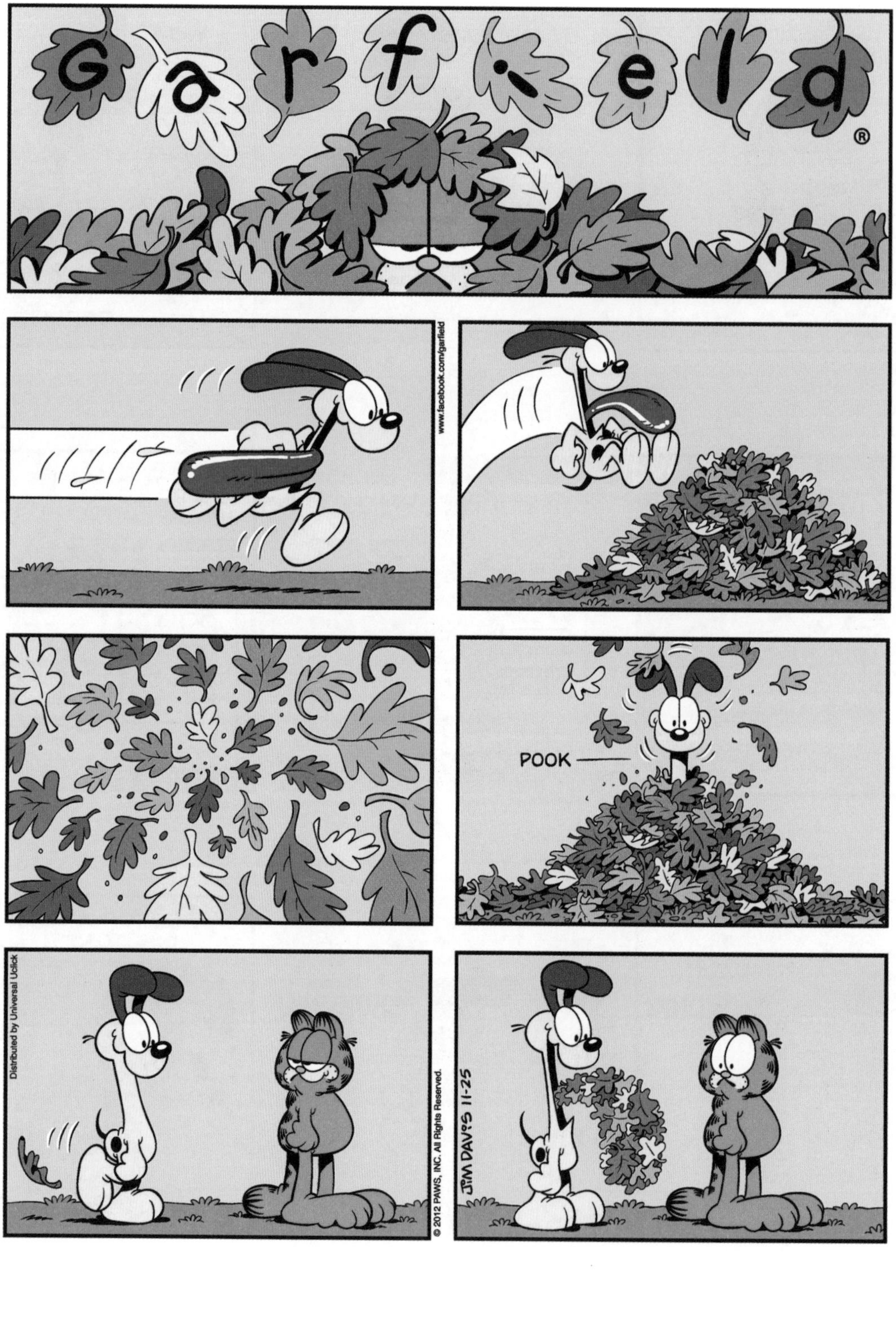
Garfield®
www.facebook.com/garfield
POOK
Distributed by Universal Uclick
© 2012 PAWS, INC. All Rights Reserved.
JIM DAVIS 11-25

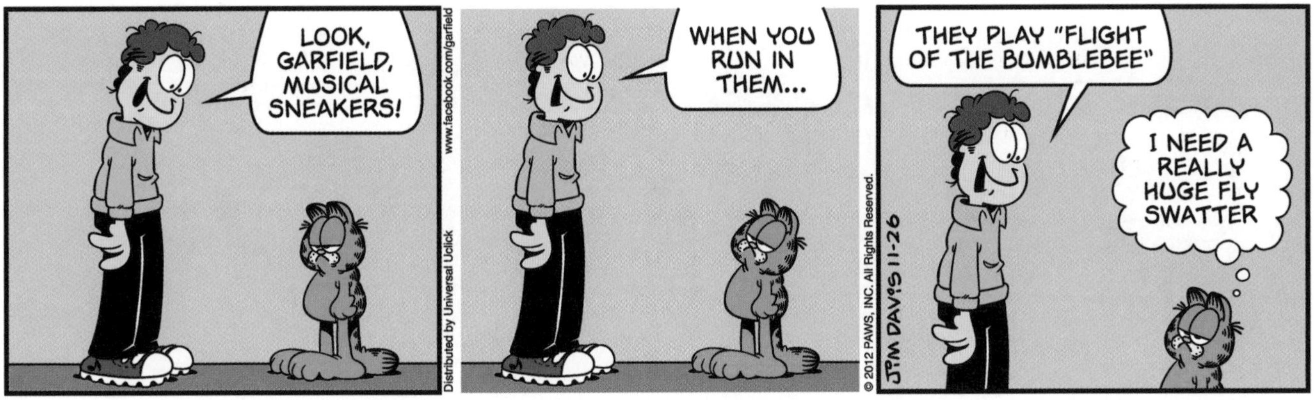
LOOK, GARFIELD, MUSICAL SNEAKERS!
Distributed by Universal Uclick www.facebook.com/garfield
WHEN YOU RUN IN THEM...
© 2012 PAWS, INC. All Rights Reserved.
JIM DAVIS 11-26
THEY PLAY "FLIGHT OF THE BUMBLEBEE"
I NEED A REALLY HUGE FLY SWATTER

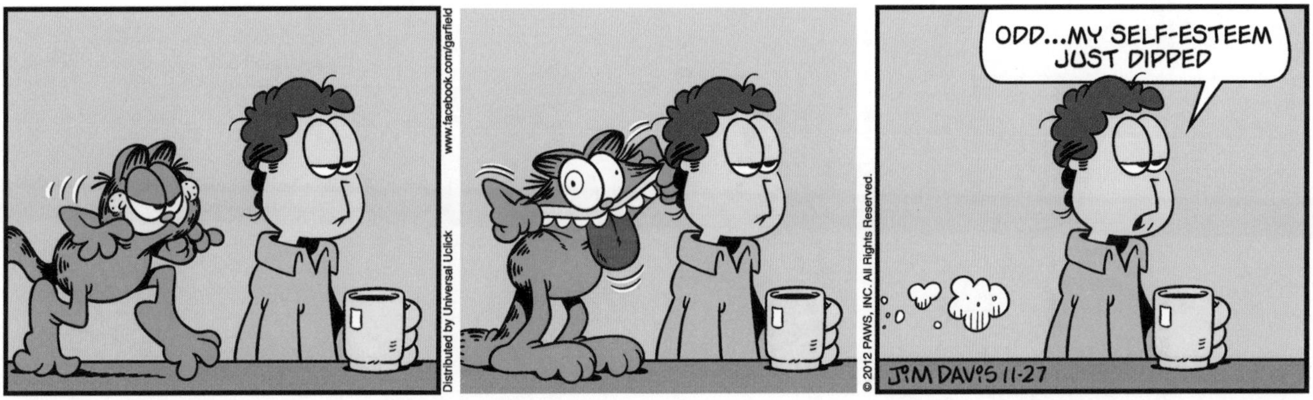
Distributed by Universal Uclick www.facebook.com/garfield
© 2012 PAWS, INC. All Rights Reserved.
ODD...MY SELF-ESTEEM JUST DIPPED
JIM DAVIS 11-27

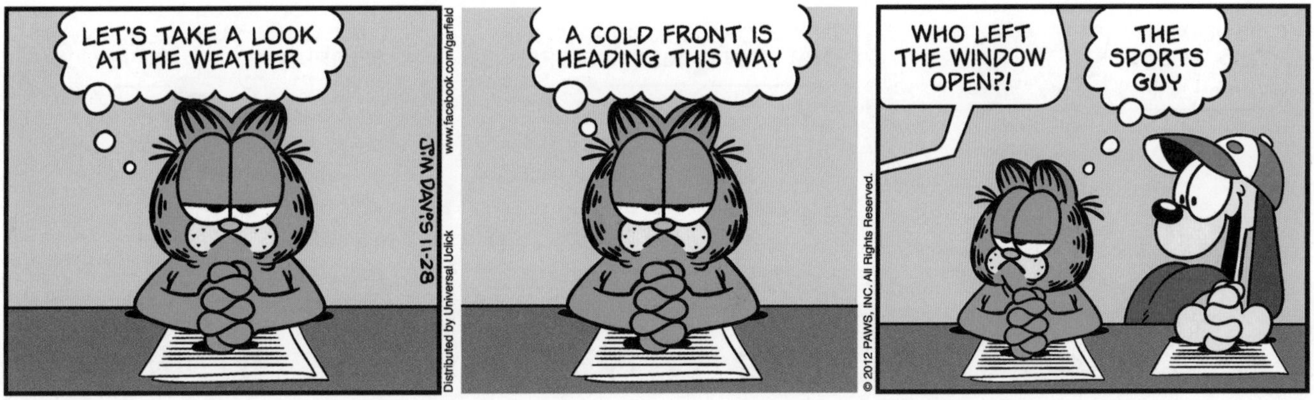
LET'S TAKE A LOOK AT THE WEATHER
JIM DAVIS 11-28
Distributed by Universal Uclick www.facebook.com/garfield
A COLD FRONT IS HEADING THIS WAY
© 2012 PAWS, INC. All Rights Reserved.
WHO LEFT THE WINDOW OPEN?!
THE SPORTS GUY

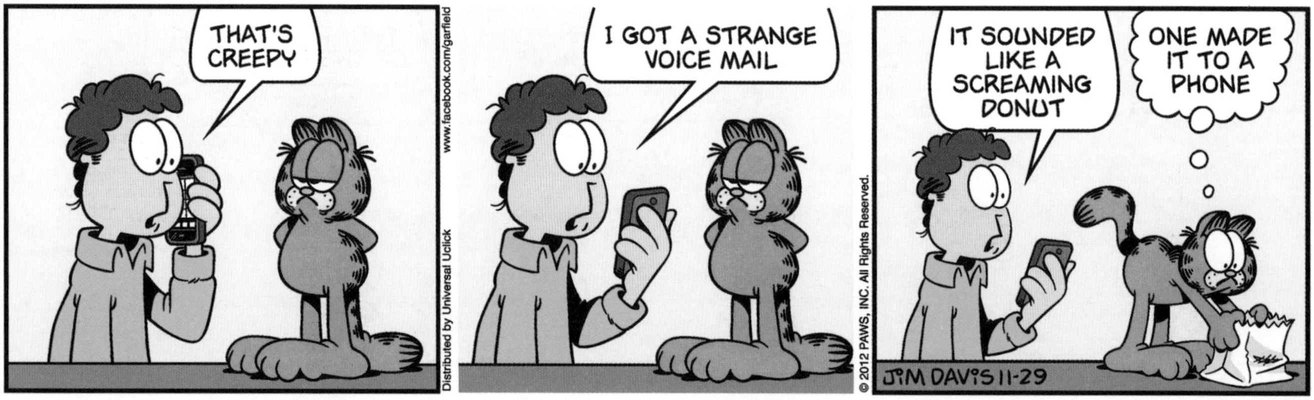
THAT'S CREEPY
www.facebook.com/garfield
Distributed by Universal Uclick
I GOT A STRANGE VOICE MAIL
© 2012 PAWS, INC. All Rights Reserved.
IT SOUNDED LIKE A SCREAMING DONUT
ONE MADE IT TO A PHONE
JIM DAVIS 11-29

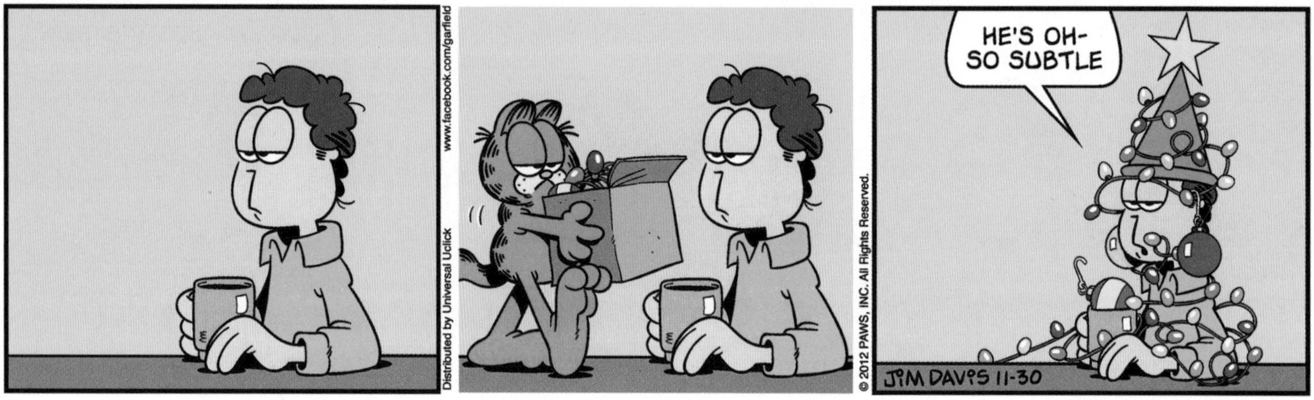
www.facebook.com/garfield
Distributed by Universal Uclick
© 2012 PAWS, INC. All Rights Reserved.
HE'S OH-SO SUBTLE
JIM DAVIS 11-30

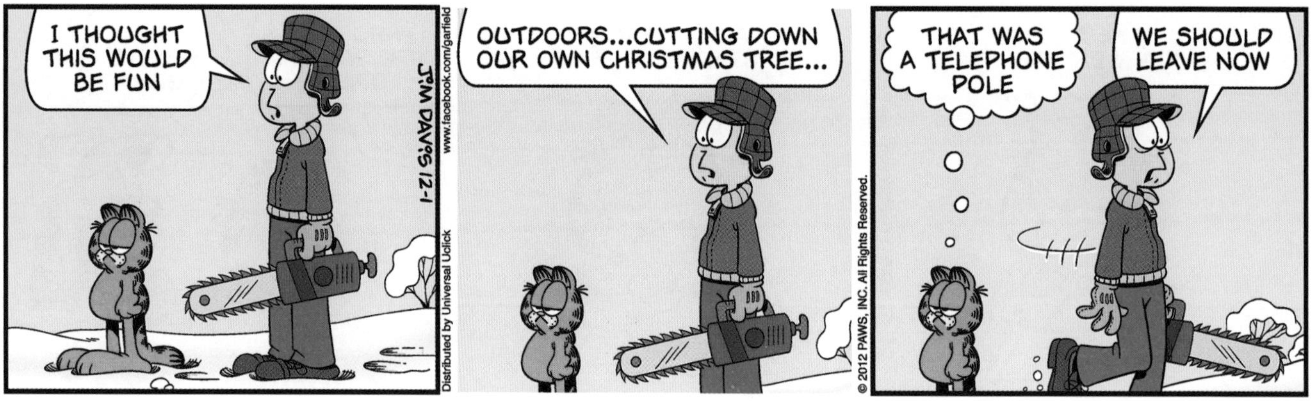
I THOUGHT THIS WOULD BE FUN
JIM DAVIS 12-1
www.facebook.com/garfield
Distributed by Universal Uclick
OUTDOORS...CUTTING DOWN OUR OWN CHRISTMAS TREE...
© 2012 PAWS, INC. All Rights Reserved.
THAT WAS A TELEPHONE POLE
WE SHOULD LEAVE NOW

More Super School Excuses

Why I Had a Bad Game...

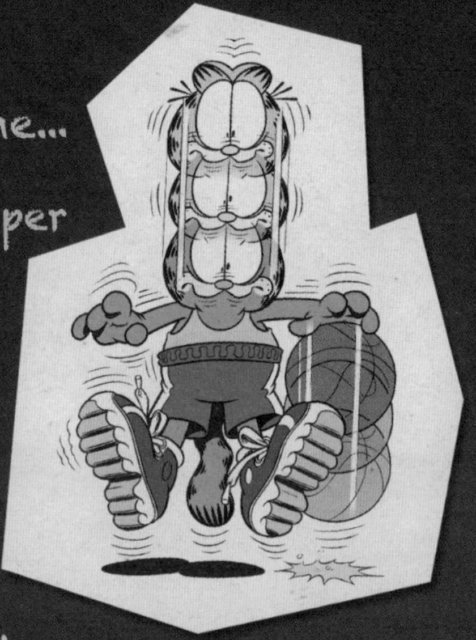

A grasshopper hopped up my nose!

Why I Was Absent...

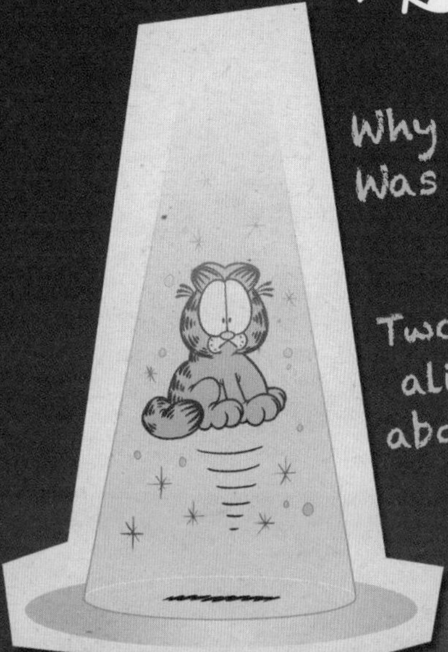

Two words: alien abduction!

Why I Need to See the Nurse...

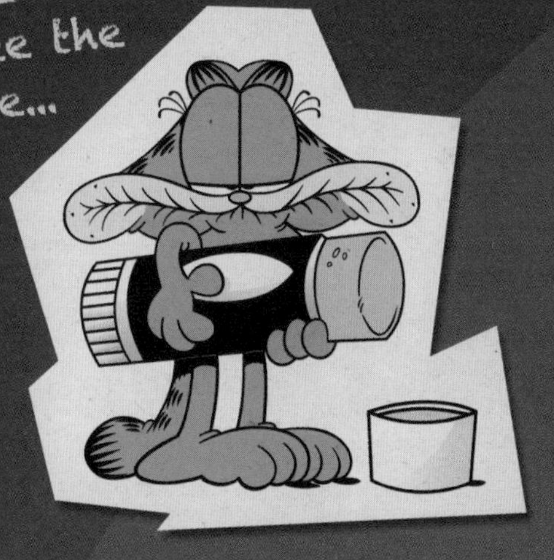

I have a chapped-lip emergency.

Why I Can't Go Out with You...

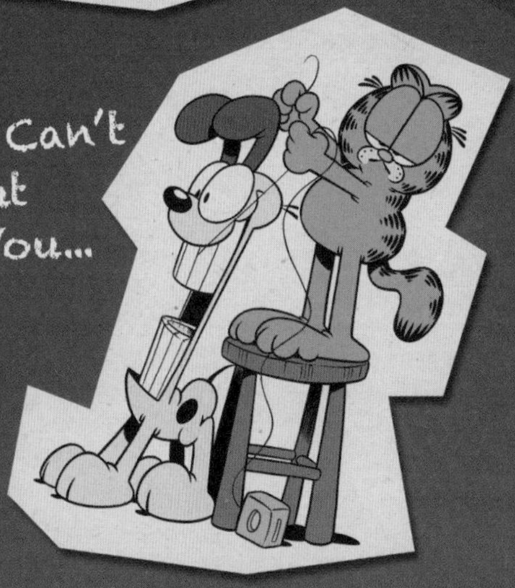

Sorry, but that's my night to floss the dog.

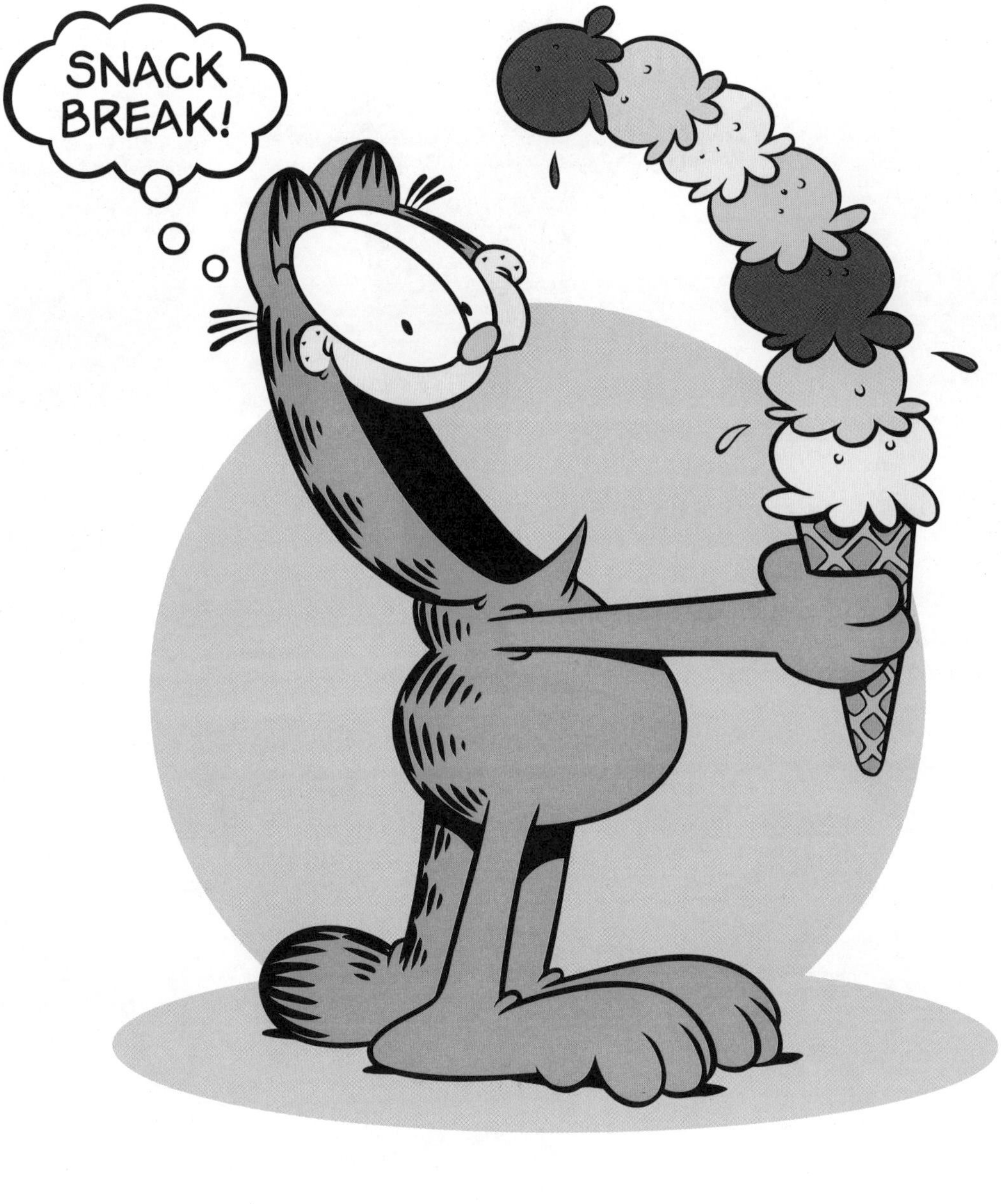
SNACK BREAK!

Garfield
CLEANS HIS PLATE

BY JIM DAVIS

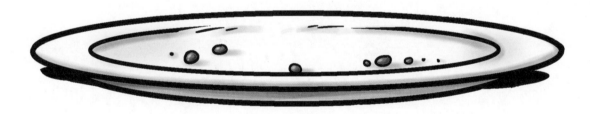

Ballantine Books • New York

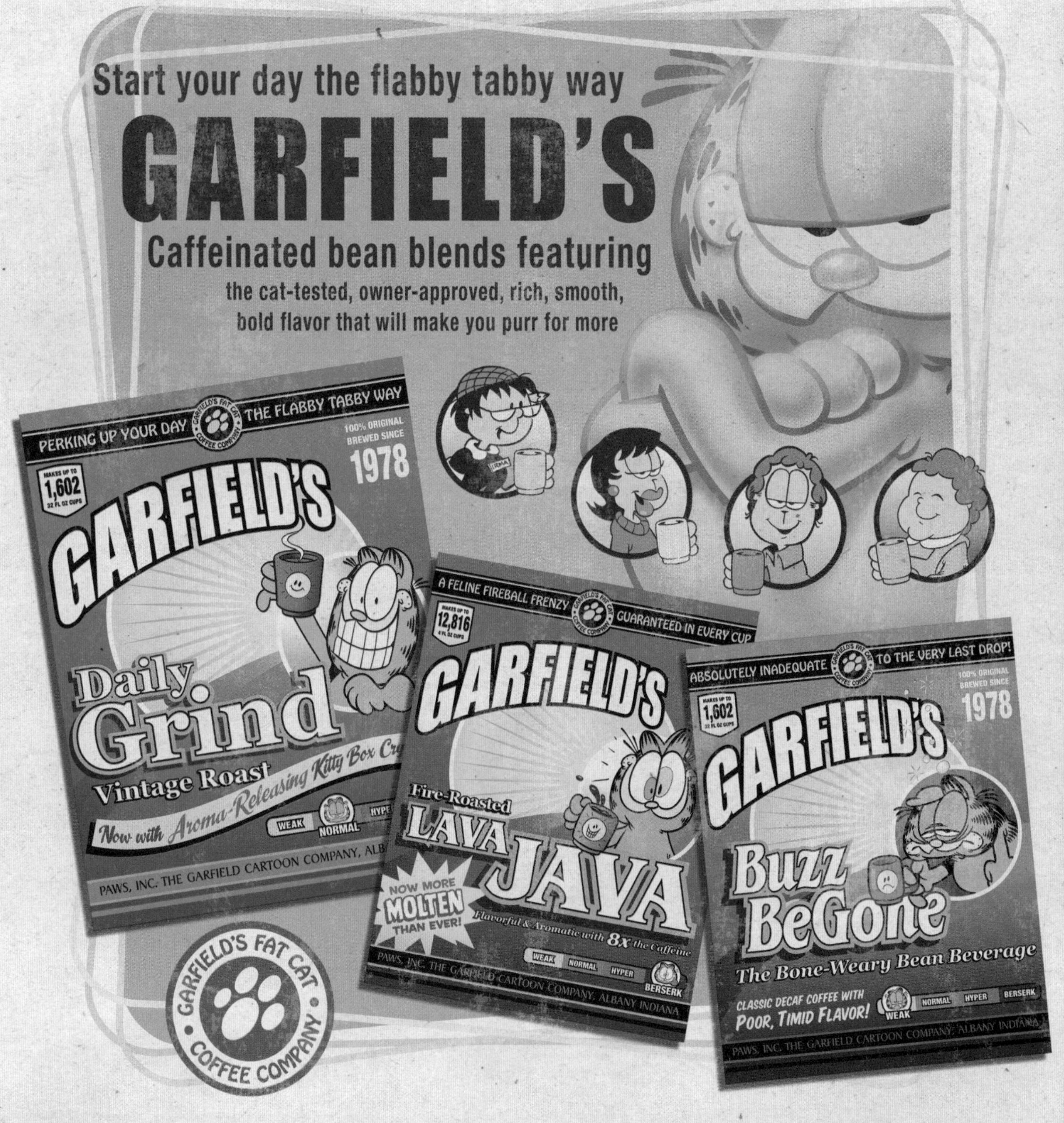
Start your day the flabby tabby way
GARFIELD'S
Caffeinated bean blends featuring
the cat-tested, owner-approved, rich, smooth, bold flavor that will make you purr for more
PERKING UP YOUR DAY
GARFIELD'S FAT CAT COFFEE COMPANY
THE FLABBY TABBY WAY
100% ORIGINAL BREWED SINCE 1978
MAKES UP TO 1,602 32 FL OZ CUPS
GARFIELD'S
Daily Grind
Vintage Roast
Now with Aroma-Releasing Kitty Box
WEAK
NORMAL
PAWS, INC. THE GARFIELD CARTOON COMPANY,
A FELINE FIREBALL FRENZY
GUARANTEED IN EVERY CUP
MAKES UP TO 12,816 4 FL OZ CUPS
GARFIELD'S
Fire-Roasted
LAVA JAVA
NOW MORE MOLTEN THAN EVER!
Flavorful & Aromatic with 8x the Caffeine
WEAK
NORMAL
HYPER
BERSERK
PAWS, INC. THE GARFIELD CARTOON COMPANY, ALBANY INDIANA
ABSOLUTELY INADEQUATE
TO THE VERY LAST DROP!
100% ORIGINAL BREWED SINCE 1978
MAKES UP TO 1,602 32 FL OZ CUPS
GARFIELD'S
Buzz BeGone
The Bone-Weary Bean Beverage
CLASSIC DECAF COFFEE WITH POOR, TIMID FLAVOR!
WEAK
NORMAL
HYPER
BERSERK
PAWS, INC. THE GARFIELD CARTOON COMPANY, ALBANY INDIANA
GARFIELD'S FAT CAT COFFEE COMPANY

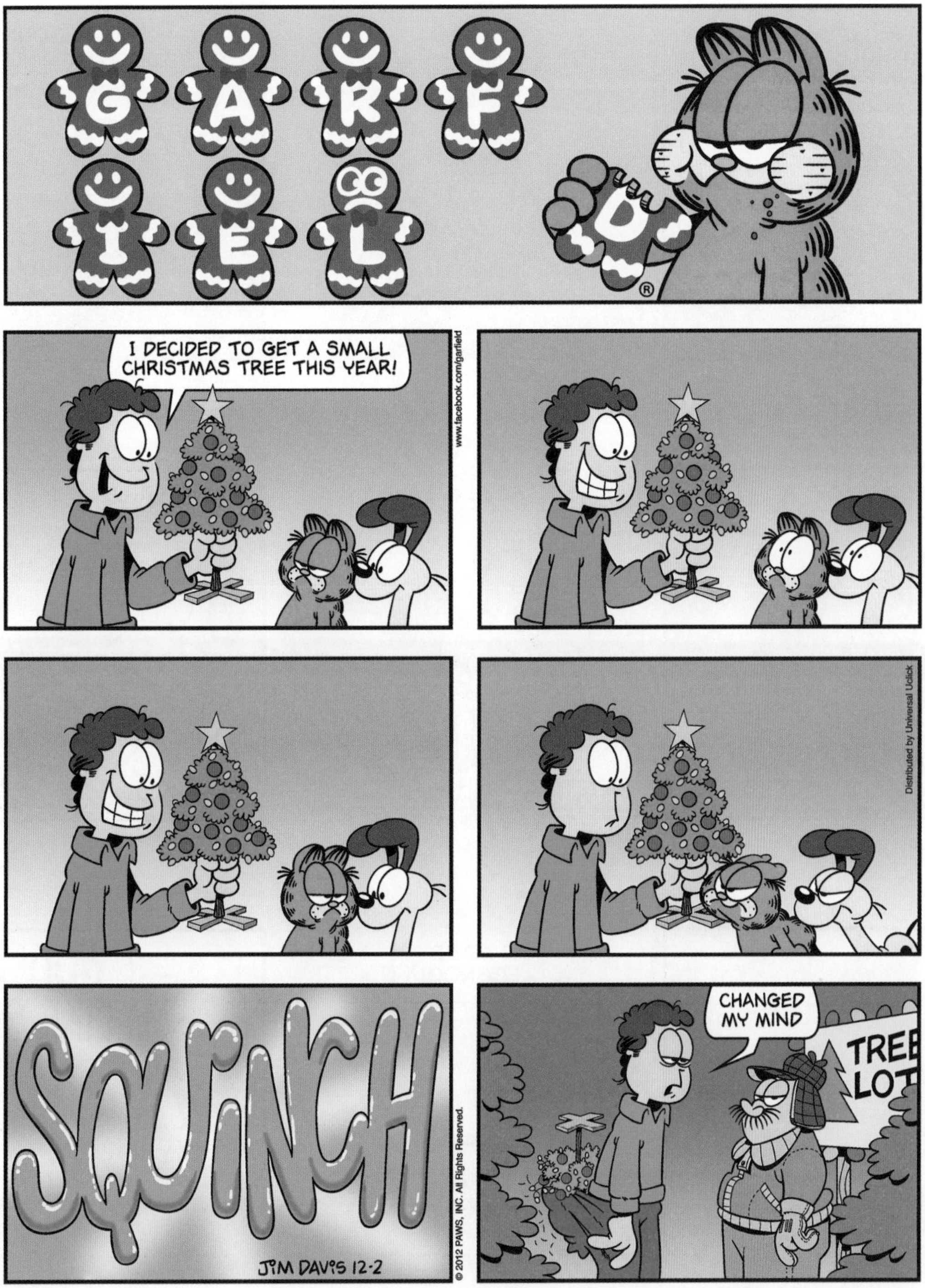
GARFIELD
I DECIDED TO GET A SMALL CHRISTMAS TREE THIS YEAR!
www.facebook.com/garfield
Distributed by Universal Uclick
SQUINCH
JIM DAVIS 12-2
© 2012 PAWS, INC. All Rights Reserved.
CHANGED MY MIND
TREE LOT

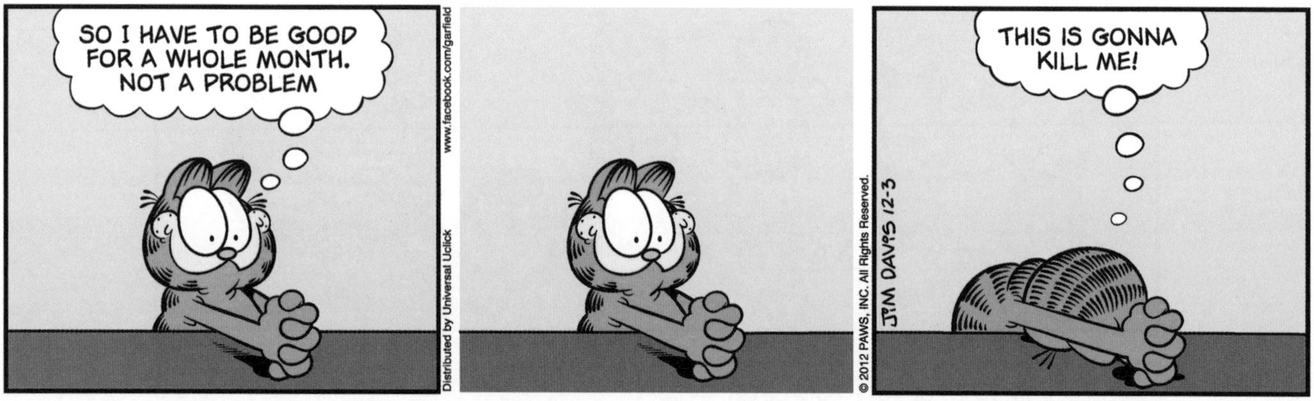
SO I HAVE TO BE GOOD FOR A WHOLE MONTH. NOT A PROBLEM
Distributed by Universal Uclick www.facebook.com/garfield
© 2012 PAWS, INC. All Rights Reserved.
JIM DAVIS 12-3
THIS IS GONNA KILL ME!

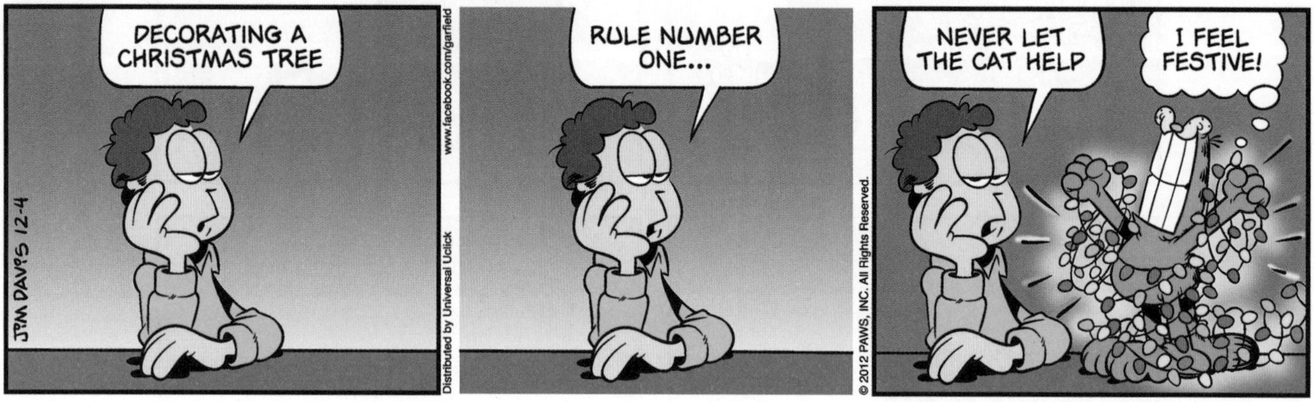
JIM DAVIS 12-4
DECORATING A CHRISTMAS TREE
Distributed by Universal Uclick www.facebook.com/garfield
RULE NUMBER ONE...
© 2012 PAWS, INC. All Rights Reserved.
NEVER LET THE CAT HELP
I FEEL FESTIVE!

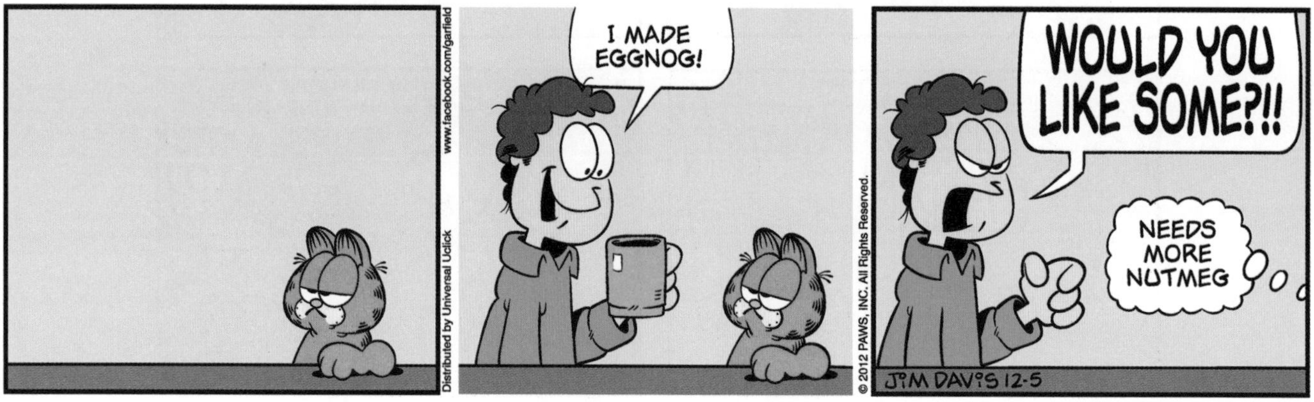
Distributed by Universal Uclick www.facebook.com/garfield
I MADE EGGNOG!
© 2012 PAWS, INC. All Rights Reserved.
WOULD YOU LIKE SOME?!!
NEEDS MORE NUTMEG
JIM DAVIS 12-5

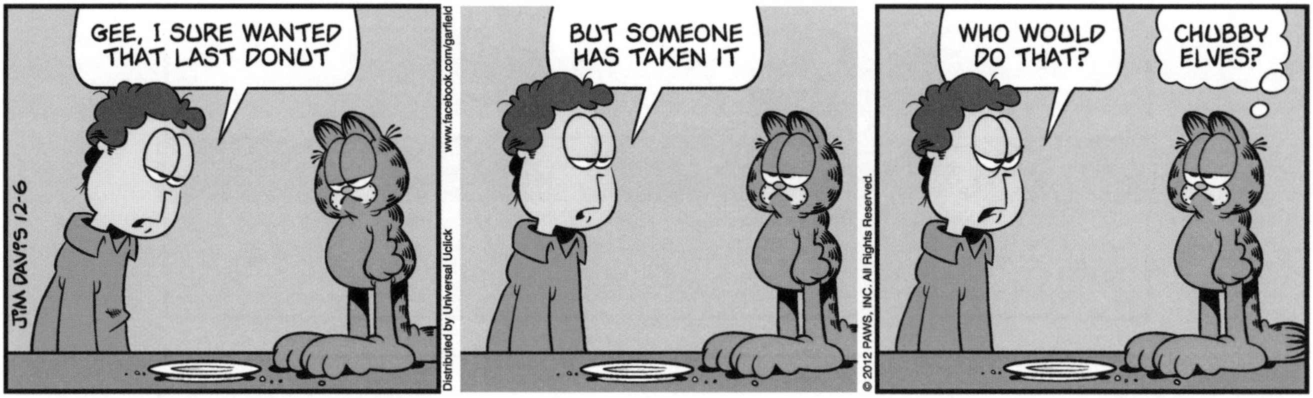
JIM DAVIS 12-6
GEE, I SURE WANTED THAT LAST DONUT
www.facebook.com/garfield
Distributed by Universal Uclick
BUT SOMEONE HAS TAKEN IT
© 2012 PAWS, INC. All Rights Reserved.
WHO WOULD DO THAT?
CHUBBY ELVES?

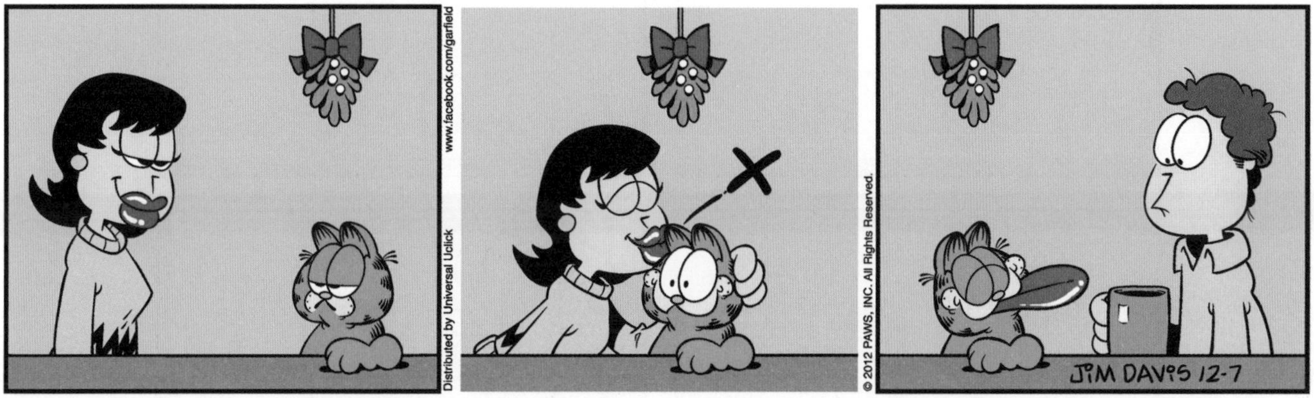
www.facebook.com/garfield
Distributed by Universal Uclick
© 2012 PAWS, INC. All Rights Reserved.
JIM DAVIS 12-7

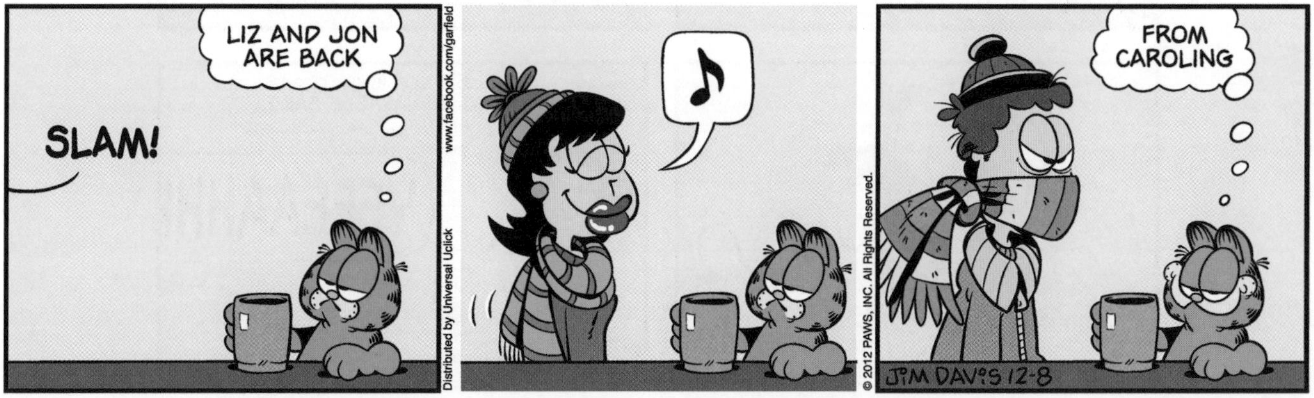
LIZ AND JON ARE BACK
SLAM!
www.facebook.com/garfield
Distributed by Universal Uclick
♪
© 2012 PAWS, INC. All Rights Reserved.
FROM CAROLING
JIM DAVIS 12-8

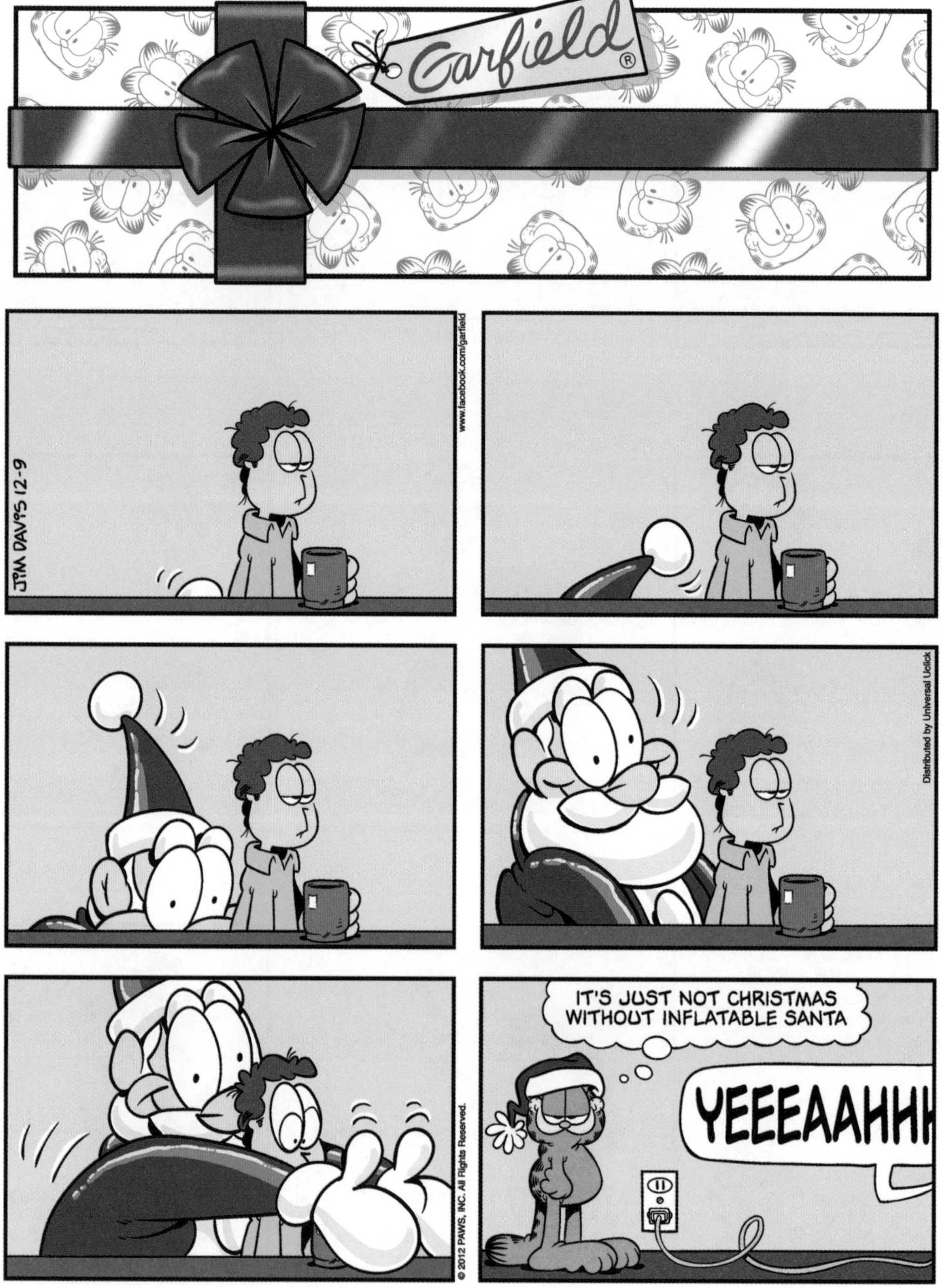
Garfield
JIM DAVIS 12-9
www.facebook.com/garfield
Distributed by Universal Uclick
© 2012 PAWS, INC. All Rights Reserved.
IT'S JUST NOT CHRISTMAS WITHOUT INFLATABLE SANTA
YEEEAAHH

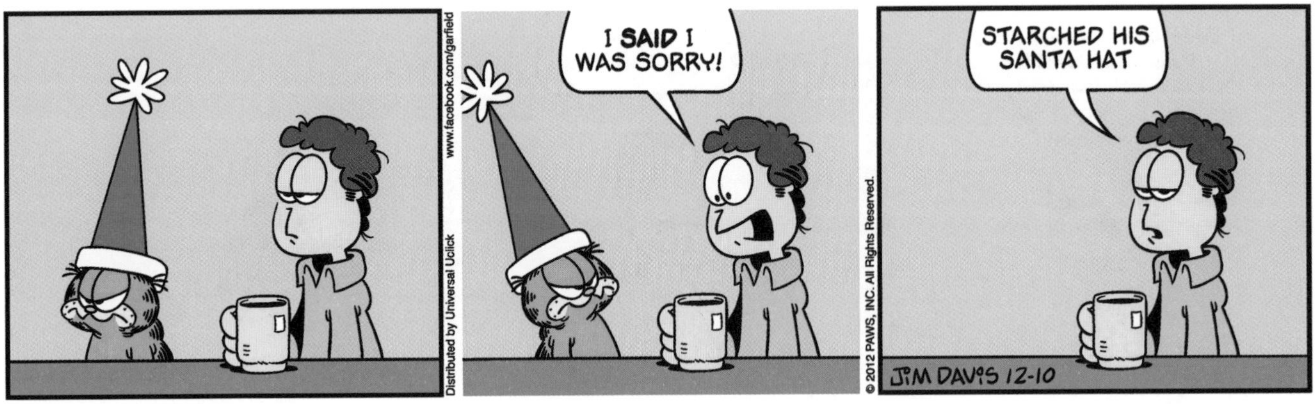
I SAID I WAS SORRY!
STARCHED HIS SANTA HAT
JIM DAVIS 12-10
Distributed by Universal Uclick www.facebook.com/garfield
© 2012 PAWS, INC. All Rights Reserved.

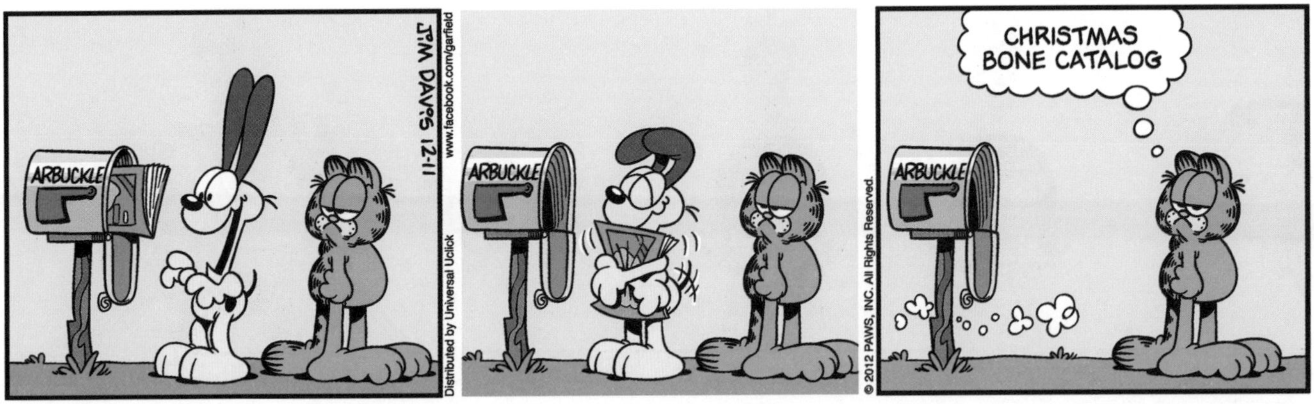
ARBUCKLE
JIM DAVIS 12-11
Distributed by Universal Uclick www.facebook.com/garfield
CHRISTMAS BONE CATALOG
© 2012 PAWS, INC. All Rights Reserved.

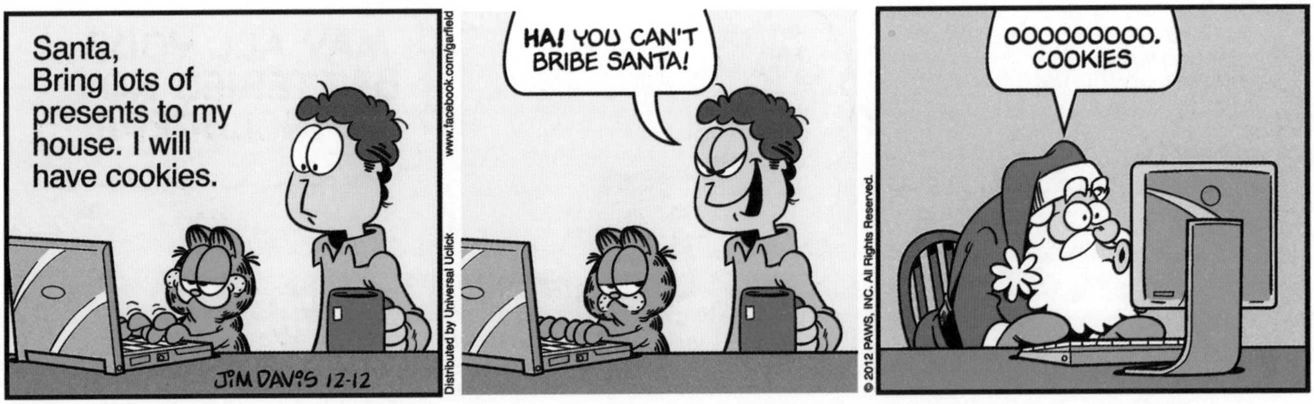
Santa, Bring lots of presents to my house. I will have cookies.
JIM DAVIS 12-12
Distributed by Universal Uclick www.facebook.com/garfield
HA! YOU CAN'T BRIBE SANTA!
OOOOOOOOO. COOKIES
© 2012 PAWS, INC. All Rights Reserved.

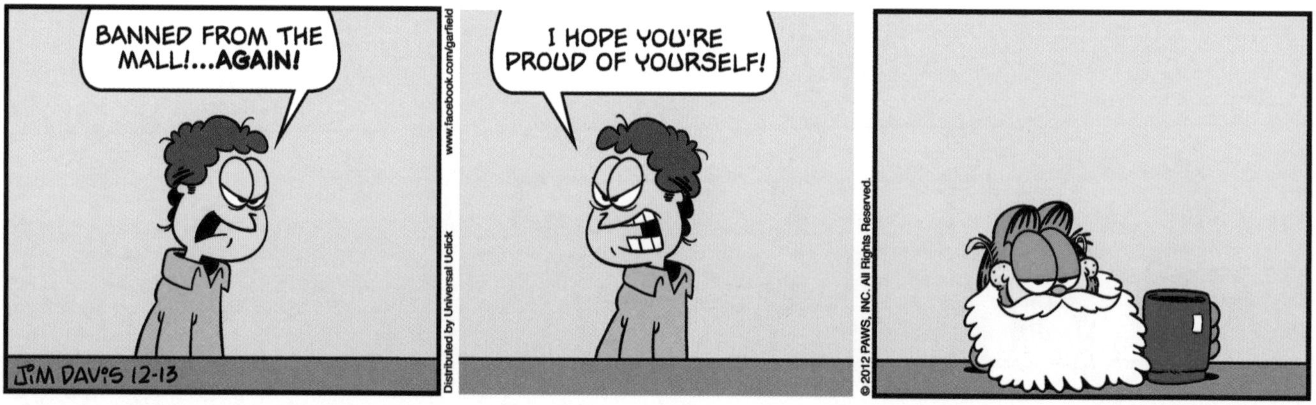
BANNED FROM THE MALL!...AGAIN!
JIM DAVIS 12-13
Distributed by Universal Uclick
www.facebook.com/garfield
I HOPE YOU'RE PROUD OF YOURSELF!
© 2012 PAWS, INC. All Rights Reserved.

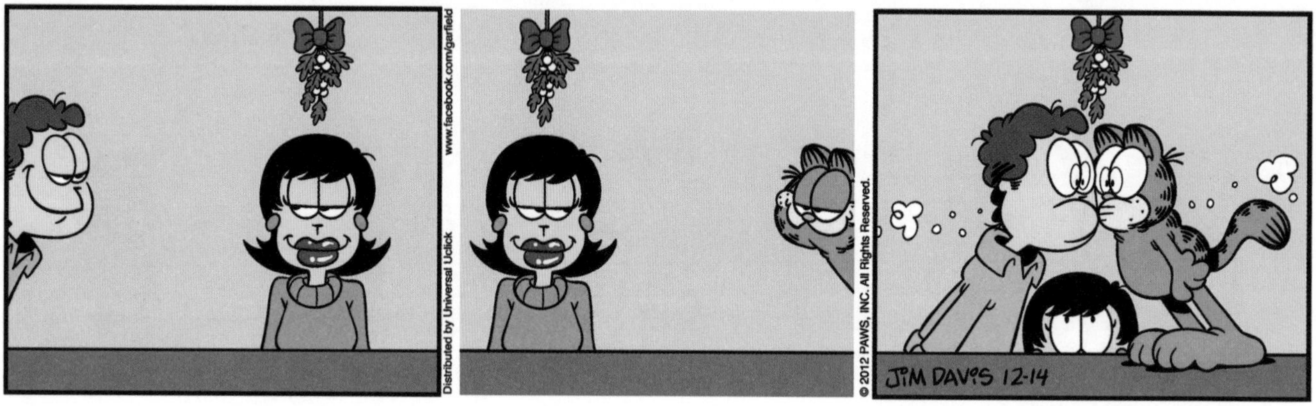
Distributed by Universal Uclick
www.facebook.com/garfield
© 2012 PAWS, INC. All Rights Reserved.
JIM DAVIS 12-14

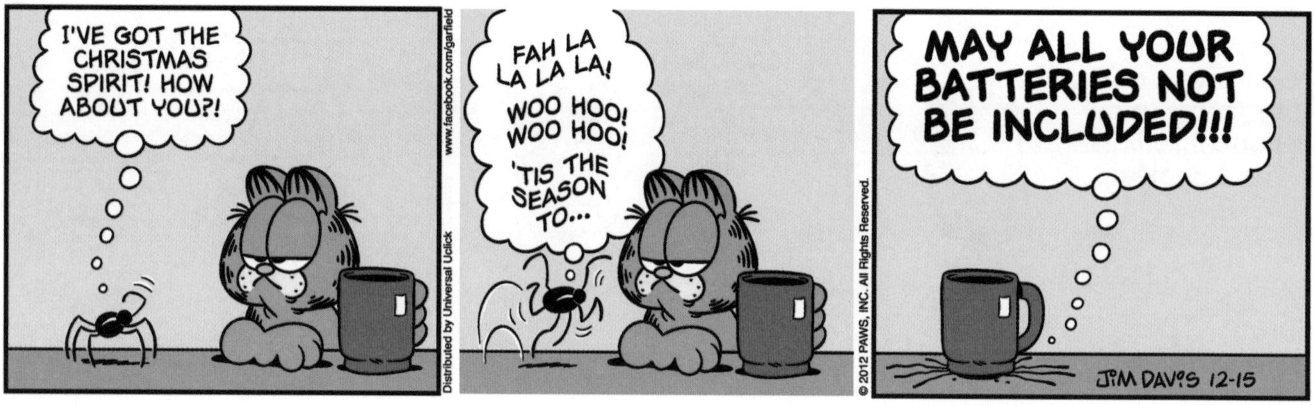
I'VE GOT THE CHRISTMAS SPIRIT! HOW ABOUT YOU?!
Distributed by Universal Uclick
www.facebook.com/garfield
FAH LA LA LA LA!
WOO HOO! WOO HOO!
'TIS THE SEASON TO...
© 2012 PAWS, INC. All Rights Reserved.
MAY ALL YOUR BATTERIES NOT BE INCLUDED!!!
JIM DAVIS 12-15

GARFIELD®
IT'S ONE OF THOSE RECORDABLE CARDS FROM EVERYONE ON THE FARM!
www.facebook.com/garfield
MOOO!
THE COW
OINK-OINK!
THE PIG
Distributed by Universal Uclick
CLUCK-CLUCK!
THE CHICKEN
BAAAA!
THE SHEEP
© 2012 PAWS, INC. All Rights Reserved.
JIM DAVIS 12-16
HEY, NEENER HEAD!
THE BROTHER

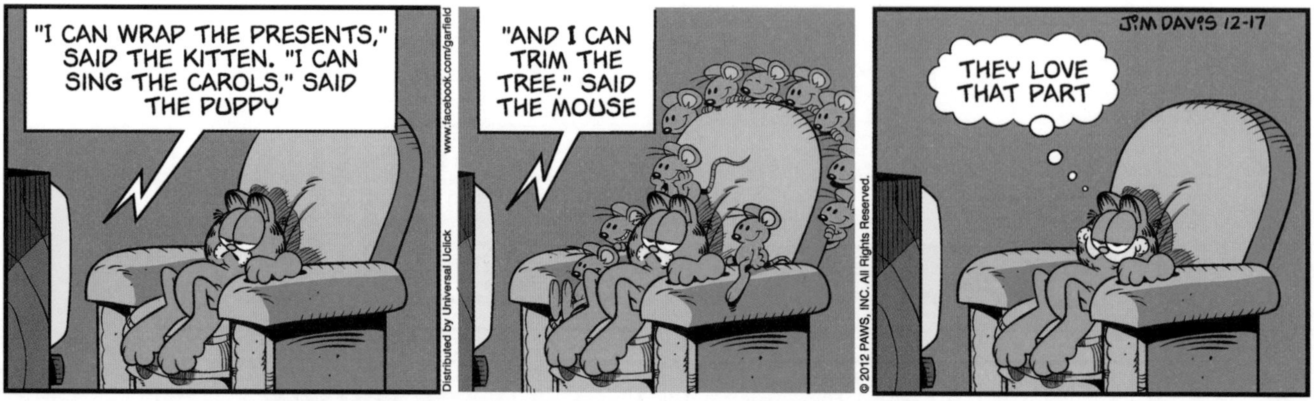
"I CAN WRAP THE PRESENTS," SAID THE KITTEN. "I CAN SING THE CAROLS," SAID THE PUPPY
"AND I CAN TRIM THE TREE," SAID THE MOUSE
THEY LOVE THAT PART
JIM DAVIS 12-17
Distributed by Universal Uclick www.facebook.com/garfield
© 2012 PAWS, INC. All Rights Reserved.

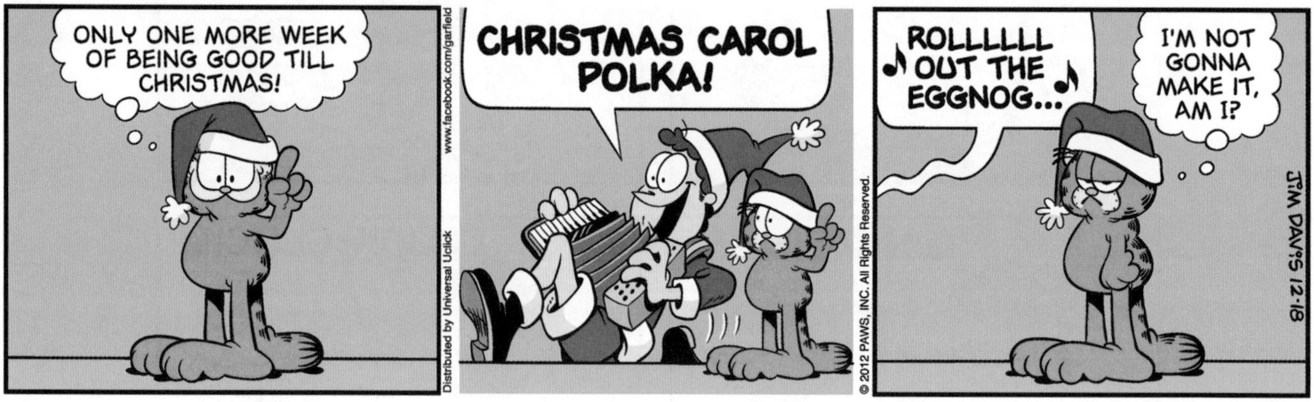
ONLY ONE MORE WEEK OF BEING GOOD TILL CHRISTMAS!
CHRISTMAS CAROL POLKA!
♪ ROLLLLLLL OUT THE EGGNOG... ♪
I'M NOT GONNA MAKE IT, AM I?
JIM DAVIS 12-18
Distributed by Universal Uclick www.facebook.com/garfield
© 2012 PAWS, INC. All Rights Reserved.

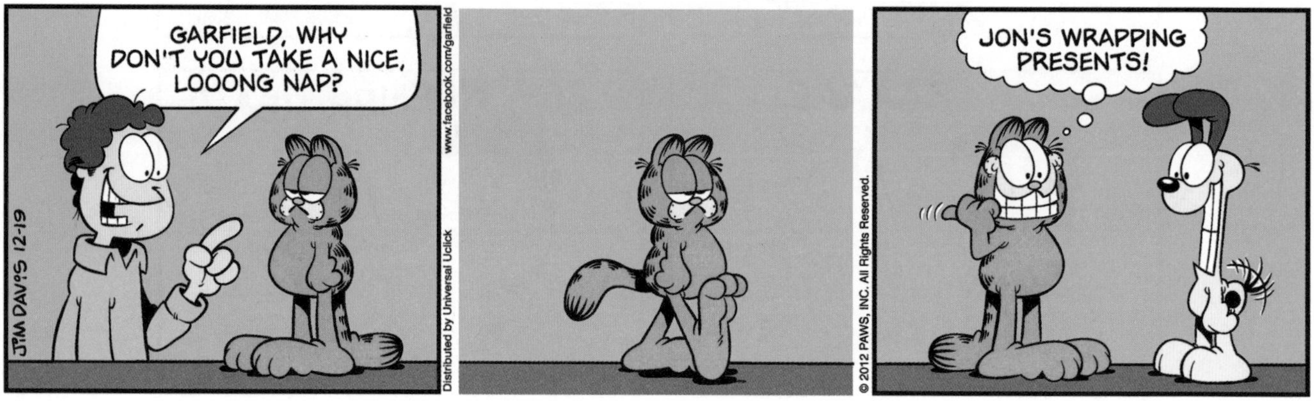
GARFIELD, WHY DON'T YOU TAKE A NICE, LOOONG NAP?
JON'S WRAPPING PRESENTS!
JIM DAVIS 12-19
Distributed by Universal Uclick www.facebook.com/garfield
© 2012 PAWS, INC. All Rights Reserved.

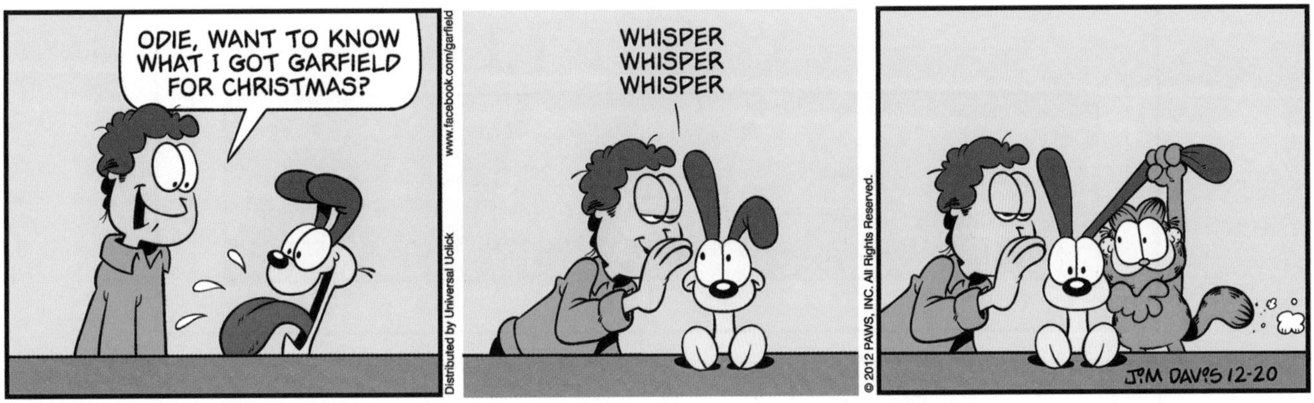
ODIE, WANT TO KNOW WHAT I GOT GARFIELD FOR CHRISTMAS?
www.facebook.com/garfield
Distributed by Universal Uclick
WHISPER WHISPER WHISPER
© 2012 PAWS, INC. All Rights Reserved.
JIM DAVIS 12-20

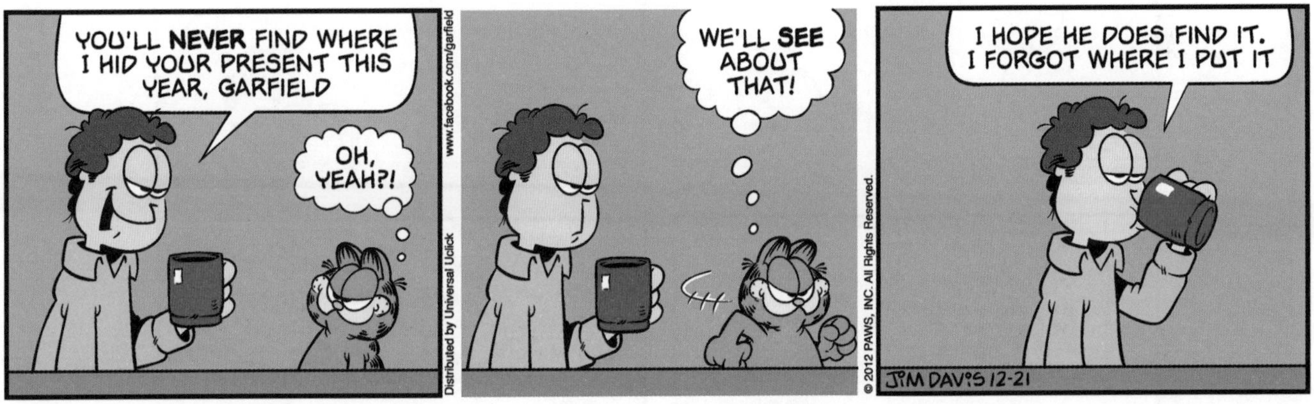
YOU'LL **NEVER** FIND WHERE I HID YOUR PRESENT THIS YEAR, GARFIELD
OH, YEAH?!
www.facebook.com/garfield
Distributed by Universal Uclick
WE'LL **SEE** ABOUT THAT!
© 2012 PAWS, INC. All Rights Reserved.
I HOPE HE DOES FIND IT. I FORGOT WHERE I PUT IT
JIM DAVIS 12-21

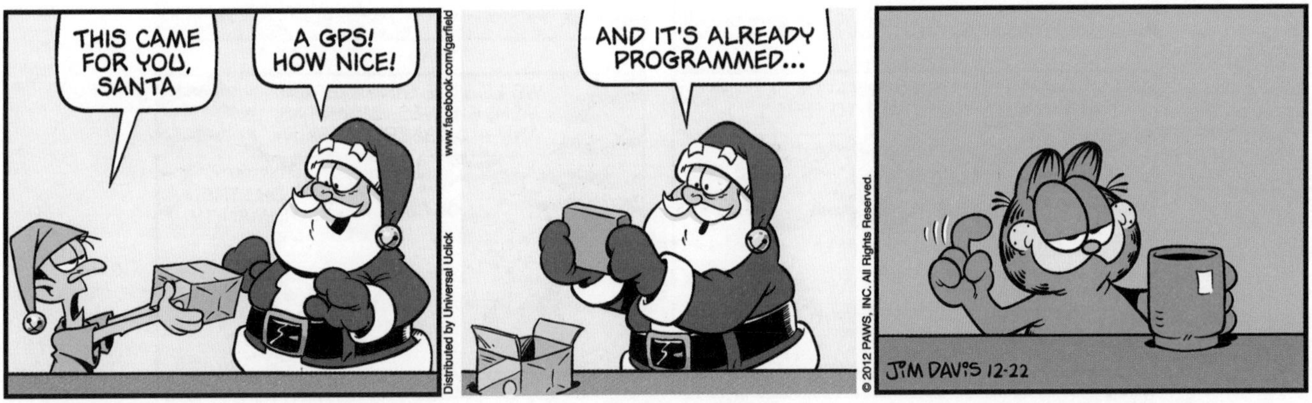
THIS CAME FOR YOU, SANTA
A GPS! HOW NICE!
www.facebook.com/garfield
Distributed by Universal Uclick
AND IT'S ALREADY PROGRAMMED...
© 2012 PAWS, INC. All Rights Reserved.
JIM DAVIS 12-22

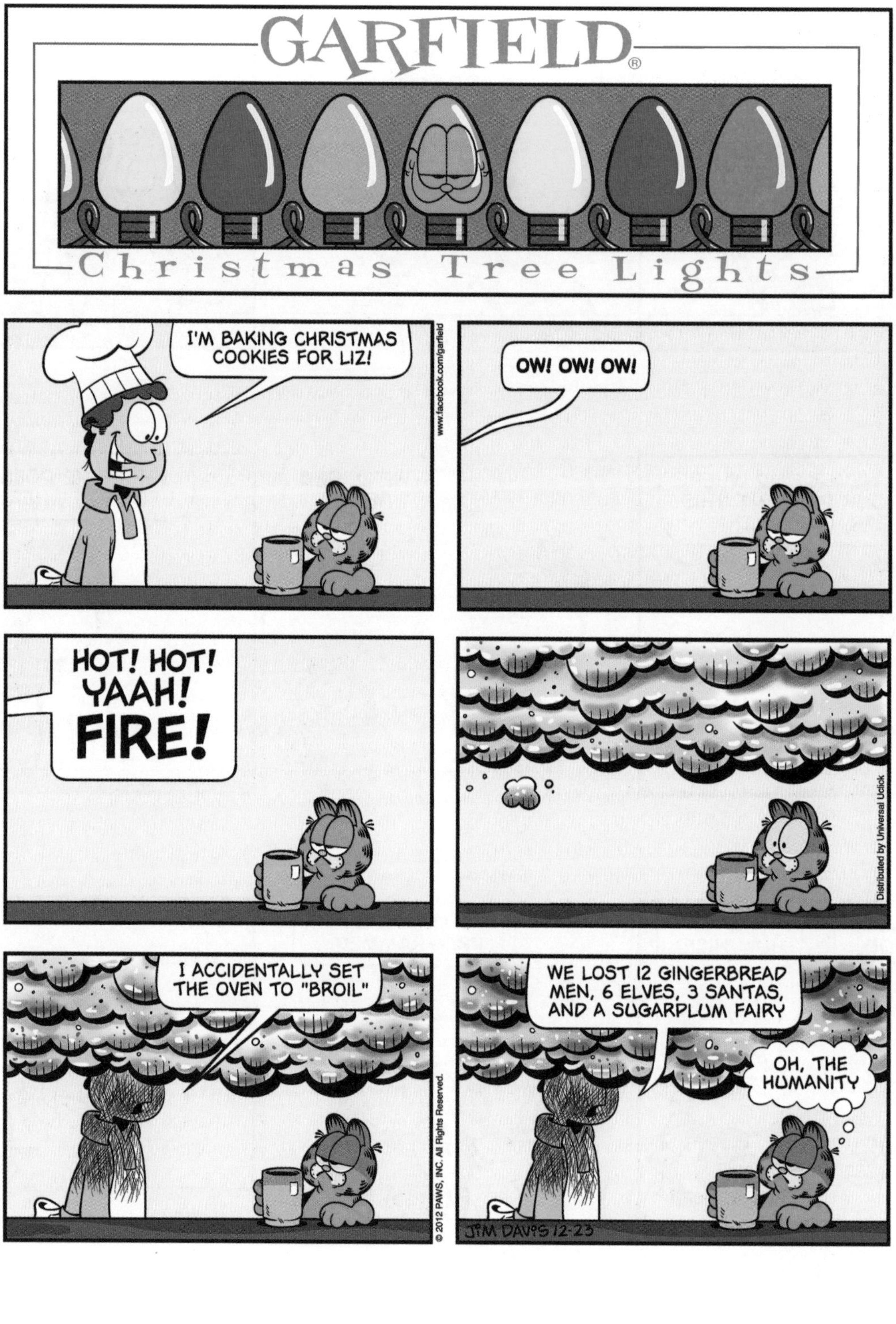
GARFIELD®
Christmas Tree Lights
I'M BAKING CHRISTMAS COOKIES FOR LIZ!
www.facebook.com/garfield
OW! OW! OW!
HOT! HOT! YAAH! FIRE!
Distributed by Universal Uclick
I ACCIDENTALLY SET THE OVEN TO "BROIL"
© 2012 PAWS, INC. All Rights Reserved.
WE LOST 12 GINGERBREAD MEN, 6 ELVES, 3 SANTAS, AND A SUGARPLUM FAIRY
OH, THE HUMANITY
JIM DAVIS 12-23

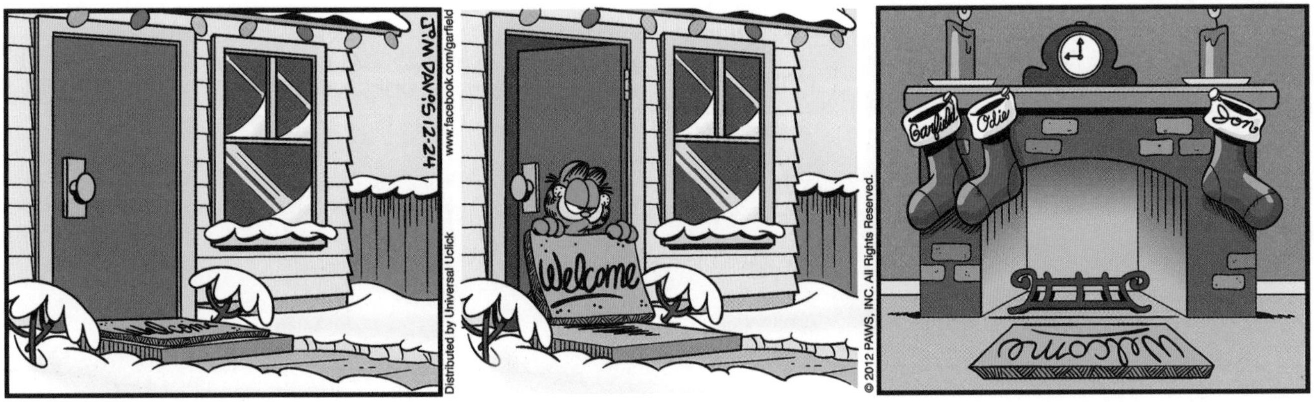
JIM DAVIS 12-24
www.facebook.com/garfield
Distributed by Universal Uclick
Welcome
© 2012 PAWS, INC. All Rights Reserved.
Garfield
Odie
Jon
Welcome

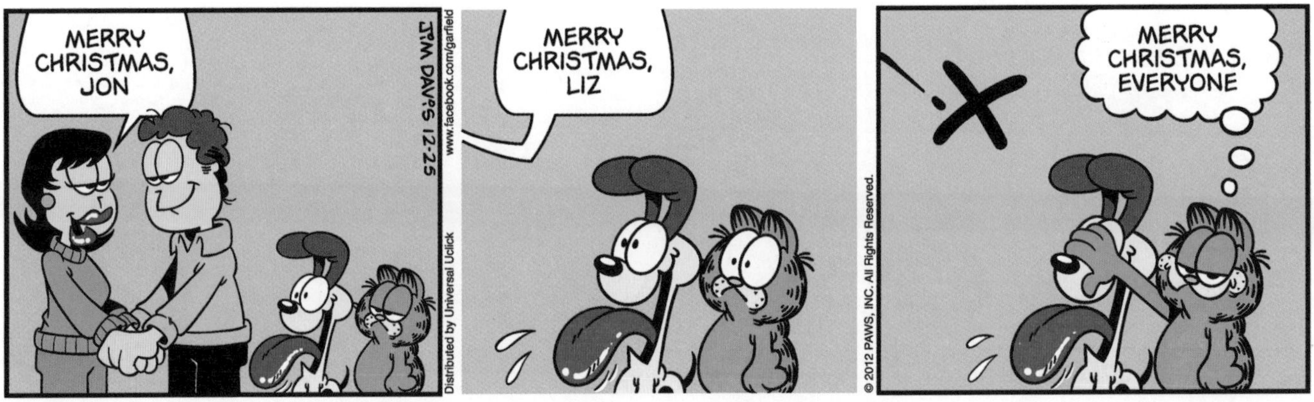
MERRY CHRISTMAS, JON
JIM DAVIS 12-25
www.facebook.com/garfield
Distributed by Universal Uclick
MERRY CHRISTMAS, LIZ
© 2012 PAWS, INC. All Rights Reserved.
MERRY CHRISTMAS, EVERYONE

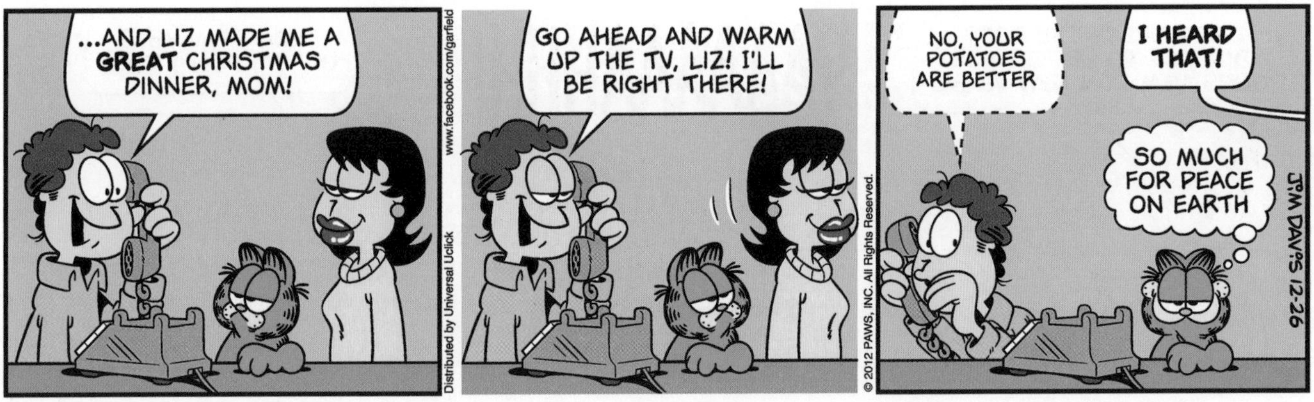
...AND LIZ MADE ME A GREAT CHRISTMAS DINNER, MOM!
www.facebook.com/garfield
Distributed by Universal Uclick
GO AHEAD AND WARM UP THE TV, LIZ! I'LL BE RIGHT THERE!
© 2012 PAWS, INC. All Rights Reserved.
NO, YOUR POTATOES ARE BETTER
I HEARD THAT!
SO MUCH FOR PEACE ON EARTH
JIM DAVIS 12-26

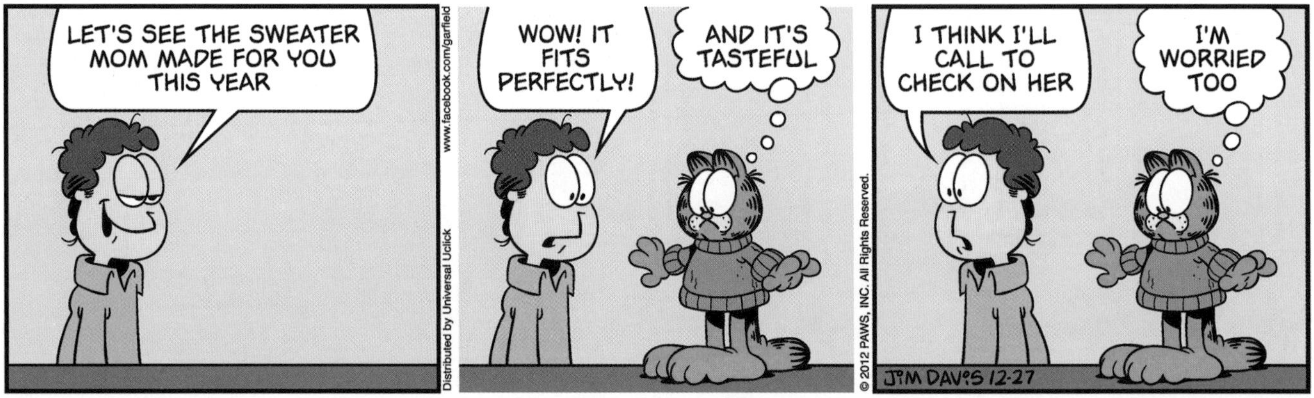

LET'S SEE THE SWEATER MOM MADE FOR YOU THIS YEAR
www.facebook.com/garfield
Distributed by Universal Uclick
WOW! IT FITS PERFECTLY!
AND IT'S TASTEFUL
© 2012 PAWS, INC. All Rights Reserved.
I THINK I'LL CALL TO CHECK ON HER
I'M WORRIED TOO
JIM DAVIS 12-27

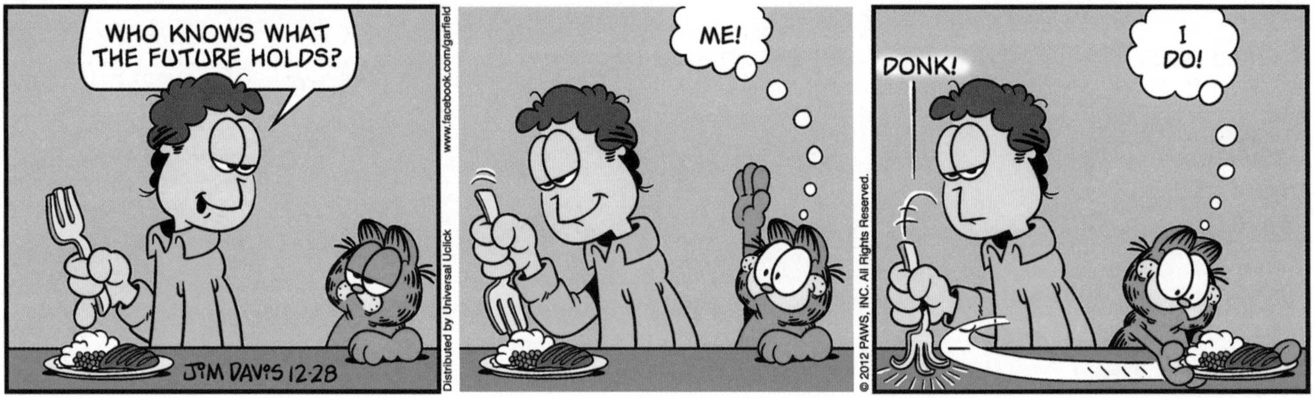

WHO KNOWS WHAT THE FUTURE HOLDS?
JIM DAVIS 12-28
www.facebook.com/garfield
Distributed by Universal Uclick
ME!
© 2012 PAWS, INC. All Rights Reserved.
DONK!
I DO!

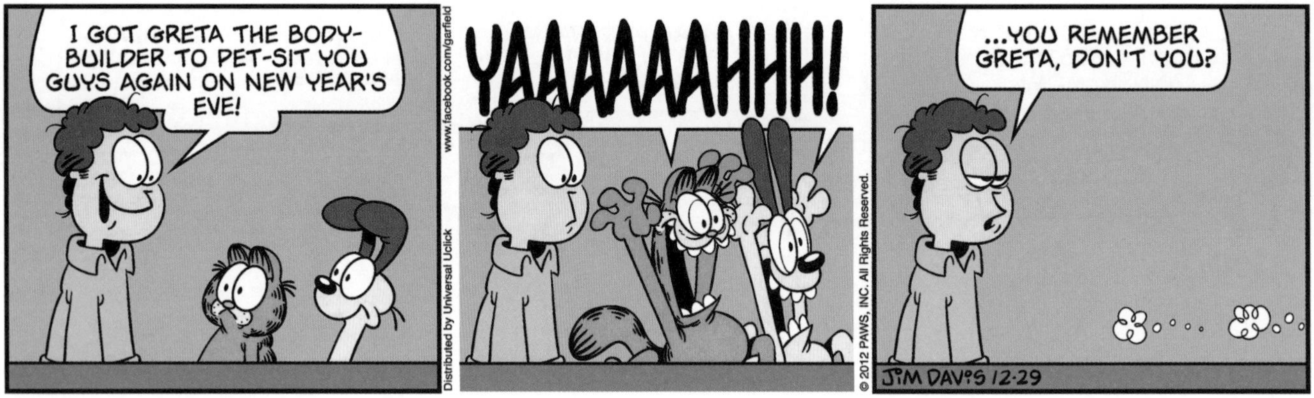

I GOT GRETA THE BODY-BUILDER TO PET-SIT YOU GUYS AGAIN ON NEW YEAR'S EVE!
www.facebook.com/garfield
Distributed by Universal Uclick
YAAAAAAHHH!
© 2012 PAWS, INC. All Rights Reserved.
...YOU REMEMBER GRETA, DON'T YOU?
JIM DAVIS 12-29

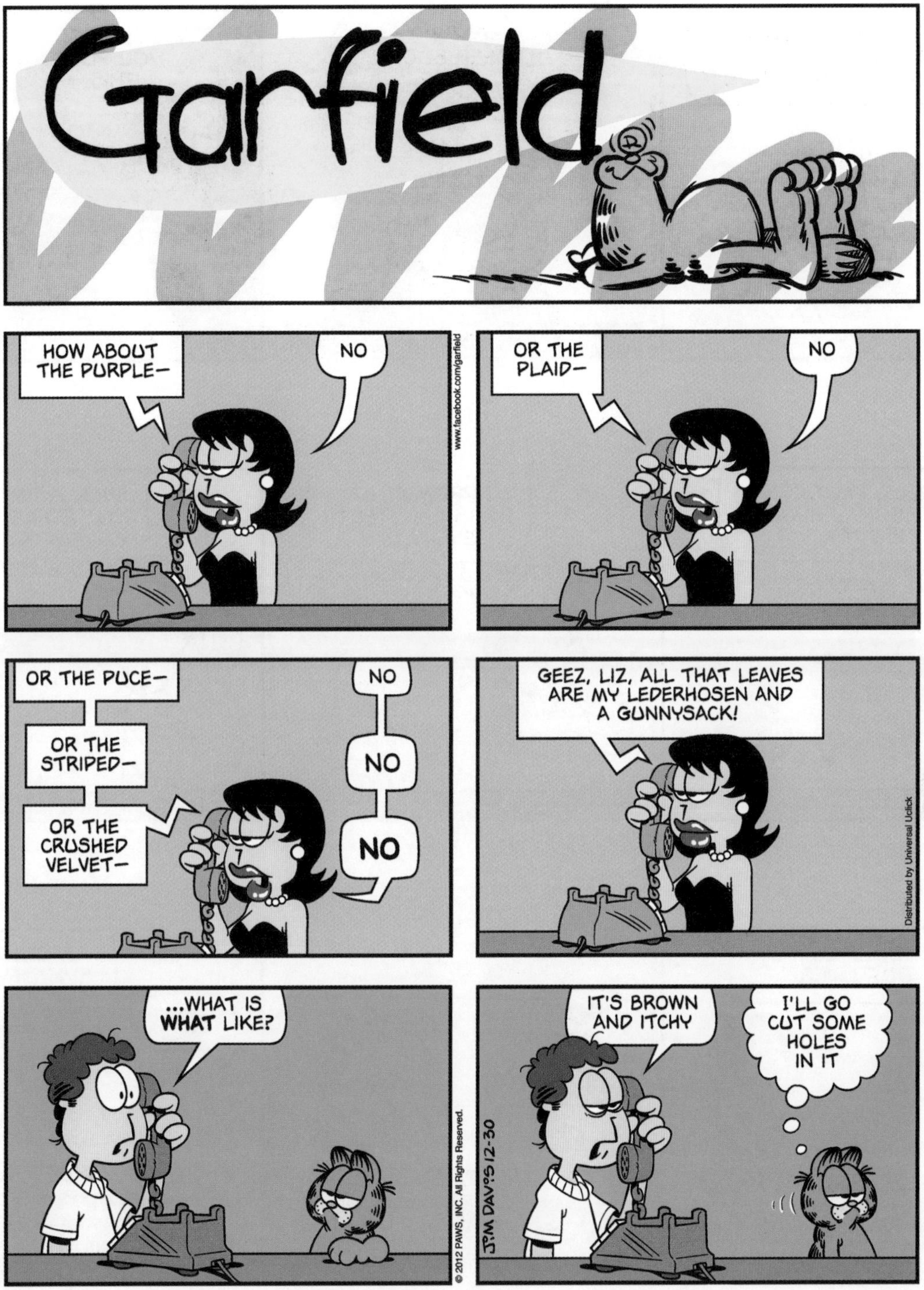
Garfield
HOW ABOUT THE PURPLE—
NO
www.facebook.com/garfield
OR THE PLAID—
NO
OR THE PUCE—
NO
OR THE STRIPED—
NO
OR THE CRUSHED VELVET—
NO
GEEZ, LIZ, ALL THAT LEAVES ARE MY LEDERHOSEN AND A GUNNYSACK!
Distributed by Universal Uclick
...WHAT IS WHAT LIKE?
© 2012 PAWS, INC. All Rights Reserved.
JPM DAVPS 12-30
IT'S BROWN AND ITCHY
I'LL GO CUT SOME HOLES IN IT

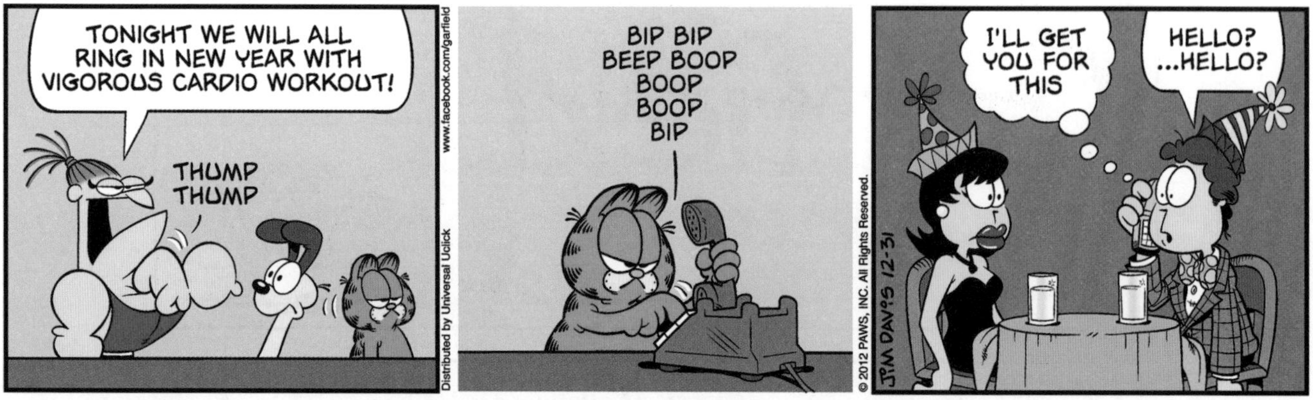
TONIGHT WE WILL ALL RING IN NEW YEAR WITH VIGOROUS CARDIO WORKOUT!
THUMP THUMP
www.facebook.com/garfield
Distributed by Universal Uclick
BIP BIP BEEP BOOP BOOP BOOP BIP
I'LL GET YOU FOR THIS
HELLO? ...HELLO?
© 2012 PAWS, INC. All Rights Reserved.
JIM DAVIS 12-31

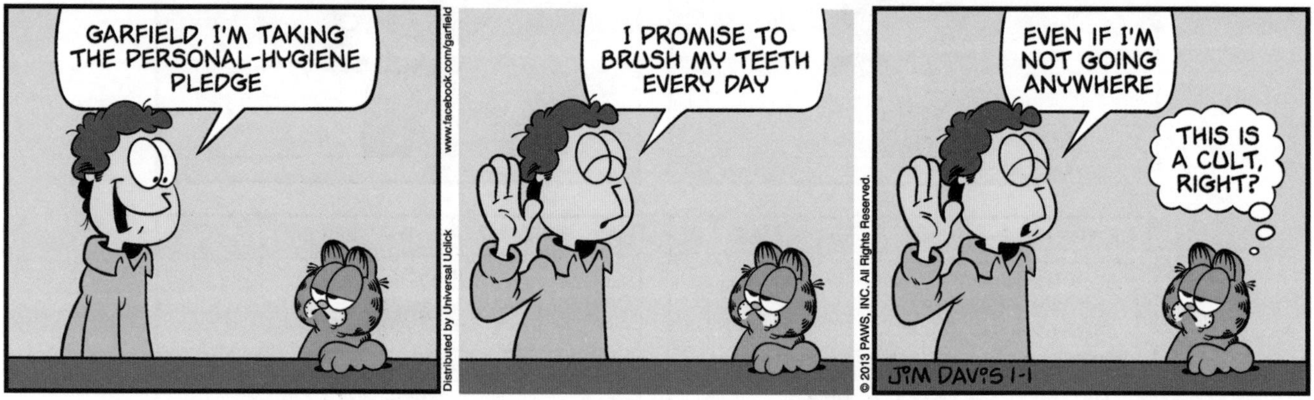
GARFIELD, I'M TAKING THE PERSONAL-HYGIENE PLEDGE
www.facebook.com/garfield
Distributed by Universal Uclick
I PROMISE TO BRUSH MY TEETH EVERY DAY
EVEN IF I'M NOT GOING ANYWHERE
THIS IS A CULT, RIGHT?
© 2013 PAWS, INC. All Rights Reserved.
JIM DAVIS 1-1

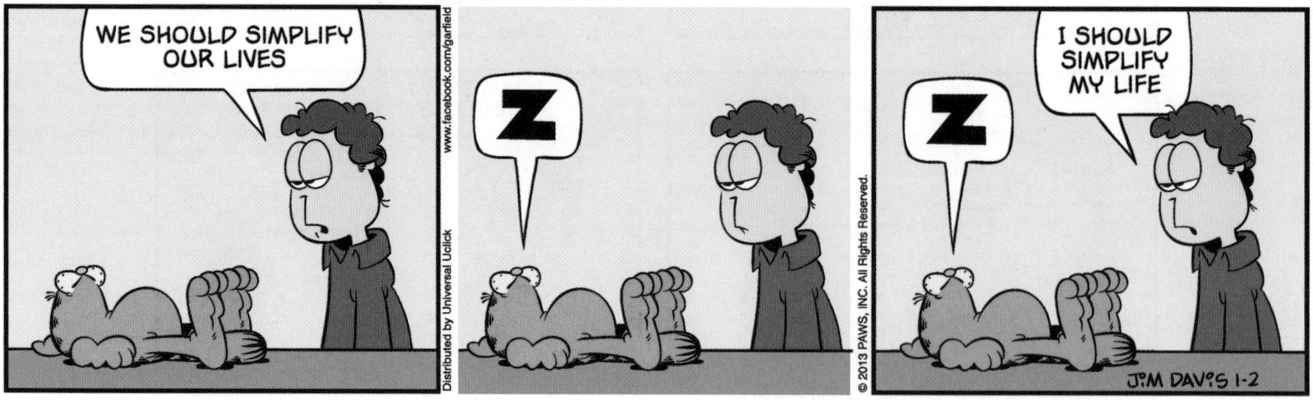
WE SHOULD SIMPLIFY OUR LIVES
www.facebook.com/garfield
Distributed by Universal Uclick
Z
Z
I SHOULD SIMPLIFY MY LIFE
© 2013 PAWS, INC. All Rights Reserved.
JIM DAVIS 1-2

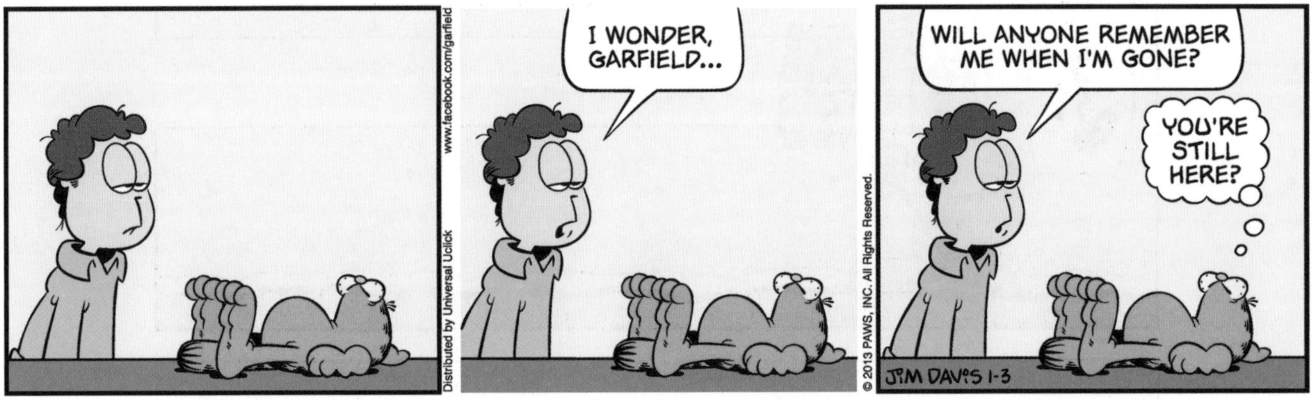
www.facebook.com/garfield
Distributed by Universal Uclick
I WONDER, GARFIELD...
WILL ANYONE REMEMBER ME WHEN I'M GONE?
YOU'RE STILL HERE?
© 2013 PAWS, INC. All Rights Reserved.
JIM DAVIS 1-3

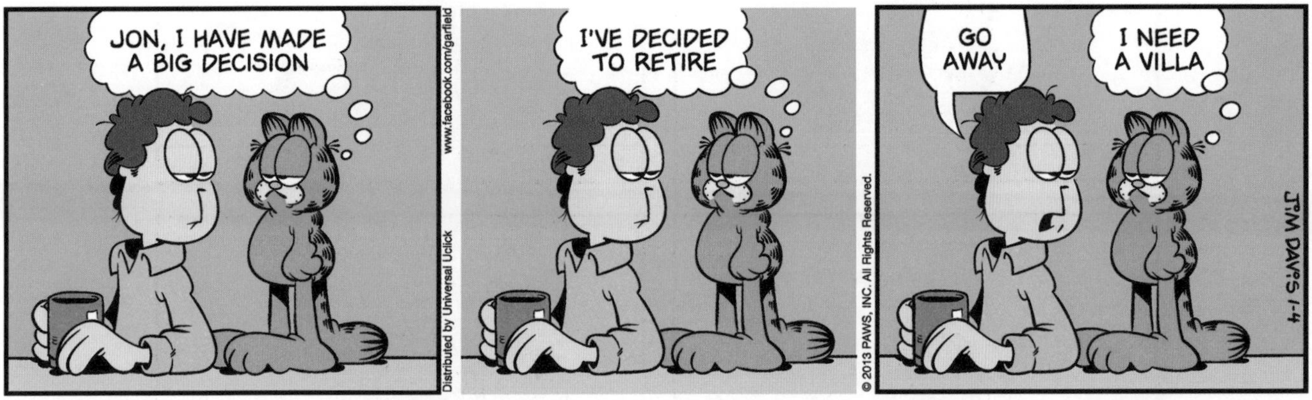
JON, I HAVE MADE A BIG DECISION
www.facebook.com/garfield
Distributed by Universal Uclick
I'VE DECIDED TO RETIRE
© 2013 PAWS, INC. All Rights Reserved.
GO AWAY
I NEED A VILLA
JIM DAVIS 1-4

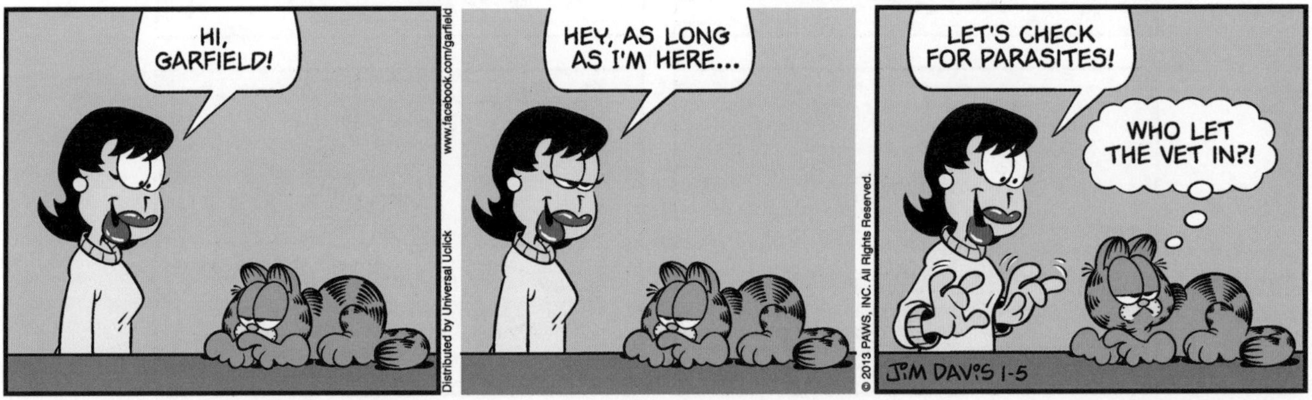
HI, GARFIELD!
www.facebook.com/garfield
Distributed by Universal Uclick
HEY, AS LONG AS I'M HERE...
LET'S CHECK FOR PARASITES!
WHO LET THE VET IN?!
© 2013 PAWS, INC. All Rights Reserved.
JIM DAVIS 1-5

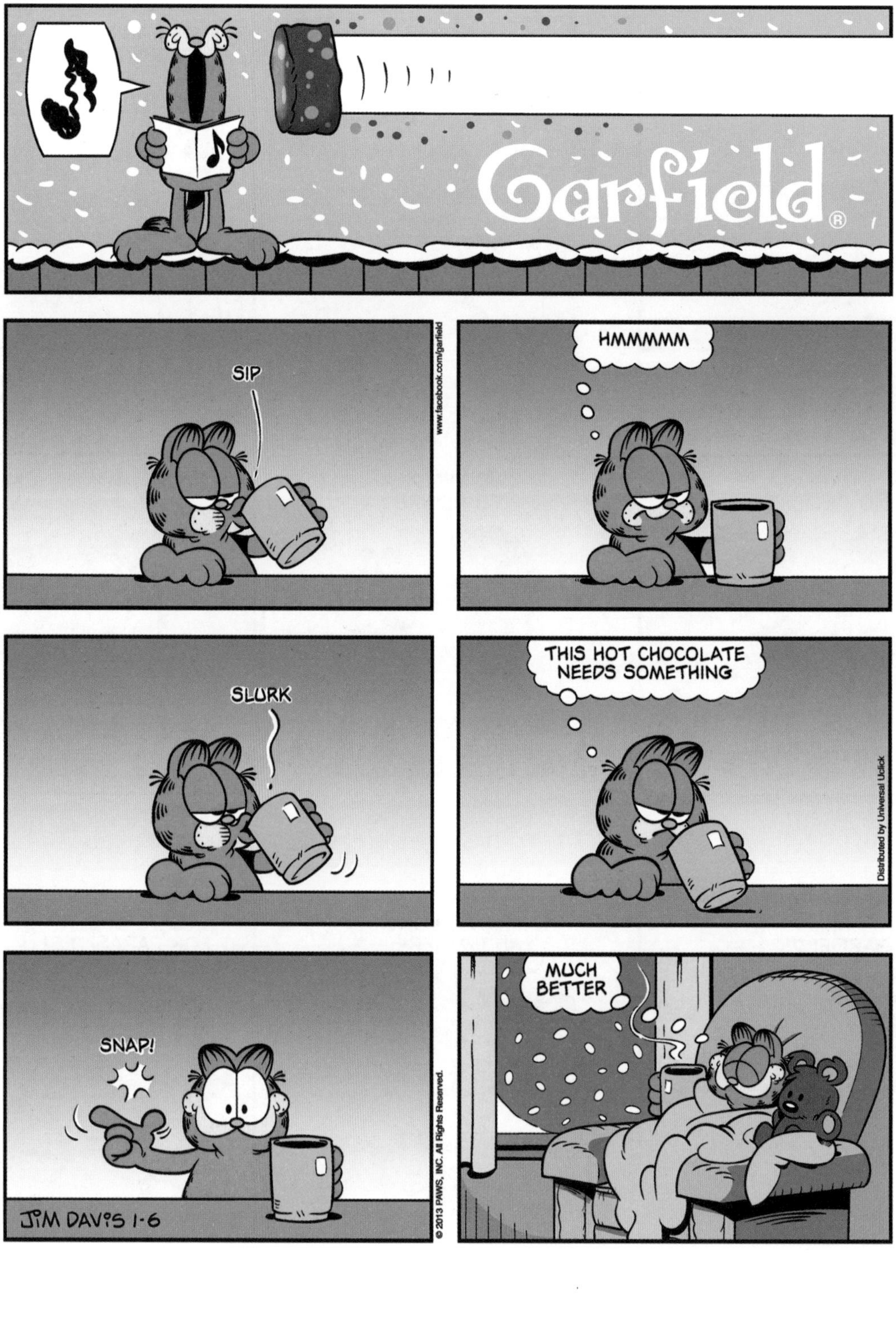
Garfield®
SIP
www.facebook.com/garfield
HMMMMM
SLURK
THIS HOT CHOCOLATE NEEDS SOMETHING
Distributed by Universal Uclick
SNAP!
JIM DAVIS 1-6
© 2013 PAWS, INC. All Rights Reserved.
MUCH BETTER

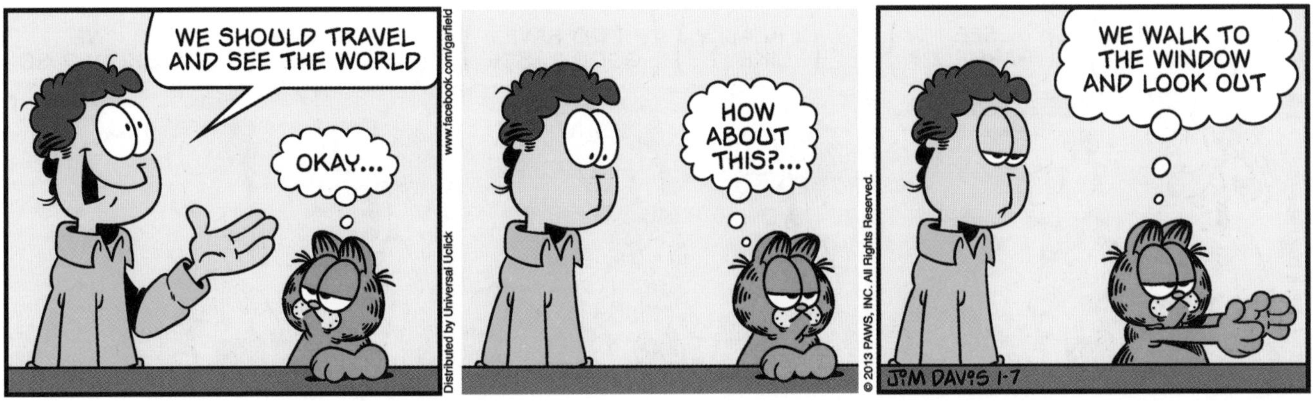
WE SHOULD TRAVEL AND SEE THE WORLD
OKAY...
HOW ABOUT THIS?...
WE WALK TO THE WINDOW AND LOOK OUT
www.facebook.com/garfield
Distributed by Universal Uclick
© 2013 PAWS, INC. All Rights Reserved.
JIM DAVIS 1-7

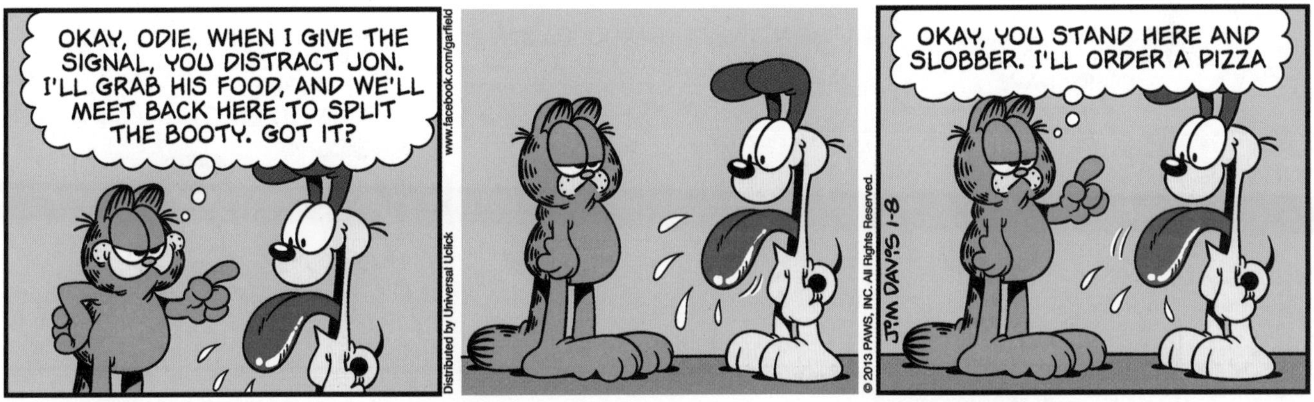
OKAY, ODIE, WHEN I GIVE THE SIGNAL, YOU DISTRACT JON. I'LL GRAB HIS FOOD, AND WE'LL MEET BACK HERE TO SPLIT THE BOOTY. GOT IT?
OKAY, YOU STAND HERE AND SLOBBER. I'LL ORDER A PIZZA
www.facebook.com/garfield
Distributed by Universal Uclick
© 2013 PAWS, INC. All Rights Reserved.
JIM DAVIS 1-8

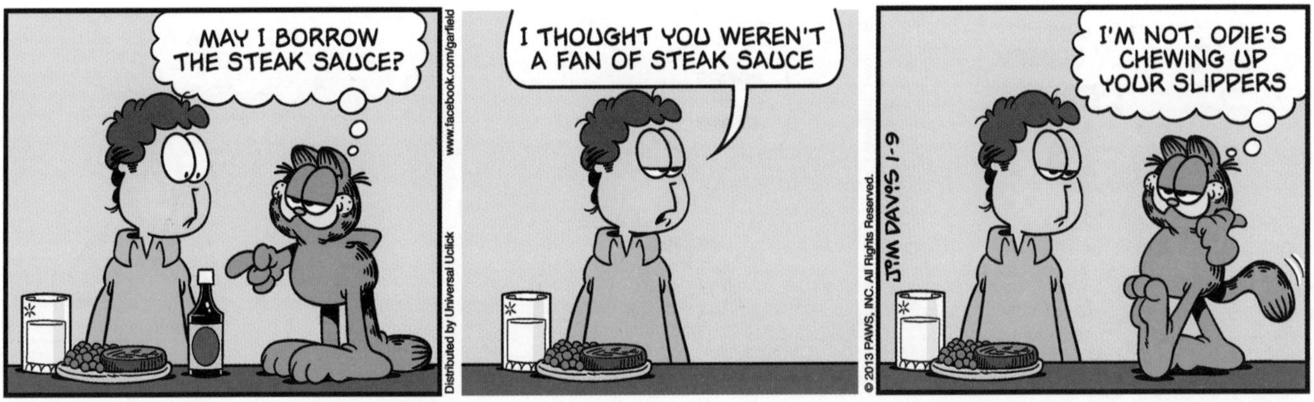
MAY I BORROW THE STEAK SAUCE?
I THOUGHT YOU WEREN'T A FAN OF STEAK SAUCE
I'M NOT. ODIE'S CHEWING UP YOUR SLIPPERS
www.facebook.com/garfield
Distributed by Universal Uclick
© 2013 PAWS, INC. All Rights Reserved.
JIM DAVIS 1-9

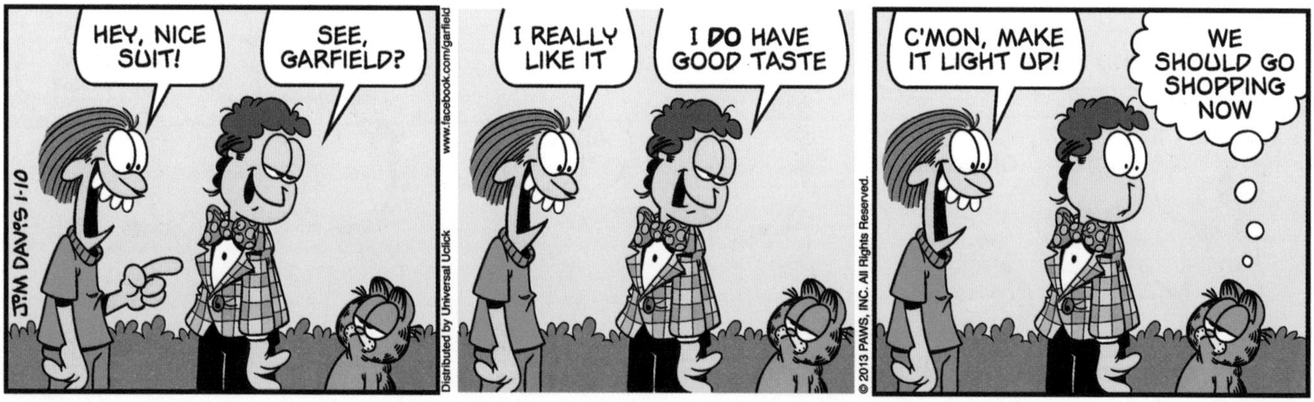
HEY, NICE SUIT!
SEE, GARFIELD?
JIM DAVIS 1-10
www.facebook.com/garfield
Distributed by Universal Uclick
I REALLY LIKE IT
I DO HAVE GOOD TASTE
© 2013 PAWS, INC. All Rights Reserved.
C'MON, MAKE IT LIGHT UP!
WE SHOULD GO SHOPPING NOW

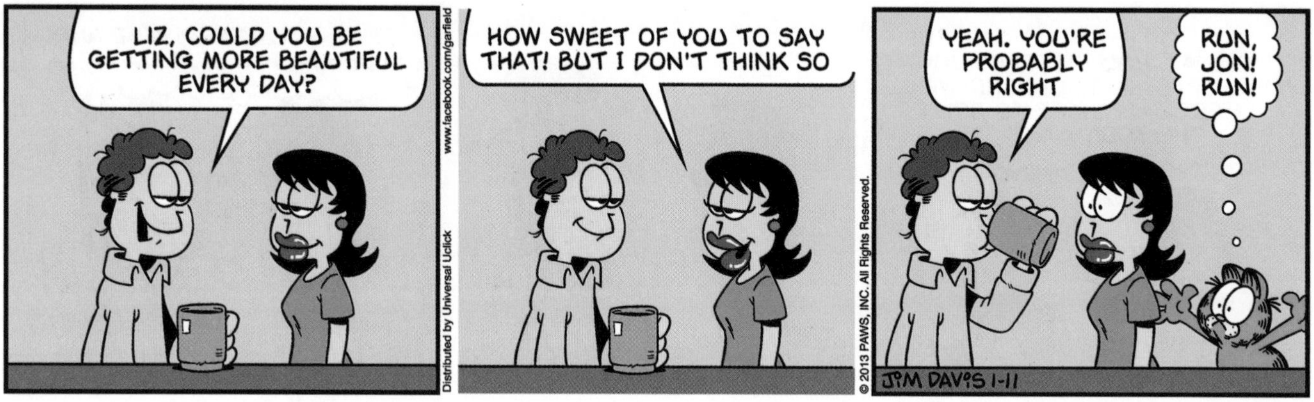
LIZ, COULD YOU BE GETTING MORE BEAUTIFUL EVERY DAY?
www.facebook.com/garfield
Distributed by Universal Uclick
HOW SWEET OF YOU TO SAY THAT! BUT I DON'T THINK SO
© 2013 PAWS, INC. All Rights Reserved.
YEAH. YOU'RE PROBABLY RIGHT
RUN, JON! RUN!
JIM DAVIS 1-11

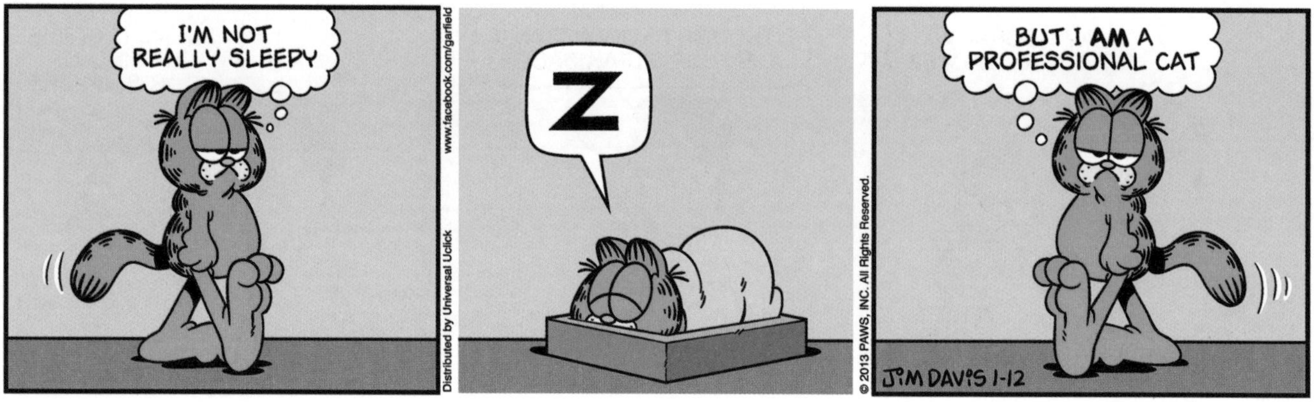
I'M NOT REALLY SLEEPY
www.facebook.com/garfield
Distributed by Universal Uclick
Z
© 2013 PAWS, INC. All Rights Reserved.
BUT I AM A PROFESSIONAL CAT
JIM DAVIS 1-12

GARFIELD
www.facebook.com/garfield
PAT PAT PAT
PAT PAT PAT
JIM DAVIS 1-13
DIG DIG DIG DIG DIG DIG DIG DIG
Distributed by Universal Uclick
© 2013 PAWS, INC. All Rights Reserved.

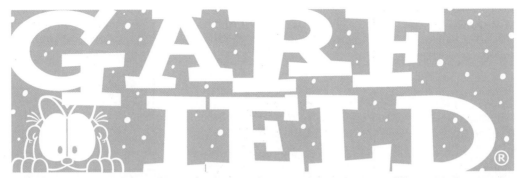

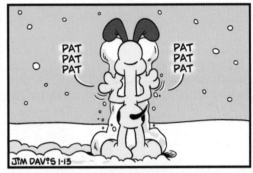

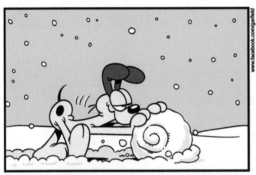

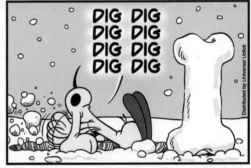

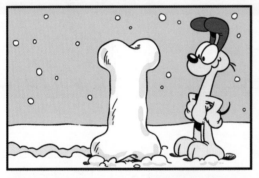

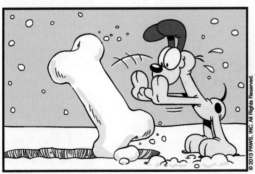

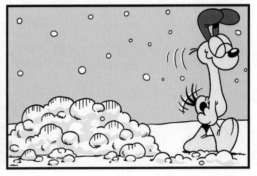

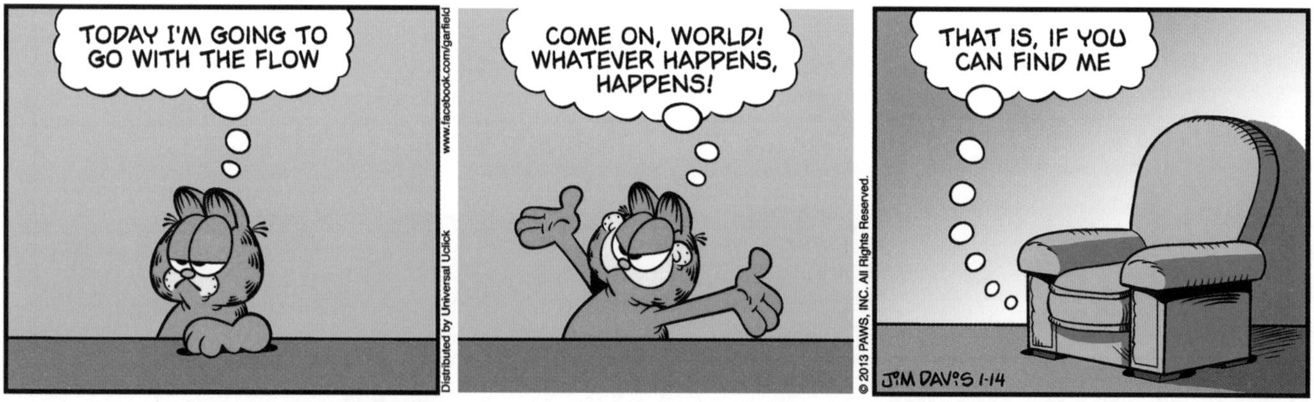
TODAY I'M GOING TO GO WITH THE FLOW
Distributed by Universal Uclick www.facebook.com/garfield
COME ON, WORLD! WHATEVER HAPPENS, HAPPENS!
© 2013 PAWS, INC. All Rights Reserved.
THAT IS, IF YOU CAN FIND ME
JIM DAVIS 1-14

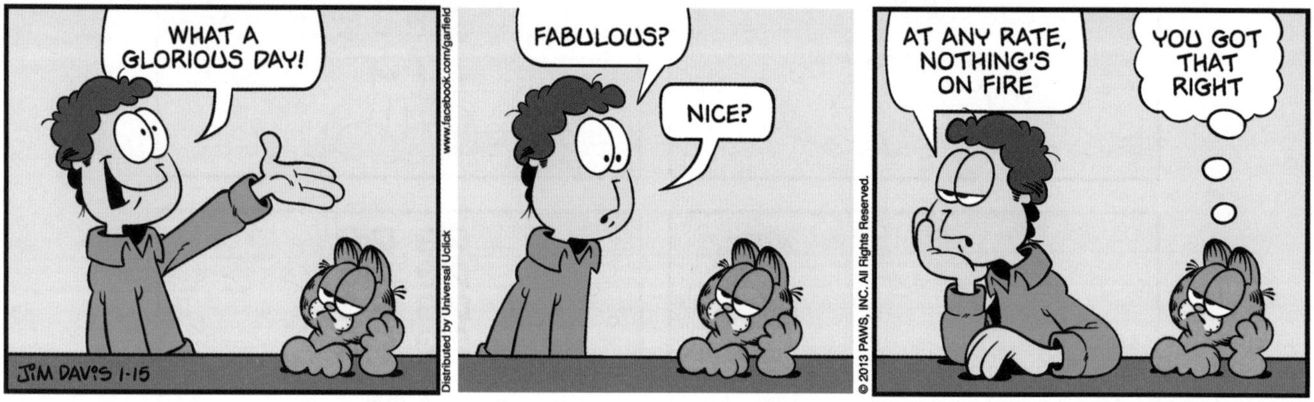
WHAT A GLORIOUS DAY!
JIM DAVIS 1-15
Distributed by Universal Uclick www.facebook.com/garfield
FABULOUS?
NICE?
© 2013 PAWS, INC. All Rights Reserved.
AT ANY RATE, NOTHING'S ON FIRE
YOU GOT THAT RIGHT

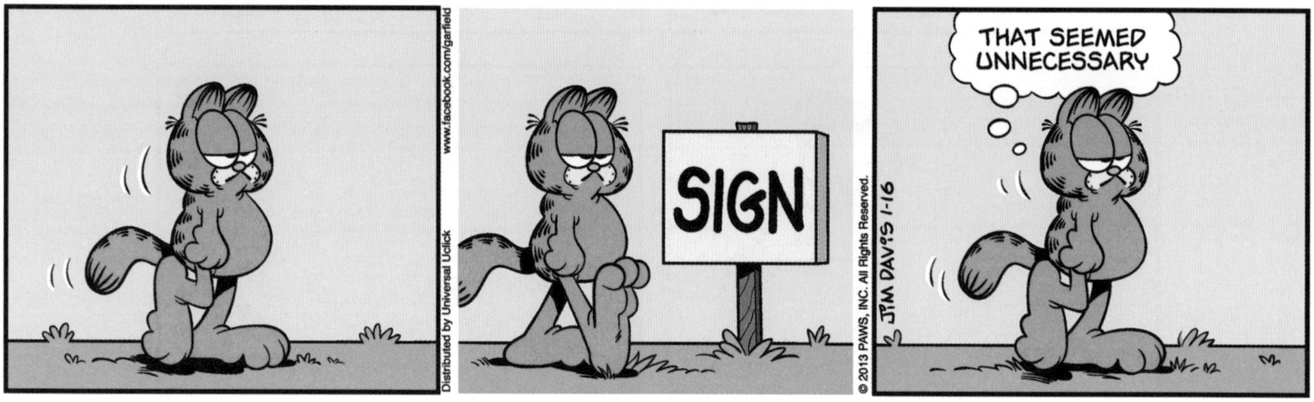
Distributed by Universal Uclick www.facebook.com/garfield
SIGN
© 2013 PAWS, INC. All Rights Reserved.
JIM DAVIS 1-16
THAT SEEMED UNNECESSARY

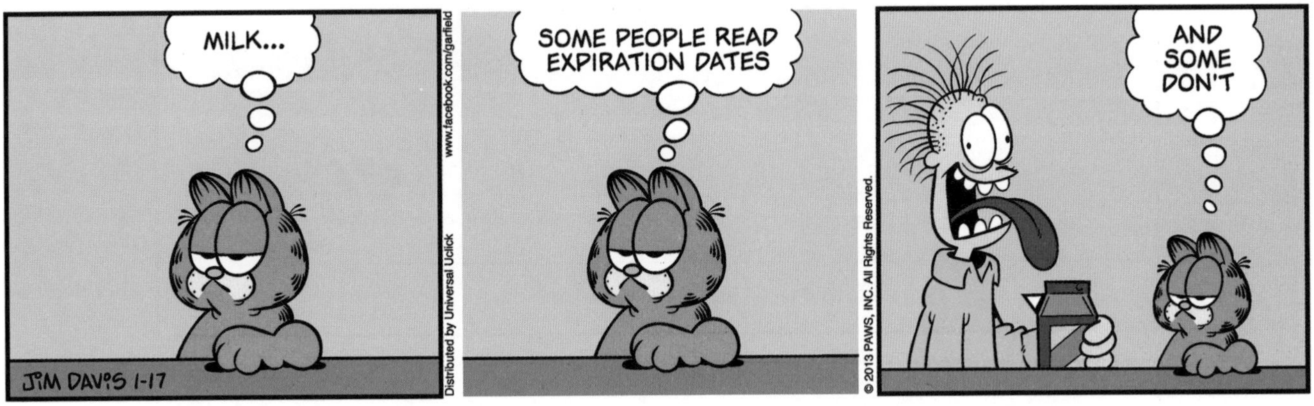
MILK...
JIM DAVIS 1-17
www.facebook.com/garfield
Distributed by Universal Uclick
SOME PEOPLE READ EXPIRATION DATES
© 2013 PAWS, INC. All Rights Reserved.
AND SOME DON'T

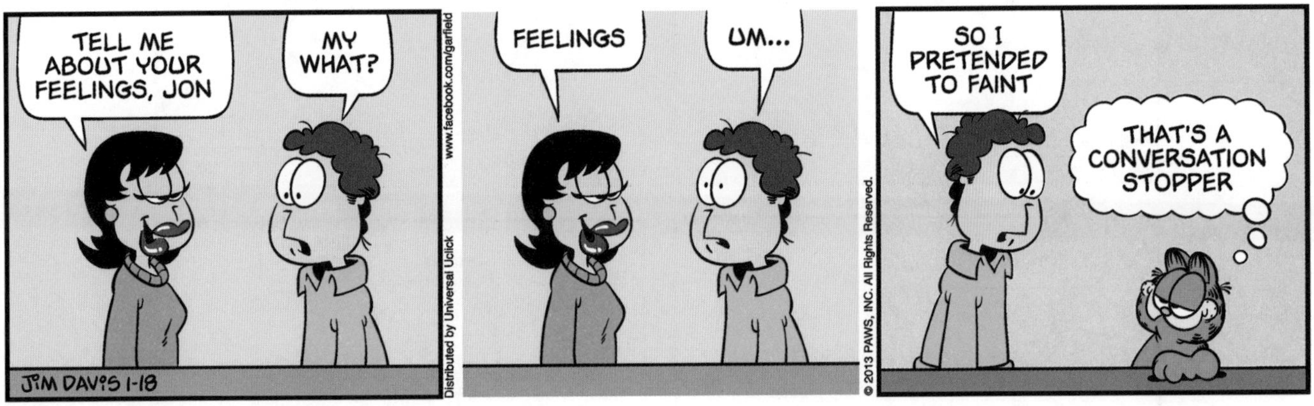
TELL ME ABOUT YOUR FEELINGS, JON
MY WHAT?
JIM DAVIS 1-18
www.facebook.com/garfield
Distributed by Universal Uclick
FEELINGS
UM...
© 2013 PAWS, INC. All Rights Reserved.
SO I PRETENDED TO FAINT
THAT'S A CONVERSATION STOPPER

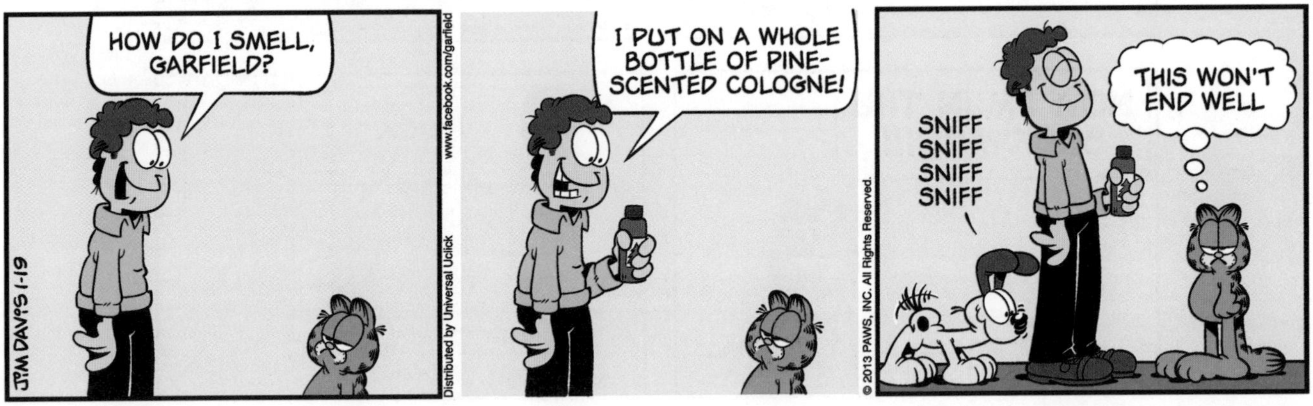
HOW DO I SMELL, GARFIELD?
JIM DAVIS 1-19
www.facebook.com/garfield
Distributed by Universal Uclick
I PUT ON A WHOLE BOTTLE OF PINE-SCENTED COLOGNE!
© 2013 PAWS, INC. All Rights Reserved.
SNIFF SNIFF SNIFF SNIFF
THIS WON'T END WELL

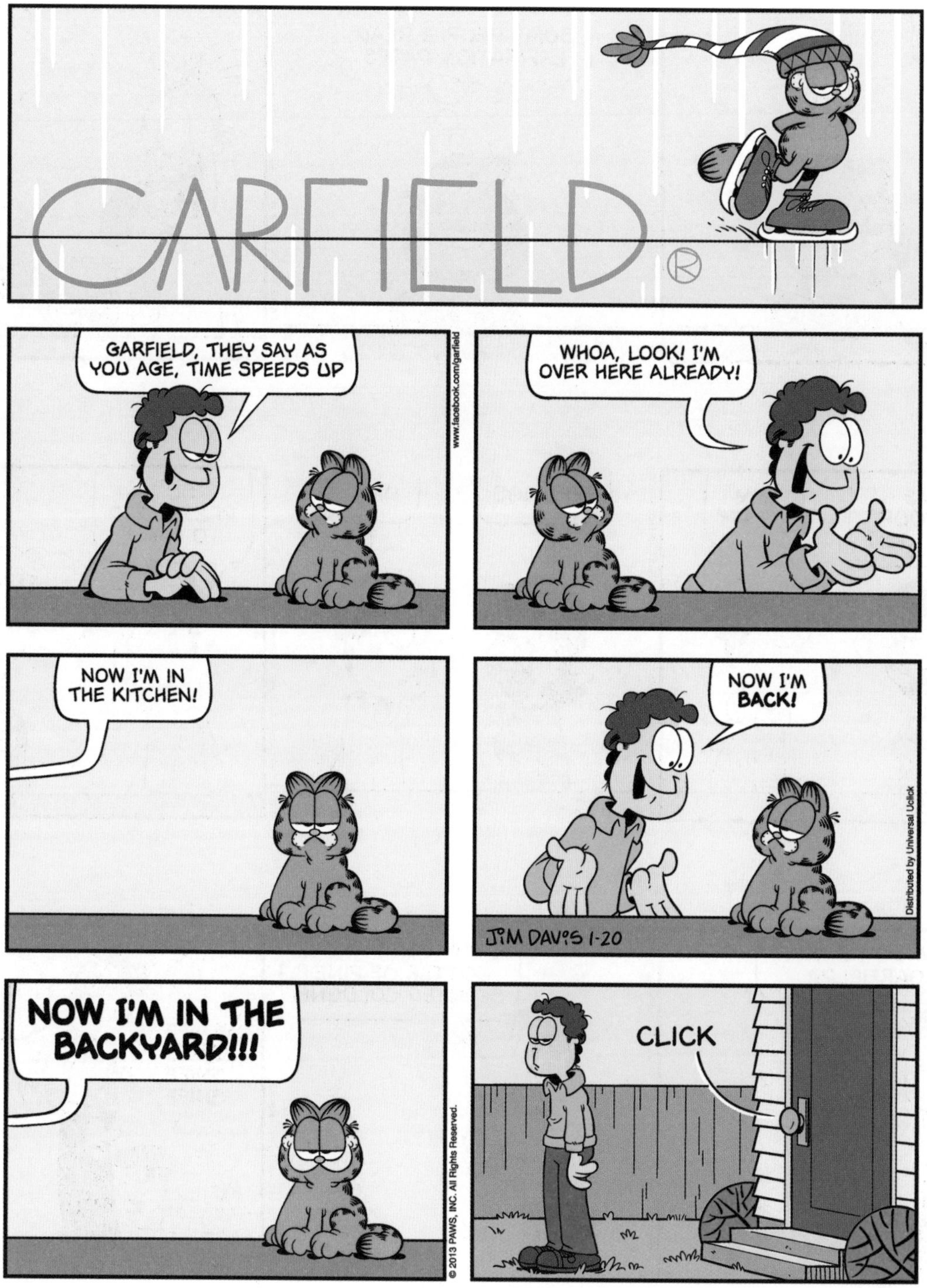
GARFIELD®
GARFIELD, THEY SAY AS YOU AGE, TIME SPEEDS UP
www.facebook.com/garfield
WHOA, LOOK! I'M OVER HERE ALREADY!
NOW I'M IN THE KITCHEN!
NOW I'M BACK!
JIM DAVIS 1-20
Distributed by Universal Uclick
NOW I'M IN THE BACKYARD!!!
© 2013 PAWS, INC. All Rights Reserved.
CLICK

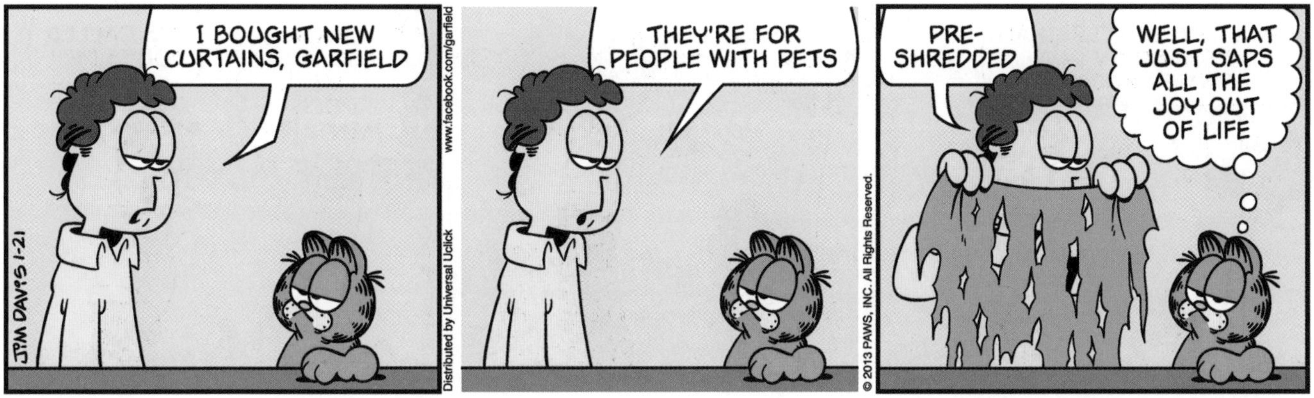
I BOUGHT NEW CURTAINS, GARFIELD
JIM DAVIS 1-21
Distributed by Universal Uclick
www.facebook.com/garfield
THEY'RE FOR PEOPLE WITH PETS
© 2013 PAWS, INC. All Rights Reserved.
PRE-SHREDDED
WELL, THAT JUST SAPS ALL THE JOY OUT OF LIFE

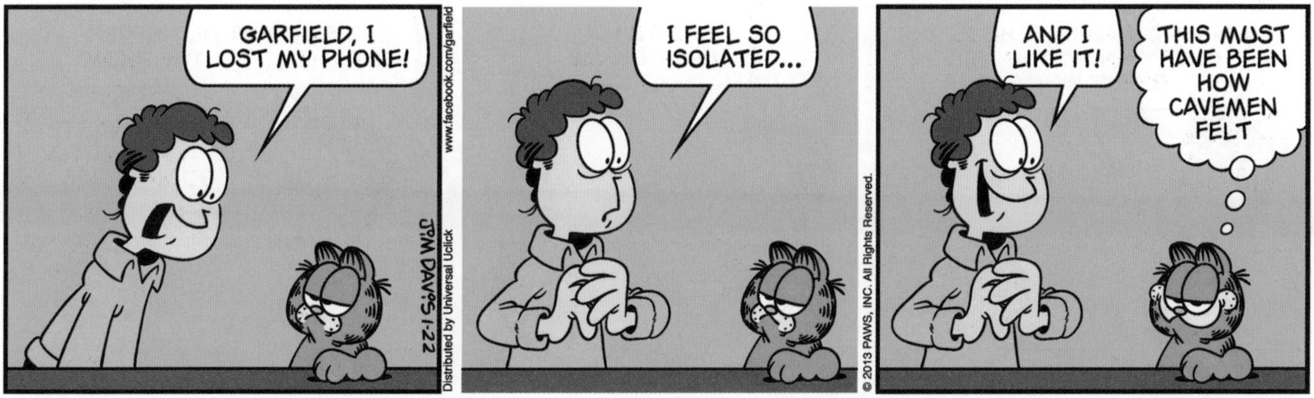
GARFIELD, I LOST MY PHONE!
JIM DAVIS 1-22
Distributed by Universal Uclick
www.facebook.com/garfield
I FEEL SO ISOLATED...
© 2013 PAWS, INC. All Rights Reserved.
AND I LIKE IT!
THIS MUST HAVE BEEN HOW CAVEMEN FELT

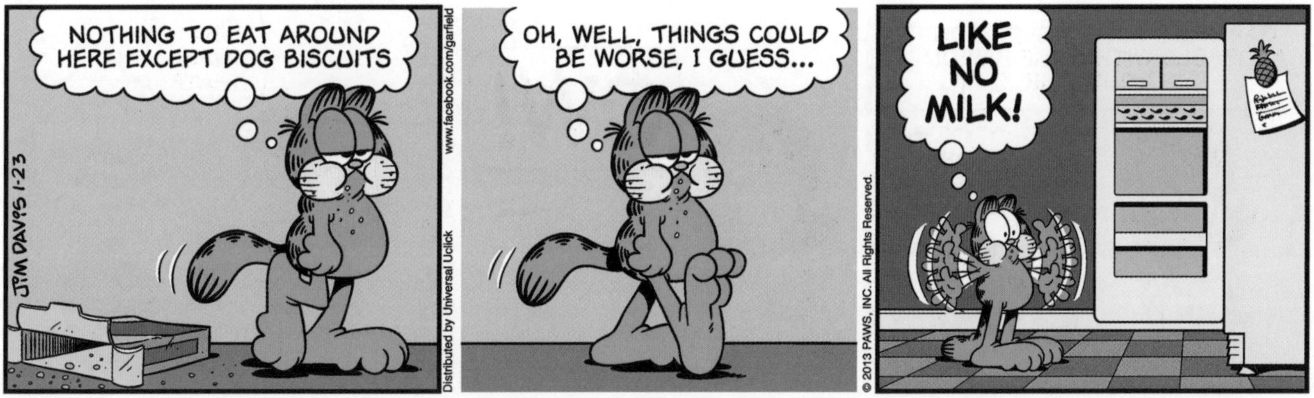
NOTHING TO EAT AROUND HERE EXCEPT DOG BISCUITS
JIM DAVIS 1-23
Distributed by Universal Uclick
www.facebook.com/garfield
OH, WELL, THINGS COULD BE WORSE, I GUESS...
© 2013 PAWS, INC. All Rights Reserved.
LIKE NO MILK!

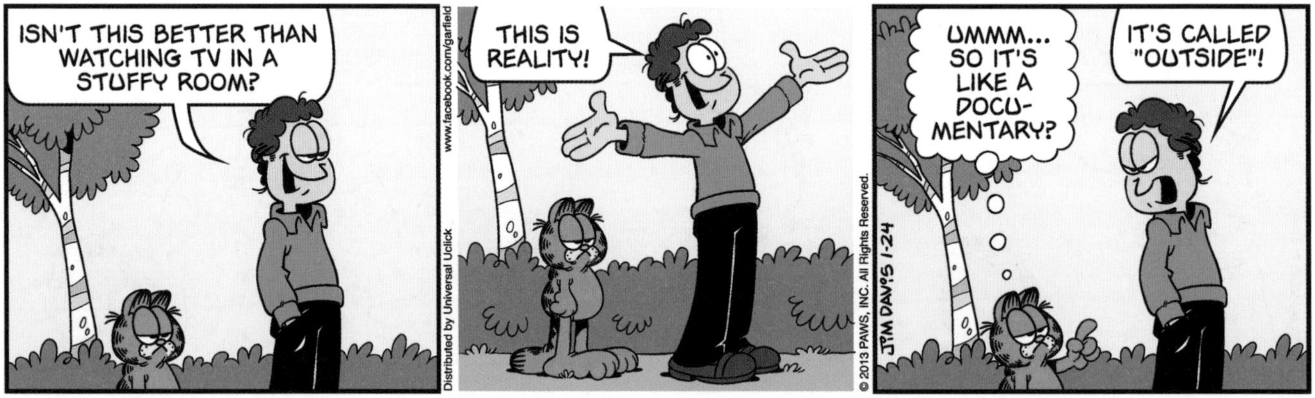
ISN'T THIS BETTER THAN WATCHING TV IN A STUFFY ROOM?
THIS IS REALITY!
UMMM... SO IT'S LIKE A DOCU-MENTARY?
IT'S CALLED "OUTSIDE"!
www.facebook.com/garfield
Distributed by Universal Uclick
© 2013 PAWS, INC. All Rights Reserved.
JIM DAVIS 1-24

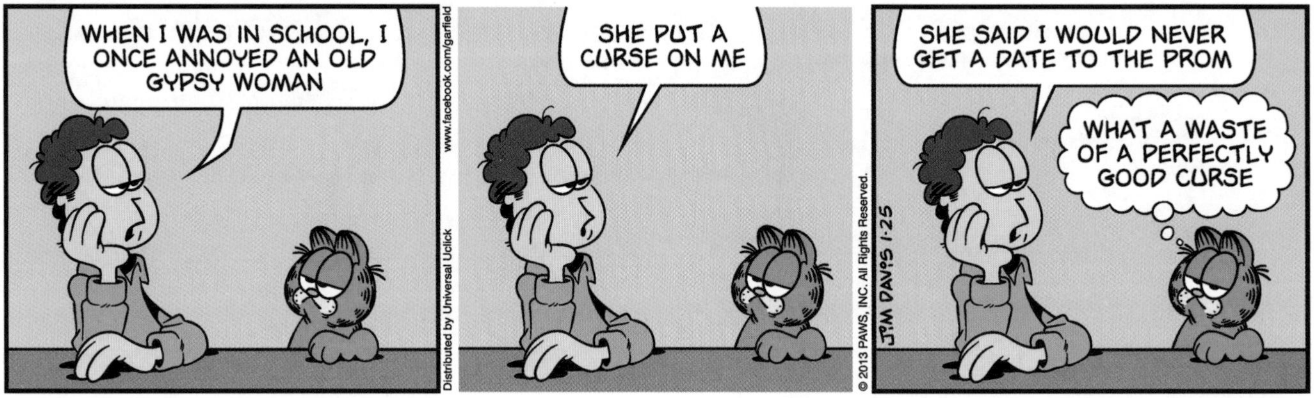
WHEN I WAS IN SCHOOL, I ONCE ANNOYED AN OLD GYPSY WOMAN
SHE PUT A CURSE ON ME
SHE SAID I WOULD NEVER GET A DATE TO THE PROM
WHAT A WASTE OF A PERFECTLY GOOD CURSE
www.facebook.com/garfield
Distributed by Universal Uclick
© 2013 PAWS, INC. All Rights Reserved.
JIM DAVIS 1-25

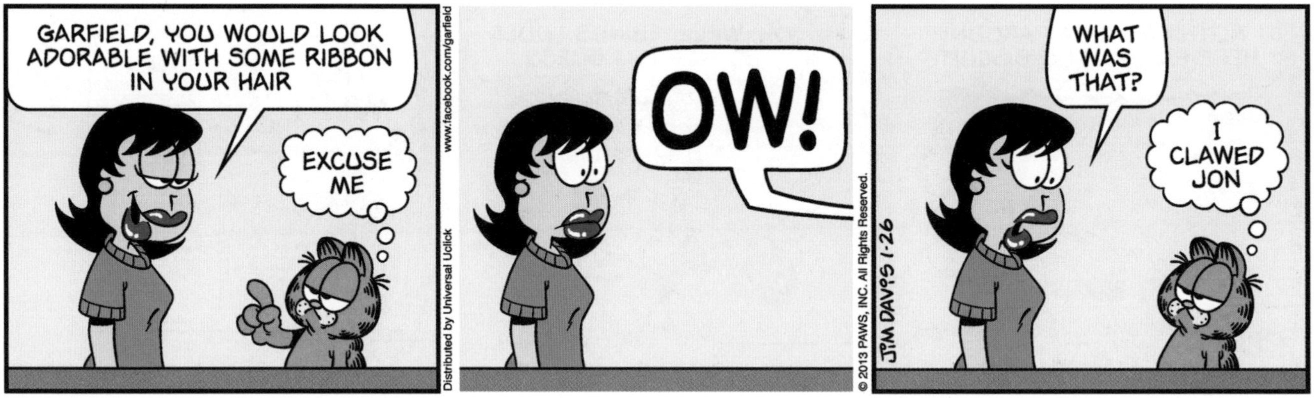
GARFIELD, YOU WOULD LOOK ADORABLE WITH SOME RIBBON IN YOUR HAIR
EXCUSE ME
OW!
WHAT WAS THAT?
I CLAWED JON
www.facebook.com/garfield
Distributed by Universal Uclick
© 2013 PAWS, INC. All Rights Reserved.
JIM DAVIS 1-26

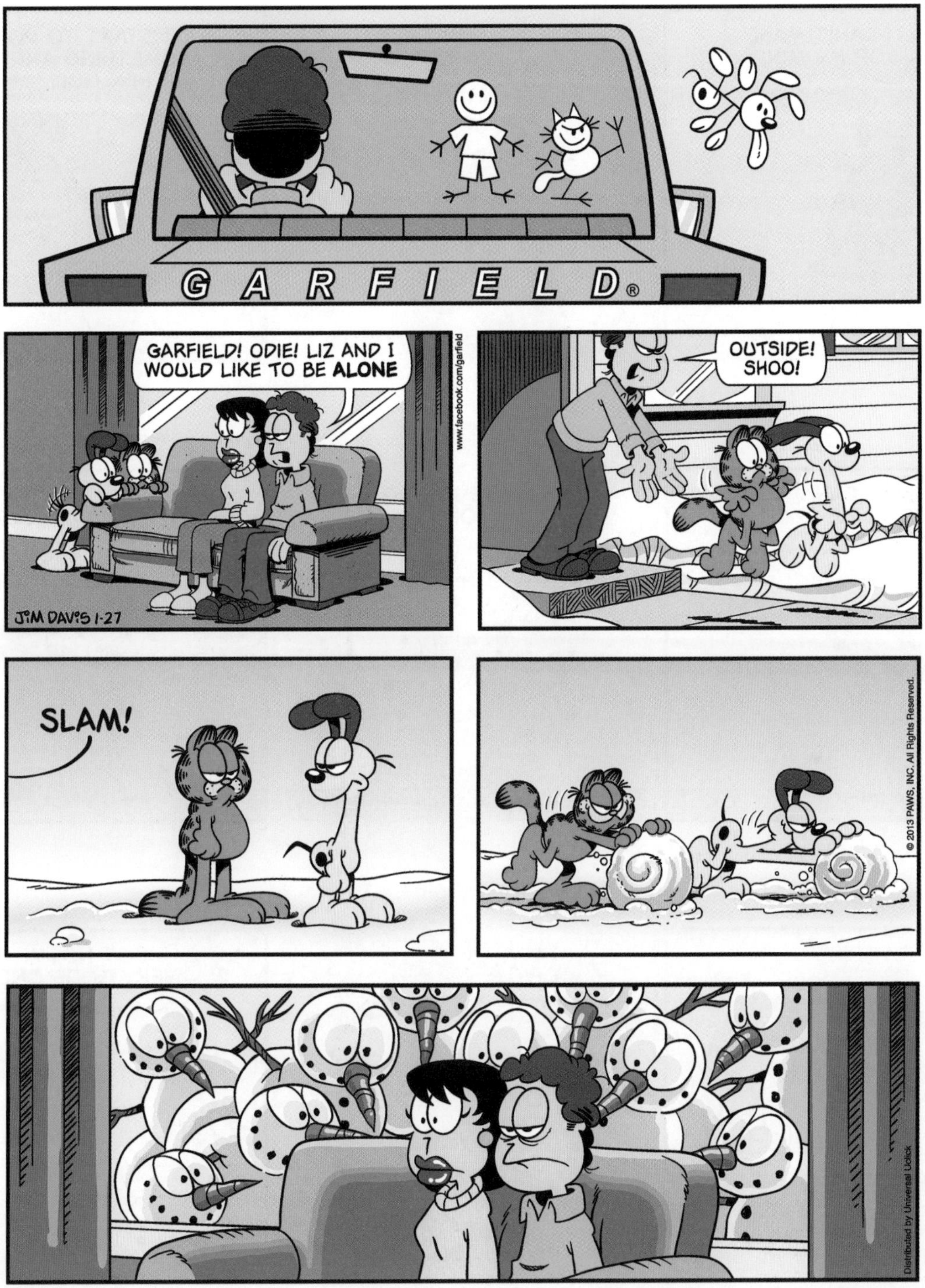
GARFIELD®
GARFIELD! ODIE! LIZ AND I WOULD LIKE TO BE **ALONE**
JIM DAVIS 1-27
www.facebook.com/garfield
OUTSIDE! SHOO!
SLAM!
© 2013 PAWS, INC. All Rights Reserved.
Distributed by Universal Uclick

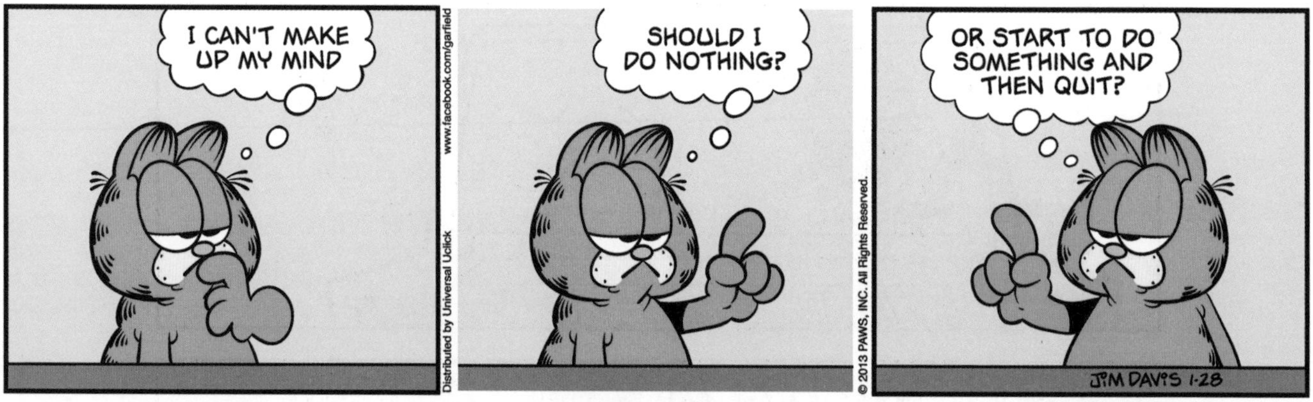
I CAN'T MAKE UP MY MIND
www.facebook.com/garfield
Distributed by Universal Uclick
SHOULD I DO NOTHING?
© 2013 PAWS, INC. All Rights Reserved.
OR START TO DO SOMETHING AND THEN QUIT?
JIM DAVIS 1-28

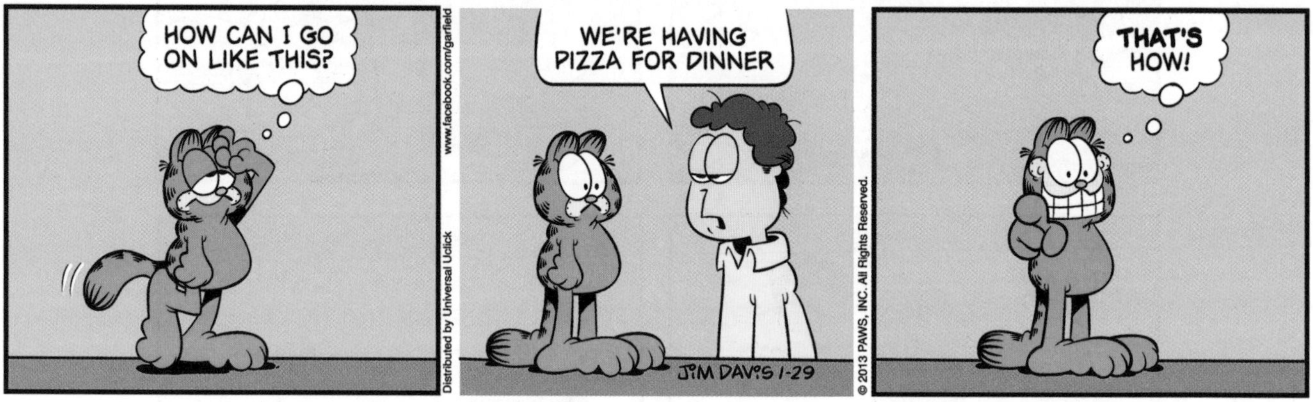
HOW CAN I GO ON LIKE THIS?
www.facebook.com/garfield
Distributed by Universal Uclick
WE'RE HAVING PIZZA FOR DINNER
JIM DAVIS 1-29
© 2013 PAWS, INC. All Rights Reserved.
THAT'S HOW!

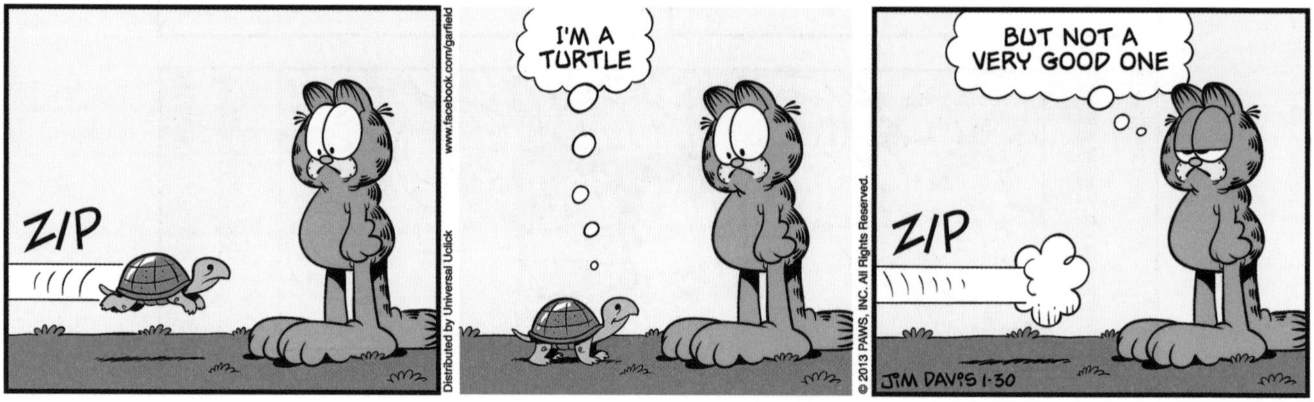
ZIP
www.facebook.com/garfield
Distributed by Universal Uclick
I'M A TURTLE
© 2013 PAWS, INC. All Rights Reserved.
BUT NOT A VERY GOOD ONE
ZIP
JIM DAVIS 1-30

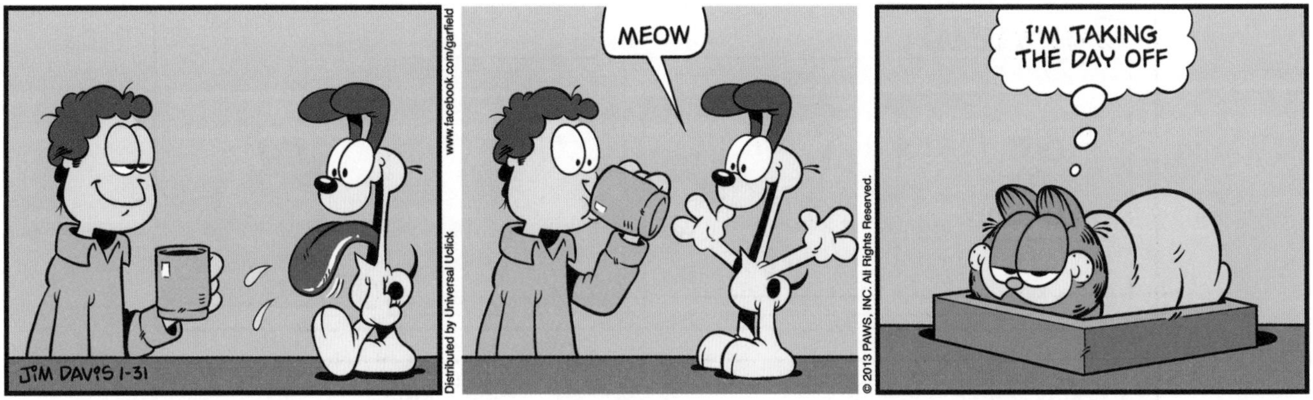
JIM DAVIS 1-31
Distributed by Universal Uclick
www.facebook.com/garfield
MEOW
© 2013 PAWS, INC. All Rights Reserved.
I'M TAKING THE DAY OFF

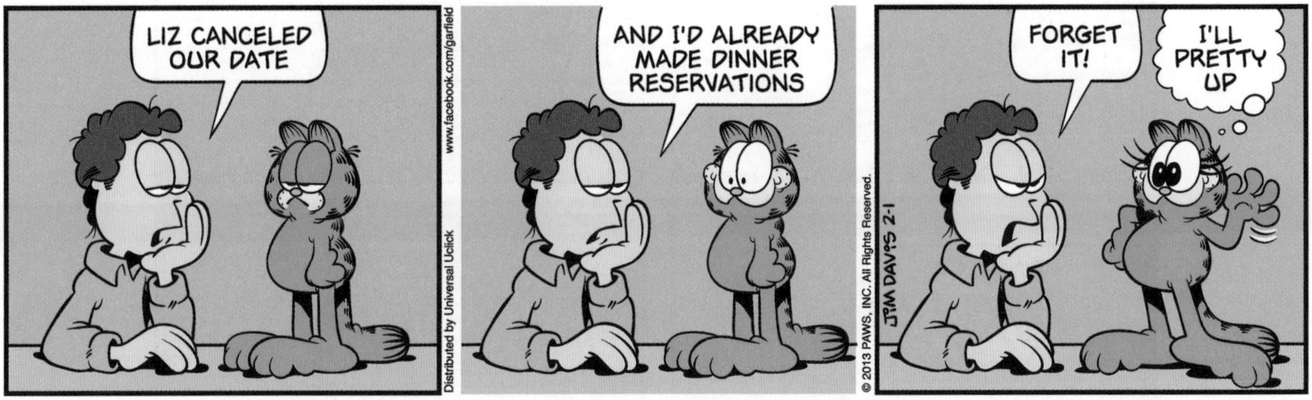
LIZ CANCELED OUR DATE
Distributed by Universal Uclick
www.facebook.com/garfield
AND I'D ALREADY MADE DINNER RESERVATIONS
© 2013 PAWS, INC. All Rights Reserved.
JIM DAVIS 2-1
FORGET IT!
I'LL PRETTY UP

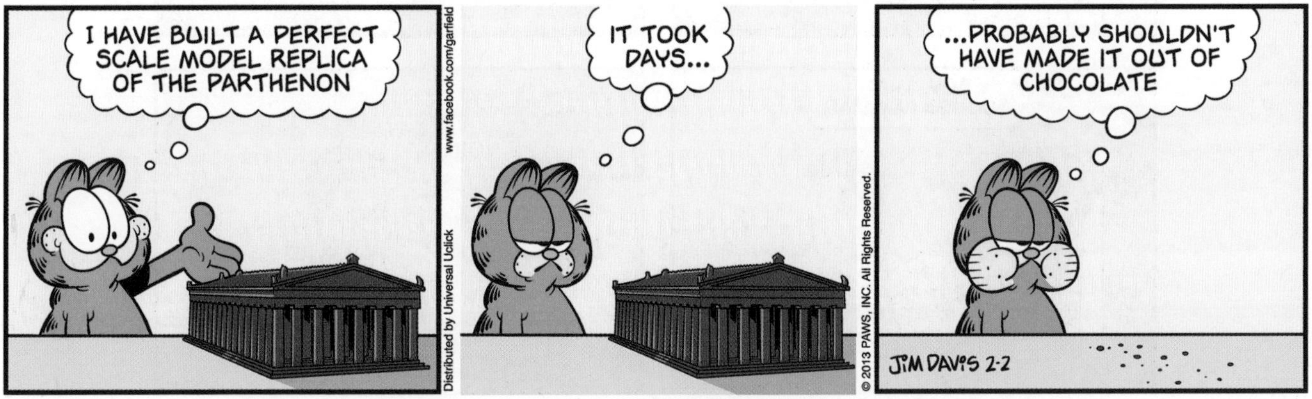
I HAVE BUILT A PERFECT SCALE MODEL REPLICA OF THE PARTHENON
Distributed by Universal Uclick
www.facebook.com/garfield
IT TOOK DAYS...
© 2013 PAWS, INC. All Rights Reserved.
...PROBABLY SHOULDN'T HAVE MADE IT OUT OF CHOCOLATE
JIM DAVIS 2-2

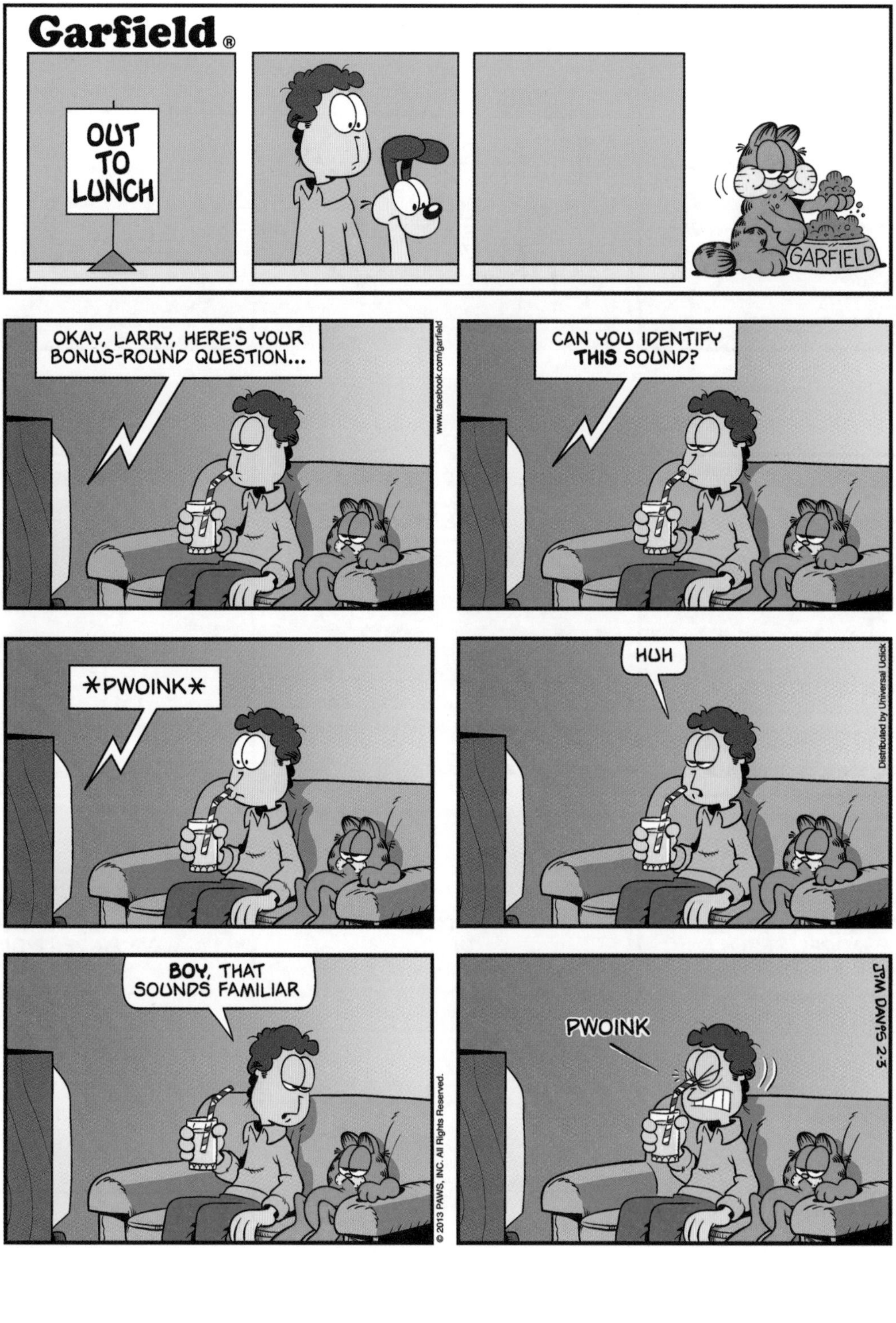
Garfield®
OUT TO LUNCH
GARFIELD
OKAY, LARRY, HERE'S YOUR BONUS-ROUND QUESTION...
www.facebook.com/garfield
CAN YOU IDENTIFY THIS SOUND?
PWOINK
HUH
Distributed by Universal Uclick
BOY, THAT SOUNDS FAMILIAR
© 2013 PAWS, INC. All Rights Reserved.
PWOINK
JIM DAVIS 2-3

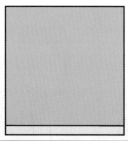

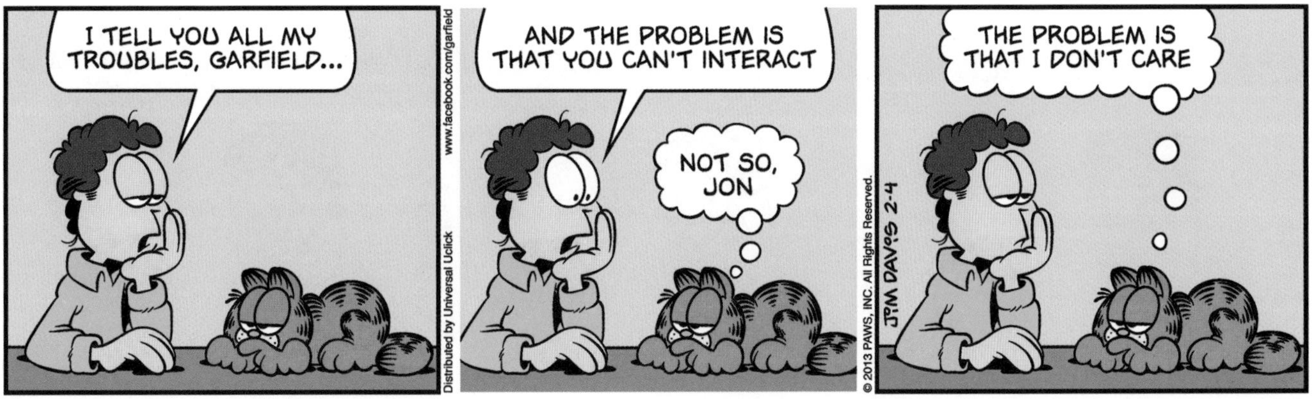
I TELL YOU ALL MY TROUBLES, GARFIELD...
Distributed by Universal Uclick www.facebook.com/garfield
AND THE PROBLEM IS THAT YOU CAN'T INTERACT
NOT SO, JON
© 2013 PAWS, INC. All Rights Reserved.
JIM DAVIS 2-4
THE PROBLEM IS THAT I DON'T CARE

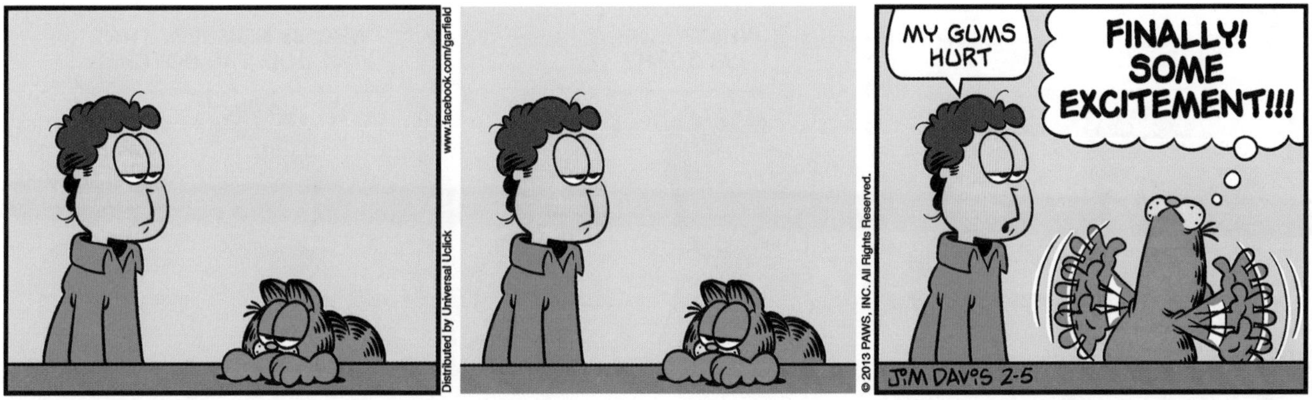
Distributed by Universal Uclick www.facebook.com/garfield
© 2013 PAWS, INC. All Rights Reserved.
MY GUMS HURT
FINALLY! SOME EXCITEMENT!!!
JIM DAVIS 2-5

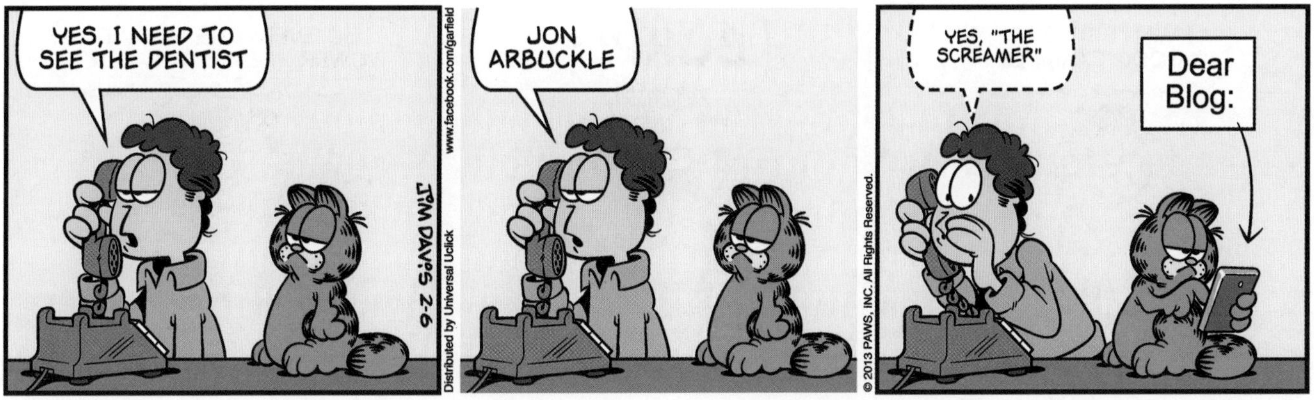
YES, I NEED TO SEE THE DENTIST
JIM DAVIS 2-6
Distributed by Universal Uclick www.facebook.com/garfield
JON ARBUCKLE
© 2013 PAWS, INC. All Rights Reserved.
YES, "THE SCREAMER"
Dear Blog:

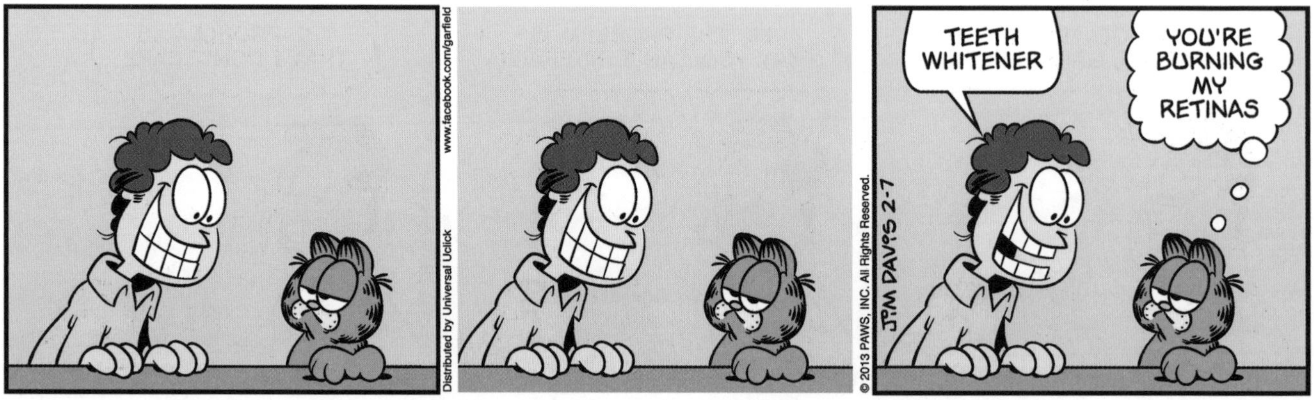
TEETH WHITENER
YOU'RE BURNING MY RETINAS
JIM DAVIS 2-7
www.facebook.com/garfield
Distributed by Universal Uclick
© 2013 PAWS, INC. All Rights Reserved.

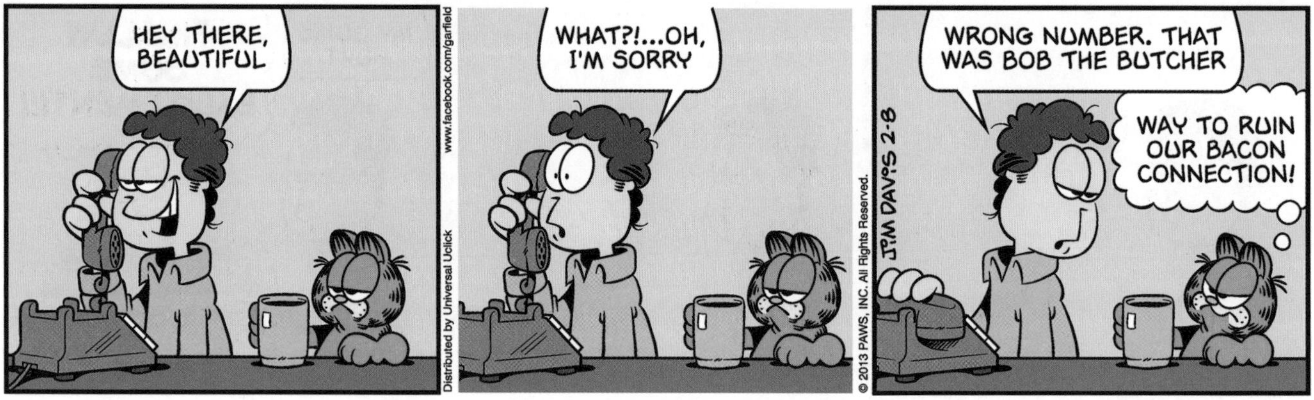
HEY THERE, BEAUTIFUL
WHAT?!...OH, I'M SORRY
WRONG NUMBER. THAT WAS BOB THE BUTCHER
WAY TO RUIN OUR BACON CONNECTION!
JIM DAVIS 2-8
www.facebook.com/garfield
Distributed by Universal Uclick
© 2013 PAWS, INC. All Rights Reserved.

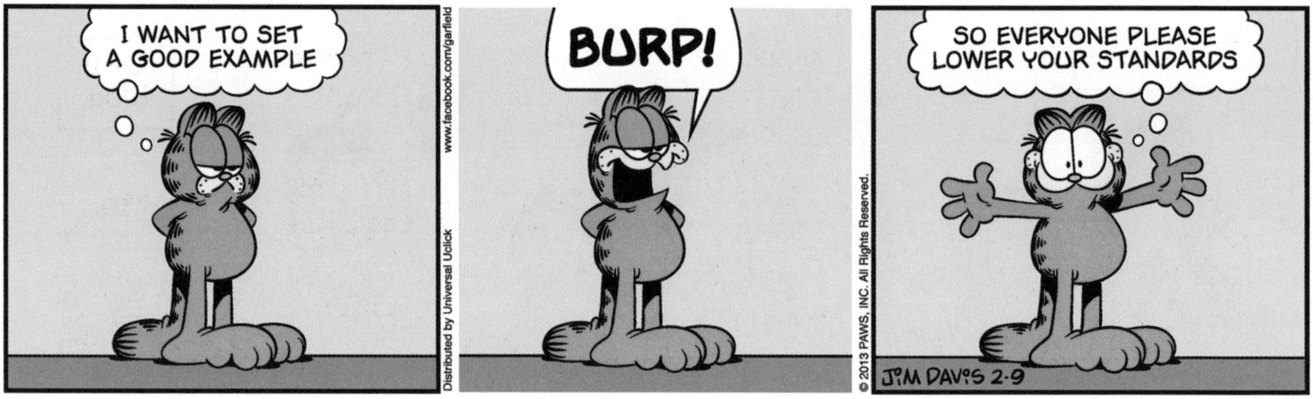
I WANT TO SET A GOOD EXAMPLE
BURP!
SO EVERYONE PLEASE LOWER YOUR STANDARDS
JIM DAVIS 2-9
www.facebook.com/garfield
Distributed by Universal Uclick
© 2013 PAWS, INC. All Rights Reserved.

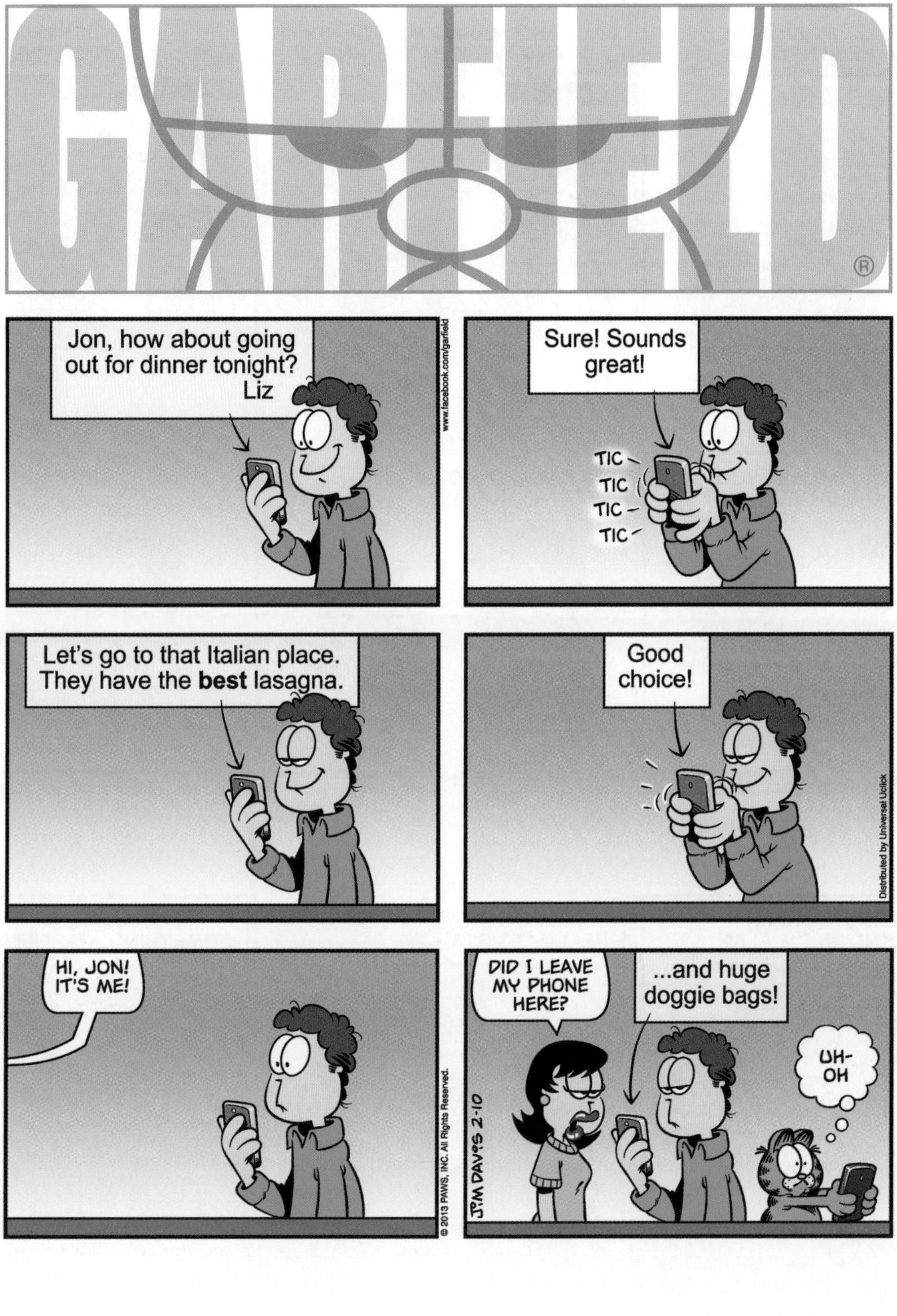
GARFIELD
Jon, how about going out for dinner tonight? Liz
www.facebook.com/garfield
Sure! Sounds great!
TIC TIC TIC TIC
Let's go to that Italian place. They have the **best** lasagna.
Good choice!
Distributed by Universal Uclick
HI, JON! IT'S ME!
© 2013 PAWS, INC. All Rights Reserved.
JPM DAVIS 2-10
DID I LEAVE MY PHONE HERE?
...and huge doggie bags!
UH-OH

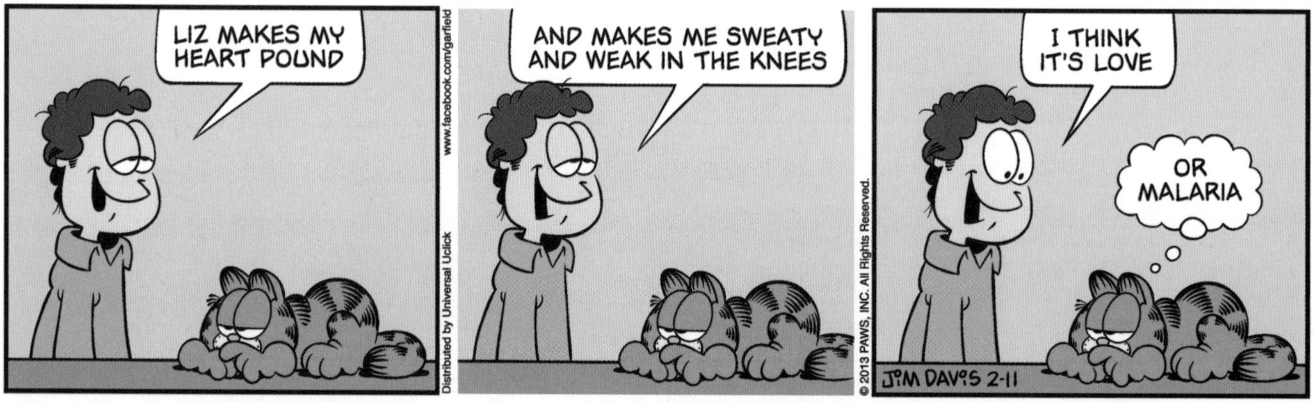
LIZ MAKES MY HEART POUND
www.facebook.com/garfield
Distributed by Universal Uclick
AND MAKES ME SWEATY AND WEAK IN THE KNEES
© 2013 PAWS, INC. All Rights Reserved.
I THINK IT'S LOVE
OR MALARIA
JIM DAVIS 2-11

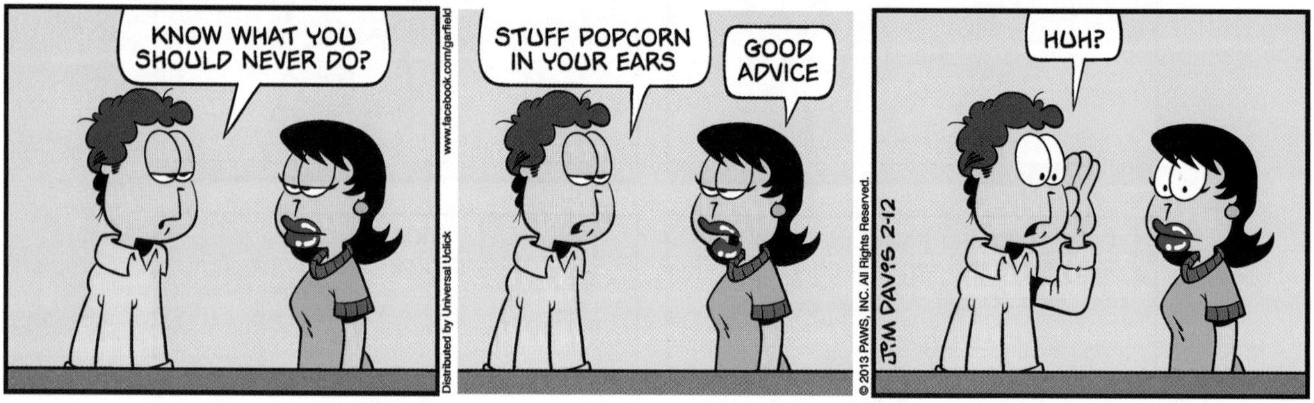
KNOW WHAT YOU SHOULD NEVER DO?
www.facebook.com/garfield
Distributed by Universal Uclick
STUFF POPCORN IN YOUR EARS
GOOD ADVICE
© 2013 PAWS, INC. All Rights Reserved.
JIM DAVIS 2-12
HUH?

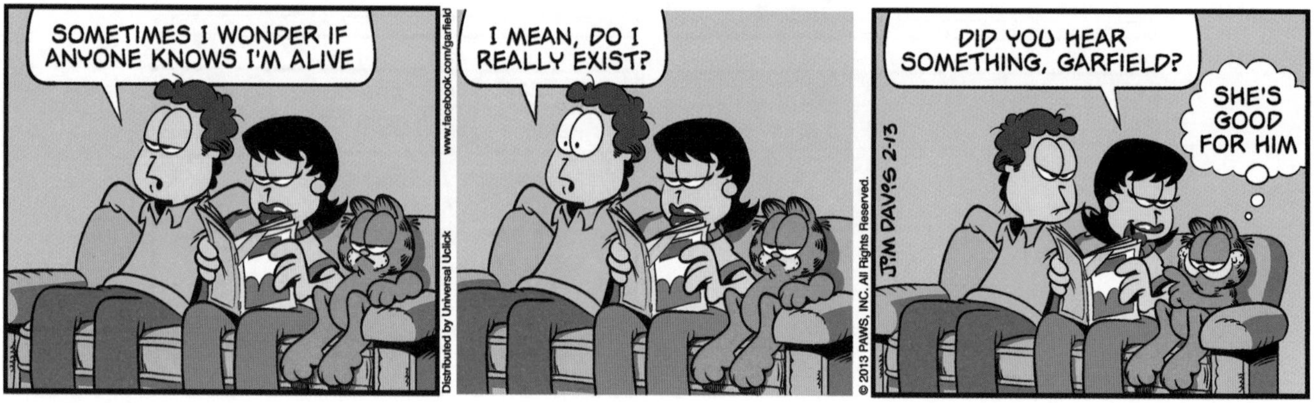
SOMETIMES I WONDER IF ANYONE KNOWS I'M ALIVE
www.facebook.com/garfield
Distributed by Universal Uclick
I MEAN, DO I REALLY EXIST?
© 2013 PAWS, INC. All Rights Reserved.
JIM DAVIS 2-13
DID YOU HEAR SOMETHING, GARFIELD?
SHE'S GOOD FOR HIM

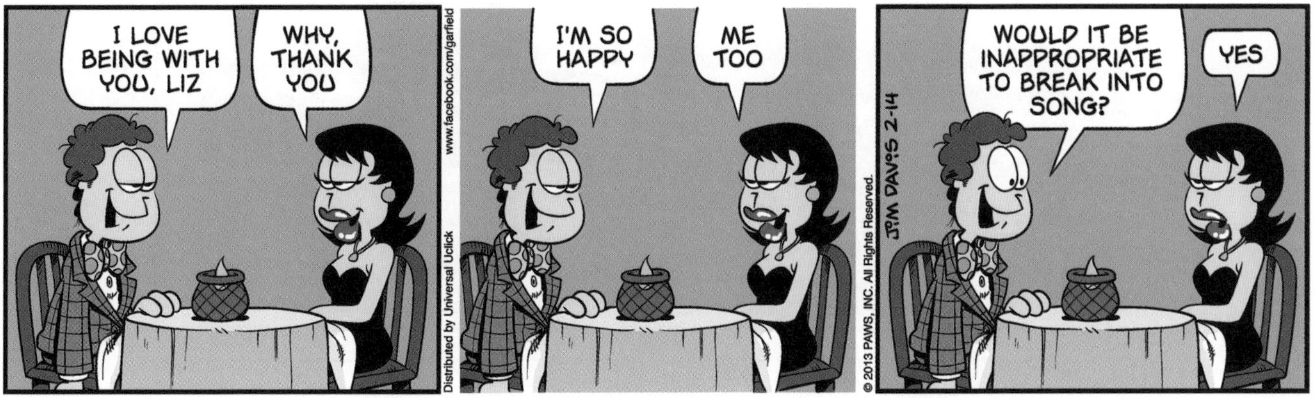
I LOVE BEING WITH YOU, LIZ
WHY, THANK YOU
www.facebook.com/garfield
Distributed by Universal Uclick
I'M SO HAPPY
ME TOO
© 2013 PAWS, INC. All Rights Reserved.
JIM DAVIS 2-14
WOULD IT BE INAPPROPRIATE TO BREAK INTO SONG?
YES

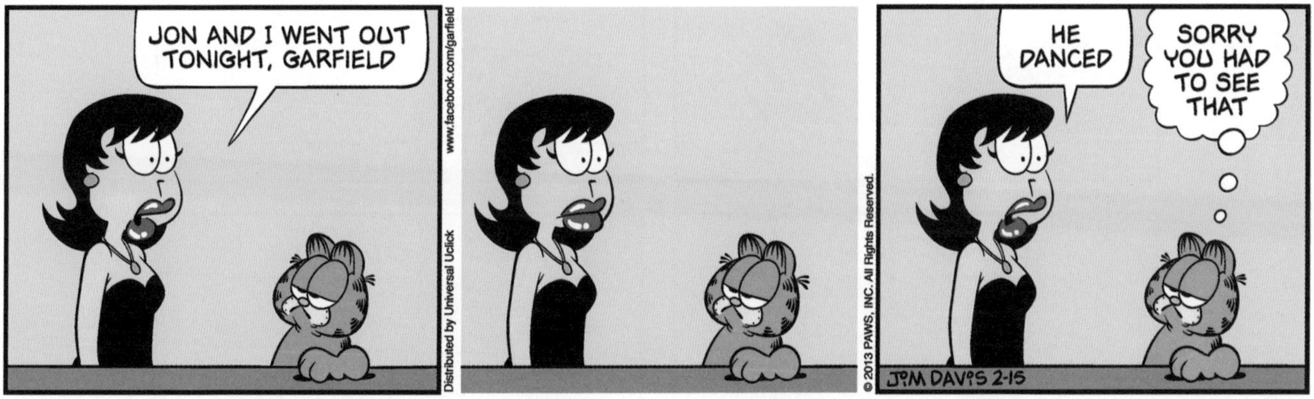
JON AND I WENT OUT TONIGHT, GARFIELD
www.facebook.com/garfield
Distributed by Universal Uclick
© 2013 PAWS, INC. All Rights Reserved.
HE DANCED
SORRY YOU HAD TO SEE THAT
JIM DAVIS 2-15

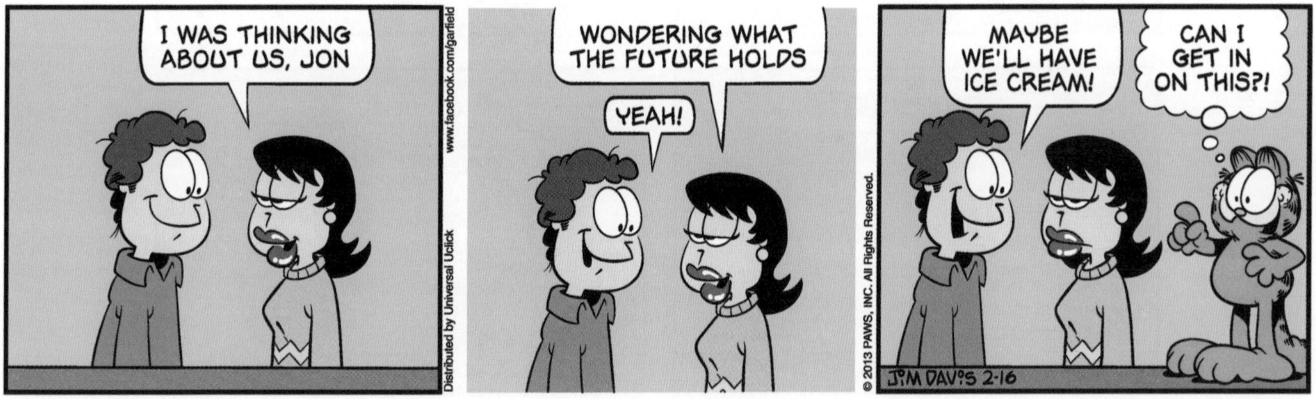
I WAS THINKING ABOUT US, JON
www.facebook.com/garfield
Distributed by Universal Uclick
WONDERING WHAT THE FUTURE HOLDS
YEAH!
© 2013 PAWS, INC. All Rights Reserved.
MAYBE WE'LL HAVE ICE CREAM!
CAN I GET IN ON THIS?!
JIM DAVIS 2-16

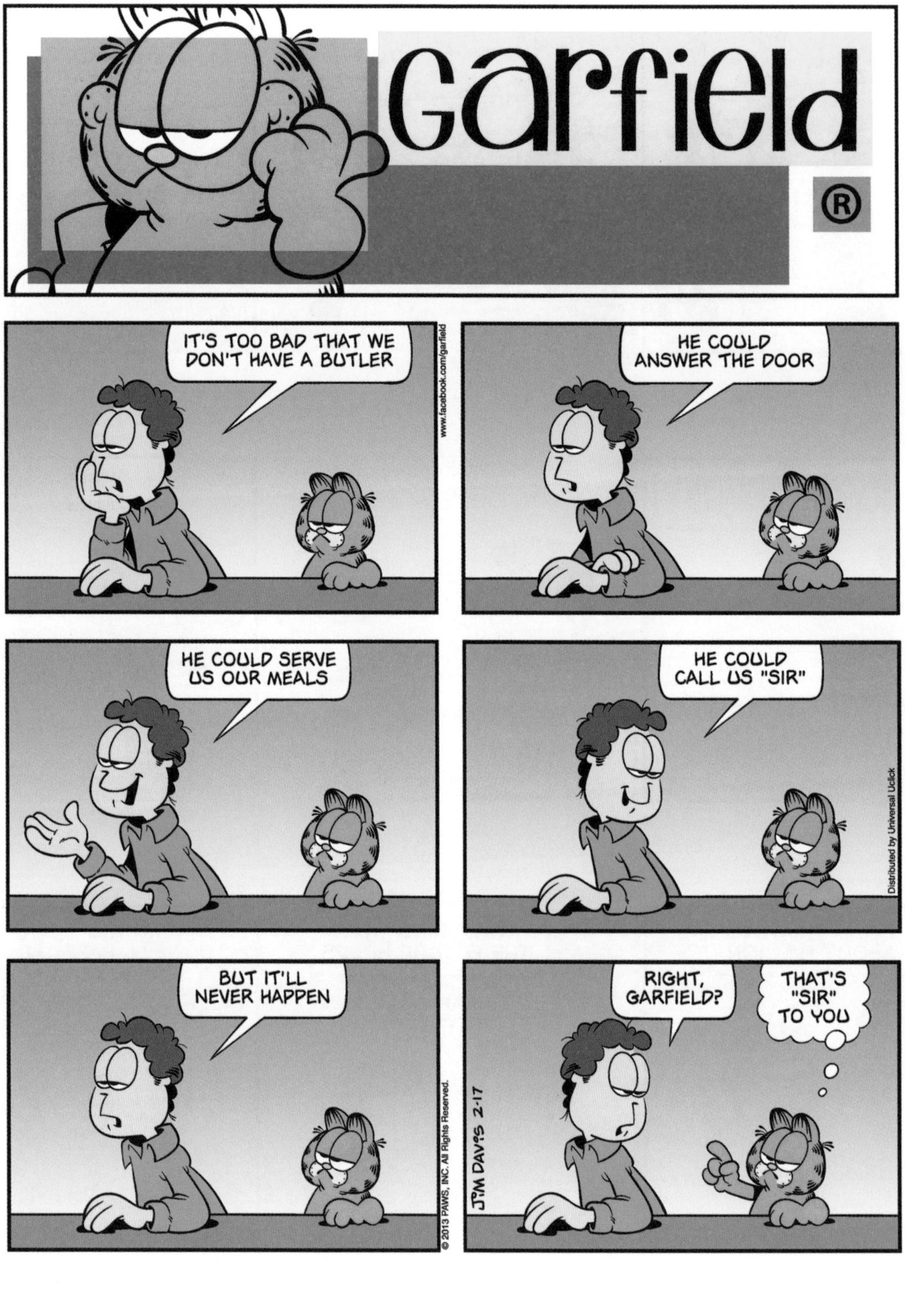
Garfield
®
IT'S TOO BAD THAT WE DON'T HAVE A BUTLER
www.facebook.com/garfield
HE COULD ANSWER THE DOOR
HE COULD SERVE US OUR MEALS
HE COULD CALL US "SIR"
Distributed by Universal Uclick
BUT IT'LL NEVER HAPPEN
© 2013 PAWS, INC. All Rights Reserved.
JIM DAVIS 2-17
RIGHT, GARFIELD?
THAT'S "SIR" TO YOU

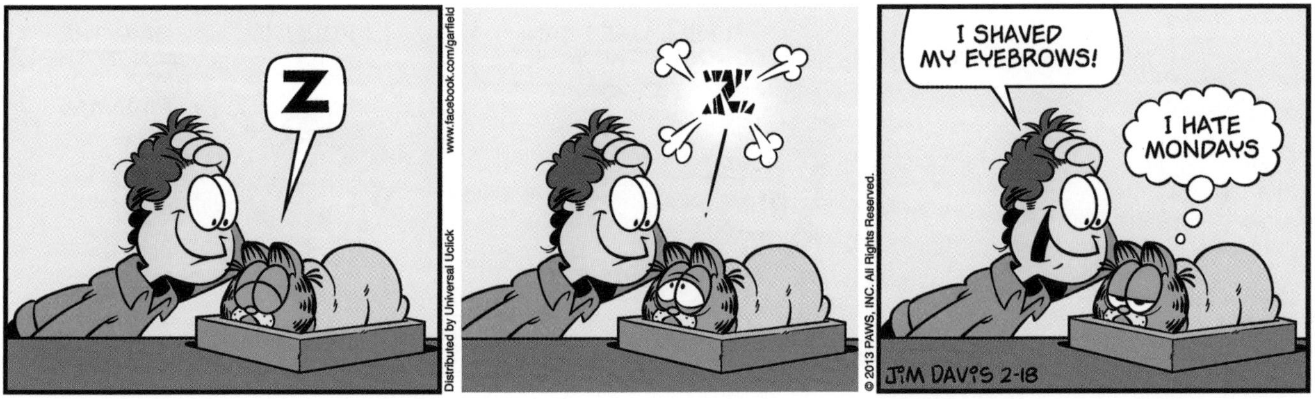
Z
Z
I SHAVED MY EYEBROWS!
I HATE MONDAYS
JIM DAVIS 2-18
www.facebook.com/garfield
Distributed by Universal Uclick
© 2013 PAWS, INC. All Rights Reserved.

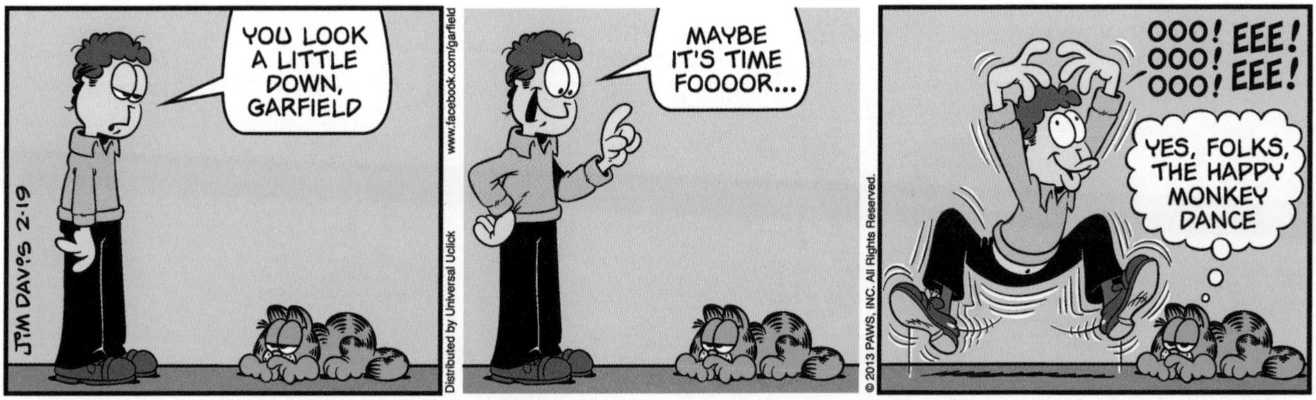
YOU LOOK A LITTLE DOWN, GARFIELD
MAYBE IT'S TIME FOOOOR...
OOO! EEE! OOO! EEE! OOO! EEE!
YES, FOLKS, THE HAPPY MONKEY DANCE
JIM DAVIS 2-19
www.facebook.com/garfield
Distributed by Universal Uclick
© 2013 PAWS, INC. All Rights Reserved.

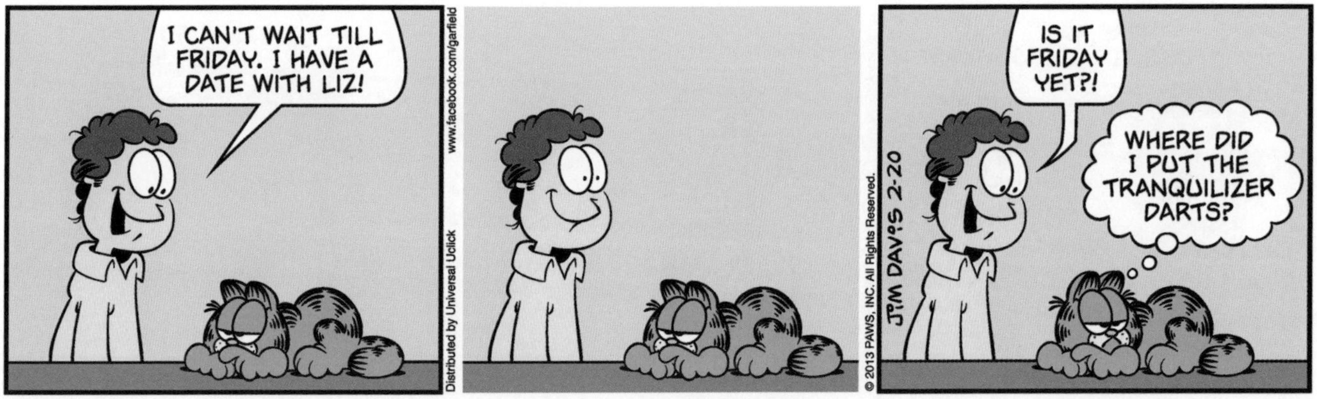
I CAN'T WAIT TILL FRIDAY. I HAVE A DATE WITH LIZ!
IS IT FRIDAY YET?!
WHERE DID I PUT THE TRANQUILIZER DARTS?
JIM DAVIS 2-20
www.facebook.com/garfield
Distributed by Universal Uclick
© 2013 PAWS, INC. All Rights Reserved.

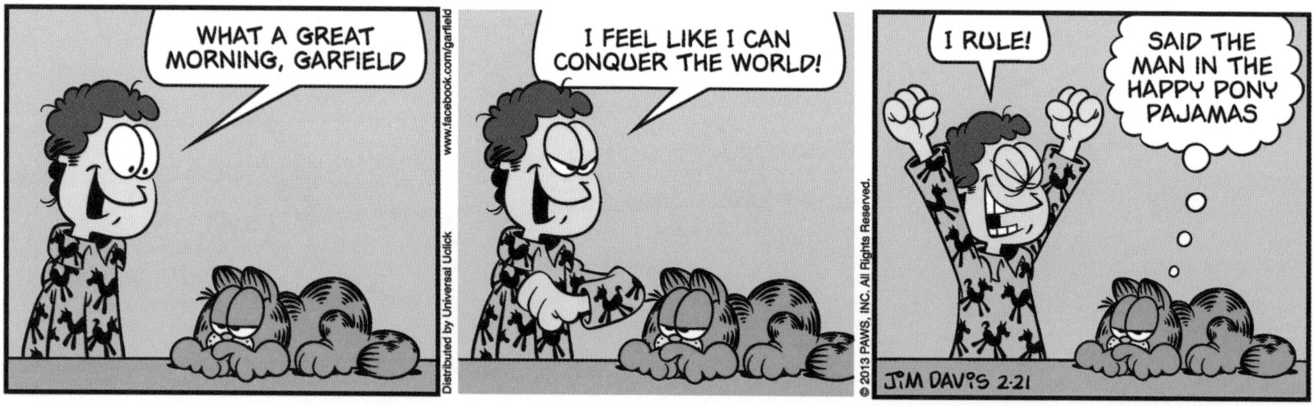
WHAT A GREAT MORNING, GARFIELD
I FEEL LIKE I CAN CONQUER THE WORLD!
I RULE!
SAID THE MAN IN THE HAPPY PONY PAJAMAS
JIM DAVIS 2-21
www.facebook.com/garfield
Distributed by Universal Uclick
© 2013 PAWS, INC. All Rights Reserved.

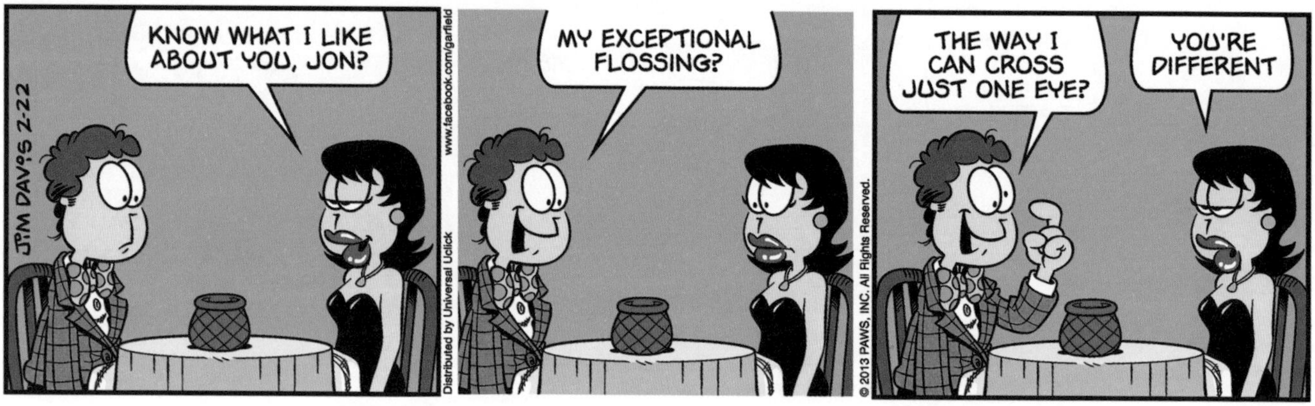
JIM DAVIS 2-22
KNOW WHAT I LIKE ABOUT YOU, JON?
MY EXCEPTIONAL FLOSSING?
THE WAY I CAN CROSS JUST ONE EYE?
YOU'RE DIFFERENT
www.facebook.com/garfield
Distributed by Universal Uclick
© 2013 PAWS, INC. All Rights Reserved.

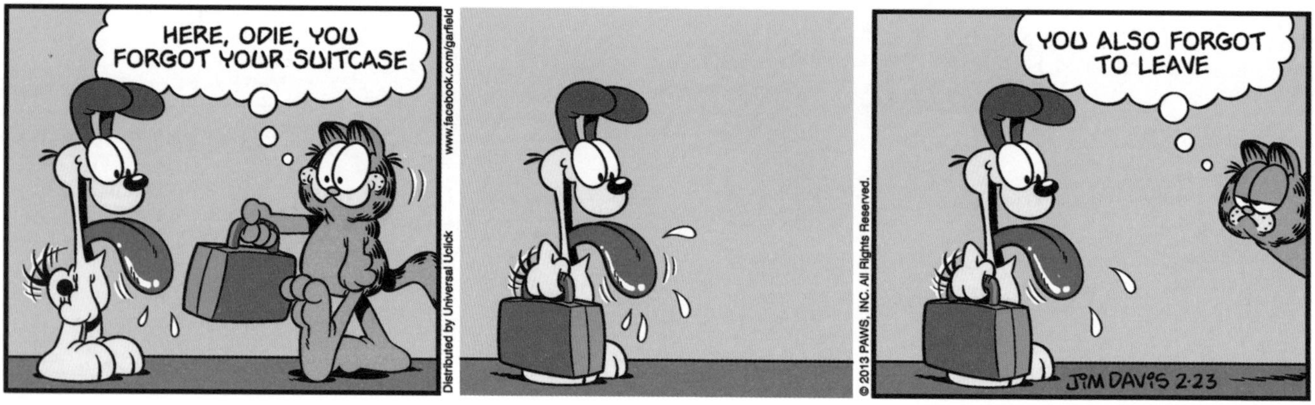
HERE, ODIE, YOU FORGOT YOUR SUITCASE
YOU ALSO FORGOT TO LEAVE
JIM DAVIS 2-23
www.facebook.com/garfield
Distributed by Universal Uclick
© 2013 PAWS, INC. All Rights Reserved.

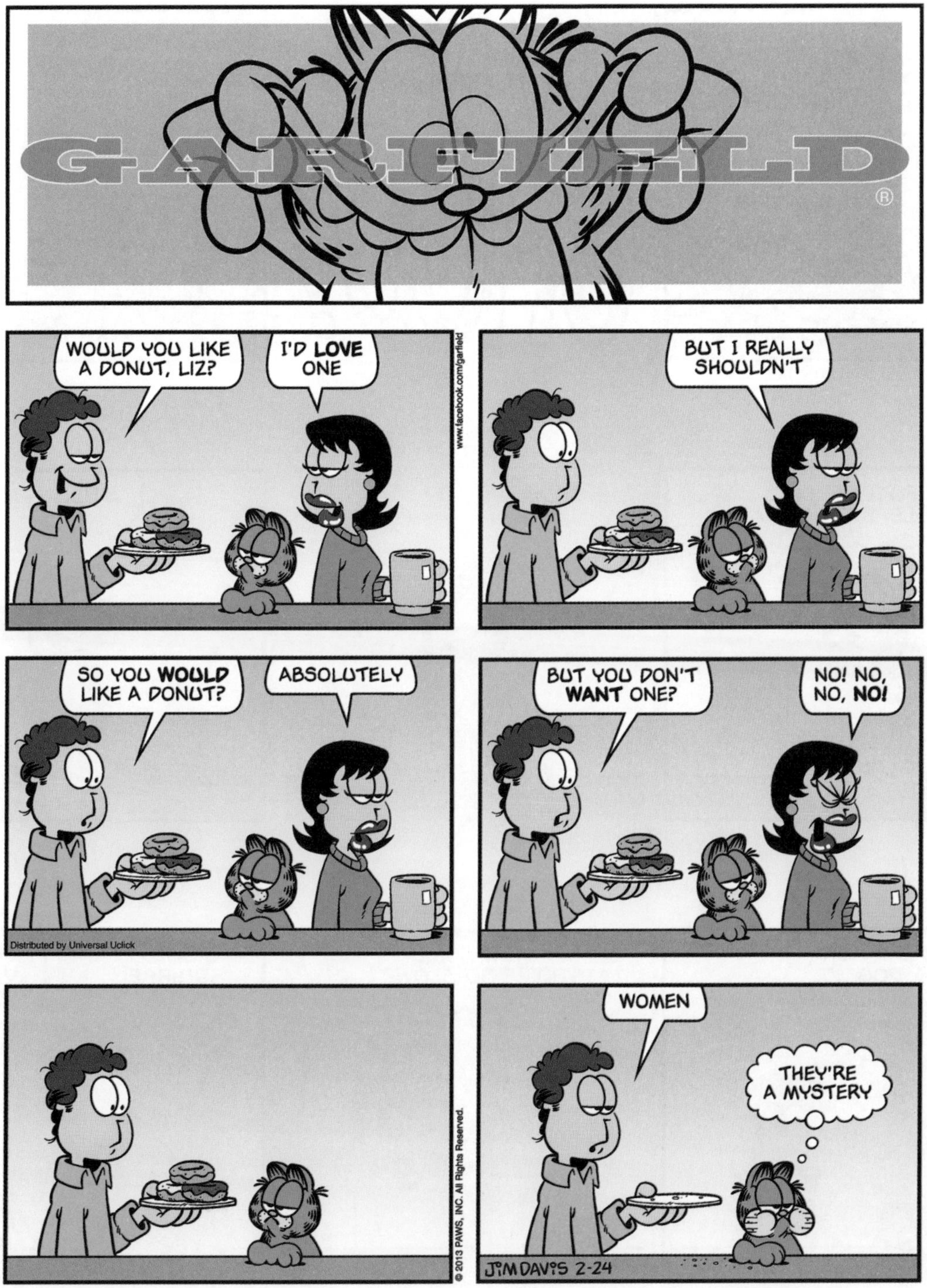
GARFIELD®
WOULD YOU LIKE A DONUT, LIZ?
I'D **LOVE** ONE
www.facebook.com/garfield
BUT I REALLY SHOULDN'T
SO YOU **WOULD** LIKE A DONUT?
ABSOLUTELY
Distributed by Universal Uclick
BUT YOU DON'T **WANT** ONE?
NO! NO, NO, **NO!**
© 2013 PAWS, INC. All Rights Reserved.
WOMEN
THEY'RE A MYSTERY
JIM DAVIS 2-24

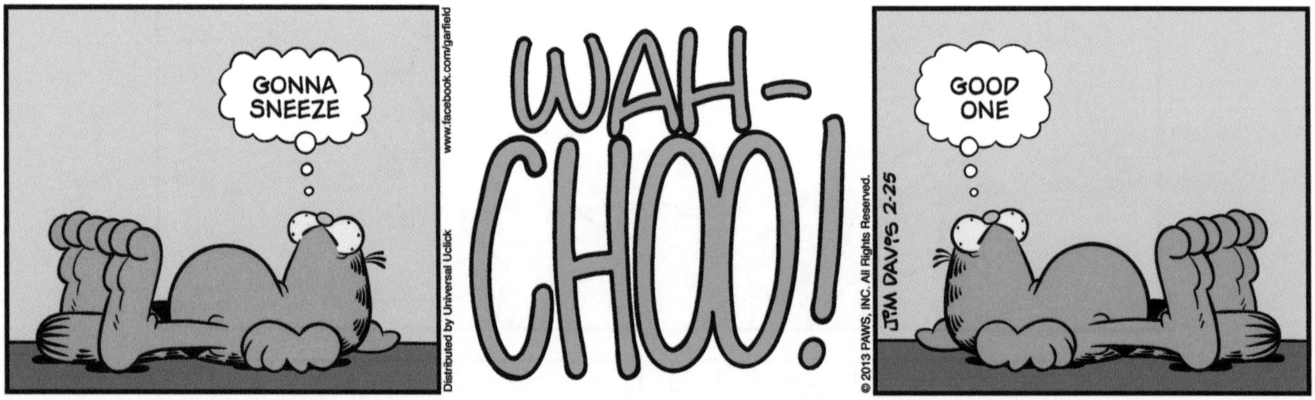
GONNA SNEEZE
WAH-CHOO!
GOOD ONE
JIM DAVIS 2-25
www.facebook.com/garfield
Distributed by Universal Uclick
© 2013 PAWS, INC. All Rights Reserved.

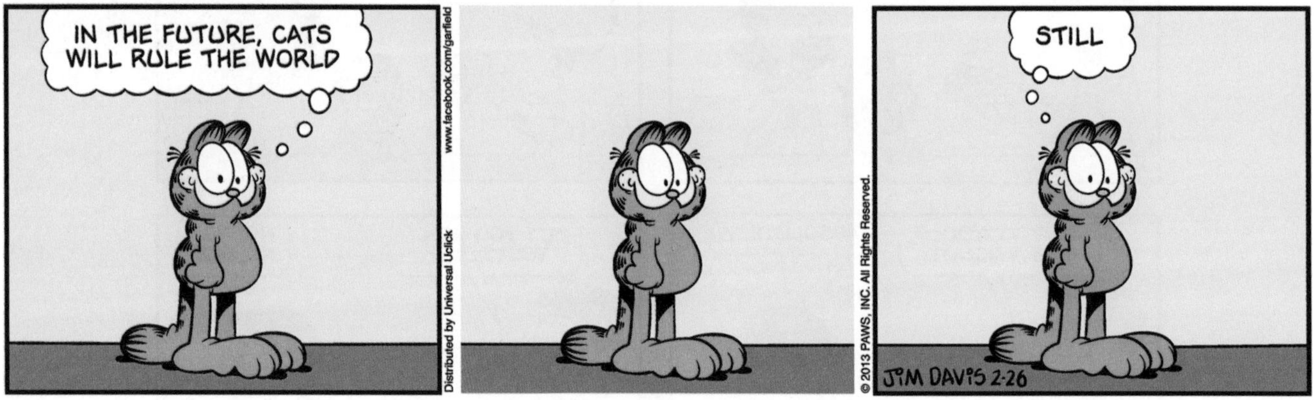
IN THE FUTURE, CATS WILL RULE THE WORLD
STILL
JIM DAVIS 2-26
www.facebook.com/garfield
Distributed by Universal Uclick
© 2013 PAWS, INC. All Rights Reserved.

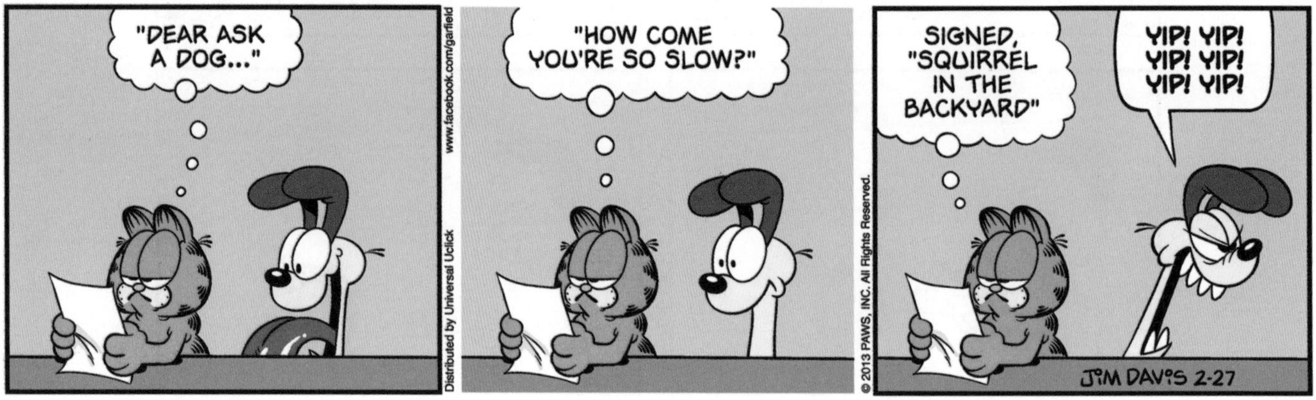
"DEAR ASK A DOG..."
"HOW COME YOU'RE SO SLOW?"
SIGNED, "SQUIRREL IN THE BACKYARD"
YIP! YIP! YIP! YIP! YIP! YIP!
JIM DAVIS 2-27
www.facebook.com/garfield
Distributed by Universal Uclick
© 2013 PAWS, INC. All Rights Reserved.

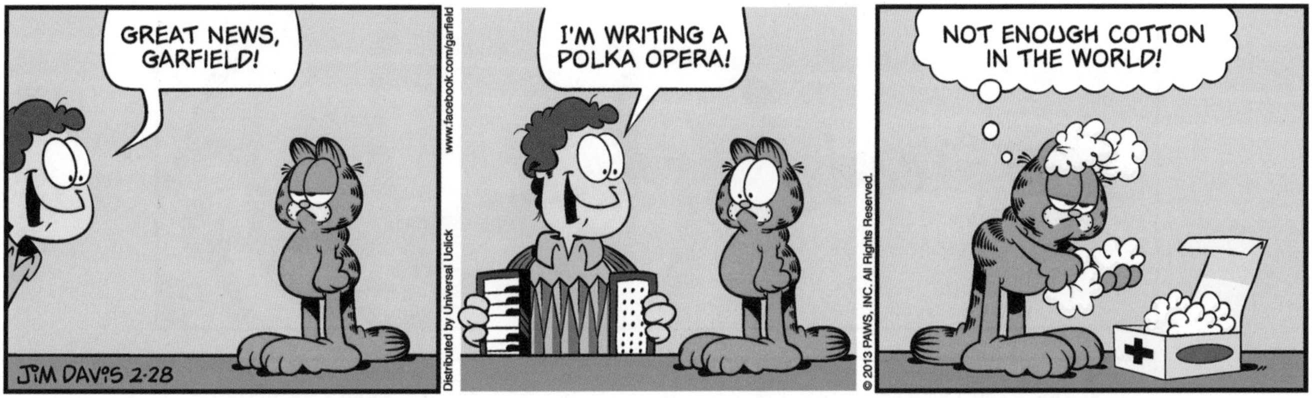
GREAT NEWS, GARFIELD!
JIM DAVIS 2-28
Distributed by Universal Uclick www.facebook.com/garfield
I'M WRITING A POLKA OPERA!
© 2013 PAWS, INC. All Rights Reserved.
NOT ENOUGH COTTON IN THE WORLD!

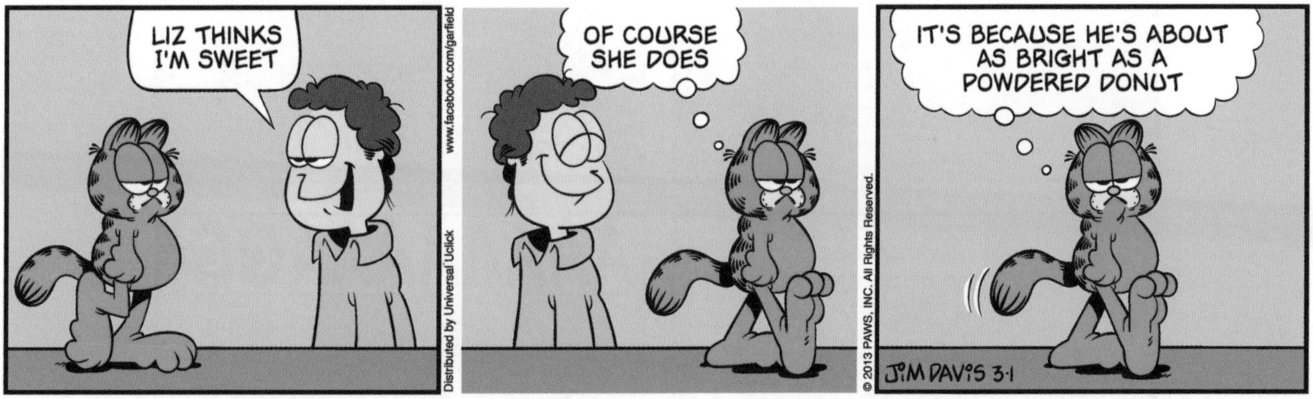
LIZ THINKS I'M SWEET
Distributed by Universal Uclick www.facebook.com/garfield
OF COURSE SHE DOES
© 2013 PAWS, INC. All Rights Reserved.
IT'S BECAUSE HE'S ABOUT AS BRIGHT AS A POWDERED DONUT
JIM DAVIS 3-1

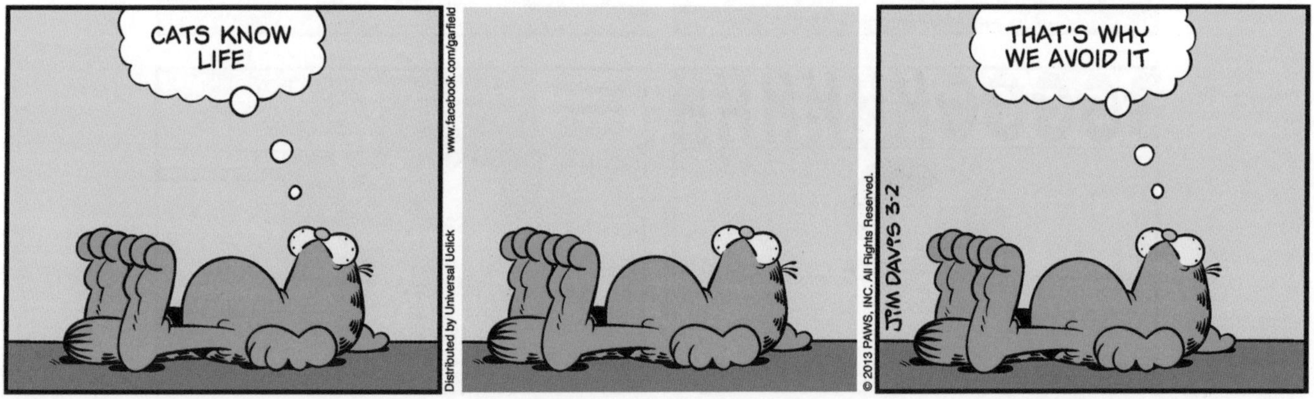
CATS KNOW LIFE
Distributed by Universal Uclick www.facebook.com/garfield
© 2013 PAWS, INC. All Rights Reserved.
JIM DAVIS 3-2
THAT'S WHY WE AVOID IT

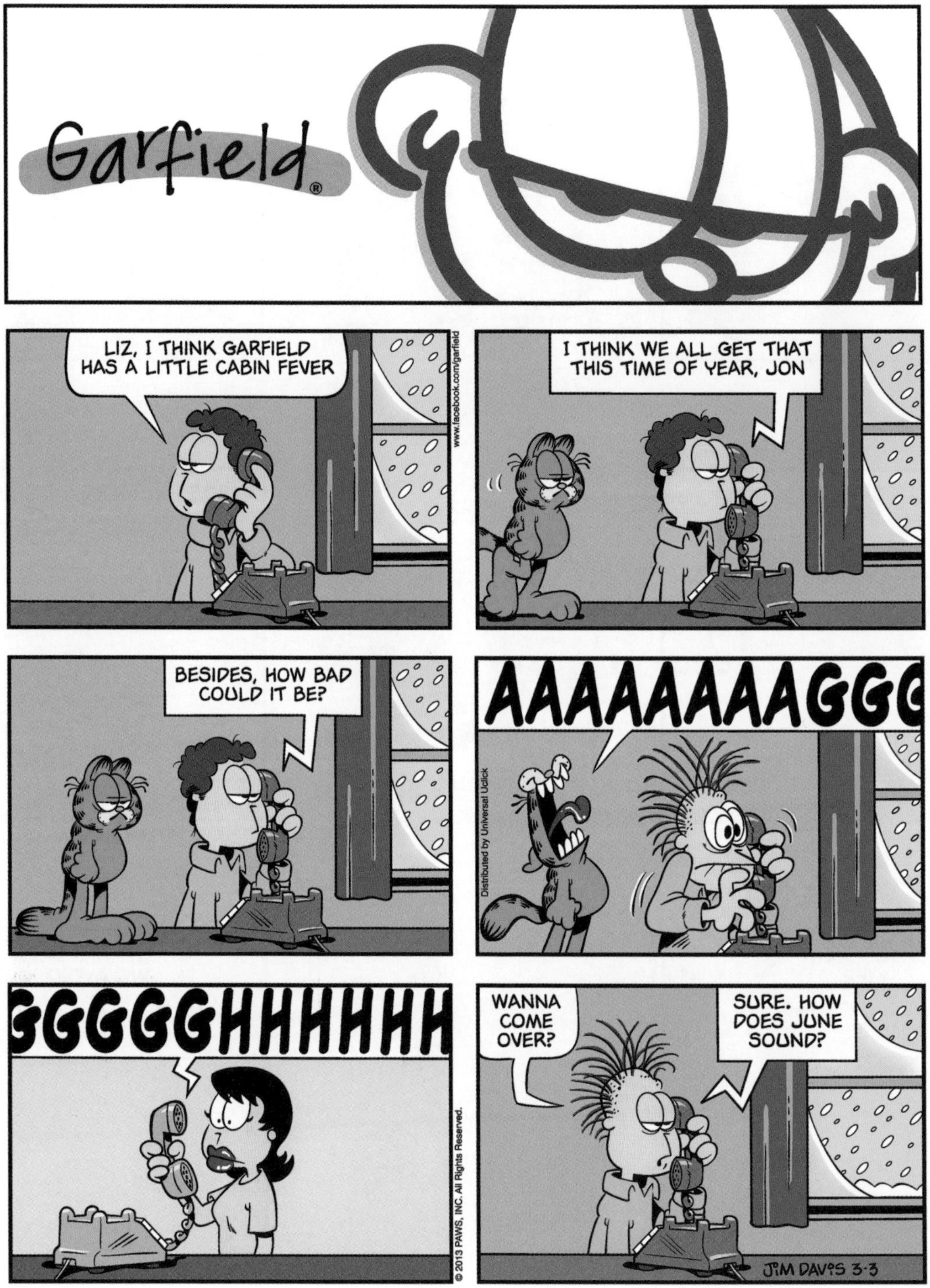
Garfield®
LIZ, I THINK GARFIELD HAS A LITTLE CABIN FEVER
www.facebook.com/garfield
I THINK WE ALL GET THAT THIS TIME OF YEAR, JON
BESIDES, HOW BAD COULD IT BE?
Distributed by Universal Uclick
AAAAAAAAGGG
GGGGGHHHHHH
© 2013 PAWS, INC. All Rights Reserved.
WANNA COME OVER?
SURE. HOW DOES JUNE SOUND?
JIM DAVIS 3-3

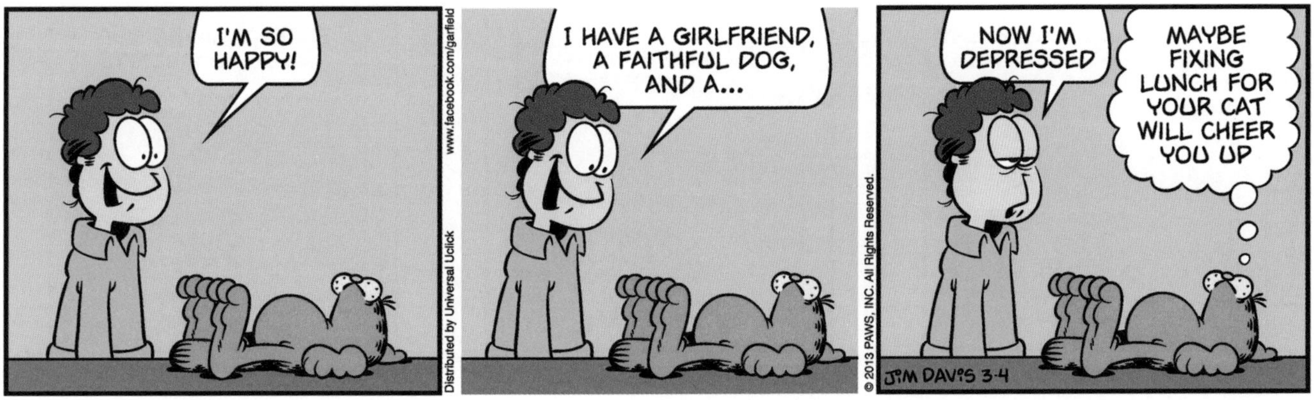
I'M SO HAPPY!
Distributed by Universal Uclick www.facebook.com/garfield
I HAVE A GIRLFRIEND, A FAITHFUL DOG, AND A...
© 2013 PAWS, INC. All Rights Reserved.
NOW I'M DEPRESSED
MAYBE FIXING LUNCH FOR YOUR CAT WILL CHEER YOU UP
JIM DAVIS 3-4

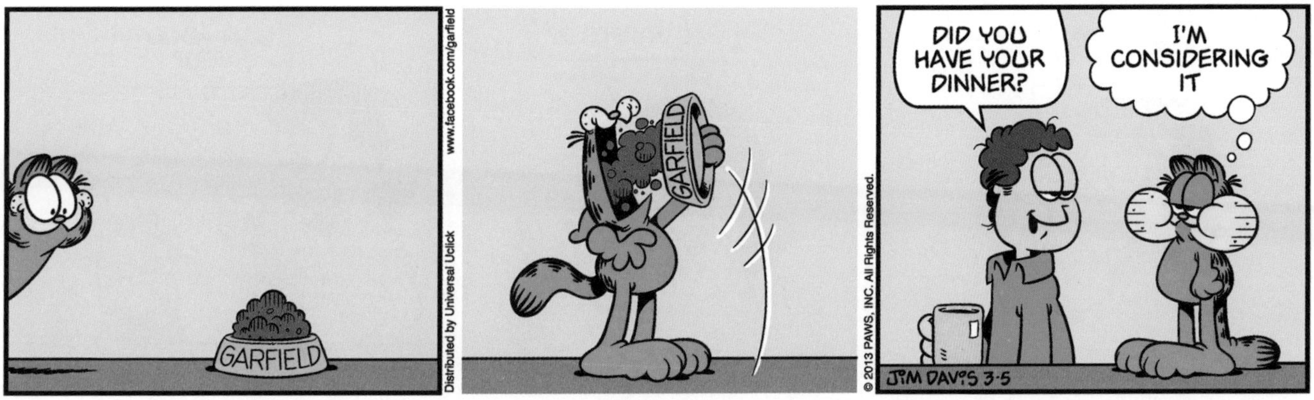
GARFIELD
Distributed by Universal Uclick www.facebook.com/garfield
GARFIELD
© 2013 PAWS, INC. All Rights Reserved.
DID YOU HAVE YOUR DINNER?
I'M CONSIDERING IT
JIM DAVIS 3-5

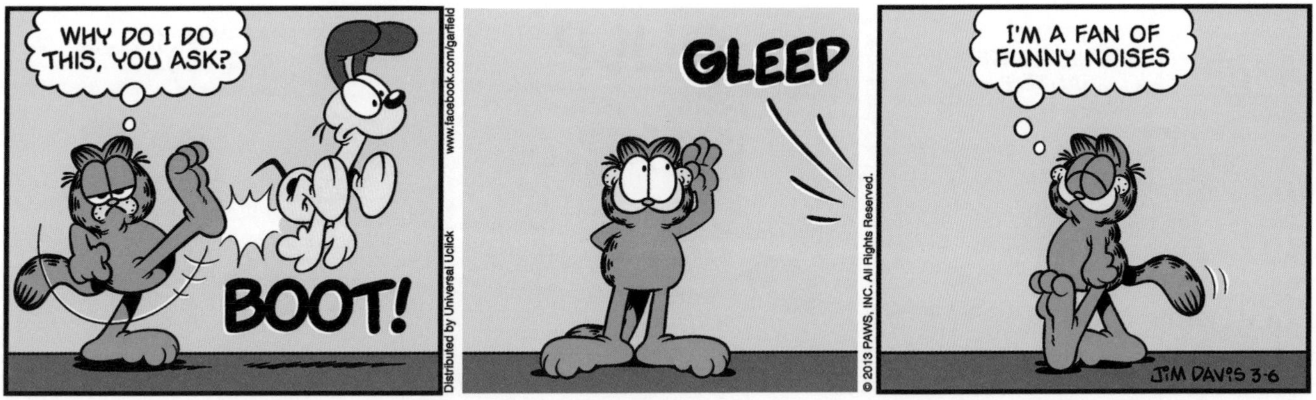
WHY DO I DO THIS, YOU ASK?
BOOT!
Distributed by Universal Uclick www.facebook.com/garfield
GLEEP
© 2013 PAWS, INC. All Rights Reserved.
I'M A FAN OF FUNNY NOISES
JIM DAVIS 3-6

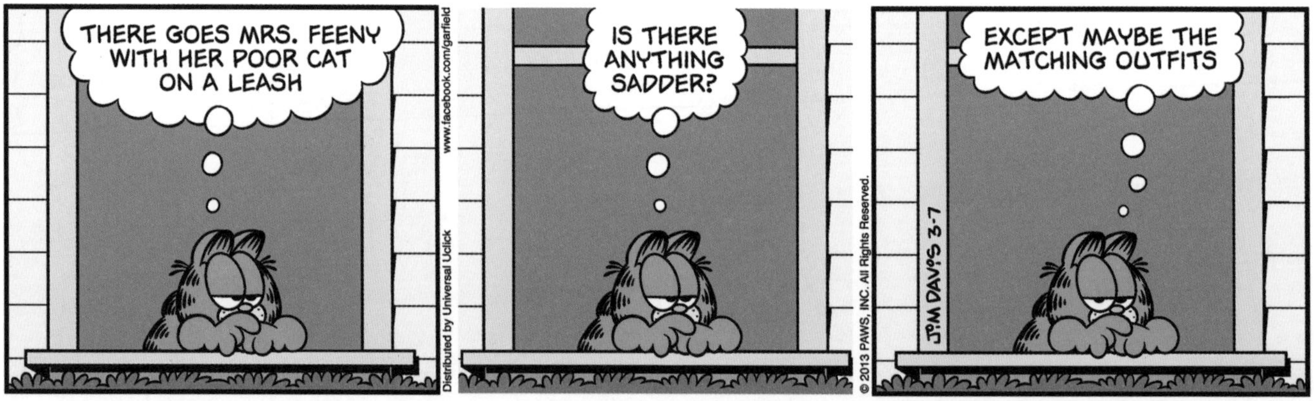
THERE GOES MRS. FEENY WITH HER POOR CAT ON A LEASH
Distributed by Universal Uclick www.facebook.com/garfield
IS THERE ANYTHING SADDER?
© 2013 PAWS, INC. All Rights Reserved.
JIM DAVIS 3-7
EXCEPT MAYBE THE MATCHING OUTFITS

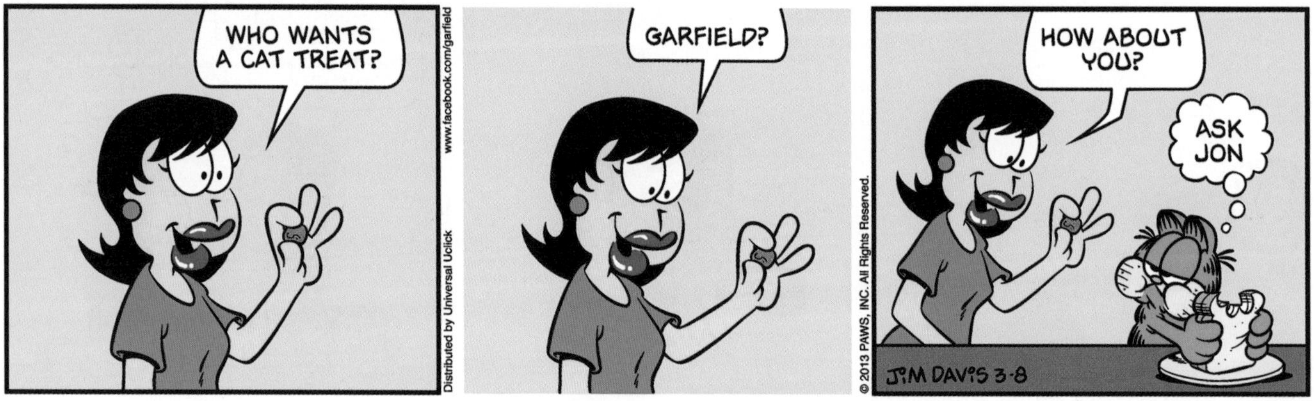
WHO WANTS A CAT TREAT?
Distributed by Universal Uclick www.facebook.com/garfield
GARFIELD?
© 2013 PAWS, INC. All Rights Reserved.
HOW ABOUT YOU?
ASK JON
JIM DAVIS 3-8

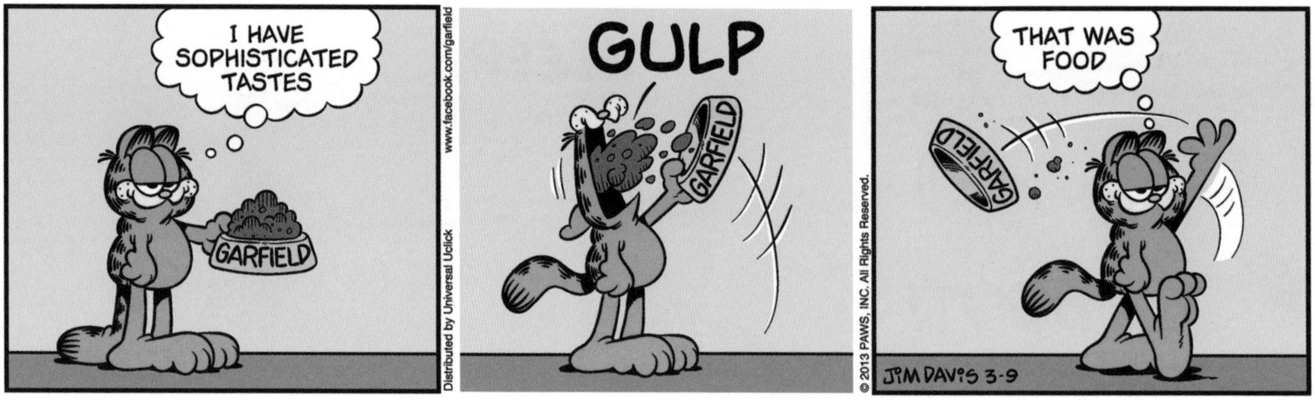
I HAVE SOPHISTICATED TASTES
GARFIELD
Distributed by Universal Uclick www.facebook.com/garfield
GULP
GARFIELD
© 2013 PAWS, INC. All Rights Reserved.
THAT WAS FOOD
GARFIELD
JIM DAVIS 3-9

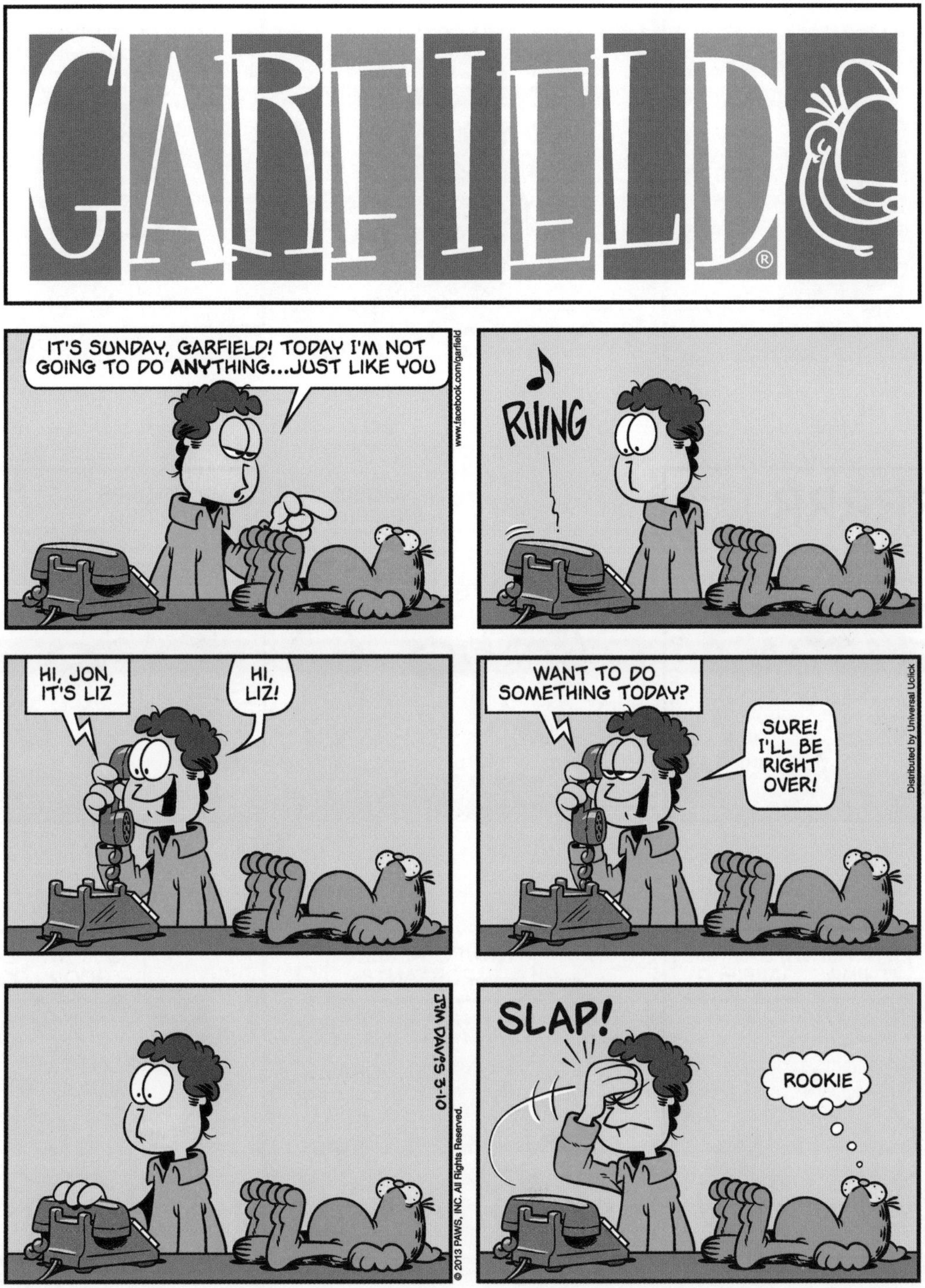
GARFIELD®
IT'S SUNDAY, GARFIELD! TODAY I'M NOT GOING TO DO ANYTHING...JUST LIKE YOU
www.facebook.com/garfield
RIIING
HI, JON, IT'S LIZ
HI, LIZ!
WANT TO DO SOMETHING TODAY?
SURE! I'LL BE RIGHT OVER!
Distributed by Universal Uclick
JIM DAVIS 3-10
© 2013 PAWS, INC. All Rights Reserved.
SLAP!
ROOKIE

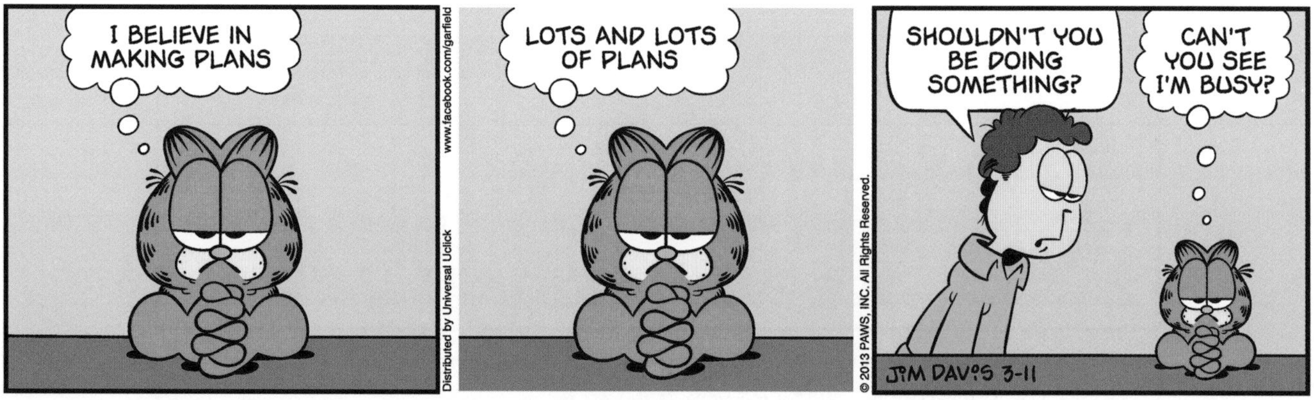
I BELIEVE IN MAKING PLANS
Distributed by Universal Uclick www.facebook.com/garfield
LOTS AND LOTS OF PLANS
© 2013 PAWS, INC. All Rights Reserved.
SHOULDN'T YOU BE DOING SOMETHING?
CAN'T YOU SEE I'M BUSY?
JIM DAVIS 3-11

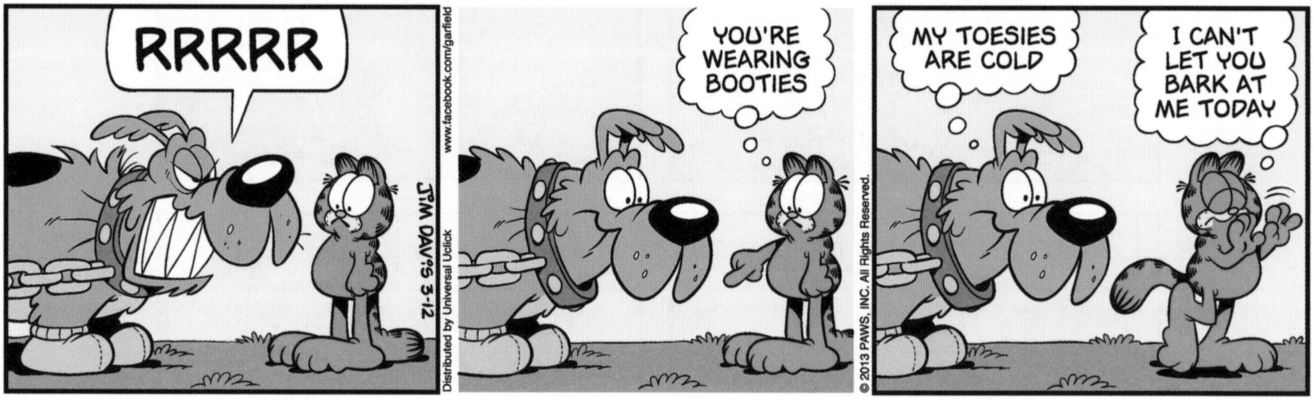
RRRRR
JIM DAVIS 3-12
Distributed by Universal Uclick www.facebook.com/garfield
YOU'RE WEARING BOOTIES
© 2013 PAWS, INC. All Rights Reserved.
MY TOESIES ARE COLD
I CAN'T LET YOU BARK AT ME TODAY

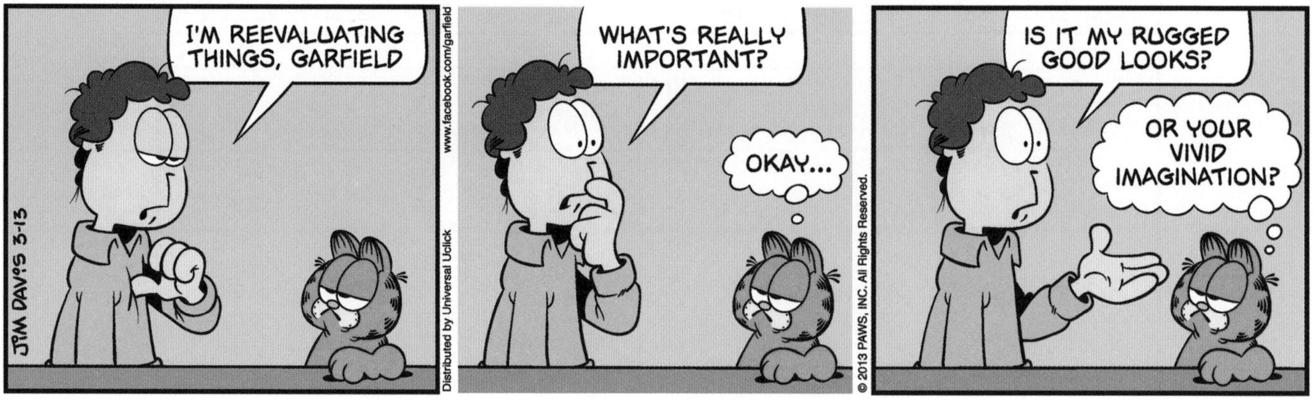
I'M REEVALUATING THINGS, GARFIELD
JIM DAVIS 3-13
Distributed by Universal Uclick www.facebook.com/garfield
WHAT'S REALLY IMPORTANT?
OKAY...
© 2013 PAWS, INC. All Rights Reserved.
IS IT MY RUGGED GOOD LOOKS?
OR YOUR VIVID IMAGINATION?

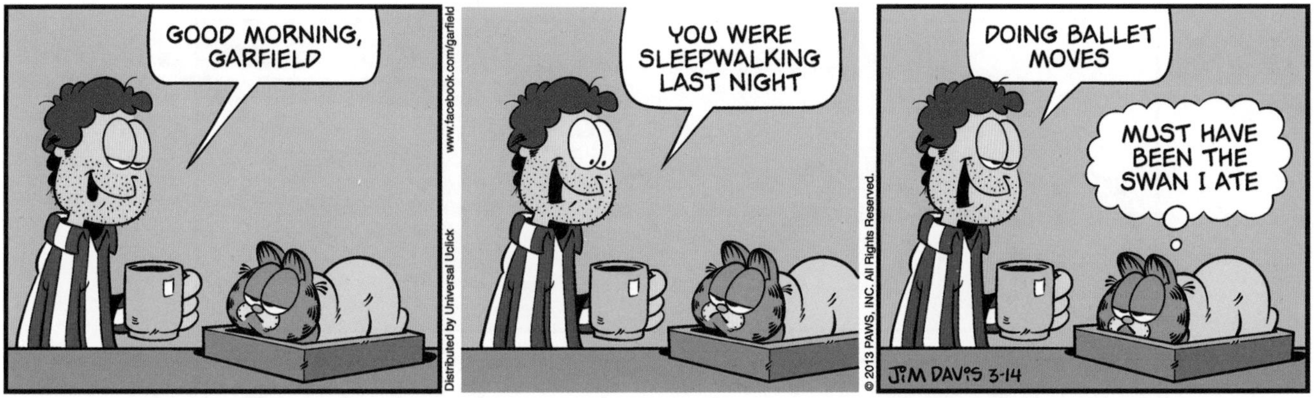
GOOD MORNING, GARFIELD
YOU WERE SLEEPWALKING LAST NIGHT
DOING BALLET MOVES
MUST HAVE BEEN THE SWAN I ATE
Distributed by Universal Uclick www.facebook.com/garfield
© 2013 PAWS, INC. All Rights Reserved.
JIM DAVIS 3-14

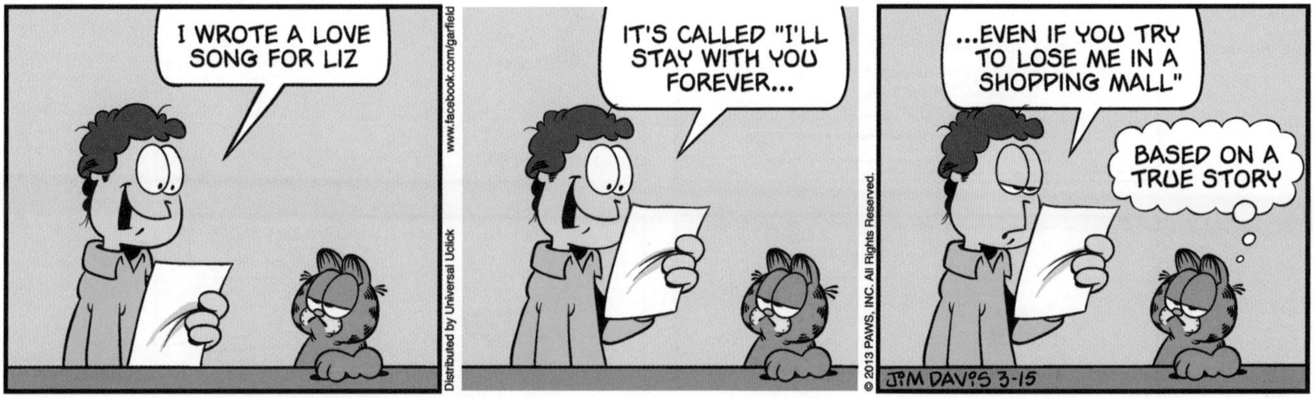
I WROTE A LOVE SONG FOR LIZ
IT'S CALLED "I'LL STAY WITH YOU FOREVER...
...EVEN IF YOU TRY TO LOSE ME IN A SHOPPING MALL"
BASED ON A TRUE STORY
Distributed by Universal Uclick www.facebook.com/garfield
© 2013 PAWS, INC. All Rights Reserved.
JIM DAVIS 3-15

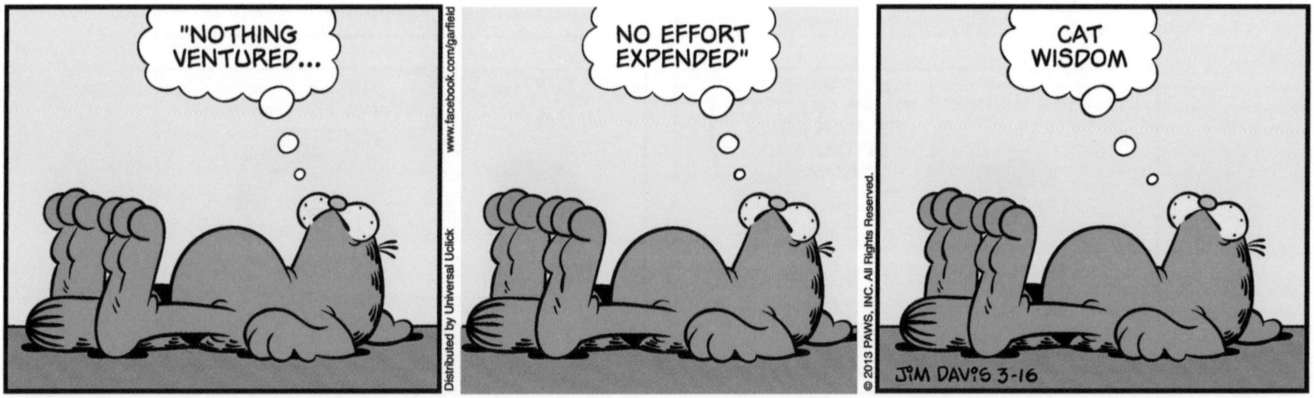
"NOTHING VENTURED...
NO EFFORT EXPENDED"
CAT WISDOM
Distributed by Universal Uclick www.facebook.com/garfield
© 2013 PAWS, INC. All Rights Reserved.
JIM DAVIS 3-16

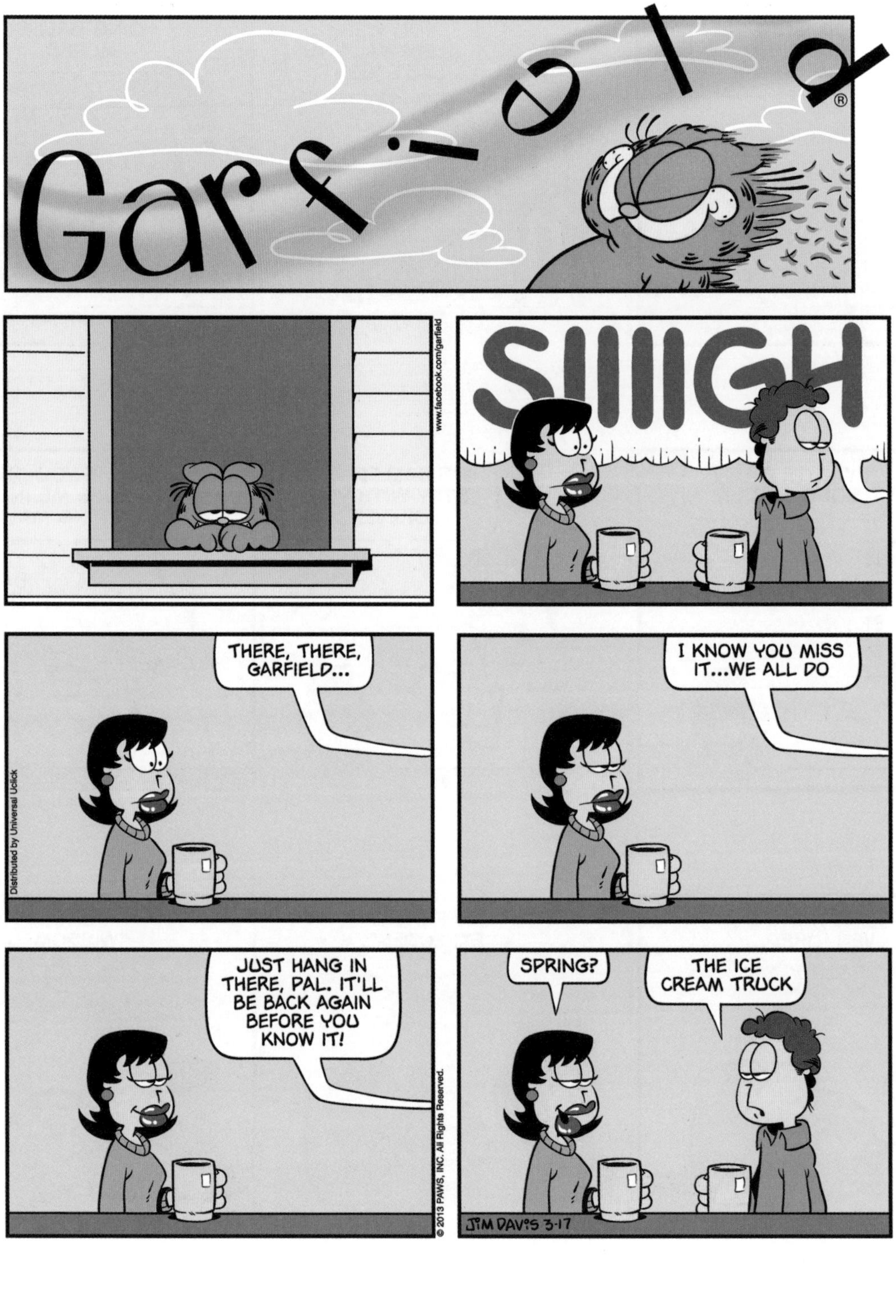
Garfield®
www.facebook.com/garfield
SIIIGH
Distributed by Universal Uclick
THERE, THERE, GARFIELD...
I KNOW YOU MISS IT...WE ALL DO
JUST HANG IN THERE, PAL. IT'LL BE BACK AGAIN BEFORE YOU KNOW IT!
© 2013 PAWS, INC. All Rights Reserved.
SPRING?
THE ICE CREAM TRUCK
JIM DAVIS 3-17

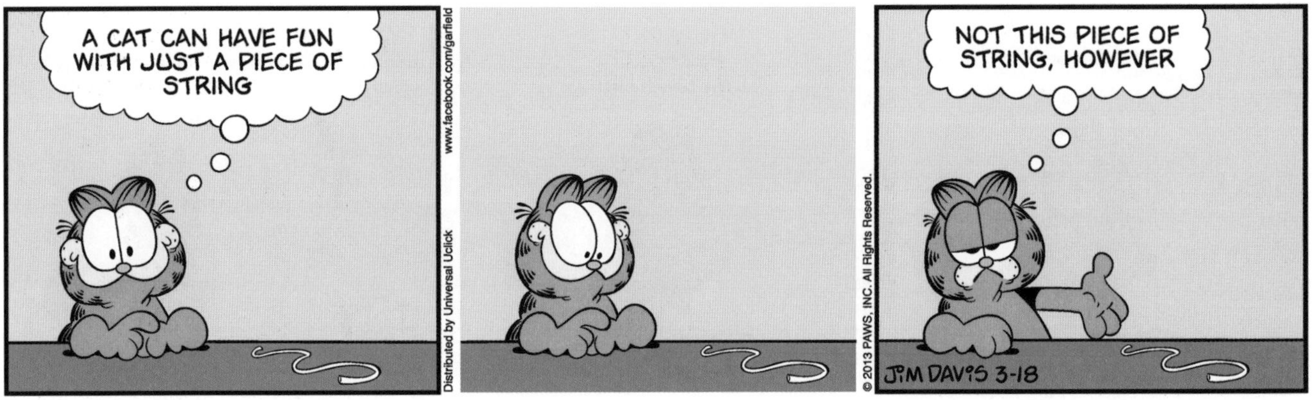
A CAT CAN HAVE FUN WITH JUST A PIECE OF STRING
Distributed by Universal Uclick www.facebook.com/garfield
© 2013 PAWS, INC. All Rights Reserved.
NOT THIS PIECE OF STRING, HOWEVER
JIM DAVIS 3-18

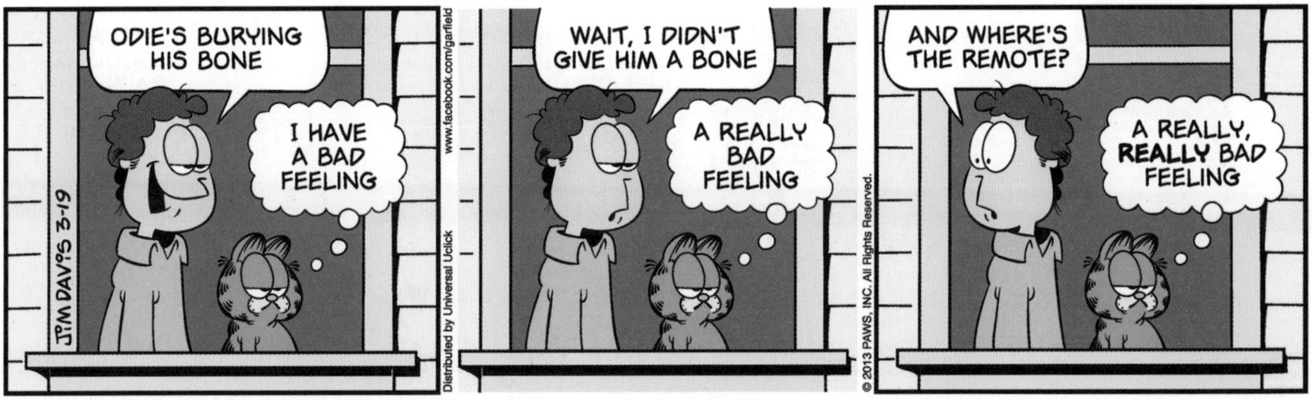
JIM DAVIS 3-19
ODIE'S BURYING HIS BONE
I HAVE A BAD FEELING
Distributed by Universal Uclick www.facebook.com/garfield
WAIT, I DIDN'T GIVE HIM A BONE
A REALLY BAD FEELING
© 2013 PAWS, INC. All Rights Reserved.
AND WHERE'S THE REMOTE?
A REALLY, **REALLY** BAD FEELING

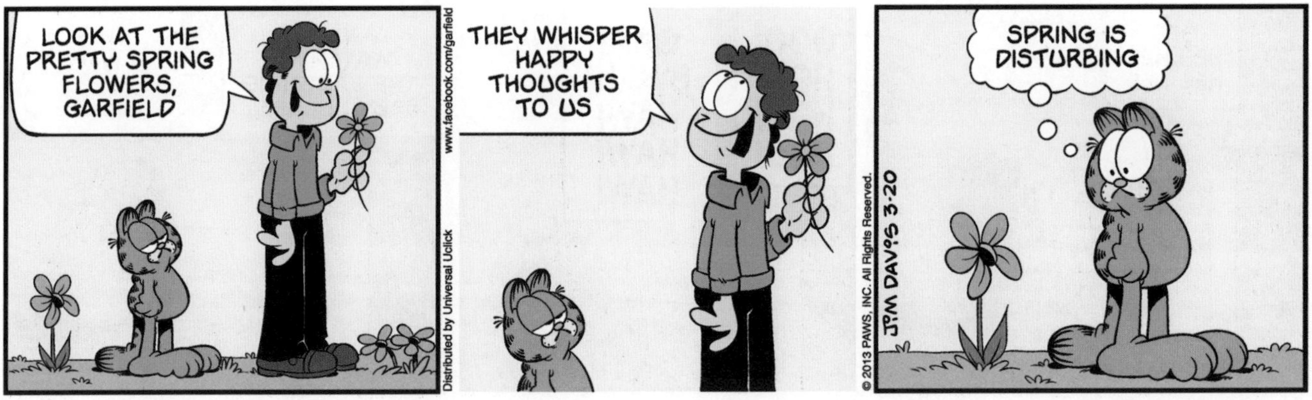
LOOK AT THE PRETTY SPRING FLOWERS, GARFIELD
Distributed by Universal Uclick www.facebook.com/garfield
THEY WHISPER HAPPY THOUGHTS TO US
© 2013 PAWS, INC. All Rights Reserved.
JIM DAVIS 3-20
SPRING IS DISTURBING

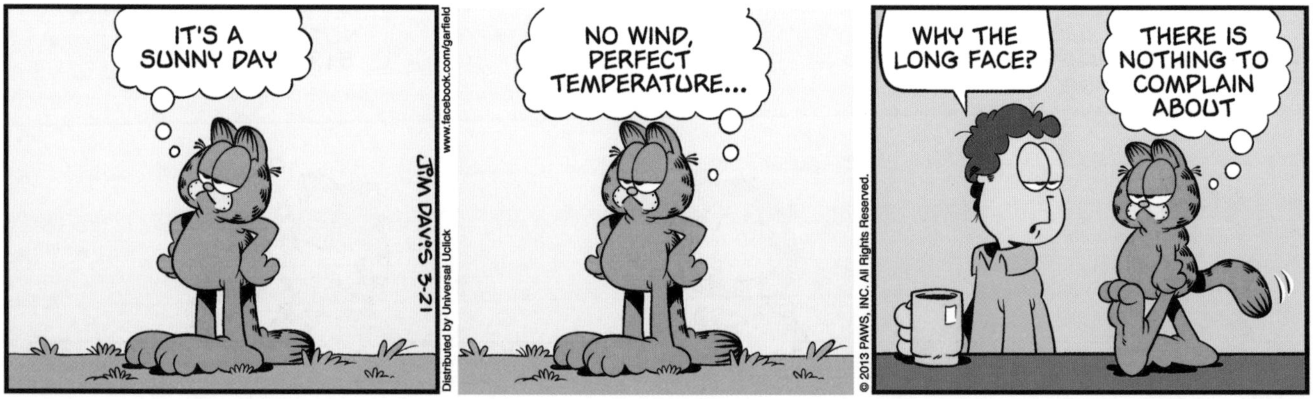
IT'S A SUNNY DAY
JIM DAVIS 3-21
Distributed by Universal Uclick www.facebook.com/garfield
NO WIND, PERFECT TEMPERATURE...
© 2013 PAWS, INC. All Rights Reserved.
WHY THE LONG FACE?
THERE IS NOTHING TO COMPLAIN ABOUT

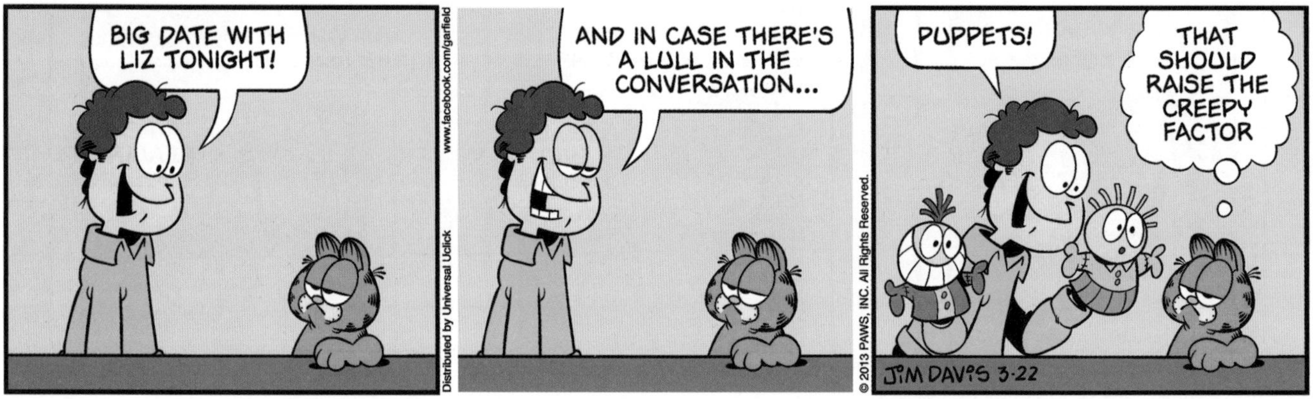
BIG DATE WITH LIZ TONIGHT!
Distributed by Universal Uclick www.facebook.com/garfield
AND IN CASE THERE'S A LULL IN THE CONVERSATION...
© 2013 PAWS, INC. All Rights Reserved.
PUPPETS!
THAT SHOULD RAISE THE CREEPY FACTOR
JIM DAVIS 3-22

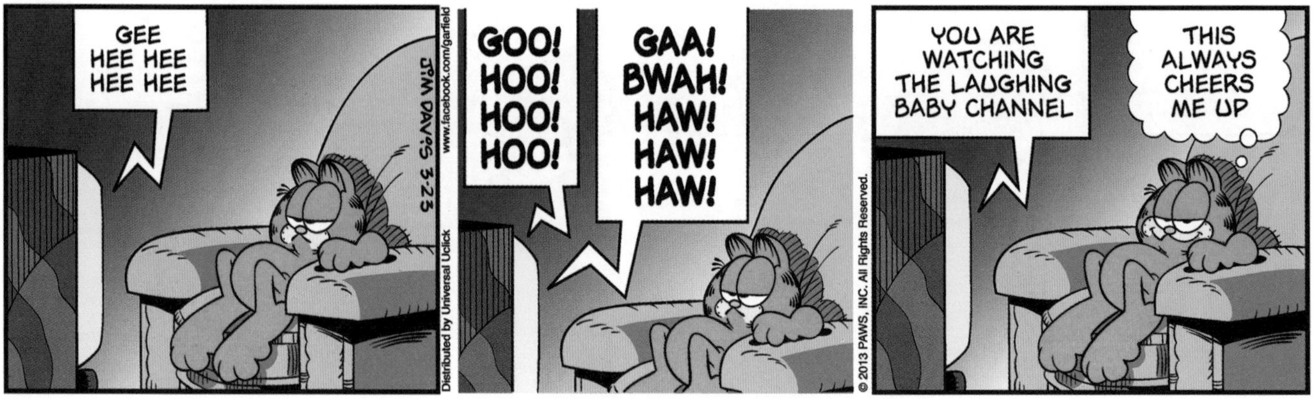
GEE HEE HEE HEE HEE
JIM DAVIS 3-23
Distributed by Universal Uclick www.facebook.com/garfield
GOO! HOO! HOO! HOO!
GAA! BWAH! HAW! HAW! HAW!
© 2013 PAWS, INC. All Rights Reserved.
YOU ARE WATCHING THE LAUGHING BABY CHANNEL
THIS ALWAYS CHEERS ME UP

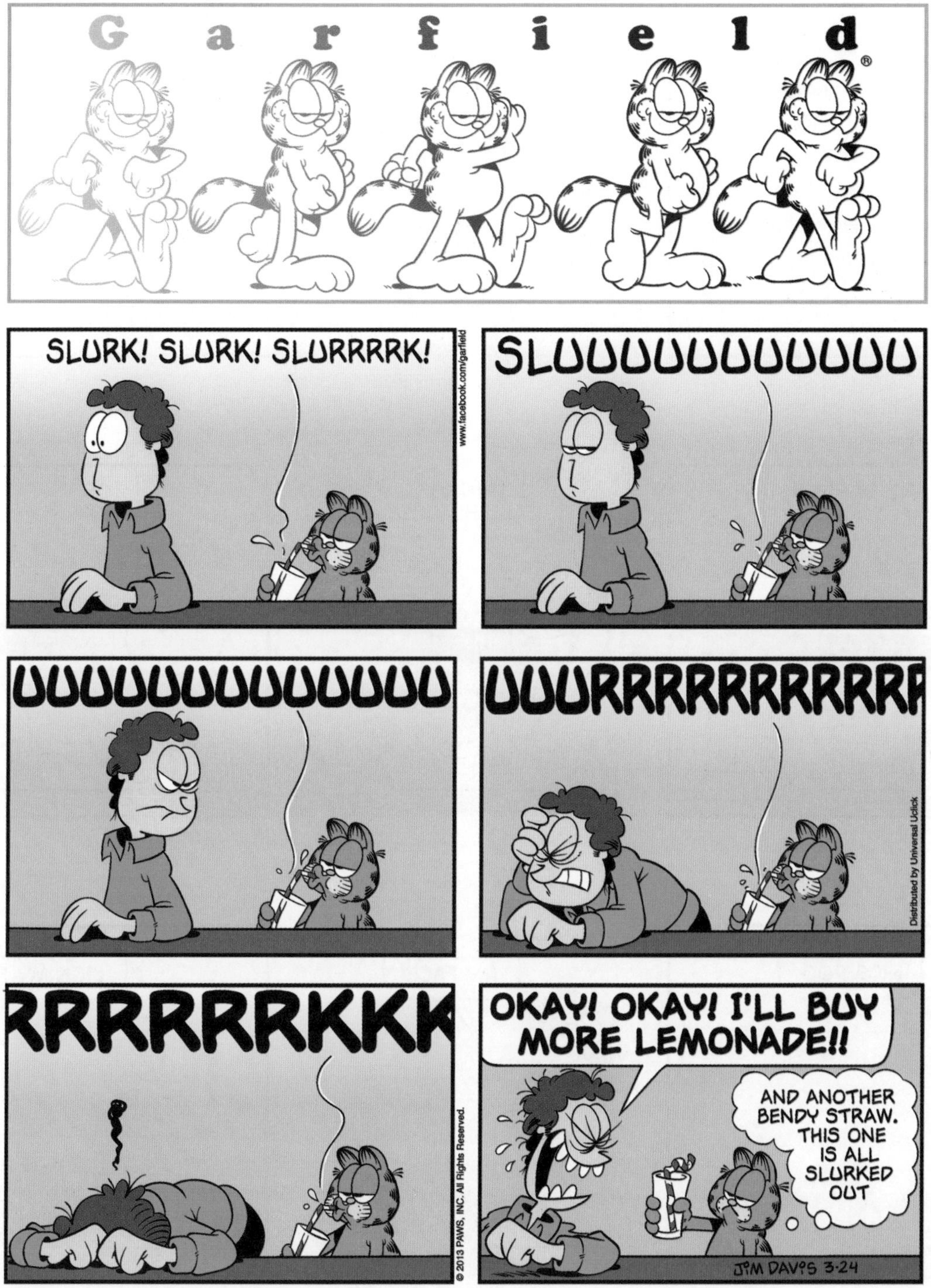
Garfield
SLURK! SLURK! SLURRRRK!
www.facebook.com/garfield
SLUUUUUUUUUUUU
UUUUUUUUUUUUUU
UUURRRRRRRRRRR
Distributed by Universal Uclick
RRRRRRRKKK
© 2013 PAWS, INC. All Rights Reserved.
OKAY! OKAY! I'LL BUY MORE LEMONADE!!
AND ANOTHER BENDY STRAW. THIS ONE IS ALL SLURKED OUT
JIM DAVIS 3-24

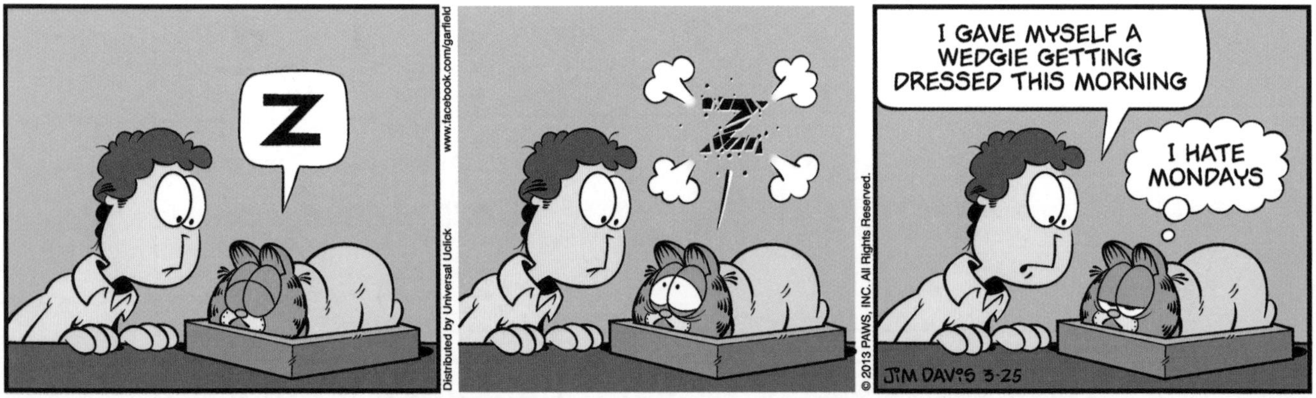
Z
I GAVE MYSELF A WEDGIE GETTING DRESSED THIS MORNING
I HATE MONDAYS
Distributed by Universal Uclick
www.facebook.com/garfield
© 2013 PAWS, INC. All Rights Reserved.
JIM DAVIS 3-25

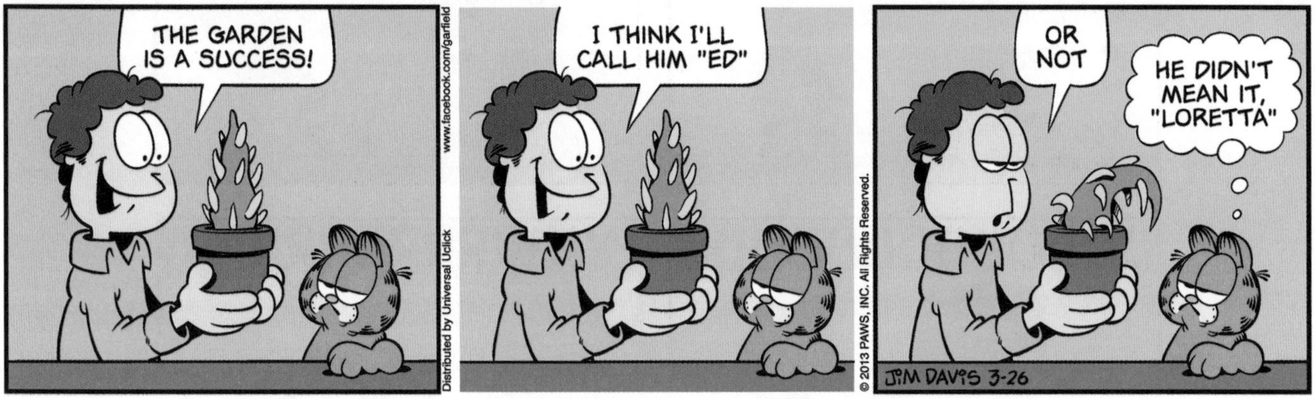
THE GARDEN IS A SUCCESS!
I THINK I'LL CALL HIM "ED"
OR NOT
HE DIDN'T MEAN IT, "LORETTA"
Distributed by Universal Uclick
www.facebook.com/garfield
© 2013 PAWS, INC. All Rights Reserved.
JIM DAVIS 3-26

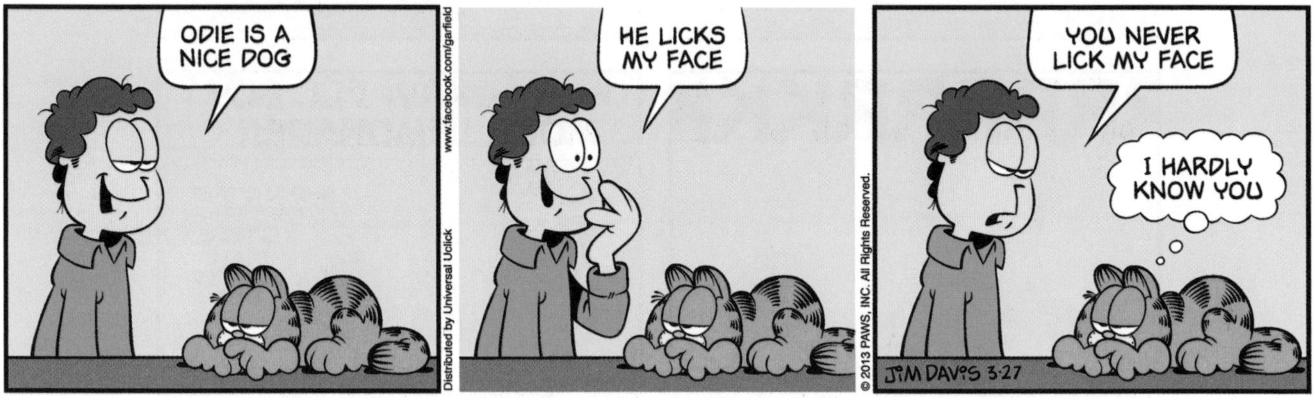
ODIE IS A NICE DOG
HE LICKS MY FACE
YOU NEVER LICK MY FACE
I HARDLY KNOW YOU
Distributed by Universal Uclick
www.facebook.com/garfield
© 2013 PAWS, INC. All Rights Reserved.
JIM DAVIS 3-27

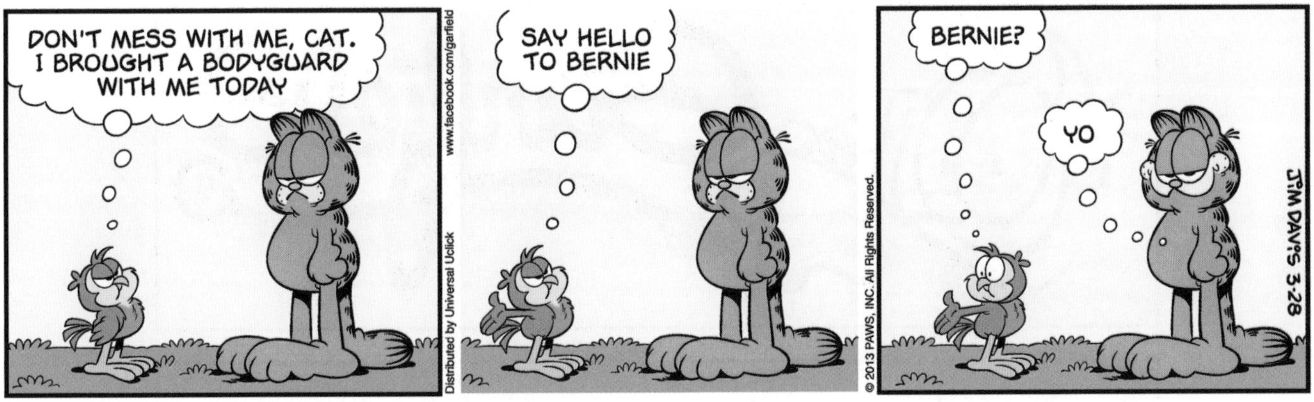
DON'T MESS WITH ME, CAT. I BROUGHT A BODYGUARD WITH ME TODAY
SAY HELLO TO BERNIE
BERNIE?
YO
JIM DAVIS 3-28
Distributed by Universal Uclick www.facebook.com/garfield
© 2013 PAWS, INC. All Rights Reserved.

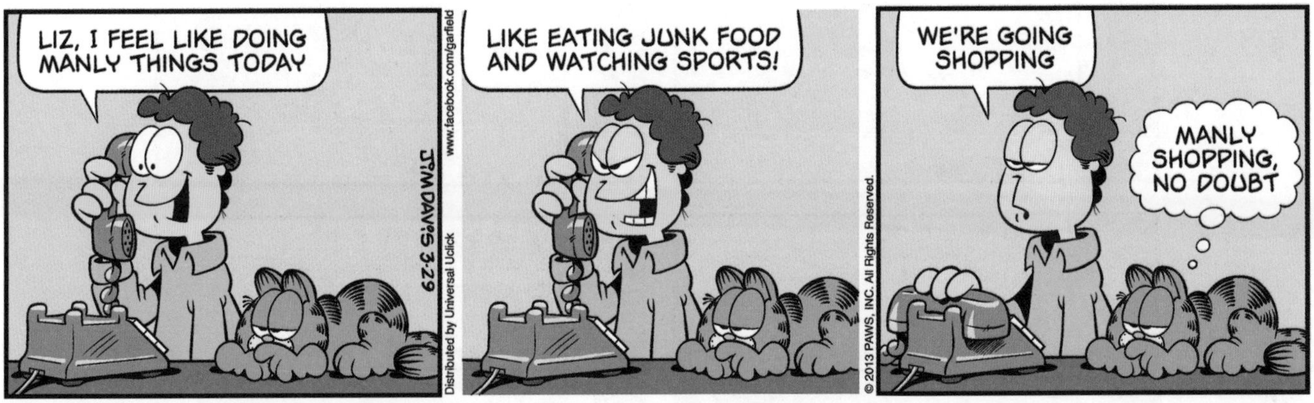
LIZ, I FEEL LIKE DOING MANLY THINGS TODAY
JIM DAVIS 3-29
LIKE EATING JUNK FOOD AND WATCHING SPORTS!
WE'RE GOING SHOPPING
MANLY SHOPPING, NO DOUBT
Distributed by Universal Uclick www.facebook.com/garfield
© 2013 PAWS, INC. All Rights Reserved.

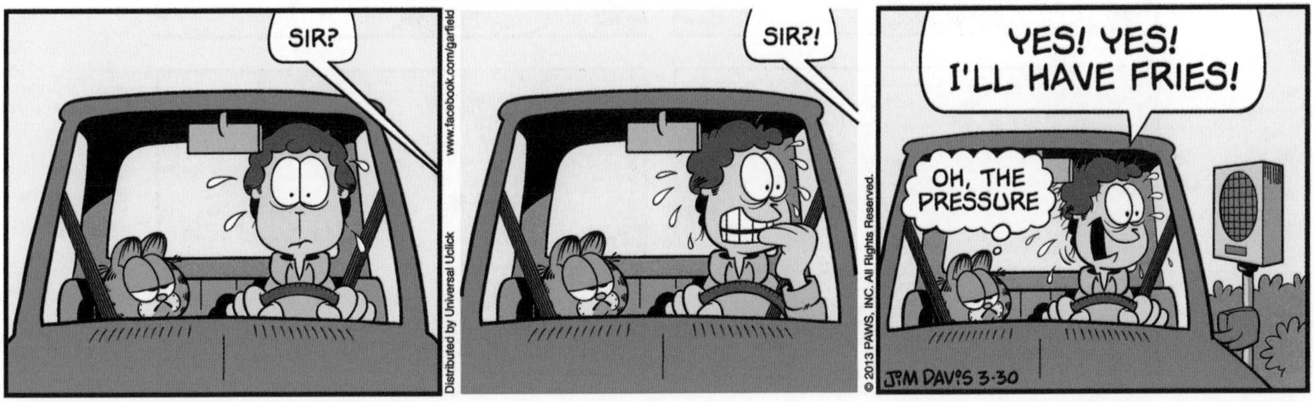
SIR?
SIR?!
YES! YES! I'LL HAVE FRIES!
OH, THE PRESSURE
JIM DAVIS 3-30
Distributed by Universal Uclick www.facebook.com/garfield
© 2013 PAWS, INC. All Rights Reserved.

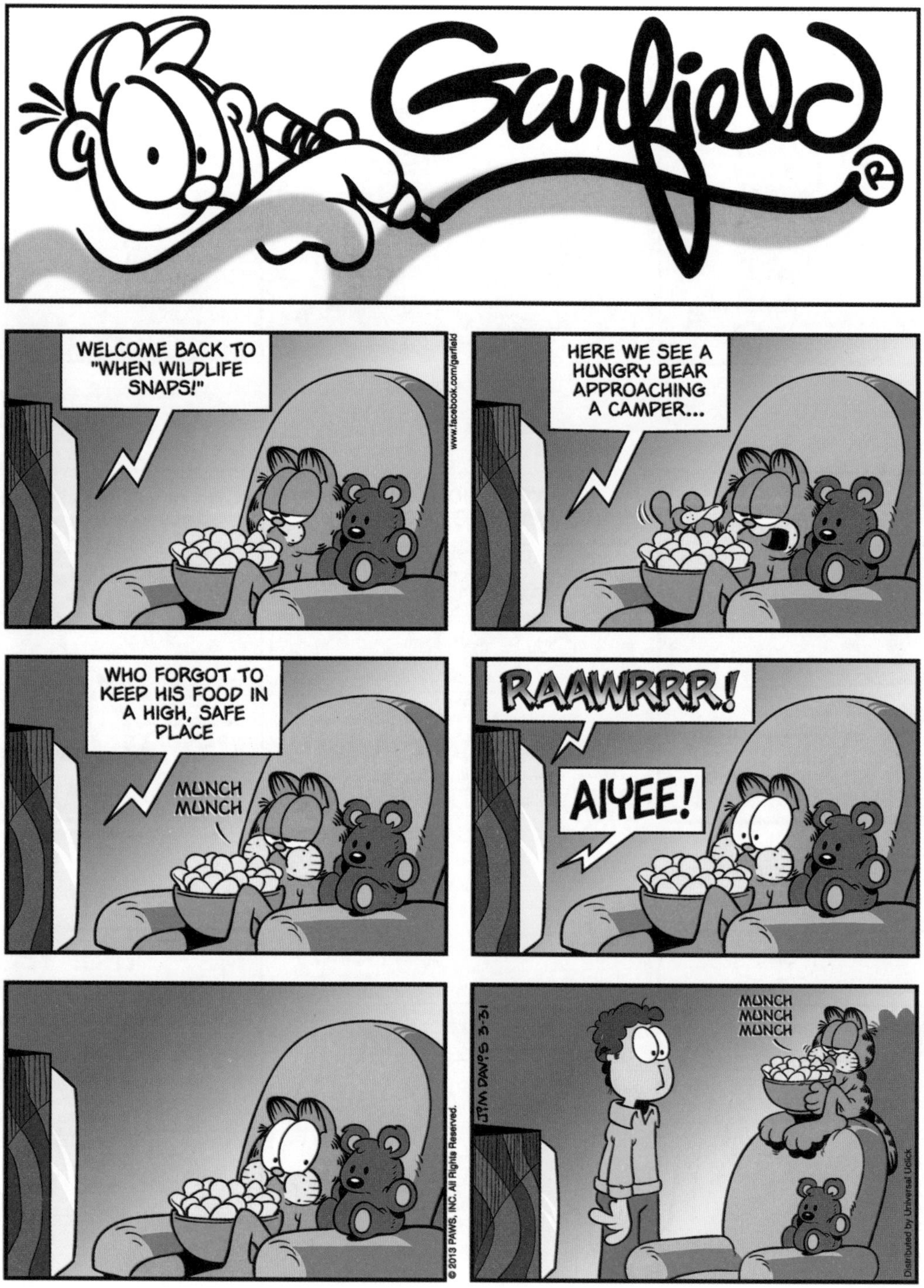
Garfield
WELCOME BACK TO "WHEN WILDLIFE SNAPS!"
www.facebook.com/garfield
HERE WE SEE A HUNGRY BEAR APPROACHING A CAMPER...
WHO FORGOT TO KEEP HIS FOOD IN A HIGH, SAFE PLACE
MUNCH MUNCH
RAAWRRR!
AIYEE!
JPM DAVPS 3-31
© 2013 PAWS, INC. All Rights Reserved.
MUNCH MUNCH MUNCH
Distributed by Universal Uclick

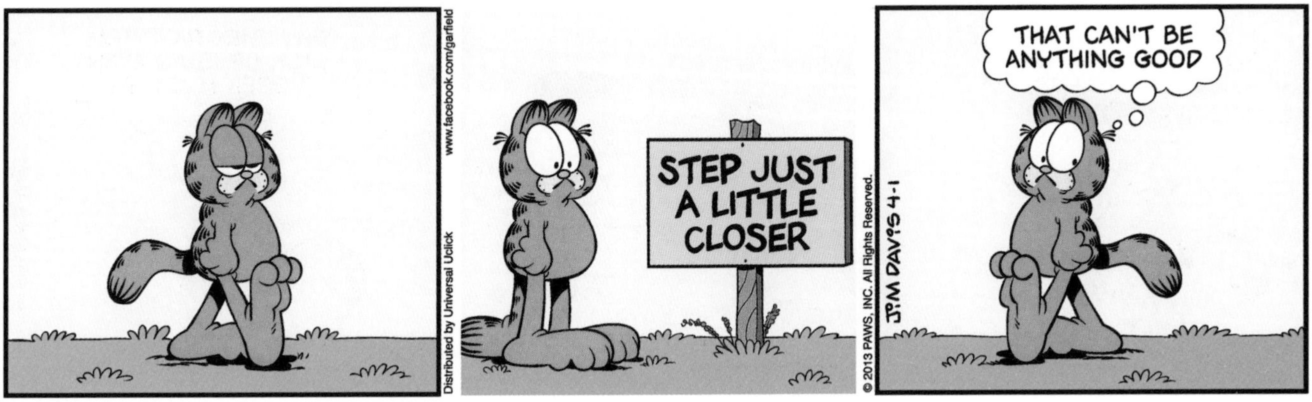
STEP JUST A LITTLE CLOSER
THAT CAN'T BE ANYTHING GOOD
JIM DAVIS 4-1
Distributed by Universal Uclick www.facebook.com/garfield
© 2013 PAWS, INC. All Rights Reserved.

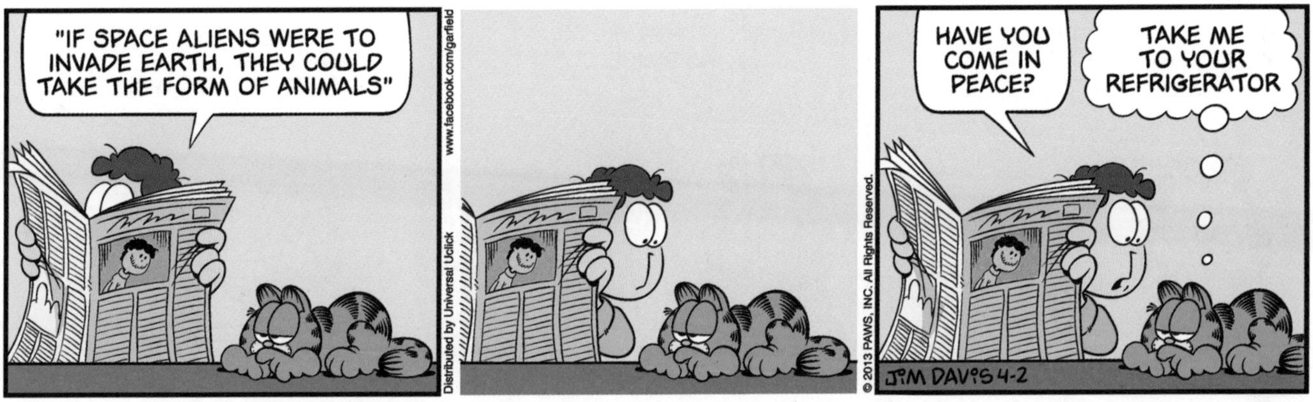
"IF SPACE ALIENS WERE TO INVADE EARTH, THEY COULD TAKE THE FORM OF ANIMALS"
HAVE YOU COME IN PEACE?
TAKE ME TO YOUR REFRIGERATOR
JIM DAVIS 4-2
Distributed by Universal Uclick www.facebook.com/garfield
© 2013 PAWS, INC. All Rights Reserved.

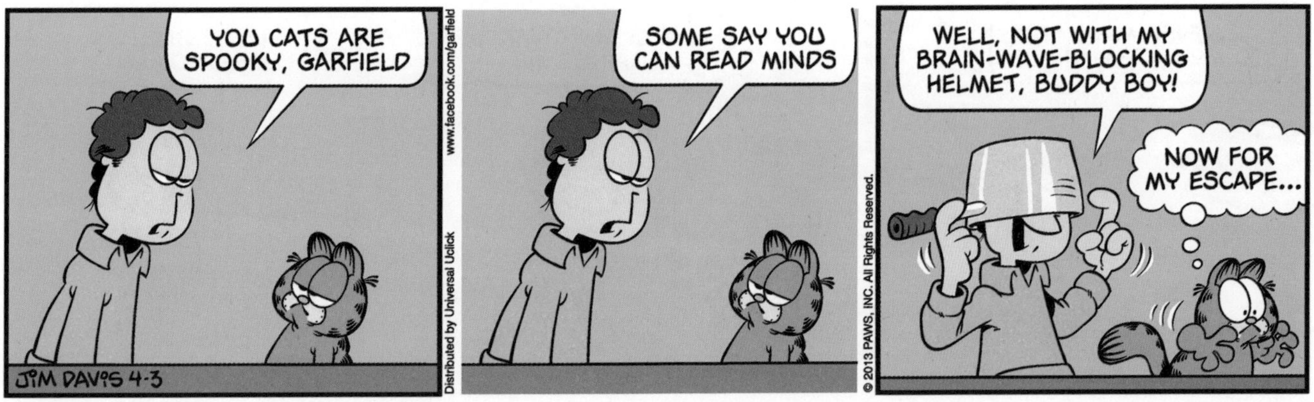
YOU CATS ARE SPOOKY, GARFIELD
SOME SAY YOU CAN READ MINDS
WELL, NOT WITH MY BRAIN-WAVE-BLOCKING HELMET, BUDDY BOY!
NOW FOR MY ESCAPE...
JIM DAVIS 4-3
Distributed by Universal Uclick www.facebook.com/garfield
© 2013 PAWS, INC. All Rights Reserved.

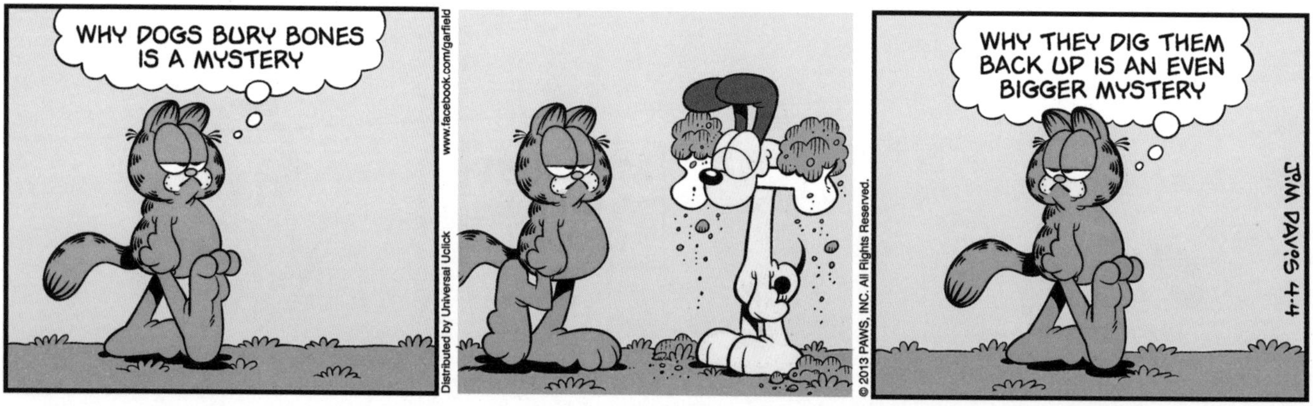
WHY DOGS BURY BONES IS A MYSTERY
WHY THEY DIG THEM BACK UP IS AN EVEN BIGGER MYSTERY
Distributed by Universal Uclick www.facebook.com/garfield
© 2013 PAWS, INC. All Rights Reserved.
JIM DAVIS 4-4

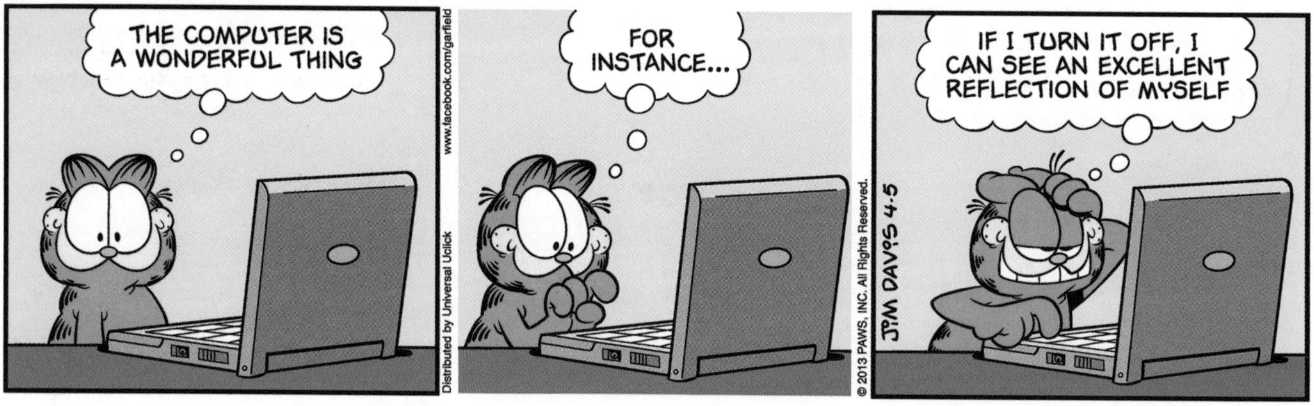
THE COMPUTER IS A WONDERFUL THING
FOR INSTANCE...
IF I TURN IT OFF, I CAN SEE AN EXCELLENT REFLECTION OF MYSELF
Distributed by Universal Uclick www.facebook.com/garfield
© 2013 PAWS, INC. All Rights Reserved.
JIM DAVIS 4-5

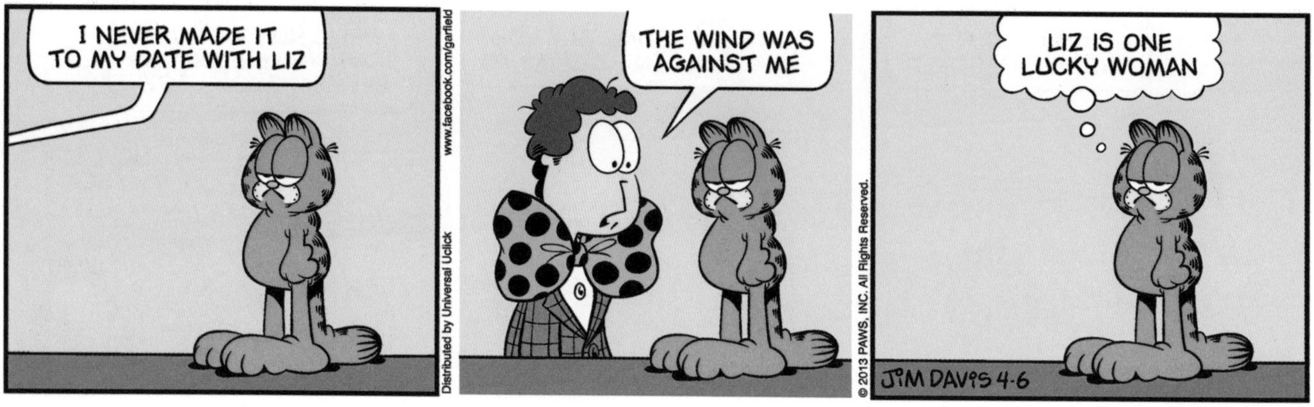
I NEVER MADE IT TO MY DATE WITH LIZ
THE WIND WAS AGAINST ME
LIZ IS ONE LUCKY WOMAN
Distributed by Universal Uclick www.facebook.com/garfield
© 2013 PAWS, INC. All Rights Reserved.
JIM DAVIS 4-6

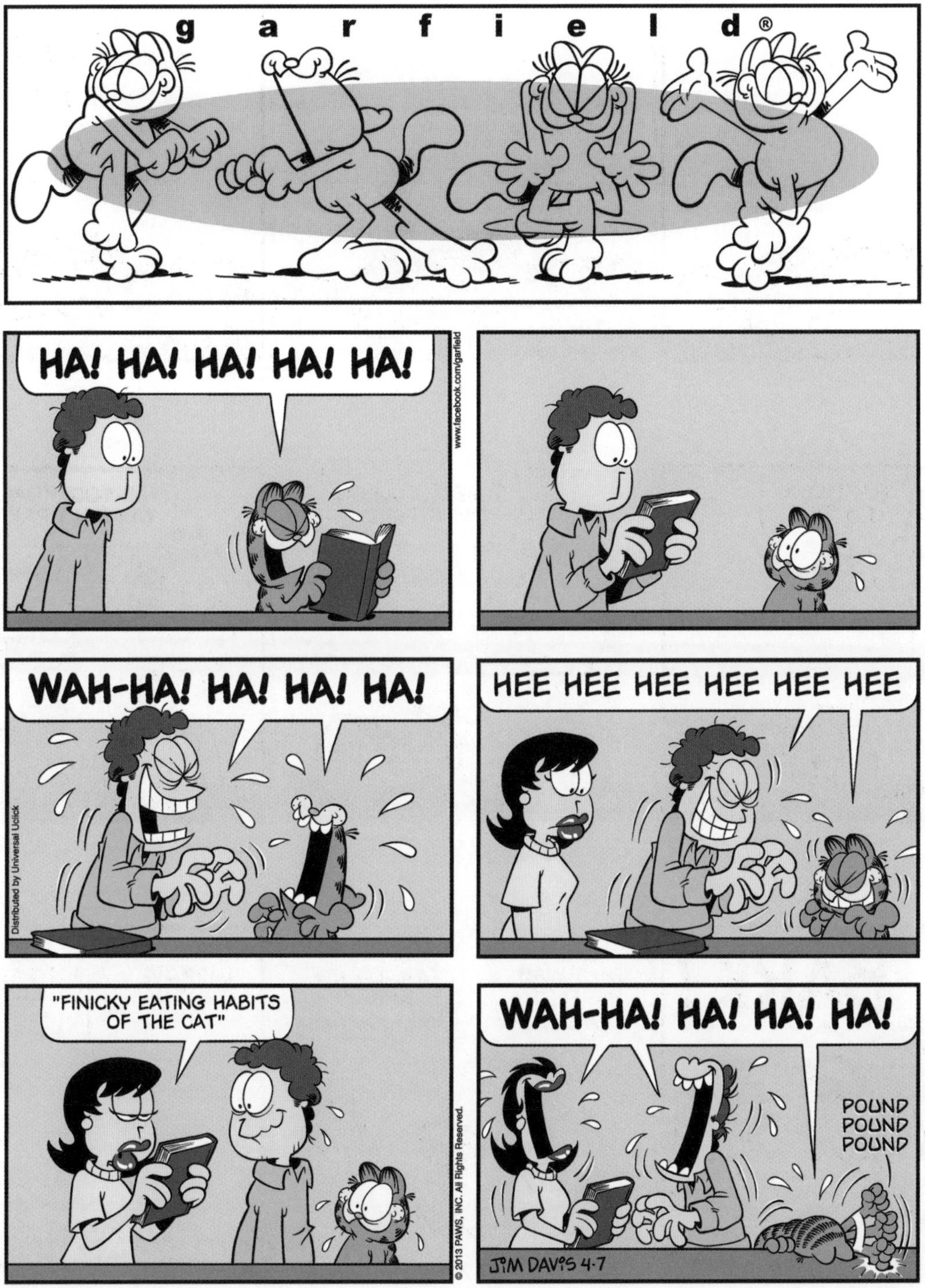
garfield®
HA! HA! HA! HA! HA!
www.facebook.com/garfield
WAH-HA! HA! HA! HA!
Distributed by Universal Uclick
HEE HEE HEE HEE HEE HEE
"FINICKY EATING HABITS OF THE CAT"
© 2013 PAWS, INC. All Rights Reserved.
WAH-HA! HA! HA! HA!
POUND POUND POUND
JIM DAVIS 4-7

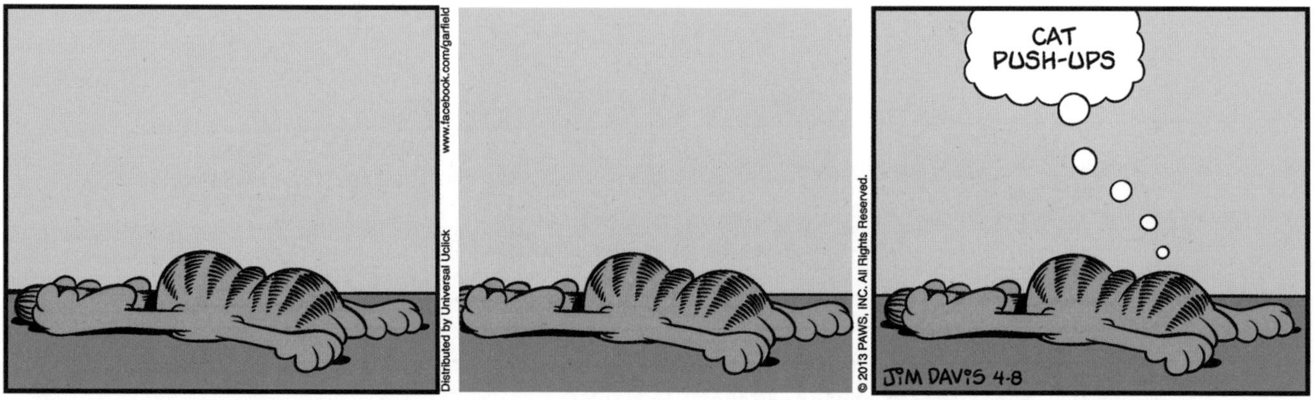
www.facebook.com/garfield
Distributed by Universal Uclick
© 2013 PAWS, INC. All Rights Reserved.
CAT PUSH-UPS
JIM DAVIS 4-8

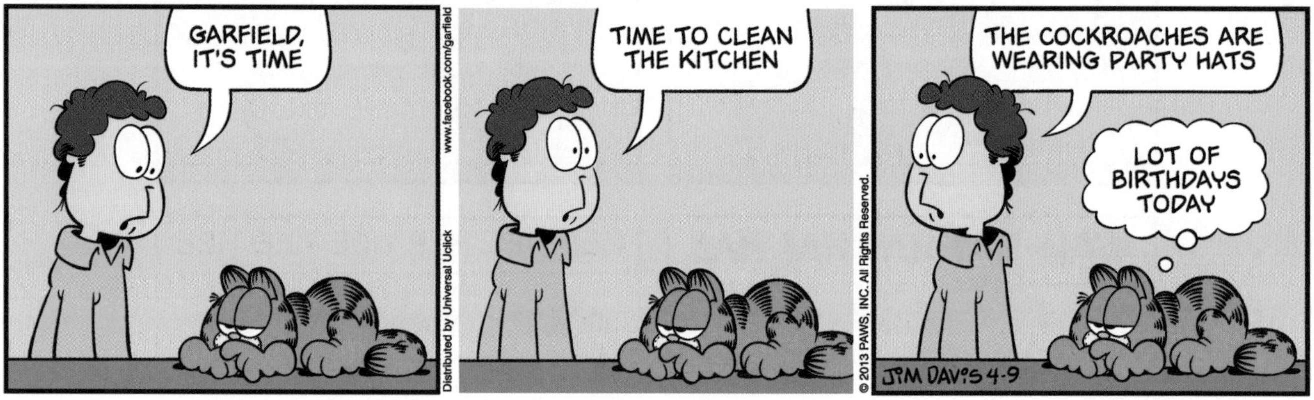
GARFIELD, IT'S TIME
www.facebook.com/garfield
Distributed by Universal Uclick
TIME TO CLEAN THE KITCHEN
© 2013 PAWS, INC. All Rights Reserved.
THE COCKROACHES ARE WEARING PARTY HATS
LOT OF BIRTHDAYS TODAY
JIM DAVIS 4-9

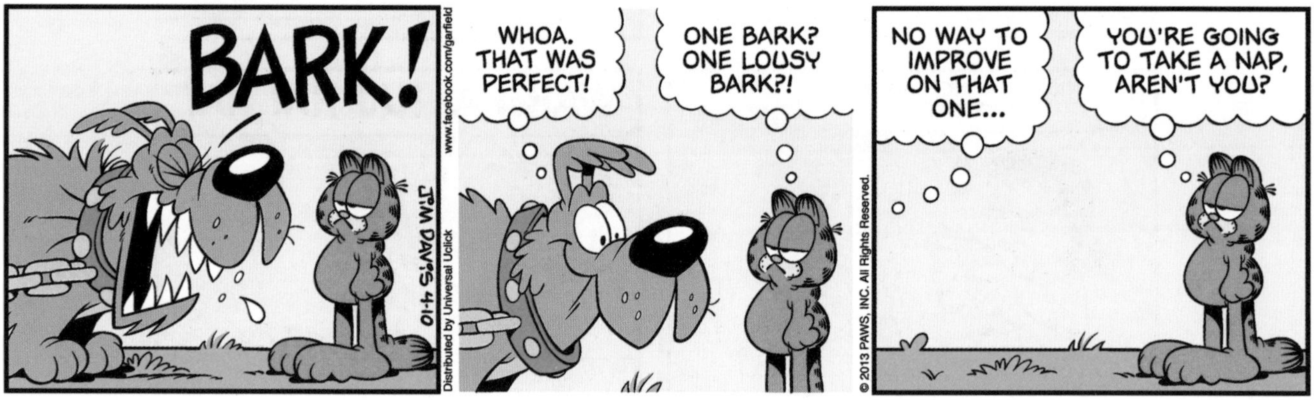
BARK!
JIM DAVIS 4-10
www.facebook.com/garfield
Distributed by Universal Uclick
WHOA. THAT WAS PERFECT!
ONE BARK? ONE LOUSY BARK?!
© 2013 PAWS, INC. All Rights Reserved.
NO WAY TO IMPROVE ON THAT ONE...
YOU'RE GOING TO TAKE A NAP, AREN'T YOU?

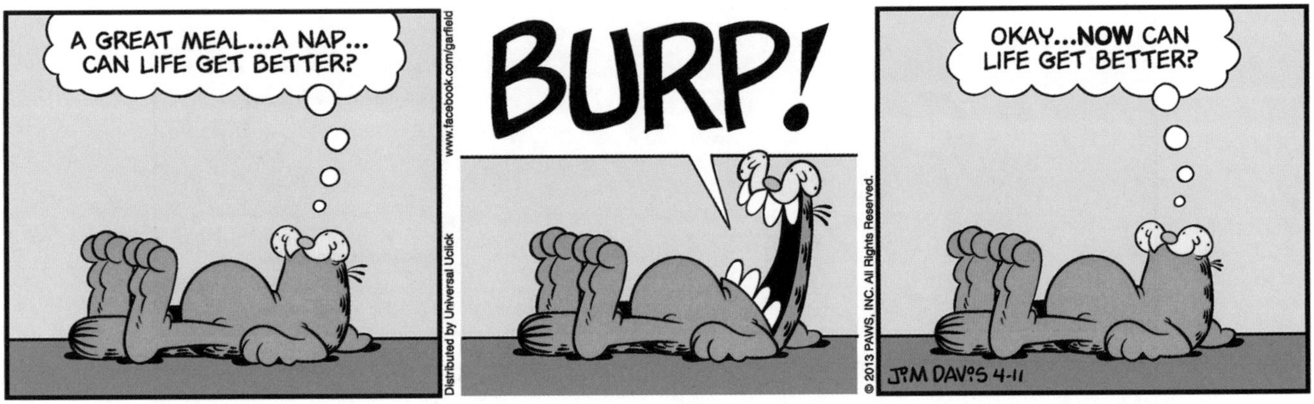
A GREAT MEAL...A NAP... CAN LIFE GET BETTER?
www.facebook.com/garfield
Distributed by Universal Uclick
BURP!
© 2013 PAWS, INC. All Rights Reserved.
OKAY...**NOW** CAN LIFE GET BETTER?
JIM DAVIS 4-11

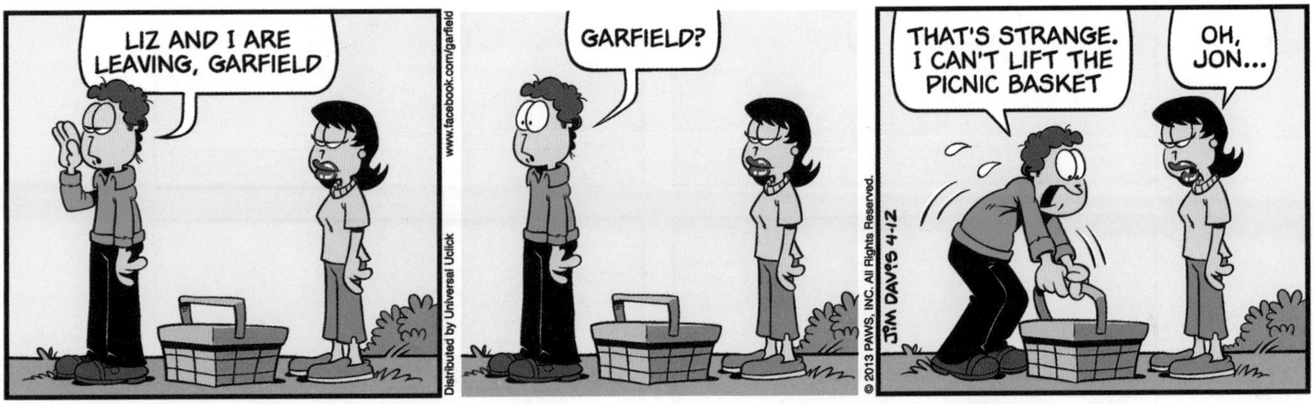
LIZ AND I ARE LEAVING, GARFIELD
www.facebook.com/garfield
Distributed by Universal Uclick
GARFIELD?
© 2013 PAWS, INC. All Rights Reserved.
JIM DAVIS 4-12
THAT'S STRANGE. I CAN'T LIFT THE PICNIC BASKET
OH, JON...

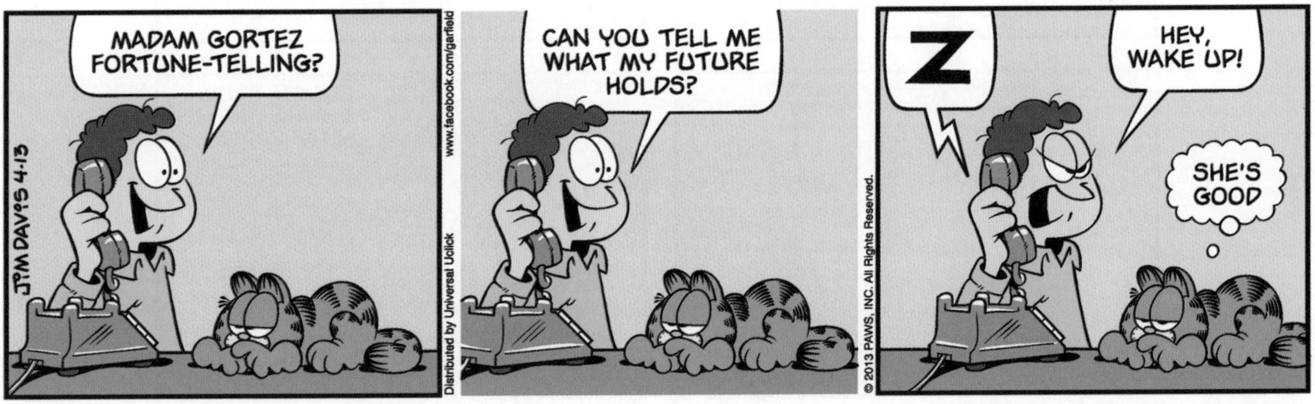
MADAM GORTEZ FORTUNE-TELLING?
JIM DAVIS 4-13
www.facebook.com/garfield
Distributed by Universal Uclick
CAN YOU TELL ME WHAT MY FUTURE HOLDS?
© 2013 PAWS, INC. All Rights Reserved.
Z
HEY, WAKE UP!
SHE'S GOOD

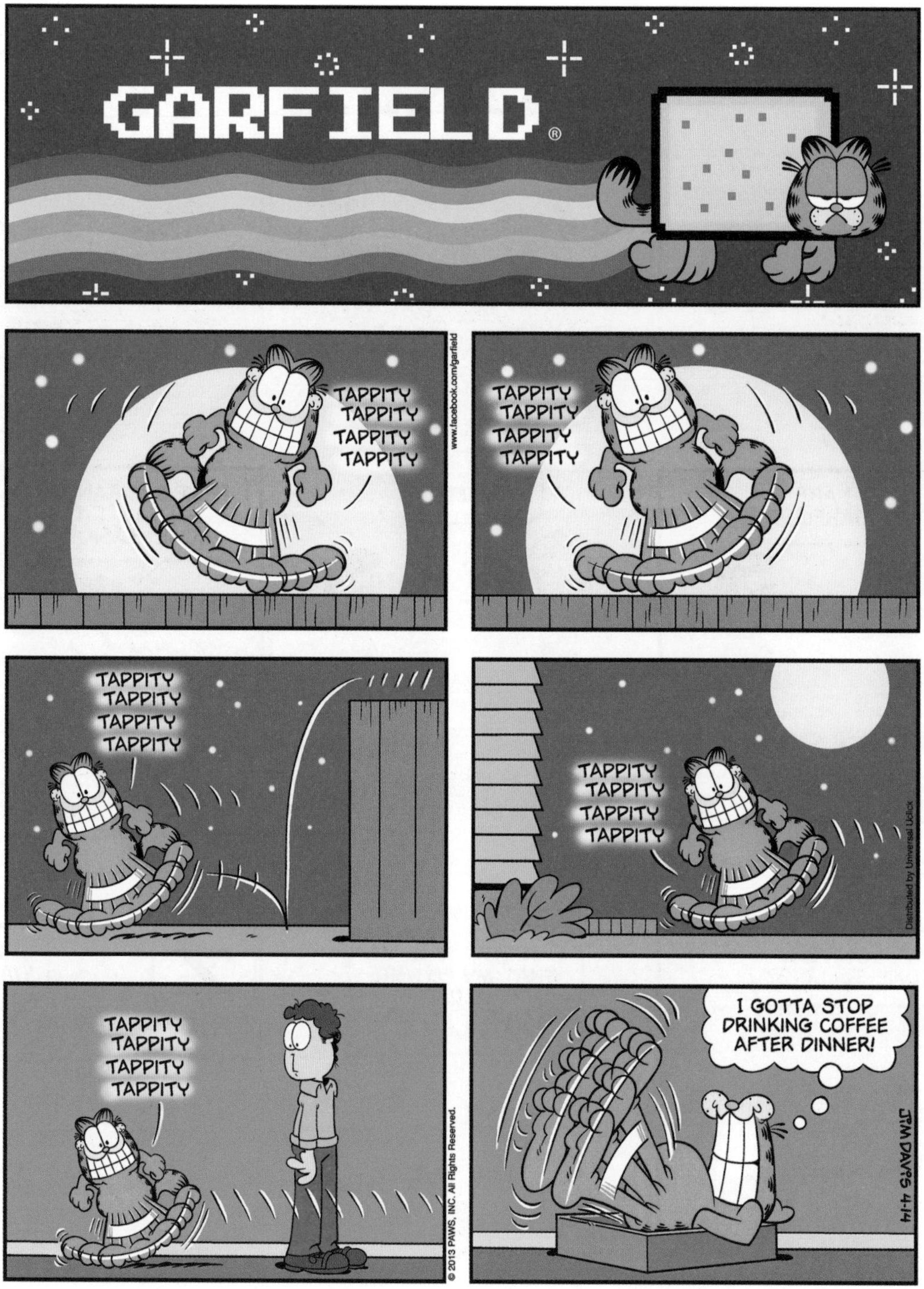
GARFIELD®
www.facebook.com/garfield
TAPPITY TAPPITY TAPPITY TAPPITY
TAPPITY TAPPITY TAPPITY TAPPITY
TAPPITY TAPPITY TAPPITY TAPPITY
TAPPITY TAPPITY TAPPITY TAPPITY
Distributed by Universal Uclick
TAPPITY TAPPITY TAPPITY TAPPITY
© 2013 PAWS, INC. All Rights Reserved.
I GOTTA STOP DRINKING COFFEE AFTER DINNER!
JIM DAVIS 4-14

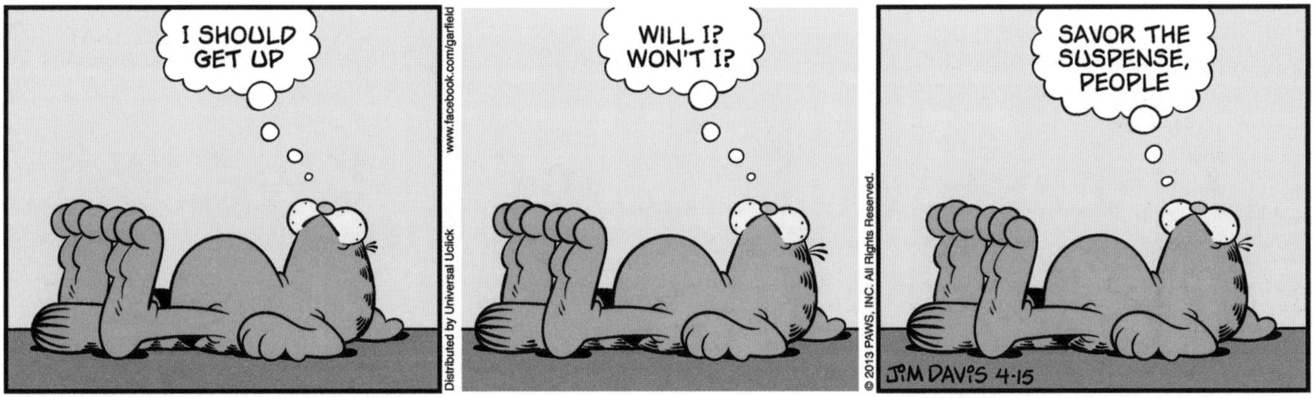
I SHOULD GET UP
WILL I? WON'T I?
SAVOR THE SUSPENSE, PEOPLE
www.facebook.com/garfield
Distributed by Universal Uclick
© 2013 PAWS, INC. All Rights Reserved.
JIM DAVIS 4-15

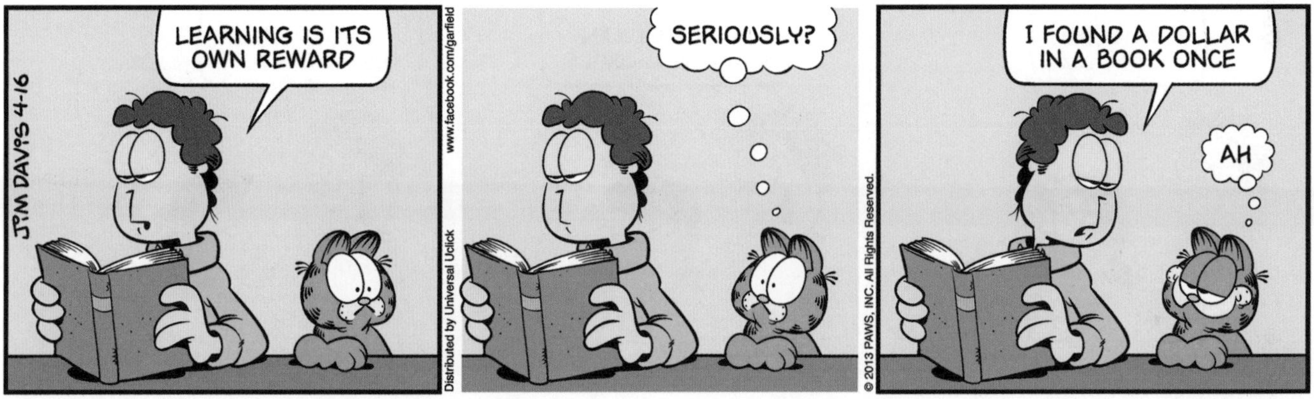
JIM DAVIS 4-16
LEARNING IS ITS OWN REWARD
SERIOUSLY?
I FOUND A DOLLAR IN A BOOK ONCE
AH
www.facebook.com/garfield
Distributed by Universal Uclick
© 2013 PAWS, INC. All Rights Reserved.

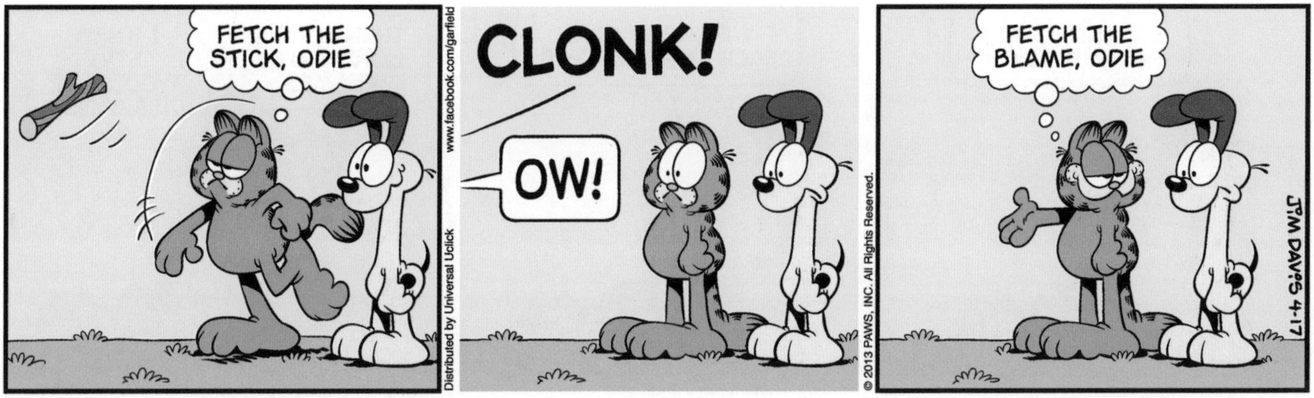
FETCH THE STICK, ODIE
CLONK!
OW!
FETCH THE BLAME, ODIE
JIM DAVIS 4-17
www.facebook.com/garfield
Distributed by Universal Uclick
© 2013 PAWS, INC. All Rights Reserved.

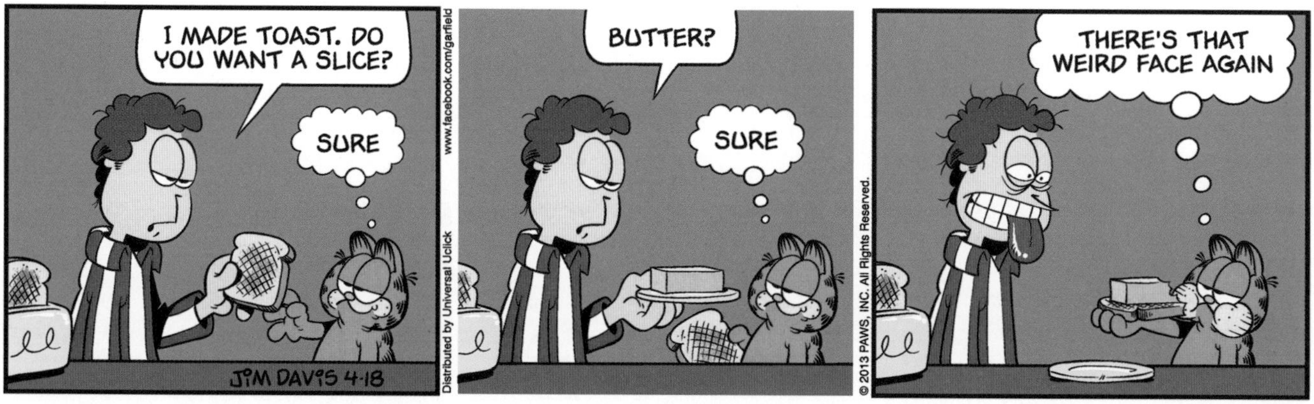
I MADE TOAST. DO YOU WANT A SLICE?
SURE
JIM DAVIS 4-18
Distributed by Universal Uclick
www.facebook.com/garfield
BUTTER?
SURE
© 2013 PAWS, INC. All Rights Reserved.
THERE'S THAT WEIRD FACE AGAIN

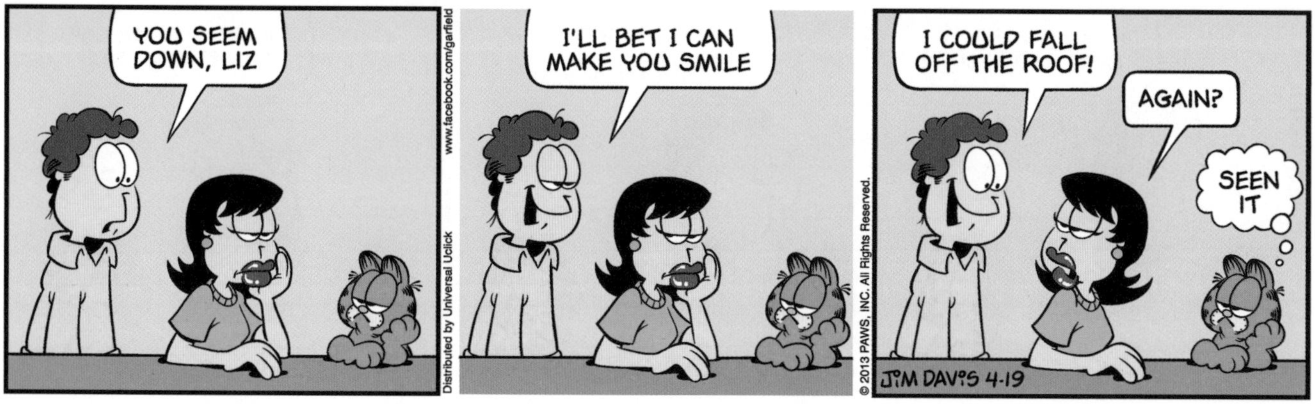
YOU SEEM DOWN, LIZ
Distributed by Universal Uclick
www.facebook.com/garfield
I'LL BET I CAN MAKE YOU SMILE
© 2013 PAWS, INC. All Rights Reserved.
I COULD FALL OFF THE ROOF!
AGAIN?
SEEN IT
JIM DAVIS 4-19

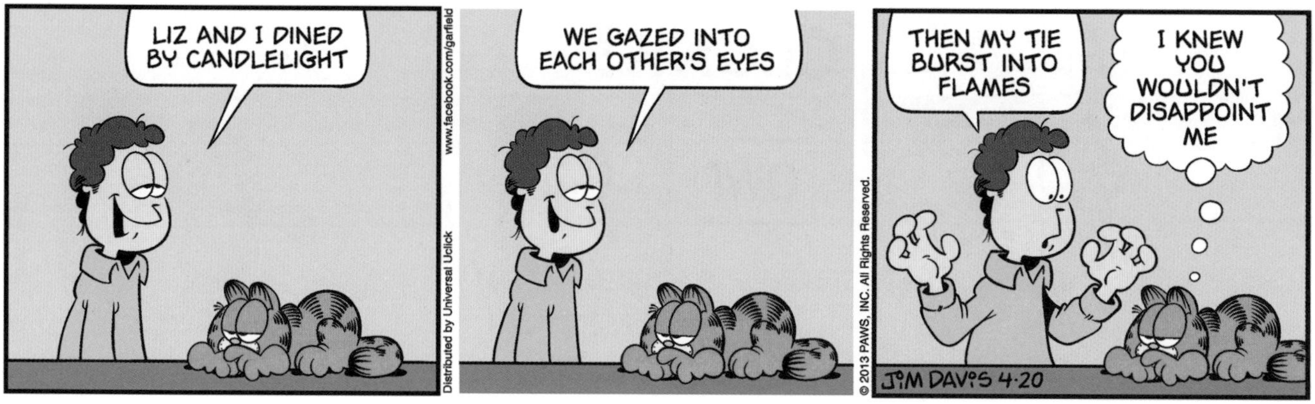
LIZ AND I DINED BY CANDLELIGHT
Distributed by Universal Uclick
www.facebook.com/garfield
WE GAZED INTO EACH OTHER'S EYES
© 2013 PAWS, INC. All Rights Reserved.
THEN MY TIE BURST INTO FLAMES
I KNEW YOU WOULDN'T DISAPPOINT ME
JIM DAVIS 4-20

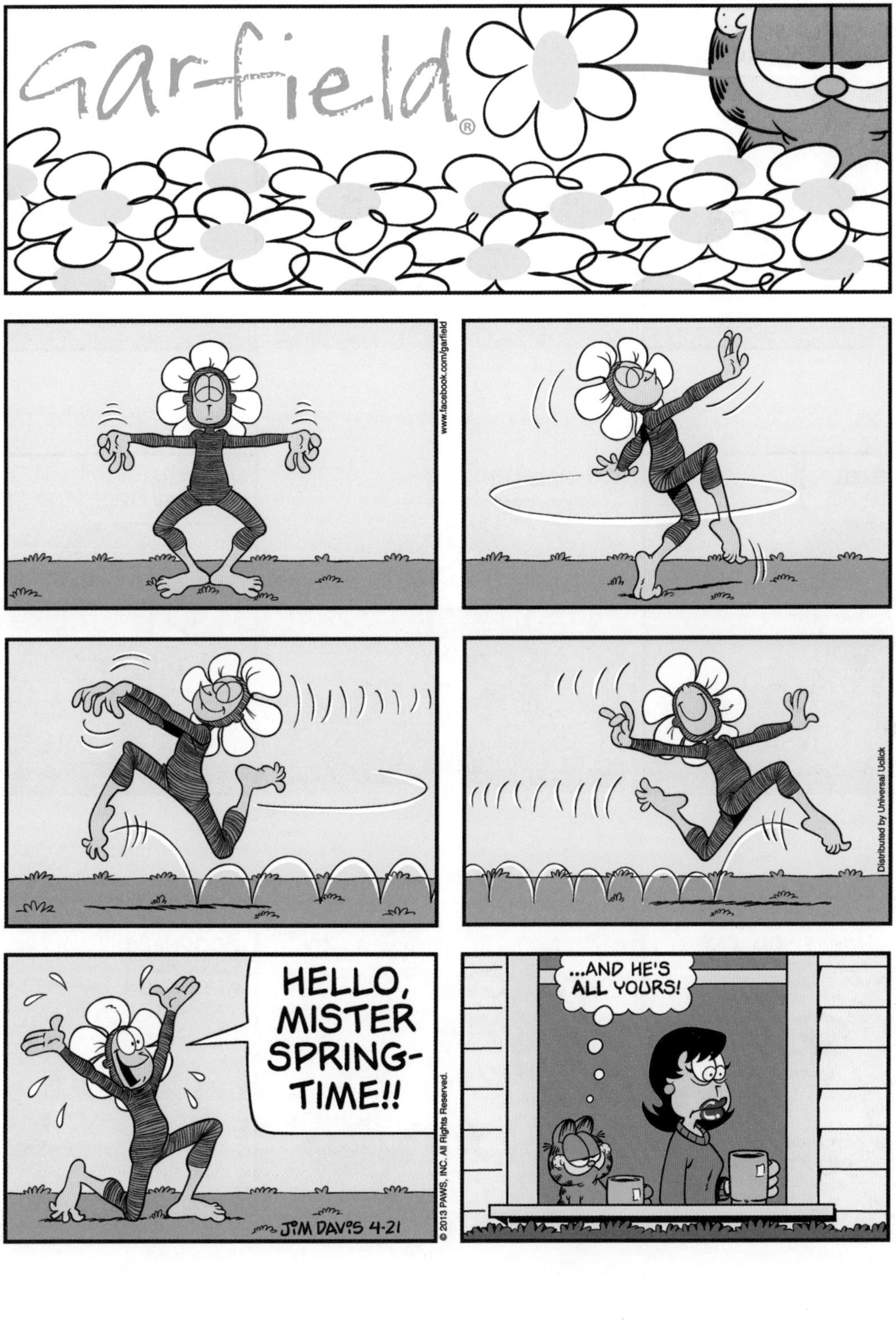
Garfield®
www.facebook.com/garfield
Distributed by Universal Uclick
HELLO, MISTER SPRING-TIME!!
© 2013 PAWS, INC. All Rights Reserved.
JIM DAVIS 4-21
...AND HE'S ALL YOURS!

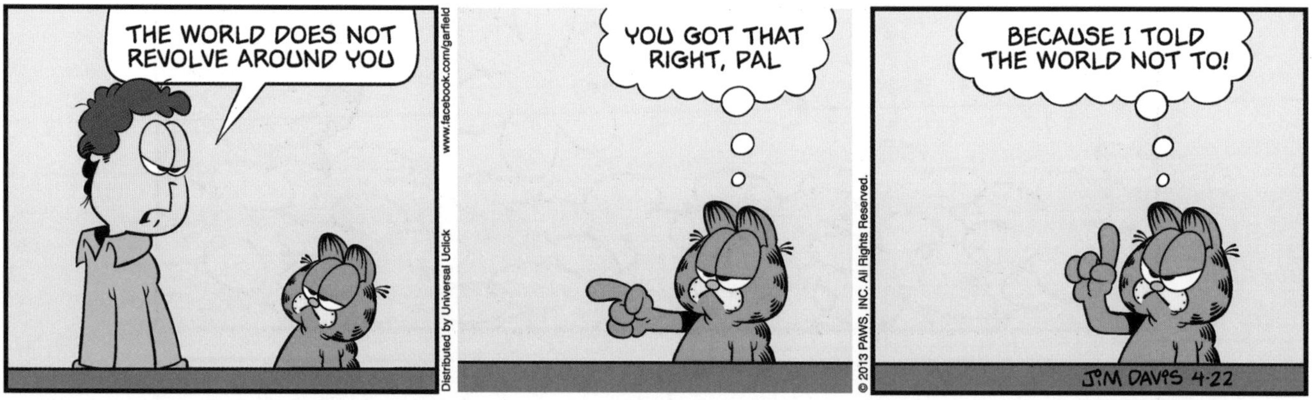
THE WORLD DOES NOT REVOLVE AROUND YOU
www.facebook.com/garfield
Distributed by Universal Uclick
YOU GOT THAT RIGHT, PAL
© 2013 PAWS, INC. All Rights Reserved.
BECAUSE I TOLD THE WORLD NOT TO!
JIM DAVIS 4·22

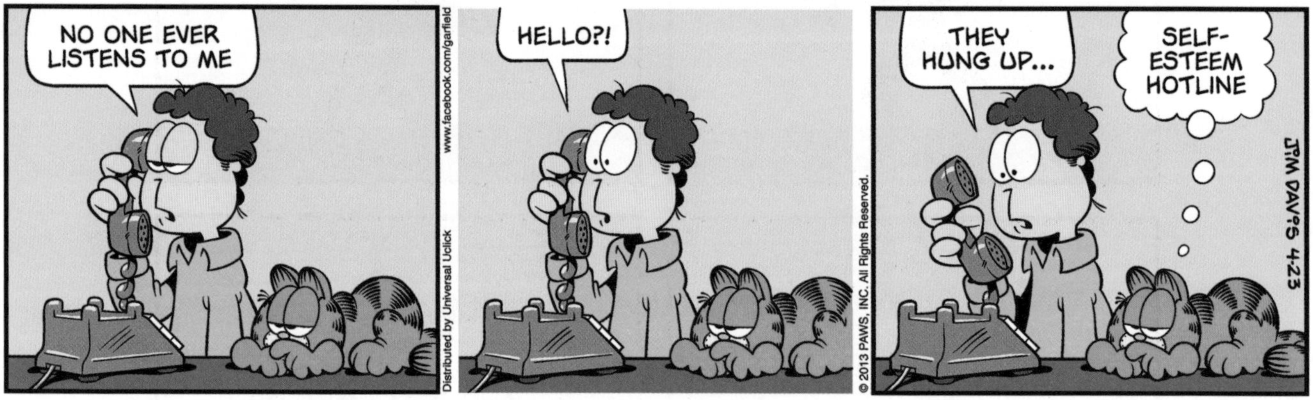
NO ONE EVER LISTENS TO ME
www.facebook.com/garfield
Distributed by Universal Uclick
HELLO?!
© 2013 PAWS, INC. All Rights Reserved.
THEY HUNG UP...
SELF-ESTEEM HOTLINE
JIM DAVIS 4·23

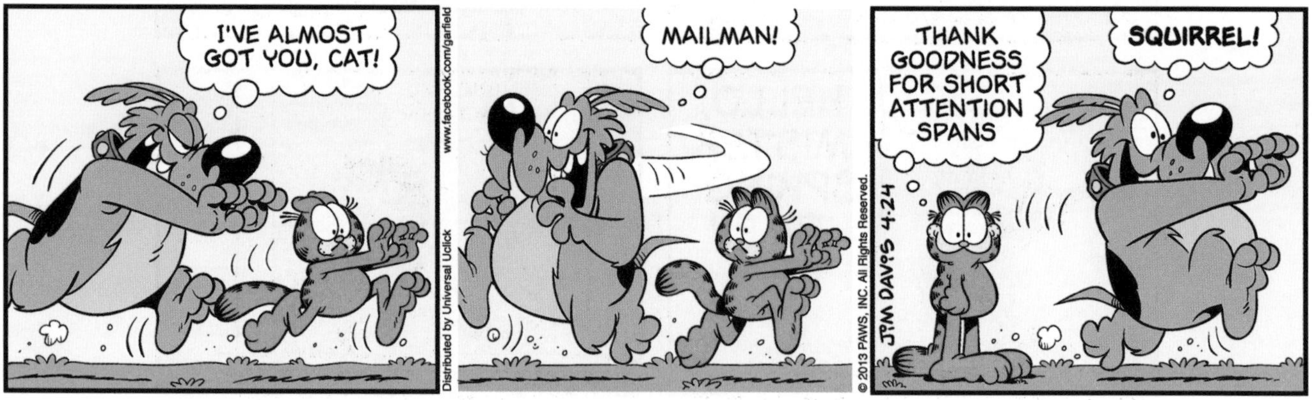
I'VE ALMOST GOT YOU, CAT!
www.facebook.com/garfield
Distributed by Universal Uclick
MAILMAN!
© 2013 PAWS, INC. All Rights Reserved.
JIM DAVIS 4·24
THANK GOODNESS FOR SHORT ATTENTION SPANS
SQUIRREL!

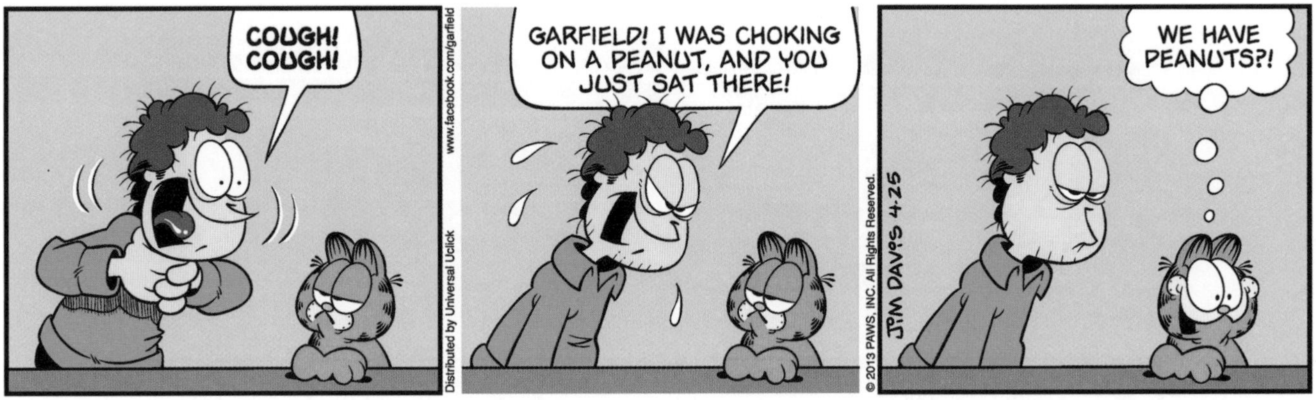
COUGH! COUGH!
GARFIELD! I WAS CHOKING ON A PEANUT, AND YOU JUST SAT THERE!
WE HAVE PEANUTS?!
Distributed by Universal Uclick
www.facebook.com/garfield
© 2013 PAWS, INC. All Rights Reserved.
JIM DAVIS 4-25

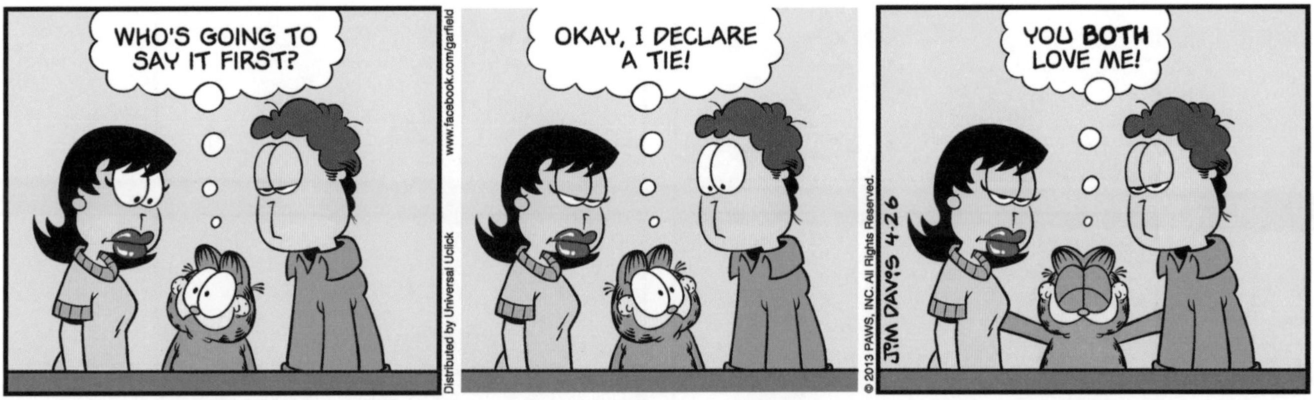
WHO'S GOING TO SAY IT FIRST?
OKAY, I DECLARE A TIE!
YOU **BOTH** LOVE ME!
Distributed by Universal Uclick
www.facebook.com/garfield
© 2013 PAWS, INC. All Rights Reserved.
JIM DAVIS 4-26

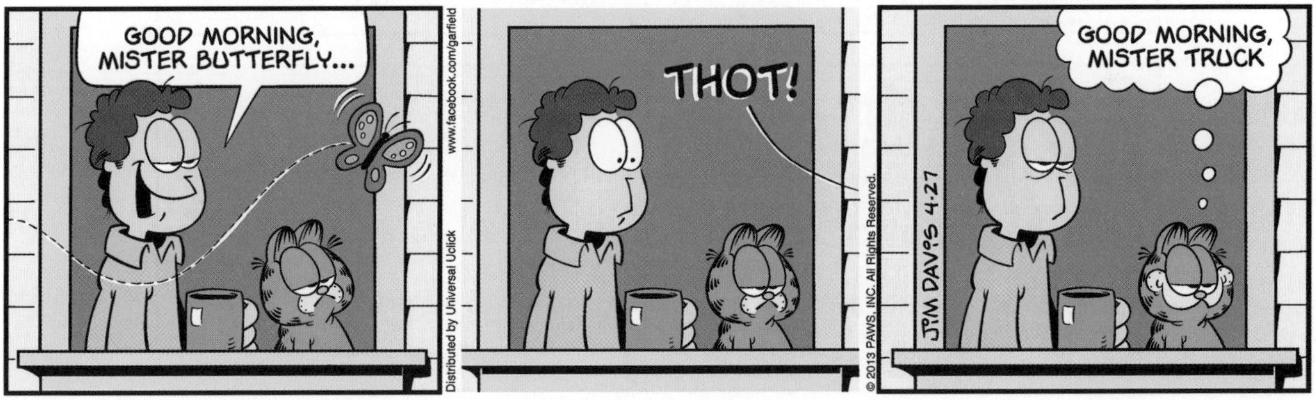
GOOD MORNING, MISTER BUTTERFLY...
THOT!
GOOD MORNING, MISTER TRUCK
Distributed by Universal Uclick
www.facebook.com/garfield
© 2013 PAWS, INC. All Rights Reserved.
JIM DAVIS 4-27

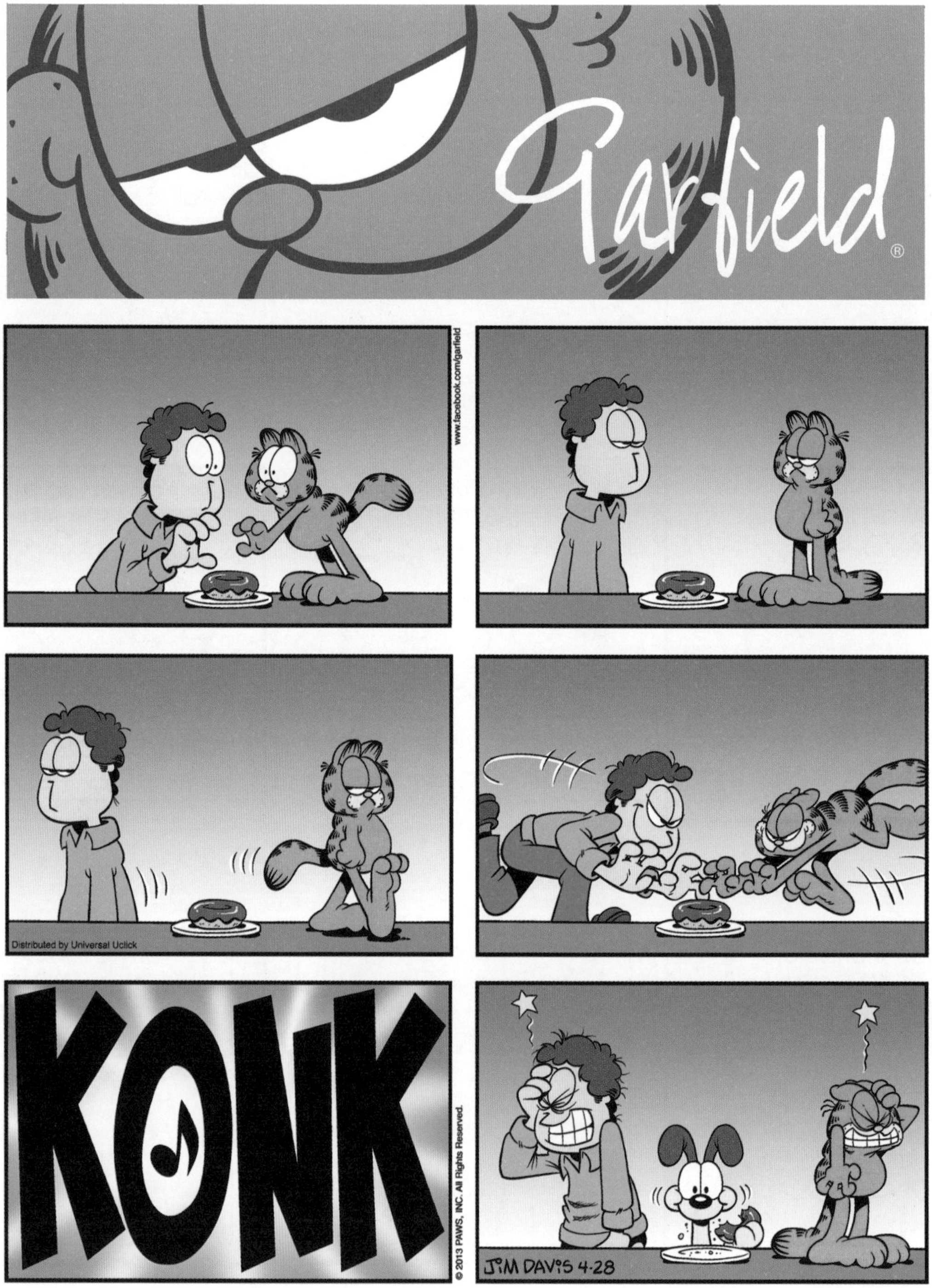
Garfield®
www.facebook.com/garfield
Distributed by Universal Uclick
KONK
© 2013 PAWS, INC. All Rights Reserved.
JIM DAVIS 4-28

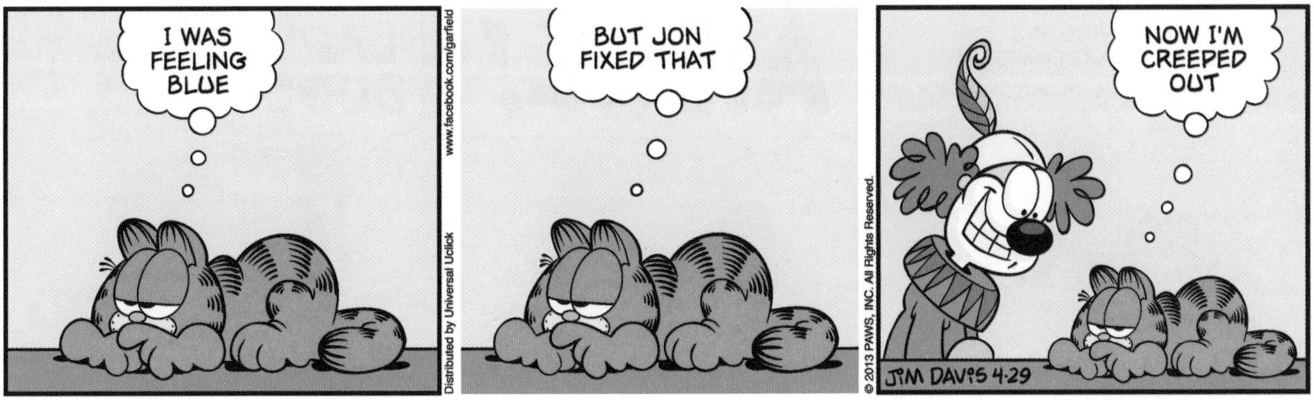
I WAS FEELING BLUE
Distributed by Universal Uclick www.facebook.com/garfield
BUT JON FIXED THAT
NOW I'M CREEPED OUT
© 2013 PAWS, INC. All Rights Reserved.
JIM DAVIS 4-29

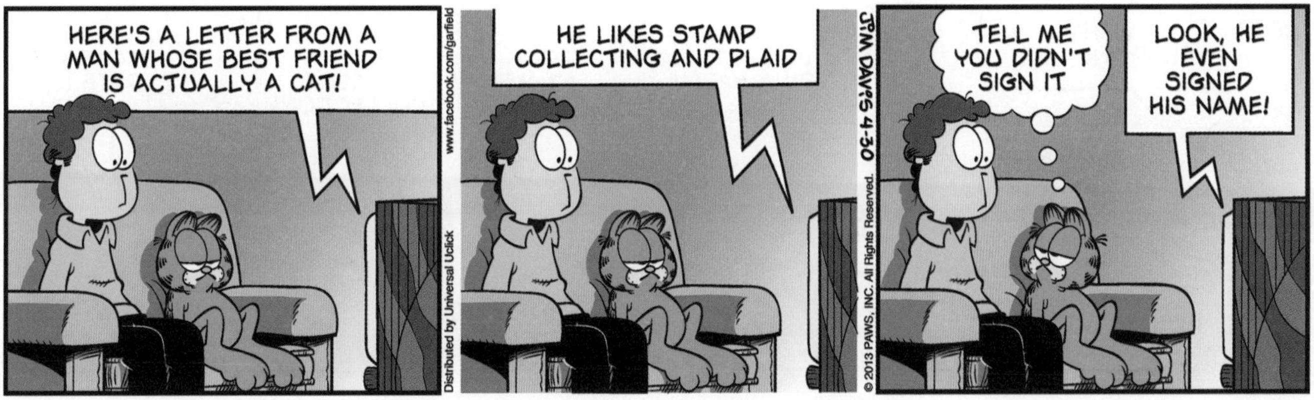
HERE'S A LETTER FROM A MAN WHOSE BEST FRIEND IS ACTUALLY A CAT!
Distributed by Universal Uclick www.facebook.com/garfield
HE LIKES STAMP COLLECTING AND PLAID
JIM DAVIS 4-30
© 2013 PAWS, INC. All Rights Reserved.
TELL ME YOU DIDN'T SIGN IT
LOOK, HE EVEN SIGNED HIS NAME!

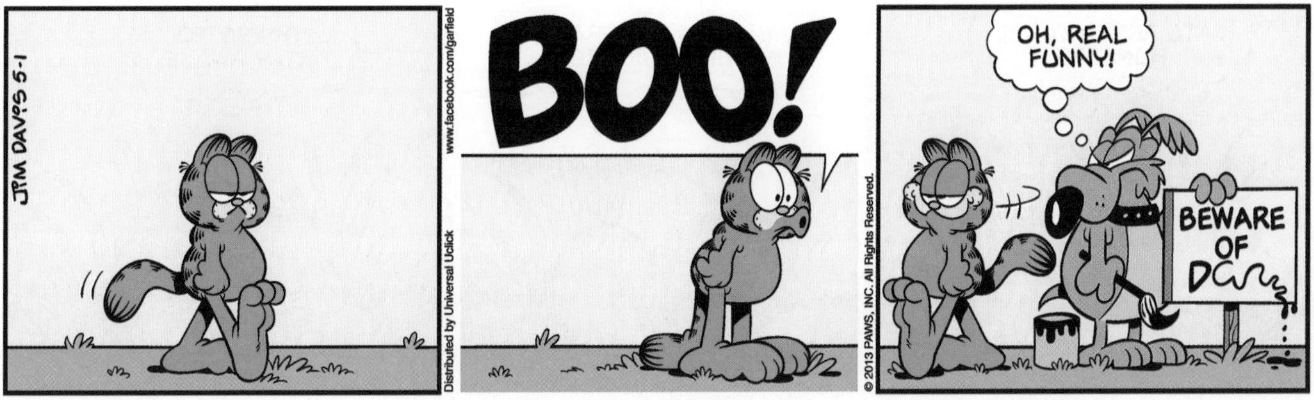
JIM DAVIS 5-1
Distributed by Universal Uclick www.facebook.com/garfield
BOO!
© 2013 PAWS, INC. All Rights Reserved.
OH, REAL FUNNY!
BEWARE OF

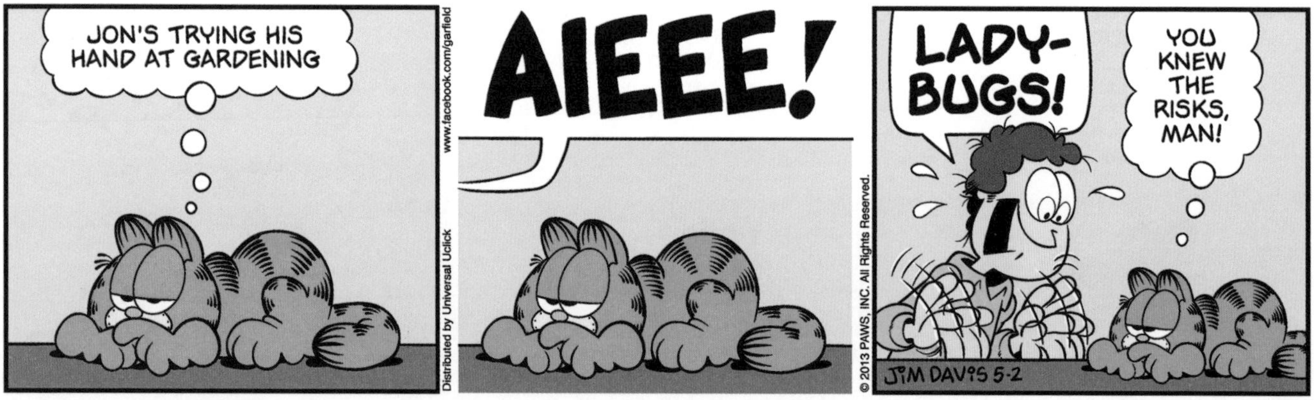
JON'S TRYING HIS HAND AT GARDENING
AIEEE!
LADY-BUGS!
YOU KNEW THE RISKS, MAN!
JIM DAVIS 5-2
www.facebook.com/garfield
Distributed by Universal Uclick
© 2013 PAWS, INC. All Rights Reserved.

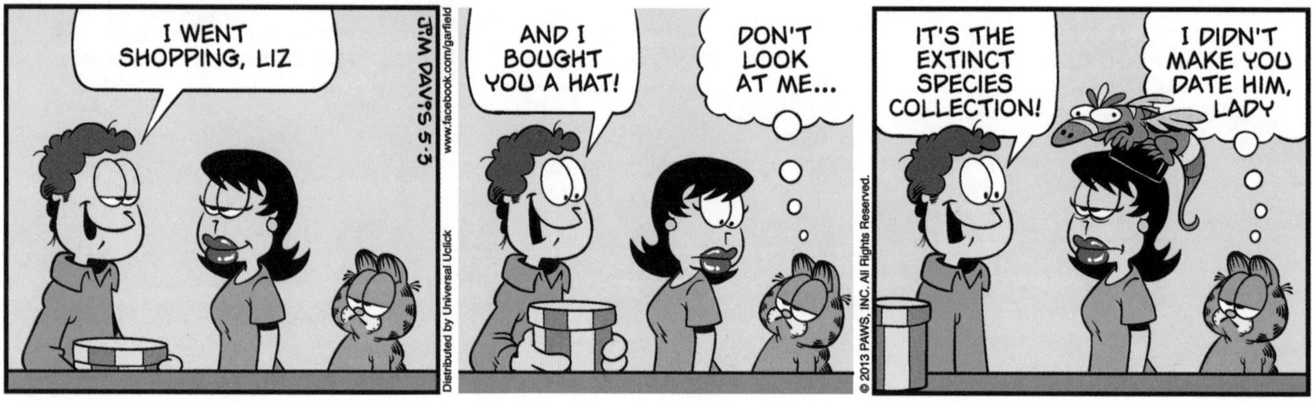
I WENT SHOPPING, LIZ
AND I BOUGHT YOU A HAT!
DON'T LOOK AT ME...
IT'S THE EXTINCT SPECIES COLLECTION!
I DIDN'T MAKE YOU DATE HIM, LADY
JIM DAVIS 5-3
www.facebook.com/garfield
Distributed by Universal Uclick
© 2013 PAWS, INC. All Rights Reserved.

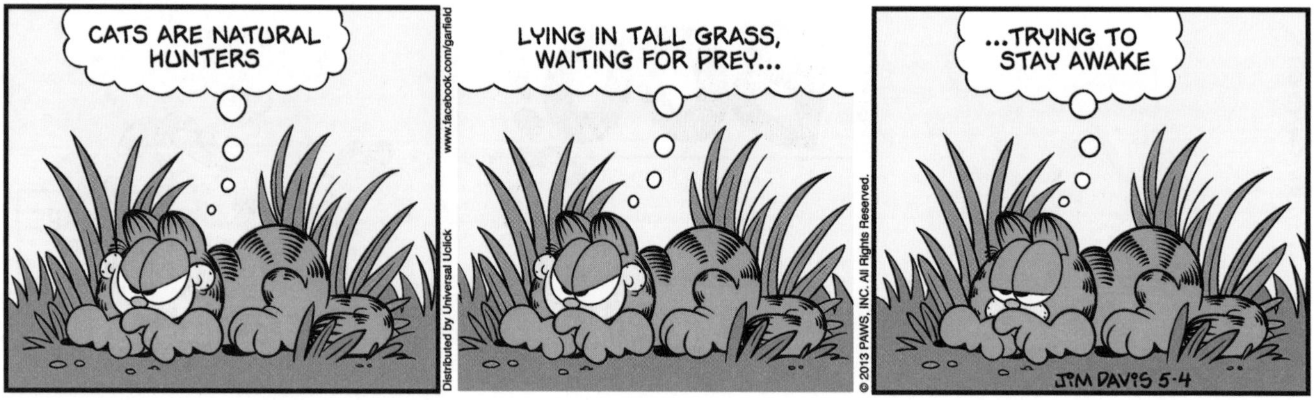
CATS ARE NATURAL HUNTERS
LYING IN TALL GRASS, WAITING FOR PREY...
...TRYING TO STAY AWAKE
JIM DAVIS 5-4
www.facebook.com/garfield
Distributed by Universal Uclick
© 2013 PAWS, INC. All Rights Reserved.

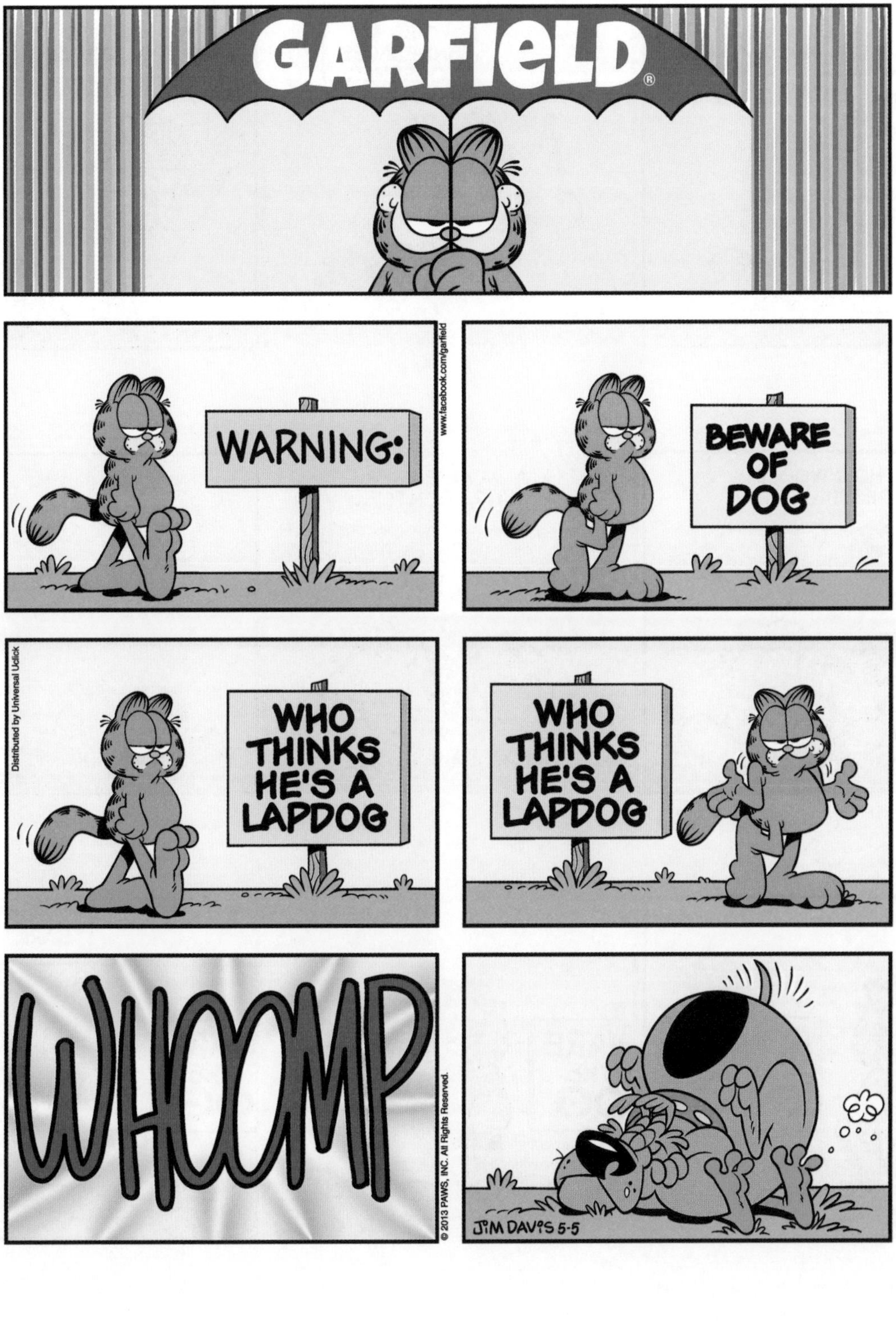
GARFIELD
www.facebook.com/garfield
WARNING:
BEWARE OF DOG
Distributed by Universal Uclick
WHO THINKS HE'S A LAPDOG
WHO THINKS HE'S A LAPDOG
WHOOMP
© 2013 PAWS, INC. All Rights Reserved.
JIM DAVIS 5-5

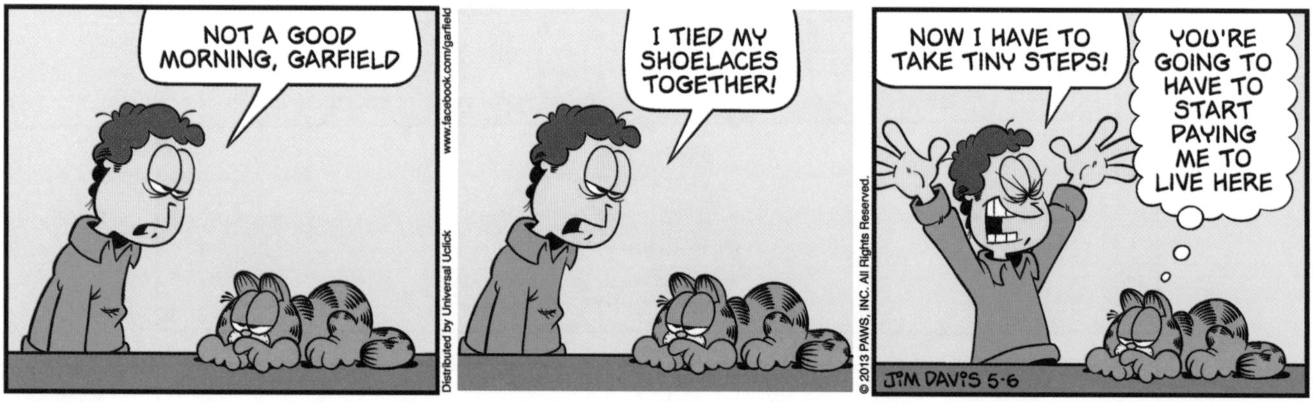
NOT A GOOD MORNING, GARFIELD
I TIED MY SHOELACES TOGETHER!
NOW I HAVE TO TAKE TINY STEPS!
YOU'RE GOING TO HAVE TO START PAYING ME TO LIVE HERE
JIM DAVIS 5-6
Distributed by Universal Uclick www.facebook.com/garfield
© 2013 PAWS, INC. All Rights Reserved.

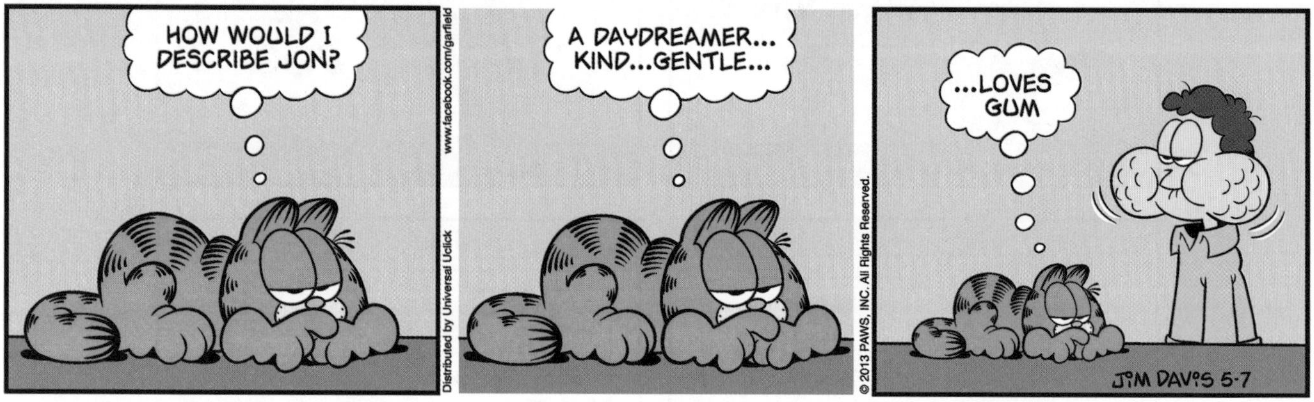
HOW WOULD I DESCRIBE JON?
A DAYDREAMER... KIND...GENTLE...
...LOVES GUM
JIM DAVIS 5-7
Distributed by Universal Uclick www.facebook.com/garfield
© 2013 PAWS, INC. All Rights Reserved.

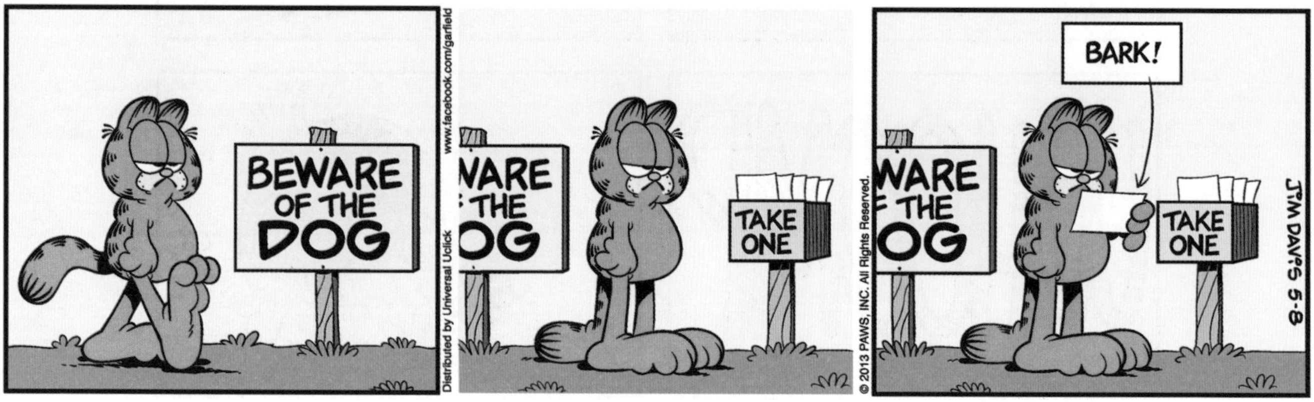
BEWARE OF THE DOG
WARE THE OG
TAKE ONE
WARE THE OG
BARK!
TAKE ONE
JIM DAVIS 5-8
Distributed by Universal Uclick www.facebook.com/garfield
© 2013 PAWS, INC. All Rights Reserved.

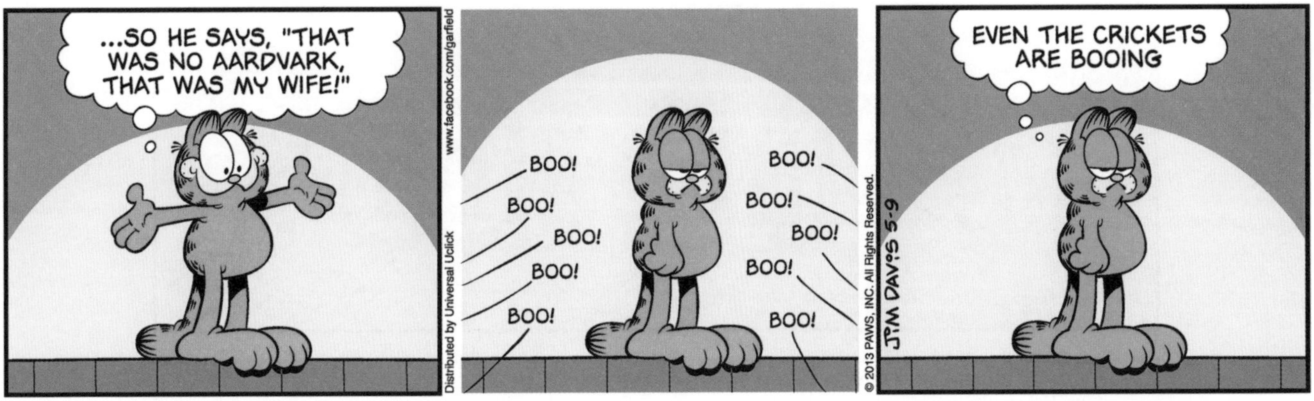
...SO HE SAYS, "THAT WAS NO AARDVARK, THAT WAS MY WIFE!"
Distributed by Universal Uclick
www.facebook.com/garfield
BOO!
BOO!
BOO!
BOO!
BOO!
BOO!
BOO!
BOO!
BOO!
BOO!
© 2013 PAWS, INC. All Rights Reserved.
JIM DAVIS 5-9
EVEN THE CRICKETS ARE BOOING

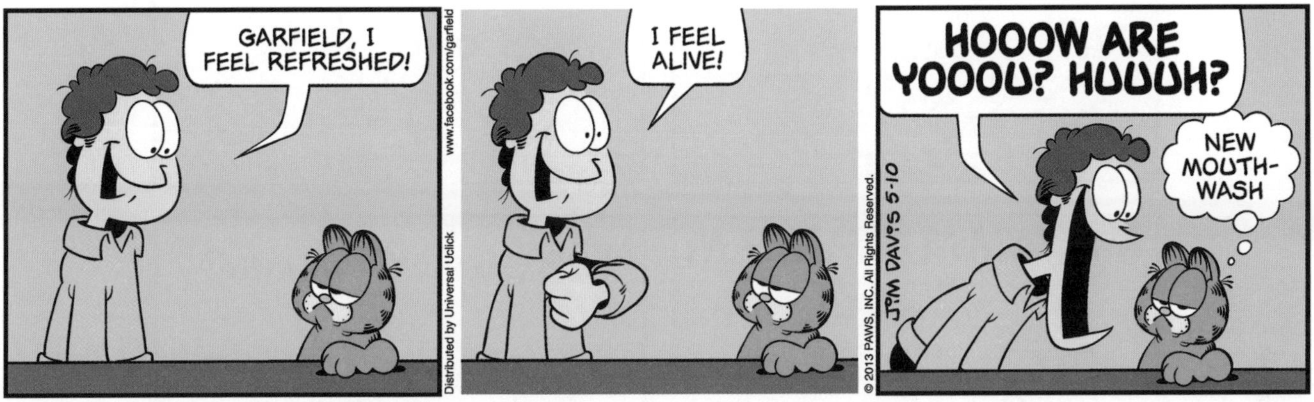
GARFIELD, I FEEL REFRESHED!
Distributed by Universal Uclick
www.facebook.com/garfield
I FEEL ALIVE!
© 2013 PAWS, INC. All Rights Reserved.
JIM DAVIS 5-10
HOOOW ARE YOOOU? HUUUH?
NEW MOUTH-WASH

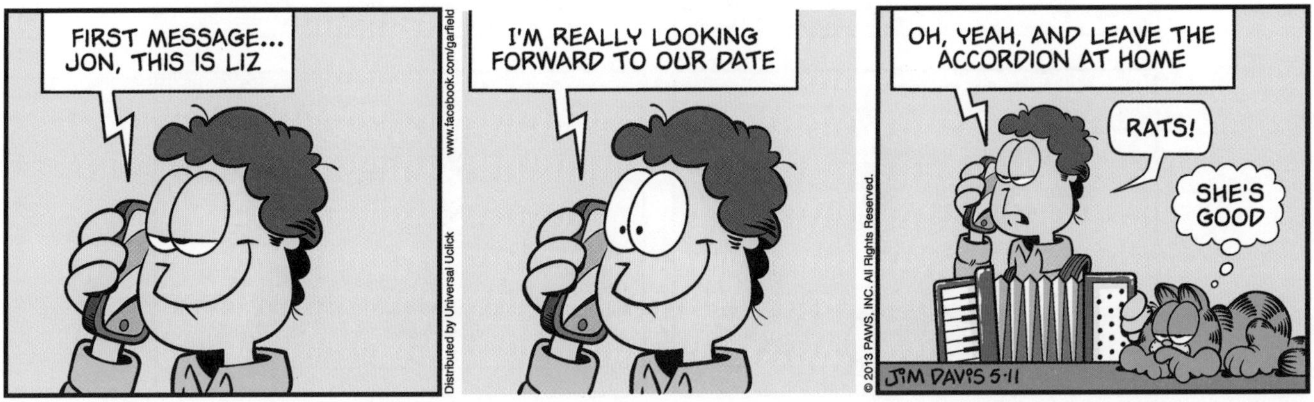
FIRST MESSAGE... JON, THIS IS LIZ
Distributed by Universal Uclick
www.facebook.com/garfield
I'M REALLY LOOKING FORWARD TO OUR DATE
© 2013 PAWS, INC. All Rights Reserved.
OH, YEAH, AND LEAVE THE ACCORDION AT HOME
RATS!
SHE'S GOOD
JIM DAVIS 5-11

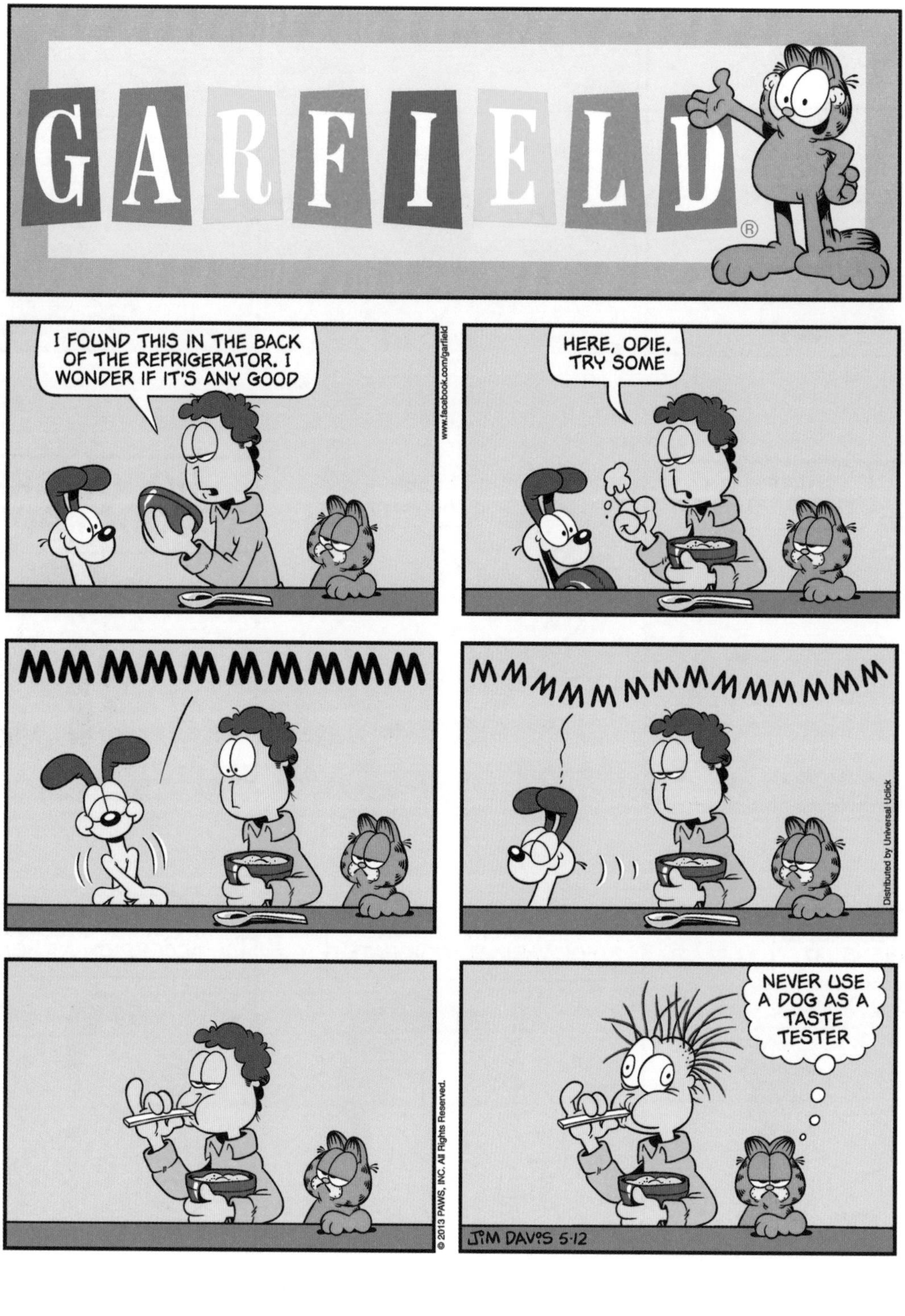
GARFIELD®
I FOUND THIS IN THE BACK OF THE REFRIGERATOR. I WONDER IF IT'S ANY GOOD
www.facebook.com/garfield
HERE, ODIE. TRY SOME
MMMMMMMMMMM
MMMMMMMMMMMMMMMM
Distributed by Universal Uclick
© 2013 PAWS, INC. All Rights Reserved.
NEVER USE A DOG AS A TASTE TESTER
JIM DAVIS 5-12

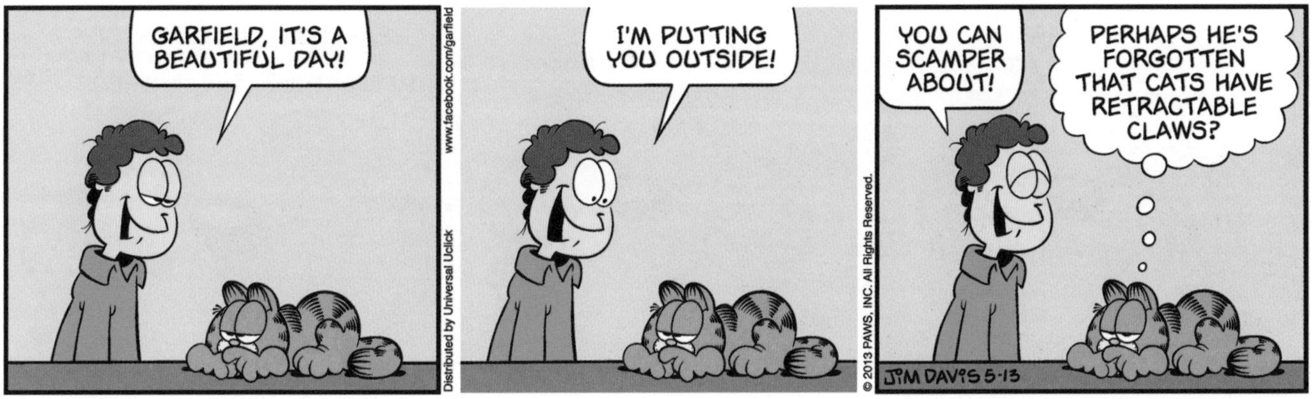
GARFIELD, IT'S A BEAUTIFUL DAY!
I'M PUTTING YOU OUTSIDE!
YOU CAN SCAMPER ABOUT!
PERHAPS HE'S FORGOTTEN THAT CATS HAVE RETRACTABLE CLAWS?
JIM DAVIS 5-13
Distributed by Universal Uclick
www.facebook.com/garfield
© 2013 PAWS, INC. All Rights Reserved.

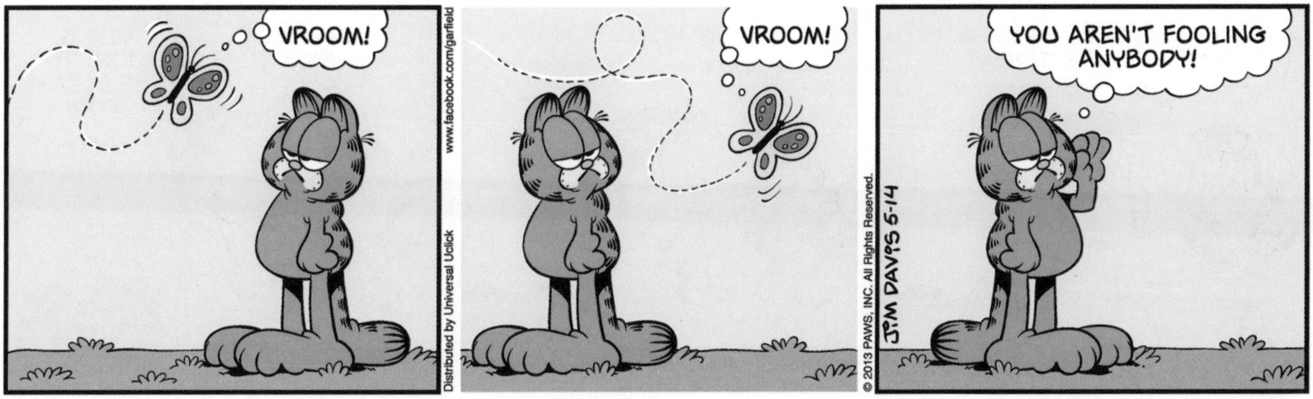
VROOM!
VROOM!
YOU AREN'T FOOLING ANYBODY!
JIM DAVIS 5-14
Distributed by Universal Uclick
www.facebook.com/garfield
© 2013 PAWS, INC. All Rights Reserved.

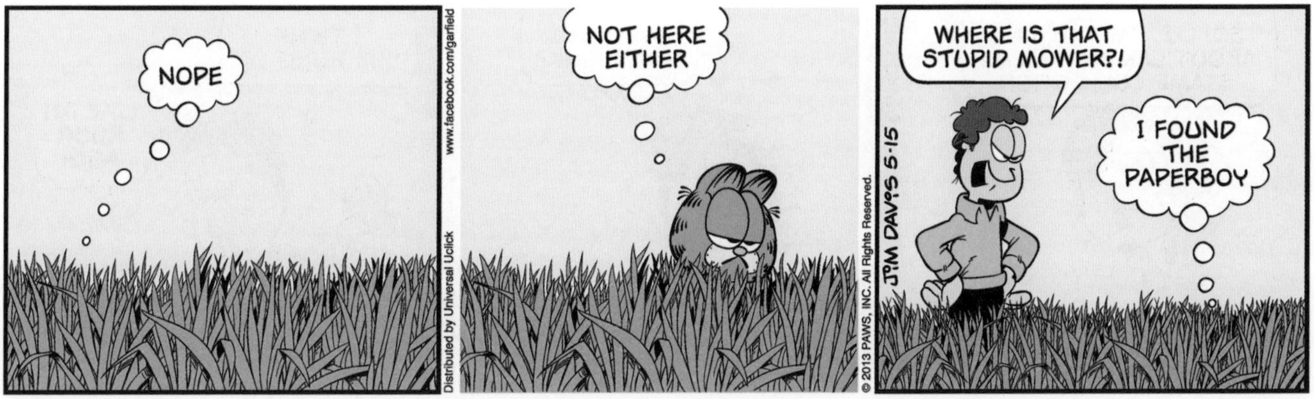
NOPE
NOT HERE EITHER
WHERE IS THAT STUPID MOWER?!
I FOUND THE PAPERBOY
JIM DAVIS 5-15
Distributed by Universal Uclick
www.facebook.com/garfield
© 2013 PAWS, INC. All Rights Reserved.

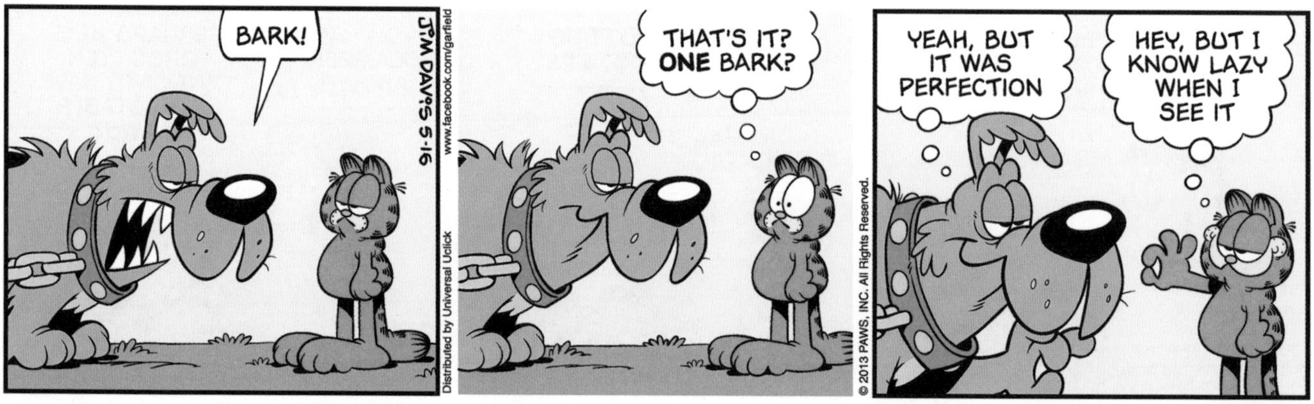
BARK!
JIM DAVIS 5-16
www.facebook.com/garfield
Distributed by Universal Uclick
THAT'S IT? **ONE** BARK?
© 2013 PAWS, INC. All Rights Reserved.
YEAH, BUT IT WAS PERFECTION
HEY, BUT I KNOW LAZY WHEN I SEE IT

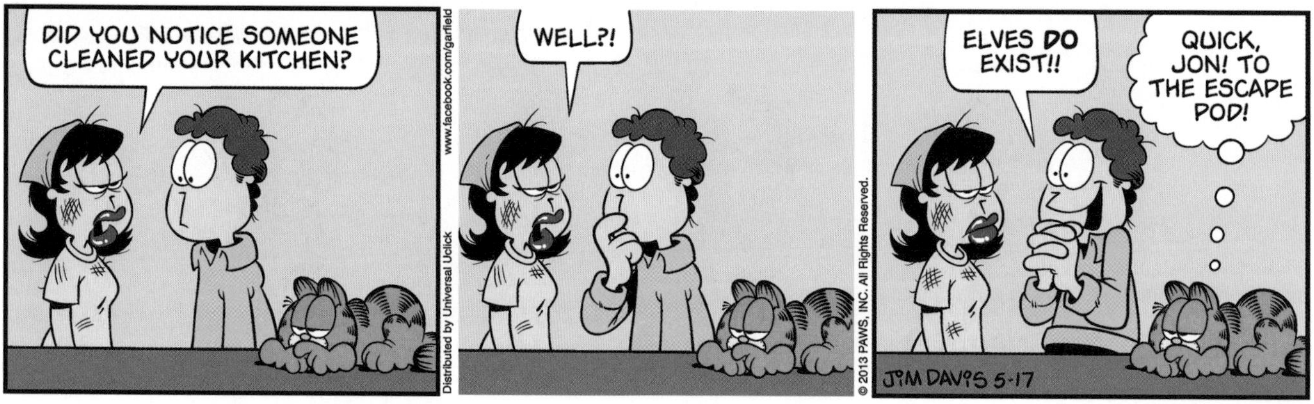
DID YOU NOTICE SOMEONE CLEANED YOUR KITCHEN?
www.facebook.com/garfield
Distributed by Universal Uclick
WELL?!
© 2013 PAWS, INC. All Rights Reserved.
ELVES **DO** EXIST!!
QUICK, JON! TO THE ESCAPE POD!
JIM DAVIS 5-17

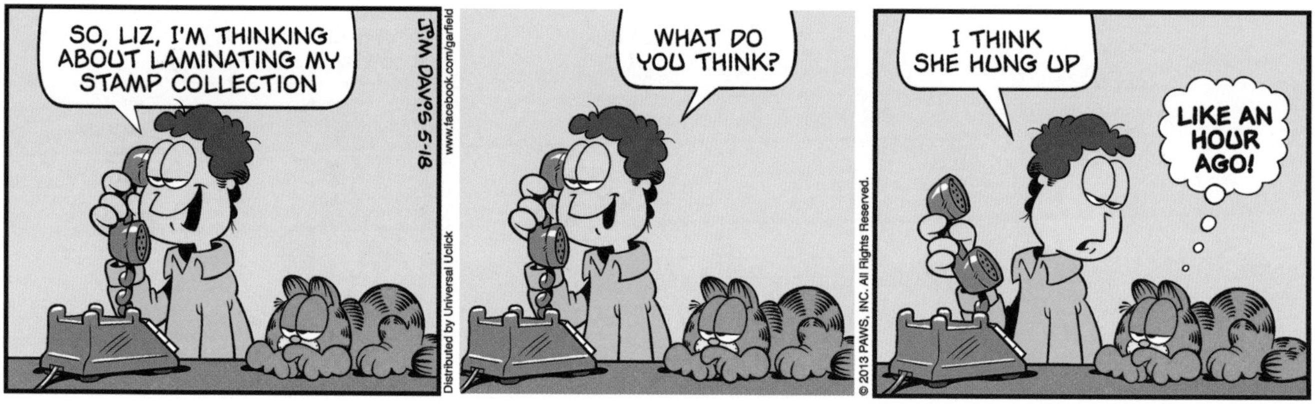
SO, LIZ, I'M THINKING ABOUT LAMINATING MY STAMP COLLECTION
JIM DAVIS 5-18
www.facebook.com/garfield
Distributed by Universal Uclick
WHAT DO YOU THINK?
© 2013 PAWS, INC. All Rights Reserved.
I THINK SHE HUNG UP
LIKE AN HOUR AGO!

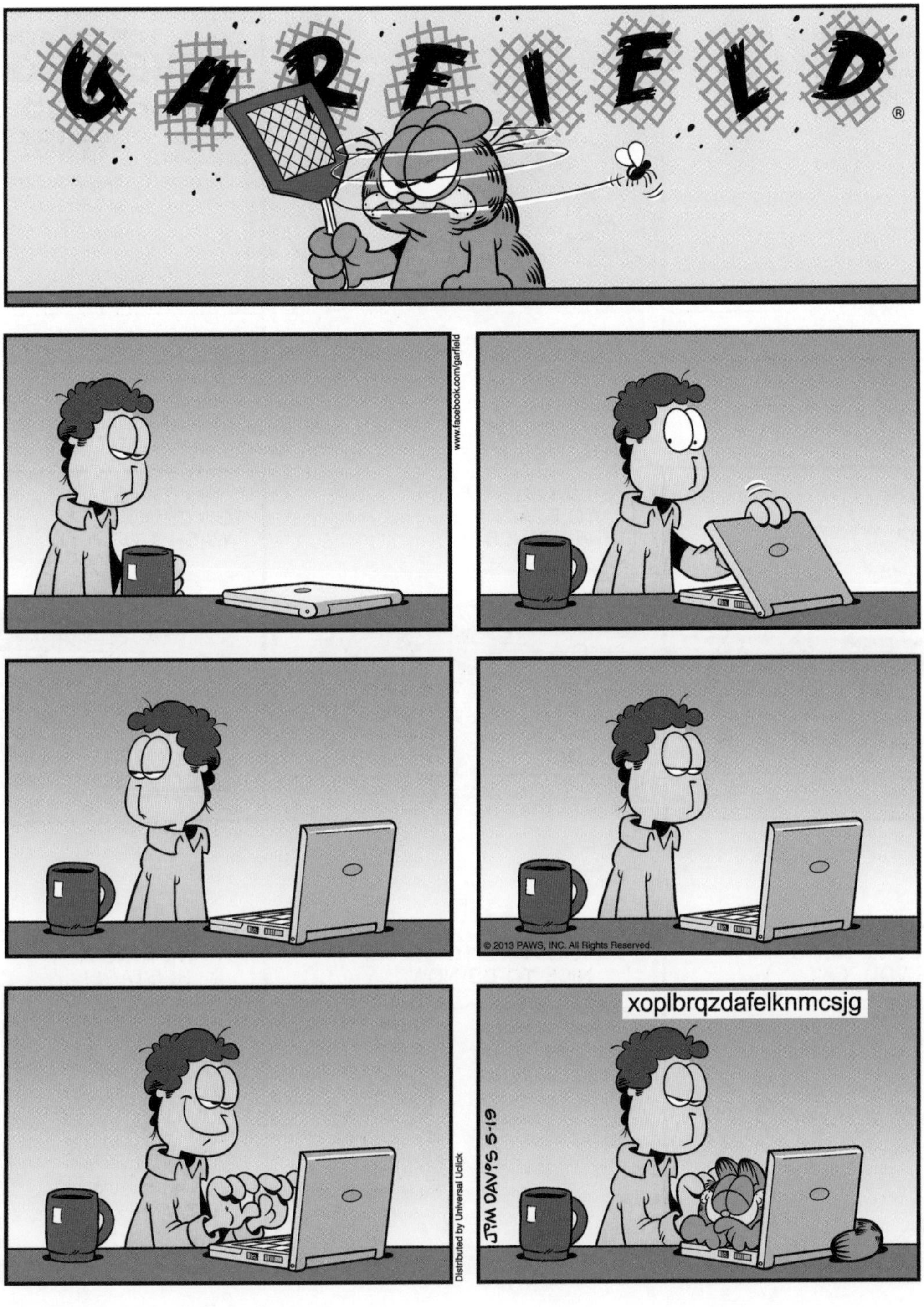
GARFIELD®
www.facebook.com/garfield
© 2013 PAWS, INC. All Rights Reserved.
xoplbrqzdafelknmcsjg
JIM DAVIS 5-19
Distributed by Universal Uclick

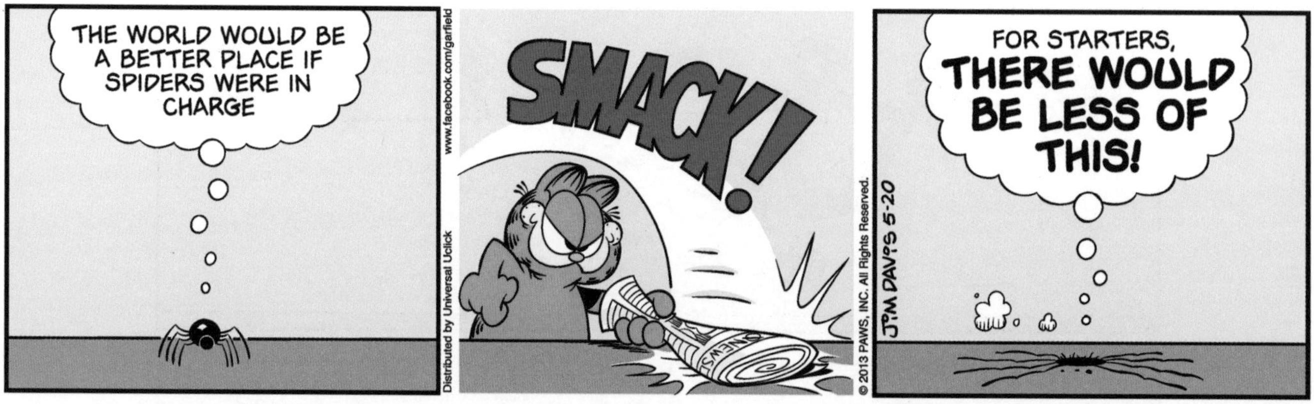
THE WORLD WOULD BE A BETTER PLACE IF SPIDERS WERE IN CHARGE
www.facebook.com/garfield
Distributed by Universal Uclick
SMACK!
NEWS
© 2013 PAWS, INC. All Rights Reserved.
JIM DAVIS 5-20
FOR STARTERS, **THERE WOULD BE LESS OF THIS!**

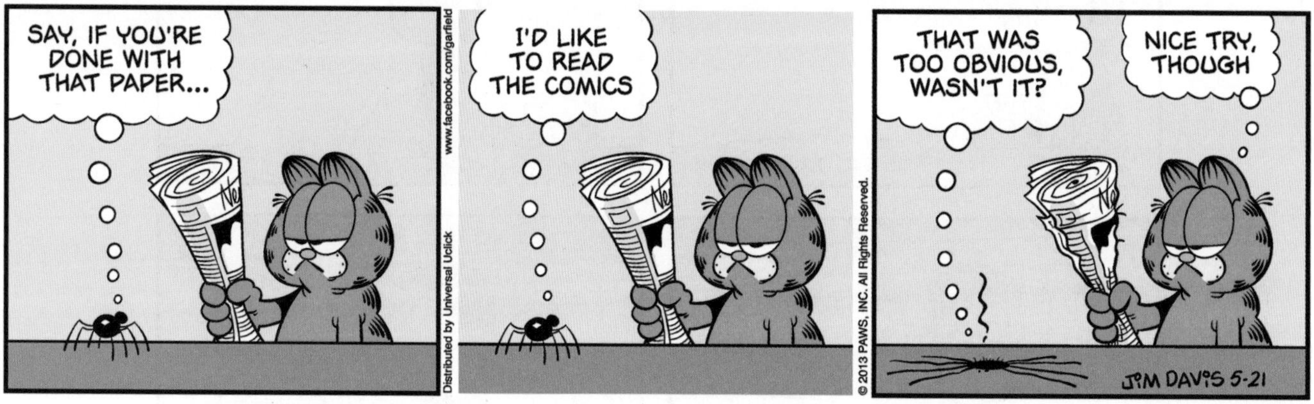
SAY, IF YOU'RE DONE WITH THAT PAPER...
www.facebook.com/garfield
Distributed by Universal Uclick
I'D LIKE TO READ THE COMICS
© 2013 PAWS, INC. All Rights Reserved.
THAT WAS TOO OBVIOUS, WASN'T IT?
NICE TRY, THOUGH
JIM DAVIS 5-21

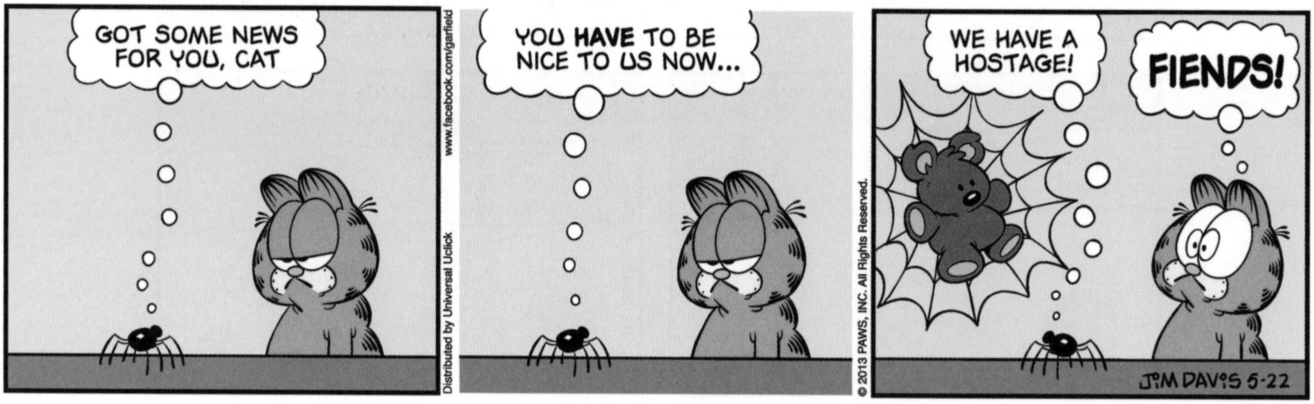
GOT SOME NEWS FOR YOU, CAT
www.facebook.com/garfield
Distributed by Universal Uclick
YOU **HAVE** TO BE NICE TO US NOW...
© 2013 PAWS, INC. All Rights Reserved.
WE HAVE A HOSTAGE!
FIENDS!
JIM DAVIS 5-22

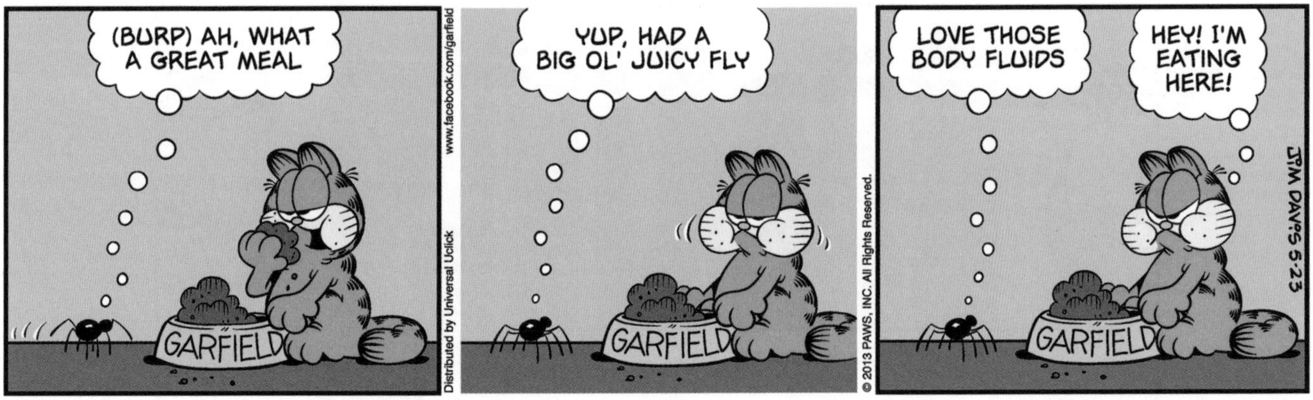
(BURP) AH, WHAT A GREAT MEAL
GARFIELD
www.facebook.com/garfield
Distributed by Universal Uclick
YUP, HAD A BIG OL' JUICY FLY
GARFIELD
© 2013 PAWS, INC. All Rights Reserved.
LOVE THOSE BODY FLUIDS
HEY! I'M EATING HERE!
GARFIELD
JIM DAVIS 5-23

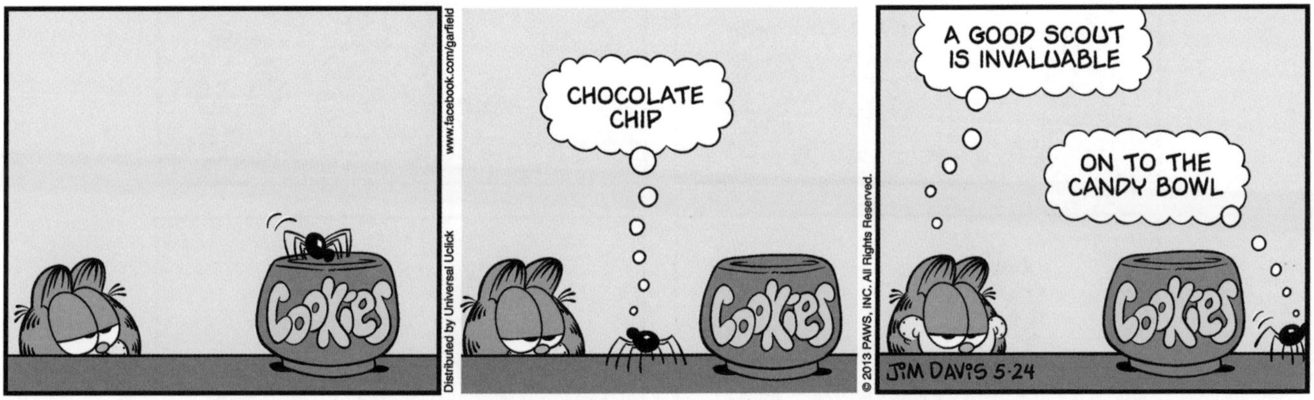
Cookies
www.facebook.com/garfield
Distributed by Universal Uclick
CHOCOLATE CHIP
Cookies
© 2013 PAWS, INC. All Rights Reserved.
A GOOD SCOUT IS INVALUABLE
ON TO THE CANDY BOWL
Cookies
JIM DAVIS 5-24

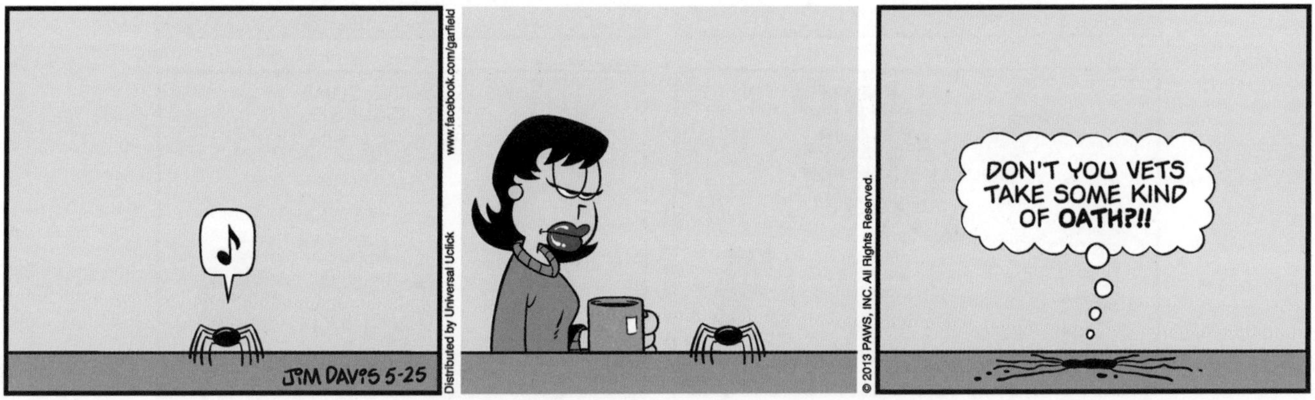
♪
JIM DAVIS 5-25
www.facebook.com/garfield
Distributed by Universal Uclick
© 2013 PAWS, INC. All Rights Reserved.
DON'T YOU VETS TAKE SOME KIND OF **OATH?!!**

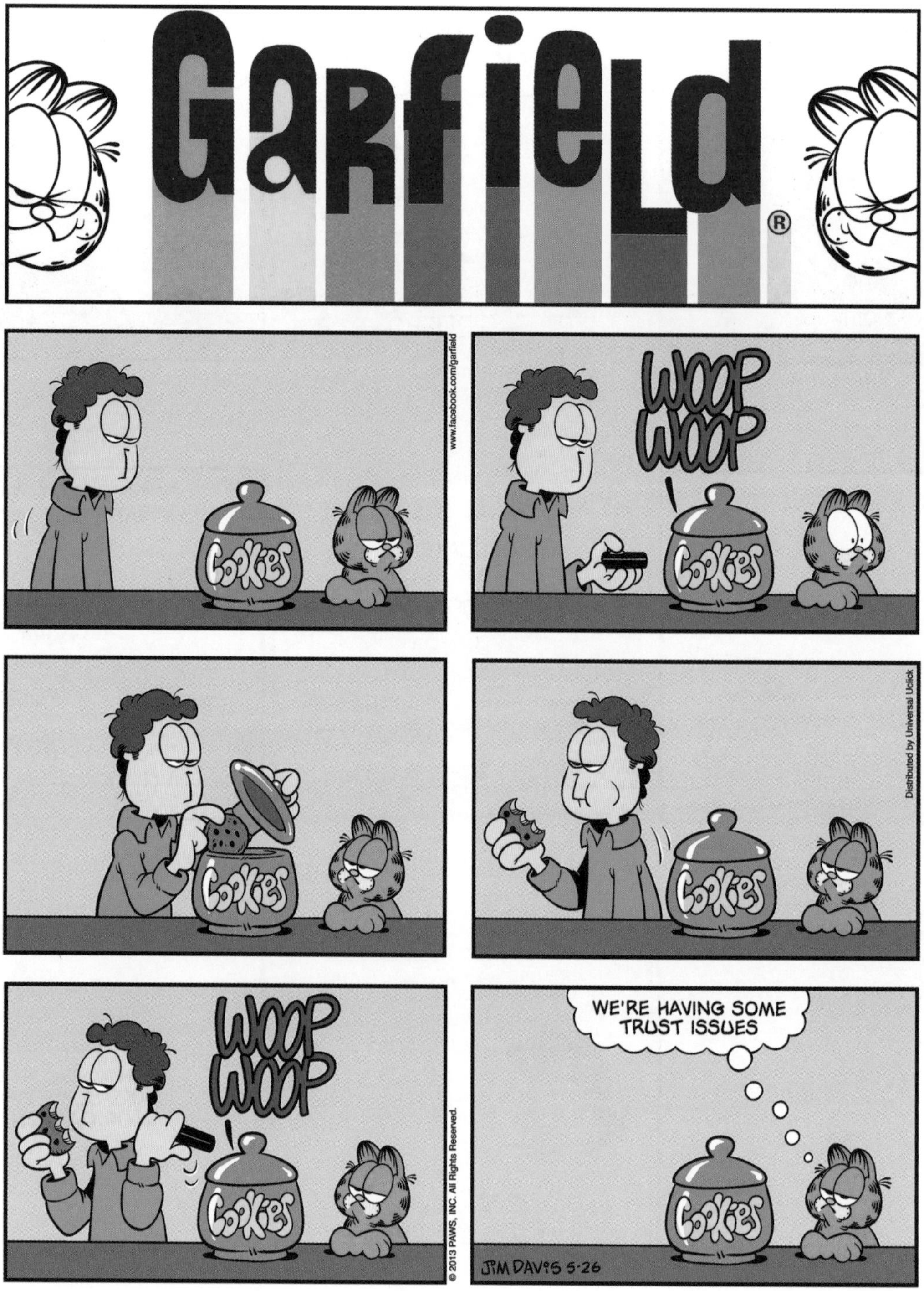
GARFIELD®
www.facebook.com/garfield
WOOP WOOP
Distributed by Universal Uclick
WOOP WOOP
© 2013 PAWS, INC. All Rights Reserved.
WE'RE HAVING SOME TRUST ISSUES
JIM DAVIS 5-26

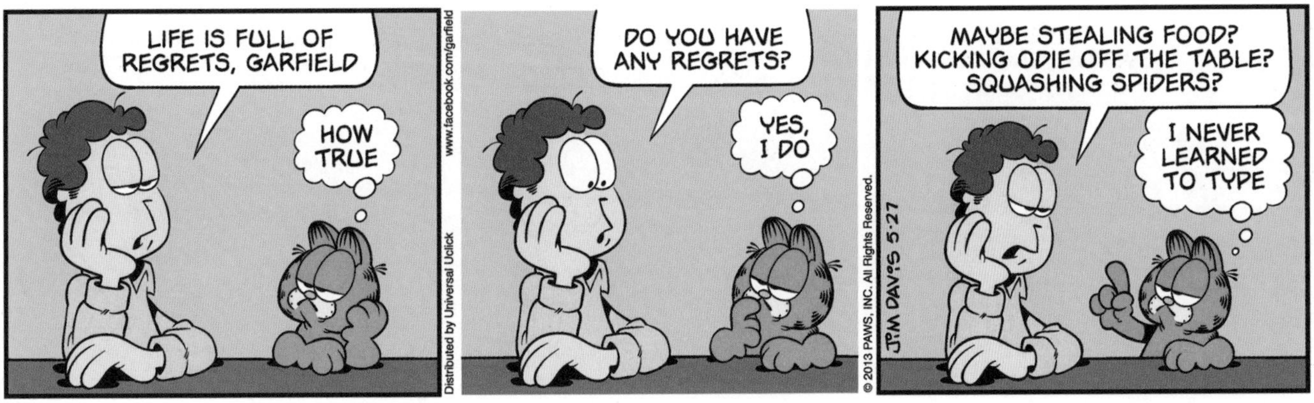
LIFE IS FULL OF REGRETS, GARFIELD
HOW TRUE
www.facebook.com/garfield
Distributed by Universal Uclick
DO YOU HAVE ANY REGRETS?
YES, I DO
© 2013 PAWS, INC. All Rights Reserved.
JIM DAVIS 5-27
MAYBE STEALING FOOD? KICKING ODIE OFF THE TABLE? SQUASHING SPIDERS?
I NEVER LEARNED TO TYPE

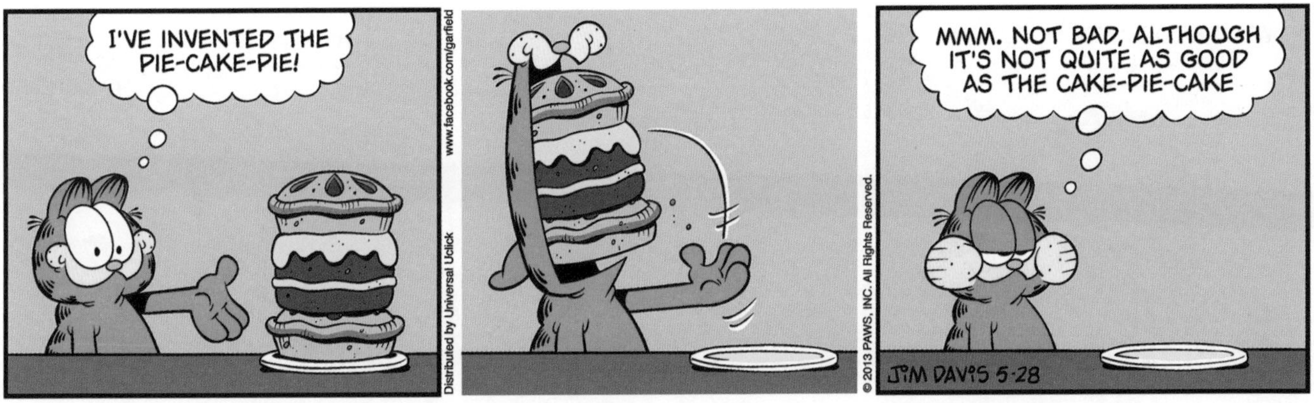
I'VE INVENTED THE PIE-CAKE-PIE!
www.facebook.com/garfield
Distributed by Universal Uclick
© 2013 PAWS, INC. All Rights Reserved.
MMM. NOT BAD, ALTHOUGH IT'S NOT QUITE AS GOOD AS THE CAKE-PIE-CAKE
JIM DAVIS 5-28

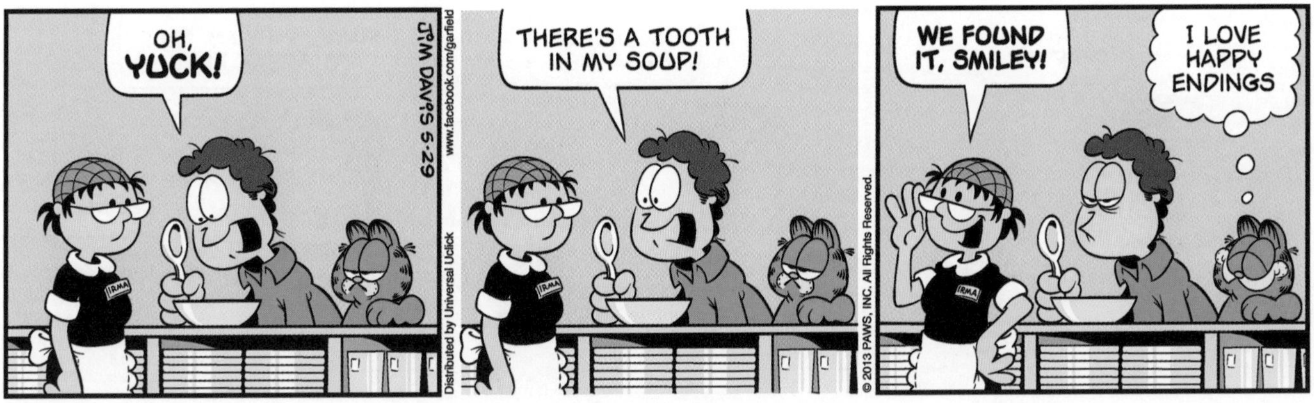
OH, **YUCK!**
JIM DAVIS 5-29
www.facebook.com/garfield
Distributed by Universal Uclick
THERE'S A TOOTH IN MY SOUP!
© 2013 PAWS, INC. All Rights Reserved.
WE FOUND IT, SMILEY!
I LOVE HAPPY ENDINGS

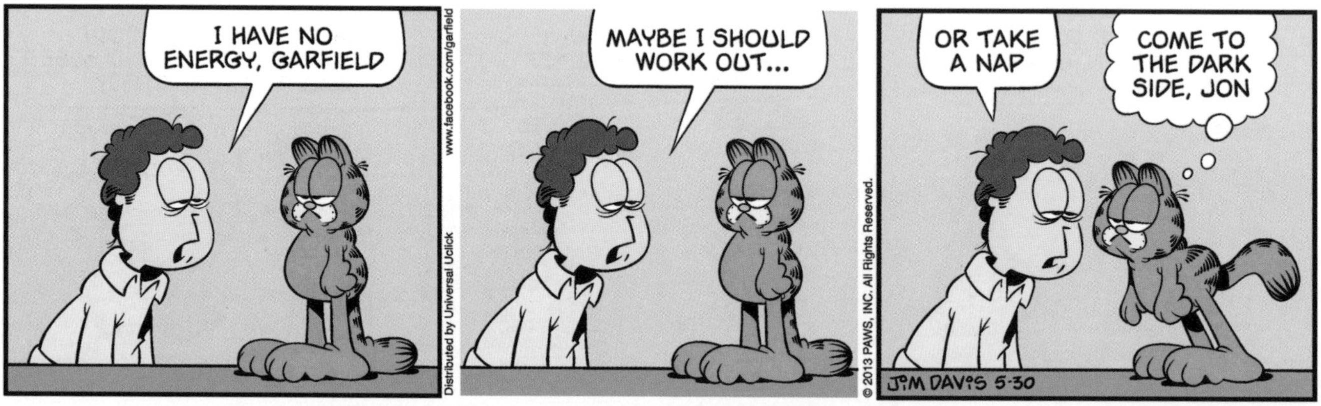
I HAVE NO ENERGY, GARFIELD
Distributed by Universal Uclick
www.facebook.com/garfield
MAYBE I SHOULD WORK OUT...
© 2013 PAWS, INC. All Rights Reserved.
OR TAKE A NAP
COME TO THE DARK SIDE, JON
JiM DAViS 5-30

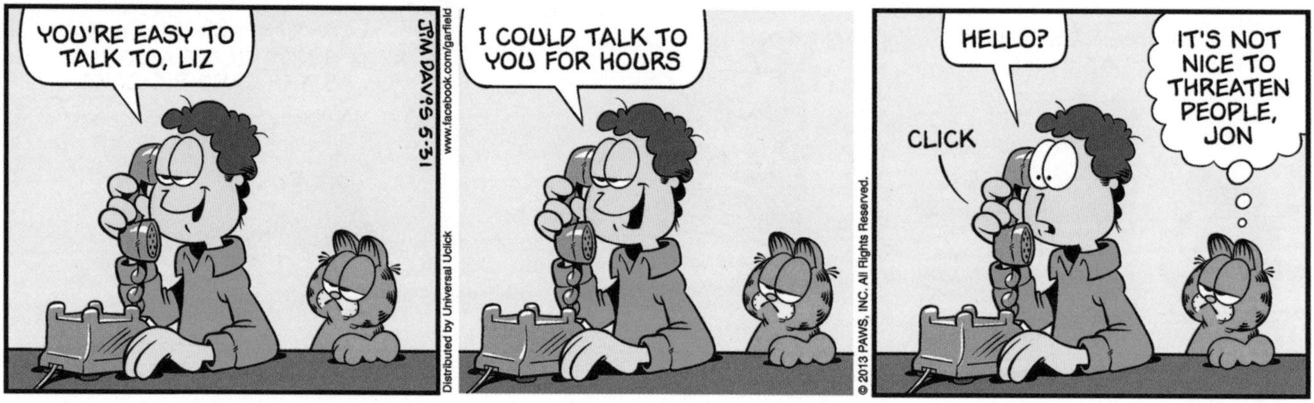
YOU'RE EASY TO TALK TO, LIZ
JiM DAViS 5-31
Distributed by Universal Uclick
www.facebook.com/garfield
I COULD TALK TO YOU FOR HOURS
© 2013 PAWS, INC. All Rights Reserved.
HELLO?
CLICK
IT'S NOT NICE TO THREATEN PEOPLE, JON

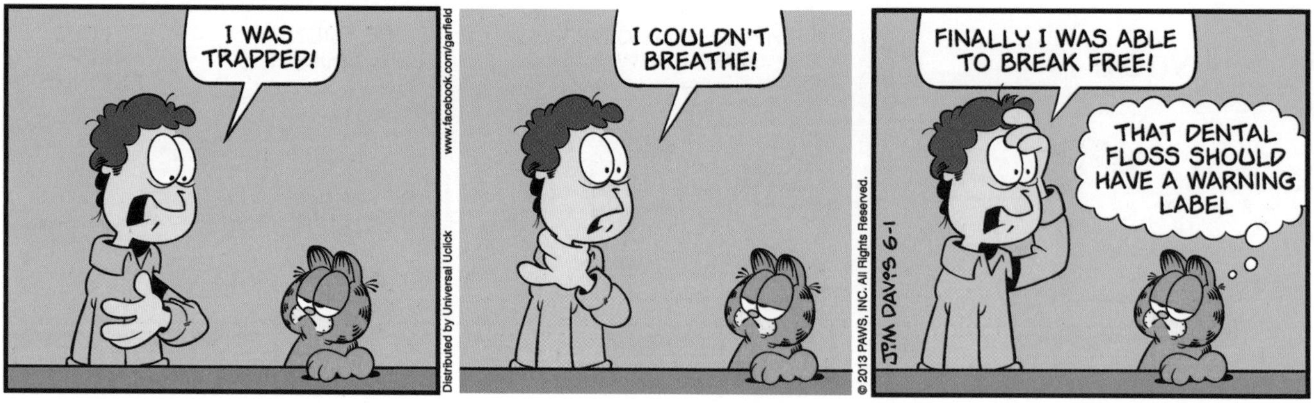
I WAS TRAPPED!
Distributed by Universal Uclick
www.facebook.com/garfield
I COULDN'T BREATHE!
© 2013 PAWS, INC. All Rights Reserved.
JiM DAViS 6-1
FINALLY I WAS ABLE TO BREAK FREE!
THAT DENTAL FLOSS SHOULD HAVE A WARNING LABEL

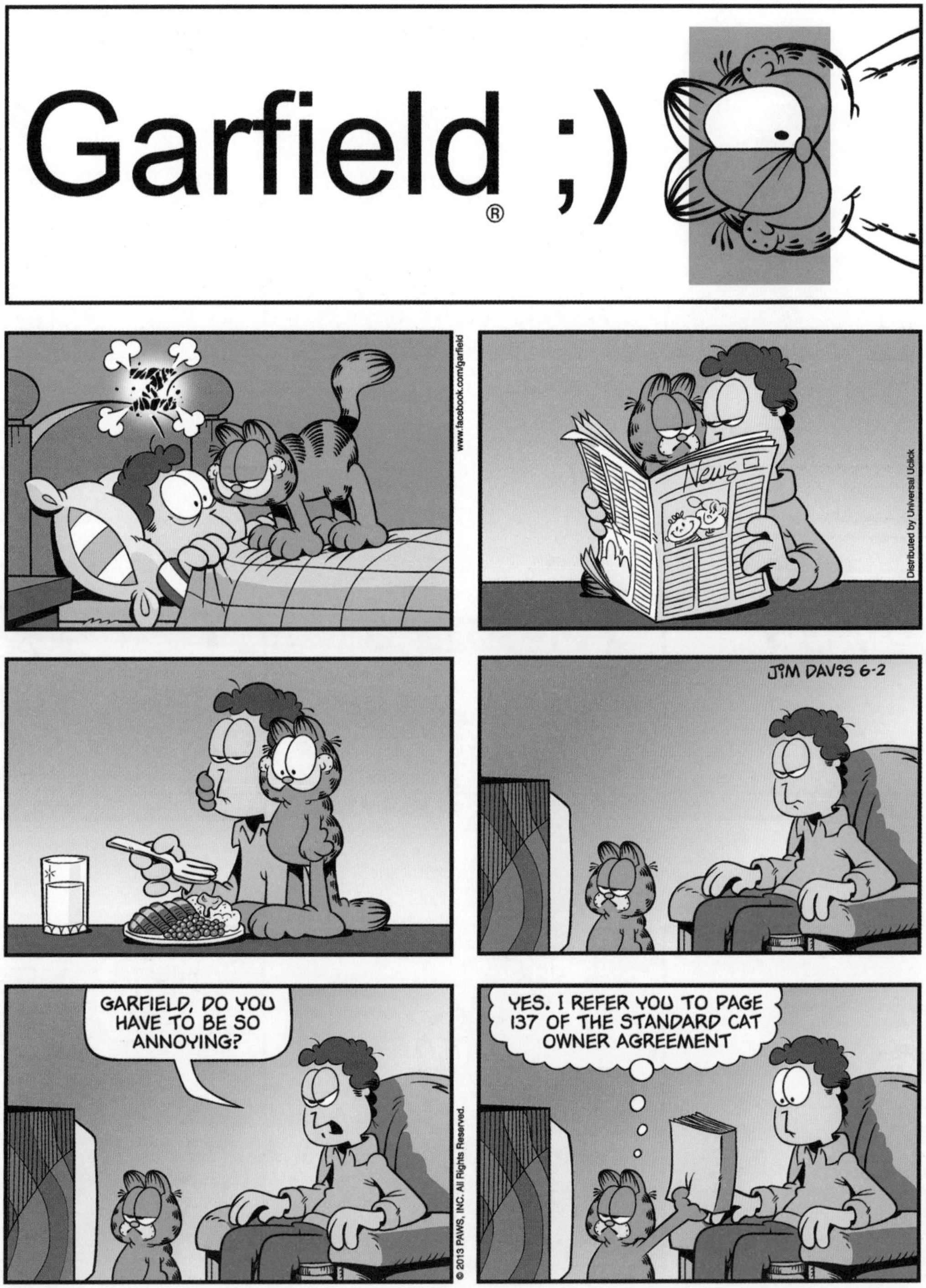
Garfield ;)
www.facebook.com/garfield
Distributed by Universal Uclick
News
JIM DAVIS 6-2
GARFIELD, DO YOU HAVE TO BE SO ANNOYING?
© 2013 PAWS, INC. All Rights Reserved.
YES. I REFER YOU TO PAGE 137 OF THE STANDARD CAT OWNER AGREEMENT

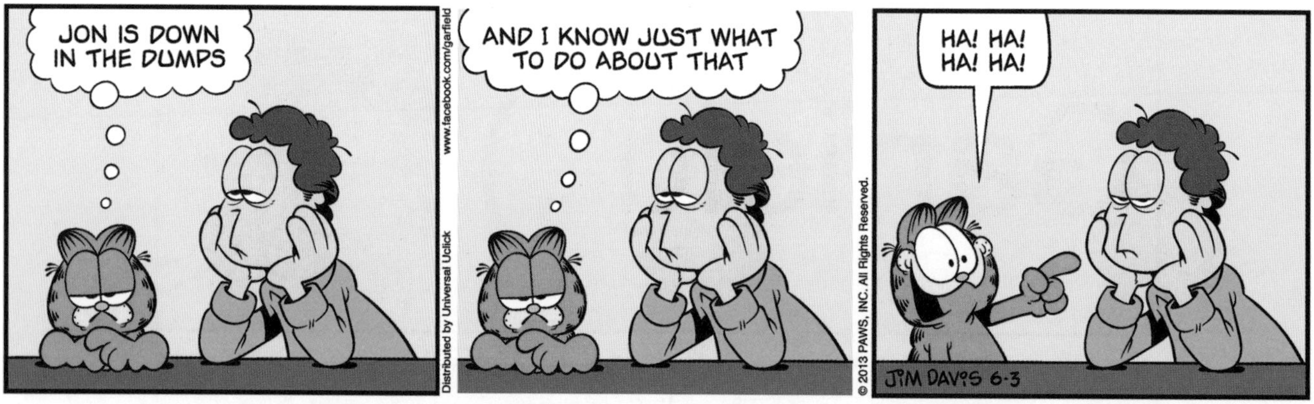
JON IS DOWN IN THE DUMPS
www.facebook.com/garfield
Distributed by Universal Uclick
AND I KNOW JUST WHAT TO DO ABOUT THAT
© 2013 PAWS, INC. All Rights Reserved.
HA! HA! HA! HA!
JIM DAVIS 6-3

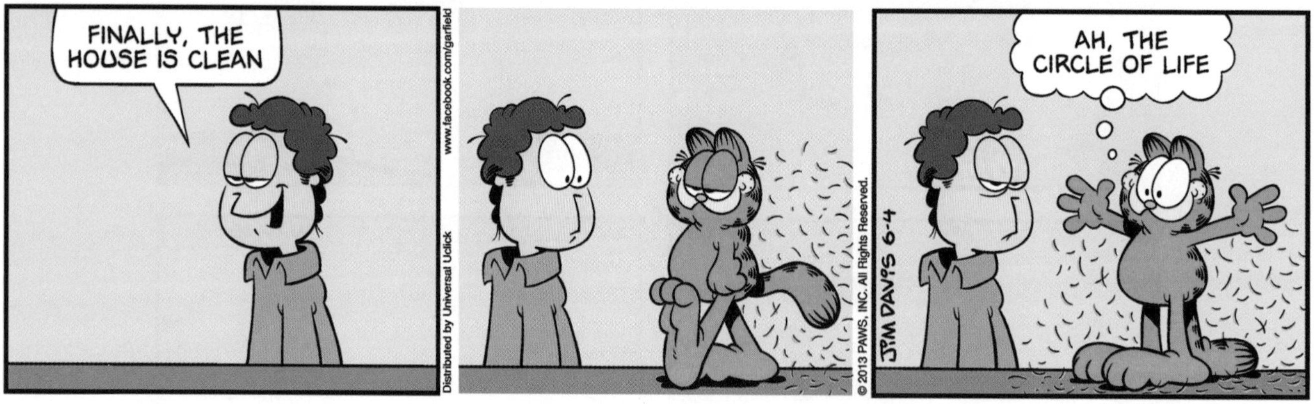
FINALLY, THE HOUSE IS CLEAN
www.facebook.com/garfield
Distributed by Universal Uclick
© 2013 PAWS, INC. All Rights Reserved.
JIM DAVIS 6-4
AH, THE CIRCLE OF LIFE

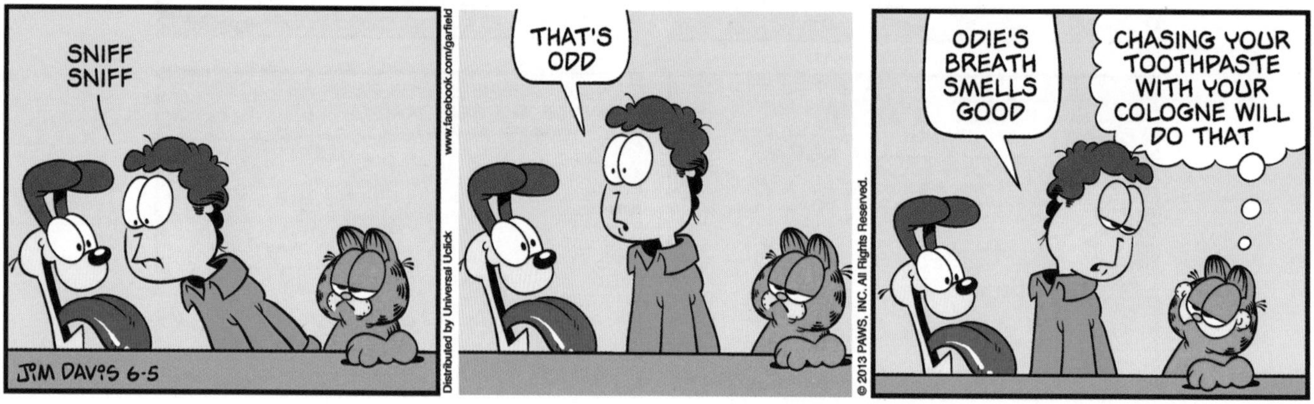
SNIFF SNIFF
JIM DAVIS 6-5
www.facebook.com/garfield
Distributed by Universal Uclick
THAT'S ODD
© 2013 PAWS, INC. All Rights Reserved.
ODIE'S BREATH SMELLS GOOD
CHASING YOUR TOOTHPASTE WITH YOUR COLOGNE WILL DO THAT

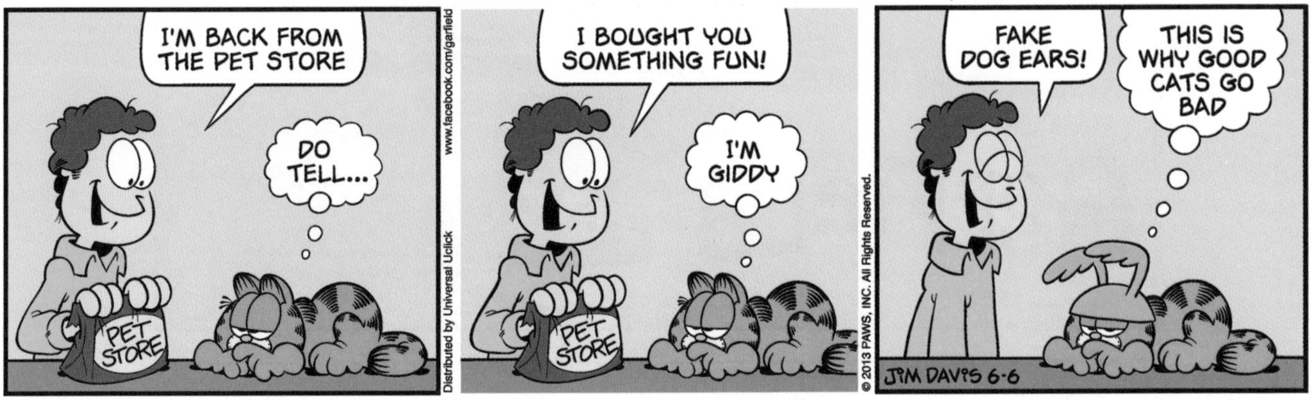
I'M BACK FROM THE PET STORE
DO TELL...
PET STORE
Distributed by Universal Uclick
www.facebook.com/garfield
I BOUGHT YOU SOMETHING FUN!
I'M GIDDY
PET STORE
© 2013 PAWS, INC. All Rights Reserved.
FAKE DOG EARS!
THIS IS WHY GOOD CATS GO BAD
JIM DAVIS 6-6

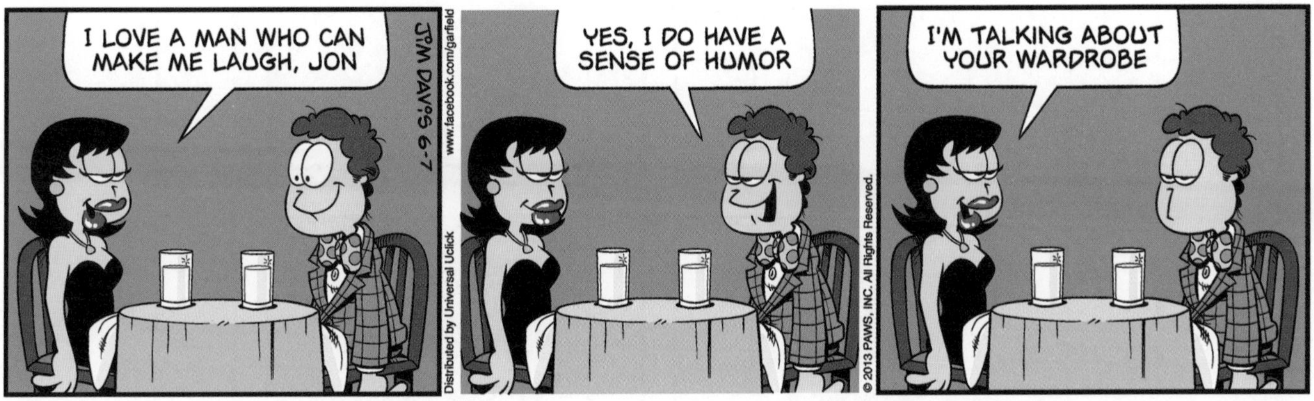
I LOVE A MAN WHO CAN MAKE ME LAUGH, JON
JIM DAVIS 6-7
Distributed by Universal Uclick
www.facebook.com/garfield
YES, I DO HAVE A SENSE OF HUMOR
© 2013 PAWS, INC. All Rights Reserved.
I'M TALKING ABOUT YOUR WARDROBE

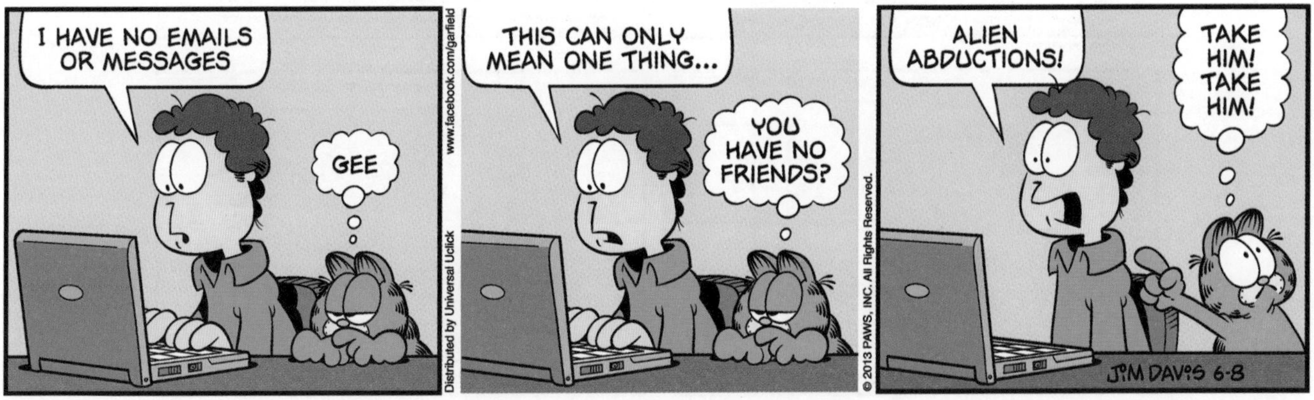
I HAVE NO EMAILS OR MESSAGES
GEE
Distributed by Universal Uclick
www.facebook.com/garfield
THIS CAN ONLY MEAN ONE THING...
YOU HAVE NO FRIENDS?
© 2013 PAWS, INC. All Rights Reserved.
ALIEN ABDUCTIONS!
TAKE HIM! TAKE HIM!
JIM DAVIS 6-8

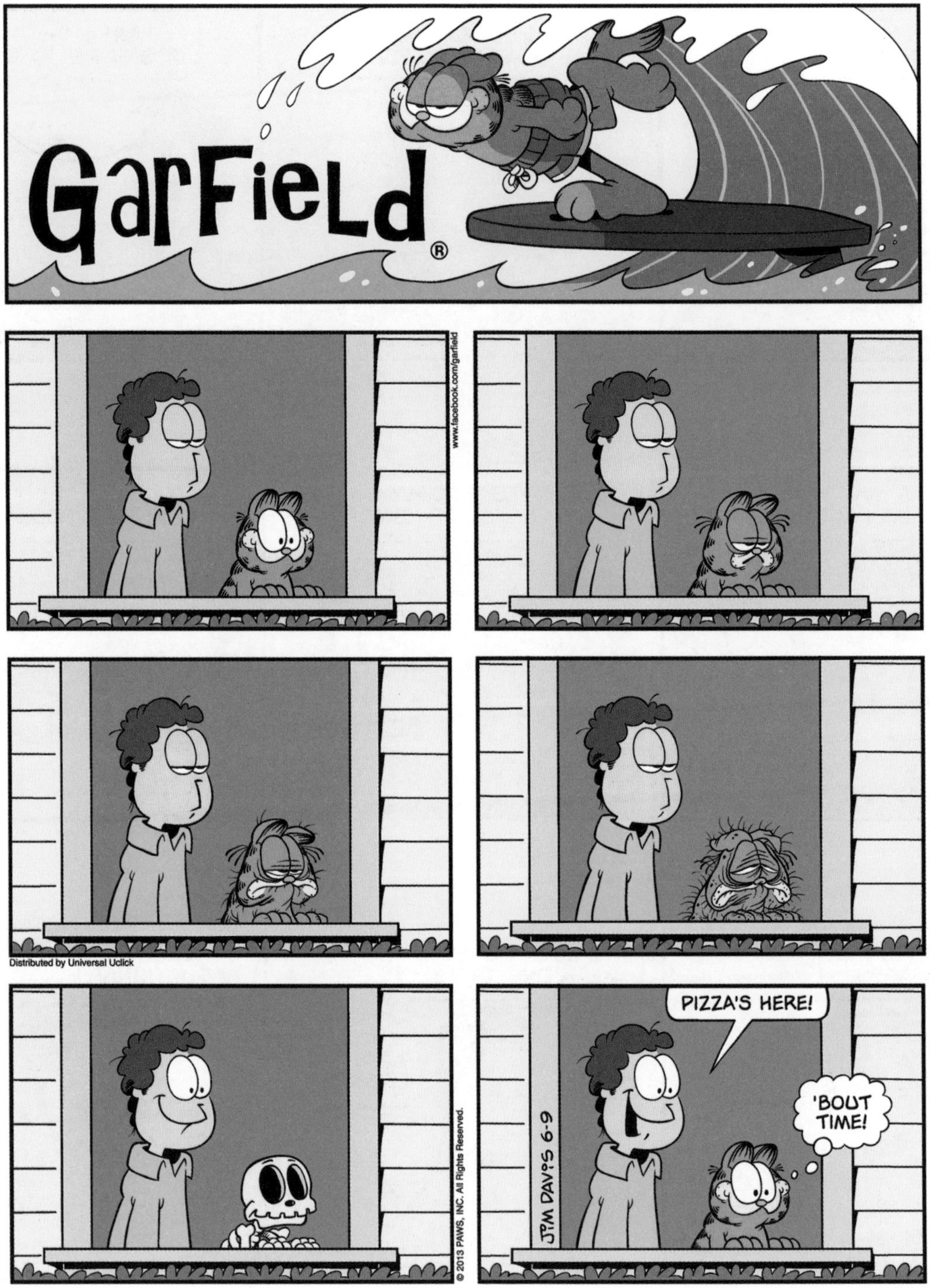
GarField®
www.facebook.com/garfield
Distributed by Universal Uclick
© 2013 PAWS, INC. All Rights Reserved.
JPM DAVIS 6-9
PIZZA'S HERE!
'BOUT TIME!

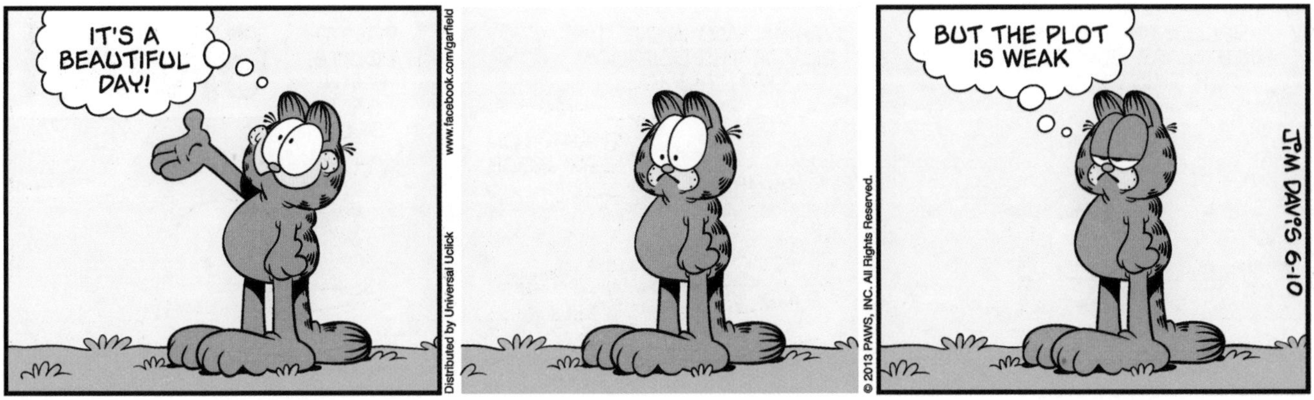
IT'S A BEAUTIFUL DAY!
BUT THE PLOT IS WEAK
JIM DAVIS 6-10
Distributed by Universal Uclick www.facebook.com/garfield
© 2013 PAWS, INC. All Rights Reserved.

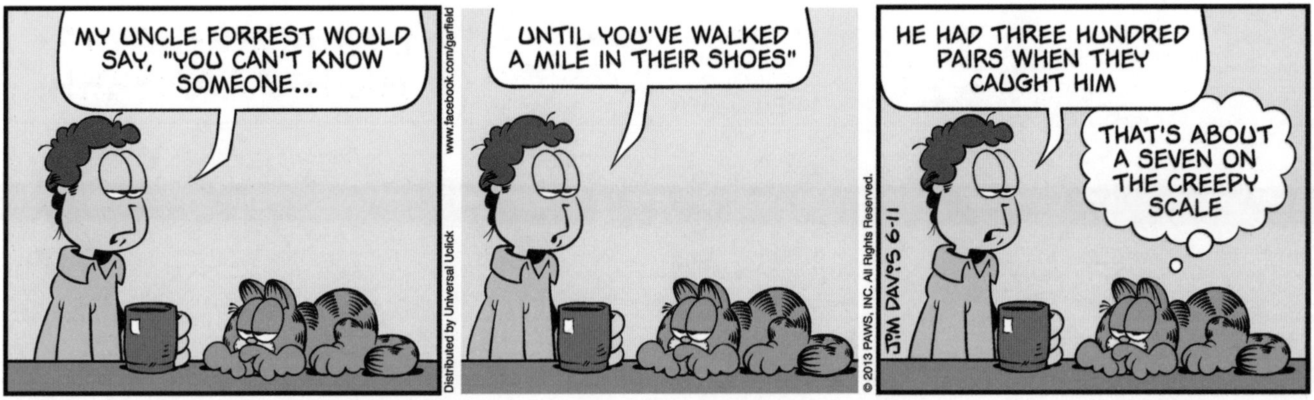
MY UNCLE FORREST WOULD SAY, "YOU CAN'T KNOW SOMEONE...
UNTIL YOU'VE WALKED A MILE IN THEIR SHOES"
HE HAD THREE HUNDRED PAIRS WHEN THEY CAUGHT HIM
THAT'S ABOUT A SEVEN ON THE CREEPY SCALE
JIM DAVIS 6-11
Distributed by Universal Uclick www.facebook.com/garfield
© 2013 PAWS, INC. All Rights Reserved.

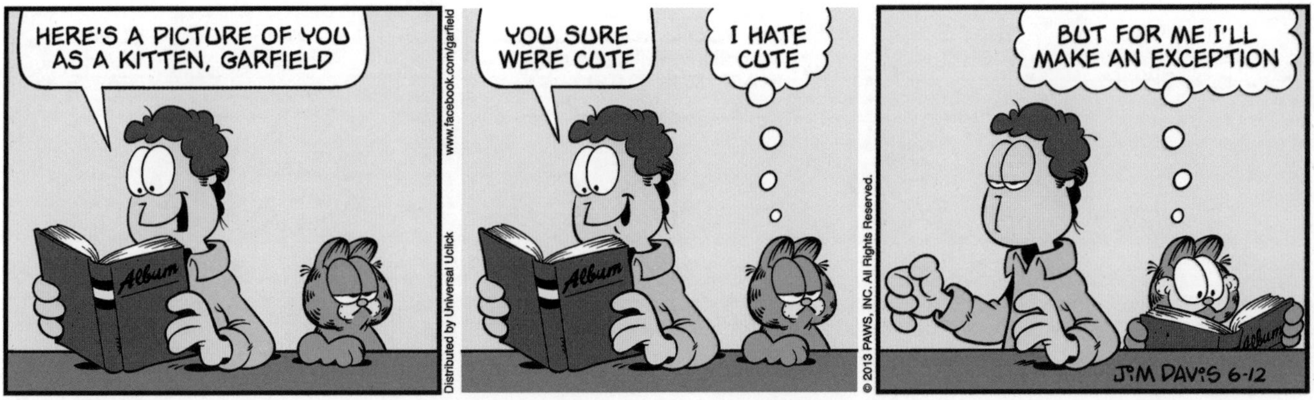
HERE'S A PICTURE OF YOU AS A KITTEN, GARFIELD
Album
YOU SURE WERE CUTE
I HATE CUTE
BUT FOR ME I'LL MAKE AN EXCEPTION
JIM DAVIS 6-12
Distributed by Universal Uclick www.facebook.com/garfield
© 2013 PAWS, INC. All Rights Reserved.

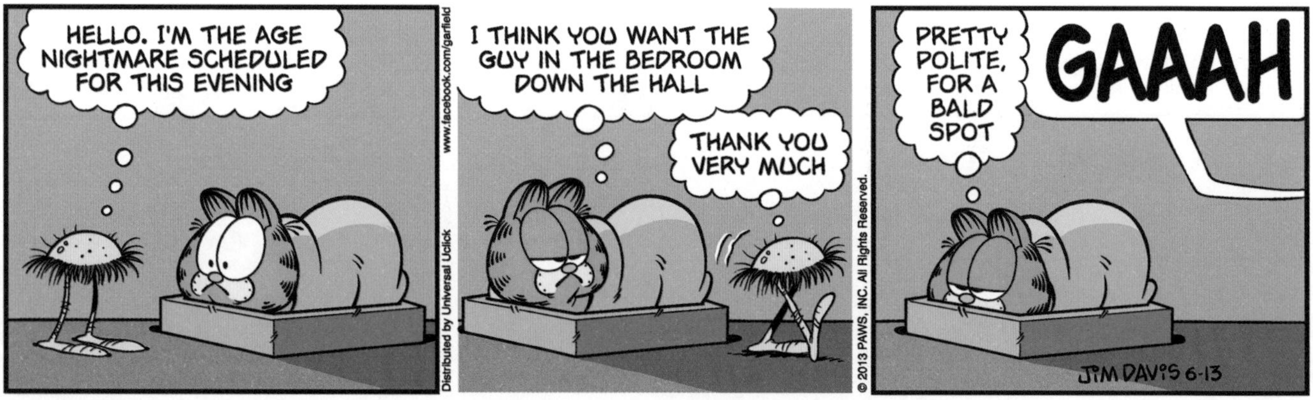
HELLO. I'M THE AGE NIGHTMARE SCHEDULED FOR THIS EVENING
I THINK YOU WANT THE GUY IN THE BEDROOM DOWN THE HALL
THANK YOU VERY MUCH
PRETTY POLITE, FOR A BALD SPOT
GAAAH
JIM DAVIS 6-13
Distributed by Universal Uclick www.facebook.com/garfield
© 2013 PAWS, INC. All Rights Reserved.

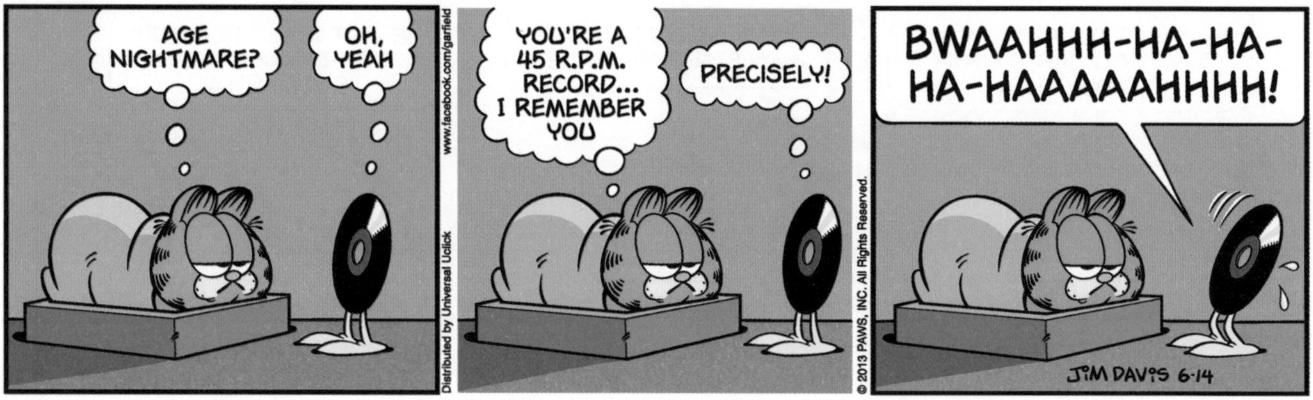
AGE NIGHTMARE?
OH, YEAH
YOU'RE A 45 R.P.M. RECORD... I REMEMBER YOU
PRECISELY!
BWAAHHH-HA-HA-HA-HAAAAAHHHH!
JIM DAVIS 6-14
Distributed by Universal Uclick www.facebook.com/garfield
© 2013 PAWS, INC. All Rights Reserved.

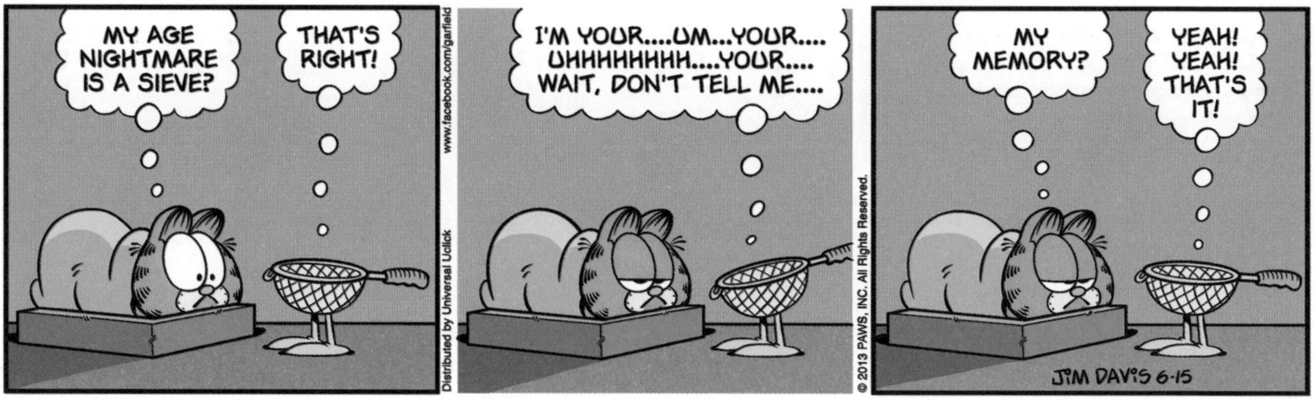
MY AGE NIGHTMARE IS A SIEVE?
THAT'S RIGHT!
I'M YOUR....UM...YOUR.... UHHHHHHHH....YOUR.... WAIT, DON'T TELL ME....
MY MEMORY?
YEAH! YEAH! THAT'S IT!
JIM DAVIS 6-15
Distributed by Universal Uclick www.facebook.com/garfield
© 2013 PAWS, INC. All Rights Reserved.

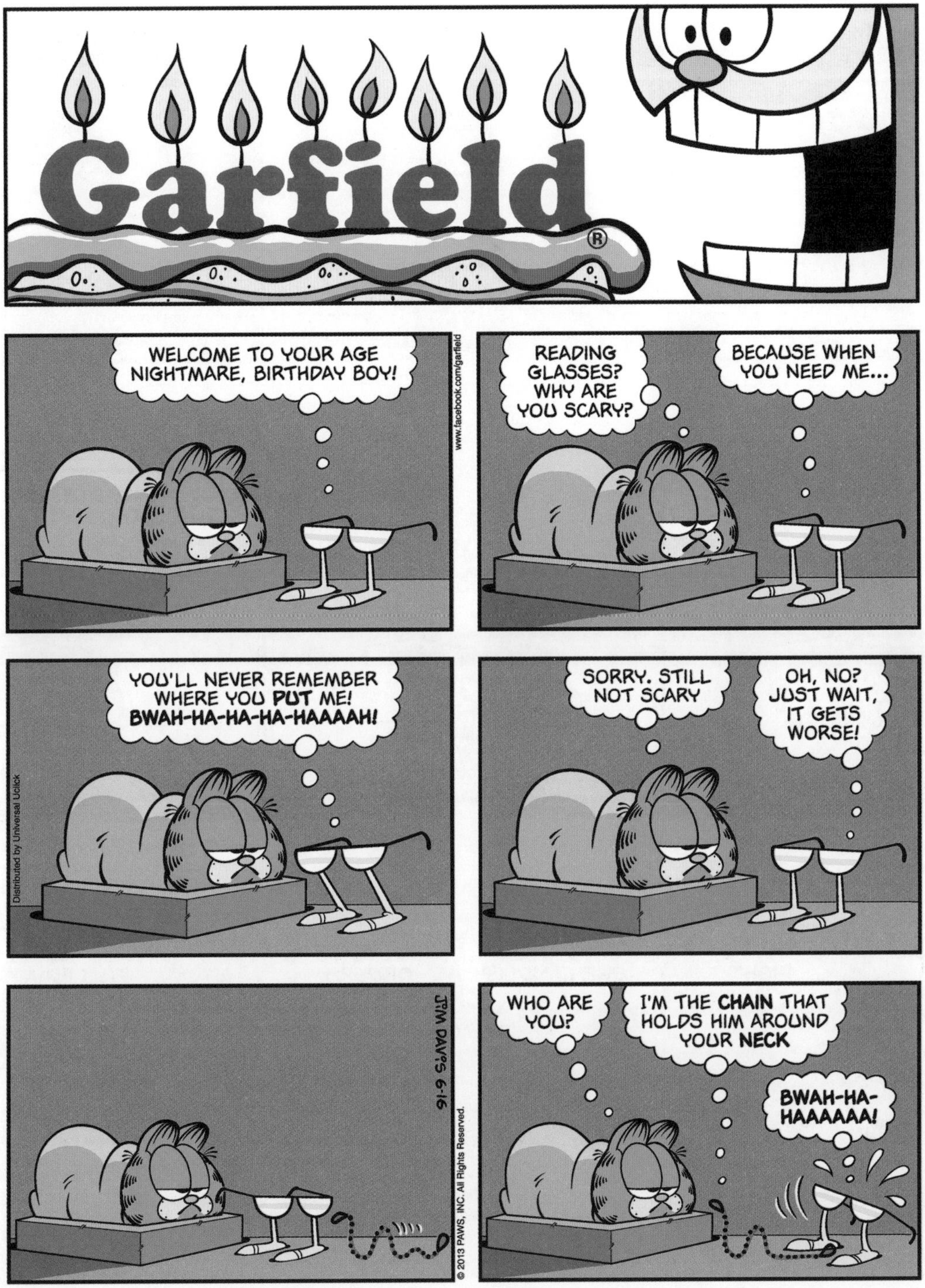
Garfield®
www.facebook.com/garfield
WELCOME TO YOUR AGE NIGHTMARE, BIRTHDAY BOY!
READING GLASSES? WHY ARE YOU SCARY?
BECAUSE WHEN YOU NEED ME...
Distributed by Universal Uclick
YOU'LL NEVER REMEMBER WHERE YOU **PUT** ME! **BWAH-HA-HA-HA-HAAAAH!**
SORRY. STILL NOT SCARY
OH, NO? JUST WAIT, IT GETS WORSE!
JPM DAVIS 6-16
© 2013 PAWS, INC. All Rights Reserved.
WHO ARE YOU?
I'M THE **CHAIN** THAT HOLDS HIM AROUND YOUR **NECK**
BWAH-HA-HAAAAAA!

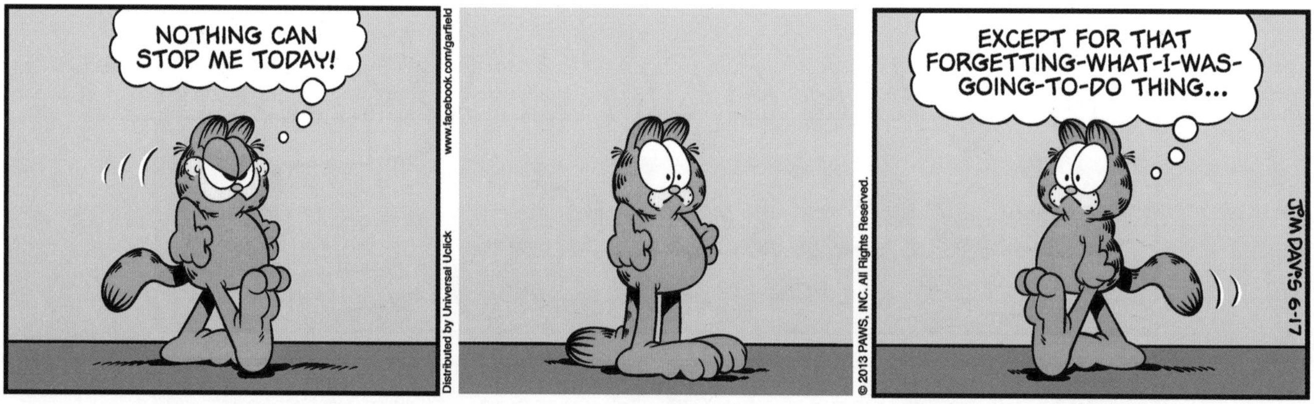
NOTHING CAN STOP ME TODAY!
Distributed by Universal Uclick
www.facebook.com/garfield
© 2013 PAWS, INC. All Rights Reserved.
EXCEPT FOR THAT FORGETTING-WHAT-I-WAS-GOING-TO-DO THING...
JIM DAVIS 6-17

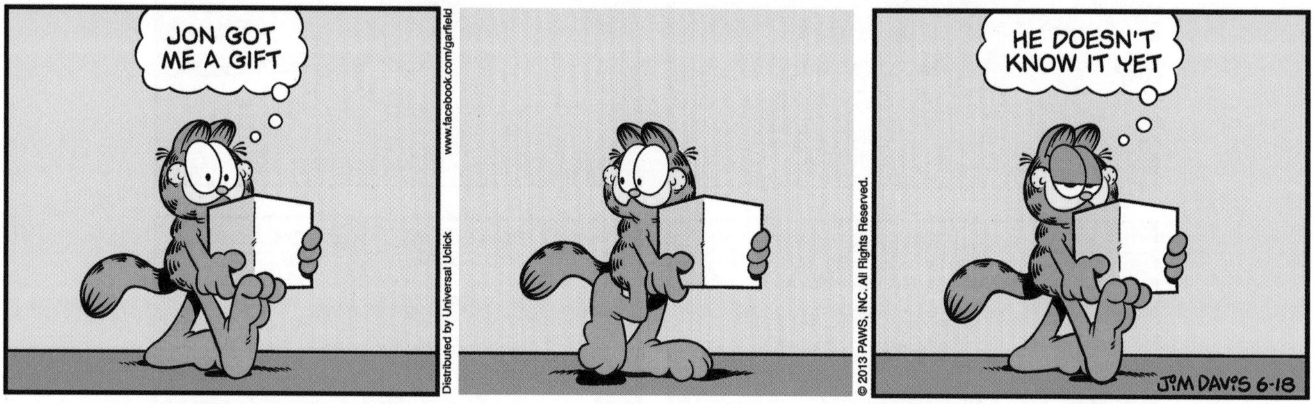
JON GOT ME A GIFT
Distributed by Universal Uclick
www.facebook.com/garfield
© 2013 PAWS, INC. All Rights Reserved.
HE DOESN'T KNOW IT YET
JIM DAVIS 6-18

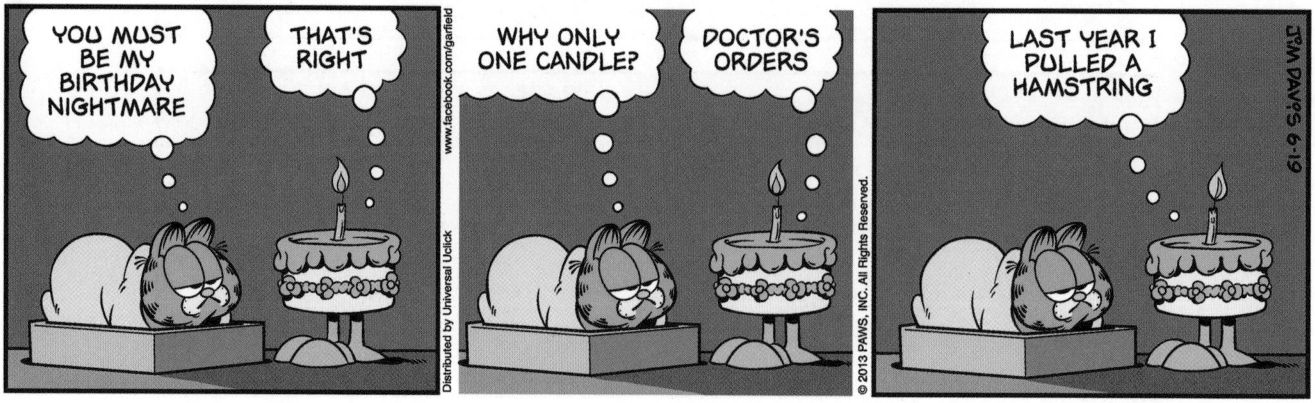
YOU MUST BE MY BIRTHDAY NIGHTMARE
THAT'S RIGHT
Distributed by Universal Uclick
www.facebook.com/garfield
WHY ONLY ONE CANDLE?
DOCTOR'S ORDERS
© 2013 PAWS, INC. All Rights Reserved.
LAST YEAR I PULLED A HAMSTRING
JIM DAVIS 6-19

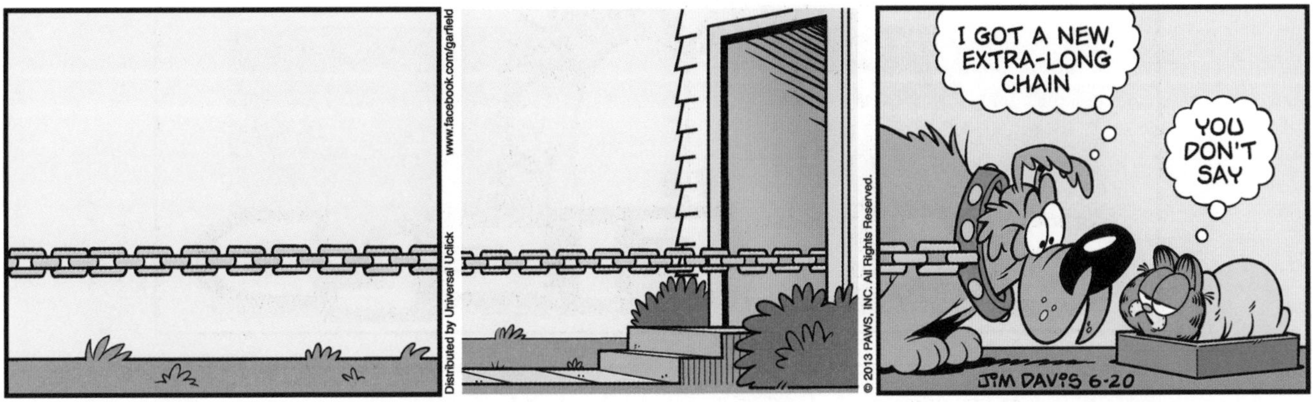
Distributed by Universal Uclick www.facebook.com/garfield
© 2013 PAWS, INC. All Rights Reserved.
I GOT A NEW, EXTRA-LONG CHAIN
YOU DON'T SAY
JIM DAVIS 6-20

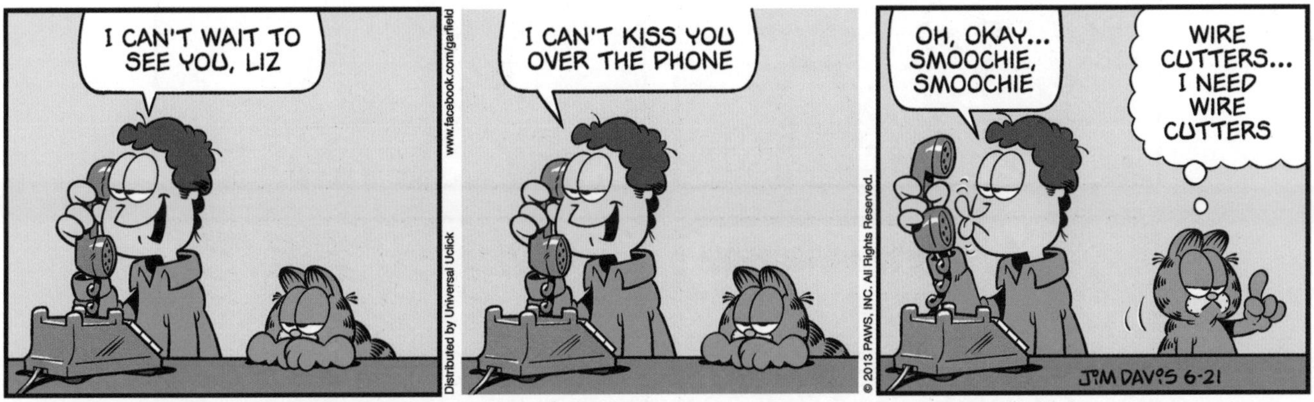
I CAN'T WAIT TO SEE YOU, LIZ
Distributed by Universal Uclick www.facebook.com/garfield
I CAN'T KISS YOU OVER THE PHONE
© 2013 PAWS, INC. All Rights Reserved.
OH, OKAY... SMOOCHIE, SMOOCHIE
WIRE CUTTERS... I NEED WIRE CUTTERS
JIM DAVIS 6-21

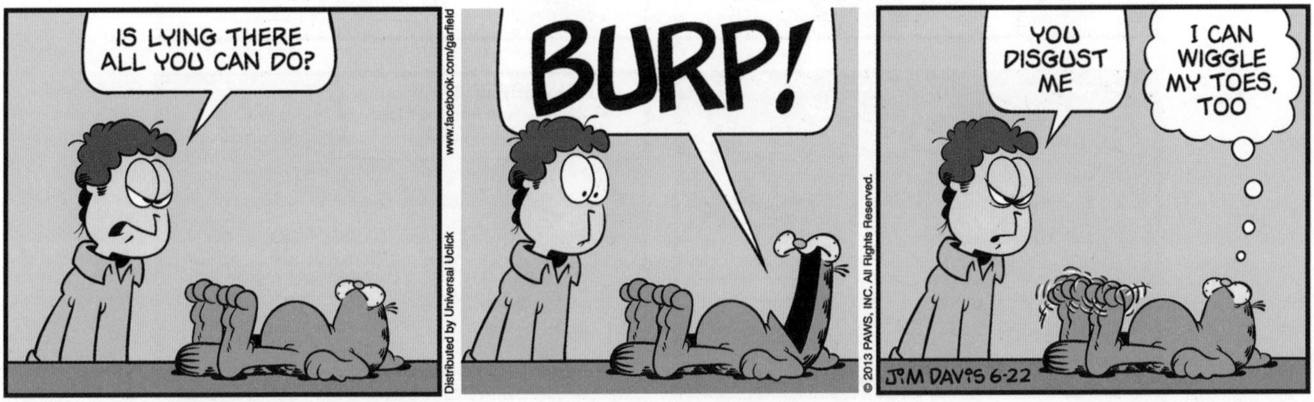
IS LYING THERE ALL YOU CAN DO?
Distributed by Universal Uclick www.facebook.com/garfield
BURP!
© 2013 PAWS, INC. All Rights Reserved.
YOU DISGUST ME
I CAN WIGGLE MY TOES, TOO
JIM DAVIS 6-22

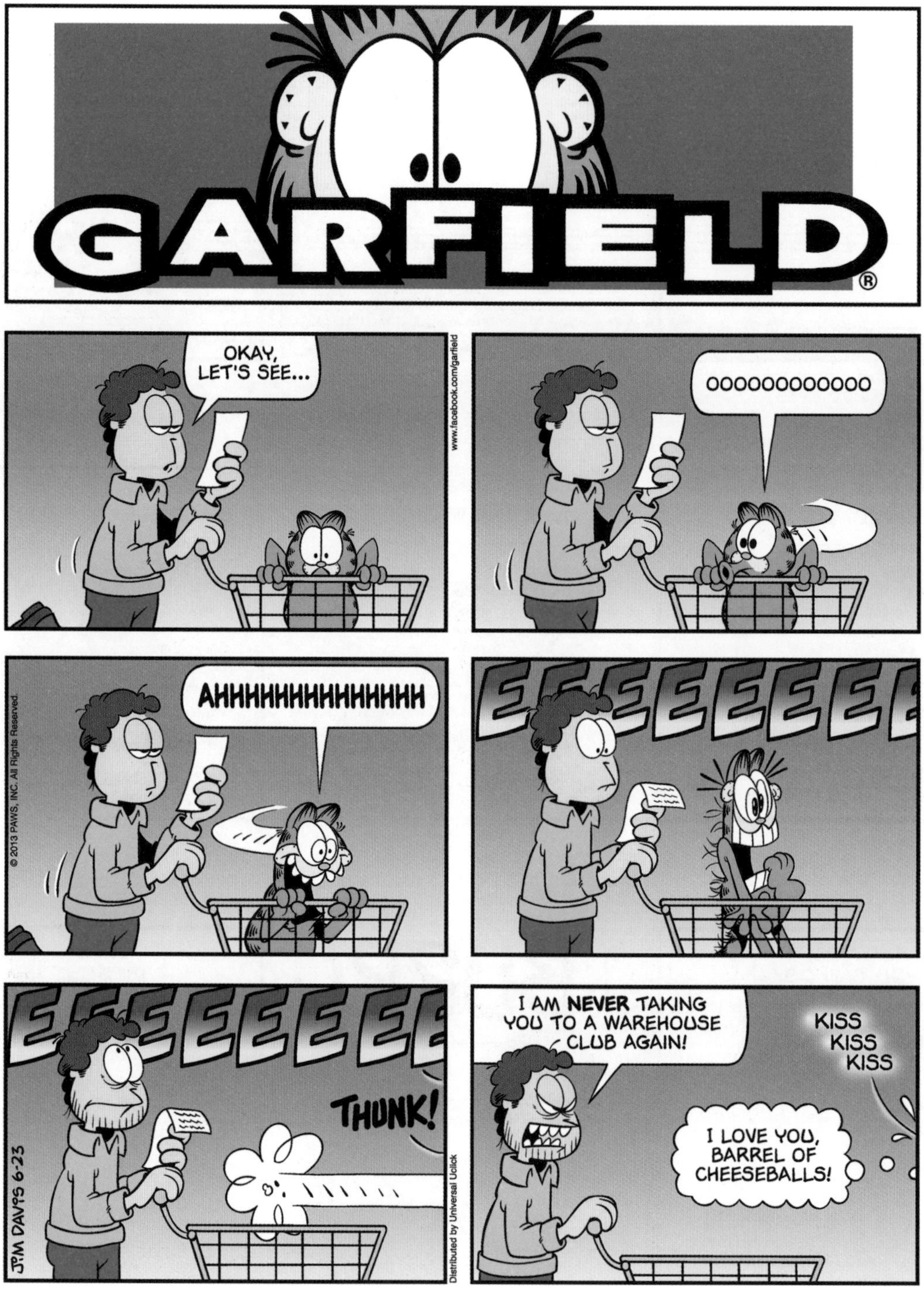
GARFIELD
OKAY, LET'S SEE...
www.facebook.com/garfield
OOOOOOOOOOOO
AHHHHHHHHHHHHHH
© 2013 PAWS, INC. All Rights Reserved.
EEEEEEEEE
EEEEEEEEE
THUNK!
JPM DAVIS 6-23
Distributed by Universal Uclick
I AM **NEVER** TAKING YOU TO A WAREHOUSE CLUB AGAIN!
KISS KISS KISS
I LOVE YOU, BARREL OF CHEESEBALLS!

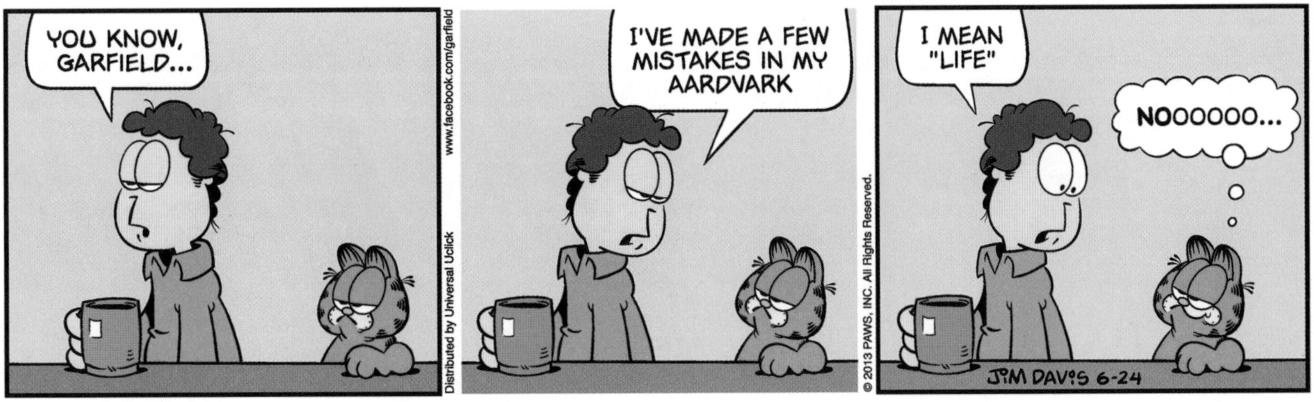
YOU KNOW, GARFIELD...
Distributed by Universal Uclick www.facebook.com/garfield
I'VE MADE A FEW MISTAKES IN MY AARDVARK
© 2013 PAWS, INC. All Rights Reserved.
I MEAN "LIFE"
NOOOOOO...
JIM DAVIS 6-24

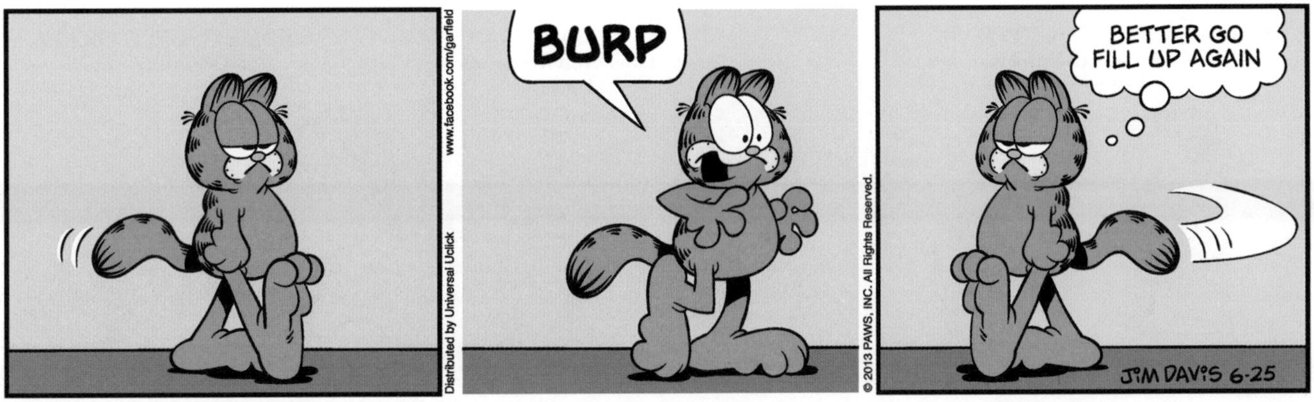
Distributed by Universal Uclick www.facebook.com/garfield
BURP
© 2013 PAWS, INC. All Rights Reserved.
BETTER GO FILL UP AGAIN
JIM DAVIS 6-25

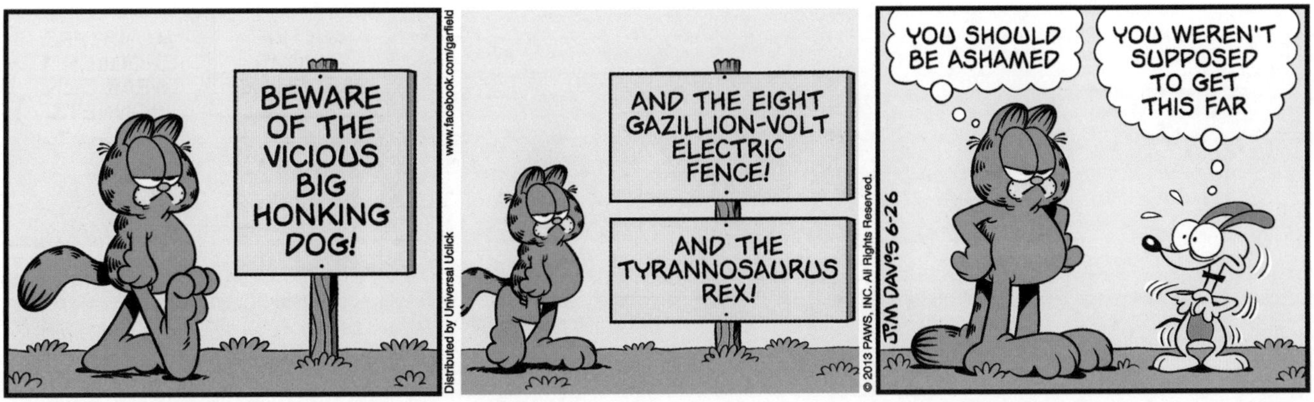
BEWARE OF THE VICIOUS BIG HONKING DOG!
Distributed by Universal Uclick www.facebook.com/garfield
AND THE EIGHT GAZILLION-VOLT ELECTRIC FENCE!
AND THE TYRANNOSAURUS REX!
© 2013 PAWS, INC. All Rights Reserved.
JIM DAVIS 6-26
YOU SHOULD BE ASHAMED
YOU WEREN'T SUPPOSED TO GET THIS FAR

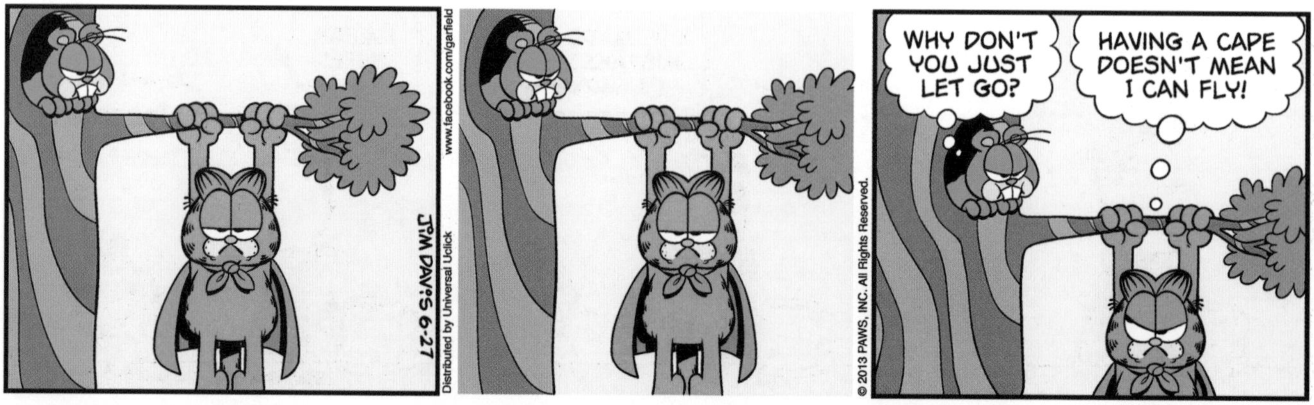
JIM DAVIS 6-27
www.facebook.com/garfield
Distributed by Universal Uclick
© 2013 PAWS, INC. All Rights Reserved.
WHY DON'T YOU JUST LET GO?
HAVING A CAPE DOESN'T MEAN I CAN FLY!

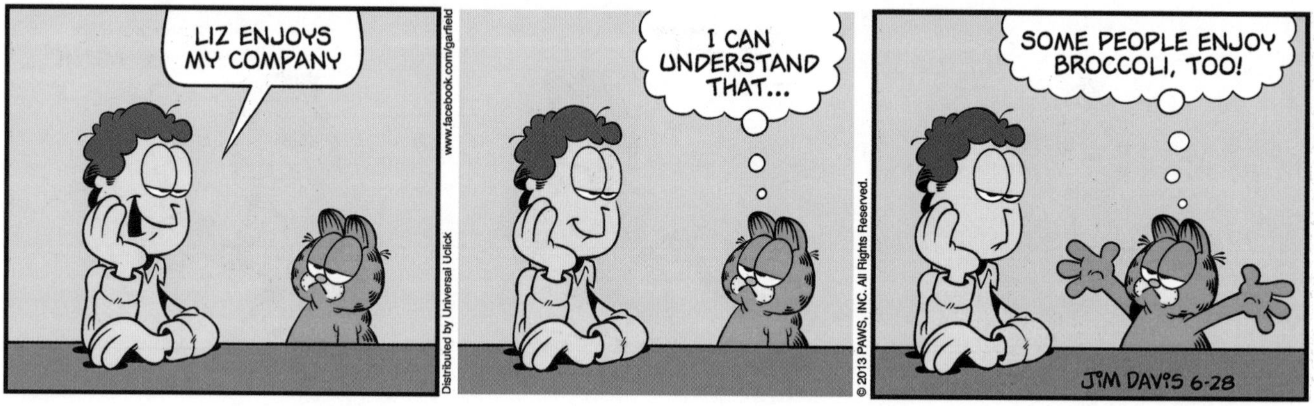
LIZ ENJOYS MY COMPANY
www.facebook.com/garfield
Distributed by Universal Uclick
I CAN UNDERSTAND THAT...
© 2013 PAWS, INC. All Rights Reserved.
SOME PEOPLE ENJOY BROCCOLI, TOO!
JIM DAVIS 6-28

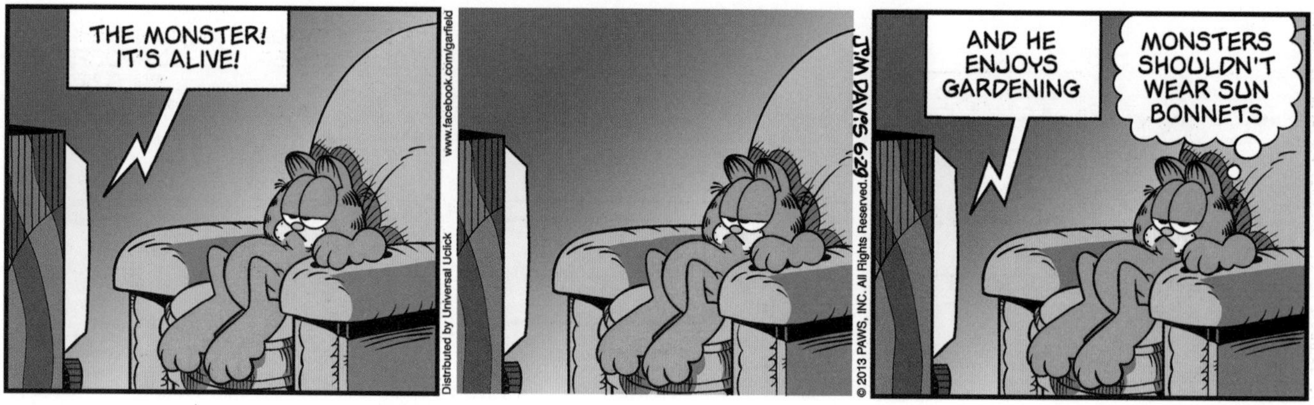
THE MONSTER! IT'S ALIVE!
www.facebook.com/garfield
Distributed by Universal Uclick
JIM DAVIS 6-29
© 2013 PAWS, INC. All Rights Reserved.
AND HE ENJOYS GARDENING
MONSTERS SHOULDN'T WEAR SUN BONNETS

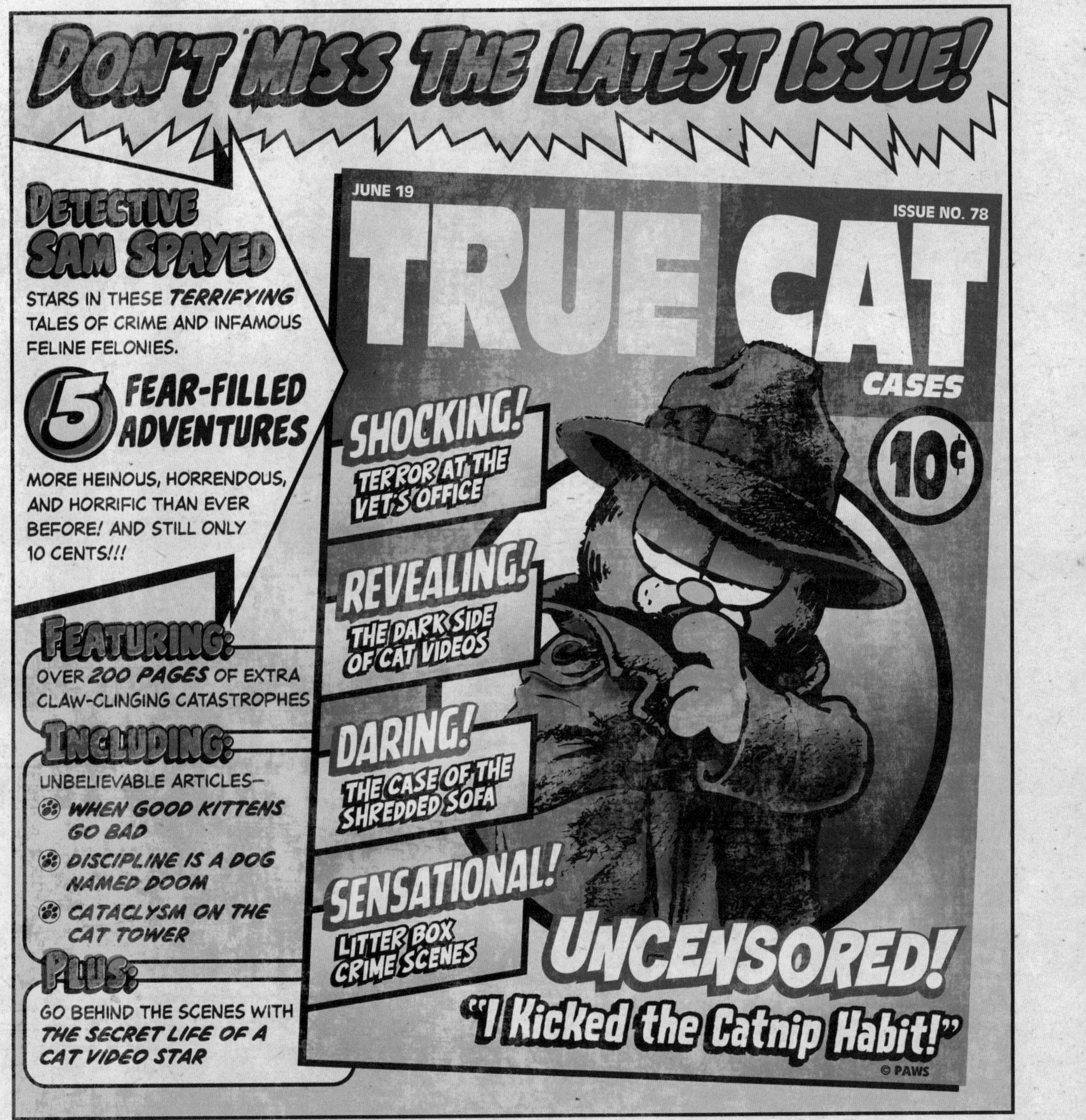
DON'T MISS THE LATEST ISSUE!
DETECTIVE SAM SPAYED
STARS IN THESE TERRIFYING TALES OF CRIME AND INFAMOUS FELINE FELONIES.
5 FEAR-FILLED ADVENTURES
MORE HEINOUS, HORRENDOUS, AND HORRIFIC THAN EVER BEFORE! AND STILL ONLY 10 CENTS!!!
FEATURING:
OVER 200 PAGES OF EXTRA CLAW-CLINGING CATASTROPHES
INCLUDING:
UNBELIEVABLE ARTICLES—
WHEN GOOD KITTENS GO BAD
DISCIPLINE IS A DOG NAMED DOOM
CATACLYSM ON THE CAT TOWER
PLUS:
GO BEHIND THE SCENES WITH THE SECRET LIFE OF A CAT VIDEO STAR
JUNE 19
ISSUE NO. 78
TRUE CAT CASES
10¢
SHOCKING!
TERROR AT THE VET'S OFFICE
REVEALING!
THE DARK SIDE OF CAT VIDEOS
DARING!
THE CASE OF THE SHREDDED SOFA
SENSATIONAL!
LITTER BOX CRIME SCENES
UNCENSORED!
"I Kicked the Catnip Habit!"
© PAWS

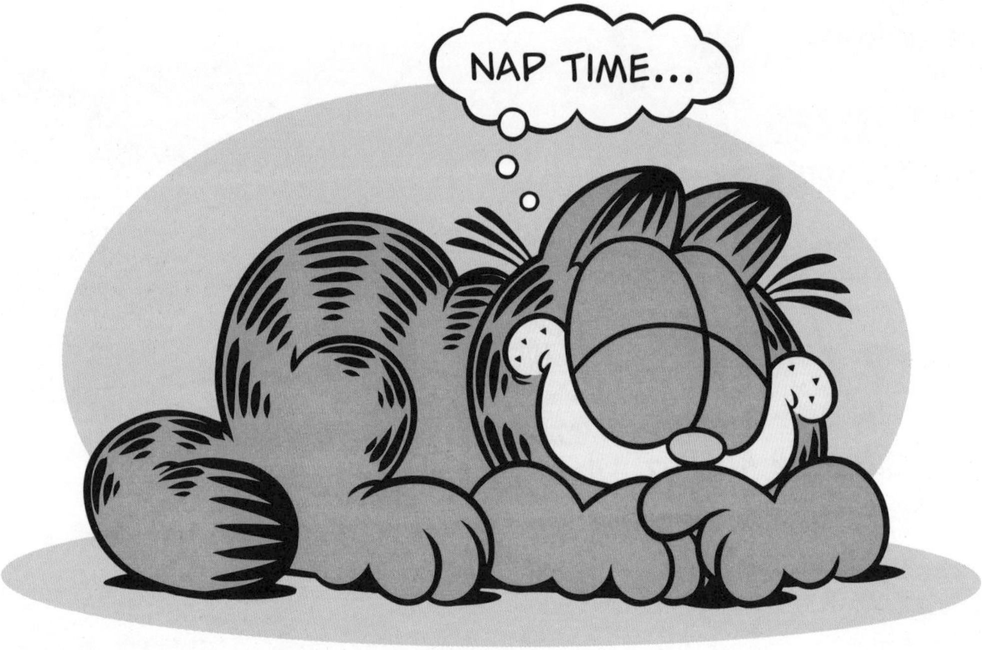
NAP TIME...